The Jury Under Fire

American Psychology-Law Society Series

Books in the Series

Trial Consulting
Amy J. Posey and Lawrence S. Wrightsman

Death by Design
Craig Haney

Psychological Injuries
William J. Koch, Kevin S. Douglas, Tonia
L. Nicholls, and Melanie L. O'Neill

Emergency Department Treatment of the
Psychiatric Patient
Susan Stefan

The Psychology of the Supreme Court
Lawrence S. Wrightsman

Proving the Unprovable
Christopher Slobogin

Adolescents, Media, and the Law
Roger J.R. Levesque

Oral Arguments Before the Supreme Court
Lawrence S. Wrightsman

God in the Courtroom
Brian H. Bornstein
and Monica K. Miller

Expert Testimony on the Psychology of
Eyewitness Identification
Edited by Brian L. Cutler

The Psychology of Judicial Decision-Making
Edited by David Klein
and Gregory Mitchell

The Miranda Ruling: Its Past, Present,
and Future
Lawrence S. Wrightsman
and Mary L. Pitman

Juveniles at Risk: A Plea for Preventive
Justice
Christopher Slobogin
and Mark R. Fondacaro

The Ethics of Total Confinement
Bruce A. Arrigo, Heather Y. Bersot, and
Brian G. Sellers

International Human Rights and Mental
Disability Law
Michael L. Perlin

Applying Social Science to Reduce Violent
Offending
Edited by Joel Dvoskin, Jennifer L. Skeem,
Raymond W. Novaco, and Kevin S. Douglas

Children Who Resist Postseparation
Parental Contact
Barbara Jo Fidler, Nicholas Bala,
and Michael A. Saini

Trauma, Stress, and Wellbeing in the
Legal System
Edited by Monica K. Miller
and Brian H. Bornstein

Psychology, Law, and the Wellbeing of
Children
Edited by Monica K. Miller,
Jared C. Chamberlain,
and Twila Wingrove

Murder in the Courtroom: The Cognitive
Neuroscience of Extreme Violent Behavior
Brigitte Vallabhajosula

Rational Suicide, Irrational
Laws: Examining Current Approaches to
Suicide in Policy and Law
Susan Stefan

International Perspectives on Violence Risk
Assessment
Edited by Jay P. Singh, Stål Bjørkly, and
Seena Fazel

Adolescence, Privacy, and the
Law: A Developmental Science Perspective
Roger J.R. Levesque

The Ethical Practice of Forensic Psychology:
A Casebook
Edited by Gianni Pirelli, Robert A. Beattey,
and Patricia A. Zapf

The Jury Under Fire: Myth, Controversy,
and Reform
Brian H. Bornstein and Edie Greene

The Jury Under Fire

Myth, Controversy, and Reform

Brian H. Bornstein

and

Edie Greene

OXFORD
UNIVERSITY PRESS

Oxford University Press is a department of the University of Oxford. It furthers the University's objective of excellence in research, scholarship, and education by publishing worldwide. Oxford is a registered trade mark of Oxford University Press in the UK and certain other countries.

Published in the United States of America by Oxford University Press
198 Madison Avenue, New York, NY 10016, United States of America.

Library of Congress Cataloging-in-Publication Data
Names: Bornstein, Brian H., author. | Greene, Edie, author.
Title: The jury under fire : myth, controversy, and reform / Brian H. Bornstein and Edie Greene.
Description: Oxford ; New York : Oxford University Press, 2017. |
Series: American psychology-law society series | Includes bibliographical references and index.
Identifiers: LCCN 2016039507 (print) | LCCN 2016039722 (ebook) | ISBN 9780190201340 |
ISBN 9780190201364 (ebook)
Subjects: LCSH: Jury—United States. | Jurors—United States—Psychology.
Classification: LCC KF8972 .B67 2017 (print) | LCC KF8972 (ebook) | DDC 347.73/752—dc23
LC record available at https://lccn.loc.gov/2016039507

To John and Sandy Emler, in-laws extraordinaire
—BHB

To Larry and Roz Greene, in loving memory
—EG

Contents

Series Foreword   ix
Acknowledgments   xi

1. Introduction   1

2. Avoid Jury Duty at All Costs   17

3. Jury Selection Can Effectively Identify Biased Jurors   37

4. 6 = 12 and They Don't All Have to Agree   58

5. Jurors Can Distinguish Accurate from Inaccurate Eyewitnesses   82

6. Jurors Can Distinguish True from False Confessions   106

7. Jurors Overvalue Expert Testimony   128

8. Jurors Treat Juvenile Defendants Fairly   152

9. Compensatory Damage Awards Are Excessive and Unpredictable   173

10. Punitive Damage Awards Are Excessive and Unpredictable   200

11. Jurors in Criminal Cases Can Fairly Punish Wrongdoers   222

12. Jurors Can Control Their Emotions   242

13. Just Let the Judge Do It   271

14. Jurors Don't Need Any Special Help   288

15. Conclusion   309

References   321
About the Authors   385
Index   387

Series Foreword

This book series is sponsored by the American Psychology-Law Society (APLS). APLS is an interdisciplinary organization devoted to scholarship, practice, and public service in psychology and law. Its goals include advancing the contributions of psychology to the understanding of law and legal institutions through basic and applied research; promoting the education of psychologists in matters of law and the education of legal personnel in matters of psychology; and informing the psychological and legal communities and the general public of current research, educational, and service activities in the field of psychology and law. APLS membership includes psychologists from the academic, research, and clinical practice communities as well as members of the legal community. Research and practice are represented in both the civil and criminal legal arenas. APLS has chosen Oxford University Press as a strategic partner because of its commitment to scholarship, quality, and the international dissemination of ideas. These strengths will help APLS reach its goal of educating the psychological and legal professions and the general public about important developments in psychology and law. The focus of the book series reflects the diversity of the field of psychology and law, as we published books on a broad range of topics.

In the latest book in the series, *The Jury Under Fire: Myth, Controversy, and Reform*, Brian Bornstein and Edie Greene review 13 different myths or controversial beliefs about juries that have been prevalent in recent years, provide a discussion of relevant empirical research that calls the beliefs into question, and consider the implications for justice system reform. The chapters cover both criminal and civil trials and include detailed discussions of jury duty (Chapter 2), jury selection (Chapter 3), and jury structure (Chapter 4); types of evidence, including eyewitness testimony (Chapter 5), confession evidence (Chapter 6), and expert testimony (Chapter 7); the defendant's age (Chapter 8); compensation (Chapter 9) and punishment (Chapter 10) in civil trials; criminal punishment (Chapter 11); law and emotion (Chapter 12); decision making by judges versus juries (Chapter 13); jury reforms (Chapter 14); and the reasons why myths about the jury persist (Chapter 15).

Bornstein and Greene begin by providing an introduction to the topic of jury trials, including the historical context as well as a primer on methodology used in jury research. Each chapter then highlights a different myth about juries, and provides a discussion of both the relevant empirical research that has accumulated on the topic as well as a discussion of the implications for reform. Bornstein and Greene provide unique insights into jury-related issues and justice system reforms.

The Jury Under Fire: Myth, Controversy, and Reform presents a comprehensive and detailed analysis of issues most relevant to improving the jury system and justice system reforms. Scholars, researchers, policymakers, and practitioners will undoubtedly find that this book has the potential to help to shape the future of interactions with the legal system.

Patricia A. Zapf
Series Editor

Acknowledgments

We published our first book on jurors in 2003. Since that time, a wealth of new research has been conducted, and courts and policymakers have debated and implemented a number of reforms. As active jury researchers, we are pleased by the growing academic and public interest in juries, but we have occasionally been dismayed by the shortsightedness and false assumptions of some of the reform efforts. Juries are not a perfect social institution, but they are an important one, and attempts to improve jury behavior should be made only after a great deal of thought and consideration of empirical evidence. Our goals in writing this book have been to summarize that evidence and to reflect deeply on the jury, in order to inform reform efforts and counter widespread myths about the jury. Ultimately, of course, our objective is to enhance the chances that jury trials will deliver true justice.

Writing is often described as a solitary endeavor, and in many ways it is. But many people contribute to the final product, either directly or indirectly. Colleagues provide feedback; students challenge our thinking; editors smooth the rough edges and oversee the production process; and friends and family members offer encouragement and respite. We benefited enormously from the contributions of all of these people, and our book is the better for it.

We are especially indebted to Patty Zapf, editor of the American Psychology-Law Society book series, and Sarah Harrington, editor for Oxford University Press. We also thank Oxford associate editor, Andrea Zekus, and production editor, Devi Vaidyanathan. Portions of the work were presented in invited talks at the Cornell University Department of Human Development,

University of Alabama in Huntsville Department of Psychology, University of Nevada, Reno Criminal Justice Department, New York University School of Law, and University of Wyoming School of Law. We received valuable feedback from colleagues and students at each place, and we thank Valerie Hans and Valerie Reyna (Cornell), Jeff Neuschatz (UAH), Monica Miller (UNR), Cathy Sharkey (NYU), and Narina Nuñez (Wyoming) for arranging the visits. Monica Miller's jury class at UNR provided a number of insightful comments on drafts of several chapters.

We are also indebted to one another. Although it seems strange to acknowledge one's co-author—it feels like thanking oneself—the book is much better for being the product of two heads rather than one. Working on the book together has also strengthened an already gratifying personal and professional relationship, and for that we are appreciative.

For part of the time while working on the book, Brian Bornstein was supported by a Faculty Development Leave from the University of Nebraska-Lincoln.

As always, we are grateful for our families—Christie, Lillian and Melissa, and Alan, David and Becca—whose love and support sustain us.

The Jury Under Fire

1

Introduction

"No matter how strong the objections to the American jury system, it is not going away. It is firmly ensconced in our state and federal constitutions, history, and traditions.... The American jury system will endure. The most important debates are the ones that discuss how to make that system better."

(Jonakait, 2003, p. xxiv)

Jury trials are something of a paradox. They are central to the American form of government—mentioned in the Bill of Rights and existing in England for centuries before that—yet heavily criticized for their perceived flaws and imperfections. They are being adopted by countries around the world but are steadily declining in the United States. Many people dread being called for jury duty and do what they can to get out of it, but those who serve find the process rewarding and subsequently show higher rates of civic engagement. Juries capture the public imagination and media attention like few other public phenomena (witness, for instance, the long-running *Law and Order* television shows), but most trials are nothing like the ones most Americans hear the most about. Attorneys who are successful at trying cases before a jury, like Clarence Darrow, Gerry Spence, Melvin Belli, Morris Dees, Johnnie Cochran, and William Kunstler, are legendary (and even judges in celebrated jury trials attain a measure of fame—quick, who was the judge in O.J. Simpson's murder trial?[1]), but most attorneys nowadays rarely if ever see

---

[1] Answer: California Judge Lance Ito. And it is probably no exaggeration to say that people remember O.J. Simpson more for his second career as a high-profile criminal and civil defendant (murder, wrongful death, armed robbery) than for his first career as a record-setting and Hall of Fame NFL running back.

the inside of a courtroom. Many efforts to reform the criminal and civil justice systems target juries, but only a tiny fraction of legal actions go to trial, let alone involve a jury. These very contradictions are a large part of what makes the jury so fascinating.

Although the jury is often referred to as one of the bulwarks of the American justice system (Abramson, 1994; Amar, 1998; Jonakait, 2003), it regularly comes under attack. Many recent changes to trial procedures, such as reducing juries' size, allowing non-unanimous verdicts, letting jurors take notes and ask questions, and rewriting jury instructions in plain English, were designed to promote greater efficiency and adherence to the law. Other changes, such as capping damages and replacing jurors with judges as arbiters in complex trials, seem designed to restrict the role of laypeople in dispute resolution. Whether these procedural innovations are motivated by a desire to facilitate the administration of justice or a belief that juries have excessive power and make irrational decisions, they raise a host of empirical questions about the measures' effects on juries' judgments and, ultimately, about their effects on justice. They also raise psychological questions about how people—specifically, jurors—make complex and highly consequential decisions. Policymakers sometimes make assumptions about jury behavior that reflect misunderstanding, ignorance, or deliberate disregard of how people process and evaluate evidence, with the result that some reform efforts have had surprising and unintended consequences (e.g., Saks, 1989; 1992a).

This book reviews a number of controversial beliefs, or myths, about juries that have been prevalent in recent years, as well as the implications of those views for jury reform. Contemporaneously with the development and persistence of these myths, a sizeable literature using empirical methodology (e.g., jury simulations, archival analysis, field studies, juror interviews) has accrued over the last several decades, and the findings of these studies can and should challenge misguided views of the jury. They can also inform reform efforts or, alternatively, show that certain reforms are unnecessary and misguided. Most importantly, scholarly research can be marshaled to craft reforms that enhance the rationality and predictability of the jury system.

In this introductory chapter we provide a brief historical overview of the jury, including common criticisms and myths that have been prevalent over the years. We address the question of why the study of juries is important, especially in light of recent research indicating that jury trials are on the wane. Having argued that both juries and jury research are important, we then summarize the various methods by which researchers study jurors. The chapter concludes with an overview of the remainder of the book.

Juries and Jury Reform in Historical Context

The origin of jury trials is difficult to pinpoint precisely, but they go back at least as far as thirteenth-century England, if not to the Norman conquest in the eleventh century or even earlier (for historical reviews of the jury system and a discussion of many of the pros and cons of trial by jury, see Landsman, 1993; 2002; Vidmar, 2000a; Vidmar & Hans, 2007). Not surprisingly, given such a long history, the jury has evolved substantially over time, with changes in the jury's size, composition (e.g., who is eligible to serve), and procedures. As England exported its culture to its colonies, the jury system took hold around the world, including in the American colonies and subsequent United States, where it became part of the Bill of Rights.

The right to a jury trial is enshrined in the Sixth (for criminal) and Seventh (for civil) Amendments to the U.S. Constitution, which read as follows:

Sixth Amendment: In all criminal prosecutions, the accused shall enjoy the right to a speedy and public trial, by an impartial jury of the State and district wherein the crime shall have been committed, which district shall have been previously ascertained by law, and to be informed of the nature and cause of the accusation; to be confronted with the witnesses against him; to have compulsory process for obtaining witnesses in his favor, and to have the Assistance of Counsel for his defense.

Seventh Amendment: In suits at common law, where the value in controversy shall exceed twenty dollars, the right of trial by jury shall be preserved, and no fact tried by a jury, shall be otherwise re-examined in any court of the United States, than according to the rules of the common law.

Although some of the language is open to interpretation, such as the precise meaning of "speedy" and "impartial," the Amendments' gist is clear—criminal defendants and civil litigants have the right to trial by jury, and the jury's decision is, for all intents and purposes, final. These rights are not absolute. The Sixth Amendment does not guarantee jury trials for petty criminal offenses, which are operationalized as those carrying a potential punishment of less than six months in prison, or for juvenile offenders. And although the Sixth Amendment applies to both state and federal criminal trials, the Seventh Amendment applies only federally, meaning that the kinds of cases in which citizens have the right to a jury trial when resolving state civil claims is more variable, depending on each state's constitution (Jonakait, 2003). Nonetheless, jury trials in both federal and state courts, for civil and criminal matters, have clearly been an essential element of the American justice system ever since there has been an American justice system.

Longevity and entrenchment do not, in and of themselves, make a social institution either desirable or undesirable, of course. But in a system where institutions can and do change (e.g., before juries existed, disputes were resolved by methods like trial by ordeal), persistence is arguably a virtue. "The civil jury is virtually the only Anglo-American adjudicatory device to have functioned serviceably for more than 900 years. Its long history reflects not the endurance of a sanctified relic but the adaptability of a decision-making mechanism that affords society substantial and unique benefits" (Landsman, 2002, p. 873). Landsman's comment could have been made equally well about the criminal jury. Juries have existed for hundreds of years, so presumably they offer some advantages: limitations on governmental authority, citizen engagement, application of community standards, and so forth.

To be sure, this does not mean that juries are perfect arbiters of justice. As Diamond (2003, p. 155) observes, "The presence of both the civil and criminal jury in the Bill of Rights does not deny the capacity for jury error." Because of this capacity for error, as well as the perception that juries are unqualified and susceptible to bias, they have been criticized essentially for as long as they have been resolving legal disputes. For example, nineteenth-century critics, such as Matthew Deady and Mark Twain, opined that the jury had outlived its usefulness, and the corporate and commercial classes have long perceived juries as biased against them (Jonakait, 2003). As in so many things, few expressed the matter as succinctly and cleverly as Twain: "The jury system puts a ban upon intelligence and honesty, and a premium upon ignorance, stupidity and perjury. It is a shame that we must continue to use a worthless system because it was good a thousand years ago."[2] The timing of Twain's criticism is not coincidental—the Industrial Revolution in the late nineteenth century was a time of great business growth, which was associated with business-friendly legislation and efforts to expand judicial power while restricting that of juries, especially in civil cases (Landsman, 1993; Vidmar & Hans, 2007). It was also a time of growing professionalization in the judiciary and a movement to allow outsiders (women and African Americans) to serve on juries (Marder, 2013). All of these social forces contributed to criticisms of the jury and efforts to limit its reach and power.

After a quiescent period during much of the twentieth century, criticism of the jury, particularly in civil cases, picked up again in the last quarter of the century, continuing into the early twenty-first century (Bornstein & Robicheaux, 2008; Greene & Bornstein, 2003; Vidmar & Hans, 2007). As with any large-scale trend, the causes of this most recent contentiousness are complex. Leading candidates include legal developments facilitating certain kinds of litigation (e.g., class actions); increases in corporate litigation and highly publicized "mega verdicts" in civil cases (see Chapters 9 and 10); growing societal attention to the problem of false convictions in criminal cases; highly publicized cases in which many people felt the jury got it wrong (e.g., O.J. Simpson's murder trial); and gradual acceptance by courts and policymakers that some trial procedures, such as the means of summoning,

---

[2] The quotation is from *Roughing It*. For this and additional Twain quotes on the jury, see http://www.twainquotes.com/Jury.html. In a *New York Tribune* piece, he also said, "The humorist who invented trial by jury played a colossal practical joke upon the world, but since we have the system we ought to try and respect it. A thing which is not thoroughly easy to do, when we reflect that by command of the law a criminal juror must be an intellectual vacuum, attached to a melting heart and perfectly macaronian bowels of compassion."

selecting, and instructing jurors, are not very user-friendly (see Chapters 2, 3, and 14).

As a public institution it is entirely proper for the jury to receive significant scrutiny. Yet many widespread perceptions of the jury are simply wrong (Bornstein & Robicheaux, 2008; Diamond, 2003; 2006; Kozinski, 2015). These jury myths are dangerous in a number of respects. They can lead legislatures and courts to implement misguided reforms and neglect innovations that would yield demonstrable benefit; lead citizens to avoid serving on a jury or to have false expectations if they do serve; and lead criminal defendants, civil litigants, and attorneys to settle, plead, or opt for a jury or a bench trial for the wrong reasons. Sixteen years into the twenty-first century, the time is ripe for a fresh consideration of the myths and controversies surrounding jury behavior.

Some mechanisms for correcting jury error exist, such as judgment notwithstanding the verdict, *additur/remittitur* (see Chapters 9 and 10), and appeal. Courts can also implement procedural safeguards (e.g., more comprehensible instructions, bifurcation) to improve jury decision making, and legislative, judicial, and law enforcement bodies frequently promulgate reforms designed to produce fairer verdicts (e.g., caps on damages, specific procedures for conducting eyewitness lineups). Many judges, who naturally are keenly aware of the challenges facing juries, are also advocates for reform (e.g., Kaye, 2008; Kozinski, 2015). Yet the reform mechanisms are not foolproof, as the growing number of falsely convicted criminal defendants attests (see Chapters 5 and 6), and well-intentioned reforms can even have adverse, unintended consequences. There is also a tendency to scapegoat juries for more systemic problems (Bornstein & Robicheaux, 2008; Landsman, 2008; Marder, 2005). For example, popular tort reform concerns like healthcare costs, class action litigation, and science in the courtroom are perfectly legitimate but ultimately have little to do with juries (Bornstein & Robicheaux, 2008).

On the other hand, many reform concerns have a great deal to do with juries, and those concerns are often well-founded: jurors' comprehension of instructions and some kinds of testimony (e.g., expert testimony) is poor; evidence does not always matter as much as it should, and nonevidentiary factors (e.g., litigant characteristics) sometimes matter more than they should; and procedural variables, such as jury selection, size, and decision rule, can affect trial outcomes. Without a doubt, then, there is room for improvement. In criticizing some jury reforms, we do not at all mean to imply that "reform" is a dirty word. Certain evidence-based reforms, which we discuss throughout the book (and especially in Chapter 14), have yielded demonstrable benefits to jury behavior and the administration of justice.

A low opinion of the jury is so pervasive that the jury is a frequent butt of jokes. In her analysis of jury humor, Hans (2013) identifies four major themes: jurors are not the best and the brightest, juries underperform, juries apply commonsense justice, and juries are a vehicle for poking fun at the law more broadly. Notably, the first two themes explicitly cast jurors' performance in a negative light, and the last two, while more positive in one sense, still portray jurors as an integral part of a dysfunctional system. Consider, for instance, the defendant who opted for a jury trial over a bench trial because "that's where twelve ignorant people decide my fate instead of one" (Hans, 2013, p. 409). As Hans observes, such jokes reinforce a jaundiced view of the law and perpetuate myths about the jury, such as that most people try to avoid jury duty and, if they cannot avoid it, do a poor job and get little out of the experience.

These myths are perpetuated further by popular accounts. In the current information age, trials involving noteworthy parties (e.g., celebrities, athletes, politicians), those with high stakes (e.g., death penalty, punitive damages, class actions), and those tapping into important social issues (e.g., police misconduct, racial discrimination) garner considerable publicity. In twenty-first-century America we take this news coverage for granted. Consider, for example, the trial of George Zimmerman, the Florida man who was prosecuted in 2013 for second-degree murder in the 2012 shooting death of Trayvon Martin. A Google search (conducted on 10/28/15) for "George Zimmerman trial" yielded approximately 1.1 million results. The shooting, trial (Zimmerman was acquitted), and subsequent protests received an enormous amount of news coverage and commentary from a great many people, including President Barack Obama. While we by no means intend to diminish the gravity of the incident or the important discussions it spawned regarding race in the United States (Zimmerman was White, Martin was Black), self-defense laws (Zimmerman claimed that Martin attacked him), and jury procedures (e.g., jury size; see Diamond, 2013), it is worth noting that according to the Florida Department of Law Enforcement, there were 1,009 murders in the state in 2012. Martin's death, while tragic and arguably (despite the jury's verdict) criminal, was not particularly heinous. There was a single victim, and the killing was not premeditated or unusually brutal.

Why, then, did the trial receive so much attention? We would wager that if it had taken place in 1813, 1913, or even 1983 instead of 2013, it simply would not have come to the notice of many people beyond Seminole County, Florida.[3] The trial of Dr. George Webster, discussed by Vidmar and Hans (2007), provides a useful comparison. Webster was a Harvard Medical College professor who was prosecuted in 1850 for the murder and dismemberment of a friend and colleague. The trial aroused a high degree of public interest, and an estimated 60,000 people observed some portion of the 12-day trial. But if you lived away from Boston—say in Lincoln, Nebraska

---

[3] Chances are that the contested shooting death of a Black teenager by a White man would not even have been prosecuted in Florida (which became a state in 1845), or many other states, in 1813 or 1913—considered in this light, Zimmerman's trial is a clear sign of society's progress.

or Manitou Springs, Colorado, where the authors reside (in 1850, neither Nebraska [1867] nor Colorado [1876] was even a state)—if you heard about the case at all, it would probably be from a short article in a months-old newspaper; that is, if you could even read, given the higher illiteracy rate of the day. In contrast, like many other Americans, we learned ample information about the Zimmerman trial from our local and national newspapers, local and national television coverage, and the Internet as the trial unfolded, more or less in real time.

We are neither historians nor media scholars, and we recognize that the rapid and voluminous dissemination of information has many advantages— yet it has disadvantages as well. With regard to jury trials, studies show that certain types of cases, such as capital trials and civil trials with very large damage awards, receive disproportionate media coverage (Bailis & MacCoun, 1996; Haney, 2005; MacCoun, 2006; Robbennolt & Studebaker, 2003; see Chapters 10 and 11). This distorted depiction of jury verdicts contributes to the creation of urban legends, whereby people come to perceive low-frequency trials (e.g., medical malpractice) as more common than they actually are, and specific verdicts (e.g., the McDonald's hot coffee case) as more outrageous than they actually were (Bornstein & Robicheaux, 2008; Diamond, 2003; Galanter, 1998). The resultant false impressions and expectations about juries can influence the behavior of victims, plaintiffs, and defendants (e.g., in deciding whether to file a criminal complaint or civil claim), attorneys (e.g., in managing settlement and plea negotiations), judges (e.g., in empaneling a jury), and the jurors themselves (e.g., in determining what constitutes a "fair" verdict). Thus, the media contribute to jury myths, and those myths can have very dangerous consequences.

The perception of juries' inadequacy is sometimes used to turn one of the purported advantages of the jury—decision by a tribunal of laypersons, unschooled in the law—into an argument in favor of professional jurists (see Chapter 13). The purview of criminal juries has remained relatively intact, but a number of reforms have constrained the civil jury's role in dispute resolution (Landsman, 2002). In short, the jury is, and has always been, controversial. Perhaps no other institution is simultaneously as sanctified and vilified as the jury. After centuries of jury verdicts and condemnation of juries, the debate continues. Is the jury a vestigial remnant of an outmoded system that serves no useful purpose, essentially the justice system's appendix? Or is its persistence in the face of such withering criticism proof positive of its value? Empirical research on juries can help to answer these questions.

Why Study Juries?

Jury trials have always been rare. For example, of 7.4 million civil claims filed in state courts nationwide in 2005, only 26,950 were disposed of by trial; of those, juries decided approximately 70% of the cases (Langton &

Cohen, 2008). Juries hear some types of cases more than others. Tort trials are especially likely to be decided by a jury, as opposed to a judge; 90% of tort cases that go to trial are decided by a jury (Langton & Cohen, 2008). In contrast, most contract cases (64%) are decided by a judge (Langton & Cohen, 2008). The vast majority of criminal charges likewise do not wind up before a jury. In all but a small proportion of cases, the charges are dropped or the defendant pleads guilty. According to the U.S. Sentencing Commission, for instance, roughly 97% of all criminal sentences (excluding petty offenses and death sentences) result from a guilty plea (United States Sentencing Commission, 2015).

Data also show that the number of trials has diminished over the past 50 years, a trend that has accelerated since the mid-1980s, in both absolute (i.e., total number) and relative terms (i.e., as a percentage of all case dispositions; Galanter 2004; Galanter & Frozena, 2011; Langton & Cohen, 2008). For example, Langton and Cohen found that the number of general civil cases disposed of by trial (both jury and bench trials) in state courts declined by 50% from 1992 to 2005. Recent data suggest that the number of jury trials may be declining even more rapidly: Of more than 900,000 civil cases disposed of between July 2012 and June 2013 in 10 urban counties in the United States, only 4% were decided by a trial, and 97% of those were bench trials (National Center for State Courts, 2015). The proportion of cases resolved at trial in federal courts, both civil and criminal, has likewise declined over the last half-century or so (Galanter, 2004). Again, this is true for both bench and jury trials. Many factors contribute to the phenomenon, particularly an increase in alternative dispute resolution (e.g., mediation, arbitration) and other nontrial dispositions (e.g., settlement, plea agreement, summary judgment). Figures showing a decline in the number of trials arouse concern that trials in general, and civil jury trials in particular, are a vanishing breed that is nearing extinction (e.g., Galanter, 2004; Galanter & Frozena, 2011). A comparable pattern of declining jury trials exists in England (Vidmar & Hans, 2007).

Accordingly, serving on a jury is a relatively infrequent experience for most Americans, although being summoned is not so rare. Approximately 650,000 people are called for jury duty each year in New York alone (Kaye, 2008). The majority of them will not actually be empaneled on a jury, but they are nonetheless participating in the system. Rose, Diamond, and Musick (2012) investigated how often people actually are called for jury duty and the extent to which they end up participating. In their random sample of 1,380 jury-eligible Texas adults (M age = 43), only 26% had ever served on a jury. Of the remainder, 35% had never been summoned, 29% had been summoned but not questioned, and 10% had been questioned but excused (see Chapter 3). Among those who had ever served on a jury, the mean number of trials was 2.33, with a mode and median of one. If jury trials are so rare and most citizens will serve on a jury at most one time, why bother understanding how juries work?

There are a number of compelling arguments for why juries matter (Devine, 2012; Greene & Bornstein, 2003; Kovera, 2017; Vidmar & Hans, 2007). Despite their diminishing frequency in American courtrooms, hundreds of thousands of trials take place each year in federal and state courtrooms, and a significant number of those involve a jury (Galanter, 2004; Galanter & Frozena, 2011). Meanwhile, although jury trials are decreasing in the United States, their use, and related systems of lay adjudication, are increasing elsewhere (Hans, Fukurai, Ivkovich, & Park, 2017; Kaplan & Martin, 2006; Marder, 2011; Vidmar, 2000b). More than 50 countries employ jury systems, more often for criminal than for civil cases; in just the last decade they have been adopted in countries ranging from Argentina to South Korea and Georgia, with other countries adopting or increasing their use of mixed tribunals consisting of laypeople and professional judges (Hans et al., 2017; Vidmar & Hans, 2007).

One of the reasons for juries' growing popularity is that they serve an important educative function (Kaye, 2008; Marder, 2011). Serving on a jury may be rare, but for citizens whose work does not involve the legal system, other real-life encounters with the courts (e.g., as litigants or witnesses) are rarer still. Understanding how juries work can lead directly to reforms to make them work better, which will enhance this educational function. Relatedly, jury service is a form of direct democratic participation that helps to legitimize the justice system (Abramson, 1994; Amar, 1998; Gastil, Deess, Weiser, & Simmons, 2010). Following jury service, citizens show increased civic engagement, such as a greater tendency to vote (Gastil et al., 2010). This is especially true for criminal jurors (Gastil et al., 2010), as well as for some civil jurors (e.g., those who serve on 12-person juries or on juries with a unanimous decision rule; Hans, Gastil, & Feller, 2014).

A jury's reach can also extend well beyond the lives of the immediate trial participants. Potential criminals might consider their odds of being convicted at trial in deciding whether to break the law in the first place (other factors would probably be a more crucial part of the cost-benefit analysis, such as the probability of being caught and the potential punishment and benefits; see Becker, 1968). More proximally, the anticipated trial outcome almost certainly enters into a criminal defendant's decision whether to accept a plea bargain and a prosecutor's decision to offer one, as well as a civil litigant's decision whether to make or accept a settlement offer. Actual and anticipated jury trial outcomes influence the choice of decision maker (i.e., judge or jury) and even the behavior of individuals and corporations (e.g., if an automobile manufacturer anticipates paying hefty sums in products liability trials, then it might improve its products' safety). Attorneys' perceptions of the predictability of jury verdicts can shape their decisions about whether to take a case and how and where to try it (Hans & Eisenberg, 2011). From citizens' perspective, even if they do not serve on a jury themselves, the knowledge that juries are one of the mechanisms by which citizens have a voice could contribute to their general satisfaction with government.[4] Thus, it is clear that the jury casts a long shadow (Galanter, 1987).

Finally, juries are a means of gauging community sentiment toward certain behaviors (Reed & Bornstein, 2015). Some charges, such as obscenity, make explicit reference to community standards. Even when community sentiment is not explicitly invoked, the jury has the power to reject laws that it deems unjust, a process known as jury nullification (see Chapter 12). One perspective on the civil justice system, in which juries (or judges) decide whether and how much one party should pay another, is as a means of implementing community preferences about wealth (re)distribution (Hans, 2014). From this perspective, the civil jury enables citizens to serve a political function (Hans, 2014; Solomon, 2012). Precisely because juries consist of ordinary citizens, they represent the larger community and provide a vehicle for determining shifting social attitudes; the behavior of professional magistrates would offer little insight into popular sentiment.

Despite their declining numbers, jury trials globally and in the United States are far from extinct. But just how vulnerable is the jury? Under the Endangered Species Act (16 U.S.C. § 1531, Section 3), a species is endangered if it is "in danger of extinction throughout all or a significant portion of its range." It is threatened if it is "likely to become an endangered species within the foreseeable future throughout all or a significant portion of its range." By this definition, jury trials do not appear to be endangered; but at least in the American portion of their range, they are definitely threatened.

A Jury Research Methodology Primer

Jury researchers come from multiple disciplines—psychology, sociology, political science, communications, law—and they use a variety of research techniques (for review, see Devine, 2012; Kovera, 2017). Four of the most common methods use real jurors who are reaching or have already reached a verdict: direct observation of functioning juries, case studies and/or posttrial juror interviews, archival analyses of datasets of jury verdicts, and field studies. The fifth and final widespread method uses mock jurors to simulate the behavior of actual jurors. In this method, jurors are essentially role-playing and making hypothetical decisions without actual consequences for the parties involved.

Each of these research approaches has its pros and cons (Bornstein, 1999; 2017; Bornstein & McCabe, 2005; Diamond, 1997; 2006; Diamond & Salerno, 2013; MacCoun, 1989; Vidmar, 2008). Direct observation offers a window

---

[4] Compare, for example, the prospect of having your case decided by a visible and identifiable jury of your peers with the prospect of having it decided by the nameless, faceless, and inaccessible authorities in Franz Kafka's novel *The Trial.*

on jury behavior as it happens, but with rare exceptions it is impermissible. Case studies based on posttrial interviews provide rich qualitative data but do not clearly generalize to other cases and are susceptible to jurors' memory bias. Archival analyses allow inferences based on large amounts of real-world data, but they are limited to whatever variables the datasets happen to contain, and they are ultimately correlational. Experimental simulations permit rigorous experimental control and causal inferences, but they have a hard time capturing the richness and complexity of actual trials, and mock jurors might differ in systematic ways from jurors whose decisions have real consequences. Field studies, in which courts randomly assign juries to different experimental conditions, are the best of both worlds in some respects, as they retain experimental control within the context of actual trials. However, they are difficult to conduct because they require the courts' cooperation, and it might not be feasible to manipulate some variables of interest (e.g., type of charge, jury size, jury composition).

Another important way in which research techniques differ is the unit of analysis—the jury as a single group entity or as a collection of individual jurors. Case studies generally focus on feedback from individual jurors, whereas archival studies contain only the final group-level jury verdict. The other methods potentially allow researchers to examine the reasoning and verdict preferences of individual jurors as well as jury verdicts. Direct observation and experimental simulations can even provide data on the deliberation process itself, by which jurors' personal reactions are shaped into a jury verdict. Whether it is more appropriate to study individual jurors or deliberating juries depends, more than anything else, on the underlying research question (Diamond 2006; Salerno & Diamond, 2010). Some things, such as comprehension of jury instructions, can be investigated and modeled well at the individual level; other things, such as the effect on verdicts of jury size and decision rule, or the role of social influence in juries, can only be understood at the group level.

Because real juries must necessarily reach a group decision, studies providing jury-level data are more ecologically valid; however, they entail a severe reduction in statistical power (e.g., a jury of six provides one data point versus six data points from individual jurors) and are logistically more complicated (e.g., deliberation takes longer and requires a certain number of persons). Of course, they are not necessarily exclusive—one could obtain judgments from individual jurors in addition to having them deliberate, and some observational, field, and simulation studies have taken this approach. But because of the drawbacks of jury studies, research on individual jurors is more common, especially within the experimental simulation tradition.

The multiplicity of methods for studying juries is an enormous advantage. Courts and policymakers are often skeptical of social science research on juries (Monahan & Walker, 2014). Multiple methods appeal to the principle of convergence, meaning that if findings from diverse approaches are consistent, then we—researchers, courts, policymakers, and the public— can be more confident that they accurately represent the true state of affairs

(Bornstein, 2017). The jury research summarized in the succeeding chapters draws on all of these methods. As experimental psychologists, we have spent more time conducting jury simulations than engaging in the other methods. Reviews of the literature also suggest that simulations are the most widely used research approach (e.g., Devine, 2012; Nietzel, McCarthy, & Kerr, 1999), although archival studies in particular, born of the empirical legal studies movement, have increased rapidly in recent years (Eisenberg, 2011; Suchman & Mertz, 2010). Yet we wholeheartedly endorse the other methods and include research using them where it is available.

Regardless of the particular research approach taken, it is usually difficult, if not impossible, to determine whether a jury reached the "right" verdict. Even the most seemingly conclusive evidence, such as a confession (see Chapter 6) or DNA test (see Chapter 7), is not entirely foolproof. Thus, there is no gold standard for judging a jury's verdict (Bornstein & Greene, 2011a; Diamond, 2003; Kozinski, 2015). There are, however, several indirect means of assessing jury performance. A few of the most common methods are to measure jurors' comprehension, to assess their reliance on evidence vis-à-vis nonevidentiary sources of information, and to compare their decisions to those of experts (Bornstein & Greene, 2011a). In other words, do they understand what they are supposed to do (see Chapter 14), do they process information as intended (see Chapters 4–12), and do they perform as well as judges (see Chapter 13)? Research techniques vary in how effectively they address these questions. For example, archival research is very good at comparing the verdicts of judges and juries, moderately effective at gauging the effects of different factors on jury verdicts, and not so good at measuring comprehension, whereas jury simulations are very good at gauging the effects of various legal and extralegal factors, moderately effective at measuring comprehension, but not so good at comparing judges and juries. Again, having a diversity of methods at researchers' disposal is beneficial.

All of these ways of assessing jury performance are informative, but ultimately, the key questions (or two sides of the same question) are as follows: Do juries properly consider evidence they are supposed to consider and make decisions as the law intends? And do juries properly ignore factors that they are not supposed to consider? The evidence that they are supposed to consider is reasonably well circumscribed by the rules of evidence and trial procedure. The good news is that the strength of the evidence is the major determinant of jury verdicts; this has been known since Kalven and Zeisel's (1966) seminal research and reaffirmed many times since (e.g., Devine, 2012; Devine et al., 2001; Greene & Bornstein, 2003). Evidence strength influences the judgments of individual jurors as well as the jury as a group (e.g., Landsman, Diamond, Dimitropoulos, & Saks, 1998).

The not-so-good news is that procedural variations (e.g., jury size, decision rule, instructions) and extralegal factors (e.g., litigant characteristics, pretrial publicity, the manner of presenting evidence, jurors' emotional responses) matter as well, and they exert their greatest effect when the evidence is close or ambiguous (Devine et al., 2001; 2009). According to Kalven and Zeisel (1966), clear evidence (i.e., weak or strong) dictates the outcome, but when it is unclear, jurors are "liberated" from evidentiary constraints, creating room for extraneous and potentially biasing factors to operate. The rub is that virtually all cases that make it to trial are at least somewhat close; otherwise they would be dropped, dismissed, settled, or pleaded out. And once a case gets to trial, there is no limit to the number of extraneous factors that might come into play, depending on the issues at hand. The evidence that jurors should consider is carefully regulated; the evidence that they should *not* consider is, quite literally, infinite. Many of the myths about juries concern assumptions about their ability to sort factors that they should consider from those they should not.

Overview of the Book

Except for the concluding chapter, each of the book's chapters presents a widespread myth about the jury, followed by a discussion of relevant empirical research that calls the belief into question. The chapter then discusses implications for justice system reform. The chapters cover both criminal and civil trials.

Chapter 2 addresses what is perhaps the most pervasive jury myth; namely, that people dread jury duty and do what they can to get out of it. This belief has led to efforts both to penalize citizens who ignore their jury summons and to make jury service more palatable (e.g., by increasing juror compensation). The truth is that although some citizens are reluctant to serve, deliberate attempts to undermine the process are rare. Moreover, jury service produces a number of benefits, such as a high degree of juror satisfaction with their experience and greater civic engagement more broadly. This is not to say that jury service is without its costs, especially for relatively long or difficult trials (e.g., capital trials, trials with complex or gruesome evidence). This chapter reviews innovations that can make jury service a more rewarding experience for jurors and, ultimately, a more just process for those whose cases jurors decide.

Once jurors arrive for jury duty, the next step is typically jury selection (also referred to as *voir dire*), covered in Chapter 3. To provide an impartial jury as guaranteed by the Constitution, the legal system has devised procedures for identifying and removing prospective jurors who have affiliations or allegiances to the litigants, racial or gender biases, or who have been tainted by media coverage. These procedures, termed *challenges for cause* and *peremptory challenges*, rest on the assumption that prospective jurors, attorneys, and judges can accurately gauge their own and others' objectivity and impartiality. Increasingly, empirical research has challenged this assumption. Jurors are ill equipped to evaluate their own impartiality, and attorneys have difficulty deducing the predispositions and verdict leanings of prospective jurors. In addition, even though the Constitution prohibits using peremptory challenges based solely on a juror's race/ethnicity or gender, attorneys are adept at generating race- or gender-neutral explanations to justify their challenges. Reform proposals for improving jury selection procedures range from eliminating peremptory challenges altogether to increasing the amount of diagnostic information about jurors available to attorneys.

Chapter 4 addresses variations in jury structure; specifically, the belief that smaller and non-unanimous juries are just as good as (and maybe even better than) 12-person juries that have to reach a unanimous verdict. Debate about the optimal size of juries and the preferred decision rule was spawned by a series of controversial United States Supreme Court decisions in the early 1970s and has simmered since then. Six-person juries are now quite common in civil trials as well as in criminal trials for less serious offenses, and unanimity is no longer a universal requirement. But research reviewed in the chapter reveals several important differences between juries varying in size and decision rule, such as that larger juries are more likely to contain at least one member of a minority group, deliberate for a longer period, discuss more of the trial testimony, and collectively recall more of the evidence. Changes to jury size and decision rule entail both costs and benefits that policymakers should factor into their considerations.

The next three chapters focus on trials containing specific kinds of evidence: eyewitness testimony (Chapter 5), confession evidence (Chapter 6), and expert testimony (Chapter 7). Laypeople, as well as legal professionals, tend to believe that eyewitnesses are reliable. Accordingly, they fail to appreciate many of the factors that predict eyewitness performance and rely instead on nonpredictive factors, especially witness confidence. Nonetheless, courts typically assume that the fallibility of memory is a matter of common sense. Courts also tend to assume that people can distinguish between true confessions and false confessions that result from coercive interrogation methods. However, laypeople are not very adept at making this distinction, and they underestimate the probability that someone would confess to something that he or she did not do. Reform efforts related to the problems of eyewitness testimony and false confessions address improving both the quality of the information itself (e.g., using interview and interrogation techniques that are more likely to elicit accurate information) and jurors' ability to make use of the information (e.g., by jury instructions or other safeguards). Another common approach is to present expert testimony on the reliability of the eyewitness or confession evidence. Expert testimony on these and many other issues is becoming increasingly common as our society becomes more complex and technologically sophisticated. This is especially true of expert scientific testimony. Despite concerns that expert scientific testimony would be unduly influential, in many circumstances jurors underutilize scientific testimony. This research suggests that reform efforts geared toward loosening the strictures on expert testimony would be welcome.

Chapter 8 addresses a factor that is not evidence, per se, but that is none-theless apparent to jurors and can affect their decisions—the defendant's age. Since the mid-1990s states have instituted policies that allow juvenile offend-ers to be tried in adult criminal court, with some states allowing waivers from juvenile to criminal court for juveniles as young as 10 years old for cer-tain offenses. But juveniles transferred from the rehabilitation-oriented juve-nile justice system to the punishment-oriented criminal court system may be at a notable disadvantage, being evaluated more harshly than juveniles tried in juvenile court, or even more harshly than adult offenders charged with the same crime. A system in which juveniles are tried as adults without any acknowledgment of developmental differences may be especially unfair.

Chapters 9 and 10 address the leading myths about civil juries, that their damage awards are excessive and unpredictable in terms of both compensa-tion (Chapter 9) and punishment (Chapter 10). These myths motivate a num-ber of reform efforts, such as caps on damages, increased use of *remittitur* (judicial reduction of an award), and giving only a part of a punitive damage award to the plaintiff (known as *split recovery schemes*). Although jurors might not engage in explicit calculations to arrive at a specific damages award, their approach to quantification is, for the most part, rational and evidence-based, taking into account relevant evidence such as the severity of the plaintiff's injury (for compensation) and the reprehensibility of the defendant's conduct (for punitive damages). In addition, the vast majority of awards are modest in size. Nevertheless, some awards are extremely large, substantial variability exists, and juries sometimes allow evidence that is relevant to one decision to influence another decision (e.g., allowing evidence of the defendant's conduct to influence compensatory damages). Thus, although there is little support for the claim that jury damage awards are either excessive or unpredictable, there is room for improvement. Yet some of the reforms that are designed to accom-plish these goals, such as caps and split recovery schemes, can have unintended consequences under some circumstances, such as undercompensating plaintiffs and paradoxically increasing the size and variability of awards.

Chapter 11, on criminal punishment, parallels Chapter 10's discussion of civil punishment. Although jurors do not sentence the majority of criminal defendants whom they find guilty, they determine sentencing for the most serious crimes, namely capital murder, where the importance of their role has been continually reaffirmed. Granting this power to juries suggests a belief that they can be fair in administering criminal sanctions. Research makes it clear, however, that they struggle with the task. In capital trials, for example, both procedural (e.g., "death qualification") and attitudinal variables can introduce bias. Jurors also have difficulty understanding capital jury instruc-tions, especially with regard to weighing aggravating and mitigating factors, which has led to efforts to revise the instructions (see also Chapter 14). Given the limited effectiveness of instruction revision, more radical reforms might be necessary, such as revamping the death qualification process.

Deciding to sentence a defendant to death is, understandably, an emotional process. Moreover, much evidence in capital trials is likely to arouse jurors' emotions, such as heinousness, remorse, graphic evidence of the victim's injuries, victim impact statements, or a hate crime charge. Emotion is by no means limited to capital trials. Practically any civil or criminal case could include emotional testimony from victims, plaintiffs, or witnesses; emotional pretrial publicity; jurors whose emotional state is affected by the trial or something entirely unrelated (e.g., coming to court in a foul mood because their car would not start); or jurors who are unusually empathetic. Chapter 12 reviews the complex relationship between law and emotion. On the one hand, courts and policymakers often assume that jurors can, and do, make decisions dispassionately, considering only the factual evidence and checking their emotions at the door. Yet on the other hand, there are many instances in which the law allows, and even seems to require, emotion to be part of the decision-making calculus—but only in a carefully circumscribed manner. The chapter considers descriptive, normative, and prescriptive perspectives on the role of emotion in juror decision making. That is, *does* emotion influence jurors (descriptive); *should* emotion influence jurors (normative); and what procedural reforms might improve the ways in which emotion does or does not influence jurors (prescriptive)?

Following up on the preceding chapters, which document some of the ways in which jury decision making is less than ideal, there is often a presumption that judges would do better. Chapter 13 reviews empirical research comparing judges and juries. There is little basis for reform attempts that would remove certain cases from the province of the jury or for holding up judges as the "gold standard" for legal decision making.

A theme running through the previous chapters is that by and large it is not that hard being a juror, and jurors can follow the law. The research shows that is often not the case; rather, jurors struggle with many aspects of their jury service. Some of the reforms we discuss are designed to improve the quality of juror decision making; some of them do have that effect, but others have unintended consequences. A number of traditional safeguards exist to aid jurors, such as cross-examination, jury instructions, and the deliberation process. There are also more innovative techniques, such as bifurcated trials and allowing jurors to ask questions, take notes, or discuss the case prior to deliberation. Chapter 14 reviews research on these reforms and the findings' implications with respect to both the jurors themselves (e.g., their satisfaction and comfort with the process) and trial outcomes (i.e., more just verdicts).

The concluding chapter (Chapter 15) explores reasons why myths about juries persist, summarizes the major themes from the foregoing chapters, highlights areas where future research is needed, and discusses public policy and reform implications. It also identifies the most promising reforms having a strong empirical foundation.

2

Avoid Jury Duty at All Costs

"I will be overjoyed if I can get out of jury duty today. I have zero interest in being a juror. And I'm pretty damn sure that my feelings are shared by most of the other people in this room." (http://hinessight.blogs.com/hinessight/2012/11/i-hate-jury-duty-heres-why.html)

"It is never a good time to serve on a jury."

(Marder, 2015, p. 939)

There is a common belief that jury duty is a burden best avoided, and excoriations of the jury system are easy to find. Just one example will suffice: Josh Barro, a contributor to *Forbes*, posted an article online in 2012 entitled "This is why people hate jury duty." It garnered more than 6,000 views and multiple repostings, and in response several people derived lists of their own reasons to hate jury duty. Indeed, many citizens are reluctant to serve, and others deliberately undermine the jury selection process in order to be excused. But these choices have consequences for court personnel, litigants, and prospective jurors alike. Jury commissioners have difficulty scheduling trials, and litigants are forced to deal with delays and complain that they are not tried by juries of their peers. Avoidant prospective jurors are denied the opportunity to immerse themselves in one of the few forms of participatory democracy that exists, and, ironically, those who *do* serve report that it can be engaging, educational, and enjoyable. Serving on a jury has unanticipated effects on people's willingness to engage in other civic institutions as well. Suffice to say that the general consensus that serving on a jury is an onerous experience begins to fade in the light of empirical scrutiny.

In this chapter, we explain why it matters what the public thinks about jury service and how their opinions affect their willingness to show up, how and why individuals have tended to avoid serving, what people who actually serve on juries report about their experiences, and how court personnel have responded to some of the concerns these jurors have raised. In recent years, with an eye toward improving public perceptions of jury duty, court officials have instituted a number of innovations in the way they communicate with prospective jurors and stage trials for selected jurors. We review what is known about the effectiveness of these reforms. Finally, we describe more broad-based efforts to enhance the image of the jury in the eyes of the public.

Why Public Perceptions of Jury Duty Matter

People tend to act in line with their beliefs. If environmental concerns are important, they opt to recycle and purchase smaller vehicles. If charity is valued, they offer time and money to help others. If patriotism is paramount, they pledge allegiance to and fly the flag, support the troops, and serve in the military. Behaviors are usually, though certainly not always, consistent with attitudes. The same is true of beliefs concerning civic responsibilities and democratic institutions, including the legal system and, by extension, jury trials. If people perceive the jury system as a valued institution that calls on citizens to judge the conduct of their peers and believe that each person has a moral obligation to undertake that responsibility, or if they simply appreciate that the jury is a "bridge between community values and the law" (Abramson, 1994, p. 61), then they would tend to act in accordance with those beliefs and appear at the courthouse when summoned for jury service. If they perceive the jury system as a lawless institution, culturally biased, or mired in formality and legal complexity, then they stay away. Most people fall somewhere between these two extremes.

Long before jurors arrive at a courthouse for *voir dire*, though, most have been exposed to unflattering portrayals of juries and descriptions of juries run amok. Criminal juries are criticized for bringing in unpopular verdicts (Speegle, 2012–13; Uelmen, 1996), and civil juries are routinely attacked by business and insurance interests for awarding excessive damages that inflate insurance rates. These depictions inflame public opinion and influence citizens' evaluations of the jury system, reducing the willingness of some to serve.

Still, nearly 32 million jury summonses are issued each year to approximately 15% of adults in the United States (National Center for State Courts, 2014), and up to one-third of all citizens will serve on juries at some point in their lives (Mize, Hannaford-Agor, & Waters, 2007; Rose, Diamond, & Musick, 2012). The impressions these jurors take from such experiences can have a ripple effect in their communities. If jurors feel that their time was poorly used, facilities were inadequate, the trial process was unclear, or they were not treated respectfully, they will avoid service in the future and share these unfavorable reactions with family, friends, and colleagues (Diamond, 1993). If their involvement was positive, others will learn of it. Given that jury service represents one of the only means by which many people have contact with the legal system, personal experiences and knowledge of others' time in the jury box will inform broader beliefs about the fairness and predictability of the law.

Concerns that prospective jurors express about their service, such as the financial hardship and time commitment, difficulties understanding nuances of the law, and the physical discomfort of prolonged sitting in a sterile courtroom, erode public support for the jury system. But they also point to remediable flaws that court personnel can address (Diamond, 1993). In that regard, juror dissatisfaction can lead to improved experiences for juries in the future, so long as reforms are developed from empirical testing and finely calibrated to encompass jurors' strengths and weaknesses.

There are other, more practical reasons that public perceptions of jury service, particularly among reluctant citizens, matter. Across the country, responses to jury summonses have declined in recent years. In some large cities, including New York City and Los Angeles, only approximately 10% of summoned jurors report for jury selection (Losh & Boatright, 2002). The result is that there are insufficient numbers of jurors for some trials.

One notable occurrence, in Bolivar County, Mississippi, prompted court officials to organize a community gathering to find out why people were reluctant to serve on juries. The impetus for the gathering was a capital murder trial in which the judge had to declare a mistrial and reschedule the case because too few jurors were available for the trial. Of the 250 summonses that were mailed 30 days prior to jury selection, 26% were returned by the U.S. Postal Service as undeliverable. Many prospective jurors were excused for statutorily approved reasons. On the day the trial began, 21% of summoned jurors failed to appear. That left a total of 60 people (24% of those summoned) from whom to select a capital jury. But after a number of them were dismissed for cause, only nine remained (Bolivar County Circuit Court Task Force, 2014), and a capital jury trial requires 12 people and two or three alternates. Clearly, low compliance rates are a serious problem as any civic institution that cannot muster sufficient community support to function effectively (or, as in this case, function at all) is unsustainable. Bolivar County officials wanted to know why, and what they learned can illuminate how the system should change to bring sufficient numbers of jurors to courthouses in the future so that justice may proceed (Bolivar County Circuit Court Task Force, 2014).

Anticipating a poor response from summoned jurors, court officials have had to over-recruit, summoning more prospective jurors than they need. Obviously, this requires more effort on the part of court staff and, in an ironic twist, has the potential to result in a glut of jurors and a wasting of their time.

Scenarios of Evasion

Perceptions of the jury system as an institution are generally negative, and it is easy to find ways that jurors and juries are disparaged in popular culture. In a cartoon drawn by Dan Rosendich, two older men adorned with angels' wings and halos meet in heaven. One says to the other, "It took an accident to get me out of jury duty." In one of Marty Buchella's cartoons, an irate judge leans across his bench and bellows at the defendant "Let me get this straight. You committed the crime to get out of jury duty?"

As mentioned in Chapter 1, cartoons and jokes about juries are so plentiful that Hans (2013) was able to accumulate sufficient numbers to categorize them according to their theme: failures of individual jurors including poor character, low intellect, and lack of civic mindedness; and failures of juries including acquitting guilty defendants, opting not to decide, and erring in the calculation of damages. In general, jury jokes tend to demean the system of trial by jury.

Tweets regarding jury service, most of them lamenting the writer's fate, abound on Twitter (#juryduty). For example:

> Got jury duty in the am I hope I don't get picked !!! :(#juryduty #am #nofun #dontpickmeplz
> Closing in on 2.5 hours of nothing, other than my time being wasted. #juryduty
> Closing out hour 3 here and still absolutely nothing has happened. Civic duty? No like civic punishment. #juryduty
> So far my contribution to jury duty is reading with bad posture and hurting my neck. #juryduty

Disregard for the jury system has become practically normative in television shows and social media. Because of the way that media images saturate our consciousness—millions of Americans watched the evasion tactics of Tina Fey (as Liz Lemon) on "30 Rock" or Larry David on "Curb Your Enthusiasm"—the derogatory messages are both widespread and difficult to challenge. Prospective jurors can get advice on avoiding jury duty at the website Wikihow (http://www.wikihow.com/Get-Out-of-Jury-Duty), which provides eight "secrets for getting out of the obligation." The secrets include playing smart, mentioning jury nullification, and explaining to the judge that one has a pressing, urgent commitment. The site also provides a sample excuse letter that we suspect judges have become rather familiar with by now.

Reluctant jurors can also read books that offer a variety of humorous techniques for evading jury duty (Dustin, 1986; TheAnonymousAttorney. com, 2008). Or they can peruse a blog entry entitled "The Idiot's Guide to Getting out of Jury Duty" which begins with this disclaimer: "By reading the following, I understand that Marshall R. Isaacs [the attorney-blogger] is not encouraging me to attempt to get out of jury duty. To the contrary, Marshall

R. Isaacs has informed me that jury duty is my civic responsibility and has encouraged me to gleefully sit in a crowded room with a bunch of cranky people, many of whom reek of body odor, while my co-workers steal my clients by telling them I've run off with their life savings" (http://theununi-fiedcourtsystem.blogspot.com/2009/03/idiots-guide-to-getting-out-of-jury.html). Derogation of jury service in popular culture, as illustrated by these examples, is likely to have strong and lasting effects on people's willingness to serve. Indeed, in courtrooms all across the United States, these "scenarios of evasion" (Sams, Neal, & Brodsky, 2013, p. 4) thrive.

Many prospective jurors simply disregard their jury summons and fail to show. In a study entitled "The vanishing juror," Seltzer (1999) determined that approximately 20% of Washington D.C. jurors ignore the jury qualification questionnaire altogether (and another 40% did not receive it at all). A study of nearly 2,000 prospective jurors conducted by the Washington State Center for Court Research from late 2006 to early 2008 found that only 46% of respondents complied with their jury summons, and the rate was approximately half that for Latinos and people of Asian descent (Bloeser, McCurley, & Mondak, 2012).

To discern why compliance rates are so low, Losh, Wasserman, and Wasserman (2000) questioned approximately 1,000 Florida residents as they entered the jury assembly room. Respondents included people who had previously tried to postpone or be excused from jury service and failed to appear, as well as others who reported for jury duty without objections. Only 26% said they were glad to be summoned and only one-third anticipated serving as jurors. Nearly half mentioned that jury duty was an inconvenience. Given that this sample was biased toward jurors who actually showed up, the poor showing indicates clearly that jury service has a bad reputation. Still, more than 60% thought they could learn from the experience and agreed that juries represent the voice of the people.

Why People Avoid Serving as Jurors

Inconvenience is an obvious disincentive, with some prospective jurors forecasting that jury duty will be a waste of time because they will be rejected by all parties (Diamond, 1993). Young people are more skeptical of the court system as a whole and less tolerant of the inconvenience of jury duty than older people (Boatright, 2001), presumably because many have childcare responsibilities or are starting careers. Also, older adults have accumulated more personal experiences with the legal system that may bring higher regard for jury service (Losh & Boatright, 2002). Those who are retired also obviously have more time.

Others, particularly those of lower socioeconomic status, cite economic hardships including time away from work and difficulty finding dependent care (Boatright, 1999). People with higher incomes are more likely to comply

(Bloeser et al., 2012), probably because they are more likely to be salaried or to have flexible working hours and have resources to rely on for alternate caregiving and transportation.

Some prospective jurors raise concerns about physical handicaps they associate with jury duty (e.g., difficulty with prolonged sitting, claustrophobia, hearing impairment) and expect that these conditions would hinder their ability to serve. Judges occasionally excuse prospective jurors who have physical ailments and impairments, though sometimes, in an effort to keep them in the jury pool, offer modifications such as longer breaks, more comfortable seating, and the opportunity to stand during the trial. According to common lore, a judge once asked a juror who complained about claustrophobia whether her living room was larger than the courtroom. She remained in the jury box.

Cultural barriers are significant for some summoned jurors, as evidenced by the low rates of minorities who answer their jury summons. Language proficiency can be an issue, in terms of both the language in which the summons is written and anticipated difficulties in understanding testimony and communicating with other jurors, though courts sometimes provide translators for non–English speaking jurors. People who live in ethnic enclaves and who have relatively little direct contact with the broader society may be wary of jury service because they lack confidence in their abilities to serve or anticipate they would not be treated with respect by court personnel (Bloeser et al., 2012; Rose et al., 2012).

Confidence in one's ability to serve on a jury is an important determinant of summons responses. Tracking the responses of more than 400 randomly chosen jury summons recipients in four jurisdictions, Boatright (2001) found that feelings of personal efficacy affected the decision about whether to respond. Specifically, those with a low sense of personal efficacy—who questioned whether they had sufficient knowledge for jury service and would be respected by court personnel and attorneys, and who thought trials would be too complicated—were less likely to respond to their summons than those with a higher sense of efficacy.

Yet another factor, distrust of government, is often associated with lack of political awareness and involvement, making its proponents unlikely to rush to the courthouse when called for jury duty. There may be little personal motivation for jury service among individuals who distrust the government and who devalue the institution that requests their assistance (Burns, Schlozman, & Verba, 2001). Data suggest that political engagement can be a potent factor because people who are apolitical, even if they are otherwise conscientious, tend to steer clear of jury duty (Bloeser et al., 2012). Racial and ethnic minorities have a less trusting opinion of governmental institutions, including the legal system, than whites (Rose, Ellison, & Diamond, 2008) and therefore are less willing to serve. Conversely, people who volunteer in the area of public service—including, for example, service groups like the Rotary, issue-oriented causes like civil rights or women's equality, and community improvement organizations—express more willingness to serve (Musick, Rose, Dury, & Rose, 2015).

Reluctance to serve on a jury may reflect the broader "slipping sense of duty" documented in an Associated Press-Gallup Poll of 1044 adults in the United States conducted in July, 2014 (Associated Press, 2014). Commitment to civic virtues such as reporting crime, volunteering, keeping informed about the news, and serving on a jury has slipped considerably since a similar survey was conducted in 1984. Young people in particular feel less obligation than their counterparts from the past.

Lack of sanctions for failure to respond to a jury summons will also influence compliance rates, and most people do not expect any significant penalty for noncompliance (Bloeser et al., 2012). Sometimes they are surprised. In 2003, Massachusetts residents were fined $2000 each for repeated failure to appear for jury duty, and Los Angeles County officials have issued over $940,000 in fines to reluctant prospective jurors (Wojdacz, 2009). But most of the time, these avoidant citizens are correct to assume they will suffer no consequences: court personnel tend not to punish nonresponders because enforcement costs can be steep and because sanctions such as criminal complaints, fines, community service, or, in rare instances, jail time might cause jurors to become resentful or vengeful.

Consequences of Jury Service Evasion

These scenarios of evasion and the varied reasons that underlie them pose serious problems for the jury system. They reduce the number and diversity of citizens from whom to select a jury. Even among the prospective jurors who *do* respond to a summons there are many reluctant citizens, more worried about completing an important project at work, picking up a child after school, or getting to the grocery store than about the proceedings at hand. Yet some trials, particularly those of any length or that involve complicated transactional or technological issues, require concentrated effort from factfinders. Jurors who are eager to escape from the courthouse will hardly provide the careful and critical attention to the evidence or the thoughtful deliberation that litigants, attorneys, and judges alike hope for.

The evasion scenarios also raise deeper concerns about the representativeness of selected jurors with regard to their age, class, and ethnicity, and, in turn, about the breadth of juries' fact-finding abilities and the quality of their discussions. These factors—representativeness, careful fact-finding, and thorough deliberation—signal the legitimacy of jury verdicts. To outside observers, the composition of a jury, including its mix of ages, genders, and races, is typically all they can see because the public is not privy to most trial evidence and is forbidden from watching a jury deliberate. Thus, prospective jurors' beliefs about the fairness of the courts, and by extension their willingness to respond when asked to serve, are informed by whether they think juries are representative of the breadth and depth of their communities.

Those with doubts will shy away from the courthouse when summoned themselves, further eroding public trust in this important civic institution.

So, as lighthearted and humorous as the media examples might seem, they cast a long and penetrating shadow over the institution of the jury and should serve as a wake-up call to court personnel that jurors' time and energy are both precious and limited. To attract prospective jurors to the courthouse, court officials need to remedy the negative beliefs many people have about jury duty. Ironically, the experience of serving on a jury may help.

Jurors' Perceptions of Their "Time Served"

Considerably less research has assessed jurors' perceptions of their experiences as jurors than their competence or bias (Cutler & Hughes, 2001). But some researchers have conducted post-trial interviews of jurors, and others have undertaken larger scale surveys of those who served and those who were dismissed during jury selection. Because jury duty varies considerably, usually requiring only a few days but occasionally lasting weeks or months, reactions to the experience of serving as a juror are somewhat varied. Some find jury duty excruciatingly dull and boring, and a very few suffer lingering adverse consequences. But for most people the experience is surprisingly satisfying, edifying, and even enjoyable. We describe these varied reactions, beginning with some adverse effects of jury service for some jury members and moving on to the positive consequences experienced by many. We explore the reasons that jury service can be affirming, and discuss implications of these findings for challenging the negative views of jury duty in the broader culture.

The Experience of Being a Juror has Adverse Consequences for Some

The vast majority of jurors experience little if any serious stress from serving. Still, those who serve in trials that involve heinous crimes, emotional testimony, or gut-wrenching decisions may suffer adverse consequences for a period of time after the trial has ended. In the Boston Marathon bombing trial jurors were moved to tears on multiple occasions by seeing horrific scenes of death and injury. In the Aurora, Colorado theater shooting trial jurors saw comparably shocking images and heard victims' and survivors' unbearable stories of grief and loss (on the effects of such testimony, see Chapter 12), consistent with the district attorney's proclamation that the case would be "a roller coaster through the worst haunted house you can imagine" (Wirthman, 2015).

But the common source of dissatisfaction for jurors is not this stressor as, thankfully, most trials do not have such graphic and gut-wrenching evidence. Rather, jurors dislike the inconvenience and financial hardship associated with jury duty. By questioning more than 4,600 venirepersons across 82 counties in North Carolina, Cutler and Hughes (2001) found that although most jurors were quite satisfied with the way that trials were conducted, the deliberation process, and the resulting verdict, 25% found jury service inconvenient and 16% said that it was difficult to manage financially. A National Center for State Courts (NCSC) survey of 400 jurors in both civil and criminal cases found that disruptions to daily routines were among the top sources of stress for jurors (NCSC, 1998).

Bornstein, Miller, Nemeth, Page, and Musil (2005) surveyed 159 jurors from 28 different trials of varying complexity and diverse charges (e.g., narcotics possession, contract disputes, manslaughter, child abuse). As part of a three-phase project in which participants completed a post-trial survey, experienced a debriefing session (some participants only), and a follow-up survey one month later, jurors were asked about potential sources of stress including evidence factors (e.g., photographs or videos of crime scenes), process variables (e.g., lengthy delays during trial, disruptions to daily routines), interactions with other jurors (e.g., being in a voting minority during deliberation), and decision consequences (e.g., knowledge of what the verdict could mean for the victim/plaintiff or defendant). Responses to the post-trial survey showed that although nearly 40% of jurors reported at least some stress, the intensity of the stressors was relatively low. On a 5-point scale that averaged all the items pertaining to a particular stressor, the highest mean score, from the category "decision consequences," was only 2.02. The greatest amount of stress resulted from the decision-making task itself. The next most stressful concerns were comprehension difficulties (mean response of 1.92) and disruption to daily life (mean response of 1.85). Jurors were least likely to report experiencing stress from external factors such as media presence or concerns about their safety during or after the trial. The researchers also took measures of depression and anxiety but found that levels fell short of clinical significance.

National Center for State Court data tend to mirror these findings (NCSC, 1998). In addition to disruptions to their daily routines, jurors questioned in this study experienced some level of stress from the fear of making mistakes and from dissension in the jury room, typically associated with differences in verdict preferences among jurors.

Jurors have expressed other sources of dissatisfaction with their experiences in a courtroom. They are irked when they feel they have not been treated with respect or are viewed as passive and compliant participants who simply absorb the evidence and produce a verdict. They are bothered by the lack of explanation from the judge about substantive and procedural issues that confuse them (Diamond, 1993). Some resent the fact that during *voir dire* they have to answer questions about their private lives in a public setting (NCSC, 1998). They wish they had more assistance with legal terminology (Sicafuse, Chomos, & Miller, 2013) and advice on how the deliberations should proceed (Bornstein et al., 2005).

Experiencing some arousal while seated in the jury box is not necessarily a bad thing, as it can enhance psychological and physical functioning by helping jurors to focus on the trial evidence, to take the task seriously, and to deliberate more effectively. Many people experience this sort of engagement (Hannaford-Agor, 2012). Fortunately, very few jurors (the NCSC estimates less than 10%) have high levels of stress that can lead to anxiety, depression, sleeplessness, nightmares, and, on rare occasions, physical symptoms such as nausea, shortness of breath, and elevated blood pressure (NCSC, 1998). Some observers suggest that these symptoms can be triggered by vicarious trauma, a situation that occurs when people empathize with and experience symptoms similar to those of crime or accident victims (Robertson, Davies, & Nettleingham, 2009). Typically, these symptoms disappear once the trial has ended, though in rare instances they can last for several months (Shuman, Hamilton, & Daley, 1994). Courts are beginning to provide resources to assist jurors whose symptoms linger. Later in the chapter we describe these programs.

The Experience of Being a Juror is Perceived Positively by Many

Given the negative image that jury duty connotes in the minds of many and the adverse effects experienced by a few, it may be surprising that people who serve on juries are often quite satisfied by the experience, even as they grumble about the inconvenience (Simon & Marcus, 1991). Results of several surveys challenge the belief that jurors regret the expenditure of their time and talents in a courtroom. Rather, they show that although jury duty *is* perceived as inconvenient for many and stressful for some, most jurors value the opportunity to be part of a jury and would serve again eagerly (Bornstein et al., 2005; NCSC, 1998).

By and large, being a juror enhances perceptions of the jury system and elicits positive regard for the experience. People who serve on juries or know someone who has served are more likely than those without court contact to believe that juries reach fair and just verdicts (Hans, 1993). More importantly, their opinions of the jury system and the criminal justice system improve (Boatright, 2001; O'Brien, Goodman-Delahunty, Clough, & Pratley, 2008). According to Boatright, "once citizens have served as jurors they tend to walk away holding the institution of the jury in higher esteem than they did before" (p. 302). One caveat, though: Prior service may have less salutary effects on attitudes toward the jury among Black jurors than White jurors (Rose, 2005; Shuman & Hamilton, 1992).

What evidence is there of enhanced respect for the jury system after serving? Although Cutler and Hughes (2001) found that jurors' opinions about jury duty were generally positive both before and after serving, approximately 11% rated the system in a more positive way after serving than before, and the percentage giving a neutral rating declined. Among the reasons for the swing was that the initial experience as jurors (presumably the summons and jury selection process) were informative and positive. The next most important reason: The judge and courtroom staff behaved in a respectful and helpful manner. Importantly, 82% of these jurors agreed that they would be willing to serve if summoned in the future.

Other studies have shown similar results. Despite some indication of mild stress among a few respondents, nearly all jurors surveyed by Bornstein et al. (2005) thought that the jury selection and trial proceedings were fair and that they were treated well by court staff. The vast majority were proud of what they accomplished, felt that jury duty was *not* a waste of time, and would volunteer again if asked to serve. More than half had a more positive attitude toward the justice system after serving than before, and respondents were seven times more likely to say that the next time they were summoned they would actually try to be selected than to say they would evade jury duty.

Sicafuse et al. (2013) analyzed 705 open-ended responses from 303 jurors drawn from 80 different trials in federal court, all conducted before the same judge in Iowa over a 12-year period. The majority of jurors enjoyed the experience and had a positive perception of jury service. Similarly, over 60% of jurors interviewed by Gastil, Deess, Weiser, and Simmons (2010) rated their overall courtroom experience as very good or excellent.

Even those who merely show up at the courthouse and never serve as jurors are affected by the experience, and some of them also express more favorable attitudes by the end of their "service" than beforehand (Diamond, 1993). Relative to jury-eligible citizens with no jury experience, those who reported for jury duty in one of three states in Australia but were not impaneled had increased confidence in the criminal justice system (O'Brien et al., 2008). Perhaps seeing the system in action, learning how trials are conducted, and (ideally) being treated with respect—even if not selected to decide a case—is sufficient to enhance laypeople's attitudes.

These attitudes may be mediated by jurors' beliefs about the reasons they were dismissed during *voir dire*, however. When Rose (2003) questioned jurors who were excused about why they thought they had been dismissed, and their willingness to return to jury duty in the future, she found that those who believed they had been dismissed because of their legally relevant experiences were more accepting of the *voir dire* process than those who assumed they were dismissed because of their personal characteristics. Overall, though, their willingness to serve in the future was not associated with beliefs about why they had been excused.

There are conflicting data on the effect of jury service on jurors from racial and ethnic minority groups. Although some data indicate less endorsement of the jury system by Black former jurors than White former jurors (e.g., Shuman & Hamilton, 1992), more recent findings reach a different conclusion. Rose et al. (2008) asked a representative sample of Texas residents to imagine four scenarios and to say whether, for each scenario, they would prefer a jury or a judge to decide the case. The scenarios included "If you wanted a decision to be the most accurate," "If you were accused of a crime," "If you were suing someone because you had been injured in an automobile accident," and "If you were being sued for causing an injury in an automobile accident." Prior jury service and respondents' race influenced responses to the two civil lawsuit scenarios: African Americans with prior jury service were more likely than Whites to choose a jury over a judge in the civil plaintiff scenario, and both African Americans and Hispanics were more likely than Whites to choose a jury over a judge in the civil defendant scenario. Also, African-American former jurors were more likely than African-American nonjurors to opt for a jury, and the effects of prior jury service were much greater among African Americans than among Whites. As Rose and her colleagues note correctly, they cannot be sure whether jury service improved minority jurors' views of jury trials or whether respondents who actually served on juries differed in some ways from those who did not. Regardless, support for the institution of the jury is greater among minorities who have been jurors than among those who have not.

Taken together, these studies show that jurors generally have a more positive attitude about the jury system after serving. The logical question is why. More than 20 years ago, Diamond (1993) pointed out that researchers had generally not addressed that issue, and little has changed since then. But a few hints from former jurors and a rather large dose of speculation yield three factors that can explain the ameliorative effects of jury service: the opportunity for learning, the chance to broaden one's perspectives via exposure to a heterogeneous group of fellow citizens, and feelings of efficacy that come from participating in a process in which one has invested resources.

Jury duty provides an opportunity for learning. Two-thirds of jurors interviewed by Consolini (1992) reported that they learned something factual or positive about the legal system while serving as jurors. Some of the learning is a byproduct of being immersed in a system of formal rules and procedures that most jurors are not familiar with. These include jury instructions that detail the elements of crimes, requirements of proof necessary for prosecutors and civil plaintiffs to prevail, and legal definitions of terms that laypeople may have heard but do not fully understand (e.g., circumstantial evidence, beyond a reasonable doubt). The need to synthesize evidence produced at the trial with the legal requirements provided by the judge can be cognitively taxing yet ultimately stimulating for many participants. Formulating and articulating an argument for one verdict preference over others requires cognitive skills of rhetoric and persuasion that some people enjoy using (Weinstock, 2005).

Jury service brings together people of varying ethnicities, ages, socioeconomic strata, political persuasions, and religions. In fact, serving on a jury may provide access to the most heterogeneous community that most Americans will ever experience closely. Exposure to diverse others can broaden one's perspectives, sources of information, and social interactions, and hearing contrasting points of view can cause people to sharpen their own beliefs and articulate them more clearly (Ferguson, 2013). Various aspects of a criminal trial allow jurors to see things from the perspective of others: "to not only understand what it is like to be in their shoes, but also to see what the world looks like through their eyes" (Clark, 2014; p. 422). Diversity within a group results in novel strategies of dialogue, which tend to enhance the quality of decisions and increase satisfaction with the group process (Abdel-Monem, Bingham, Marincic, & Tomkins, 2010; Clark, Anand, & Roberson, 2000).

Finally, participating in a trial may promote satisfaction by fostering responsibility-taking and enhancing feelings of efficacy. Assuming responsibility for our actions is both a key human trait and an important civic virtue (Clark, 2014), which a jury trial promotes by forcing jurors to see the litigants and be seen by them, emphasizing agency in jurors' decisions. Taking part in a group decision results in commitment to a process and outcome of that decision (Bazerman, Giuliano, & Appelman, 1984; Whyte, 1993) and increases feelings of usefulness. In particular, the extent to which individuals participate influences their sense of satisfaction with the group (Cooper & Wood, 1974). This can explain why jurors who are more engaged in the deliberation glean more value from the experience than those who are not. But it also suggests that the group experience can result in some level of fulfillment and gratification for most jurors.

The Experience of Being a Juror Has Broader Implications for Civic Attitudes and Involvement

The experience of serving on a jury can change attitudes and behaviors well beyond the confines of any particular courtroom. Early support for the notion that jury service enhances general trust in courts came from a series of statewide surveys conducted by judicial branches in 24 states between 1984 and 1998. The surveys focused on public trust and confidence in the courts and on how experience with those courts affected those attributes (Rottman, 1998). One of the most ambitious was a survey conducted in Louisiana in 1997 (Howell, 1998). Approval of the courts was highest among former jurors and three other categories of court users: traffic defendants, court employees, and lawyers. Jurors and witnesses gave the most positive assessment of fairness, and more than three-quarters of jurors agreed that judges were fair and impartial. Other convincing data come from state surveys that compared the attitudes of various categories of court users to those who lacked court contact. In most surveys, jurors had the most positive attitudes regarding courts' performance relative to people who lacked court experience (Rottman, 1998).

Similar findings have emerged from Australia. O'Brien et al. (2008) surveyed 628 impaneled and 1,048 non-impaneled jurors and found that the former expressed higher levels of confidence in the capacity of juries, judges, and prosecutors to do their jobs, and the ability of defense attorneys to represent their clients. People who served on a jury were more satisfied with the experience of jury duty than non-impaneled jurors, and the more satisfied jurors were with their experience the more confidence they expressed in the broader criminal justice system.

A study on the influence of jury experience, race, and ethnicity involved telephone interviews of a random sample of people from across the United States who had been jurors, litigants, or witnesses during the preceding 12 months (Rottman, Hansen, Mott, & Grimes, 2003). Of the respondents, 147 were former jurors including 85 Whites, 41 African Americans, and 21 Latinos. Regardless of race or ethnicity, jurors held more positive beliefs about the fairness of trial outcomes and procedures and had more positive views of how respectfully they were treated than did litigants or witnesses. Rose et al. (2008) have speculated that enhanced views of judges may be an especially important consequence of jury service among African Americans, who are generally more critical of the judiciary than Whites (Overby, Brown, Bruce, Smith, & Winkle, 2005).

The most interesting consequences of jury service are the collateral effects it has on civic engagement, including voting frequency, attentiveness to politics, and even volunteerism. Evidence for these changes comes from an exhaustive project undertaken by Gastil et al. (2010), who analyzed official records of jury service and the voting history of over 10,000 impaneled jurors from eight counties across the United States. The analysis of jury and voting records was supplemented with surveys of thousands of prospective jurors in King County (Seattle) Washington, and in-depth interviews with a subset of them. Gastil and his collaborators found that jurors who reached verdicts in criminal cases and who had previously been infrequent voters were 4%–7% more likely to vote in subsequent elections than jurors who did not deliberate, either because the case was settled via plea or ended in a mistrial. This effect was amplified for jurors who decided multiple charges and thus experienced a more complex deliberation. Jury service apparently enhances civic engagement when jurors have a consequential and conclusive experience.

The boost in civic engagement post–jury service, as measured by voting frequency, also applies to those who serve in civil trials, although the effects depend on a range of trial-related variables (Hans, Gastil, & Feller, 2014). It is most apparent among jurors who served in trials that included at least one organization rather than private individuals only, and is more potent among jurors who had a unanimity rather than majority decision rule and a jury size of 12. Deliberating as part of a larger group in which all members must agree on a verdict and discussing issues of weightiness that extend beyond individual claims apparently fosters a civic awakening among infrequent voters, prompting them to go to the polls more often.

Serving on a jury also increases attention to the news and results in more frequent conversations with friends and neighbors about community issues. It even influences people's charitable actions, as jurors who reached guilty verdicts in criminal trials become more active in charitable group activities (Gastil et al., 2010), perhaps because they aligned themselves with the government or perhaps because they need a way to assuage any residual doubts about siding with the prosecution. Finally, the experience of serving as a juror tends to strengthen one's faith in government and in fellow citizens and to modify one's self-concept as someone who is more politically capable and self-confident (Consolini, 1992; Gastil et al., 2010).

Innovations to Increase Participation in Jury Service

As we have shown, the reported reactions of jurors run counter to the negative portrayals of the jury system in popular culture. This suggests that once people have the experience of serving as jurors, their support for the jury and the broader legal system will be enhanced. But getting them to the courthouse to witness the rewards and satisfaction of serving has proven to be a daunting task for court officials. The solution may come from innovations that have begun to make the process more efficient, effective, and enjoyable for citizen-jurors.

Over the past 35 years, nearly all states have undertaken steps to enhance their jury trial systems. Some of the efforts are aimed at increasing participation rates, while others strive to improve the in-court experiences of jurors. The Center for Jury Studies at the National Center for State Courts has been a leading proponent and resource for these efforts. The Center provides training and online information on topics ranging from jury system technology to new media and trial management strategies for both mundane and notorious trials.

Some of the reforms aimed at increasing participation rates attempt to broaden the base of prospective jurors. Although a number of states are mandated to use only designated source lists (typically voter registration lists and/or licensed driver lists), other states also take names of prospective jurors from income or property tax rolls and from lists of people receiving public assistance and/or unemployment compensation (NCSC, 2007).

Other innovations focus on undeliverable summonses. These include using only "active" records from jury source lists, sending a second summons, and combining juror qualification questionnaires typically sent via mail with the summonsing process (NCSC, 2007) to reduce the problems related to undeliverable mail.

Still other reforms focus on nonresponders and involve the use of technology to remind jurors of their responsibility to serve and to provide information to assist them in getting to the courthouse. In New Jersey, for example, 57% of the 200,000 jurors summoned each year now respond to online juror questionnaires. Those jurors also receive text messages reminding them of the days they are expected to appear and letting them know each night during their service term whether they need to come to the courthouse the next morning. The New Jersey judiciary has also developed a "NJ Juror App" that provides user-friendly details about the location of the courthouse, parking, nearby restaurants, and details about jury service.

Some jurisdictions have tried a punitive approach. In California, no-shows without good excuses have been held in contempt of court, fined, and even jailed, and the state legislature passed a law making it clear that jury duty is a mandatory responsibility of its citizens (Judicial Council of California, 2009). In Dallas, where turnout is a paltry 19%, court officials tested a pilot program in 2011 in which people who failed to respond to their summons were fined and ordered to appear. Participation rates increased 2%. Judges are now requesting funding to establish a jury duty court that formalizes the sanctions previously tested, citing similar programs that have proven effective in El Paso County, Texas, and Orange County, California (Watkins, 2014). In some locales, sheriff's deputies have been enlisted to enforce summons responses, knocking on the doors of nonresponders (Boatright, 1999). But as we have noted, such heavy-handed enforcement is expensive, results in only token efforts, and runs the risk of casting the jury system in a very negative light (Losh et al., 2000).

Some data suggest that a softer approach that focuses on reminding jurors of their civic duty may be more effective. Borrowing from the success of "get out the vote" efforts of political parties and nonprofit organizations, one group of researchers assessed the effectiveness of "get out the juror" direct mail methods to increase juror yields (Bowler, Esterling, & Holmes, 2014). These researchers mailed postcard reminders to citizens who had been summoned for jury duty. Some of the randomly selected citizens received a simple reminder that they had been issued a jury summons, others received a "civic duty message" that detailed the importance of jury service to the community, and still others also got an enforcement message informing them of possible civil penalties for failure to appear. A fourth group did not receive any postcard. Turnout increased in all groups that received reminders, and it increased the most in the group that was reminded of the penalties they would face for not responding.

These findings are consistent with data on the effectiveness of written reminders to misdemeanor defendants about the negative consequences of failure to appear, with the greatest effectiveness shown for misdemeanants with low levels of trust in the courts (Bornstein, Tomkins, Neeley, Herian, & Hamm, 2013). Despite the many differences between prospective jurors and misdemeanor defendants, the subtle processes of persuasion inherent in these reminders may be similar. Specifically, a direct mail statement of potential sanctions might mobilize jurors and defendants alike, because it provides a clear signal of the costs relative to the benefits of not responding. It may also evoke an "obedience to authority" effect, which has been shown to be effective in tax compliance (Bowler et al., 2014). A message about enforcement leverages the coercive power of the government and apparently impels both prospective jurors and recalcitrant defendants to respond.

Innovations to Enhance the Experience of Serving on a Jury

Other innovations focus on making the experience of jury duty more pleasurable or at least less onerous. These include providing childcare, improving the comfort level of courtrooms and access to parking and food, enabling Wi-Fi in jury assembly rooms, and increasing jurors' pay. Responding to the frustrations that many prospective jurors feel about the hardships of schedule disruptions and wasted time, approximately one-third of local courts now operate a one-day, one-trial system in which respondents serve for either one day or one trial.

Although it seems logical to expect benefits, we could find no evidence that the provision of childcare, increased comfort in the courthouse, or access to the Internet increased jurors' willingness to appear or the pleasure they took from jury duty. Whether increased pay reaps benefits also is unclear. In Washington State, yields did not rise markedly when juror pay was increased from $10/day to $60/day, even among prospective jurors with work-related constraints or lower incomes (Bloeser et al., 2012). On the other hand, fewer jurors have asked to be excused in courts where juror compensation exceeds the national average than in courts where pay is below the national average (Mize et al., 2007). Courts that have implemented one-day or one-trial terms of service also have lower excusal rates than courts with longer service terms (Mize et al., 2007).

Once jurors arrive at the courthouse, and especially after they are selected to serve on a jury, they may experience a different set of innovations intended to enhance their experience. Courts now routinely provide juror orientation programs that typically consist of a judge's welcome as well as a video that details basic information about trial procedures and laws, jurors' responsibilities, and the qualifications for service (Miller & Bornstein, 2013). Orientations of this sort increase both jurors' knowledge about the legal system and their level of comfort with their role as jurors (Bradshaw, Ross, Bradshaw, Headrick, & Thomas, 2005), and they are easy to implement and cost-effective. Alaska's juror orientation video, "You, the Alaska Juror" features former jurors discussing their experiences, including the care and seriousness of the enterprise, the value they gleaned from having served, and their desire to serve again (https://www.youtube.com/watch?v=GwyokdgJhbA).

Judges have become attentive to the need to protect jurors' privacy, particularly in high-profile cases and in trials that concern sensitive issues such as child maltreatment, domestic violence, or mental illness and in which jurors' personal experiences are relevant but not easily shared in public (NCSC, 1998). Courts are making more use of individualized *voir dire* in these situations and, as we note in Chapter 3, have been able to obtain important information from jurors that might not be divulged in open court (Miller & Bornstein, 2013).

A variety of innovations to the trial process itself address the stressors that jurors experience during a trial. These stressors stem from the difficulties jurors have remembering the evidence, lingering questions they would like to ask the witnesses, and the complexity they must grapple with in applying their jury instructions. Reforms in this realm have been in place for many years, and jurors in most jurisdictions can now take notes and receive a written copy of the jury instructions. In approximately 15% of trials jurors can submit written questions to the witnesses, and a number of jurisdictions now provide simplified jury instructions. Although some inconsistencies exist, these modifications generally facilitate more informed decision making and improve the experience for most jurors (see Chapter 14).

At the conclusion of especially stressful trials and those with significant consequences for the litigants, a few jurors may experience the physical and psychological ailments we have described. Some courts provide informational brochures that alert jurors to symptoms of stress and give tips on how to cope after jury duty. Occasionally, debriefing sessions or group counseling sessions, led either by the judge or by mental health professionals, are offered. Jurors who participate in high-stress federal trials are eligible for mental health benefits through the Employee Assistance Program administered by the U.S. Department of Health and Human Services (Hannaford-Agor, 2012).

Theoretically, debriefing and counseling sessions can inform jurors of the symptoms commonly associated with juror stress and give them the chance to explore their reactions to the trial. But many jurors are physically and emotionally exhausted and eager to leave the courthouse at the end of a trial and may only experience symptoms in the hours or days after their service has ended. And evaluation data show that although jurors deem them helpful, debriefing sessions may be of limited use in reducing stress-related symptoms (Bornstein et al., 2005).

Still, these innovations signal a radical transformation in the way that jurors are viewed by court officials. In the past, jurors were treated as passive recipients of evidence who were accorded little concern and few accommodations. In recent years they have become increasingly active participants in trials, and not just because they can ask questions of witnesses. Attorneys and judges alike now understand that jurors actively assess witness credibility, scrutinize the evidence, and typically strive to provide justice for all parties. As this shift in perspective has occurred, judges and other court officials have learned that they must continue to find ways for citizens to feel that their time has been spent wisely in service to the courts and their fellow citizens.

Enhancing the Image of the Jury System

Away from the courthouse and in the larger sphere of public life, other methods for improving perceptions of jury service come into focus. Commentators have proposed improving public education about jury duty, including media announcements, coverage in social studies and civics courses, and publicized mock trials (Losh et al., 2000), as well as partnerships between schools, attorneys, and law students to inculcate attachment to the structures and functions of our courts and justice system (Royal & Hofman, 2013). The major thrust of these efforts has been to stress the importance of having a diverse set of citizens available and willing to serve on juries. Former New York Chief Justice Judith Kaye once pointed out that jury duty provides an ideal vehicle for enhancing the reputation of the courts:

> Each year we summon more than 500,000 citizens to jury duty. That's more than half a million chances every year to educate the public about our courts. Half a million chances to draw in every segment of society, to show people firsthand that the system really does work. Half a million chances a year to counteract pervasive public negativism and cynicism about courts and lawyers (Kaye, 1999, p. 1495).

Some legal professionals have taken up the call. Both the Marshall-Brennan Constitutional Literacy Project and Street Law, Inc. involve law students and attorneys in educating the public through experiential and informational sessions about the rights and responsibilities of Americans and modeling the skills and dedication necessary for successful jury service.

Legal groups and court organizations have also launched online campaigns to broaden the appeal of jury service. For instance, the website "Save Our Juries: It's Your Constitutional Right" (www.saveourjuries.org) strives to uphold the Seventh Amendment right to a jury in civil cases by educating the public about current issues and the history and value of the right to trial by jury. The American Bar Association's Commission on the American Jury Project has collaborated with courts, state legislatures, and bar organizations to implement jury innovations to enhance the trial experience of jurors and to encourage more citizens to serve. Its website features a photograph of Harrison Ford, superimposed with the words "Answer the call to jury service. Harrison Ford did" (www.americanbar.org/groups/judicial/american_jury.html). Politicians including Secretary of State John Kerry and former New York City mayor Rudolph Giuliani have both served on juries, and celebrities including Oprah Winfrey, Tom Hanks, and Madonna have all done their civic duty.

Conclusions

As Hans (2013) correctly notes, citizens have tended to avoid jury duty "like the plague" (p. 394). Yet, ironically, those who *do* serve come away from the experience with quite different—and typically improved—opinions of trial by jury as well as the broader criminal and civil justice systems. Importantly, they also become more engaged in corollary aspects of civic life, perhaps because the experience of serving as a juror heightens their sense of civic obligation and causes them to view themselves as more efficacious, reliable, and responsible citizens.

In his book *Why Jury Duty Matters,* Ferguson (2013) suggests that jury duty provides an opportunity for people to reflect on their right and responsibility to assume an ongoing identity as a constitutional actor, much like an elected official or a voter. He argues that involvement in jury service benefits citizens by reconnecting them to a larger participatory democracy, creating and reinforcing habits of concentration, deliberation, and purpose, and bridging differences in race, class, political beliefs, and educational attainment. From this vantage point, serving on a jury profits ordinary citizens on whom the legal system relies as much it benefits the system itself. Admittedly, some work is needed to trumpet these attainments to the public. But if public education efforts mount, court officials continue their innovative ways, and people come away from courtrooms with positive regard for the experience, scenarios of evasion should begin to taper off and be replaced by scenes of engagement. One can so hope.

3

Jury Selection Can Effectively Identify Biased Jurors

"No, it is not disturbing that voir dire accomplishes so little. What is disturbing is that we expect voir dire to accomplish so much."
(Kerr, Kramer, Carroll, & Alfini, 1991, p. 699)

The essence of trial by jury as enshrined in the Sixth and Seventh Amendments is the selection of fair and impartial jurors, and various jury selection processes exist to achieve that goal. The questioning of prospective jurors, termed *voir dire*, has a rich and turbulent history as attorneys, judges, and legislators have attached varying desires and objectives to this first phase of a trial. Although most agree that *voir dire* has both practical and symbolic importance, it has, over the years, also garnered ambivalence, contentiousness, and derision—much of this caused by perceptions that it does not work. The core objection to *voir dire* as currently practiced in the United States is that it fails to deliver on the promise of impartiality; that is, it fails to identify prospective jurors whose experiences and beliefs impair their abilities to serve in a just and open-minded way. In this chapter we explore that objection, the reasons why it exists, and some ways to make jury selection more effective.

Multiple Goals of *Voir Dire*

Jury selection is multifaceted. Its main objective is to select impartial jurors. Principle 11 of the American Bar Association (ABA) *Principles for Juries and Jury Trials* (2005) makes that clear: "Courts should ensure that the process used to empanel jurors effectively serves the goal of assembling a fair and impartial jury." But assuring impartiality is not the sole objective of *voir dire*. There are, in fact, at least three judicially sanctioned purposes of *voir dire*: determining whether a prospective juror meets the statutory requirements to serve (generally these include citizenship, age, residency in the jurisdiction, and lack of a felony conviction); ascertaining whether the juror can participate in the deliberation by relying solely on the evidence and the law presented during the trial; and providing information that allows attorneys to decide which jurors to challenge and excuse (Suggs & Sales, 1981). Less obviously, *voir dire* also serves to transform reluctant laypeople into "responsible jurors" (Marder, 2015, p. 929) by taking them away from their quotidian concerns and into an event of public note. But attorneys would say that, above all, *their* goal in *voir dire* is to weed out jurors who would be biased against their client.

Procedural rules in almost all jurisdictions allow for prospective jurors to be questioned by judges, attorneys, or both, though practices vary significantly between federal and state courts. In federal courts *voir dire* is dominated by judges, whereas attorneys take a much more active role in state courts (National Center for State Courts, 2007). Exactly how the questioning unfolds depends on who is doing the asking: Judges tend to pose questions to the entire panel of prospective jurors and follow up with individual jurors in a very limited way, whereas attorneys tend to ask more questions of individuals and pursue a line of inquiry in greater depth. Not infrequently, jury selection involves some combination of judge-based and attorney-based questions. Reports from nearly 12,000 trials conducted in state and federal courts across the country between 2002 and 2006 showed that attorney-conducted *voir dire* could last up to two hours longer than *voir dire* that was shared equally by judge and attorneys (National Center for State Courts, 2007).

As the questioning unfolds, a prospective juror may be challenged and eliminated *for cause*. A for-cause challenge arises when jurors' views or experiences prevent or impair them from performing their duties in accordance with the law and their oath to consider the evidence fairly and impartially. Jurors are struck for cause if they have an affiliation with any of the witnesses set to testify or have personal or professional experiences akin to the issues that will arise during the trial (e.g., they have been victimized in a way that affects their ability to remain open-minded or have specialized knowledge about an aspect of the evidence that would influence their judgment). They are also struck for cause if they are unwilling to follow the law or purport to have beliefs at odds with notions such as the presumption of innocence in criminal cases or plaintiffs' right to seek damages or injunctions in civil cases.

Attorneys often ask the judge to dismiss prospective jurors for cause, and they must provide an explanation for that request. The judge then has to determine whether that juror should be released, taking into account the nature of the case and the juror's responses to questions, assessment of his or her own ability to be fair, and demeanor. As we will show, judges are reluctant to dismiss jurors out of hand, believing that if they can elicit a promise from a challenged juror to decide the facts and reach a verdict in an open-minded way, they have met the spirit of the impartiality requirement. So challenges for cause are sustained rather infrequently.

At the end of *voir dire*, the attorneys have another opportunity to deselect potential jurors and remove them from the panel. Each side may exercise a certain number of *peremptory challenges* without providing any explanation, thereby striking jurors whom they believe would be unfavorable to their position. The number of peremptory challenges is determined by statute, and these challenges are entirely attorney-driven; judges are not involved in these choices.

This brief overview of *voir dire* practices shows why it is complicated and sometimes contentious, and why it may not meet the goal of identifying biased jurors. In order for decisions to be made about who should remain in the jury box and who should be dismissed, all parties involved in the dialogue—prospective jurors, attorneys and their clients, and trial judges—are required to make judgments of fairness. Occasionally that decision is quite clear-cut, as when a prospective juror professes beliefs or attitudes that reveal deep-seated prejudices or biases. But usually it is not so obvious, because a fair number of prospective jurors conceal or distort their true beliefs—occasionally to remain on the jury, though more often to be released.

To complicate matters further, the factors that determine whether people can be fair are typically hidden from themselves, let alone from others. In fact, all of us have implicit biases that, without being apparent to us, influence how we make sense of the world and of other people's actions. All prospective jurors come to the jury box with a full complement of experiences and attitudes that predispose them to think about the evidence in a particular way and that affect their ability to be objective. As Gabriel (2015) notes, these beliefs are "borne of years of driving cars, working in various employment situations, or using products." This means that despite protestations to the contrary, no prospective juror can be completely neutral; there are no *tabulae rasae*. Implicit biases also influence judges' beliefs about which jurors will be more and less objective, and whom to dismiss for cause. And they inform attorneys' choices about which jurors will be unfavorable to their side and whom to challenge peremptorily. In short, implicit as well as explicit biases abound in the early stages of a trial.

Unfortunately, the process of juror questioning does little to expose implicit biases to the light of day. Instead, biases endure due to problems of self-awareness and self-disclosure. They are tacitly sustained via notions like judicial discretion and appellate oversight, and, some allege, behind a series of winks and nods (e.g., Marder, 2012). But research in the field of social cognition, focusing on how we perceive, think about, and make sense of the actions of ourselves and others in our social environment, has begun to illuminate the many ways that bias—particularly implicit bias—plays a role in jury selection. In this chapter we focus on what research in social cognition has revealed about implicit biases and the extent to which jury selection can yield unbiased factfinders. But before doing so, we consider some of the reasons that it is difficult to learn even about jurors' *explicit* biases—the predilections and beliefs about which they are fully aware. Various elements of *voir dire* make it difficult for jurors to share these sentiments openly and honestly.

Recognizing Explicit Biases in Prospective Jurors

The problem of recognizing and identifying any sort of bias during jury selection starts with the fact that jurors do not readily self-disclose, as Broeder noted after interviewing jurors involved in one of the 23 trials he studied extensively in the late 1950s (Broeder, 1965). Several jurors admitted to him that they deliberately hid or distorted information about their personal history and attitudes during *voir dire* questioning. Because attorneys failed to probe sufficiently, and instead devoted most of the *voir dire* to indoctrinating jurors or ingratiating themselves, this information went untold.

There are various reasons that jurors do not disclose, and many involve structural aspects of jury selection. Conducted in a public setting with a black-robed judge perched above the proceedings, a court reporter taking down every word, and an armed deputy guarding a criminal defendant, jury duty can be a stressful experience (see Chapter 2). Prospective jurors may be too nervous or shy to recognize, reflect on, and articulate any relevant experiences, particularly if those experiences involve illicit behavior or difficult-to-discuss personal issues (Hans & Jehle, 2003). Imagine jurors in a case of alleged financial abuse being asked whether they had been involved in any sort of financial transgression.

Being questioned by a judge imposes a status differential that can further intimidate prospective jurors and influence their responses. When the social distance between an interviewer and respondent is sufficiently large, respondents feel pressure to answer in a manner that conforms to the interviewer's expectations. Attorneys may be better at this task since they occupy a moderate social distance from jurors, though some attorneys (i.e., prosecutors) are still agents of the state, and even private attorneys might be intimidating because of their specialized knowledge and jargon, formal attire, and socioeconomic status. But it stands to reason that on balance, jurors will feel more comfortable and provide more information when questioned by attorneys than by judges (Jones, 1987).

As we noted, judges typically question a panel of prospective jurors as a group. These questions might take the form of "Would any of you be unable to be fair and impartial toward the defendant because of the media coverage which has surrounded this case?" If no one admits to any concerns, the judge simply moves on to another question. This situation is hardly one that facilitates honest disclosure, because no particular individual is obligated to respond, and there are enormous social pressures to say nothing. Suggs and Sales (1981) describe it this way: "Even when relatively mundane questions are addressed to the prospective jurors as a group ... they squirm in their seats and look around to see if anyone else is going to volunteer information; if they discover that no other hands are raised, they settle back in their chairs and refuse to respond" (p. 260). Any jurors brave enough to speak up might be asked a few additional questions to reveal the extent of their concerns. Judges justify this practice of *en masse* questioning by the time it saves and by the assumption that it will reveal relevant biases in group members. But neither group inquiry nor individual-within-a-group interviews promote honest self-disclosure. As Johnson has stated, "it is easier to stay quiet untruthfully than to respond untruthfully" (Johnson, 1985, p. 1675).

All of these factors combine to put pressure on prospective jurors who *do* speak up. But rather than providing honest responses, these jurors typically insist that they can be impartial, in part because they know that that is the "correct" or "appropriate" answer. So, for example, although 60% of the public will tell a stranger on the phone that they do not agree with the presumption of innocence, hardly anyone would express that opinion when questioned in a courtroom (Horowitz, 1990). Prospective jurors are particularly reluctant to convey any inkling of prejudice, since such admissions would be met with social disapproval and derision (Johnson, 1985), yet these sentiments almost certainly influence jurors' verdicts in the jury room.

Oftentimes jurors remain silent in response to *voir dire* questions because they are simply not certain whether any pretrial sentiments or experiences might affect their judgment. In the example concerning a financial transgression, one juror might wonder whether writing a check on a bank account with insufficient funds constitutes a financial transgression while another might interpret it to mean theft. But, lacking clarity, neither may speak up. Iowa federal judge Mark Bennett had presided for more than 15 years when he wrote, "I find it remarkable when a juror has the self-knowledge and courage to answer that he or she cannot be fair in a particular case, and even more remarkable when the juror's explanation for that inability is based on a factor that neither I, nor the parties, have raised" (Bennett, 2010, p. 160).

Before we explore implicit biases in more detail, we can reach some tentative conclusions about better ways to structure *voir dire* to bring explicit biases to light. If we assume that jury selection should enable individuals to communicate their true beliefs about their ability to serve, then, minimally, people need to be questioned out of the presence of fellow jurors, particularly in cases that involve sensitive issues such as victimization (especially sexual assault). Such individualized questioning would also reduce any reticence to express firmly held but unpopular attitudes and any pressure to conform responses to those of the group. Prospective jurors need to be asked clear and unambiguous questions with follow-up as necessary to overcome the natural reluctance to express their true sentiments and to describe personally relevant experiences.

The Role of Implicit Bias in Jury Selection

Although the expression of explicit biases and prejudices has, without a doubt, declined in contemporary American society, implicit biases endure, operating without people's awareness, intent, or control. Implicit biases are unconscious attitudes that affect our assumptions about other people and distort our judgment and behavior. Over the past few decades it has become apparent that these biases permeate the criminal and civil justice systems, and even those who insist that they harbor no preconceptions, prejudices, or ill will toward others exhibit this subtler form of bias. The selection of jurors is not immune from its reach.

Research has shown that implicit biases are distinct from explicit bias (Nosek et al., 2007), pervasive and widespread (Lane, Kang, & Banaji, 2007), and predictive of certain kinds of actions (see, e.g., Krieger & Fiske, 2006). Studies have used subliminal priming paradigms and reaction time measures to reveal attitudes that escape self-awareness and social-desirability biases. One of the best known experimental techniques is the Implicit Associations Task, or IAT, in which people make a series of rapid judgments about pairs of words to assess the strength of association between concepts such as gay people or African Americans and evaluative terms such as good or bad, smart or athletic. Faster responses to particular pairings are interpreted to indicate stronger associations in memory, revealing attitudes that people are unaware of (see, e.g., Greenwald, McGhee, & Schwartz, 1998; Greenwald, Nosek, & Banaji, 2003). Results of these studies generally show that people maintain unconscious biases against stigmatized groups that they would never reveal in public. Even members of bias-affected groups show these predilections (Banaji & Greenwald, 1995).

Another popular methodology for demonstrating implicit bias, particularly regarding race, is the shoot–no shoot paradigm in which participants play videogames under instructions to shoot "perpetrators"—characters holding guns—as fast as possible, but not to shoot innocent "bystanders" who are unarmed but holding nonlethal objects. Results generally reveal that viewers shoot Black perpetrators more quickly and frequently than White perpetrators and refrain from shooting White bystanders more quickly and frequently than Black bystanders (Correll, Park, Judd, & Wittenbrink, 2002; Payne, 2001).

Implicit biases allow us to categorize others rapidly on some salient dimension like race, age, or gender, enabling us to recognize and respond to people or situations more efficiently: "the ability to understand new and unique individuals in terms of old and general beliefs is certainly among the handiest tools in the social perceiver's kit" (Gilbert & Hixon, 1991, p. 509). But these categorization schemes come packaged with stereotypes that affect our perceptions and judgments of others and that lead to prejudiced treatment. In the context of jury selection they affect what prospective jurors know about their own justice-relevant attitudes, and what attorneys and judges presume about prospective jurors' beliefs. Stereotype activation is especially likely when people have limited information about others (Sherman, Stroessner, Conrey, & Azam, 2005) and when they make decisions under time constraints (Kunda, Davies, Adams, & Spencer, 2002) or high cognitive load (Wigboldus, Sherman, Franzese, & Van Knippenberg, 2004). Because jury selection incorporates these very conditions (Sommers & Norton, 2008), implicit biases are quite likely to come into play.

So even as lay jurors purport to being unbiased when questioned about their beliefs during *voir dire*, they probably maintain prejudices and partialities of which they are unaware. (Implicit biases also influence the way that jurors interpret and remember evidence, discuss their interpretations with other jurors, and ultimately decide on verdicts and awards, though these topics are outside the scope of this chapter.) Decisions that judges make during *voir dire* about which jurors to dismiss will be influenced by their own implicit biases, though with sufficient motivation judges can apparently compensate for these biases (Rachlinski, Johnson, Wistrich, & Guthrie, 2009; as described in Chapter 13, judges are susceptible to other sorts of biases). Further, attorneys will also be influenced by implicit biases—for example, by assuming that prospective Black jurors will be suspicious of police and that prospective White jurors will be willing to overlook corporate malfeasance (Sommers & Norton, 2007). We provide more details about the nature and consequences of implicit bias on each of these players and on various *voir dire* decisions in the sections that follow.

The Role of Implicit Bias in Challenges for Cause

When Boston Marathon bombing suspect Dzhokhar Tsarnaev went on trial in early 2015, his attorneys argued that because the bombing had affected so many Bostonians the trial should be moved to a different location. But Judge George O'Toole denied their recurring requests, firmly committed to the notion that "the time tested method for determining whether a juror can actually set aside his beliefs and apply the presumption of innocence is *voir dire*" (Boeri & Sobel, 2015). In other words, the judge assumed that he would simply ask jurors whether they could be fair and impartial and then use their responses to decide which jurors should be retained and whom to dismiss.

Judge O'Toole is hardly alone in this belief. The shared wisdom in the legal system is that prospective jurors can identify and report on their own biases and assess their own objectivity. Even the United States Supreme Court has expressed this position: "[S]urely one who is trying as an honest man to live up to the sanctity of his oath is well qualified to say whether he has an unbiased mind in a certain matter" (*Smith v. Phillips*, 1982, p. 217). According to Hannaford-Agor and Waters (2004), who observed *voir dire* questioning of more than 700 prospective jurors in 18 criminal trials in California, jurors' self-assessments of bias were the most predictive factor in whether they were removed for cause by the judge. As long as jurors stated that they were at least *somewhat* confident they could be fair and impartial, the judge did not excuse them. But, as we have hinted, jurors have limited powers of introspection, and they want to think of themselves as and show others that they are fair and open-minded. As a result, they maintain an unwarranted illusion of objectivity (Norton, Vandello, & Darley, 2004; Wilson & Brekke, 1994).

Even those jurors who express doubts about their objectivity are not immediately disqualified from jury service. Hannaford-Agor and Waters (2004) observed that of the prospective California jurors who said they were not sure they could be fair, only 50% were removed for cause. And Judge O'Toole did not automatically dismiss Boston jurors who presumed that Tsarnaev was guilty, either. Rather, following standard procedures, he asked jurors whether they could set aside their opinions and decide the case on the basis of the evidence they would hear and the instructions he would provide.

Although judges and appellate courts appear to put a great deal of weight on the answers to that question, jurors "do not come equipped with an on/off switch, and they cannot escape such a bias just by making a solemn promise" (Broda-Bahm, 2013, p. 1). This point became clear from interviews of 15 jurors who served in one of four felony trials in Santa Cruz, California in 1988 (Johnson & Haney, 1994). When asked to reflect on the jury selection process and on whether they were really able to set aside their biases during the trial, nearly half said they were not, and all of these jurors felt compelled to explain why (e.g., "No person alive could do that," "I felt them creeping in," and "It's a worthwhile goal, but cannot be achieved" [Johnson & Haney, p. 499]).

In the Boston bombing trial, Judge O'Toole went a bit further than to ask jurors whether they could be impartial. He reminded each and every one of them that the law *requires* that they set aside their opinions before hearing the evidence. To one woman he asked, "Would you be able to discipline your mind so that you can make a decision based on the evidence presented at trial rather than ideas you came in with?" (Boeri & Sobel, 2015). This process goes by the term "rehabilitation" because under increasing pressure to expedite trials, judges are hesitant to dismiss jurors and begin the selection process anew with different jurors. They prefer to try to rehabilitate a juror who expresses doubts about his or her objectivity. (One of the judges that Johnson and Haney [1994] observed, rather than dismissing jurors who admitted to a bias, insisted that the juror "take his or her biases and set them on a shelf during the trial" [p. 503]).

Recently rehabilitation has been taken to a new level, as judges have begun a practice that one set of commentators call premature rehabilitation or "prehabilitation" (Hamilton, Lindon, Pitt, & Robins, 2014). Even before a juror can admit to concerns about potential bias, the judge signals the legally and socially desired response concerning jurors' responsibilities to be impartial, set aside their biases, and follow the law by presuming innocence. So judges have told jurors, "This is the portion of the trial that talks about pretrial publicity … about what you heard and its effect on your ability to keep from forming a preconceived notion, and your ability to look at the other side of the story," and "Keep in mind that it is your duty to presume that the defendant is innocent unless his guilt is proven beyond a reasonable doubt" (Hamilton et al., p. 50).

Content analysis of more than 600 *voir dire* interviews of jurors in 11 high-profile cases showed that all 11 judges gave prehabilitation introductions, typically reminding jurors of their obligation to remain fair and impartial (Hamilton et al., 2014). It is difficult to imagine that anyone, when questioned in this manner, would admit to holding any preconceived notions about a defendant's guilt or liability, regardless of his or her actual sentiments. Instead, jurors must either hide the fact that they are biased or claim falsely to be free of biases.

One criminal defense attorney commented on Judge O'Toole's response to jurors who said they thought Tsarnaev was guilty. The judge reminded them that the law required them to set aside those opinions before hearing the evidence, and he asked, again, whether they would be able to do this. The commentator called that "browbeating" and asked rhetorically why judges think they can browbeat people out of a bias (Boeri & Sobel, 2015). Indeed, biases stemming from associations in semantic memory (for instance, the confirmation bias, overconfidence, and, presumably, prospective jurors' prejudgments of Tsarnaev's guilt) are relatively undiminished by entreaties or instructions that warn of the bias (Arkes, 1991), probably because these associations occur outside of awareness (Ratcliff & McKoon, 1981). De-biasing is especially difficult when there are strong motivations at play (Markman & Hirt, 2002).

Jurors have difficulty gauging their own impartiality. It is, in fact, very difficult for jurors to recognize their own biases, even more difficult to bring them to the attention of the judge (Marder, 2012), and probably impossible to browbeat them away. Research in social cognition shows that our judgments and decisions are guided by sophisticated, flexible, and adaptive processes of which we are unaware (Bargh, 2006). These include belief perseverance (e.g., Anderson, Lepper, & Ross, 1980), conformity to others' attitudes (e.g., Wilder, 1977; 1990), and confirmation biases (e.g., Swann & Read, 1981). And despite our lack of conscious awareness of the factors that influence our behavior, we can generate compelling explanations for why we do what we do (Nisbett & Wilson, 1977; Shafir, Simonson, & Tversky, 1993).

Limitations in our understanding of the factors that influence our thoughts are even more pronounced when we are questioned about our biases. In a society that values rationality and predictability, we are loath to admit to such a pejorative trait, and we remain blind (or at least visually impaired) to our biases. In fact, we tend to believe that we are more objective than our peers, and we put greater credence on our own introspections about the forces on our judgment than on similar introspections by other people (Ehrlinger, Gilovich, & Ross, 2005; Pronin, Gilovich, & Ross, 2004).

If jurors are not aware of the factors that influence their thoughts or of the capacity for their predilections to influence decision making, then they surely cannot report accurately on their ability to be fair and impartial. Even if they acknowledged their biases, they would have difficulty forecasting how they might respond in the future and how their biases would affect their actions (Mallett, Wilson, & Gilbert; 2008; Wilson & Gilbert, 2003). Moreover, unless they were motivated and had the cognitive capacity to counteract their biased attitudes, even those who recognize their biases may not correct for them (Kawakami, Dovidio, & Van Kamp, 2007; Wilson & Brekke, 1994). So assertions that jurors can be fair may have little relationship to whether they can indeed be fair, and any trial judge who happens to believe otherwise would, according to Bennett (2010), be "delusional."

Mock jury research in both the criminal and civil realms makes these points clear. At least four simulation studies have examined the effectiveness of *voir dire* questioning in a criminal case with pretrial publicity (Dexter, Cutler, & Moran, 1992; Kerr et al., 1991; Ogloff & Vidmar, 1994; Sue, Smith, & Pedroza, 1975). In the most extensive of these, Kerr et al. exposed mock jurors to various forms and amounts of prejudicial pretrial publicity including information about a previous conviction for a similar offense and discovery of incriminating evidence in the defendant's girlfriend's apartment. Next they questioned jurors about what effect, if any, the publicity would have on their ability to serve as impartial jurors. They classified the responses as indicating that the juror definitely could not be fair, possibly could be fair, or definitely could be fair. Jurors then watched a videotaped reenactment of an armed robbery trial that included all the standard elements of a trial, and they deliberated to a verdict. In addition, a large and diverse sample of experienced criminal defense attorneys, prosecutors, and judges viewed the filmed juror questioning and made various judgments including challenges for cause, peremptory challenges, and change of venue rulings.

Not surprisingly, mock jurors were affected by exposure to the prejudicial pretrial publicity, convicting more often when so exposed. In terms of for-cause challenges, judges would have excused jurors who said they definitely could not be fair. But they tended not to dismiss those with concerns about their impartiality. And jurors who asserted that they could try to disregard the publicity and base their judgments solely on the evidence—the jurors who typically would *not* be excused during *voir dire*—were just as likely to convict as those who expressed serious doubts about whether they could set the publicity aside. These findings raise questions about both jurors' awareness of their thought processes and judges' reliance on those assertions of fairness. In terms of peremptory challenges, prosecutors' choices would have resulted in a group of jurors that was more conviction-prone, but defense attorneys' intuitions were no better than judges'—they would have been as likely to reduce conviction proneness by simply flipping a coin.

A recent study used similar methodology to test jurors' ability to self-diagnose bias in the context of a civil trial. Robertson, Yokum, and Palmer

(2013) exposed some mock jurors to prejudicial pretrial publicity concerning the defendant, a doctor on trial for medical malpractice. Jurors were then asked a variety of *voir dire* questions that have been endorsed by the United States Supreme Court in *Skilling v. United States* (2010). These included questions about whether any opinion related to the publicity would prevent them from impartially considering the evidence at trial and whether they could base their verdicts only on the evidence presented in the courtroom. Although jurors who said "Yes" to the first question and "No" to the second would have been disqualified, all jurors in the study watched a realistic medical malpractice trial video. The researchers surmised that if jurors can accurately gauge the influence of prejudicial publicity on their judgments, then those who doubted their impartiality would be likely to find the defendant liable after hearing the publicity, but that the defendant's liability would be reduced if these people were removed from the analysis (i.e., as if they had been challenged for cause).

As expected, exposure to prejudicial publicity significantly influenced jurors' judgments, doubling the odds of a verdict against the defendant and more than tripling their damage awards. But these effects did not disappear when jurors who acknowledged some bias were removed from consideration. When all jurors were included in the analysis, 52% of those exposed to the prejudicial publicity deemed the defendant liable. But data from only those jurors who asserted their impartiality was essentially identical: 53% of those exposed to the prejudicial publicity found the defendant liable. So, as Robertson and his colleagues (2013) noted, banking on jurors' self-diagnoses of impartiality may not provide courts with a reliable way to sort biased jurors from unbiased jurors. A Harry Potter-esque "sorting hat" might prove to be just as reliable (for additional discussion of pretrial publicity, see Chapter 12).

Amidst all this attention to jurors' inability to self-diagnose, we need to ask whether there are, in addition to bias blind spots, any structural factors in *voir dire* that inhibit accurate forecasting of bias. One reason that jurors may have difficulty estimating their impartiality is that they get only a barebones description about what they will hear and see during the trial. With such minimal detail about the issues and only a cursory overview of what is expected of them, jurors cannot be expected to provide a good assessment of their capacity to be impartial (Rose & Diamond, 2008). At the end of the chapter we provide some suggestions for how this situation can be remedied.

Judges use heuristics to gauge jurors' impartiality. Whether a prospective juror says that she can be fair or claims that she cannot be fair, it is up to the judge to decide what to do next. This decision requires the judge to determine whether, given the juror's background and opinions, she is being honest (to the extent that she can be), is misrepresenting herself or being unnecessarily modest, or has some ulterior motive like getting out of jury service. In other words, the judge has to interpret the juror's demeanor and words—a tough task given the limited amount of information available. In making that decision, judges are likely to rely on simplifying strategies called *heuristics*.

Researchers Mary Rose and Shari Diamond (2008) evaluated whether the confidence with which jurors express their impartiality serves as a heuristic for judges' decisions about for-cause challenges. They suspected that judges would be less likely to excuse jurors who confidently stated their impartiality than jurors with identical backgrounds and attitudes who lacked confidence in their ability to be fair. In an experiment, they presented to real judges a series of vignettes in which prospective jurors had a problematic background (e.g., in a sexual molestation case the juror's daughter had been sexually abused, in a drunk driving case the juror's niece had been killed by a drunk driver) but in which the jurors reported, using more or less confident language, that they could be fair. Judges read an exchange between the hypothetical juror and judge that tried to clarify whether the juror could maintain an open mind and follow the instructions. Later, when asked whether they would have excused each prospective juror for cause, the judges tended to focus on jurors' certainty, perceiving those who gave a firm response as more likely to be fair than those who equivocated. Obviously, a juror's confidence can stem from various sources, including dispositional self-assurance, familiarity with a courtroom, and verbal fluency, that are unrelated to one's actual ability to be impartial. But as Rose and Diamond suggest, even an imperfect cue is preferable to no cue at all.

The Role of Implicit Bias in Peremptory Challenges

Judges sometimes sidestep the messy business of deciding whether to remove jurors for cause by rationalizing that attorneys can dismiss them peremptorily. Peremptory challenges allow attorneys to eliminate prospective jurors who were not dismissed for cause and others whom they suspect would be disinclined toward their side. Peremptory challenges also ensure the parties a measure of autonomy and independence from the judge because these strikes are in their hands, beyond the control of any judge. As Morrison suggests, "For one brief moment during jury selection, even the humblest litigant can wield the autocratic power of the Queen of Hearts, dismissing anyone who displeases her" (2014, p. 15–16). The autonomy that peremptory challenges afford to litigants may actually help legitimate the jury's verdict.

But peremptory challenges rest on the assumption that attorneys can identify jurors' biases—which, given their inaccessibility, is rather unlikely. Without such information, attorneys must rely on their own stereotypes and presumptions. And even though, as we will explain, attorneys are forbidden from challenging prospective jurors solely because of their gender or race, in practice those factors often drive their choices. Finally, when judges are positioned to circumvent gender- or race-based challenges, as is required of them, their own blind spots can get in the way. As a result, the implicit biases of both attorneys and judges can go unchecked during the exercise of peremptory challenges.

Attorneys have difficulty identifying biased jurors. Our legal system adheres to the tradition of peremptory challenges for reasons of autonomy and independence from the judge, but also because it assumes that lawyers can identify jurors who are biased. But *voir dire* is sometimes remarkably short, particularly in federal court, leaving attorneys with few insights about the leanings of prospective jurors. In addition, attorneys rarely get formal training in this task or feedback on the wisdom of past choices. So, as Hastie has noted, "[a]n attorney's ability to predict appears limited by a very low ceiling of precision" (Hastie, 1991, p. 712).

Empirical studies show that lawyers have difficulty detecting bias and determining which jurors would be more and less sympathetic to their side, which is what they really want to do, of course. In an early study, Zeisel and Diamond (1978) compared the decisions of actual juries and of juries consisting of people who had been excused through peremptory challenges and randomly selected venirepersons, and found that attorneys were only minimally effective in using peremptory challenges to their advantage. One reason seems to be that attorneys use fairly simple rules of thumb—as unsophisticated as those of college sophomores—to assess juror desirability (Olczak, Kaplan, & Penrod, 1991). Another reason is that attorneys exercise peremptory challenges in criminal cases without fully exploring the most relevant attitudes of prospective jurors. Johnson and Haney (1994) observed *voir dire* in state trial courts in California and compared the criminal justice attitudes of retained jurors in each case to those of a randomly selected group of 12 prospective jurors and the first 12 jurors questioned in the case. They found that although attorneys *mostly* used peremptory challenges to their advantage, still, some jurors who had extreme beliefs were retained even though the attorneys could have struck them. In the end, the actual juries did not differ markedly in terms of their criminal justice–relevant attitudes from these other groups. Lacking useful information about jurors' true inclinations, attorneys' decisions about whom to excuse apparently were informed by their own stereotypes.

The Batson framework. Although attorneys are not skilled at detecting bias in jurors, prosecutors, plaintiffs' lawyers, and defense counsel alike have suspicions about the types of jurors who would be favorable and hostile to their side. These suspicions often turn on jurors' appearance, age, gender, and particularly their race. But in 1986 the United States Supreme Court held that the 14th Amendment's Equal Protection Clause forbids the prosecutor in a criminal case from striking "black veniremen on the assumption that they will be biased in a particular case simply because the defendant is black" (*Batson v. Kentucky,* p. 97). In the years since *Batson,* the Court has extended the ban on the discriminatory use of peremptory challenges to criminal defense attorneys (*Georgia v. McCollum,* 1992) and civil trials (*Edmonson v. Leesville Concrete Co.,* 1991), and to cases in which Latinos (*Hernandez v. New York,* 1991) and Hispanics (*Allen v. Hardy,* 1986) have been challenged. The Court has ruled that the Equal Protection Clause also prohibits the discriminatory use of peremptory challenges based solely on jurors' gender (*J.E.B. v. Alabama ex rel. T.B.*, 1994), and federal appellate courts have issued conflicting rules on whether the prohibition extends to jurors' sexual orientation (*SmithKline Beecham Corp dba GlaxoSmithKline v. Abbott Laboratories,* 2014; *United States v. Blaylock,* 2005), signaling the possibility of review by the United States Supreme Court.

In *Batson*, the Court established a three-step process for assessing whether peremptory challenges were based on discriminatory intent. In step one, a defendant raises the inference that a prosecutor's challenge was race-based. In step two, the prosecutor is required to provide a race-neutral explanation for the challenge (one of only two instances in which an attorney must justify a peremptory challenge; the other requires a gender-neutral explanation when it appears that a juror has been challenged because of his or her gender). In step three, the trial judge decides whether the prosecutor's challenge reflects purposeful discrimination.

Various behavioral theories underlie the *Batson* decision, and most assume that racial considerations are conscious and explicit. For example, the *Batson* framework assumes that attorneys will be aware of their reasons for striking particular jurors and that they can honestly report these motivations to the judge. It assumes that judges can correctly distinguish between honest and dishonest rationales. In short, it rests on the "psychologically naïve" belief (Morrison, 2014, p. 30) that race-based judgments can simply be purged from *voir dire* through honest reporting and evaluation.

But a large body of research shows that most of us have implicit biases against racial minorities even when we assume that we are unbiased (see, e.g., Dovidio & Gaertner, 1998) and that a wide gap exists between what we think about our beliefs on this subject and what they actually are. The dissociation occurs because we want to think of ourselves, and we want others to think of us, as unbiased and open-minded (Norton et al., 2004). But even as people deny that race factors into their thoughts, implicit biases linger below the surface, outside of awareness, and thus difficult to report (Sommers & Norton, 2008). Attorneys are not immune.

Attorneys can justify biased peremptory challenges. But when required to justify their biased choices in step two of the *Batson* process, attorneys—like other people—are quite facile at generating reasonable and neutral-sounding explanations. Michael Norton and his colleagues (2004) termed this phenomenon "casuistry," the "specious reasoning in the service of justifying questionable behavior" (p. 819) and, along with Samuel Sommers, showed evidence of it in jury selection.

In one study, Sommers and Norton (2007) presented the summary of a robbery and assault case involving a Black defendant to three groups of participants: college students, law students, and trial attorneys, all of whom were asked to take on the role of the prosecutor. They were told that they would exercise their final peremptory strike by choosing between two prospective jurors, both of whom were unfavorable to the prosecution. (Juror A was familiar with police misconduct and Juror B was skeptical about forensic evidence that the prosecution would rely on in the case.) Researchers varied the race of the prospective jurors: In one condition, Juror A was Black and Juror B was White, and in a second condition their races were reversed. Results showed that participants' choices varied by jurors' race: The Black juror was challenged significantly more often than the White juror, and the effect was stronger for the trial attorneys than the students. But when asked to explain their decisions to a judge, participants rarely cited jurors' race. Rather, they were overwhelmingly likely to mention the reason the juror was believed to be unfavorable to the prosecution in the first place. So even without knowing about *Batson*, participants were loath to admit any influence of jurors' race and were easily able to generate plausible, race-neutral explanations.

Similar results occurred when Norton, Sommers, and Brauner (2007) varied prospective jurors' gender. That is, when the defendant was a woman on trial for murdering her abusive husband, participants acting as prosecutors were more likely to challenge female jurors and, despite the clear impact of jurors' gender on their choices, they were able to generate gender-neutral explanations.

Worth noting is the obvious fact that when attorneys *are* aware that they exercised a peremptory challenge on the basis of a juror's race or gender, they have a big incentive to deny it. Because they want to win at trial, they will shroud their biased choices with neutral-sounding justifications. According to one trial lawyer when asked to justify his peremptory strike, "you are tempted to engage in that thing which is absolutely horrible: lying in the courtroom. You have an ethical duty to be candid to the court, and yet we all know that pretext is the name of the game here" (Brown, 1994, p. 1209).

In light of these findings, the *Batson* formulation seems fraught with problems. Asking lawyers to identify their own implicit biases seems hopelessly naïve because these biases are, by definition, hidden from view. Attorneys who happen to be aware that race informed their decisions to strike particular jurors will deny it, and if questioned about their peremptory challenges they know what reasons to give and which to avoid. As some commentators have noted, "jurors are more likely to be struck by lightning than by a violator of the Equal Protection Clause" (Bellin & Semitsu, 2011, p. 1102). And not least, judges' assessments of attorneys' intentions also are prey to unconscious beliefs and stereotypes.

Judges accept attorneys' race- and gender-neutral explanations. In the third stage of a *Batson* challenge, judges have discretion to accept or reject attorneys' justifications for peremptory strikes. As Justice Stephen Breyer noted in his concurring opinion in *Miller-El v. Dretke* (2005), this obligation requires "judges to engage in the awkward, sometimes hopeless, task of second-guessing a prosecutor's instinctive judgment—the underlying basis for which may be invisible even to the prosecutor exercising the challenge" (pp. 267–268). Justice Breyer essentially acknowledged the difficulty of recognizing implicit bias.

More than 80% of the time, judges opt to accept the prosecutor's explanation for the peremptory strike (Melilli, 1996). In fact, the United States Supreme Court recently held it "harmless error" for a judge to accept prosecutors' explanations for excusing all of the minority jurors even when the explanations were given in a hearing at which defense attorneys were not present (*Davis v. Ayala*, 2015).

There are several reasons why judges are so likely to affirm prosecutors' justifications, including their own implicit biases. Having no objective way to measure the rationale behind an attorney's peremptory strike, judges must fall back on their intuitions about what is reasonable. Believing, like most of us, that they are fair and objective (and, in fact, socialized to appear that way), judges may have little access to the hidden forces on their thoughts and behaviors. Seeing no reason to question their own motivations or neutrality, they may simply assume that their instincts in accepting prosecutors' explanations are above reproach. It helps that their in-court decisions are infrequently appealed and even more rarely overturned by appellate justices.

Judges may also tend to accept gender- and race-neutral explanations because they do not wish to question or impugn the integrity of the prosecutor. Another reason is that the United States Supreme Court has held that prosecutors' race-neutral justifications need not be "persuasive or even plausible" (*Purkett v. Elem*, 1995, p. 768) so long as the trial judge deems them race-neutral. Thus, courts have found these explanations to be acceptable: "I don't like the way he's dressed. He looks like a drug dealer to me" (*State v. Crawford*, 2004); the juror "had dyed-red hair" (*Jackson v. State*, 2008); and the juror "had a hat on, kind of a large white hat, with sunglasses on" and "would have brought some attention to herself" (*State v. Tyler*, 2006). These examples suggest that nearly any justification will do so long as it does not mention race, rendering compliance with *Batson* mostly a formality (Morrison, 2014).

But in one recent case (*Foster v. Chatman*, 2016), United States Supreme Court ruled that prosecutors ultimately went too far in their efforts to remove Black jurors from a jury. In the 1987 trial of Timothy Foster, a Black man, prosecutors struck all four Black prospective jurors, and Foster was convicted of capital murder and sentenced to death by an all-White jury. This case is unusual because a "smoking gun" turned up in a public records request made years after Foster's trial: Prosecutors had taken notes during jury selection, highlighting and marking the names of all Black prospective jurors with a "B" and ranking them in case they had to select one to serve on the jury. Yet when they were called upon to explain their peremptory strikes, they denied that race was a factor. Instead, they said that the Black prospective jurors seemed disrespectful, nervous, hostile, and did not make sufficient eye contact, and the trial judge accepted this rationale despite the defense's objections. During oral arguments in *Foster v. Chatman*, Justice Elena Kagan asked, "Isn't this as clear a *Batson* violation as this court is likely to see?" So the *Foster* case may be an exception to the largely "toothless and symbolic" *Batson* framework which has allowed lawyers to give pretextual explanations of their peremptory challenges (Liptak, 2015).

At this point it is worth asking whether peremptory challenges serve their intended purpose of providing the parties some independence from the judge and an opportunity to sculpt the jury as they prefer. And it is worth considering whether the costs associated with peremptory challenges—eliminating prospective jurors because of their age, gender, sexual orientation, and especially race, and the lack of recognition by counsel and judges that these decisions are driven by implicit biases—justify their continued existence. It is beyond the scope of this chapter to describe the many arguments in favor of and opposed to eliminating peremptory challenges, or the many tweaks to the *Batson* framework that have been proposed over the years (e.g., Morrison, 2014; Ogletree, 1994). But much ink has been spilled on this topic, so a brief summary is in order. Proponents of elimination (e.g., Hoffman, 1997; Page, 2005) argue that, among other things, peremptory challenges are not constitutionally mandated, result in wasteful litigation, invite invidious discrimination, and deny citizens the opportunity to serve as jurors. Just as passionately, various groups of lawyers, academics, and judges, including the ABA (2005), the Arizona Supreme Court Committee on More Effective Use of Juries (1994), and attendees at a joint ABA–Brookings Institution conference (Litan, 1993) support the status quo. They contend, generally, that peremptory strikes provide an essential safeguard of litigants' rights and allow parties some autonomy to assemble the most favorable jury possible. Suffice to say that for the foreseeable future, peremptory challenges are going nowhere, as trial lawyers "would sooner dispense with a few amendments to the Constitution" (Hoffman, 2000, p. 136) than give them up, and to date no U.S. jurisdiction has eliminated them.

Remedies and Reforms

The core promise of trial by jury is that an assemblage of impartial laypeople can dispassionately judge the affairs and conduct of their fellow citizens. What do we make, then, of the fact that *voir dire*, the crucial first stage of a trial when the biases of prospective jurors should be addressed, falls woefully short of this ideal? Various remedies and reforms have been proposed, aimed mostly at improving the ability of attorneys and judges to detect bias in prospective jurors. But it is important to remind ourselves that these techniques are really only effective at uncovering stated, explicit bias (which might not even correspond to actual biased judgments) and at screening out jurors with the most extreme attitudes and beliefs related to the facts of the case. Implicit biases are likely to remain concealed from prospective jurors, attorneys, and judges alike, while affecting their conduct during jury selection and their assessment of the process when it is complete.

With that caveat in mind, we describe several means by which jury selection can be made more effective and move closer to the promise of providing a panel of impartial arbiters. First, it certainly cannot hurt for judges to become more knowledgeable about how various biases operate in prospective jurors and how their own actions (and inactions) promote withholding information and lack of candor. The National Center for State Courts (NCSC) has designed an intervention that uses a combination of hands-on activities (e.g., judges take the Implicit Associations Test) and research-based materials to increase judges' understanding of the science on implicit social cognitions (Kang et al., 2012). The program has now been pilot-tested in three states; its goal is to increase judges' motivation to adopt sensible countermeasures to address both explicit and implicit biases in prospective jurors. If nothing else, we hope that it encourages judges to remove the concepts of "set aside" and "rehabilitation" from their jury-selection vocabulary (Macpherson, 2014).

Among the countermeasures proposed is an increased reliance on juror questionnaires prior to in-court questioning. Principle 11 of the ABA *Jury Principles* recommends using written questionnaires to improve information gathering and dissemination, particularly on sensitive topics like criminal history, substance use, and personal finances that jurors might feel uncomfortable discussing in public and with strangers. Completing juror questionnaires gives respondents some time to contemplate their responses, searching their memories for relevant experiences and sentiments (Hans & Jehle, 2003). Questionnaires have the additional advantage of pinpointing topics that can be explored in subsequent in-court inquiries.

But according to a survey of state and federal court practices conducted by the NCSC (Mize & Hannaford-Agor, 2008), as of 2007 very few judges were utilizing pretrial juror questionnaires. This is unfortunate, because although there are costs in time and resources associated with creating a questionnaire, having jurors answer questions before trial may actually speed up jury selection. Simple details like demographics, educational and work histories, and legal experiences can be easily shared via questionnaire, leaving more time during *voir dire* for questions that probe prospective jurors' beliefs and attitudes. Hearing the responses to these sorts of nuanced questions will enable attorneys and judges to make better decisions about which jurors to challenge and excuse.

The NCSC survey revealed that another technique promoted by Principle 11 and intended to reveal information that jurors may be reluctant to disclose—individual *voir dire*—is also used only rarely. As we have noted, expecting jurors to volunteer sensitive information when questioned en masse, in the formal setting of a courtroom and in the presence of strangers, is quite unrealistic. This procedure may actually discourage jurors from identifying and disclosing their biases. But judges tend to view individual *voir dire* as burdensome, so unless a juror requests a private conversation they rarely use it.

Judges in a handful of states allow attorneys to give mini–opening statements, sometimes called "*voir dire* openings," at the start of jury selection. These statements, typically no more than 5–7 minutes long, provide prospective jurors some modicum of information about the dispute and the key issues in the case. Their purpose is to allow lawyers to explain "why we're here" (the explanation of "why we're right" is reserved for actual opening statements). As trial consultant Susan Macpherson correctly points out, asking jurors whether they can be fair and impartial when they do not yet know what they should be fair and impartial *about* may not lead to useful responses. She wrote, "there are very few jurors who have the nerve or the self-awareness to give the response that I recently heard from the back row of the jury box: 'Depends on what you guys got for me to decide!'" (Macpherson, 2013).

When jurors have a sense of what the case will entail, they can more effectively identify personal experiences and attitudes that may affect their ability to be fair. Providing a frame of reference for the tasks ahead may be especially necessary in a civil trial that involves concepts like antitrust and trademark infringement that are opaque to most laypeople. Macpherson (2014) gives the example of an eminent domain case that, when introduced using those terms, may mean little to prospective jurors. (Eminent domain refers to the power of the government to seize private land for public uses.) But when the issues are unpackaged and jurors learn that a key dispute concerns the potential use of property for a retail site and whether its value is diminished when access from a main road is removed, they will be better positioned to know whether their experiences or attitudes will matter. Macpherson has heard jurors say these sorts of things after hearing mini-openings: "I'm not sure if it matters, but given what you said about the case I thought I should tell you that . . . ." and "This situation is just too close to an experience that left a really bad taste in my mouth—I'm already leaning in favor of one side" (Macpherson, 2013).

Some New York state trial judges and attorneys took part in a field experiment in 2005 in which attorneys spoke to potential jurors about the case for 5 minutes at the outset of *voir dire*. In posttrial questionnaires, both judges and attorneys thought the practice was valuable. They agreed that it enhanced jurors' candor, improved their understanding of why they were being questioned, and perhaps most importantly increased their willingness to serve (Krauss, 2005).

Another remedy would broaden *voir dire* beyond its current scope. When *voir dire* is limited to relatively few questions put to an entire panel and even fewer follow-up questions to individual jurors, and when those questions come primarily from a judge, jurors are unlikely to provide a full and honest reporting of their sentiments. Expanding *voir dire* by giving attorneys the chance to pose questions, including follow-up and clarification questions, and allowing them greater latitude in what questions they may ask, would encourage candor. For one thing, it would eliminate jurors' tendency to give the socially desired responses (Bennett, 2010). For another, attorneys who are more familiar than the judge with the facts and issues in the case could ask more relevant questions. And the more that prospective jurors speak out, the better the chances that they will reveal biases and preconceptions that could inform judges' and attorneys' decisions (Marder, 2015).

Finally, we consider a questioning technique that encourages prospective jurors to reflect more deeply on their ability to judge a case that involves minority defendants. Schuller, Kazoleas, and Kawakami (2009) compared the effects of the standard close-ended challenge currently used in Canada and a more reflective strategy that required mock jurors to comment on *how* their ability to judge the case would be affected by the fact that the defendant was Black. The open-ended format resulted in a reduction in racial bias, perhaps because it reminded jurors that it was important to consider the evidence with an open mind to the extent possible. This finding is consistent with Sommers' (2006) demonstration that when racial issues are addressed head-on during *voir dire*, forcing jurors to ponder how their race-based attitudes might influence their reactions to the evidence, White jurors are less likely to convict a Black criminal defendant than if *voir dire* does not touch on race. Apparently, despite difficulties people have in knowing their biases and forecasting their future actions, if, during *voir dire*, they reflect on how they might respond to a socially sensitive topic during the trial, those biases are attenuated.

Conclusions

We began with the premise that the Constitution requires impartial jurors, and throughout the chapter raised various concerns about whether reality squares well with this ideal. In many respects, *voir dire* as currently practiced in the United States comes up short. Several of the problems we identified stem from the fact that all of us are biased in particular ways that influence our attention, preferences, assumptions, inferences, and judgments. (This in itself raises the interesting question of whether "bias" is even the appropriate term for this package of preconceptions and predilections!)

One implication of our conclusion is that the notion of a truly impartial juror is mythical, and the best that one can hope for are jurors and judges who *strive to be* open-minded, dispassionate, and even-keeled. Another is that attorneys and judges who must interpret jurors' statements about their beliefs should cast a wary eye on their conclusions. Attorneys wish to identify jurors who are hostile to their position, of course, and to protect those inclined in their favor, and judges try to detect those who seem less than fair-minded. But because most jurors lack awareness of what actually motivates and influences them, both attorneys and judges have only half-truths and limited insights to work with, and both must rely on their own suspicions and intuitions in making decisions during jury selection.

But we also believe that there are several "structural defects" in jury selection procedures which, if addressed directly, could expose jurors' partisan leanings and bring us closer to the ideal. We acknowledge that it will take longer to formulate pretrial juror questionnaires, query jurors in depth and in private once a trial commences, and provide mini–opening statements. We acknowledge that if judges eschew asking jurors to set aside their biases and opt out of rehabilitating—or worse, prehabilitating—them, *voir dire* might have to begin anew with a fresh crop of prospective jurors. But if the promise of impartial lay arbiters is to have any real meaning for litigants and for the legitimacy of the justice system, we should expect nothing less.

4

6 = 12 and They Don't All Have to Agree

".. . the reliability of the jury as a factfinder hardly seems likely to
be a function of its size"

(*Williams v. Florida*, 1970, p. 100–101)

"We have no grounds for believing that majority jurors, aware of
their responsibility and power over the liberty of the defendant,
would simply refuse to listen to arguments presented to them . . .
terminate discussion, and render a verdict"

(*Johnson v. Louisiana*, 1972, p. 361)

".. . no offense, but we are going to ignore you"

(Diamond, Rose, & Murphy, 2006, p. 216)

We explore two myths in this chapter: that smaller juries are functionally
equivalent to larger juries, and that juries allowed to reach a majority verdict
work essentially like juries whose verdict must be unanimous. These beliefs
stem from a series of United States Supreme Court rulings in the early 1970s
in which the justices made various assumptions about juror and jury behavior. Their decisions, and particularly their rationales, impelled psychologists
to conduct empirical studies to test those assumptions. And though what
they learned about optimal jury size and decision rule challenges the conclusions of the Court, their efforts may have been too little or too late, as
the rulings from the early 1970s still stand and six-person juries and non-
unanimous verdicts are commonplace in the United States (though unconstitutional in combination). We explore the consequences of these moves
for jury fact-finding, representativeness, and legitimacy, beginning with the
impact of varying jury size.

Does 6 *Really* Equal 12? The Effects
of Jury Size on Decision Making

One of the most sensational legal cases in recent years culminated in the July 2013 murder trial of neighborhood watch volunteer George Zimmerman, accused of killing unarmed teenager Trayvon Martin (see Chapter 1). The trial took place in Florida, where only six jurors are required to decide cases of serious felonies including murders. After a three-week trial, Zimmerman was acquitted of both second-degree murder and manslaughter by a six-member, all-female jury that included a lone non-White juror.

Perhaps it is no coincidence that the leading United States Supreme Court case on constitutional requirements regarding jury size also emanated from Florida. In that case—*Williams v. Florida* (1970)—the Court upheld the constitutionality of a six-member jury that tried and convicted Johnny Williams of robbery in 1967. Despite the fact that for seven centuries of common-law history and two centuries of U.S. constitutional history the accepted view was that a "jury" meant a 12-person jury, the *Williams* decision deemed a six-member panel equivalent in all respects to a 12-member panel and consistent with the requirements of the Sixth Amendment that "the accused shall enjoy the right to a speedy and public trial, by an impartial jury of the state and district wherein the crime shall have been committed." The practice of using six-member juries has been in place in Florida ever since.

In deciding essentially that "6 = 12" regarding the number of jurors required to try a case, the Court made various behavioral assumptions about how differently sized groups function and concluded that there would be few differences. In this chapter we describe these assumptions and the empirical research spawned by the *Williams* decision and its progeny. But first we return to the George Zimmerman trial and consider whether the verdict might have been affected by the fact that only six jurors deliberated his fate.

Several distinctions between six-member and 12-member juries could arguably have played a role in Zimmerman's acquittal (Diamond, 2013). The likelihood that the jury will be a representative sampling of the community is cut in half when there are only six as opposed to 12 jurors, and surely the all-female makeup of Zimmerman's jury is not representative of the community, even if the jury pool had been majority female. It is also noteworthy that in this racially charged case, only one member of the jury was non-White. In addition, with a smaller jury comes a narrower set of experiences and beliefs that can affect how the panel interprets and discusses the evidence. Finally, larger juries tend to deliberate more thoroughly and remember the evidence more accurately. Of course we cannot know whether a larger jury would have discussed the evidence more completely or reached a different verdict in this specific case, but as Diamond contends, a serious charge demands the highest procedural considerations. This may be especially true when the serious charge is tinged with racial considerations and inflames the nation, as this one did.

After much media scrutiny of the fact that Florida is one of just two states (Connecticut is the other) that allow six-person juries in murder cases, Florida state legislators introduced two relevant bills during their 2014 session. One bill (SB94) would have required 12 jurors in felony cases, though only when the charge carries the possibility of a life sentence, and sought to have juries reflective of the demographics of the county. The second bill (HB39) was broader, requiring 12-person juries in all felony cases and six-member panels in all other criminal cases. Both bills were killed in committee.

Jury Size in Historical Context

From where did the convention of having 12 people on a jury originate? In the twelfth century Henry II, King of England, established a system in which 12 free men were charged with the task of resolving land disputes. Blackstone's *Commentaries* on English common law, originally published in 1765–1769, clearly identified 12 as the proper number of people to constitute a jury:

> "'[T]he truth of every accusation, whether preferred in the shape of indictment, information, or appeal, should afterwards be confirmed by the unanimous suffrage of twelve of his equals and neighbours, indifferently chosen and superior to all suspicion'" (*Duncan v. Louisiana*, 1968, p. 151–152, quoting Blackstone).

The custom of having 12 people—at the time, only men—serve on a jury was passed on and practiced by early American colonists and persisted after the Revolution. It was enshrined in the Sixth Amendment for criminal cases and the Seventh Amendment for civil cases, though neither explicitly states that a jury must include 12 people. Nonetheless, that had been the tradition in this country since the Constitution was ratified. In an 1898 case, *Thompson v. Utah,* the Supreme Court interpreted the Sixth Amendment to require that in criminal cases, "a jury [be] comprised of twelve persons, neither more nor less" (p. 349).

Yet by the middle of the twentieth century, jury trials had undergone various transformations including reevaluation of the size requirement in response to concerns about the frequency of hung juries. The practice of lowering the minimum size of the jury was justified by the belief that smaller juries would be less likely to contain outliers who could impede agreement on a particular verdict preference. This practice and subsequent disputes about the constitutionality of juries with fewer than 12 members culminated in the 1970 case, *Williams v. Florida*, and the 1973 case, *Colgrove v. Battin,* both ultimately decided by the United States Supreme Court.

Supreme Court Decisions Relevant to Jury Size

In *Williams v. Florida* (1970) the petitioner argued that implicit in his Sixth Amendment right to a jury trial was a panel composed of 12 jurors. But the

Court rejected this argument, noting that there was no explicit reference to jury size in either the language or legislative history of the Constitution. The opinion declared that the traditional 12-member jury was an "historical accident unrelated to the great purposes which gave rise to the jury in the first place" (p. 101–102) and determined that a jury of six could satisfy the requirements of the Sixth Amendment. As a result, state courts have reduced the size of juries in both felony and misdemeanor cases ever since.

In its decision the Court developed a set of criteria to assess whether a six-person jury would function like a 12-person jury. These included questions about whether any reduction in size would adversely affect the quality of the deliberations, accuracy of jurors' fact-finding, verdict preferences, inclusion of a fair cross-section of the community on the panels, and ability of jurors holding minority perspectives to resist pressure from the majority. Concluding, without substantive empirical evidence, that the size of the jury would have no impact on these matters, the Court opined that six-person juries were functionally equivalent to 12-person juries. On what foundation *had* the Court relied? According to a recent analysis, it relied on: "1) what it claimed were empirical studies but which were not empirical studies at all; 2) actual studies, the findings of which the Court read exactly backwards; and 3) its own speculation" (Smith & Saks, 2008, p. 455). One source of empirical support (Cronin, 1958) was an interview of "a court clerk and three attorneys involved in trials in the district court, and these four persons said that the smaller juries seemed to behave the same as larger juries" (Smith & Saks, 2008, p. 456).

The decision in the *Williams* case was derided by jury scholars (e.g., Zeisel, 1971), who were quick to point out that the Court had cited studies that did not deal directly with jury size and, therefore, their conclusion was not empirically based. They also set about conducting research to examine differences between six-person and 12-person juries, and these studies were cited by the Court three years later in *Colgrove v. Battin* (1973), which focused on the constitutionality of six-member juries in federal civil trials. This time, the court claimed retrospective support from the empirical "evidence" it cited in *Williams* and current support from "four very recent studies [that] provided convincing empirical evidence of the correctness of the *Williams* conclusion that 'there is no discernible difference between the results reached by the two different-sized juries'" (*Colgrove v. Battin*, 1973). Jury scholars (e.g., Zeisel & Diamond, 1974) scoffed again, this time because the studies on which the Court relied had so many shortcomings that their conclusions were unreliable.

There were a few more developments in the Court's decision making regarding jury size and in researchers' responses to this line of cases. Perhaps anticipating that their ruling in *Williams* could be taken to an extreme, the Court decided in *Ballew v. Georgia* (1978) that the Constitution prohibited juries with fewer than six members because such small juries would not be representative of their communities. No major Supreme Court case has considered jury size since the 1970s.

This string of cases, decided by the highest court in the land yet seemingly unmoored from empirical support, launched a number of more sophisticated studies in the 1970s and 1980s that pointedly examined the effects of changing jury size. They focused on the criteria "relied on" by the *Williams* Court including the quality of the deliberations, reliability of jurors' fact-finding, verdicts, and minority representation. They also assessed the likelihood of hung juries in panels of varying sizes. Although research on jury size per se has subsided in the past few decades, recent studies of group decision-making processes are arguably relevant, as are forays into game-theoretic approaches to determining the effects of group size on trial outcomes. We review some of these studies in the following sections.

The Status Quo Regarding Jury Size

There is currently a patchwork of policies in place regarding jury size. Criminal trials in federal courts normally require 12 jurors. But nearly four-fifths of state courts currently use juries composed of fewer than 12 jurors in misdemeanor cases, and six states permit that in felony cases. Of the states that allow fewer than 12 jurors in felony cases, all require 12 jurors in capital cases, although Connecticut and Florida allow capital defendants to stipulate to smaller-sized juries (Rottman & Strickland, 2006).

In civil trials, federal courts and more than half of state courts allow fewer than 12 but at least six jurors. In states that do not require a full complement of 12, jury size is dependent on the judge's discretion and such issues as the nature of the claims and monetary value of the case. In some jurisdictions, smaller juries are used if both parties agree (Rottman & Strickland, 2006).

What Research Has Shown Regarding the Effects of Jury Size

The extant research on the effects of varying jury size can be broadly categorized into those studies that examine how the *processes* of decision making (e.g., consideration of minority viewpoints, memory of the evidence) change with the size of the jury, and other studies that focus on how trial *outcomes* (e.g., verdicts and damage awards) are affected. We use that dichotomy to guide our analysis here. Across all studies, researchers have tended to compare "larger" juries—typically consisting of 12 members—with "smaller" juries consisting of six or eight members. Some studies examine features of criminal cases and others look at factors in civil cases. The methodologies range from controlled, laboratory-based simulations to archival studies of actual trials. Some studies use correlational designs, and others employ experimental methodology. A meta-analysis of 17 studies (Saks & Marti, 1997) examined research published between 1972 and 1990 involving approximately 2,000 juries and 15,000 individual jurors. Nine of these studies used archival analysis and eight analyzed mock jury experiments.

How jury size influences decision-making processes. Conventional wisdom and sampling theory both suggest that smaller groups are less likely than larger groups to include a variety of perspectives, experiences, and beliefs. Larger groups are more likely to reflect the diverse array of individuals in a community. Saks (1996) provided a stark example by noting that "[i]f we draw juries at random from the population consisting of 90% one kind of person and 10% another kind of person (categorized by politics, race, religion, social class, wealth, or whatever), 72% of juries of size twelve will contain at least one member of the minority group, compared with only 47% of juries of size six" (p. 264).

In a criminal trial setting, concern focuses on whether smaller juries will contain members of minority groups—primarily racial/ethnic minorities—and jurors who are like criminal defendants in ways that enable them to provide a sociocultural or subcultural context in which to judge the defendant's conduct. This issue was articulated in *Ballew v. Georgia* (1978), when the Supreme Court recognized the importance of heterogeneity in criminal juries, particularly in jurisdictions that opt to use smaller panels. A parallel concern is whether members of minority groups will be able to voice their perspectives effectively to other jurors. Sampling theory predicts that a larger jury is more likely than a smaller group to include more than one minority group member. This is important because having allies with similar perspectives enables those jurors with diverse viewpoints to align themselves and assert their opinions in the face of opposition from the majority. Moreover, diverse juries provide other benefits in that they consider more case facts, make fewer factual errors, and deliberate for longer than juries that are less diverse (Sommers, 2006).

Empirical analyses support the notion that as group size increases, so too does the likelihood that individuals holding minority points of view will be represented (e.g., Tindale et al., 1996). The meta-analysis, which included three field studies of actual juries, showed that larger juries are more likely than smaller groups to contain at least one non-White member (Saks & Marti, 1997). Another study assessed the likelihood that African-American and Hispanic jurors were represented in eight-person and 12-person juries in actual trials in Los Angeles Municipal Court (Munsterman, Munsterman, & Penrod, 1990). Findings showed that of the eight-person juries tracked in this study, 20% included no African Americans and 31% included no Hispanics, although by population estimates the expected percentages were 6% and 20% respectively. Minority representation on 12-person juries was somewhat greater: 16% lacked African Americans and 18% lacked Hispanics. In short, reducing the size of the jury reduces the representativeness of that jury.

Jury deliberations suffer when viewpoints of racial minorities are not considered, particularly in cases that are tinged with racial overtones or that involve members of racial or ethnic minorities. Jurors belonging to different racial groups may process evidence differently (Taylor-Thompson, 2000), broadening the perspectives brought to the deliberation table. Not only do diverse juries consider a wider set of information, but they also tend to remember trial-related information more accurately, as evidenced by the fact that White jurors make fewer inaccurate statements as members of diverse juries than as members of homogeneous (i.e., all-White) juries (Sommers, 2006).

It is also reasonable to assume that larger (and theoretically more heterogeneous) juries are preferable to smaller (and theoretically more homogeneous) juries because the viewpoints represented by additional members will cancel out any extreme positions staked out by a few. Legal scholar Cass Sunstein (2002) articulated this assumption by suggesting that "homogeneity can be breeding grounds for unjustified extremism, even fanaticism, [and that to] work well, deliberating groups should be appropriately heterogeneous and should contain a plurality of articulate people with reasonable views" (p. 4). But there may be a downside to heterogeneity that bears mentioning: Although groups comprised of people with diverse perspectives may make more moderate decisions, they may also experience more difficulty than homogeneous groups of the same size in reaching consensus. (Note that this reflection concerns group heterogeneity and not group size per se, though as we note the two are intertwined.) The woeful legislative record of the United States Congress, composed in the recent past of lawmakers with increasingly divergent positions, is an all too real example of this problem. We consider the problem of gridlock—hung juries—as a function of group size later in this chapter.

Jury size can also affect the quality of the group's deliberation as measured by deliberation time. Presumably, larger groups will generate more discussion than smaller groups (Smith, 1997), and longer deliberations should be more thorough and wide-ranging than shorter deliberations. Larger juries do tend to deliberate longer than smaller groups (Davis et al., 1997), though the differences are surprisingly small. Saks and Marti (1997) found, in three studies that involved actual jurors, that larger groups deliberated an average of 45 minutes longer than smaller groups. In a more recent study that involved analysis of over 11,000 jury trials (Mize, Hannaford-Agor, & Waters, 2007), researchers showed an even smaller time differential: 12-member juries deliberated just 18 minutes longer than six-member groups. Whether these modest differences mean that larger groups engage in more substantive deliberations is somewhat unclear because factors other than group size per se may be implicated. It simply takes more time for a larger group to "get its act together," so process inefficiencies could explain the differences (Horowitz & Bordens, 2002), as could the possibility that larger groups are saddled with more complex decisions.

The most conclusive study on the effects of jury size on deliberation time (Brunell, Dave, & Morgan, 2009) underscores this last point. The dataset included the length of deliberations in 1,159 trials conducted in Portland, Oregon during the period 1973–1976 and examined a good mix of six-person ($n = 203$) and 12-person ($n = 931$) juries. Approximately half of the six-juror cases were civil trials, as were approximately 60% of the 12-juror cases. Researchers hypothesized that smaller juries would come to a decision more rapidly, and the raw data supported their prediction: The average deliberation lengths were 82 minutes for six-member panels and 122 minutes for 12-member juries. But once researchers controlled for other factors such as the severity of the crime and case complexity, the difference in deliberation time disappeared.

Yet another way to gauge the effects of jury size on deliberation quality is to assess whether juries composed of a larger number of people remember more of the evidence and recall it more accurately than juries composed of fewer people. Indeed, one crucial reason that we entrust important decisions to a group of jurors rather than any single individual is that we assume group members will possess nonshared information—knowledge unique to each of them—that they can transfer to the group, increasing the likelihood that the group will reach a well-informed consensus. According to a recent meta-analysis, information sharing positively predicts team performance (Mesmer-Magnus & DeChurch, 2009). So there is little doubt that for many kinds of decisions, involving more people brings more resources to the task.

Relevant data show that groups do recall trial-related information better than their individual members (Vollrath, Sheppard, Hinsz, & Davis, 1989), and larger juries tend to recall more information collectively and discuss it more accurately than smaller juries (Saks & Marti, 1997). What's more, the additional information recalled by larger groups appears to be highly relevant to evidence presented during the trial: When Horowitz and Bordens (2002) asked jurors to recall as much information as possible about a mock civil trial involving work-related injuries to the plaintiff, they found that 12-member juries recalled more probative facts than six-member juries. When they assessed reporting of information that was not probative—either because it was unrelated to the trial or was incorrect—they determined that six-member panels elicited more nonprobative statements when jurors were under high cognitive load, a finding that can be explained by the inability of jurors in these groups to provide proper checks on each other's memories.

But this pooling of resources may be beneficial only up to a point when returns begin to diminish, a situation well known to those who have tried to cook with too many others in the kitchen. In fact, smaller juries do have one advantage over larger juries in terms of the contribution of individuals to the judgment process. If equal participation by all jurors and optimal interaction among group members are desirable attributes of deliberative discussion, then smaller juries may be preferable to larger juries because a given individual has more opportunity to make a mark on the former than on the latter. Equal participation is, in fact, a goal of deliberation because each juror possesses unique information that can aid the group process. But just as there can be too many cooks in the kitchen, there can be too many jurors on a jury because, as Smith and Saks (2008) put it, "in larger juries, the talkative talk even more and the less talkative talk even less" (p. 465).

Studies of naturally occurring conversations show that regardless of the number of people present, there is an upper limit to the number who can converse effectively at any one time. Larger groups tend to splinter naturally into smaller groups that consist of four people—a speaker whose position rotates among group members and three listeners (Dunbar, Duncan, & Nettle, 1995). This would suggest that without an explicit or systematic process to include all members, a small contingent of a larger group will come to dominate discussion. The perspectives of quieter members, as in 12-person juries, may be lost altogether.

There is considerable support for the idea that jury members rarely contribute equally to the deliberation. In mock jury studies that used participants from actual jury pools, Strodtbeck, James, and Hawkins (1957) found that just three jurors accounted for more than half of the discussion in 82% of the deliberations. Others (e.g., Hastie, Penrod, & Pennington, 1983) have shown that a quarter of jurors actually remained silent during the entire jury discussion. More recently, observers determined that 33% of mock jurors were infrequent contributors to the discussion and 25% never spoke at all (Shestowsky & Horowitz, 2004). Some jurors reported feeling bullied or intimidated (Tinsley, 2002), sentiments that surely do not promote involvement and inclusiveness. Tracking the contributions of more than 2,000 criminal jurors in 302 juries, Cornwell and Hans (2011) showed that jurors of higher social status were more likely than their lower-class counterparts to participate.

Other research has shown that the size of the jury affects the likelihood of individual participation. In comparing deliberations from larger and smaller juries, Velasco (1995) found that at least one juror remained silent during the entire deliberation in more than half of large juries, whereas all members of smaller juries contributed to the discussion. When Waller and colleagues (2011) compared the experiences of mock jurors in a group of 12 with jurors subdivided into small groups that mirrored optimally-sized conversational sets (i.e., three groups of four), they found that individuals in small groups felt less intimidated and contributed more to the group discussion. Compared with members of 12-person juries, those on six-person juries reported that both they and fellow jurors contributed more to the deliberations in a mock civil trial (Horowitz & Bordens, 2002).

The silence of some members of larger juries does not stem from the lack of opportunity to speak up, however. In fact, 98% of jurors questioned in a recent survey said they had ample opportunity to participate (Gastil, Burkhalter, & Black, 2007). Rather, reduced participation in larger groups is likely because individuals can rely on the contributions of fellow members to put in the cognitive effort required to complete a task, a concept related to diffusion of responsibility and known as *social loafing* (Najdowski, 2010). It can be unclear to members of a large group—a 12-person jury, for example—how much any one person contributes to the final product, the verdict. So jurors on larger juries can essentially hide in the crowd, whereas members of smaller juries have less opportunity to conceal themselves. As a result, those in smaller groups are more conscientious about matching their performance to that of others in the group.

A conclusion one might reach from studies of social loafing is that juries should be composed of fewer than the 12 people currently required by federal and many state statutes. But that would be a mistake, as a simple cost-benefit analysis can show. Indeed there are costs associated with a 12-person jury including, as we just described, the lack of full participation from all members as well as the inefficiencies associated with organizing a discussion that involves 12 people (to say nothing of the added time it takes to select 12 rather than six jurors during *voir dire*). But the benefits we have already outlined regarding broader minority representation and enhanced recall of the evidence on 12-member panels are significant for both symbolic and practical reasons that we expand on later in the chapter.

Moreover, there are ways that individual jurors can be nudged to contribute to the deliberations, even on larger juries. Although jury deliberations are sometimes characterized by fervent disagreement, the tone of the discussion can be modulated by directives from judges, and to the extent that this guidance can enhance group cohesion, more jurors are likely to participate. Gordon (2015) urges that jurors be trained in decision making, information sharing, and procedural matters, and she provides concrete examples of what such training might entail. Juror orientation materials can enhance group solidarity even before the trial begins, assuring individual members of their value to the entire panel (see Chapter 2). Finally, posttrial polling when the verdict is delivered in court allows for each juror's voice literally to be heard, which can increase jurors' feelings of instrumentality and sense that they are being evaluated (Najdowski, 2010). To our mind, these remedies are far preferable to a reduction in jury size.

How jury size influences decision-making outcomes. We now ponder how, if at all, the size of the jury affects verdicts—guilt judgments in criminal cases and liability and damages decisions in civil cases. We also consider the likelihood that the jury will be unable to reach consensus in both kinds of cases. Sampling theory provides a basis for deriving expectations about how and when jury size should matter. According to this theory, larger juries will produce correct verdicts more often than smaller juries because larger samples result in less variable outcomes. This obviously begs the question of what is a "correct" verdict. Although there is no clear benchmark of correctness, one can gauge accuracy by assuming that, absent some community-wide hysteria or mob mentality (e.g., witchcraft, lynching), a correct verdict is the one the entire community would have chosen had the community constituted the jury. As discussed in Chapter 1, a key function of juries is to embody and express community sentiment. If we choose citizens for juries who are representative of their community, then larger samples (juries) will come closer than smaller samples to approximating the community's sentiments because with a larger number of community members making decisions, the margin of error associated with those decisions decreases.

The true test of this theory will never be conducted, as it would require multiple samplings of juries of varying sizes and, more problematically, a sense from the entire community of what the correct verdict might be. So rather than dwell on the question of whether larger juries are more likely than smaller juries to issue *correct* verdicts, researchers have asked whether groups of different sizes issue *different* verdicts. On this question, the data are fairly clear: juries of different sizes do not produce verdicts that differ significantly (Saks & Marti, 1997). Further, smaller and larger juries reach similar verdicts in criminal cases regardless of whether the cases tend to favor conviction or are more evenly balanced (Kerr & MacCoun, 1985).

But there is an interesting footnote to this general finding: Although verdicts issued by large and small juries are essentially equivalent, those coming from six-person juries may be less predictable than those issued by 12-person juries because the verdict preferences of members of smaller juries will be more dispersed, and the group norm will be weaker and more variable. As proof, Snortum and colleagues (1976) planted confederates with extreme viewpoints into both six-person and 12-person juries and found that the outlier was able to have more impact in smaller groups, shifting the group verdict from 24% guilty to 45% guilty in 12-person juries and from 30% guilty to 72% guilty in six-person juries. Because group norms and pressure to align with those norms are weaker in smaller groups, a person who espouses an extreme position will have more power in a smaller jury.

Similar forces prevail in the realm of civil cases. Awards from smaller juries will be less predictable and more variable than those from larger juries. Again, sampling theory can explain why. According to the law of large numbers, larger groups give more reliable estimates of population parameters—in these cases, consensus about an appropriate damage award. Thus, awards from large juries will be more tightly clustered around the population average, whereas awards from small juries will be more dispersed and include both very small and very large awards, rendering them both more variable and less predictable (Hans, 2001).

The results of two mock civil jury studies support these suppositions. Davis and his colleagues (1997) had six-person and 12-person mock juries decide a product liability case and found that awards from six-member juries were both larger and more variable than awards from 12-member juries. Similar findings came from a study in which six-member and 12-member juries viewed a trial involving a plaintiff who sued an employer for injuries sustained on the job (Horowitz & Bordens, 2002). Mean damage awards were higher in six-person than in 12-person juries, and awards from smaller juries were more variable.

These findings are rather troubling because, unlike criminal juries that typically involve 12 members (at least for felonies), the size of civil juries varies substantially from state to state (Rottman & Strickland, 2006), meaning that plaintiffs and defendants in different jurisdictions will receive different treatment as a function of the number of jurors deciding their cases, among other factors. The increased variability and reduced predictability in awards from smaller juries could also affect settlement practices because in jurisdictions with smaller civil juries, attorneys will be less able to anticipate how a jury would decide a case. When attorneys lack that knowledge, settlement negotiations may break down sooner and more cases will be passed on to the trial stage (Saks, 1996). As Valerie Hans (2001) notes, "[p]aradoxically, attempting to promote efficiency by reducing jury size might actually increase the burden on our courts" (p. 14).

Sampling theory also makes very straightforward predictions about the likelihood of hung juries as a function of group size. A larger group should deadlock more often than a smaller group because individuals with minority perspectives are more likely to have allies on larger juries, allowing them to resist pressures to conform and resulting in more gridlock.

What do the studies reveal about the incidence of hung juries in groups of varying sizes? Although a few early studies hinted that impasse might be more likely in larger juries, there are reasons to be skeptical of their results. For example, although jurors in mock armed robbery trials deadlocked more often in larger juries than in smaller groups (Kerr & MacCoun, 1985), this result can easily be explained by the very restricted time (10 minutes) they were allowed to deliberate. The meta-analysis finding (Saks & Marti, 1997) that 12-member juries were more likely than smaller groups to end in hung juries can also be called into question. Here, the effect appears to be associated with simulations in which trial evidence was intentionally ambiguous and limitations on deliberation time were often imposed. Either of these factors, rather than jury size, could explain why juries deadlock. In fact, simulated studies included in the meta-analysis resulted in hung juries 19% of the time, while only 1% of archival studies involving actual juries did.

More recent studies (e.g., Eisenberg et al., 2005; Hannaford-Agor, Hans, Mott, & Munsterman, 2002) have failed to show any differences in hung-jury rates as a result of jury size, and the widespread reduction in jury size from 12 to six that began after the *Williams* decision (1970) has not reduced the mistrial rate in the United States (Luppi & Parisi, 2013). It bears keeping in mind, though, that the diminution in jury size has occurred predominantly in the civil arena, and civil cases are significantly less likely than criminal cases to end in deadlock (Hans, 2001).

But there are other reasons that, contrary to sampling theory predictions, larger juries are no more likely than smaller juries to hang. Normative social influences are more powerful in larger groups, meaning that a lone holdout or two will have a harder time maintaining that position on a 12-member jury than on a six-member jury (Devine, 2012).

Two economists provide another explanation of the so-called hung-jury paradox. By examining group polarization and cascade behavior that occur during deliberations, Luppi and Parisi (2013) noted that jury decision making involves dependent or correlated decisions in which group members speak sequentially, with the goal to influence the choices and decisions of others in the group. As the deliberation unfolds and the opinions of other jurors are made clear, people tend to become less confident of their prior beliefs and ever more convinced that one conclusion—the group consensus—is the correct one. This sequential exchange of information—informational cascading—means that hearing others' verdict preferences renders each juror less responsive to his or her own beliefs and, therefore, less informative to others. This dynamic is sometimes referred to as contamination of the jury deliberation process. In time, informational cascading propels the group to coalesce around a shared outcome, and it does so more consistently in larger groups than smaller groups.

So there may be countervailing forces at work as jury size changes. The probability of a hung jury should increase with jury size because there are more people with diverse beliefs in a larger group. But normative influence is stronger in larger groups, and cascade behavior means that jurors' judgments are attuned to the sentiments expressed by others and adjusted by what others have said. As a result, by the time a juror with divergent views is able to express an opinion, his or her perspective already may have changed in response to other people's opinions. In many situations, informational cascading takes precedence and a larger group will come to consensus more often than a smaller group.

Is there an optimal jury size? One might reasonably ask why comparisons of jury size focus almost exclusively on the numbers six and 12. The simplest answer is that Johnny Williams was convicted by a Florida jury that included just six members, whereas juries had historically involved 12 jurors. His case then launched a series of empirical studies in the 1970s and 1980s that assessed differences between juries with six and 12 members. But are either of those the optimal size of a jury? If a jury of 12 is an "historical accident," then why not consider eight or nine or 10 jurors? Although slightly smaller juries may be less likely to include minority representation, they may not function less effectively than 12-person juries (whether they do is an empirical question, of course), and reducing the number below 12 could result in savings associated with jury selection and possibly shorten the length of the deliberation. Might the cost of reduced representativeness be worth the benefit of efficiency?

In recent years, economists have brought game-theoretic approaches to the question of the optimal jury size. The research by King and Nesbit (2009) is especially clear in laying out the alternatives and the costs of using juries of various sizes. King and Nesbit note that most studies attempting to determine the optimal size of a jury have concentrated on the cost of two errors in jury verdicts—convicting the innocent and acquitting the guilty—and have failed to account for the cost to jurors themselves, mainly in their time. Thus, they modeled the expected *total* social cost of a jury decision by taking into consideration both the costs associated with judgment errors and juror-related costs. The data were derived from the 2001 Civil Justice Survey of State Courts, which included details from civil cases tried in the

75 most populous counties in the United States in 2001 (Bureau of Justice Statistics, 2001). Although the methodological details are beyond the scope of this chapter, the general objective was to use regression analyses (including a variable number of jurors) to estimate the expected total costs of the average jury decision and the cost-minimizing that occurs with juries of different sizes. Results showed that a model which reduced the social costs of convicting an innocent person and acquitting a guilty person, as well as the opportunity cost of jurors' time, involved a jury of nine members. A nine-person jury (or any other odd number) also has implications for trials that do not require a unanimous verdict, as discussed below. Interestingly, only North Dakota uses nine-member jury panels and even there, only in civil trials.

What Can We Conclude About the Effects of Jury Size?

Court officials often cite efficiency concerns and the desire to speed trials along as justification for reducing the size of juries. Implicit in this perspective is the expectation that with fewer jurors, *voir dire* will be shortened, jury deliberations will be completed more quickly, and the prospect of a mistrial stemming from a hung jury will be reduced, all without any deleterious effect on the decision-making process itself. In the *Williams* case, the Supreme Court went even further in stating unequivocally that a jury of six is equivalent in nearly all respects to a jury of 12.

Our review of the relevant empirical data suggests that at best there is minimal support for these assumptions. In fact, there is good reason to believe that larger juries outperform smaller juries on several dimensions. They also have symbolic and practical value that their smaller counterparts lack. Larger juries collectively remember the trial evidence more completely and accurately and award damages that are less variable and, hence, more predictable. And although individual jurors may be more involved in deliberations that involve fewer participants, the verdicts that emanate from smaller juries are not different in substantive ways from those that come from larger groups. Nor do smaller juries deliberate for less time or hang less often than their more densely populated cousins. After reviewing the empirical evidence on jury size, Smith and Saks (2008) conclude succinctly that "six- and twelve-person juries are not functionally equivalent and thus six-person juries impair the constitutional purpose and function of the jury" (p. 463).

All of this might be sufficient to challenge preferences for smaller juries, but concerns about minority representation should seal the deal. There is clear evidence that community members from racial or ethnic minority groups and those whose perspectives are different from the mainstream are underrepresented on smaller panels. This imbalance affects the way in which a jury makes its decisions, as homogeneous groups tend to consider a narrower set of perspectives than heterogeneous groups. But the more significant impact of underrepresentation may have little to do with what occurs behind the closed doors of a deliberation room. Underrepresentation on juries can have a profound effect on how minority communities perceive fairness or lack thereof in the court system. Community members come to trust the process and outcome of legal dispute-resolution forums to the extent that they believe their interests and those of their friends and neighbors are represented and respected (Tyler & Jackson, 2014). Being excluded or disregarded as arbiters of criminal charges or civil claims, even if the intent to exclude is lacking, renders people less trusting of the courts and the outcomes that occur there. Whatever minuscule savings may be realized by a reduction in jury size is surely not offset by the practical and symbolic losses associated with reduced minority representation.

Should They All Have to Agree? The Effects of Decision Rule on Jury Judgments

In criminal trials in Texas, all 12 members of a jury must agree on a verdict. That seemingly simple concept was questioned in October 2014 when jurors deliberating the fate of Ed Graf, being retried 28 years after an arson conviction in the deaths of his two young stepsons, sent a question to the judge. The question provided a moment of levity in an otherwise deadly serious matter because it asked how many jurors would have to vote for a verdict to make it unanimous. As expected, the judge replied that all 12 would have to concur.

Setting aside this rather odd inquiry, there is serious contentiousness about the proper decision rule for both criminal and civil trials: whether unanimous verdicts should be required or whether verdicts based on majority rule can suffice. As with the debate over the appropriate size of a jury, this issue presents a balancing test between efficiency and accuracy. Proponents of majority rules argue that they reduce the likelihood of hung juries and thus the costs associated with retrials. Costs are also reduced in majority-rule juries because deliberations tend to be shorter. Furthermore, majority rules deprive "one oddball, crank, or corrupt person" (Abramson, 1994, p. 201) from derailing the thoughtful discussion of those in the majority. But critics claim that majority rules undermine serious deliberation by silencing jurors with thoughtful minority positions and thereby threaten the legitimacy of the jury's verdict (Diamond et al., 2006).

This issue has many similarities with the jury size debate. After centuries in which unanimity was the norm, traditions began to weaken in the twentieth century, and cases questioning the constitutionality of less-than-unanimous verdicts eventually made their way to the United States Supreme Court. The rulings in these cases claimed support from empirical research, though that support was essentially vapid. And, like the jury size rulings, they spawned a number of more sophisticated research efforts that now allow us to assess some clear differences in how juries deliberate as a function of their decision rule. In elucidating the effects of different decision rules, these endeavors point to both *process* and *outcome* changes. Accordingly, we structure subsequent sections of the chapter along those lines. But first we provide an historical context and describe patterns in decision rules currently in place in courts across the United States.

Decision Rule in Historical Context

The Sixth Amendment provides for an impartial jury in the jurisdiction in which a crime was committed; it says nothing about how many jurors must agree on a verdict. The Seventh Amendment, guaranteeing the right to a trial by jury in suits at common law, says even less. Regardless, prior to the twentieth century there had been a long history of unanimous verdicts in the Anglo-American legal system. The rule was established in 1367 by King Edward III, has been the norm in England for six centuries, was adopted by most of the American colonies, and soon after became common practice. Blackstone's *Commentaries* explicitly mention the virtue of unanimity:

> "[i]t is the most transcendent privilege which any subject can enjoy, or wish for, that he cannot be affected either in his property, his liberty, or his person, but by the unanimous consent of twelve of his neighbors and equals" (1979, p. 379).

Supreme Court Decisions Relevant to Decision Rule

United States Supreme Court rulings of the late nineteenth century implied that unanimity was an essential feature of trials in this country. In 1897 the Court ruled that unanimity was required in civil trials (*American Publishing Company v. Fisher*) and the following year held that it applied in all federal trials, both civil and criminal (*Thompson v. Utah*, 1898). As Riordan (2012) states, "there lies an almost unbroken line of decisions that canonized the virtues of jury unanimity" (p. 1422).

But that lineage was severed in 1972 when the Court issued rulings in a pair of cases—*Johnson v. Louisiana* and *Apodaca v. Oregon*—that deemed constitutional jury verdicts that had been rendered by a majority of state court jurors. (Frank Johnson had been convicted of armed robbery by a 9–3 vote—the minimum level of agreement for conviction in Louisiana at the time, and Robert Apodaca was found guilty of assault with a deadly weapon by a vote of 11–1 after a 41-minute deliberation. The minimum number of votes to sustain conviction in Oregon at the time was 10.) In both cases, and eerily similar to the jury size decisions, the majority ruling included behavioral assumptions about how juries would function under varying contexts. In *Johnson,* Justice White opined that under majority rule, majority jurors would thwart discussion only *after* it ceased to be effective and further, because these jurors are "aware of their responsibility and power over the liberty of the defendant" (p. 361), they would not simply refuse to listen to arguments presented by the minority holdouts. Likewise, in *Apodaca*, Justice White rejected the notion that under majority rule, jurors in the minority would be unable to represent their viewpoints, reasoning that they would be present throughout the deliberations so their opinions would be considered. He concluded that neither the quality of the deliberation nor the reliability of the verdict is compromised by majority rule and approvingly noted the reduction in hung juries when unanimity is not required. Unsurprisingly, perhaps, these intuitions about how juries function are contradicted by current jury research—findings that we illuminate in this chapter.

Also in parallel with its rulings on jury size (i.e., *Ballew v. Georgia*, 1978), the Supreme Court drew a line regarding the minimum level of agreement that the Constitution requires. In *Burch v. Louisiana* (1979), it decided that convictions by a non-unanimous six-member jury were unconstitutional. This is essentially the last word about constitutionally allowable decision rules from the highest court in the land. In 2014 the Court denied *certiorari* in *Jackson v. Louisiana*, a case that once again challenged the constitutionality of the framework for decisions by Louisiana juries.

The Status Quo Regarding Decision Rule

The movement away from jury unanimity after the *Johnson* and *Apodaca* decisions has not been nearly as consequential as the move to reduce jury size, at least in serious criminal cases (Hans, 2001). The one exception— not surprising, perhaps, given the jury size requirements—is Florida, where the most consequential decision, to recommend the death penalty, can be made by a simple majority of jurors. In terms of decisions about a defendant's guilt in a criminal trial, Oregon and Louisiana remain the only states that allow non-unanimous verdicts, and even their requirements have become more stringent in the intervening years. Oregon law allows for conviction by a 10–2 vote in most criminal cases but requires an 11–1 verdict for conviction in murder cases and a unanimous verdict in a capital murder case. Louisiana law now also requires at least 10 votes in the majority for conviction and unanimity in capital cases. (Federal criminal trials have always required a unanimous verdict.) Despite the fact that just two states currently allow non-unanimous verdicts in criminal cases, loosening the requirements for agreement is not a moot issue. Legislators from California, Colorado, and New York have introduced bills to rescind unanimity requirements in criminal trials. Although these proposals are couched as anticrime initiatives, Riordan (2012) offers a different rationale, suggesting that "there is obvious and powerful political capital to be gained from increasing conviction rates, regardless of the means by with one does so" (p. 1405).

Quite a different picture emerges regarding unanimity requirements in civil trials, with great variability across jurisdictions. Approximately half of the states allow non-unanimous verdicts in civil cases, and the majority of these use either a 3/4 or a 5/6 decision rule. Iowa law requires a 7/8 majority and Montana law demands just a 2/3 majority (Rottman & Strickland, 2006). As in criminal cases, verdicts in federal civil trials must be unanimous.

What Research Has Shown Regarding the Effects of Decision Rule

Scholarly interest in the effects of varying decision rules began in earnest after the Supreme Court decisions of 1972 (e.g., Davis et al., 1975; Kerr et al., 1976; Nemeth, 1977), continued through the 1980s (e.g., Hastie et al., 1983; Miller, 1985), and, with a few recent exceptions, subsided in the 1990s. But as with jury size effects, some clarity has been provided recently by theoretical studies of group decision making (e.g., Rijnbout & McKimmie, 2014) and economic modeling of jury-like situations (e.g., Coughlan, 2000; Neilson & Winter, 2005). Many early studies involved mock jury methodology in which researchers manipulated the voting rules (requiring agreement of 2/3, 3/4, 5/6, or all jurors) and then assessed how individual verdict preferences were translated into group decisions. In particular, they examined the thoroughness and accuracy of deliberations, jurors' subjective impressions of the deliberations, the likelihood that all jurors have an opportunity to contribute, the nature of the verdicts, and the incidence of hung juries.

The most sophisticated mock jury study (Hastie et al., 1983) had participants watch a reenactment of a murder trial and deliberate in 12-person juries under one of three decision rules: 2/3 (eight of 12 jurors had to agree), 5/6 (agreement among 10 of 12), or unanimity. Researchers filmed and content-analyzed the deliberations, focusing particularly on how decision rules affected the duration and quality of the deliberations. Two other studies merit attention. Diamond et al. (2006) provided a unique perspective on deliberations under majority rule by analyzing the content of actual jury discussions in 50 civil trials conducted in Arizona, where six of eight jurors must agree on a verdict. The cases were fairly typical of those tried by juries: half involved motor vehicle claims, and a third involved other sorts of torts. Plaintiffs won 65% of these cases with damages ranging from $1,000 to $2.8 million. And quite recently, in the first jury study ever conducted in Taiwan, Huang and Lin (2014) focused on how decisions are affected by two deliberation rules under consideration for newly implemented lay panels that deliberate and issue advisory decisions to professional judges. Huang and Lin manipulated the decision rule (majority or unanimity) and filmed the deliberations of 39 juries in a phone fraud case. They were especially interested in how deliberating under these two rules affected jurors' aversion to wrongful convictions and other post-deliberation decisions. Like efforts from the 1970s, these

studies all addressed the fundamental question of how voting requirements affect the deliberation process and whether, as Justice White pos-
ited, juries operating under different voting rules function in roughly
equivalent ways.

How Decision Rule Influences Deliberation Processes

Simulation studies have shown that jury deliberations are generally shorter
under majority rules than when unanimity is required (Hastie et al., 1983;
Kerr et al., 1976; Miller, 1989; Vollrath & Davis, 1980). Hastie and colleagues
observed that unanimous juries deliberated an average of 138 minutes,
whereas those operating under a 10–2 rule deliberated 103 minutes on average, and juries using an 8-4 rule deliberated an average of only 75 minutes.
Under non-unanimous voting rules, juries tend to cease deliberating when
the necessary quorum is reached. According to Hastie et al. (1983), in juries
that can return 8–4 verdicts, "little occurs after the faction size reaches eight
. . . Deliberation continues for a few minutes, typically less than five" (p. 95).
However, when groups were required to be unanimous, approximately 20%
of the deliberation occurred after the majority faction reached eight persons,
and fully one-third of juries operating under a unanimity rule failed to agree
on a verdict.

But the data on deliberation length as a function of decision rule are actually rather murky. Worth noting is the analysis of more than 1,000 Oregon
jury trials conducted from 1973 to 1976: The average unanimous jury deliberated for 91 minutes, whereas the average non-unanimous jury deliberated
for 133 minutes (Brunell et al., 2009). A large-scale project of real juries, the
"State-of-the-States" project (Mize et al., 2007), also found that juries reached
a verdict faster under unanimity than majority rule. These findings may be
related to structural rules that govern majority-rule jury deliberations. In a
jurisdiction that allows 10–2 verdicts, it is reasonable to assume that any jury
issuing a unanimous verdict was rather likely to be unanimous from the outset of deliberations. (After all, with a majority vote option the group has no
need to struggle to reach full consensus.) In contrast, a jury that issues a 10–2
verdict was probably split at the initial vote with fewer than 10 jurors on one
side or the other (e.g., 6–6 or 7–5), and had to continue to deliberate to reach
the 10 votes minimally required for a verdict.

Within reason, lengthier deliberations are preferable to shorter ones
because with time, jurors scrutinize the evidence more carefully and apply
their instructions more conscientiously. Furthermore, in approximately 10%
of trials the verdict favored by a majority of jurors at the beginning of deliberations is *not* the verdict that the jury eventually issues (Kalven & Zeisel,
1966). Had these juries been operating under a majority decision rule, they
would have terminated their discussions prematurely.

The thoroughness and accuracy of deliberation—factors inherent to the
duration of deliberations—also vary with decision rule. By various metrics,

unanimous juries are more thorough than majority juries: They discuss key facts to a greater extent, cover more of the evidence, correct mistaken assertions more often, and pay greater attention to the law (Hastie et al., 1983). Working under unanimity rules increases the pooling of uniquely held information and reduces the negative effects of outliers, as dealing with deviant positions becomes an accepted part of the decision-making process (Rijnbout & McKimmie, 2014). When questioned about their deliberations after trial, members of Arizona juries that reached a unanimous verdict (69 of 167 juries examined by Hannaford, Hans, & Munsterman [2000]) reported that their deliberations were of higher quality than did those that reached a majority verdict. The former were more likely to say that the deliberations focused on critical issues and that jurors' collective memory of the evidence was good.

Decision rules can also affect the nature of the deliberations, including how the discussions and votes unfold. Operating under majority voting rules, juries are likely to take their first formal vote within 10 minutes of beginning deliberations, and they tend to vote often until they reach a verdict. These verdict-driven deliberations are generally less thorough and serious than evidence-driven deliberations which characterize discussions under a unanimity requirement (Hastie et al., 1983). Groups that must reach a unanimous decision tend to discuss the evidence at some length prior to taking their first vote.

Closely related to the thoroughness of the deliberation is its inclusiveness; that is, whether it encompasses the perspectives of *all* jurors. Inclusiveness can be thought of in at least two respects: considering the input of jurors in the voting minority (holdout jurors), and attending to and valuing the perspectives of jurors from ethnic and racial minority groups. We consider these processes in turn.

In his dissent from the majority in *Johnson v. Louisiana* (1972), Justice Douglas conceded that although a majority with the requisite votes might deign to listen to the minority, there are important differences between "courtesy dialogue" (p. 389) and the robust arguments necessary to sway other jurors. Group theory predicts that eliminating the unanimity requirement will diminish contributions from holdout jurors because when only a majority vote is required, jury members can give short shrift to the viewpoints of the minority. Both mock jury studies (Hans, 1978; Hastie et al., 1983) and analyses of actual jury deliberations (Diamond et al., 2006) show unequivocally that participation of minority-view jurors is reduced when unanimity is not required. Once jurors in majority-rule contexts have the votes, they essentially disregard any member with opposing views by terminating attempts to resolve differences. One of the jurors in the Arizona study made this very explicit, informing another, ". . . no offense, but we are going to ignore you" (Diamond et al., 2006, p. 216). Obviously, this sort of outright dismissal means that any possibility of compromise is eliminated and that alternative perspectives and interpretations of the evidence and the law are not considered. It does nothing good for the snubbed juror's feelings about having performed a civic duty.

Non-unanimous decision rules can also thwart the input of jurors from racial and ethnic minority groups, despite the fact that juries are to represent a cross-section of the community. This was one of the arguments made by the petitioners in *Johnson* and *Apodaca*, namely that majority rules interfere with the application of the fair cross-section requirement of jury trials. In response, Justice White reasoned that not "every distinct voice in the community has the right to be represented on every jury and a right to prevent conviction of the defendant in any case" (*Apodaca v. Oregon*, p. 413). Taylor-Thompson (2000) counters that a majority-decision rule will have a disproportionate impact on jurors of color and female jurors because their perspectives and verdict preferences often diverge from other jurors'. She argues that this rule essentially eliminates "the voice of difference" on a jury (p. 1264). As far as we know, this claim has not been examined empirically.

The operative decision rule also has an effect on jurors' subjective impressions of their trial-related experiences. According to Jeffrey Abramson (1994), "[t]his is so intuitively plausible that we probably did not need fancy mock jury studies to prove it: jurors not voting in favor of the majority's verdict are hardly likely to think justice was done" (p. 200). Such mock jury studies exist and they *do* show that jurors who deliberate under unanimity rules are more satisfied with the process and confident of their verdict (Hastie et al., 1983), and unanimous-rule jurors who were initially in the minority express stronger support for the final verdict than majority-rule jurors in the minority (Huang & Lin, 2014). A similar pattern emerges from actual juries (Diamond et al., 2006), as jurors in the Arizona study whose jury reached unanimous verdicts were more satisfied with the experience than those whose deliberations ended with a majority verdict. Interestingly, even when their opinion ultimately prevailed, those in majority juries rated the experience as less positive than jurors who reached unanimous verdicts, perhaps because they observed dismissive treatment of the holdouts. So although it may be somewhat more difficult to reach a unanimous verdict, jurors are more satisfied with the experience when they do.

How Decision Rule Influences Deliberation Outcomes

Next we ask whether the decision rule is systematically related to the frequency of convictions and acquittals in criminal cases and to liability judgments and damage awards in civil cases. Because outcomes in simulated criminal trials are typically limited to guilty and not-guilty verdicts (though lesser-included options are not uncommon in real trials) and verdicts in simulated civil trials involve continuous alternatives, it is easier to predict and evaluate the effect of varying decision rules on criminal verdicts.

One might suspect that juries operating under majority rules require less evidence to convict and do so more often, thereby increasing the likelihood of both correct and mistaken convictions. The petitioner in *Johnson v. Louisiana* (1972) alleged that a non-unanimous rule led to his wrongful conviction because guilt beyond a reasonable doubt was not proven if three jurors harbored doubts about his guilt. (Johnson was convicted by a 9–3 majority.) There is some support for this idea: Modeling studies have shown that the probability of conviction under a 5/6 decision rule is higher than under a unanimous decision rule (Friedman, 1972), as is the probability of convicting an innocent person (Nagel & Neef, 1975). They have also shown that as unanimity requirements are weakened, the probability of both correct and wrongful convictions increases (Neilson & Winter, 2005).

But many studies have found that criminal verdicts (i.e., the distribution of guilty and not-guilty verdicts) are not affected by the operative decision rule (Devine, 2012). Rather, juries tend to return the verdict that is favored by the majority of jurors at the beginning of deliberation (Stasser, Kerr, & Bray, 1982), though this effect is somewhat stronger in majority-rule juries than in unanimous-rule juries (Huang & Lin, 2014).

When jurors initially in the minority on unanimous-rule juries change their vote, they switch more often from conviction to acquittal than the opposite, consistent with the defendant leniency effect (MacCoun & Kerr, 1988). This suggests that unanimous voting requirements will reduce the probability of convicting an innocent defendant. Game-theoretic approaches that model the effects of voting rules on the likelihood of trial errors—convicting the innocent and acquitting the guilty—tend to support this suspicion (Coughlan, 2000).

Decisions are structured differently in civil cases, requiring contingency responses that criminal trial verdicts do not. The issue is not conviction versus acquittal, but rather whether a defendant is liable on a particular claim and if so, how much money the plaintiff should receive. To complicate matters further, civil jurors are often asked to allocate the percentage of liability between the plaintiff and defendant and must pool their damage assessments in some way to reach a consensus judgment. They receive only rudimentary instructions on these matters (Greene & Bornstein, 2000; see also Chapter 9 of the present volume) and no directive whatsoever about what role, if any, an outvoted dissenter on liability should have during the discussion about damages (Diamond et al., 2006). Thus, predicting how unanimity and majority requirements will affect the win rates and award levels in civil trials is a tricky business.

In terms of the effects of decision rules on liability judgments, there exist various beliefs about their impact but little hard data. For example, Diamond et al. (2006) note that plaintiffs are expected to fare better under majority rules because when unanimity is required, pro-plaintiff jurors may be forced to compromise on the size of the award in order to bring pro-defense jurors into agreement on liability. In addition to being a clear violation of judge's instructions to determine liability and damages separately, this assumes, of course, that holdout jurors tend to favor the defense—a questionable assumption, according to analyses of the Arizona jury deliberations.

As we noted previously, sampling theory predicts that decisions based on a larger number of individual inputs will be more stable and predictable than decisions that involve fewer. This suggests that majority rule may lead to larger or smaller awards than unanimous rule. But the few existing studies of effects of decision rules on damage award decisions show something a bit different, at least in situations where pre-discussion preferences are skewed—as is usually the case when money is the issue. Here, juries operating under unanimity rules must accommodate any outliers who advocate for extreme awards. This means that awards will be higher or lower (depending on the direction of skewness of the initial preference distribution) under unanimity than majority rule. This expectation has been confirmed by Kaplan and Miller (1987), who found that mock juries' punitive damage awards were higher when unanimity was required, and partially confirmed by Ohtsubo, Miller, Hayashi, and Masuchi (2004), who found that the most extreme award preferences correlated with the jury's verdict under unanimity rules but not under majority rules.

Finally we address the question of how decision rules affect the likelihood of hung juries. Theoretically, hung jury rates should be lower among majority-rule juries because jurors in the majority can simply outvote the minority holdouts. Studies show that this is true (Miller, 1985; Vollrath & Davis, 1980). There are at least two ways to consider this fact: in terms of cost savings and verdict accuracy. First, regarding cost savings: Hung juries are an infrequent occurrence—roughly 2% of federal trials, between 4% and 6% of state trials, and just one of the 50 juries filmed in the Arizona project (Diamond et al., 2006)—and many cases are dropped or settled after a hung jury. Since jury verdicts constitute such a small proportion of total dispositions in the first place, there is probably little to be gained in cost savings by reducing the small number of hung juries that occur when unanimity is required (Van Dyke, 1977). Regarding verdict accuracy: Not all hung jury verdicts result in dropped charges or settlements, of course; some lead to retrials. And modeling has shown that when these retrials are taken into account and verdicts are eventually reached in criminal cases, unanimous jury rules tend to result in more accurate verdicts than non-unanimous jury rules, primarily by leading to the conviction of guilty defendants (Neilson & Winter, 2005). After all, because the evidence against a defendant must have been strong for the trial to hang, hung juries are more likely to occur for guilty than for innocent defendants. In sum, unanimous rules add relatively minor costs and a bit more accuracy to criminal trials.

What Can We Conclude about
the Effects of Decision Rule?

As it did when reasoning about acceptable jury size, the Supreme Court beat psychologists to the punch regarding the appropriate decision rule, though their conclusions seem misguided in retrospect. The rulings in *Johnson v. Louisiana* and *Apodaca v. Oregon* concluded, with little more than intuition to back them up, that eliminating unanimity would have a negligible effect on the nature or outcome of jury deliberations. Psychological research that challenged that assumption came only later.

But now we understand the costs associated with less-than-unanimous verdicts: Majority rule reduces both the breadth of perspectives and the depth of analysis in deliberations, quiets the voices of holdouts and racial and ethnic minority jurors whose views on the case may differ from majority jurors, reduces satisfaction with the deliberation process and confidence in the verdict among *all* jurors, and renders judgments less predictable and accurate. In general, the effects of eliminating unanimity mirror the impact of reducing jury size by undermining the quality, completeness, and accuracy of the jury's deliberation and rendering their verdicts less defensible and hence, less legitimate.

Conclusions: The Optimal Framework
for Jury Decision Making

We value the collective wisdom of a jury to settle matters of grave importance to society. As Abramson (1994) notes, a key function of the jury system is to legitimize the state's exercise of coercive power in the eyes of the citizenry by allowing "ordinary persons like ourselves" (p. 203) to determine verdicts. So it is perplexing that we structure jurors' task—at least in terms of the rules they use to make decisions and the number who must agree—in ways that lead to questionable outcomes. If inclusion of varying perspectives heightens the legitimacy of the jury, then the bulk of the data favor 12-person unanimous juries, as they ensure that ethnic and racial minorities and those outside the mainstream are represented, have allies, and get heard. If predictability in verdicts heightens the legitimacy of the jury, then 12-person unanimous juries should be the norm, as they remember the evidence more accurately, discuss it more thoroughly, and rein in extremism. In this light, the costs associated with larger and unanimous juries, such as slightly increased trial times and minimally higher rates of hung juries, seem slight and inconsequential. The weight of the evidence strongly favors 12-member unanimous juries.

5

Jurors Can Distinguish Accurate
from Inaccurate Eyewitnesses

> "It is common knowledge that eyewitnesses may make mistakes
> and may forget what they have seen."
>
> *(State v. McClendon*, 1999, p. 1115)

In March 1985 a student at Texas Tech University in Lubbock, Texas, named Michele Mallin, was raped at knifepoint and robbed. She got a good look at her assailant, who drove her, in her car, outside of town to commit the assault before returning to Lubbock. Ms. Mallin told the police that the perpetrator was a young African-American man, described his clothing, and said that he had smoked cigarettes during the attack.

Two weeks after the crime, police arrested Timothy Cole, a 26-year-old Army veteran and student at Texas Tech. Ms. Mallin positively identified Cole in a photo lineup and subsequent live lineup. She identified him again at his trial for aggravated sexual assault. Fortunately for Timothy Cole, he had a pretty good defense. Witnesses testified that on the night of the rape they had observed him studying at home, where his brother was hosting a card game. He had severe asthma and did not smoke. Victims of previous similar rapes did not pick him out of the same lineup viewed by Ms. Mallin (police believed that a serial rapist was responsible for all the attacks). Similar attacks continued to occur after his arrest. Forensic evidence, such as serology and hair testing, did not exclude him but was not very conclusive, either.

Unfortunately for Timothy Cole, none of that mattered much in light of the victim's positive identification. The jury deliberated for six hours before convicting him of aggravated sexual assault, and he was sentenced to 25 years in prison. After the statute of limitations had passed, another Texas prisoner confessed to the crime, but Cole died in prison in 1999 before any-thing came of it. DNA testing posthumously exonerated Cole and implicated the other man. Texas Governor Rick Perry pardoned Cole in 2010, and the state created the Timothy Cole Advisory Panel on Wrongful Convictions and passed the Timothy Cole Act to provide services to the exonerated and com-pensation to them or their families. Ms. Mallin, the victim, now works to raise awareness about misidentifications and wrongful convictions (http://www.innocenceproject.org/Content/Timothy_Cole.php; other eyewitnesses whose identifications turned out to be erroneous have also taken this brave step; see, e.g., Thompson-Cannino, Cotton, & Torneo, 2009).

Like the Connecticut Supreme Court cited above (*State v. McClendon*, 1999), everyone knows that memory is fallible. We all experience this every day when we fail to remember an acquaintance's name, forget to pick up something at the store, or miss an item on a test. Most memory errors are fairly benign. But others are not, and in the legal arena, their consequences can be catastrophic. Misidentifications are involved in approximately 75% of all convictions determined to be false by DNA testing, and in many cases they were the only evidence against the defendant (Garrett, 2011; Gross et al., 2005; Wells, Memon, & Penrod, 2006; for details on individual cases, the Innocence Project, http://www.innocenceproject.org, has compiled a wealth of information).

If people know that memory is fallible, then why are they so believing of eyewitnesses? The major reason, we propose, is that (as in the case of Timothy Cole) by the time eyewitnesses make it all the way to trial, they are highly confident. And jurors—who themselves believe that when they are sure of something, they are more likely to be correct—use eyewitness confidence as an indicator of accuracy. People naturally assume that individuals who are more confident are more knowledgeable, even when greater confidence does not mean greater accuracy (Price & Stone, 2004). Although eyewitness confi-dence is a better predictor of accuracy under some circumstances than others (e.g., Sporer, Penrod, Read, & Cutler, 1995), it is a relatively weak predictor overall (Leippe & Eisenstadt, 2007). The irony is that witnesses who are low in confidence might be just as reliable as highly confident witnesses. Yet wit-nesses whose confidence is shaky rarely testify, in part because those cases are dropped at earlier stages in the process.

Laypeople, who are prospective jurors, tend to believe that eyewitnesses are reliable (Benton, McDonnell, Ross, Thomas, & Bradshaw, 2007; Boyce, Beaudry, & Lindsay, 2007; Read & Desmarais, 2009). Accordingly, they fail to appreciate many of the factors that predict eyewitness performance and rely instead on nonpredictive factors, especially witness confidence. Nonetheless, courts typically assume that the fallibility of memory is a matter of "common sense" and use this assumption to exclude expert testimony on eyewitness issues (Benton et al., 2007; we cover this topic in depth in Chapter 7). The present chapter reviews research on what jurors know, or think they know, about eyewitness memory. As we will show, the situation is not as simple as "jurors understand the limitations of eyewitness memory," but it is also not as clear-cut as "jurors are out in left field." Moreover, others involved in the trial process, such as judges and attorneys, suffer from some of the same biases.

A common distinction in talking about eyewitness factors is between system variables, which are under the legal system's control (e.g., how to conduct lineups), and estimator variables, which are not (e.g., characteristics of the witness, perpetrator, or event; see Wells et al., 2006). There is some evidence that laypeople are more aware of estimator than system variables (Shaw, Garcia, & McClure, 1999), yet that awareness does not necessarily translate to proper reliance on factors that predict eyewitness performance and dismissal of those that do not. For both classes of variables, some factors that should influence jurors' judgments—because they have an empirically documented impact on eyewitness performance—do exert an effect, but others do not. Conversely, certain factors that should not influence jurors' judgments— because they lack an empirically documented impact—appropriately do not have an effect, whereas others do (Boyce et al., 2007).

Methods for Measuring Beliefs About Eyewitnesses

Researchers have developed several techniques for assessing laypeople's beliefs about eyewitnesses and measuring how those beliefs, as well as eyewitness testimony itself, influence juror decisions. Boyce et al. (2007) identify three principal techniques: questionnaires, in which laypeople (or others) are surveyed about their beliefs regarding the various factors that do and do not affect eyewitness performance; prediction studies, in which participants observe eyewitness testimony or read about an eyewitness situation and evaluate the eyewitness's accuracy or credibility; and jury simulation studies, similar to studies that we have covered in other chapters but where one of the key variables of interest is eyewitness testimony. As always, each technique has its pros and cons. For example, questionnaires are susceptible to wording bias (Read & Desmarais, 2009), prediction studies are fraught with ethical and practical complications (Boyce et al., 2007), and simulations might fail to capture important aspects of a real trial (see Chapter 1). For that reason it is important to compare across methodologies in order to obtain convergent validity; or, alternatively, to determine that results obtained using one particular method do not generalize to others.

Questionnaire Assessment of Eyewitness Beliefs

Questionnaires are perhaps the most common means of assessing what people believe about eyewitness memory (Desmarais & Read, 2011). They have been used with a variety of populations: laypeople, judges, attorneys, law enforcement, and experts. Experts are a valuable population to study for two reasons: first, they are not infrequently called to testify as expert witnesses in cases involving eyewitness testimony, a topic we discuss in depth in Chapter 7. Second, assessing the knowledge of experts is one of the best ways available for determining the truth regarding the various factors that do and do not affect eyewitness performance. Although the research is not always conclusive, a consensus has developed among eyewitness researchers on the impact of a number of variables (Kassin, Ellsworth, & Smith, 1989; Kassin, Tubb, Hosch, & Memon, 2001). Thus, the beliefs of experts can be compared to those of other populations to assess how much the other groups know about eyewitness reliability. Our focus here is on laypeople, especially in comparison to experts; later in the chapter we consider the various categories of legal professionals.

In what is probably the most heavily cited eyewitness expert survey, Kassin and colleagues (2001) asked 64 eyewitness memory researchers their opinions on 30 eyewitness phenomena (see Box 5.1). For each topic, the experts indicated whether (and how strongly) the evidence supported a statement about the phenomenon (e.g., "Very high levels of stress impair the accuracy of eyewitness testimony," "Eyewitnesses have more difficulty remembering violent than nonviolent events"), and they also indicated (yes/no) whether the phenomenon "was reliable enough for psychologists to present it in courtroom testimony" (Kassin et al., 2001, p. 407–408). For 16 phenomena (indicated by * in Box 5.1), more than 80% of the experts believed that the research was reliable enough to testify on in court, which Kassin et al. took as a strong endorsement of the reliability of the phenomenon. Such surveys can then be used as the standard by which to judge others' beliefs.

Box 5.1 Eyewitness Phenomena in the Kassin et al. (2001) Survey

1. Stress	2. Weapon focus*	3. Showups
4. Lineup fairness	5. Lineup instructions*	6. Exposure time*
7. Forgetting curve*	8. Accuracy-confidence*	9. Postevent information*
10. Color perception	11. Wording of questions*	12. Unconscious transference*
13. Trained observers	14. Hypnotic accuracy	15. Hypnotic suggestibility*
16. Attitudes & expectations*	17. Event violence	18. Cross-race bias*
19. Confidence malleability*	20. Alcoholic intoxication*	21. Mugshot-induced bias*
22. Long-term repression	23. False childhood memories	24. Discriminability
25. Child witness accuracy	26. Child suggestibility*	27. Description-matched lineup
28. Presentation format*	29. Elderly witnesses	30. Identification speed

Direct comparisons of experts and laypeople have found considerable disagreement between the two groups. For example, Kassin and Barndollar (1992) asked a sample of college students and community adults whether a subset of the statements used by Kassin et al. (2001; drawn from an earlier version of the expert survey; see Kassin et al., 1989) were "generally true" or "generally false." There was little difference in the beliefs of students and nonstudents; however, lay participants' opinions differed from the experts' opinions on 13 of 21 topics. In some instances laypeople were less aware than experts that some factor affected performance (e.g., lineup instructions, exposure time, cross-race bias), whereas in other instances laypeople overestimated the impact of a factor (e.g., the confidence-accuracy relationship, gender differences, hypnosis). Put another way, laypeople knew what the experts knew on only eight of the 21 topics. Similar studies comparing experts and laypeople have likewise found an unimpressive level of layperson knowledge (e.g., Benton, Ross, Bradshaw, Thomas, & Bradshaw, 2006). On the one hand, this should come as no surprise: If laypeople know as much as the experts, then the experts are not really very expert. On the other hand, it is problematic if the supposedly commonsense nature of eyewitness memory phenomena serves as grounds for restricting jurors' access to information that could correct their misconceptions, such as via expert testimony (see Chapter 7) or jury instructions (see Chapter 14).

Other eyewitness belief surveys have used somewhat different methods but with largely comparable results (Lindsay, 1994; Boyce et al., 2007). For example, in one of the earliest studies in the genre, Deffenbacher and Loftus (1982) administered the Knowledge of Eyewitness Behavior Questionnaire (KEBQ) to several samples: two groups of college students drawn from institutions in different states (Washington and Nebraska) and a group of citizens in Washington, D.C., some with experience serving on a jury and some without. Rather than asking whether a certain statement is supported by the evidence, or whether participants agree with the statement, the KEBQ contains 14 multiple-choice questions, each with a "right" answer according to expert consensus. Across all samples, participants scored better than chance (i.e., > 25% accuracy on the 4-choice questions) on about half the items. The pattern of responding was largely the same across the different groups, except that the D.C. participants were consistently less knowledgeable. This finding is noteworthy not only because this was the most diverse and "jury-like" sample, but also because respondents with prior jury experience had, indeed, just completed their jury service. Not only does experience as a juror fail to improve laypeople's knowledge of eyewitness issues (Magnussen, Safer, Sartori, & Wise, 2013), but prior experience acting as a witness in a real legal case does not help either (Noon & Hollin, 1987).

Overall, then, laypeople—both students and adult community members—display an unimpressive level of knowledge about eyewitness memory. The major caveat to this conclusion is that methodological issues in the questionnaires' construction can influence respondents' performance. Put another way, laypeople might have more accurate knowledge than the questionnaire is able to tap. Persuasive evidence in favor of this possibility comes from a study conducted by Read and Desmarais (2009), who surveyed three community samples of jury-eligible Canadian participants. In their first study, they asked participants to rate their agreement, on a 4-point scale (from strongly disagree to strongly agree), with 29 of the 30 statements used by Kassin et al. (2001; Read and Desmarais deleted one item because it lacked a clear expert consensus). Respondents could also answer "Don't Know." Although laypeople's beliefs fell somewhat short of experts' knowledge (based on the Kassin et al. findings), their overall rates of agreement were nonetheless considerably higher than those in previous surveys (e.g., Benton et al., 2006; Kassin & Barndollar, 1992). For example, for items on which there was a strong expert consensus (>75% agreement), lay participants agreed with the experts roughly two-thirds of the time. On items where the participants fared worse, there was correspondingly less agreement among the experts.

It is tempting to conclude that the Canadian participants in Read and Desmarais' (2009) study were simply smarter or better informed than the American participants included in other eyewitness knowledge surveys; however, they likewise outperformed Canadian respondents in previous studies (Yarmey & Jones, 1983), and surveys of laypeople in other countries yield findings that are essentially comparable to data from American samples (e.g., Houston, Hope, Memon, & Read, 2013; Magnussen, Melinder, Stridbeck, & Raja, 2010; Noon & Hollin, 1987). Moreover, national comparisons have yielded few significant differences (Desmarais & Read, 2011). Interestingly, in the minority of instances where national differences do emerge, Canadian respondents do better than both American and British respondents (Desmarais & Read, 2011), perhaps mirroring the fact that Canadian detectives are more knowledgeable about accepted procedures for dealing with eyewitnesses than their American counterparts (Greene & Evelo, 2015). Racial and ethnic differences might also exist, at least for select topics. For example, African Americans are more likely to be aware of the cross-race effect than Whites (Abshire & Bornstein, 2003).

Read and Desmarais (2009) attribute the differences to greater public awareness of wrongful convictions, false memories, and investigative procedures (Desmarais, Price, & Read, 2008). Consistent with this interpretation, a recent meta-analysis of eyewitness knowledge surveys found that laypeople are becoming more knowledgeable over time, at least for some topics (Desmarais & Read, 2011). Read and Desmarais also point to the possible influence of methodological differences among the various studies, which they explored in two follow-up surveys. In these additional questionnaires, they attempted to increase comprehensibility of the items by rewording statements and reducing technical jargon (Surveys 2 and 3), or by adding contextual information through the inclusion of brief case vignettes (Survey 3). These changes increased accuracy and reduced the frequency of "Don't Know" responses, suggesting that laypeople know more about eyewitness memory than they sometimes show, depending on how their knowledge is assessed (see also Desmarais & Read, 2011; Houston et al., 2013). The improvement when providing case vignettes is particularly noteworthy, as other research has similarly found that people are more sensitive to factors predicting eyewitness performance when judging concrete scenarios than when evaluating abstract statements (Alonzo & Lane, 2010).

Predicting Eyewitness Performance

Many judges believe that jurors can tell the difference between accurate and inaccurate eyewitnesses (e.g., Houston et al., 2013; Wise & Safer, 2004). This belief underlies judges' reluctance, in many trials, to implement safeguards that might aid jurors in evaluating eyewitness testimony (Wise & Safer, 2004). The critical question, then, is: *Can* jurors (or laypeople in general) distinguish accurate from inaccurate witnesses?

Scientists have tried to answer this question by using various methodologies, but the most common type of eyewitness prediction study consists of two phases (Boyce et al., 2007). In the first phase, participants witness some event, often a staged crime, and subsequently recall details of the event and/ or attempt to make an identification. This procedure produces both accurate and inaccurate eyewitnesses. Researchers sometimes also vary the witnessing conditions during this phase. In the second phase, other participants observe the eyewitnesses from Phase 1 as they make an identification or testify about what they saw; they then judge (i.e., predict) whether the eyewitnesses were accurate or not. Some prediction studies couch the task as part of a trial, in which the Phase 2 participants also reach a verdict based on the eyewitness (and usually other) testimony.

One of the earliest, and still one of the best, exemplars of a prediction study was conducted by Lindsay, Wells, and Rumpel (1981). In the first phase, students who were participating in an experiment witnessed a theft, staged under conditions designed to elicit relatively low, moderate, or high levels of accurate eyewitness identifications (accomplished by varying exposure time to the thief and whether he wore a hat). The witnessing conditions had the expected effect on eyewitness accuracy (33%, 50%, and 74% in the low, moderate, and high conditions, respectively). The experimenter then showed witnesses a six-person lineup and, if they made a positive identification, filmed them being cross-examined about their memory of the perpetrator (e.g., "Describe what the person was wearing," "How long was the person in the room?" etc.).

In the second phase of the study, Lindsay et al. (1981) showed a separate group of participants ("evaluators") videotapes of four different cross-examinations. They viewed accurate or inaccurate witnesses from one of the three witnessing conditions (i.e., all four witnesses viewed by a participant came from the same cell produced by the 2 [accuracy] × 3 × [witnessing conditions] design). In addition, each evaluator viewed witnesses who had relatively high and relatively low confidence in their identification. For each witness, evaluators indicated whether they believed the witness had made an accurate identification.

Witnesses' actual accuracy had no effect on evaluators' judgments of their accuracy (Lindsay et al., 1981). However, the evaluators were more likely to believe witnesses who expressed high confidence in their identification, even though the Phase 1 data yielded only a weak (but statistically significant) relationship between confidence and accuracy. They were also more likely to believe witnesses who had seen the theft under conditions relatively conducive to accurate perception. But the effect of witnessing conditions was limited to judgments of low-confidence witnesses; evaluators believed witnesses who expressed high confidence about three-quarters of the time regardless of the circumstances under which they viewed the crime.

Wells and Lindsay (1983) replicated these findings in several other studies. Consistently, evaluators were unable to distinguish accurate from inaccurate witnesses, and eyewitness confidence had a pronounced effect on their judgments of eyewitness accuracy. Moreover, the effect—more properly the absence of an effect—is quite robust. Telling evaluators to ignore an eyewitness's confidence did eliminate the effect of confidence, and it made them less likely to believe an eyewitness's testimony overall; however, it made them no more successful at distinguishing accurate from inaccurate witnesses (Wells, Lindsay, & Tousignant, 1980). In addition, the effect held even when witnesses were questioned by actual lawyers in a real courthouse, and videotapes of their testimony were shown to mock jurors as part of a simulated trial (Lindsay, Wells, & O'Connor, 1989). Lindsay et al. found that accurate and inaccurate eyewitnesses produced roughly equal conviction rates (68% vs. 70%), whereas there was a significant correlation between witnesses' perceived confidence and mock jurors' verdicts.

Although most prediction studies have found that evaluators are poor at discriminating accurate from inaccurate witnesses, there are exceptions (e.g., Martire & Kemp, 2009; Smalarz & Wells, 2014). For example, Smalarz and Wells followed the standard two-phase paradigm, with the exception that Phase 1 participants viewed a video of a simulated crime rather than witnessing a live staged crime. In addition, they manipulated whether or not witnesses received confirming feedback after their identifications ("Good job! You got the guy") but before they gave testimony. Such postidentification feedback has been shown to increase eyewitnesses' confidence, as well as to distort their retrospective judgments related to their perception and memory of the event (Douglass & Steblay, 2006). Smalarz and Wells found that when witnesses were not given feedback, evaluators were quite successful at distinguishing between accurate (70.3% believed) and mistaken eyewitnesses (35.9% believed). However, their ability to discriminate between accurate and mistaken witnesses disappeared when the witnesses had been given confirming feedback. Importantly, mistaken witnesses who received confirming feedback are also perceived as more accurate, confident, and credible than those who did not (Douglass, Neuschatz, Imrich, & Wilkinson, 2010; MacLean, Brimacombe, Allison, Dahl, & Kadlec, 2011).

Smalarz and Wells (2014) caution that certain aspects of the postidentification feedback paradigm, such as not giving witnesses the option to reject the entire lineup, might have made discrimination easier than it would normally be in actual cases. Nonetheless, their study yields two important conclusions: First, laypeople are capable of discriminating between accurate and inaccurate witnesses under some circumstances; and second, there are things that lineup administrators can do to make discrimination worse. This is a strong argument for implementing procedures, such as double-blind lineups, to avoid the possibility of postidentification feedback.

Eyewitness Jury Simulation Studies

As the previous section makes clear, some prediction studies ask participants to act as jurors in the second phase of the study (e.g., Lindsay et al., 1989). Jury simulation studies naturally do that as well. The principal difference between the two kinds of studies is that prediction studies present evaluators (sometimes mock jurors) with real witnesses, whereas jury simulations present evaluators (always mock jurors) with eyewitness testimony that has been created—and often manipulated—for purposes of the study. Prediction studies often contain little, if any, information about the case besides the eyewitness testimony; jury simulations, on the other hand, typically include other evidence, as well as attorney arguments, jury instructions, and other features that would ordinarily be found in a trial. The mock jurors usually render a verdict, although sometimes they merely evaluate the credibility of the eyewitness (e.g., Alonzo & Lane, 2010; Martire & Kemp, 2009; our focus is primarily on studies including verdict judgments, as those have greater ecological validity). The advantage of using real witnesses is that their behavior corresponds more closely to real-world situations; the disadvantage is that their behavior can vary in an uncontrolled fashion, making it harder to draw causal inferences (Boyce et al., 2007). The advantage of using a more fleshed-out trial is that it corresponds better to the task engaged in by actual jurors; variables affecting judgments of an eyewitness might be diluted in the broader context of a trial.

A number of jury studies have examined jurors' beliefs about eyewitness memory by manipulating aspects of the eyewitness testimony. These variables could relate to system variables, estimator variables, or the eyewitness's testimony at trial. In all cases one can infer mock jurors' beliefs about a given eyewitness factor from an observation of whether or not it influences their trial judgments. The first question, of course, is whether the presence of eyewitness testimony influences jurors' verdicts compared to its absence. There seems to be little question that it does, and that eyewitness testimony is one of the most compelling kinds of evidence that can be presented at trial, if not the most compelling (Benton et al., 2007; Boyce et al., 2007; Lindsay et al.,

1986, Experiment 1; Spanos, Myers, DuBreuil, & Pawlak, 1992–93). This is also true for other kinds of identification evidence, such as that based on a voice identification (i.e., earwitness testimony; van Wallandael, Surace, Hall Parsons, & Brown, 1994).

The next question is whether various aspects of eyewitness testimony influence jurors' verdicts, and here the matter is less clear-cut. For example, Cutler, Penrod, and Dexter (1990) presented mock jurors with a videotaped armed robbery trial that involved an eyewitness identification. They manipulated ten factors associated with the crime and the eyewitness identification (i.e., both system and estimator variables): disguise of robber (knit cap vs. no hat), weapon presence (visible vs. hidden), violence (present vs. absent), retention interval (2 days vs. 14 days), mugshot search (conducted vs. not conducted), lineup instructions (biased vs. unbiased), lineup size (6 vs. 12), foil bias (similarity of lineup members to the robber high vs. low), voice samples during the lineup (present vs. absent), and eyewitness confidence (80% vs. 100%). With the exception of confidence, all of these variables have a demonstrable relationship to eyewitness performance. One might hope that they would affect judgments of the eyewitness's reliability, but none of the variables known to matter did, in fact, influence participants' judgments, whereas eyewitness confidence did: Participants placed greater weight on the eyewitness's testimony when she was highly confident. Other research has consistently shown that eyewitness confidence, despite being only weakly predictive of accuracy, has a pronounced effect on mock jurors' evaluation of eyewitness testimony (e.g., Bradfield & Wells, 2000; Brewer & Burke, 2002; Cutler, Dexter, & Penrod, 1989; Fox & Walters, 1986).

Cutler and colleagues (1990, p. 190) concluded that "jurors are insensitive to the factors that influence eyewitness memory"; that is, they fail to consider factors that they should take into account, and they do consider one (confidence) that they should not consider. Using a different mock trial, subsequent research has largely replicated Cutler et al.'s findings in terms of verdicts with respect to the system variables of foil and instruction bias, while demonstrating that mock jurors are also not sensitive to lineup presentation (simultaneous vs. sequential; Devenport, Stinson, Cutler, & Kravitz, 2002). In addition to being insensitive to lineup procedures, jurors' judgments are not influenced by variations in witness interviewing techniques (Fisher, Mello, & McCauley, 1999).

Estimator variables, unlike system variables, cannot be controlled in order to improve eyewitness performance directly. However, a proper appreciation of their relationship to eyewitness accuracy is still important, especially when it comes to judging eyewitness credibility at trial. Unfortunately, jurors are not much more sensitive to estimator variables than they are to system variables. For example, their verdicts do not reflect differences in the viewing conditions under which an eyewitness witnesses a crime (Bradfield & Wells, 2000; Lindsay, Lim, Marando, & Cully, 1986, Experiment 4); the duration of exposure to the criminal (Lindsay et al., 1986, Experiment 4) or the retention interval (Bradfield & Wells, 2000); or the relationship between the race of the eyewitness and the race of the perpetrator (Abshire & Bornstein, 2003). About the only estimator variable to which mock jurors are sensitive is the degree of attention that the witness paid to the culprit: They are more willing to convict when the eyewitness reports paying close attention than when the eyewitness's attention is focused elsewhere (Bradfield & Wells, 2000); however, self-reported attention is not necessarily a reliable indicator of actual cognitive processing (Wells & Quinlivan, 2009). In the absence of safeguards, even strong manipulations of estimator variables combining multiple factors (e.g., retention interval, disguise, exposure time) have little to no effect on mock jurors' verdicts (Cutler, Dexter, & Penrod, 1989, 1990; Cutler, Penrod, & Dexter, 1989; Laub, Kimbrough, & Bornstein, 2015).

Other jury simulation studies focus not on system or estimator variables but on characteristics of the eyewitness's testimony at trial (in a sense these might still be thought of as a subset of estimator variables, given their potential relationship to eyewitness accuracy; we consider them separately because they deal with the testimony per se, as opposed to aspects of the witnessed event). Two such testimonial variables that have been examined are the level of detail it contains and the consistency of the eyewitness's testimony. Bell and Loftus (1988) manipulated the degree of detail in eyewitness testimony in both a civil (Experiment 1) and a criminal case (Experiment 2). The criminal case concerned a robbery-murder that took place in a small grocery store. The eyewitness testified that prior to the murder, the culprit either "requested a few store items" or "requested a six-pack of Diet Pepsi, Kleenex, and Tylenol." A high-detail witness was perceived as more credible than a low-detail witness, whether testifying for the prosecution or the defense, largely due to inferences about the quality of the witness's memory. Degree of detail had a corresponding effect on verdicts. In truth, more detail does not inevitably translate to greater accuracy (Wells & Quinlivan, 2009), and research shows that there is little correlation between the two (Meissner, Sporer, & Schooler, 2007).

There are multiple ways in which a witness's trial testimony can be consistent with other aspects of the evidence. It can be consistent with the testimony of other witnesses, with the witness's own pretrial statements (e.g., police reports), with other evidence (e.g., the witness's description of the perpetrator vs. the defendant's actual appearance), or within the witness's trial testimony itself (Boyce et al., 2007). Undoubtedly some kinds of inconsistency are indicative of unreliability; for example, if two witnesses make contradictory statements, or the same witness contradicts himself or herself on separate occasions, then at least one person (or the same person on one occasion) must be wrong. However, not all inconsistencies—for example, a discrepancy between person description and identification—are necessarily probative (Meissner et al., 2007). Nonetheless, mock jurors tend to take any kind of inconsistency as a sign of poorer reliability, and inconsistency thus leads to diminished perceptions of the defendant's guilt (Berman & Cutler,

1996; Berman, Narby, & Cutler, 1995; Lindsay et al., 1986, Experiment 2; Semmler & Brewer, 2002).

Inconsistency does not invariably lead to a lower conviction rate, however (Brewer & Burke, 2002; Lindsay et al., 1986, Experiment 3). This finding might reflect the variety of methods used to manipulate consistency, or additional factors, such as whether or not jurors actually detected the inconsistencies (Semmler & Brewer, 2002), their mood (Semmler & Brewer, 2002), the eyewitness's age (Leippe & Romanczyk, 1987), or the role of eyewitness confidence (Brewer & Burke, 2002). For example, an eyewitness whose testimony conflicts with that of another witness is evaluated more favorably (leading to a correspondingly higher conviction rate) when the eyewitness's confidence is relatively low than when it is relatively high (Tenney, MacCoun, Spellman, & Hastie, 2007). According to Tenney and colleagues, that is because the low-confident, erroneous eyewitness is better calibrated (error-prone but aware of the possibility)—and therefore more credible—than the high-confident, erroneous eyewitness (error-prone but not aware of it). A unique feature of the Tenney study is that the eyewitness's testimony was not only inconsistent but demonstrably erroneous, based on other evidence presented at trial. In many cases inconsistency requires jurors to weigh competing versions of the same story, but the truth is unknown. In such cases calibration is much harder to demonstrate, likely leaving jurors to fall back on the eyewitness's stated confidence level.

Explaining Divergent Findings across Methods: Beliefs Versus Decisions

All of the methods for assessing laypeople's beliefs about eyewitness memory show that they labor under a number of misconceptions about eyewitness phenomena. Nonetheless there are subtle differences, with laypeople professing to know about certain factors but not being influenced by those factors in specific cases, and vice versa (e.g., Alonzo & Lane, 2010; Cutler, Penrod, & Dexter, 1989; Lindsay, 1994; Lindsay et al., 1986). For example, Devenport et al. (2002) found that mock jurors rated foil-biased lineups as more suggestive and less fair than unbiased lineups; however, lineup bias had no effect on verdicts. Mock jurors also rated simultaneous lineups as less fair, but lineup presentation exerted no effect on either verdicts or defendant culpability ratings. Meanwhile, other studies show that people actually know more about eyewitness topics than they can say, depending on how their beliefs are measured (Houston et al., 2013; Read & Desmarais, 2009).

Although mock jurors' decisions might not follow directly from their beliefs, in some instances beliefs and eyewitness evidence interact. One of us (BHB) has conducted several studies exploring this possibility (Abshire & Bornstein, 2003; Bornstein, O'Bryant, & Zickafoose, 2008; Neal, Christiansen, Bornstein, & Robicheaux, 2012). For example, Bornstein et al. (2008, Experiment 1) measured participants' beliefs about the relationship between eyewitness arousal and performance with the question, "I believe that in an emotionally arousing event, an eyewitness is *more likely/less likely* (circle one) to remember the details of that event." Although the relationship is complex, arousal generally has a negative effect on eyewitness memory (Deffenbacher, Bornstein, Penrod, & McGorty, 2004), a position with which most experts agree (Kassin et al., 2001). Participants were roughly evenly split between those who believed arousal helps memory and those who believed it hurts. Participants also acted as mock jurors in a robbery-murder trial that manipulated the arousal level of the eyewitness. Participants' belief and the evidence interacted, such that the eyewitness testimony was more persuasive when it corresponded to their expectations. Specifically, participants who believed arousal helps memory voted guilty more often in the high-arousal than the low-arousal condition (98% vs. 78%), whereas participants who believed arousal hinders memory voted guilty more often in the low-arousal than the high-arousal condition (53% vs. 44%; this latter comparison was not statistically significant).

Neal et al. (2012, Experiment 1) obtained analogous interactions between mock jurors' beliefs regarding eyewitness age and weapon focus and experimental manipulation of those factors in a simulated trial, although the effects did not hold across all dependent measures. Specifically, in some cases the interaction was statistically significant for judgments of eyewitness credibility but not verdict, and in other cases the reverse was true. Moreover, the belief × eyewitness evidence interaction does not occur for all eyewitness factors: The influence of the estimator variables of decision latency in making an identification (Neal et al., 2012, Experiment 2) and the cross-race effect (Abshire & Bornstein, 2003) does not vary depending on participants' expectations regarding those variables. Nonetheless, the general pattern of results shows that it is not enough to measure participants' beliefs or their judgments in response to evidentiary manipulations alone; rather, the interaction between the two is important. Mock jurors are swayed more by an element of eyewitness testimony when it conforms to their prior expectation than when it does not.

Special Cases: Bystander Versus Victims and Child Witnesses

Nearly all of the studies discussed previously involve bystander witnesses— that is, eyewitnesses who are not themselves victims of the crime. However, in many cases the most important and compelling witness is the victim himself or herself. Little research has directly compared victim witnesses and bystander witnesses, as it is hard to equate them while holding other factors constant. They necessarily differ in terms of their vantage point, proximity to the criminal, duration of exposure to the event and perpetrator, arousal level, and many other factors (Christianson & Hübinette, 1993). The victim's testimony is, and naturally should be, incredibly important to factfinders. Nonetheless, insofar as victims are testifying based on their recollection of events, their memories are as susceptible to error as those of any other eyewitness. To the extent that factors having an adverse impact on eyewitness memory, such as arousal (Deffenbacher et al., 2004), are more prominent among victims than among bystanders, we might even expect victims to be poorer eyewitnesses, all else being equal. When using formal interview protocols, victims and bystanders provide comparable amounts of information (Lamb et al., 2003), although whether they provide comparably accurate information is somewhat less clear.

In at least some kinds of cases, mock jurors appear to weigh bystander-witness testimony more heavily than testimony from a victim-witness (Holcomb & Jacquin, 2007). However, the effect on credibility of a witness's relationship to the crime might vary depending on other factors, such as the witness's age. For example, Pozzulo and Dempsey (2009) found that mock jurors perceived a child and adult victim as equally credible, but they viewed a child bystander-witness as less credible than an adult bystander. Thus a witness's age can have a significant effect on how the witness is perceived. The credibility of child victim-witnesses is of special concern, given children's unique vulnerability to victimization, growing awareness in society of child maltreatment (e.g., child sexual abuse), and issues related to children's competency as witnesses (e.g., cognitive limitations). As with eyewitnesses in general, those credibility issues reflect prior beliefs that laypeople have about child witnesses.

In criminal cases where the victim is a child, and especially in cases of child sexual abuse (CSA), jurors cite the child's testimony as the most important evidence (Bottoms et al., 2007; Myers et al., 1999). Child victims are more credible when testifying about sexual abuse than when testifying about other (nonsexual) crimes, presumably because of inferences related to children's honesty about and experience with different kinds of events (McCauley & Parker, 2001)—even though many adults' expectations about CSA are erroneous (Goodman-Delahunty, Cossins, & O'Brien, 2010). To some extent laypeople are aware that age is an important determinant of eyewitness accuracy and that children are, at least in many respects, less reliable eyewitnesses than adults (Golding, Dunlap, & Hodell, 2009; Holcomb & Jacquin, 2007; Newcombe & Bransgrove, 2007; Pozzulo & Dempsey, 2009; Ross, Dunning, Toglia, & Ceci, 1990). Nonetheless, expert surveys suggest that laypeople are less knowledgeable about the relationship between eyewitness age and reliability than they should be (Benton et al., 2006; Kassin et al., 2001).

Prediction studies for child witnesses are analogous to those described previously for adult witnesses, with the exception that evaluators attempt to discriminate between accurate and inaccurate child witnesses as opposed to adults. The results are mixed, with some studies finding that evaluators can discriminate between accurate and inaccurate child witnesses (Leippe, Manion, & Romanczyk, 1992), others finding that they cannot (Leichtman &

Ceci, 1995), and still others finding that it depends on things like whether a child is being compared to another child of the same age or a different age (Newcombe & Bransgrove, 2007), the type of assertion made by the witness (Block et al., 2012), and participants' age (Block et al., 2012). For example, Block et al. found that adult evaluators were better at judging accurate reports, accurate denials, and false reports (i.e., a false assertion that an event had in fact occurred) than they were at judging false denials (i.e., a false assertion that an event had not occurred). Older adults did better than younger adults, although this difference was not explained by a difference in experience with children. Regardless of discrimination ability, adult evaluators are generally more reluctant to believe the word of a young child than an older child (Golding et al., 2009; Newcombe & Bransgrove, 2007).

A frequently manipulated variable in simulation studies of child witnesses is the child's age (for a review, see Bottoms et al., 2007; Golding et al., 2009). Several studies show that younger children testifying about CSA are perceived as more credible than older children, and that cases with younger victims are more likely to result in convictions (e.g., Holcomb & Jacquin, 2007; Ross et al., 1990). Other simulation studies, however, have found little effect of child witness age (e.g., Golding et al., 1997; McCauley & Parker, 2001). The same inconsistency occurs in studies of real jurors, who report perceiving child witnesses of different ages more or less the same (Myers et al., 1999). However, in what is perhaps the largest and most comprehensive archival analysis of CSA cases (over 2,000 criminal complaints, including 466 jury trials), Read, Connolly, and Welsh (2006) found that convictions were less likely when complainants were 13 or older at the time the alleged abuse began (a conviction rate of 86.1%), compared to younger complainants. For groups younger than 13, the complainant's age was not related to the conviction rate (97%–98% for all groups; the researchers divided complainants into four quartiles based on age: 1–6, 7–9, 10–12, and 13–19).

These inconsistent results might stem from competing inferences (Bottoms et al., 2007; Leippe & Romanczyk, 1987). On the one hand, younger children are usually perceived as more sexually naïve and therefore less likely to fabricate an allegation of CSA, as well as less likely to lie in general; on the other hand, they are seen as less cognitively competent. For these reasons the relationship between child witness age and juror decisions could be nonlinear. Child witnesses' perceived honesty is a stronger predictor of mock jurors' CSA verdicts than perceived cognitive ability (Ross, Jurden, Lindsay, & Keeney, 2003), which would explain why, when age differences are found, younger children are viewed as more credible. As Ross and colleagues observe, in other types of cases, where the victim's honesty is less salient, cognitive ability might be a stronger predictor. This seems to be the case in trials where the child witness is a bystander rather than a victim; in such cases children often are perceived as less credible than adults, and younger children as less credible than older children (e.g., Goodman et al., 1987;

Leippe & Romanczyk, 1987; Neal et al., 2012; Pozzulo, Lemieux, Wells, & McCuaig, 2006; but see Holcomb & Jacquin, 2007; Ross et al., 1990).

The victim's age can be a factor, not only at the time of the alleged crime but also at the time of reporting and/or testifying about the crime. The distinction often arises in claims of recovered memory, where a substantial delay invariably exists; but a delay can also be relevant in cases involving continuous memories of abuse (Connolly & Read, 2006; 2007; Pozzulo, Dempsey, & Crescini, 2010). In their analysis of more than 2,000 claims of "historic" CSA—which they defined as two years or more having elapsed from the end of the offense to trial—Connolly and Read (2006) found that the mean age at which the alleged abuse ended was 12.39 years, but the mean age of the complainant at trial was 26.09, a difference of nearly 14 years. In the vast majority of recovered memory cases, the victim was a child when the alleged incident occurred but did not report it until adulthood, or in some cases adolescence (for review, see Geraerts, Raymaekers, & Merckelbach, 2008; Piper, Lillevik, & Kritzer, 2008).

Claims of recovered memory of CSA often involve allegations that the traumatic memory was repressed, but recovered memory and repression do not necessarily go together. Other cognitive processes might cause individuals to lose access to memories temporarily, only to regain it later, and in some cases individuals simply forget previous instances of remembering (Belli, 2012; Geraerts et al., 2008). By some accounts, most delayed CSA prosecutions do not involve a claim of repression (Connolly & Read, 2006). Nonetheless, recovered memory cases have garnered a great deal of popular, media, and legal attention (e.g., changes to statutes of limitations); consequently a number of studies have examined laypeople's beliefs about recovered memory, as well as mock juror decisions in cases involving recovered memory claims.

Although the public is generally accepting of the concepts of repression and recovered memory (e.g., Golding, Sanchez, & Sego, 1996), jurors tend to be skeptical of recovered memory claims at trial (e.g., Bornstein & Muller, 2001; Clark & Nightingale, 1997; ForsterLee, Horowitz, Ho, ForsterLee, & McGovern, 1999; Loftus, Weingardt, & Hoffman, 1993), especially when the jurors are men (e.g., Golding, Sanchez, & Sego, 1999; Loftus et al., 1993), the alleged victim is male (Clark & Nightingale, 1997), or the victim claims homosexual abuse (Bornstein & Muller, 2001). These results again show a disjunction between beliefs and trial judgments. The research we reviewed previously showed that laypeople are sometimes aware that some factor influences eyewitness performance, but it does not affect their verdicts (e.g., Devenport et al., 2002); whereas here they tend to believe (erroneously) in the reality of repression, but a claim of repression does not make them more likely to find the defendant guilty. If anything, they are less likely to convict a defendant who has been accused based on a recovered memory than one whose alleged victim remembered all along.

Beliefs of Legal Professionals

Despite jurors' importance to the criminal justice system, they are not the only players. In evaluating eyewitness testimony, jurors, such as those in the Timothy Cole trial, naturally rely on their intuitions, which, alas, turn out to be less than perfectly accurate. And one can hardly fault victims like Michele Mallin, a victim of a brutal crime, for making a memory error. But what about the professionals who deal with eyewitnesses all the time, like police, defense attorneys and prosecutors, and judges—shouldn't they know better? Although such individuals are unlikely to serve as jurors themselves, their beliefs are relevant to jury decision making in eyewitness cases because they are the ones deciding how to interact with eyewitnesses in the field, how to prepare them for and question them during trial, and whether to implement potential safeguards that can potentially help jurors make better use of eyewitness testimony. Thus, legal professionals' beliefs about eyewitnesses have clear implications for whether jurors hear eyewitness testimony at all, as well as how that testimony is presented at trial. Several studies have measured what these diverse groups of legal professionals know about eyewitness memory.

Police

Police officers' knowledge of eyewitness memory is crucial. Understanding which factors do and do not predict eyewitness performance can allow them to weigh eyewitness reports properly, which could in turn aid them in their search for the perpetrator, as well as in judging the likelihood that a given suspect is actually guilty. If the Lubbock police knew that high levels of stress tend to have a negative effect on eyewitness memory, then they might have been less accepting of Michele Mallin's identification of Timothy Cole, which could have prolonged their search for alternative suspects. But once investigators settle on a particular suspect, they tend to seek additional confirming evidence and ignore other possibilities (Simon, 2012). A better understanding of eyewitnesses should also, of course, contribute to the police administering fairer and more effective interviewing and identification procedures. In the course of their work, police undoubtedly come into contact with a range of eyewitnesses, and they also receive training on how to question witnesses and administer lineups. It is therefore reasonable to expect that police officers would be fairly knowledgeable about eyewitness performance.

Unfortunately, that does not appear to be the case. In what is perhaps the largest study of police officers' beliefs regarding eyewitness memory, Wise, Safer, and Maro (2011) surveyed 532 officers, drawn from several regions of the United States. Some of the officers worked in departments that had instituted eyewitness reforms, whereas others did not. They rated their (dis)agreement with 11 statements, most of which were borrowed from the Kassin et al. (2001) survey, about eyewitness factors for which there was strong empirical evidence. Officers in both reform and nonreform jurisdictions were correct on slightly more than half of the items (means of 6.11 and 5.68 out of 11, respectively; the difference between the two groups was marginally significant). Greater experience (i.e., being a detective as opposed to a patrol officer) was not associated with greater knowledge of eyewitness factors. Other studies have corroborated Wise et al.'s finding that law enforcement officers have limited knowledge of eyewitness issues, although at least one direct comparison did find that officers were more knowledgeable than a sample of adults summoned for jury duty (Benton et al., 2006). Benton and colleagues found that police officers agreed with experts (from the Kassin et al., 2001 data) on 12 of 30 items (40%), compared to only four of 30 items (13.3%) for jurors.

Attorneys

Police are usually the first representatives of the criminal justice system to interact with eyewitnesses, but attorneys spend more time working with them. They observe lineups, they depose eyewitnesses, they prepare them for trial, and they question them as part of the trial. Thus one might expect that attorneys, at least those who practice criminal law, would be more knowledgeable about eyewitness behavior than police. Correct knowledge would help them in either establishing or attacking an eyewitness's credibility, whereas erroneous expectations could lead to misguided trial strategy, misrepresenting eyewitnesses to juries, and miscarriages of justice—notably, not merely prosecuting the innocent, but also failing to defend them adequately.

Thirty-five years ago, before misidentifications and false convictions were as well publicized as they are today, Brigham (1981) conducted a survey of lawyers' beliefs about eyewitness memory (see also Brigham & Wolfskeil, 1983). He surveyed 235 Florida attorneys who worked in public defender's offices, state attorney's offices, and private criminal defense practice, about the effects of several eyewitness factors (e.g., stress, confidence, witness and suspect characteristics). The principal finding was that prosecutors were less knowledgeable than defense attorneys, and they concomitantly felt that eyewitness memory was more accurate. For example, in response to the question "About what percent of the eyewitness identifications you have observed were probably correct," 83% of prosecutors answered "90% or more." Defense attorneys were somewhat less sanguine, but most still responded that "about 75%" of identifications were correct. Thus even defense attorneys, who were more sensitive than prosecutors to the fallibility of eyewitness memory, tended to accept eyewitness identifications at face value.

More recent work has confirmed Brigham's (1981) findings that attorneys are aware of some eyewitness factors but have misconceptions about others (Stinson, Devenport, Cutler, & Kravitz, 1996; Wise, Pawlenko, Safer, & Meyer, 2009). Prosecutors continue to know less about eyewitness performance than defense attorneys; correspondingly, they are less skeptical about eyewitness testimony, as well as about jurors' knowledge of the factors that predict eyewitness accuracy. They are also more skeptical about the necessity of various legal safeguards to ensure that jurors use eyewitness testimony properly (Wise et al., 2009). As with police officers, greater experience is not associated with more accurate beliefs about eyewitnesses among attorneys (Wise et al., 2009).

Judges

Judges' beliefs about eyewitness memory are important for a number of reasons. In addition to weighing eyewitness testimony themselves and reaching verdicts in bench trials, trial court judges determine whether certain eyewitnesses (e.g., children) are competent to testify at all; they make evidentiary rulings such as whether to suppress a potentially biased identification (Stinson, Devenport, Cutler, & Kravitz, 1997); and they rule on the permissibility of other legal safeguards that might help jurors evaluate eyewitness testimony (e.g., expert testimony, jury instructions). At the appellate court level, judges' decisions provide the legal criteria for determining whether identification procedures were unduly suggestive. If judges have erroneous beliefs about eyewitness memory, then judge-made law can be at odds with empirical data (Wells & Quinlivan, 2009). It is therefore extremely important that judges be well informed about the vagaries of eyewitness performance.

Several eyewitness belief surveys have included a sample of judges. Benton and colleagues (2006) found that judges did about as well as police officers, agreeing with experts on 12 of 30 items (40%)—a less than stellar level of performance but considerably better than the jurors in the same study. Wise and Safer (2004) obtained slightly worse results, with 80% or more of their judge sample giving the correct response on only 3 of 14 items (21.4%). Judges' knowledge varied widely depending on the topic, and, as with police officers and attorneys, greater experience was not associated with better performance. However, knowing more about eyewitness performance was associated with a greater willingness to permit legal safeguards in eyewitness cases, a greater appreciation of jurors' limited eyewitness knowledge, and a reluctance to convict defendants based solely on eyewitness testimony. These findings are significant because of judges' gatekeeping role and control over virtually all trial procedures (Stinson et al., 1997).

Legal Professionals Outside the United States

Needless to say, legal systems outside the United States, especially outside the British common law system, can be quite different from American practice. This is particularly true in terms of the evidentiary rules and whether the countries employ juries or other lay adjudicators. Nonetheless, legal professionals in any country must deal with eyewitnesses in investigating, prosecuting, and adjudicating crimes, and, as discussed above, those individuals' beliefs can significantly affect the administration of justice. A handful of studies have addressed the eyewitness knowledge of legal professionals in countries other than the United States.

For example, Granhag, Strömwall, and Hartwig (2005) examined the eyewitness beliefs of three groups of Swedish legal professionals: 104 police officers, 158 prosecutors, and 251 judges. Their questionnaire asked about 13 empirically well-established topics, such as those in the Kassin et al. (2001) expert survey, in a multiple choice format. Participants' beliefs were in accord with research findings and expert consensus on some topics (e.g., weapon focus, completeness of children's vs. adults' testimony) but not others (e.g., simultaneous vs. sequential lineup presentation, the forgetting curve). When differences between the groups emerged, judges tended to do some-what better than the other groups, and they were also more likely to profess ignorance (i.e., they were more likely to choose the "don't know" response option). Experience had little relationship with beliefs for any of the groups. Other studies of non-U.S. legal professionals have yielded comparable find-ings, with samples of Italian defense attorneys (Magnussen et al., 2013), Australian defense attorneys (Martire & Kemp, 2008), Norwegian judges (Magnussen et al., 2008; 2010), Scottish judges (Houston et al., 2013), and Chinese judges (Wise, Gong, Safer, & Lee, 2010).

Overall, then—at least in those countries where the topic has been stud-ied so far—judges and police officers tend to know more than jurors and the general public, and defense attorneys know more than prosecutors. However, knowledge of eyewitness issues is relatively modest for all groups of legal professionals in the United States and abroad, and the professionals know considerably less than eyewitness experts. Moreover, for none of the groups does greater professional experience appear to lead to superior knowledge.

Improving Jurors' Assessments of Eyewitness Testimony

A number of techniques or "safeguards" have been proposed to aid jurors in evaluating eyewitness testimony (Devenport, Kimbrough, & Cutler, 2009; van Wallendael, Cutler, Devenport, & Penrod, 2007). The most common strategies include (in the order in which they appear at trial): *voir dire*, cross-examination, testimony from an expert in the field, closing arguments, and jury instructions provided by the judge. In deciding which safeguards to use, it is important to consider not only their potential effectiveness but also their costs. Expert testimony, because it introduces additional witness(es), length-ens a trial, and experts require payment. The cost is usually borne by the party calling the expert—in eyewitness cases almost always the defense—but the court can retain an expert, and in the case of indigent defendants the state often pays. Addressing eyewitness issues in jury instructions costs little in additional trial time, as instructions are part of the case anyway; but there can be a cost if deviating from standard, pattern jury instructions increases the chance of an appeal. *Voir dire* and cross-examination are inherent in the trial structure itself and therefore carry essentially no costs, though as with the other safeguards, using them to address eyewitness issues specifically can lengthen the trial somewhat. Because we cover expert testimony (see Chapter 7) and jury instructions (see Chapter 14) elsewhere, our focus here is on the other safeguards.

Voir Dire

Voir dire can be an effective safeguard if jurors who are unable or unwilling to make proper use of eyewitness testimony can be identified and rehabilitated or excluded. Most questioning by attorneys and judges during standard *voir dire* is too cursory to identify case-specific attitudes and beliefs, but more extensive *voir dire* is sometimes an option (see Chapter 3). Narby and Cutler (1994) developed an Attitudes Toward Eyewitnesses Scale (ATES) that could be used during extensive *voir dire* to screen for jurors' eyewitness attitudes. The ATES includes nine items rated on a Likert (dis)agreement scale, such as "Eyewitnesses are reliable witnesses" and "Eyewitnesses frequently misidentify innocent people just because they seem familiar." Although Narby and Cutler showed the scale to have good internal consistency, research on its ability to predict mock jurors' judgments has yielded mixed results (Devenport & Cutler, 2004; Narby & Cutler, 1994).

Cross-Examination

Like *voir dire*, cross-examination is part and parcel of jury trials. Presumably, if an eyewitness's memory is shaky or the procedures used to elicit that memory were overly suggestive, skillful questioning by counsel will expose any shortcomings. Counsel's ability to do that, however, is limited by attorneys' own limited knowledge of the witnessed event and misconceptions about eyewitness memory (van Wallandael et al., 2007). And even if attorneys are able to highlight factors known to influence eyewitness performance through cross-examination, the raising of those factors is unlikely to be very effective if jurors—the ones weighing the credibility of the eyewitness—lack the requisite knowledge (Devenport et al., 2002; van Wallandael et al., 2007). As the first part of this chapter demonstrates, jurors' knowledge of eyewitness memory leaves much to be desired.

Closing Arguments

Defense attorneys have the opportunity to caution jurors about an eyewitness's reliability when they make closing arguments, and some data suggest that they do so effectively. Geiselman and colleagues (2002) found that when the attorneys' closing arguments reiterated the contents of expert testimony about eyewitness memory, guilty verdicts were reduced. Furthermore, the presence of information in the closing arguments that called eyewitness reliability into question led jurors to be more skeptical of eyewitness evidence, to discount the eyewitness evidence, and to base their decisions on the other (circumstantial) evidence instead. In a follow-up study, Geiselman and Mendez (2005) discovered that closing arguments alone (i.e., without expert testimony) led mock jurors to be more skeptical of the eyewitness evidence, but they also showed worse discrimination between good and poor witnessing conditions compared to when there was expert testimony. In contrast, a study by Laub and colleagues (2015) found that closing arguments were capable of sensitizing jurors to circumstances of the witnessing situation. Thus, there is evidence that closing arguments addressing problems with eyewitness memory can make jurors more skeptical of eyewitness testimony and might even enhance their evaluation of that testimony (i.e., by sensitizing them to relevant factors).

Educating Jurors: A New Approach

Overall, the traditional, relatively low-cost safeguards such as *voir dire*, cross-examination, and closing arguments have not been shown to be particularly effective, although closing arguments appear to have some potential for sensitizing jurors, or at least making them more skeptical about eyewitness testimony. The lackluster effect of these safeguards, along with the legal complications associated with expert testimony on eyewitness memory (see Chapter 7), have led to some novel reform efforts. One of the most promising developments is a teaching aid for educating jurors (Pawlenko, Safer, Wise, & Holfeld, 2013).

Pawlenko and colleagues (2013) tested whether teaching jurors about the interview-identification-eyewitness (I-I-Eye) method for analyzing eyewitness accuracy would sensitize them to the quality of eyewitness evidence in a given case. The I-I-Eye provides evidence-based guidelines for evaluating eyewitness accuracy, taking into account interviewing and identification procedures (i.e., system variables like open-ended vs. closed-ended or leading questions, lineup size and composition, etc.), as well as estimator variables associated with crimes that could affect eyewitness accuracy (e.g., alcohol, stress, age, disguise, etc.; see Wise, Fishman, & Safer, 2009). Training consists of a 15-minute PowerPoint slide show.

To assess its effectiveness, Pawlenko et al. (2013) had student mock jurors reach a verdict in a robbery trial that presented either a strong or a weak eyewitness case, based on a number of system variables that were involved (e.g., 8-person vs. 5-person lineup, unbiased vs. biased lineup instructions, blind vs. nonblind lineup administration). Prior to the jury simulation, they viewed the I-I-Eye or one of two control presentations related to being a juror: either general information about jury duty or a description of eyewitness factors identified as important in United States Supreme Court jurisprudence (i.e., the so-called *Biggers* factors; *Neil v. Biggers*, 1972). There was a marginally significant effect of case strength on verdicts, with 37% of participants finding the defendant guilty in the strong case compared to 27% in the weak case. More importantly, there was a significant interaction between teaching aid and case strength. Case strength exerted a substantial effect on participants' verdicts in the I-I-Eye condition (55% vs. 16% guilty for the strong and weak case, respectively), but participants in the two control conditions failed to discriminate between strong and weak evidence.

The I-I-Eye is a promising tool for helping jurors make proper use of eyewitness testimony. There is a small cost in terms of the time that it takes to administer (albeit relatively brief), but that time could be saved by incorporating it into the general juror orientation process (see Chapter 2) rather than making it part of the trial. Additional studies on its effectiveness need to be conducted—to see, for instance, if it generalizes to other kinds of trials and nonstudent samples—but it obviates the legal concerns associated with expert testimony (see Chapter 7) and is therefore an encouraging sign for ameliorating mistaken beliefs that jurors might have about eyewitnesses.

Conclusions

Jurors' knowledge and expectations about eyewitness memory have been measured in various ways. Estimates of jurors' knowledge are only as good as the methods used to assess that knowledge, and the research has yielded somewhat disparate findings. Some methods may underestimate how much jurors know (e.g., Desmarais & Read, 2011; Read & Desmarais, 2009), and jurors' beliefs about abstract topics do not necessarily comport with their reliance on those beliefs in concrete cases (Alonzo & Lane, 2010). Legal professionals know somewhat more than laypeople about eyewitness memory, but their knowledge is still limited, and greater professional experience confers no additional advantage. This means that they may make ill-informed decisions about how to deal with eyewitness issues before and during trial, thereby leaving jurors to struggle on their own with the complexity of eyewitness evidence.

Even if research conducted since the earlier surveys of laypeople's eyewitness beliefs does seem to suggest that people know more than we give them credit for, the more recent studies still indicate, quite clearly, that there are some topics on which most people are misinformed (Desmarais & Read, 2011). Moreover, jury simulation research shows that jurors are less sensitive to a variety of system and estimator variables than they should be, while they overweigh other factors such as confidence. Safeguards are only modestly effective. And jurors' evaluation of eyewitness evidence interacts, albeit imperfectly, with their prior expectations. When eyewitness behavior is congruent with jurors' expectations, the eyewitness evidence has a greater impact.

When evaluating the behavior of others, beliefs and expectancies are hard—if not impossible—to set aside. Thus it should come as no surprise that they influence legal decision making, just as they influence judgment in other areas of life (McAuliff & Bornstein, 2012). Indeed, a reliance on prior beliefs can be efficient and adaptive (Ariely, 2009; Hastie & Dawes, 2009). Problems only arise when those beliefs are erroneous or applied in the wrong situation. To a large extent, that is what occurs with laypeople's—hence prospective jurors'—beliefs about eyewitnesses. But unlike in other situations, the belief-holders themselves do not pay the price of their erroneous beliefs—innocent defendants like Timothy Cole do.

6

Jurors Can Distinguish True
from False Confessions

"Why would Chuck [Erickson] implicate himself in a crime and agree to serve 25 years in jail if he didn't commit the crime? That just didn't make any sense to us. Who makes a confession that will send them to prison if they're innocent?"

The words that open this chapter came from a Columbia, Missouri juror who, in 2005, relied on Erickson's confession implicating himself and his 20-year old friend, Ryan Ferguson, in the strangulation death of *Columbia Daily Tribune* sportswriter Kent Heitholt. Persuaded by Erickson's testimony, the jury convicted Ferguson, and Erickson pled guilty in a deal that shortened his sentence. But in light of extensive media coverage, Erickson's story slowly unraveled as it became apparent that his confession and trial testimony resulted from pressure by police and prosecutors. According to confession expert Richard Leo, Erickson's admission had all "the hallmarks of a persuaded false confession" (Innocence Project, 2008), and in a 2010 recantation Erickson acknowledged that he incriminated himself and Ferguson only after reading a newspaper article about the crime, dreaming that they killed the victim, and being coerced into confessing by police threats and fabricated evidence. Ferguson never wavered from his claim of innocence, and his conviction was vacated in 2013 after he had spent nearly 10 years in prison.

The words of this juror serve as our focal point as we assess how jurors and juries evaluate evidence gleaned from police interrogations of suspects. Among other questions, we ask why the jury in the Ferguson trial relied so heavily on Erickson's interrogation despite seeing video of detectives feeding him key details about the crime scene and the murder weapon, and despite the fact that none of the hair, blood, or fingerprint evidence found at the scene matched Ferguson. A hint comes from this juror's seemingly reasonable query, "Who makes a confession . . . if they're innocent?" and the implication that innocent people would never confess to a crime that they did not commit.

In fact, though, innocent people *do* confess to crimes they did not commit. They do so to protect other people, sometimes confessing to crimes actually committed by others and occasionally taking responsibility for crimes that never happened at all. They do so because they believe—incorrectly— that a prosecutor will release them from custody or a judge will grant them leniency if they cooperate. And they do so because they accede to interrogators' coercive questioning techniques. Some people (e.g., the mentally disabled and mentally ill, juveniles, those who are intoxicated or addicted) are especially vulnerable and more likely to falsely confess. However, we should acknowledge several other truths about interrogations and confessions: The vast majority of suspects who confess to interrogators are likely to be guilty of the act they admitted to or some variant of that act, and their confessions serve to expedite cases through the criminal justice process, promote public safety, and provide a sense that justice has been done. Indeed most of the time, detectives who work to gain confessions and prosecutors who pursue charges and gain convictions based on those confessions are serving the public well.

But not all confessions should be taken at face value, and some sizeable minority are false. So an important question is how often this occurs. Precise prevalence rates of false confession cannot be known, of course, because many are rejected prior to trial and others result in guilty pleas. Even the terms "correct" and "false" confession are not as clear-cut as one might imagine, because some suspects give truthful confessions but then, when pressed by interrogators to deliver more, fabricate additional violations. Still other suspects provide confessions that contain elements of the truth and falsehoods (Reisberg, 2014).

Yet, some data can approximate an answer: Gudjonnsson (2003) reports that 12% of Icelandic prisoners he interviewed said they gave false confessions to police. The incidence may be considerably higher when the suspects are young. In their interviews of 193 teenage males incarcerated for serious crimes, Malloy, Shulman, and Cauffman (2014) learned that 35% had apparently made a false statement (either a false confession or false guilty plea) to law enforcement officials. The Innocence Project has determined that roughly 30% of its DNA exonerations involved evidence of confessions.

Although it is commonly understood that police might suspect innocent people and subject them to interrogation, what happens next is not commonsensical and can explain why people erroneously confess and why others— including jurors—seem to believe them. People who confess falsely tend to be confident that their innocence will set them free once it becomes clear to investigators, prosecutors, and jurors. As a result, they cooperate with police and, against their self-interest, waive their *Miranda* rights and subject themselves to questioning (Kassin, 2005). Along the way, and as a result of subtle powers of coercion, they naively and unknowingly transform themselves from innocent interviewees to guilty suspects.

After a confession has been extracted, it begins to take on a life of its own and to define the case against a defendant because detectives, prosecutors, defense attorneys, and (as we show in this chapter) jurors assume that a confession—especially one that contains detailed information—is true. The presence of a confession influences detectives' subsequent actions, prosecutors' and defense attorneys' strategies, the weight that jurors attach to both that confession and to other evidence presented at trial, and even affects judges' sentencing decisions, as judges tend to punish defendants who claim innocence and fail to express remorse (Leo, 2008). A confession overshadows evidence proving a suspect's innocence (Leo, 2008). So people who give, and then retract, confessions are sadly misguided if they think that their mistaken acknowledgments of guilt will be set aside.

In cases involving contested confessions, defendants typically retract the confession after meeting with an attorney or considering its consequences, then plead not guilty and proceed to trial. From here on, the legal system places considerable faith in juries to determine the authenticity of the confession and to recognize false confessions as such. But, as we explain in this chapter, *any* confession that is introduced at trial is likely to be believed by jurors who lack insight into the strong situational pressures of an interrogation room, the dispositional factors that make some suspects especially susceptible to such pressures, and the sequence of events that transpire once a confession has been offered. Thus the jury system provides no obvious safeguard to suspects who falsely confess. That counterintuitive fact was underscored in the dissenting opinion of United States Supreme Court Justices Brennan and Marshall in *Colorado v. Connelly* (1986): "Triers of fact accord confessions such heavy weight in their determinations that the introduction of a confession makes the other aspects of trial in court superfluous, and the real trial, for all practical purposes, occurs when the confession is obtained" (p. 182).

In this chapter we focus on what social scientists, lawyers, and judges assume and know about jurors' use of confession evidence. The essence of their findings is that jurors and juries have difficulty distinguishing true and false confessions. This means that they convict both those who confess to crimes they committed and those who admit to acts they did not commit. In fact, the odds for false confessors who come before juries are not good: By delving into the details of sixty cases of false confessions, Leo and Ofshe (1998) determined that 73% of false confessors who opted to take their cases to trial were convicted. In subsequent analyses of 125 different defendants whose confessions were proven to be false, Drizin and Leo (2004) determined that 81% of the false confessors whose cases went to trial were convicted, and that convictions occurred even when the confession was contradicted by other evidence or lacked corroboration. Obviously, every time a jury mistakenly convicts a false confessor, the actual perpetrator escapes prosecution and remains unaccounted for.

In the sections that follow, we describe the ways that scientists and lawyers have studied jurors' impressions of confession evidence and what this research has revealed. We propose various psychological processes, including attribution errors and confirmation biases, to account for jurors' difficulties in distinguishing between true and false confessions. Finally, we detail various attempts to ameliorate these judgmental errors and improve jurors' discrimination in cases that involve confession evidence.

Studying the Impact of Confession Evidence on Jurors and Juries

Psychologists and legal scholars use three different kinds of research methods to assess the impact of confessions on jurors: surveys, mock trials, and archival analyses. Surveys are perhaps the easiest to do because they involve asking general opinion questions of a group of citizens who are not connected in any way to a particular case. Mock trials typically entail exposing groups of jury-eligible adults to simulated trial testimony involving a confession (and sometimes other forms of controversial testimony) to gauge the impact of that evidence on their judgments. For example, mock jurors' perceptions of confessions extracted by means of fabricated evidence have been examined via mock jury methodology. Archival analyses usually involve *post hoc* assessments of trial-related information in cases of known wrongful convictions. Researchers who undertake these studies ask whether and how a false confession might have tainted the police investigation and jury trial. We explore the impact of confession evidence on jurors and juries by describing scientific research that uses these distinct methodologies.

General Beliefs about Interrogations and Confessions

At least five survey studies on the impact of confession evidence have been published since 2008. The earliest (Chojnacki, Cicchini, & White, 2008; Henkel, Coffman, & Dailey, 2008) asked respondents whether an innocent person would falsely confess to a crime and whether a confession was an indication of guilt. People tended to believe both that false confessions occur and that confessions connote guilt. In an online survey of 502 adults from 37 states, two-thirds expressed the belief that an innocent person might falsely confess to a crime after strenuous interrogation by police (Chojnacki et al., 2008). Nearly that same proportion of the 169 adults from Connecticut, New York and New Jersey surveyed by Henkel et al. assumed that a person who confessed to a crime was probably guilty. Interestingly, though, these participants were quick to say that they *personally* would not confess to a crime they did not commit; only 14% acknowledged that the pressures inherent in an interrogation would cause them to make a false confession. A newer study showed that only 8% of the 461 participants from across the country agreed that they might falsely confess if interrogated by the police (Costanzo, Shaked-Schroer, & Vinson, 2010). Apparently people can understand that others might succumb to the pressures of harsh interrogation tactics, but most believe that they would be immune.

Some surveys have asked questions pertaining to beliefs about specific interrogation practices, including their coerciveness and the likelihood that they would elicit true and false confessions. Responses show important gaps in laypersons' knowledge. In Leo and Liu's (2009) survey of 264 university students, participants acknowledged that psychological pressure and other nonphysical interrogation techniques such as confronting a suspect with incriminating false polygraph or DNA evidence would be coercive, and that these so-called false evidence ploys are considerably more coercive than true evidence ploys. Respondents were quite likely to say that psychological interrogation methods would elicit true confessions, but considerably less likely to acknowledge that they would elicit false confessions unless the interrogations involved direct threats of beatings or violence. (But, as we point out later, false admissions of guilt in response to fabricated evidence ploys are actually quite common.) When questioned about the coerciveness of various interrogation techniques, the 126 actual jurors studied by Blandón-Gitlin, Sperry, and Leo (2011) rated the presentation of false evidence as only slightly less coercive than actual or threatened violence by interrogators, yet they too deemed false evidence ploys significantly less likely to elicit a false confession than a true one. So even though laypeople believe that threats of harm and presentations of false evidence can be highly coercive, they assume that truly innocent people can somehow resist these pressures and maintain their innocence.

Survey results reveal another unfortunate and compelling fact: Jurors' beliefs about the techniques that police use in interrogations differ as a function of their race. For approximately half of the questions asked by Constanzo and his colleagues (2010), there were statistically significant differences in responses from White and non-White jurors. On all of these items, the latter expressed less confidence in the police and a greater willingness to believe that false confessions are possible. So, for example, non-Whites were more likely than Whites to agree that if interrogated by police, they would falsely confess to both a minor and a serious crime. And they were less likely to agree that in order to help police persuade suspects to confess, interrogators should be permitted to threaten a longer sentence. These beliefs are consistent with other data showing that minority racial and ethnic groups have more negative perceptions of the police than Whites, particularly concerning police misconduct and use of force (Weitzer, Tuch, & Skogan, 2008). These sentiments—whether accurate or not—are likely to shape how minority jurors process and evaluate confession evidence.

The Impact of Confession Evidence on Mock Jurors

An empirical question that is especially well suited to mock jury research is how confession evidence compares with other common and powerful forms of evidence, such as eyewitness testimony and character evidence, in terms of its impact on jurors. Kassin and Neumann (1997) conducted a simulation study to assess whether, as the majority of United States Supreme Court justices expressed in *Arizona v. Fulminante* (1991), confession evidence is essentially "similar in degree and kind" to other forms of evidence. To test this notion the researchers varied the nature of the evidence in murder and assault trials by including a confession, an eyewitness identification, and negative character testimony, either alone or in combination, and evaluating verdicts and responses to case-relevant questions. The confession evidence presented alone garnered the highest conviction rates, and when presented in combination with other evidence was deemed the most incriminating, showing that it is indeed a potent form of evidence.

In their decision in the *Fulminante* case, Supreme Court justices also suggested that the admission into evidence of coerced confessions should be considered harmless error because jurors can correctly evaluate and, when necessary, reject testimony detailing a coerced confession. Were they correct? This question is also ripe for a mock jury simulation. In one of the first studies to address the issue experimentally, Kassin and Wrightsman (1980) showed that participants were strongly swayed by a confession even when they knew it had been given in response to an offer of leniency, and they relied on it to convict. More recently, Kassin and Sukel (1997) had participants read one of several versions of a transcript from a murder trial. In the low-pressure versions the defendant had confessed to the police immediately upon the start of questioning. In the high-pressure versions he was in obvious pain during the interrogation and confessed only after the detective yelled in an aggressive manner and waved his gun around. A third group of participants had no confession evidence. Results showed that regardless of pressures exerted on the suspect during the interrogation, mock jurors who knew about the confession convicted more often than those who did not, and the effect persisted even after a judge gave an admonition to discount the confession if it appeared to be coerced.

So confession evidence is apparently powerful stuff. But don't jurors pay attention to the circumstances that gave rise to the confession, as the *Fulminante* majority implied? Although they appeared to discount the confession in the high-pressure interrogation—judging it to be involuntary and stating that it did not influence their judgments—this appearance was illusory. In fact all groups who heard the confession, including those in the high-pressure condition, were more likely to convict than those who did not, regardless of whether the judge instructed them to disregard confessions that had been coerced. People have difficulty discounting confession evidence, even when it has been extracted under coercive circumstances and when it is legally appropriate to do so. So on this point, justices in the majority in the *Fulminante* case got it wrong.

A few mock jury studies have examined the impact on jurors of evidence that the police fabricate during an interrogation (e.g., Forrest et al., 2012; Woody & Forrest, 2009; Woody, Forrest & Yendra, 2014). This controversial tactic is one of many techniques that police investigators are trained to use (Inbau, Buckley, Reid, & Jayne, 2001) and involves presenting to the suspect seemingly incontrovertible evidence of his or her guilt, such as fingerprint or DNA evidence, an eyewitness identification, or the results of a "failed" polygraph when such evidence does not actually exist. The rationale is that presenting this "evidence" can reduce the anxiety associated with admissions of wrongdoing and make a confession more likely. Courts in the United States, including the Supreme Court (*Frazier v. Cupp*, 1969), are generally accepting of police deception during interrogations. Consequently, such tactics are used routinely. In a survey of 631 police interrogators, 92% claimed they fabricated evidence when interrogating individuals (Kassin et al., 2007).

Fabricated evidence or so-called false evidence ploys can be grouped into three categories. *Demeanor* false evidence ploys claim that the suspect's appearance or demeanor during the interrogation suggests that he is guilty (though there is no reason to believe so). *Testimonial* false evidence ploys indicate to the suspect that an eyewitness, co-conspirator, or surveillance camera has placed him at the scene of the crime. *Scientific* false evidence ploys suggest that scientific analysis of evidence recovered at the scene of the crime, such as DNA or other forensic testing, implicates the suspect (Leo, 2008).

Interrogators use these ploys to convince suspects that because incriminating evidence exists, their best course of action is to admit to the wrongdoing. And despite claims by proponents that false evidence ploys are diagnostic, causing guilty suspects to confess but having no effect on innocent suspects (Inbau et al., 2001), the bulk of the evidence suggests otherwise, leading Kassin and his colleagues (2010) to conclude that false evidence ploys "have been implicated in the vast majority of documented false confession cases" (p. 12). These tactics work because they apparently lead to a sense of hopelessness in interviewees, a precondition for many false confessions (Ofshe & Leo, 1997).

How do mock jurors react to confessions that stem from these sorts of fabricated evidence? Forrest and her colleagues (2012) addressed that question by embedding the three types of false evidence ploys into transcripts of actual interrogations. Participants read portions of these interrogations, which included Miranda warnings, references to previous discussions between detectives and suspects, the false evidence ploy, and the resulting confessions. They also learned whether the confessions were later proven to be true or false. Mock jurors rated the testimonial ploys as more coercive and deceptive than the demeanor ploys and, not surprisingly, the veracity of the confession affected their perceptions of the false evidence. They deemed the evidence ploys to be more justified when they learned that the confession turned out to be true.

Some false evidence ploys involve explicit, direct claims of nonexistent evidence (e.g., "We have your DNA"), whereas others are implicit and merely suggest that fabricated evidence exists (e.g., "What if I told you we have your DNA?"). Proponents of false evidence ploys recommend that detectives make implicit rather than explicit claims, because explicit ploys can backfire if a suspect knows that evidence is surely false (e.g., when the suspect fled on foot and the evidence ploy mentions use of a vehicle). Under such circumstances suspects may stop responding and the interrogation may terminate abruptly (Inbau et al., 2001).

But can jurors distinguish between confessions gleaned through explicit ploys and those that emanate from implicit ploys? Presumably the latter would seem less deceptive than the former (Perillo & Kassin, 2011), leading jurors to deem their use less coercive and resulting in higher conviction rates of suspects who confess. But when Woody and his collaborators (2014) exposed 208 mock jurors to trial summaries that included transcripts of interrogations involving explicit, implicit, or no false evidence ploys, they found that *both* sorts of evidence ploys were viewed as deceptive and coercive, though whether the ploy was implicit or explicit had no effect on verdicts.

The ubiquitous nature of false evidence ploys, the fact that suspects are more likely to confess falsely in the face of fabricated evidence (Perillo & Kassin, 2011), and the finding that jurors sometimes convict these suspects with little regard for the deception they experienced, raise various concerns. First and most obviously, a jury trial will not provide an adequate safeguard for defendants who falsely confess, because even though prospective jurors may express distaste for coercive interrogation tactics (Leo & Liu, 2009), they tend to accept them if they believe that a confession is true (Wallace, 2010). Second, implicit false evidence ploys are apparently perceived by jurors as just as deceptive as explicit ploys, debunking the notion that they can be helpful in distinguishing between confessions from innocent and guilty suspects. Worth noting is the fact that interrogators in the United Kingdom are forbidden from lying to suspects (Gudjonsson, 2003), and some data suggest that this method results in fewer false confessions than the accusatory-type interrogations common in the United States (Meissner et al., 2014).

Not all confessions come directly from people under suspicion; some come from others associated in one way or another with a suspect. In contrast to a suspect admitting his or her own guilt, these so-called "secondary confessions" are statements by a third party (e.g., a cellmate of the suspect acting as a jailhouse informant, commonly referred to as a "snitch") who purportedly heard the suspect confess and passed that information along to law enforcement officials. What impact do secondary confessions have on factfinders?

A variety of evidence shows that secondary confessions, even when false, are persuasive. When mock jurors were exposed to a secondary confession from a jailhouse informant who either did or did not receive an incentive (a 5-year sentence reduction) for testifying, their conviction rates were significantly higher than in a no-confession control condition. Moreover, they made little distinction between confessions from incentivized informants and those without incentives (Neuschatz et al., 2008), suggesting that they are insensitive to the motives underlying secondary confessions. Nor did mock jurors differentiate between the secondary confessions of incentivized informants who had testified 20 times in the past and those who had never done so, rating the informants as equally trustworthy and truthful (Neuschatz et al., 2012).

So secondary confessions must impress jurors as truthful, regardless of the circumstances in which they arise. Are they also more persuasive than other forms of trial testimony? The answer, apparently, is yes. In a recent study mock jurors read trial summaries that included one of three types of testimonial evidence: an eyewitness who was present at the scene of a murder, a character witness who testified about the reputation of the defendant, or a jailhouse informant who claimed that the defendant confessed to committing the murder (Wetmore, Neuschatz, & Gronlund, 2014). They rated the secondary confession as more persuasive than either the eyewitness or character testimony, and they were most likely to convict after hearing the secondary confession. When testimony of a secondary confession was directly pitted against testimony of a primary confession and testimony from an eyewitness, mock jurors perceived a secondary confession to be as indicative of guilt as a primary confession, and significantly more indicative of guilt than an eyewitness. These findings suggest that jurors are impressed by the very existence of confession evidence and do not discount even those confessions that come to officials indirectly and from individuals with incentives to lie.

Bringing together these strands of research on the impact of confession evidence on mock jurors leads to the following conclusions: Confession evidence is more influential than other form of testimonial evidence including eyewitness identifications, regardless of whether it emanates directly from a suspect or from a third party who claims to have heard a suspect's confession; jurors pay little heed to the situational factors present during interrogations and have difficulty discounting confessions that were given under duress, even when instructed to do so; and they regard false evidence ploys by interrogators as both coercive and deceptive, particularly when the ploys involve lies about testimonial evidence, but they tend to look beyond these tactics and convict suspects who have been tricked.

The Impact of Confession Evidence on Real Juries

Consistent with findings from jury simulation studies, Leo (2008) claims that no piece of erroneous evidence, if placed before a jury, will lead to more wrongful convictions than false confessions. This means, of course, that false confessors who proceed to trial will often be convicted. Indeed, there is ample evidence from actual criminal cases that jurors convict on the weight of false confessions.

We have already hinted at some numbers: According to the Innocence Project, 30% of its DNA exonerations have involved confessions given by suspects themselves or by jailhouse informants and snitches. Details of the cases, including those of the infamous Central Park Five, are provided on the Innocence Project website (www.innocenceproject.org). Other case examples are documented on the websites of the Center for Wrongful Convictions at Northwestern Law School (www.law.northwestern.edu) and the National Registry of Exonerations at the University of Michigan Law School (www.law.umich.edu).

In addition to these anecdotal examples, miscarriages of justice involving false confessions have been systematically documented since the 1980s. Bedau and Radelet (1987) identified 350 wrongful convictions in potential capital cases in the United States between 1900 and 1987, and determined that in 14% of them false confessions played a causal role. After the introduction of DNA testing in criminal investigations, some defendants who claimed they were innocent now had a definitive way to test those claims. The first account of cases in which DNA testing conclusively proved a prisoner's innocence was published in 1996 (Connors, Lundregan, Miller, & McEwen, 1996). It provided descriptions of 28 wrongful convictions, of which 18% were attributable to false confession evidence. Two years later, Leo and Ofshe (1998) conducted detailed analyses of 60 cases of police-induced false confessions where the confessions were not supported by any physical or other significant credible evidence and were recanted by defendants. Leo and Ofshe determined that a false confessor was approximately three times more likely to be convicted than acquitted, underscoring the fact that for lay jurors, evidence of a confession often outweighs strong evidence of a defendant's innocence.

Accounts of wrongful convictions and false confessions became much more frequent after the year 2000, although not all came from jury trials. These include a study of miscarriages of justice in homicide prosecutions in Illinois between 1970 and the early 2000s, in which 25 of the 42 cases involved convictions of defendants who had falsely confessed (Warden, 2003); a review of 111 individuals released from death row between 1973 and 2004 which showed that 46% of these cases involved a false secondary confession from a jailhouse informant (Warden, 2004); an analysis of a cohort of 125 proven false-confession cases which showed that virtually all false confessions came in the face of false evidence ploys (Drizin & Leo, 2004); and an examination of 340 official exonerations of wrongfully convicted individuals, of which 15% involved false confessions (Gross et al., 2005).

Taken together these studies illuminate an important problem of police-induced false confessions: They occur primarily in more serious cases such as homicides and other high-profile felonies, including capital cases (Gross, 1996). There are several reasons why. Homicide cases often lack eyewitnesses—obviously, because the victim is dead—and many would go unresolved without a confession. In addition, the police work harder to resolve serious and high-profile cases, investing more resources such as the time necessary to conduct longer and more intense interrogations. Detectives who attempt to elicit confessions in such cases are more likely to use psychologically coercive techniques that can wear down a suspect and presumably lead to a false confession.

Despite the fact that both case studies and larger field studies provide incontrovertible proof of the existence of false confessions and subsequent wrongful convictions, the frequency with which these occur will never really be known. Leo (2008) contends that these documented examples probably understate the problem, because many false confessions are unacknowledged by police and prosecutors, disbelieved even by defense attorneys, treated as probative by jurors, and overlooked by researchers.

But the totality of the evidence regarding false confessions is now clear: They are perilous when put before juries because they profoundly bias jurors' evaluations of the case in favor of conviction. In essence they transform an innocence-presumptive ritual into a guilt-presumptive process and override jurors' analysis and consideration of exculpatory evidence (Leo & Ofshe, 1998). Yet the legal system uses a liberal standard for admitting contested confessions into evidence, placing faith in jurors' abilities to recognize a false confession as such (Simon, 2012). That faith seems not well placed.

We have alluded to multiple real-life examples of wrongful convictions based on false confessions. We end this section by describing a clever experimental study that shows why jurors have trouble recognizing false confessions as such. In this study, male prison inmates gave videotaped or audiotaped statements that provided either true confessions to the crimes for which they were incarcerated or false confessions about crimes they did not commit (Kassin, Meissner, & Norwick, 2005). Laypeople and police investigators were then exposed to these statements and asked to say whether the confessions were true or false. Their discrimination abilities were poor, and the police (48% accurate) were even less able than laypeople (59% accurate) to make this important distinction. These numbers are actually rather startling, given that chance accuracy is 50%. A follow-up study examined the kinds of errors made and showed that 46% of the time, laypeople incorrectly identified a false confession as true. In the next section we explore why jurors are so willing to believe defendants who have confessed.

Why Jurors Believe Confessions

One broad explanation for jurors' difficulty recognizing false confessions is that they are notably poor deception detectors. Neither laypeople (Bond & DePaulo, 2006; Vrij, 2008) nor legal professionals (Ekman & O'Sullivan, 1991) can distinguish truth from lies at very high levels of accuracy because the commonsense cues that people use to make this judgment (e.g., averting one's gaze) are not very useful. In fact, laypeople are only slightly more accurate than chance at distinguishing truth from deception. When they err they tend to do so in predictable ways, taking most assertions at face value and assuming that they are true (the so-called "truth bias" [Bond & DePaulo]). But there are additional factors unique to interrogations and confessions that can account for jurors' erroneous beliefs.

A Dearth of Knowledge

Jurors' dearth of knowledge about some of the nuances of interrogations—in particular the institutional pressures on the police to solve serious crimes and the resulting situational pressures they place on interviewees—are surely crucial factors. Lacking such knowledge means that jurors walk into a courtroom with naïve beliefs that the police would not interrogate innocent suspects (Blandón-Gitlin et al., 2011) and that they would follow various rules of common decorum (e.g., not lying to suspects, presuming their innocence) as they and other law enforcement officials prepare the case for trial. Laypeople may be unaware that detectives typically close their investigations after gleaning a confession and overlook alternative suspects and other possible leads, even when the confession is contradicted by other evidence (Drizin & Leo, 2004). Because they maintain the belief that they themselves would never admit to a crime they did not commit, most laypeople probably conclude that only guilty suspects would confess (Simon, 2012). And because most confessions are not videotaped, jurors have little information about whether the factors that promote false confessions occurred prior to trial.

This dearth of knowledge is made worse by laypeople's misconceptions. So, for example, lacking knowledge about the nature of the interrogation process, laypeople may assume that the truly innocent would be able to fend off even the most strong-armed interrogation techniques and that only those who are mentally disabled, mentally ill, or physically threatened would falsely confess (Leo & Davis, 2010). On the latter point they would clearly be wrong, as the bulk of data show that most false confessions come from cognitively intact adults (Drizin & Leo, 2004; Leo & Ofshe, 1998).

Attribution Errors

With little understanding of the coercive nature of most interrogations, laypeople fall prey to the fundamental attribution error: the psychological phenomenon by which people over-rely on dispositional factors and underestimate situational forces when inferring the causes of others' behavior (Ross, 1977). In cases involving confessions, jurors tend not to acknowledge the role of coercive interrogation techniques, such as suggestive questioning and the strong pressures on suspects to comply and "come clean," or they tend to discount suspects' physical states including hunger, exhaustion, and drug use prior to the interrogation. Instead they tend to assume that a confession is a voluntary exercise of free will, and that suspects who confess make conscious decisions to admit their guilt.

This bias toward internal attributions of behavior is strengthened by jurors' tendency to believe statements that people make against their own self-interest. They might ponder why, unless he was guilty, a person would opt to incriminate himself. This means that jurors are more likely to trust suspects' admissions of guilt than their denials (Levine, Kim, & Blair, 2010). If jurors fail to notice or discount the external factors operating on suspects during interrogations, if they assume that people do not confess to acts they did not commit, and if they pay added attention to statements against a person's self-interests, they will accept most confessions as valid and diagnostic of guilt.

Confessions Contain Contextual Details

A cue commonly used in assessing the truthfulness of a confession is the amount of detail it contains, and confessions replete with detail are presumed to be true, particularly when those details are not publicly known. The assumption is that only actual perpetrators and not innocent suspects would be privy to the specifics of a crime. So jurors who learn that suspects' confessions contained precise details about the crime would be inclined to believe them.

But because interrogators are typically very familiar with those details and trained to confront suspects with indications of their guilt, false confessions also "come fully packaged with detailed accounts of the confessor's purported criminal deeds" (Simon, 2012, p. 162). The process typically unfolds in this way: During questioning, interrogators expose suspects to purported evidence against them such as photos of the crime scene and descriptions of victims' injuries. By way of leading questions, visits to the crime scene, or comments from secondhand sources, they convey vivid tidbits about the crime to suspects. Eventually, savvy and prolonged questioning of this sort can elicit descriptions and details about the crime—both of which have been fed to suspects—along with statements of motives such as jealousy, vengeance, and rage; explanations such as alcohol and drug intoxication, peer pressure, and provocation; and apologies and expressions of remorse. It can also yield false memories of actually committing the crime (Gudjonsson & MacKeith, 1982).

When provided with this sort of specific evidence, complete with a compelling and coherent storyline, jurors have little reason to doubt the veracity of the confession. They are especially impressed by a suspect's knowledge of nonpublic facts (Simon, Stenstrom, & Read, 2008), unaware that the confession could have been scripted by the police in a manner consistent with their theory of the case and rehearsed with the suspect for hours on end. Jurors will not learn that when the suspect seemed especially weary and resigned to the police's theory, he or she was asked to sign a written statement—itself often generated by the police—or to be filmed "reenacting" the crime. Jurors will have little understanding that over time, this process transforms a suspect's halting admission into a fully formed narrative in what Leo (2008) refers to as the *confession-making* phase of interrogation.

Analyses of the confessions given by 38 people later exonerated through DNA testing revealed the impressive quality and quantity of detail included in their statements (Garrett, 2010). In all but two of these cases the innocent confessor provided specific details, and in half of the cases the prosecutors emphasized these details during the trial, often noting that they included nonpublic information that could only be known to the actual perpetrator. (One prosecutor claimed that it was a "mathematical impossibility" that an innocent suspect could have guessed correctly on so many details.) In 27 of these 38 cases, the detective-interrogator denied under oath that he disclosed any facts about the crime to the suspect.

A subsequent study focused on 20 false confessions included in the Innocence Project database (Appleby, Hasel, & Kassin, 2013). All involved serious crimes including rape and murder, and all of the innocent confessors were eventually exonerated. Using the most popular interrogation training manual to derive a set of distinct conceptual categories, the researchers coded the content of the confessions. They noted the presence of visual details, references to victim's behavior, details of victim's appearance and mental state, and mention of the time and location of the crime.

Results showed that all of the confessions recounted the facts of who, what, how, and why the crimes occurred—sometimes in remarkable detail. All contained visual details (e.g., "There was blood all over the walls") and descriptions of how the victim acted before, during and after the crime (e.g., "She tried to run away"). Eighty percent described what the victim had said during the crime (e.g., "Leave me alone, let me out"), and 75% provided details about what the victim looked like or was wearing (e.g., "She had on a blue denim dungaree jacket, I think a dark top, dark pants, and white high top sneakers").

Other aspects of the false confessions may have enhanced their credibility. Fully 85% of the innocent confessors commented on the thoughts or feelings they "experienced" at the time of the crime, and 80% provided a full-blown motive for committing the crime (most of the innocent "rapists" mentioned the desire or need for sex and the innocent "murderers" tended to mention provocation). A sizeable number of the false confessions provided details such as self-defense, victim-blaming, or alcohol intoxication that minimized the seriousness of the offense—excuses often provided by interrogators to reduce a suspect's anxiety and normalize his behavior. Finally, 40% of the confessors expressed sadness or remorse and 25% gave outright apologies. This level of detail coupled with insights into the confessor's motivations at the time of the crime and remorse afterwards would cause most jurors to accept these statements at face value. One can certainly presume that the juries that wrongly convicted all of these defendants were impressed by the details.

To assess the effects of detailed confessions on jurors, Appleby and colleagues (2013) conducted a mock jury experiment in which they varied the presence of crime details, motive statements, and apologies in the written confession of an alleged murder that was part of a trial summary. Results showed that it took very little evidence to convince jurors that the confessor was guilty: A simple admission of guilt, later retracted, was typically sufficient. But the confession had added impact when it provided details of how the crime was committed and included the confessor's motives. When jurors hear a detail-rich statement admitting to some wrongdoing, they will have little reason to doubt its authenticity and evidently use it to support their decision to convict.

Confirmation Biases

One infamous case of false confessions involved the so-called Norfolk (Virginia) Four—four men who confessed to and were convicted of a brutal 1997 rape and murder despite exculpatory DNA evidence that was presented at their trials (Wells & Leo, 2008; see also www.norfolkfour.com). The foreman of one jury remarked on the clout of the defendant's confession, explaining that the confession "just washed everything else away . . . That was the supernova circumstance of the entire trial. It overwhelmed everything else" (Wells & Leo, 2008, p. 228). Like jurors in many other trials involving contested confessions, these jurors apparently allowed the power of the confession to sculpt their reactions to the rest of the evidence, causing them to focus on guilt-supportive evidence and to ignore and discount evidence of innocence.

The tendency to seek out and interpret information in a manner that confirms one's suspicions or beliefs and to avoid or reject information that counters it is termed *confirmation bias* (Gilovich, 1991). It courses throughout the investigation of cases that involve false confessions (and through most investigations, in fact), beginning with erroneous assumptions by the police that an innocent person is guilty. These hunches lead them to look for evidence that affirms their suspicions and reject evidence that does not (Simon, 2012). During interrogations, confirmation biases cause investigators to assume guilt and to validate statements from suspects that support their assumption and to discourage denials or statements of innocence. As a result, the evidence that emerges at trial has been filtered by prior actors in ways that are consistent with their beliefs.

There is ample indication that the admission of a confession also causes jurors to selectively filter the evidence. They pay attention to and remember details of the confession and other pieces of evidence that are consistent with it and with their beliefs about how and why the crime occurred. They ignore or discount evidence that is inconsistent with these narratives. As the

Norfolk foreman noted, confessions provide such powerful evidence of guilt that they can radically transform jurors' evaluation of evidence and decision-making processes.

Confirmation biases set in motion by confession evidence can taint how jurors as well as other witnesses or experts interpret other, presumably independent, evidence that might be presented at trial including fingerprint evidence (Dror & Charlton, 2006), exculpatory DNA evidence (Appleby & Kassin, 2011), and handwriting analysis (Kukucka & Kassin, 2014). In essence the confession provides a frame of reference that transforms observers' presumption of innocence into assumptions about guilt, and that guides how they evaluate other pieces of a forensic puzzle. So, for example, prior to hearing about a confession actual fingerprint analysts deemed certain evidence to be "ambiguous." But after learning that the suspect had confessed, they concluded that the prints in question matched the suspect's prints (Dror & Charlton, 2006). And a majority of eyewitnesses who learned that a suspect had confessed subsequently picked that person out of a lineup, even though they had previously identified someone else or rejected the lineup altogether (Hasel & Kassin, 2009). A similar process can play out among jurors. Kukucka and Kassin (2014) asked research participants to read a case summary that, for some, included a confession. These participants were more likely than those without evidence of a confession to conclude that a handwriting sample from the defendant matched a sample from the perpetrator and to deem the defendant guilty. Knowledge of the confession allowed laypeople to perceive a "match" that did not exist for those who had no confession evidence.

In theory, a verdict should emanate from the gradual accumulation of inferences as jurors piece together evidence fragments to reach a judgment. But introducing a confession into evidence seems to arouse such a strong inference of guilt that it affects the weight attributed to other evidence items. As these pieces of evidence are reevaluated or perhaps examined for the first time in light of the confession, that admission begins to gather support from these seemingly independent sources of information. This process is motivated by decision makers' striving to make the evidence and ultimate decision fit into a coherent whole (Simon, 2012). Importantly, though, the entire process has been transformed by the introduction of a defendant's confession into the mix of evidence.

How to Remedy Overreliance on Confession Evidence

It should now be clear that suspects who confess are more likely than others to be charged with a crime and if they are tried, more likely to be convicted by jurors who lack the ability to discriminate between true and false confessions. Attorneys, researchers, and commentators have proposed various reforms to this imperfect system.

Some recommendations focus on reducing the incidence of false confessions in the first place. These include prohibiting the use of certain interrogation approaches (Kassin et al., 2010) and developing more diagnostic questioning tactics (Hartwig, Granhag, Stromwall, & Kronkvist, 2006) to increase the probative value of confession evidence. Other recommendations aim at keeping unreliable confession evidence out of court. Arguing that traditional safeguards for screening confession evidence have been inadequate because "too often judges simply 'kick' the confession to the jury," Leo and his colleagues (Leo, Neufeld, Drizin, & Taslitz, 2013, p. 799) have called for pretrial reliability hearings in which judges gauge the reliability of confession evidence prior to trial. As active gatekeepers, judges would be required to analyze the fit between a defendant's narrative and the objective facts of the crime to determine the veracity of informant testimony and to exclude any untrustworthy confession evidence.

More pertinent to our concerns are reforms surrounding confessions that *have* been admitted into evidence and whether these reforms can increase jurors' abilities to discriminate true from false self-incriminations. Reformers have proposed three mechanisms to counter the commonsense notions that innocent suspects would not make statements counter to their own interests, and that confessions full of crime details must be true. The reforms include making an electronic recording of all confessions that would provide juries with an objective record of how the statements were gleaned; educating jurors via expert testimony about the processes, techniques, and outcomes of interrogative questioning; and enhancing jury instructions to increase jurors' sensitivity to confession evidence. We discuss these suggestions in turn.

Electronic Recordings of Interrogations

Of the proposed reforms, calls for recording all custodial interviews and interrogations have been the most vociferous ("Without equivocation, our most essential recommendation is to lift the veil of secrecy from the interrogation process in favor of the principle of transparency" [Kassin et al., 2010, p. 25]). Although the vast majority of interrogations are not recorded, the practice is gaining momentum. By 2012, 17 states were requiring recordings of custodial interrogations in major felony investigations, and many more jurisdictions were recording interrogations voluntarily (Sullivan, 2012).

In addition to increasing accountability among law enforcement officials, recordings can provide putative benefits to jurors. Through access to a factual record of the questioning process, their ability to determine a confession's authenticity should improve. In many cases recordings will provide assurance that the interrogation was conducted in an appropriate manner. In fact, recordings may actually increase jury conviction rates because a recorded confession will appear to be more credible and convincing evidence of guilt than the mere testimony of the police officer who extracted the confession or a written statement by the suspect (Sullivan, 2004), particularly in urban settings where the police are distrusted by various segments of the population.

Electronic recordings are presumed to be effective because they allow observers to determine whether police used aggressive or suggestive questioning tactics and to examine suspects' verbal and nonverbal behaviors for signs of intimidation, coercion, or exhaustion, though jurors may benefit only to the extent that they know what they should be looking for (Lassiter, 2010). In recent years it has become increasingly clear that two recording procedures enhance the value of electronic records, namely recording the interrogation in its entirety and focusing the camera equally on suspect and interrogator.

Why should interrogations be filmed from start to finish, and how is access to the full record likely to affect jurors' decision making? Partial and selective recordings generally do not reveal any contaminating influences that occurred during questioning. On the other hand, a full record discourages the practice of providing secondhand information or motive statements to suspects, subtly encouraging them to incorporate these details into their confessions and then, when the camera is turned on, extracting statements replete with these innuendos and suggestions. One jury simulation study demonstrated the value of presenting video of a complete interrogation (Kassin, Leo, Crocker, & Holland, 2003). Mock jurors who watched the full interrogation were more likely than those who saw only the final confession to make accurate judgments about the confession and to reach the "correct" verdict: convicting guilty confessors and acquitting innocent "confessors." Jurors' judgments are aided by access to information about the conditions under which the confessions originated.

In most filmed interrogations in the United States, the camera is focused entirely on the suspect (Lassiter, Ware, Ratcliff, & Irvin, 2009). That this is the default arrangement is understandable, since this person's demeanor and statements are arguably most informative to factfinders (Lassiter, Ware, Lindberg, & Ratcliff, 2010). But positioning the camera only on the suspect can impair observers' ability to understand the dynamics at work during interrogations, leading them to conclude that suspects' incriminating statements were volitional rather than a consequence of coercive pressures from interrogators. This phenomenon, known as *illusory causation*, has been documented extensively by Lassiter and his colleagues, who have examined the effects of mock and authentic interrogations filmed from three camera angles: suspect-focused, interrogator-focused, and equal-focus. Viewers who see suspect-focused interrogations deem them the most voluntary (Lassiter & Irvine, 1986) but underestimate the pressures exerted on suspects by detectives. Viewers are considerably more attentive to the situational factors that lead to confessions when the camera encompasses both suspect and interrogator (e.g., Lassiter et al., 2002; Lassiter & Geers, 2004). The camera perspective also influences viewers' judgments of suspects' guilt: Participants who viewed suspect-focused versions of authentic interrogations judged the suspect more likely to be guilty than did participants who viewed interrogator-focused versions (Lassiter et al., 2009).

An equal-focus perspective should protect defendants from salience biases aroused when observers attribute a greater causal role to more salient individuals in a social interaction. But some recent data suggest that even with an equal-focus perspective, certain suspects may still be vulnerable. Specifically, when mock jurors viewed an equal-focus (retracted) confession embedded in a murder trial, those who perceived a defendant as a member of a minority group compared to those who believed he was a majority group member paid more attention to him, rated his confession as more voluntary and incriminating, and were more likely to convict (Pickel, Warner, Miller, & Barnes, 2013). Suspects who stand out visually or whose race makes them seem distinctive apparently receive more attention from viewers even when an equal-focus perspective is used. Given the disproportionate representation in the criminal justice system of members of minority groups and their heightened susceptibility to false confession (Davis, Leo, & Williams, 2014), this salience bias is cause for concern for minority suspects who retract confessions and are tried by largely majority-group jurors.

Expert Testimony

We have shown that laypeople are rather poorly equipped to evaluate the authenticity of confessions that contain vivid and accurate details about a crime. They may naturally wonder why a person who claims to be innocent would have confessed to a crime that he did not commit. To minimize the ripple effects of those misconceptions on jury verdicts, some commentators have argued that experts should be allowed to testify about the processes and outcomes of interrogations, including the psychological and social factors that can lead a suspect to falsely confess (e.g., Costanzo & Leo, 2007; Kassin, 2008). This testimony can educate jurors on the reality of false confessions, the manner in which specific interrogation techniques can induce confessions, and factors that put particular suspects at risk (see Chapter 7). Experts can review and provide analysis of any audio and video recordings of interrogations presented during trial (Costanzo, Blandón-Gitlin, & Davis, 2016).

Courts in the United States are divided about whether to admit this type of expert testimony (Fulero, 2010), prompting the American Psychological Association (APA) to advocate for its admission. The APA notes that experts have a sizeable set of research studies on which to rely, and that without guidance juries tend to overvalue suspects' confessions (e.g., American Psychological Association, 2013a). The APA also claims that expert testimony would assist jurors in assigning the appropriate weight to a suspect's confession, allowing them to make more informed and accurate evaluations of a prosecutor's claim that a confession is true and a defendant's claim that it is not.

To be admissible in court, expert testimony must concern a subject matter that is beyond the common knowledge of most jurors and must aid or assist the triers of fact. On the first point Kassin (2008) contends there is little debate: "it seems clear that there are few, if any, phenomena of human behavior that are less intuitive than that of false confessions" (p. 211). On the second point, jurors themselves tend to believe that expert testimony would be useful: Approximately three-quarters of respondents in the studies by Costanzo et al. (2010) and Chojnacki et al. (2008) thought it would be helpful to hear an expert explain how interrogation techniques can lead to a false confession.

A recent experimental study showed that expert testimony can have a modest effect on mock jurors' decision making (Blandón-Gitlin et al., 2011; see also Chapter 7). Mock jurors read the transcript of a trial involving a police murder, judged the defendant's guilt, and rated the coerciveness of various interrogation tactics before and after being exposed to expert testimony on the potential coercive nature of popular interrogation tactics and other situational factors that arise in interrogations. The proportion of participants who found the defendant guilty decreased from 90% prior to exposure to the expert testimony to 76% after exposure. Ratings of the coerciveness of interrogation tactics increased after the expert testified, and participants who changed their verdicts identified specific features of the expert's testimony that influenced their decisions. An implication of this study is that an expert can effectively alert jurors to situational factors they may not have considered on their own.

Enhanced Jury Instructions

Jury instructions are given at the end of every trial and thus have the potential to affect many jury verdicts. The instructions can, and very often do, address specific types of evidence or elements of the law that might be difficult for jurors (e.g., eyewitness testimony or aggravation and mitigation in death penalty cases; see Chapter 14). Unfortunately, jury instructions in general are the reform of last resort because they affect only the small percentage of cases that go to trial and involve little systemic change or novelty (Leo, 2008). Furthermore, it is rare for judges to provide any specific instructions on how confession evidence should be evaluated or what weight it should be accorded, as they generally assume that jurors are capable of determining whether a witness is lying (e.g., *Commonwealth v. Alicia*, 2014) and believe that instructions regarding witness credibility apply. But some empirical research showed that those generic instructions had little effect on mock jurors' judgments in a simulated trial involving a disputed confession (Gomes, Stenstrom, & Calvillo, 2012).

Recent developments may signal a bit of change in judges' behavior, however. In *Commonwealth v. DiGiambattista* (2004), the Massachusetts Supreme Judicial Court ruled that defendants are entitled to a cautionary jury instruction when confessions are obtained without being electronically recorded, and a similar instruction is now mandated in New Jersey (Sullivan, 2006).

It is conceivable that reforms to jury instructions on confessions will follow the trajectory of eyewitness jury instructions, becoming more useful to jurors as they become more specific and scientifically grounded (see Chapter 14). For many years judges were unwilling to provide cautionary instructions on the pitfalls of eyewitness memory and were especially resistant to instructions that gave any scientifically derived conclusions about factors that influence the reliability of an eyewitness's identification. But that resistance began to erode in 2012 after the New Jersey Supreme Court adopted enhanced jury instructions based on generally accepted research on the reliability of eyewitness memory (*New Jersey v. Henderson*, 2011). Since then, other courts have followed suit (Turgeon, Francis, & Loftus, 2014). Someday, jurors in cases with retracted and disputed confessions may receive detailed guidance on how they should evaluate the situational and dispositional factors inherent in those admissions, with the objective to enhance their ability to distinguish true and false confessions, convict the guilty, and acquit the innocent. As often occurs with eyewitness instructions, instructions on confession evidence might simply make jurors more skeptical about the confession and not enable them to do a better job of distinguishing true from false confessions (see Chapter 14); but in light of their natural tendency to over-rely on confessions, a little additional skepticism is not necessarily a bad thing.

Conclusions: Looking Ahead

Recording custodial interrogations, improving the utility of jury instructions, and providing expert testimony when appropriate are helpful steps in reforming jury decision making in confession cases. But the latter two reforms especially seem like small, stopgap measures that fail to address the real problems that stem from the pressures and suggestive influences that suspects feel in interrogation rooms, and from jurors' intuitive but incorrect beliefs that confessions replete with details and emotions must be authentic and true.

Perhaps it is time to consider another approach. One possibility is to borrow from the innovative efforts in England and Wales that have changed the very nature of police interviews in those countries over the past two decades. Rather than operating under a guilt-presumptive model that strives to glean confessions via confrontational tactics, these procedures seek information from interviewees to move investigations along, and interviewers are not allowed to lie or present fabricated evidence. A detailed analysis of the methodology is beyond the scope of this chapter, but some preliminary results are promising. A meta-analysis of five observational field studies and 12 experimental studies assessed the influence of information-gathering versus accusatorial methods in eliciting true and false confessions and revealed that the former produces fewer false confessions and more true confessions than the latter (Meissner et al., 2014). If one's objective is to improve jury decisions in confession cases like Ryan Ferguson's that opened this chapter, then reducing the incidence of false confessions in the first instance is surely the place to start.

7

Jurors Overvalue Expert Testimony

"Jurors have determinable attitudes and beliefs about experts.
Do they serve as an accurate guide to how much weight to give
testimony?"

(Saks & Wissler, 1984, p. 448)

As our society becomes more complex and technologically sophisticated, the
civil and criminal justice systems necessarily become more complex as well.
This is especially true in some areas of law, such as patents, antitrust, class
actions, products liability, and medical malpractice (e.g., Landsman, 1995;
1999; 2008; Lempert, 1993). Although there is a "complexity exception" in
some jurisdictions, whereby judges (in the United States and other common
law countries) can refuse to allow highly complex cases to be decided by a
jury, for the most part the right to a jury trial trumps complexity concerns
(Fordham, 2006; Landsman, 1999; Wiggins & Breckler, 1992).

Trial complexity has many facets, and each type of complex case presents its own set of problems (Wiggins & Breckler, 1992). Some of the issues
are procedural, such as the number of parties or claims, the sheer volume
of information, and whether jurors are allowed to take notes or ask questions for purposes of clarification (e.g., Heuer & Penrod, 1994a; Horowitz &
Bordens, 2000; 2002; Horowitz et al., 2001). Evidentiary factors can also contribute to trial complexity, and one of the main things that makes trials complex is evidence delivered by expert witnesses (e.g., Cutler & Kovera, 2011;
McAuliff, Kovera, & Nunez, 2009). These experts might be testifying directly
about facts in issue (e.g., a blood type match) or as a way of educating jurors
about the limitations of other testimony, such as forensic evidence, eyewitnesses, or confessions.

Expert testimony is increasingly common in both civil and criminal trials (Faigman, 1999; Faigman et al., 2014; Gross, 1991). Such increases are difficult to quantify with precision, but an analysis of one type of complex evidence—statistical evidence, which is usually introduced by expert witnesses—found that it had increased 56% from 1990 to 2004 (Koehler, 2011). In certain kinds of civil cases, such as products liability and medical malpractice, it would now be highly unusual *not* to have expert testimony (Gross & Syverud, 1991; Ivkovic & Hans, 2003; Landsman, 1995; Vidmar, 1995). And in criminal cases, expert forensic evidence has become so common that jurors may even expect it and be surprised if it is absent. Although this so-called "CSI effect" may produce expectations about and attitudes toward trial evidence, there is little indication that it affects trial outcomes (Mancini, 2011; Schweitzer & Saks, 2007).

The challenge for jurors is not merely to understand the expert testimony, which can be highly technical and deal with matters about which they likely have little, if any, familiarity; if there are experts called by both sides, they must also judge the quality of each expert's underlying knowledge base. In some cases this might require them to evaluate competing interpretations of the same data (e.g., experts might assess the same person or set of studies and reach different conclusions). This can be somewhat akin to a patient with a certain constellation of symptoms obtaining divergent opinions from two different physicians—which one is right? How is the patient supposed to decide between options (e.g., Treatment A or Treatment B, which might mean no treatment at all), when the experts themselves can't agree? In medical situations the natural tendency is to defer to a physician's recommendation. But when two expert-physicians disagree, there is a concern that the patient will be influenced by extraneous factors, such as one physician's credentials or which one of the two is more likeable. Concerns that jurors will be similarly deferential to legal experts are hence not completely out of place.

In this chapter we begin by briefly sketching the rules governing the admissibility of expert testimony. The rules necessarily differ somewhat depending on jurisdiction, but the underlying themes and concerns are pretty much the same.[1] We next consider the question of who counts as an expert and, relatedly, which factors tend to make experts more (as opposed to less) credible. Given the generality of the legal guidelines, practically anyone, under the right circumstances, could qualify as an expert; nonetheless, some kinds of experts are more common—in society at large as well as in the courts—than others. The next two sections focus on the main question of interest, namely, the effects of expert testimony on jurors. Despite a

---

[1] Our focus is on American law and trial procedures, but similar issues arise in other common law countries (Bernstein, 1996; Fordham, 2006).

widespread concern that jurors will overvalue expert testimony (for review, see Faigman, 1999; Faigman et al., 2014), empirical research indicates that this belief is yet another myth about jury behavior. Given the enormous diversity of experts, it is hardly surprising that not all kinds of experts have been studied in this regard. Much of the extant research concerns expert psychological testimony, perhaps because so much of the research itself has been conducted by psychologists. Before our review of psychological experts, we discuss the effects on jurors of other types of expert testimony.

Admissibility of Expert Testimony

The law governing the admissibility of expert testimony has evolved over time and varies somewhat depending on jurisdiction (Faigman et al., 2014). Currently, the federal courts and most state courts are governed by the Federal Rules of Evidence (as adopted and sometimes modified by the states) and the *Daubert* standard (*Daubert v. Merrell Dow Pharmaceuticals*, 1993). Rule 702 of the Federal Rules of Evidence defines expert testimony as the "scientific, technical, or other specialized knowledge" of a witness qualified "by knowledge, skill, experience, training, or education." Whereas ordinary "fact witnesses" differ from jurors solely in having had the opportunity to perceive things directly that the jurors did not, expert witnesses possess specialized knowledge that jurors lack (Faigman et al., 2014). Their testimony must be based upon sufficient data and must be the product of reliable principles and methods, and the expert witness needs to apply those principles and methods reliably to the case facts.

The key question, then, is whether the evidence is reliable. The Supreme Court has explicated the basis for making this assessment. Specifically, for scientific or technical evidence to be admissible, *Daubert* and subsequent Supreme Court jurisprudence (*General Electric Co. v. Joiner*, 1997; *Kumho Tire Co. v. Carmichael*, 1999) direct judges to consider a theory or technique's falsifiability, error rate, general acceptance within the relevant scientific community, and whether it has been subjected to peer review and publication (Pearce, 2011). The *Daubert* factors place a significant burden on judges to act as gatekeepers in ruling on the admissibility of expert testimony. A nuanced assessment of *Daubert* and its implementation suggests that it has resulted in a stricter standard for some kinds of scientific evidence but a looser standard for others (Faigman et al., 2014).

As with any other evidence, the expert testimony must also be relevant to the matter at hand. Two important aspects of relevance are "fit" and "helpfulness" (Pearce, 2011). Fit refers to the evidence's application to the specific facts of the case, whereas helpfulness refers to the evidence's capacity to "assist the trier of fact to understand the evidence or to determine a fact in issue" (Federal Rule of Evidence 702). Fit and helpfulness are often obvious and easy to demonstrate, as in a physician's testimony about the nature of a person's injury or a serologist's testimony about blood matching. However, fit and helpfulness may not be so obvious when it comes to testimony about general research findings, such as an eyewitness expert who is called to testify about the factors that tend to make eyewitness identification more or less accurate. Courts frequently exclude such testimony on the grounds that it fails to show whether a particular witness is accurate or not (i.e., lack of fit) or is a matter of commonsense (i.e., lack of helpfulness; Boyce et al., 2007).

Another commonly invoked reason for excluding expert testimony is that it will be overly influential. Federal Rule of Evidence 403 provides: "Although relevant, evidence may be excluded if its probative value is substantially outweighed by the danger of unfair prejudice, confusion of the issues, or misleading the jury, or by considerations of undue delay, waste of time, or needless presentation of cumulative evidence." Some of these elements are merely practical (e.g., delay, waste of time, cumulative evidence), but others require substantive inferences about the content and anticipated impact of the evidence (e.g., prejudice, confusion, misleading the jury). The underlying concern here is typically that jurors will grant the evidence more importance than it deserves.

Experts: Who Counts and Who's Most Credible

There is no universally agreed upon taxonomy of expertise (Faigman et al., 2014). Although anyone might have relevant "specialized knowledge," depending on the nature of the dispute, courts rely on some kinds of expertise more than others. In civil cases, medical experts are especially common (Gross, 1991; Landsman, 1995). For example, Gross (1991; Gross & Syverud, 1991) conducted a review of 529 California civil trials, 86% of which included expert testimony. Half of the expert witnesses were medical doctors, 20% were engineers and other scientists, 11% were financial or business experts, 9% were nonphysician health professionals (e.g., clinical psychologists, dentists), and 8% were experts in reconstruction and investigation. These same kinds of experts figure in criminal cases, which may also feature forensic scientists (e.g., blood, DNA, fingerprint, ballistics, and handwriting experts), epidemiologists, statisticians, toxicologists, and polygraphers, to mention but a few.

Experts in general, especially scientific experts, are overwhelmingly perceived by the public favorably (Gauchat, 2012; MacCoun, 2015). Expert witnesses in general, perhaps simply by virtue of having the label "experts," are viewed as more credible than other kinds of witnesses (e.g., Champagne, Shuman, & Whitaker, 1992; Lieberman, Carrell, Miethe, & Krauss, 2008; Saks & Wissler, 1984). Needless to say, not all experts are created equal, and the science underlying some kinds of expert testimony is more reliable than others. To some extent laypeople (i.e., prospective jurors) are aware of these differences. Saks and Wissler (1984) surveyed adults summoned for jury duty on their opinions about 10 different witnesses they might encounter in a trial. In addition to a police officer and an eyewitness, there were eight categories of witnesses who would most likely testify as experts: a medical doctor, a chemical/drug expert, an accountant/appraiser, a handwriting expert, a psychiatrist, a psychologist, a firearms expert, and a polygraph examiner. Participants indicated how likely they would be to agree with the testimony of each kind of expert and rated the honesty and competence of people in each field (these measures were highly correlated). Physicians, chemists, and firearms experts were perceived as most credible, while handwriting experts and polygraph examiners were perceived as least credible. The other categories of experts, along with eyewitnesses and police officers, were in the middle. Laypeople have an especially high opinion of DNA-profiling evidence compared even to other forms of forensic identification evidence (Lieberman et al., 2008). This creates a possibility that they might consequently be too accepting of some kinds of expert testimony, such as that regarding DNA (we discuss this possibility in the following section).

This ordering is consistent with laypeople's tendency to view the physical, environmental, and medical sciences more positively than the social and behavioral sciences (MacCoun, 2015). Psychology in particular seems to have a bit of a credibility problem, being viewed as less rigorous than other sciences (Lilienfeld, 2012). Notably, all of the witnesses examined by Saks and Wissler (1984) received relatively high ratings (i.e., means above the midpoint of the rating scale), perhaps reflecting an assumption that if the court allows a witness to testify—especially an expert—then the witness must have something valuable to say, and the judge must have already evaluated it and given it his or her seal of approval. Indeed, laypersons are less critical of, and more persuaded by, expert evidence when it is presented as part of a trial, compared to the same evidence presented outside the courtroom context (Schweitzer & Saks, 2009).

As the preceding discussion shows, experts, by their very nature and role at trial, tend to be perceived as credible witnesses. Yet although expert witnesses start at a relatively high level of presumed credibility, many factors can raise or lower the impact of an expert witness's testimony (apart from variations in the precise content of the testimony, as discussed in greater detail in the following sections). Considerable research has specifically addressed how to make an expert witness more credible (e.g., Brodsky, Griffin, & Cramer, 2010; Brodsky & Pivovarova, 2016). This research is closely linked to the field of trial consulting, because one of the tasks engaged in by consultants is to help attorneys prepare witnesses to make them powerful and persuasive (Brodsky, 2009; Posey & Wrightsman, 2005).

Expert Characteristics Related to Credibility

What characteristics make an expert witness more credible? The factors that enhance an expert's credibility vary, to some extent, depending on the type of expert. The things that make a physician more credible (e.g., type and location of training) are not the same as those that make an automobile mechanic more credible (e.g., experience and success working with different vehicles). Thus many characteristics of an expert witness (e.g., the person's credentials and type of work conducted) covary, making it hard to isolate the possible impact on jurors of individual factors. For example, if a neurologist who presents brain images is more credible than a psychologist who presents findings from a clinical interview, are jurors responding to the expert's training and credentials (MD vs. PhD), nature of the expert testimony (brain scan vs. clinical evaluation), both, or something else altogether? Nonetheless, many aspects of an expert witness—especially those related to the witness's in-court testimony—cut across all areas of expertise.

Many factors go into public perception of experts, such as knowledge/ability, trustworthiness, integrity, likeability, and so on (Bank & Poythress, 1982; Brodsky et al., 2010; Hurwitz, Miron, & Johnson, 1992; MacCoun, 2015). A common approach to experts who testify at trial is to view the expert's role in terms of persuasion; that is, the expert (like any witness in an adversarial system, or even the attorneys) is a source of information who delivers a persuasive message to a target, in this case the jury (Bank & Poythress, 1982; McAuliff, Nemeth, Bornstein, & Penrod, 2003; see, generally, Petty & Cacioppo, 1986). More credible sources are more persuasive, and more persuasive sources come across as more credible (e.g., Pornpitakpan, 2004; Smith, De Houwer, & Nosek, 2013). Ordinarily in such situations, both central cues (i.e., the content of the message) and peripheral cues (e.g., characteristics of the source or messenger) play a part, with their relative importance varying depending on a variety of factors.

In the case of scientific expert testimony, source characteristics related to the expert's credentials (e.g., degree, training) typically make a difference (e.g., Cooper, Bennett, & Sukel, 1996; Hurwitz et al., 1992; Ivkovic & Hans, 2003; but see Schweitzer & Saks, 2009), as do features like the expert's likeability (Brodsky, Neal, Cramer, & Ziemke, 2009) and gender (Brodsky & Pivovarova, 2016; Neal, 2014). With respect to gender, for example, male experts are generally found more credible than female experts, especially when testifying on traditionally masculine topics; but female experts are less disadvantaged, and might even be perceived more favorably, when testifying about a traditionally feminine domain (e.g., children, women's clothing; see Neal, 2014; Schuller, Terry, & McKimmie, 2001). An expert's likeability also matters more for female than for male experts (Brodsky et al., 2009).

The greatest contributor to an expert witness's perceived credibility is the expert's confidence (Brodsky et al., 2010), mirroring the data on the credibility of eyewitnesses (see Chapter 5). As with eyewitnesses, an overemphasis on confidence is problematic; experts, like eyewitnesses, are not necessarily well calibrated (MacCoun, 2015). There are a number of reasons why experts might perform less well than expected, such as biases associated with expert clinical judgment, conflicts of interest, expert overconfidence, and the sheer difficulty of many of the judgment tasks that experts undertake (MacCoun, 2015).

Jurors are also not particularly sensitive to the quality of expert scientific testimony in terms of the underlying science (Kovera, McAuliff, & Hebert, 1999; Levett & Kovera, 2008). Kovera and colleagues (1999) manipulated characteristics of the experimental methodology used in the research described by an expert witness in a simulated hostile work environment case (i.e., the research's general acceptance and validity). Although the expert's testimony should be more influential when it is of relatively high quality (i.e., generally accepted and high in validity), the research characteristics exerted no effect on mock jurors' verdicts. This failure to find an effect of research quality on jurors' decisions highlights the importance of judges' gatekeeper role in determining whether scientific evidence is sufficiently reliable that it should be admitted at all. Unfortunately, however, judges are not much better than jurors at evaluating the quality of empirical research, especially in the absence of scientific training (Kovera & McAuliff, 2000).

Experts' behavior on the stand matters as well. Not surprisingly, what they say and how they say it are enormously important. Jurors place great emphasis on the clarity and accessibility of expert testimony; that is, they like experts who are good teachers (Ivkovic & Hans, 2003). Even something as simple as using too much passive voice can make an expert seem less credible (Hurwitz et al., 1992).

Expert testimony, especially when it is technical or scientific, naturally has a tendency to sound, well, technical and scientific. More scientific-sounding testimony might seem more legitimate and hence more attention-worthy (Brodsky & Pivovarova, 2016; Horowitz et al., 2001), but it is possible to go too far. When testimony becomes so technical and jargon-ridden that it is difficult to process, jurors do a poorer job of making legally relevant distinctions (e.g., among plaintiffs who vary in the severity of their injuries; Horowitz, ForsterLee, & Brolly, 1996) and recall fewer and less probative case facts (Horowitz et al., 2001). Highly technical testimony influences jurors' credibility judgments of experts (and hence verdicts) less when the case facts are ambiguous than when they clearly favor one party (Horowitz et al., 2001), and it can cause jurors to shift from attending primarily to the message to more peripheral cues, such as the expert's credentials, payment, or frequency of testifying (Cooper et al., 1996; Cooper & Neuhaus, 2000).

These findings suggest that the effects of the language used by expert witnesses are complex. Consequently, experts who testify at trial—and the attorneys and litigants who retain them—need to be very careful about the manner of expert testimony (Brodsky & Pivovarova, 2016). Nonverbal aspects of presentation style also make a difference. For example, expert witnesses (especially male experts) who make more eye contact with the questioning attorney and the jurors are perceived as more credible than experts who make less eye contact (Neal & Brodsky, 2008).

Posttrial interviews with jurors show that they are alert to the possibility of expert bias and recognize that in an adversarial system, experts are usually retained by one side because their opinion supports that side's position (Fordham, 2006; Ivkovic & Hans, 2003). Although they do not perceive experts as blatantly partial to the side that calls them (Fordham, 2006), they find court-appointed experts to be more persuasive and credible than adversarial experts (Scurich et al., 2015). They also have reservations about experts who give the impression of being hired guns who testify frequently (Ivkovic & Hans, 2003), especially if they are handsomely paid (Cooper & Neuhaus, 2000). Thus the evidence suggests that jurors pay careful attention to experts. Experts appear to be granted a default assumption of credibility, but a number of central and peripheral cues can make an expert more or less credible and persuasive. Characteristics of the jurors themselves can also influence their response to expert testimony.

Individual Differences in Jurors' Impressions of Expert Witnesses

By and large, jurors' demographic characteristics are not related to their views of expert witnesses (Bank & Poythress, 1982; Ivkovic & Hans, 2003; Shuman, Champagne, & Whitaker, 1996), although better educated jurors find expert witnesses of all kinds to be less competent and honest (Saks & Wissler, 1984). Given the unique nature and frequent complexity of expert testimony, more subtle individual differences might play a larger role. Individual jurors necessarily vary in their attitudes and the sophistication of their judgment processes (Graziano, Panter, & Tanaka, 1990). It is reasonable to suppose that jurors who have a more positive attitude toward scientific evidence, are more scientifically savvy, comfortable with numerical information, or thoughtful about processing complex information would deal with technical and complex expert testimony—especially when it has a scientific and/or numerical component—more appropriately than jurors who lack such characteristics.

Several studies have addressed this hypothesis. For example, Hans and colleagues (2011) found that mock jurors who had more formal education, especially math and science courses, and who had fewer reservations about science in general understood DNA evidence better than those with less education or more reservations. These attributes can also predict jurors' verdicts. Lieberman et al. (2008, Study 3) measured mock jurors' attitudes toward DNA evidence (e.g., "DNA is the most reliable type of physical evidence we have today"; "I would convict a defendant if the only evidence against him was DNA"). Mock jurors who were more trusting of DNA evidence were more likely to believe that a defendant who was implicated by DNA testing— an expert witness testified that based on a DNA analysis, there was a .00005% chance that the defendant was not at the crime scene—was guilty. And mock jurors who are concerned about their ability to understand statistical

reasoning are influenced less by statistical evidence that varies in its probative value than jurors who feel better about their reasoning skills (Kaasa,
Peterson, Morris, & Thompson, 2007). Conversely, those who are relatively
confident in their math or science ability are more influenced by variations
in statistical evidence (Scurich, 2015; Thompson, Kaasa, & Peterson, 2013).

Most of the studies that have addressed individual differences relevant
to expert testimony have focused on a construct known as *need for cognition*
(NFC; Cacioppo, Petty, Feinstein, & Jarvis, 1996). NFC measures "people's
tendency to engage in and enjoy effortful cognitive activity" (Cacioppo et al.,
1996, p. 197). Several studies have found a relationship between individual
mock juror judgments and NFC or similar types of cognitive processing,
across a variety of different kinds of criminal (Butler & Moran, 2007a; Kassin,
Reddy, & Tulloch, 1990; Mancini, 2011; Miller, Wood, & Chomos, 2014;
Sommers & Kassin, 2001; Wevodau, Cramer, Clark, & Kehn, 2014) and civil
cases (DeWitt, Richardson, & Warner, 1997; McCabe, Krauss, & Lieberman,
2010; Salerno & McCauley, 2009; Vinson, Costanzo, & Berger, 2008).
However, NFC does not always predict verdicts (Allison & Brimacombe,
2010; Bornstein, 2004; Graziano et al., 1990; Krauss, McCabe, & Lieberman,
2012; McCabe et al., 2010; Miller, 2006), suggesting that the relationship
varies depending on case and other individual characteristics. Indeed, the
principal effect of NFC appears to be one of moderating the impact of evidentiary variables (e.g., Butler & Moran, 2007a; Cramer, Kehn, et al., 2013;
Kassin et al., 1990). Although NFC could affect the processing of any kind
of evidence, expert testimony is an especially strong candidate, considering
that it is, by definition, "beyond the ken" of the average juror.

In support of this possibility, a few studies have found that NFC moder-
ates expert testimony's effects. Compared to jurors low in NFC, jurors high
in NFC are less influenced by anecdotal evidence (Bornstein, 2004), and
they are more sensitive to some (but not all) variations in the soundness of
the research on which an expert relies (McAuliff & Kovera, 2008; Salerno &
McCauley, 2009). However, low-NFC jurors' relatively poor sensitivity to
research quality can be improved by cross-examination and deliberation
(Salerno & McCauley, 2009). This suggests that although some jurors might
be less capable of evaluating expert testimony than others, attorneys and
other jurors can essentially educate them through the procedural safeguards
of cross-examination and deliberation.

Research on deliberation dynamics shows that contrary to their reputation for not engaging in effortful cognitive activity, jurors low in NFC are
more responsive to differences in the quality of other jurors' arguments than
are jurors high in NFC (Shestowsky & Horowitz, 2004). Left to their own
devices low-NFC jurors might not seek out or be especially adept at evaluating complex information, but they are receptive to it when another party provides it. This suggests that NFC might be measuring motivation more than
ability. For their part, high-NFC jurors are more persuasive and speak more
during deliberation (Shestowsky & Horowitz, 2004; Shestowsky, Wegener,

& Fabrigar, 1998). Importantly, high-NFC and low-NFC individuals do not differ in the quality of the arguments they produce during deliberation (Shestowsky & Horowitz, 2004). Thus individuals might differ in the processing styles that they bring to jury deliberation, but they tend to balance each other out, with some jurors taking a more active role than others and some being more responsive to variations in evidence and argument quality. It is worth pointing out that large (i.e., 12-person) juries are more likely to have this sort of healthy mix of processing styles than small juries (see Chapter 4), a mix of particular importance in cases involving complex evidence provided by expert witnesses.

Juries and Nonpsychological Experts

Probabilistic and DNA Evidence

One of the more common types of expert testimony, especially in criminal cases, is testimony about probabilistic incidence rates. In a sense, all evidence is probabilistic. Jurors' task is to determine the probability (likelihood) that a given hypothesis, such as that the defendant is guilty of the crime with which he is charged, is true. Individual pieces of evidence, which vary in their probative value, make the hypothesis more or less likely (*probative*, "*probability*", and *prove* all share the same Latin root, *probare*—to test, approve, or prove). For example, an expert might testify to the extremely low probability that someone other than the defendant could have left a fingerprint or tissue found at the scene of the crime. How low? In June, 2014, Michael Cisneros was tried for first-degree murder in the drowning death of a 20-month-old toddler in Mason City, Iowa. Blood was found on the victim's pajama bottoms.[2] At trial, a criminalist from the Iowa Division of Criminal Investigation testified that the probability the DNA profile developed from the bloodstains belonged to someone other than Cisneros was less than 1 in 100 billion. A Cerro Gordo County jury found Cisneros not guilty in December, 2014. The verdict might seem surprising in light of the DNA evidence, and we can only speculate as to the reasons for it. The defense was apparently successful in its efforts to shift suspicion to the victim's father, and the long delay between the crime and the DNA testing might also have been a factor.

Probabilistic evidence can take many forms; two of the more common are random match probabilities (e.g., 1 in 1,000,000 people share some biomarker left at the crime scene, and it is a biomarker the defendant also happens to share, producing a 1 in 1,000,000 chance of a match due to random

---

[2] The crime occurred in 1994, but the trial did not take place until 2014 for two reasons: DNA testing was not available at the time, and once it became available, Cisneros' DNA was not in the database (CODIS). The match was flagged in January, 2013.

chance) and base rates (e.g., 20% of patients taking some medication experience suicidal ideation). Courts and legal commentators have had longstanding concerns about probabilistic evidence, for example, that it lacks probative value or will be misused (see, e.g., Bernstein, 1996; Huber, 1991; Tribe, 1971; for cogent critiques of these arguments, see Kaye & Koehler, 1991; Koehler, 1992; Koehler & Shaviro, 1990). Some observers argue further that as a matter of public policy, the quantification of error is immoral, probabilities violate the defendant's right to be treated uniquely, and the public will not respect verdicts based on probabilistic evidence (for a discussion of policy concerns, see Koehler, 1992). These concerns have intensified in recent years along with the advent of DNA testing, largely because of the extremely low probabilities that DNA testing yields (Koehler, Chia, & Lindsey, 1995), which can be "vanishingly small" (Schklar & Diamond, 1999, p. 160). Random match probabilities can be so small that they are essentially taken as dispositive, leading to "a mystical aura of definitiveness" surrounding DNA evidence (Lieberman et al., 2008, p. 27).

Prospective jurors do view DNA evidence as extremely reliable (e.g., Golding et al., 2000; Hans et al., 2011; Lieberman et al., 2008; Thompson et al., 2013). Lieberman and colleagues (2008, Study 1) asked laypersons (jurors who had completed jury duty and undergraduate students) to rate the accuracy of nine different types of evidence: DNA evidence, fingerprint evidence, hair and fiber evidence, videotape surveillance pictures, alcohol and drug tests, expert testimony by scientists, a suspect's confession, victim statements, and eyewitness statements. They rated each kind of evidence on a scale ranging from 0% (not accurate at all) to 100% (completely accurate). DNA evidence was perceived as the most accurate by both jurors and students (Ms of 94.9% and 93.7%, respectively). Other forms of expert and scientific evidence were also perceived as quite accurate; all received mean ratings greater than 75% (lawyers and judges, in contrast, have less positive views of experts; see Saks & van Duizend, 1983). The various forms of non-expert testimony (confession, victim, and eyewitness testimony) received the lowest ratings but were still judged to be relatively accurate in an absolute sense (Ms ranged from 63%–76%).

Lieberman et al. (2008, Study 1) also conducted a jury simulation that included five of the different evidence types (DNA, hair, fingerprint, victim testimony, and eyewitness testimony), in addition to manipulating whether the evidence was incriminating or exonerating and the type of crime (rape or murder). There were some differences depending on the type of crime, but overall the probative value of the evidence (incriminating or exonerating) had a greater effect for the expert than for the non-expert evidence. It was especially pronounced for DNA evidence: 100% of participants voted to convict both the rape defendant and the murder defendant when the DNA evidence incriminated him, compared to 15% (in the rape condition) and 36% (in the murder condition) when the DNA evidence exonerated him. These findings show that jurors perceive DNA evidence as very powerful.

As the Cisneros case shows, DNA evidence does not trump everything else. Jonathan Koehler, one of the leading scholars of statistical evidence at trial, identifies the belief that jurors will overweigh statistics as the leading misconception about statistical evidence (Koehler, 2011). Despite concerns that jurors will be overawed by highly inculpatory probabilistic evidence, mock jury studies show that they are reluctant to make decisions based on statistical evidence alone (e.g., Niedermeier, Kerr, & Messé, 1999; Wells, 1992), can often understand it quite well (Hans et al., 2011; Thompson et al., 2013), and, if anything, give expert probabilistic testimony less weight than it deserves (Faigman & Baglioni, 1988; Kaye & Koehler, 1991; Koehler, 1992; Koehler et al., 1995; Martire et al., 2013; Nance & Morris, 2005; Thompson & Schumann, 1987). Explaining to jurors how to incorporate probabilistic evidence with other kinds of testimony, or how to combine multiple probability estimates (e.g., according to Bayes' Theorem) generally has little effect; they still underweight the probabilistic evidence (Faigman & Baglioni, 1988; Schklar & Diamond, 1999; Smith, Penrod, Otto, & Park, 1996).

Jurors are especially likely to underutilize probabilistic base-rate information when it is contrasted with salient anecdotal information. Bornstein (2004) demonstrated this in a jury simulation using a personal injury (toxic tort) case. In two studies, anecdotal expert testimony supporting the defense (i.e., three others were exposed to the same substance as the plaintiff but developed no health problems) had a greater effect on mock jurors' verdicts than experimental expert testimony supporting the defense (i.e., an animal laboratory study showing that exposure to the substance did not cause health problems). This tendency to discount probabilistic evidence in favor of individual cases reflects a general tendency to prefer anecdotal information to summary base rates (Kahneman & Tversky, 1973; Koehler, 1996; Stanovich & West, 1998), a cognitive bias known as the *base-rate fallacy* (e.g., Bar-Hillel, 1980).

Although jurors tend to underweight probabilistic testimony in general, they are often sensitive to clear differences in the probative value of probabilistic expert testimony (Kaasa et al., 2007; Kaye & Koehler, 1991; Koehler, 2001, Experiment 3; Schklar & Diamond, 1999; Scurich, 2015; Smith et al., 1996; Thompson et al., 2013; Thompson & Newman, 2015). For example, mock jurors in a study by Smith et al. heard expert testimony from a forensic serologist who testified that either 20% or 80% of the population had an enzyme type shared by the defendant and the assailant in a rape. Mock jurors in the 80% condition perceived the defendant as less guilty. Mock jurors are also much more likely to convict when expert testimony is incriminating than when it is exculpatory (Lieberman et al., 2008).

As with expert testimony in general, the manner in which an expert witness presents probabilistic evidence can make it more or less influential (e.g., Koehler, 2001; Nance & Morris, 2005; Thompson & Newman, 2015; Thompson & Schumann, 1987). For example, Koehler (2001, Experiment 1) presented participants with a summary of the facts regarding the affair (at the time of the study, not yet substantiated) between President Bill Clinton and Monica Lewinsky. Included in the evidence was that a dress worn by Ms. Lewinsky contained semen matching President Clinton's DNA. A DNA expert reported on the probability of obtaining a match if President Clinton were not the source of the genetic material. For half of the participants, the expert stated: "The probability that Mr. Clinton would match the semen stain if he were not its source is 0.1%." The other half read that "1 in 1,000 people in Washington who are not the source would also match the semen stain" (Koehler, 2001, p. 499). Although 1 in 1,000 and 0.1% are mathematically identical, participants in the probability condition (0.1%) thought it was more likely that Clinton was the source of the DNA than participants in the frequency (1 in 1,000) condition. Koehler (2001, Experiment 2) replicated this finding with a less sensationalized case in which participants gave a verdict in addition to evaluating the evidence. Koehler's interpretation was that presenting probabilistic information in terms of its frequency made it easier to imagine coincidental matches (supporting the defense's argument that despite the match, someone other than the defendant was the source of the DNA).

As researchers on probabilistic evidence have pointed out, there are many (indeed infinite) ways of presenting the same probability: 0.1% = 1 in 1,000 = 10 in 10,000 = 1,000 in 1,000,000 . . . Probabilities also can be, and often are, quantified verbally. The correspondence between verbal quantifiers and numerical probabilities, in fields ranging from medicine and law to everyday discourse, is notoriously imprecise (e.g., Reagan, Mosteller, & Youtz, 1989; Wallsten et al., 1986). Despite this lack of precision, Martire and colleagues (2013) found that expert testimony incriminating the defendant had comparable (and underutilized) effects whether it was presented in a numerical (e.g., 4.5 times more likely) or verbal (e.g., offers weak or limited support) format. Mock jurors' general tendency to underutilize such testimony might mute the effects of presentation format.

Neuroscientific Evidence

Statistical evidence has been around a long time; DNA evidence is of relatively recent vintage but is now fairly well established. One of the newest, and currently one of the more controversial, forms of expert testimony is neuroscientific expert evidence, which may include neuroimages that are the product of functional magnetic resonance imaging (fMRI) or other imaging technology (Jones, Wagner, Faigman, & Raichle, 2013; Schweitzer et al., 2011). Experts with various types of backgrounds might provide such testimony, including psychiatrists, neurologists, other physicians, neuroscientists, or neuropsychologists. Neuroscientific evidence could be used to address a number of issues, including volitional control, moral reasoning, truth telling, and various other aspects of motivation and cognition associated with brain damage or neuroanatomical abnormalities.

Expert testimony that describes fMRI data can be quite influential, exerting a greater effect on mock jurors' decisions than other expert testimony reaching the same conclusion, such as testimony based on a polygraph examination (McCabe, Castel, & Rhodes, 2011). However, the concern of some courts and commentators is that such evidence will be unduly influential not only because of the usual patina of credibility associated with the witness's expertise and professional credentials, but also because the visual images that may accompany fMRI testimony will be unusually compelling, and evidence of a malfunctioning brain will come across as unusually conclusive (e.g., Brown & Murphy, 2010; Haederle, 2010). Schweitzer et al. (2011, p. 362) refer to these presumed mechanisms as the "power of the visual" and the "power of the neurological."

To assess whether concerns about the power of neuroscientific evidence are justified, Schweitzer et al. (2011) conducted several mock jury studies that varied the extent to which neuroscientific evidence and images supported an expert witness's conclusion that a criminal defendant's mental disorder reduced his capacity to control his actions (i.e., a *mens rea* defense). For example, their first study presented mock jurors with the case of a defendant charged with armed robbery and homicide. The central issue was not whether the defendant had committed the acts in question (i.e., the *actus reus*) but whether he had formed the necessary level of intent—that is, whether he possessed the requisite *mens rea*. The defense argued that he suffered from a neurological defect in his frontal lobe that prevented him from forming the necessary intent. This defense was accompanied by one of eight different expert testimony conditions, which principally varied the type of expert testimony (e.g., neuroscientist presenting fMRI findings or clinician making a different kind of diagnosis) and accompanying image (e.g., fMRI image, graph of brain function, or a control image of a courtroom). The different forms of expert testimony had no effect on participants' verdicts or recommended sentences. Neuroimages likewise have no effect when used in support of other claims at trial, such as an insanity defense (Schweitzer & Saks, 2011), and they are no more persuasive than neuropsychological evaluations that reach the same conclusions about an individual's brain functioning but lack the supposed allure of a visual image (Greene & Cahill, 2012).

Only two studies have found an effect of neuroimages on juror decision making (Appelbaum, Scurich, & Raad, 2015; Saks, Schweitzer, Aharoni, & Kiehl, 2014), and those effects were somewhat inconsistent. For example, Saks and colleagues, using a capital trial jury simulation, found that neuroimages bolstered the argument of whichever side used it compared to other kinds of expert evidence, even including the same neuroscientific evidence without the image. However, the effect was small, and it varied depending on the defendant's diagnosis (psychopathy or schizophrenia). And Appelbaum et al. found that neuroimaging data affected mock jurors' death penalty sentencing decisions but not their sentencing decisions in a non–capital murder trial. Thus, although more research is needed as imaging techniques develop and neuroscientific evidence becomes more commonplace in court, to date there is little cause for concern that such evidence is overly influential.

Juries and Expert Psychological Testimony

Specialists from a number of psychological disciplines routinely testify in court, including clinical, cognitive, developmental, and social psychologists (Costanzo, Krauss, & Pezdek, 2007). Given this wide range of expertise, the issues that their testimony addresses also vary substantially. Psychologists who testify as expert witnesses might be quite knowledgeable about their own particular area of expertise but have limited knowledge about other psychological topics. For example, clinical psychologists (and psychiatrists) who serve as expert witnesses do not know very much about memory processes (Melinder & Magnussen, 2015). This is not a problem for the courts if judges do their job as gatekeepers and limit experts' testimony to the topics on which the experts are qualified to speak; however, subtle discriminations in expertise might be hard for judges to make.

The bulk of psychological testimony takes one of two forms. First, clinicians may perform an assessment of an individual who is going through the legal system in some capacity and testify about their clinical impressions. Many legal questions benefit from, and indeed can even require, an evaluation from a psychologist or some other mental health professional about an individual's mental state (although our discussion focuses on psychologists, the same services can be, and are, provided by psychiatrists, social workers, and other providers with various kinds and levels of mental health training). Table 7.1, though not exhaustive, provides a list of many of the capacities for which psychologists conduct evaluations for the courts and provide testimony. Notably, this work can involve both civil and criminal defendants (on topics such as, for example, competency of various types, prediction of future dangerousness, and assessment for purposes of determining sanity or a potential diagnosis such as battered woman syndrome, psychopathy, post-traumatic stress disorder); civil plaintiffs (e.g., psychological injury, malingering, existence of preexisting conditions), victims (e.g., psychological injury), other witnesses (e.g., competency to testify), and individuals not directly involved in the proceedings but whose interests are affected by them (e.g., children of parents going through divorce or a custody dispute). The assessment can focus on an individual's current or prior mental state (e.g., at the time of the offense). This kind of testimony, which involves an assessment of a specific individual, is akin to the case-specific expert testimony that might be provided by other experts, such as a physician (e.g., testifying about

Table 7.1 Issues Addressed by Clinical Psychological Expert Testimony

Competency	Other (Noncompetency)
To stand trial	Civil commitment
To waive rights (e.g., Miranda, counsel)	Future dangerousness
To plead guilty	Mental state/diagnosis at time of offense
To testify	Current mental state/functioning/diagnosis
To refuse insanity defense	Child custody/well-being
To be sentenced	Hypnotic memory enhancement
To be executed	Neuropsychological assessment
To provide consent	Guardianship
To confess	Intellectual disability
To make treatment decisions	Juvenile transfer
To make a will	

Note. Compiled from a variety of sources, especially Melton, Petrila, Poythress, & Slobogin (2007); Neal & Grisso (2014); Ogloff, Wallace, & Otto (1992); and Saks (1992b).

a plaintiff's physical injuries) or ballistics expert (e.g., testifying about a gun's properties).

The second form of expert psychological testimony involves not an individual assessment but rather testimony about a general issue that is relevant to factfinders' evaluation of other evidence. This type of testimony, often referred to as "social framework evidence" (Monahan & Walker, 2014) or "educative" testimony (Nuñez, Gray, & Buck, 2011), is usually provided by experimental psychologists who present empirical research findings that are relevant to some fact in issue. Two issues about which psychologists are often called to testify are eyewitness memory and confessions. For example, an expert might testify about the factors that are associated with better/worse eyewitness performance (see Chapter 5) or that can lead to a false confession (see Chapter 6). In such cases the expert typically does not meet with the eyewitness or defendant to make an individualized assessment about whether the eyewitness testimony or confession is reliable; in that sense, then, the expert testimony's relevance to the central issue is indirect. It is for the factfinder—judge or jury—to determine whether the expert testimony makes the eyewitness or defendant any more or less credible.

Clinical Psychological Testimony

Given the breadth of issues on which clinical psychologists can be called to testify (see Table 7.1), it is difficult to summarize the nature of clinical psychological testimony or its effects on jurors. Nonetheless, some conclusions can be drawn in terms of the form that the testimony takes and its connection, explicit or implicit, to the case at hand. One of the ongoing debates in clinical psychology is whether clinicians should perform clinical assessments and diagnosis using clinical intuition, a structured assessment tool that yields an actuarial prediction, or some combination of the two (e.g., Melton et al., 2007; Neal & Grisso, 2014). Considerable empirical evidence indicates that actuarial measures are superior to clinical judgments in making certain predictions, such as violence risk (e.g., Hanson & Morton-Bourgon, 2009). Nonetheless, many clinicians continue to rely on their subjective judgment in forensic and other mental health evaluation contexts (Neal & Grisso, 2014).

Daniel Krauss, Joel Lieberman, and their colleagues have conducted several jury simulation studies exploring jurors' reactions to clinical versus actuarial psychological testimony in different types of trials, where the expert's testimony focuses on the defendant's risk of future violence (Krauss & Lee, 2003; Krauss, Lieberman, & Olson, 2004; Krauss, McCabe, & Lieberman, 2012; Krauss & Sales, 2001; Lieberman & Krauss, 2009; Lieberman, Krauss, Kyger, & Lehoux, 2007; McCabe & Krauss, 2011; McCabe, Krauss, & Lieberman, 2010). For example, participants in the study by McCabe et al. (2010) viewed a videotaped sexually violent perpetrator (SVP) hearing and decided whether the respondent in the case was an SVP and should therefore be committed. The hearing included testimony from an expert witness who described the materials he reviewed, his opinion that the respondent was a pedophile, and his belief that the respondent was likely to reoffend. He based his conclusion on either his interview with the respondent (in the clinical expert condition) or his use of two actuarial instruments that predict recidivism in sex offenders (in the actuarial expert condition).

McCabe and colleagues (2010) found that mock jurors were influenced more by clinical than actuarial expert testimony, a finding replicated in several other studies (e.g., Krauss & Lee, 2003; Krauss et al., 2012; Lieberman et al., 2007). The advantage of clinical testimony is consistent with research showing that jurors prefer highly salient, anecdotal information to more abstract scientific evidence (Bornstein, 2004; Krauss & Sales, 2001). Although jurors' tendency to favor clinical over actuarial evidence does not always occur (Guy & Edens, 2003; 2006), it is fairly robust and persists even after cross-examination, testimony from competing experts, or cautions from the respondent's attorney to focus on the facts and avoid being swayed by emotion (Krauss & Lee, 2003; Krauss & Sales, 2001; McCabe & Krauss, 2011). Moreover, there is some indication that it is moderated by certain case characteristics (e.g., the respondent's precise clinical diagnosis; Lieberman & Krauss, 2009), as well as juror demographic characteristics such as gender and student status (e.g., Lieberman et al., 2007; McCabe et al., 2010; McCabe & Krauss, 2011). For example, testimony type predicts verdicts for nonstudents, who are older and demographically more diverse, but not for students (McCabe et al., 2010; McCabe & Krauss, 2011), perhaps because students are relatively predisposed toward more abstract actuarial information to begin with.

Several of the studies by Krauss and Lieberman also measured respondents' cognitive processing style with the Rational versus Experiential Inventory (RVEI; Pacini & Epstein, 1999). Similar to NFC (discussed above, and which the RVEI incorporates), the RVEI measures one's motivation to process information rationally or experientially (i.e., less rationally and more intuitively). More rational mock jurors were more likely to favor actuarial testimony, whereas more experiential mock jurors were more likely to favor clinical testimony (McCabe et al., 2010). However, this effect held only for college student mock jurors (McCabe et al., 2010; McCabe & Krauss, 2011) and was not replicated in a subsequent study (Krauss et al., 2012).

In addition to viewing processing style as a stable trait, the theory underlying the RVEI suggests that it has a state-based component, which suggests that it should be possible to manipulate a person's processing style in the short term, such as while serving as a juror at trial. Krauss and colleagues (2004) explored this possibility in the context of a mock death penalty trial in which an expert witness provided either clinical or actuarial testimony about the defendant's probable future dangerousness. The mock jurors were directed into either a rational or an experiential mode of processing before reading the expert testimony and rendering a verdict, by completing a set of math problems (rational) or drawing a picture to express their current emotional state (experiential). Those who were primed to process information rationally were more influenced by the actuarial testimony, whereas those who were primed to process information experientially were more influenced by the clinical testimony. Jurors' state-based processing style can be altered similarly by other means, such as through jury instructions (Lieberman et al., 2007; Lieberman & Krauss, 2009). Thus, the effectiveness of expert testimony depends not only on the content of the testimony itself, or even individual differences in processing style that the jurors bring with them to trial, but also on subtle changes in information processing that would ordinarily fluctuate naturally throughout the course of the trial.

Social Framework Testimony

Social framework testimony typically summarizes research findings that are relevant to the case at hand. Psychological experts frequently testify about research on eyewitnesses, suspects undergoing interrogation, and the experiences of victims (e.g., abused children or battered women). They also testify, though less often, about psychological factors in the workplace that can lead to discrimination (Fiske & Borgida, 2008) or about interpersonal coercion as a precursor to elder financial abuse (Gibson & Greene, 2013). Evidentiary rules may bar the expert from drawing explicit conclusions about legal issues in a case—referred to as *ultimate opinion* or *ultimate issue* testimony—such as whether a given eyewitness's memory is accurate, as judges often rule that doing so would invade the province of the jury (Malpass, Ross, Meissner, & Marcon, 2009). Even when ultimate issue testimony is allowed, expert witnesses testifying about general research findings typically do not provide it simply because, unlike clinical expert witnesses, they have not examined the individual witness. Thus an expert may be allowed to testify about research

showing that the presence of a weapon in a crime impairs subsequent identification, compared to the absence of a weapon (i.e., the weapon focus effect),
but the expert would very rarely testify that a particular eyewitness robbed
at gunpoint was therefore inaccurate; rather, it is the jury's job to connect the
dots and draw any relevant inferences.[3]

In the remainder of this section we discuss expert testimony on eyewitness memory and confessions—two areas where psychologists are frequently
retained as expert witnesses to provide social framework testimony, but
where the courts are often concerned about the likely impact of that testimony. In these situations, the expert ordinarily does not evaluate the individual witness or defendant but describes, instead, research relevant to the
reliability of the memory or confession. Our focus is on the effects on jurors
of such expert testimony at trial, but the same experts are also often called
on to testify at pretrial hearings to suppress an identification or confession.

Eyewitness experts. As we described in Chapter 5, not only is eyewitness memory fallible, but jurors (as well as legal professionals) have numerous misconceptions about the factors that do and do not predict eyewitness
performance. In addition to other safeguards used to aid jurors in evaluating
eyewitness testimony, such as *voir dire*, cross-examination, and closing arguments (see Chapter 5), expert testimony can potentially serve this function.
Eyewitness expert testimony is subject to the same standards as any other
expert testimony, and a substantial literature applies evidentiary standards,
especially *Daubert,* to the field of eyewitness research (e.g., Benton et al.,
2007; Epstein, 2009; Faigman et al., 2014). The trend nationally seems to be
a gradual loosening of restrictions on the admissibility of eyewitness expert
testimony (e.g., Faigman et al., 2014; National Academy of Sciences, 2014;
New Jersey v. Henderson, 2011), but concerns persist about the reliability and
consistency of eyewitness research and its applicability to real-world cases
(e.g., Flowe, Finklea, & Ebbesen, 2009; Malpass et al., 2008). Although courts
can, and often do, admit eyewitness expert testimony, in most jurisdictions
it is not an abuse of judicial discretion for judges to exclude it (Benton et al.,
2007; Faigman et al., 2014). The most common reasons given for excluding
eyewitness expert testimony, assuming that the expert's credentials are sat-
isfactory and the research itself is deemed generally accepted, are that the
testimony does not fit the particular case, is a matter of common sense,
invades the province of the jury, or would be prejudicial (Benton et al., 2007;
Epstein, 2009).

---

[3] No self-respecting expert would draw such a conclusion in any case. Because
the research involves comparative probabilities in large samples, it cannot speak
conclusively to an individual instance, despite strengthening or weakening a
specific hypothesis about the individual case (e.g., that the witness is accurate/
the defendant is guilty).

The question of "fit" goes to the applicability of social framework evidence in general, and it can be managed by careful argument and framing of the testimony (Benton et al., 2007; Malpass et al., 2009). As described in Chapter 5, eyewitness memory is not simply a matter of common sense; rather, laypeople's intuitions about the subject are erroneous in many respects. The questions of invading the jury's province and possible prejudice are relevant to one of the essential criteria for expert testimony, namely, that it would be helpful to the factfinders. The key question, then, is whether eyewitness expert testimony helps juries make better decisions despite its potential for prejudice or lessening jurors' decision-making authority. As with other safeguards employed to help juries deal with eyewitness testimony, expert testimony is most helpful if it does not merely make jurors more skeptical about eyewitnesses but sensitizes them to relevant eyewitness factors—that is, if it enables them to discriminate between circumstances that enhance an eyewitness's memory and those that impair it (Devenport et al., 2009). Doing so would mean placing greater weight, in determining eyewitness credibility and defendant culpability, on the testimony of "good" (i.e., more likely to be accurate) versus "bad" eyewitnesses (i.e., less likely to be accurate).

Research on the effects on jurors of eyewitness expert testimony is mixed (Benton et al., 2007; Cutler & Wells, 2009; Leippe & Eisenstadt, 2009). A number of jury simulation studies have shown that it makes jurors skeptical of eyewitness testimony (e.g., Bornstein et al., 2008; Cutler, Dexter, & Penrod, 1990; Fox & Walters, 1986; Hosch, Beck, & McIntyre, 1980; Maass, Brigham, & West, 1985; Martire & Kemp, 2011); that is, having an expert testify for the defense about the problems associated with eyewitness memory made the eyewitness seem less credible and led to fewer convictions. However, the expert testimony did not necessarily help mock jurors do a better job of discriminating between relatively good and relatively poor eyewitnesses.

Additional studies, on the other hand, have found evidence that expert testimony can sensitize jurors to relevant eyewitness factors, leading them to place more weight on "good" eyewitnesses (i.e., those who witnessed under conditions promoting relatively high accuracy) than on "bad" eyewitnesses (e.g., Cutler et al., 1989; Geiselman et al., 2002; Laub, Kimbrough, & Bornstein, 2015). It is possible that the disparate findings reflect variations in the content of the expert testimony across studies. The more detailed and specific the expert testimony is, addressing specific factors highly relevant to the case at hand and explaining why those factors have their effect, the greater the testimony's impact (Fox & Walters, 1986; Maass et al., 1985). Expert testimony might also sensitize jurors to some factors but not others (Devenport et al., 2002), and it has a greater impact when it is congruent with their expectations (Bornstein et al., 2008).

Despite the failure of eyewitness expert testimony to demonstrate a consistent sensitization effect, such testimony appears to be beneficial. Jurors tend to overvalue eyewitness testimony and place too much weight on it, especially when the eyewitness is highly confident (see Chapter 5). Thus, merely reducing jurors' reliance on eyewitness testimony—that is, a skepticism effect—is a positive outcome (one would not want expert testimony to reduce jurors' use of eyewitness testimony too much, producing *under*reliance, but the research suggests there is little risk of that happening). And sensitization does occur, at least under some circumstances. In a nutshell, skepticism is good, and sensitization is better.

Confession Experts

Similar issues arise with regard to expert testimony on interrogation practices and confessions. As described in Chapter 6, false confessions are a leading cause of erroneous convictions, and jurors have misconceptions about the frequency of false confessions, the factors that cause them, and their own and others' (e.g., police officers') ability to distinguish among true confessions, false confessions, lies, and true denials. Like expert testimony on eyewitness memory, expert testimony on interrogations and confessions is generally admissible, but it is subject to judicial discretion, and courts vary widely in how they treat it (Costanzo, Blandón-Gitlin, & Davis, 2016; Costanzo & Leo, 2007; Fulero, 2001; Kassin & Gudjonsson, 2004). When judges do not allow it, it is most often on the grounds that the topic is a matter of common sense or that expert testimony on confessions would invade the province of the jury (e.g., *United States v. Hall*, 1996).

In light of laypeople's misconceptions about false confessions, expert witnesses can educate jurors by discussing research on factors that increase or decrease the risk that a suspect will confess to a crime he or she did not commit (see Chapter 6, this volume; Costanzo et al., 2016). The expert can also analyze the record of the interrogation (i.e., audio or video recording), if one exists, though most experts refrain from providing ultimate opinion testimony about whether the specific confession at issue is true or false (American Psychological Association, 2013b; Costanzo et al., 2016).

Despite their misconceptions, laypeople are generally receptive to the idea of expert testimony on interrogation techniques and false confessions (Chojnacki et al., 2008; Costanzo et al., 2010), suggesting that they are aware, to some extent, of their limited knowledge. Unfortunately, little research has directly addressed the question of whether expert testimony on confessions improves juror decision making. What evidence exists suggests that expert testimony does more to increase jurors' skepticism about confessions than it does to sensitize them to the differences between more and less reliable confessions (Blandón-Gitlin et al., 2011; Woody & Forrest, 2009). For example, Woody and Forrest (2009; see Chapter 6) conducted a mock juror study in which the principal evidence against a homicide defendant was his confession, which he subsequently recanted. The trial summary contained evidence that the police interrogation either did or did not include a false-evidence ploy (which would make a false confession more likely) and also varied whether an expert witness testified about interrogation tactics and false confessions. The presence of expert testimony led to fewer convictions (37.5% vs. 49.7% without expert testimony), but the interaction between expert testimony and the presence of a false-evidence ploy was not statistically significant; that is, the expert testimony did not sensitize mock jurors to a factor that could make the defendant's confession more likely to be false. In light of laypeople's general failure to appreciate the risks of false confessions, one could construe the skepticism aroused by confession expert testimony as a positive outcome. Nonetheless, future research should examine ways of presenting expert testimony on confessions so that it enables jurors to do a better job of distinguishing between confessions that are more versus less likely to be genuine.

Psychological Experts: Summary and Recommendation. Psychologists and related mental health professionals make frequent appearances as expert witnesses in court. Their testimony affects jurors' verdicts, but not necessarily in an optimal fashion. Clinical psychologists who perform evaluations of individual trial participants are more influential when they testify based on their subjective intuitions than when they testify about more reliable, actuarial data. And psychologists testifying about social framework evidence are more likely to induce skepticism than they are to truly educate jurors in a way that helps them use other trial evidence more appropriately. Although increased skepticism might be desirable with respect to some of the issues about which psychologists testify, such as eyewitness memory and confessions, it leaves much room for improvement.

Taken as a whole, the research suggests that psychologists who serve as expert witnesses are in a quandary. As scientists, the majority of them presumably appreciate the greater reliability and relevance of sound scientific research (e.g., actuarial data); but as not-quite-wholly-impartial witnesses operating within the confines of an adversarial system, their testimony has less impact when it relies heavily on abstract scientific research than when it presents subjective clinical findings.

What to do? Fortunately, it is not an "either-or" situation. Expert witnesses in many cases can provide relevant information that is both general and case-specific. Schuller (1992, Experiment 1) investigated this possibility by presenting mock jurors in a homicide case, which involved a battered woman defense, with one of three different kinds of expert testimony on behalf of the defendant: none, general expert testimony, or specific expert testimony. In both expert testimony conditions, the witness (a clinical psychologist) explained the social science research pertaining to battered women. In the specific expert testimony condition, he also stated that he had personally interviewed the defendant and that she displayed the characteristics of a woman suffering from battered woman syndrome. Participants rendered more lenient verdicts (i.e., not guilty on the grounds of self-defense or guilty of manslaughter, versus guilty of second-degree murder) in the specific expert condition, where the expert linked the general research to the facts of the particular case, than in the other two conditions. Although the advantage of specific expert testimony is somewhat attenuated when the mock jurors deliberate as a group (Schuller, 1992, Experiment 2), similar effects have been obtained for other kinds of trials (e.g., child sexual abuse, rape; Brekke & Borgida, 1988; Gabora, Spanos, & Joab, 1993; Kovera, Levy, Borgida, & Penrod, 1994; Kovera et al., 1997). Concrete, specific expert testimony can "bridge the gap between the psychological research and the case evidence," thereby sensitizing jurors to relevant case characteristics in a way that more general expert testimony cannot (Kovera et al., 1997, p. 188).

Depending on the circumstances of the case, linking general testimony to the specific facts might not be feasible or appropriate. The expert might not examine the individual whose behavior is at issue, as in most eyewitness cases, and there are ethical issues associated with providing ultimate opinion testimony (American Psychological Association, 2013b). But when it is feasible, appropriate, and ethical, linking general research findings to specific elements of the case can be a powerful means to enhance the impact of expert psychological testimony.

Conclusions

As Saks and Wissler (1984) observed more than 30 years ago, jurors have identifiable attitudes and beliefs about experts, and those expectations predict, to some extent, how much weight they give to expert testimony. Yet expert testimony seems to exert paradoxical effects on jurors. On the one hand, laypeople in general, and jurors in particular, tend to view scientists and other experts as highly credible. Jurors perceive expert testimony, especially that provided by scientists (e.g., DNA, fingerprint, hair, or other scientific evidence), as more accurate than testimony provided by non-experts, such as victims or eyewitnesses (e.g., Hans et al., 2011; Lieberman et al., 2008). Nonetheless, in many circumstances jurors underutilize scientific testimony (e.g., Bornstein, 2004; Koehler, 2001), and it often fails to achieve its purpose of aiding jurors in their comprehension and use of other evidence (e.g., eyewitness testimony). Research on the impact of eyewitness and confession experts is somewhat mixed; but it typically either induces skepticism or has no effect, without "mesmerizing" jurors and leading them to overvalue it (Boyce et al., 2007; Costanzo et al., 2016). Is it possible to reconcile this apparent inconsistency?

Our proposed solution is to invoke Occam's Razor—that is, the most parsimonious explanation is the best. Jurors treat expert testimony just like they do any other evidence. They recognize experts' expertise—in essence, "This person has specialized knowledge that I don't have and that can help me make my decision"—which creates a default assumption of credibility. But rather than automatically accepting the expert's testimony, they take it—as they should—as evidence to be considered in the same light as other evidence presented at trial (Fordham, 2006). The content of expert testimony does influence jurors' decisions; unopposed expert testimony (e.g., of a DNA match) affects their verdicts, and they often (though not always) respond to variations in the testimony's probative value. Yet by its very nature, expert testimony is often complicated, and as with any evidence, jurors do not always understand it fully or use it appropriately. When that occurs, they do not simply accept the expert testimony at face value; rather, they tend to be conservative and discount it, and they may be influenced by characteristics of the messenger rather than the message. Thus jurors are not perfect consumers of expert testimony. Nonetheless, the concerns of many courts and commentators that expert witnesses would be unduly influential are unfounded.

8

Jurors Treat Juvenile Defendants Fairly

"... the unexpected intersection between childhood and
criminality creates a dilemma that most people find difficult to
resolve. Indeed, the only ways out of this problem are either to
redefine the offense as something less serious than a crime or to
redefine the offender as someone who is not really a child"

(Steinberg, 2009, p. 460)

"... the very act of trying a juvenile as an adult may deprive a
juvenile of the Sixth Amendment right to an impartial jury"

(Levine, Williams, & Valenti, 2001, p. 28)

How do jurors determine the facts of a crime, assess culpability, and reach
verdicts when the defendant is a juvenile? To what extent do they or *should*
they consider his or her age, apparent maturity level, and cognitive and psychosocial development? Does considering these factors render them more
lenient or harsher toward the youthful offender?

These are vitally pressing questions for juvenile defendants—those youth
accused of criminal violations before the age of 18—and for the jury system,
because in the early to mid-1990s a number of state legislatures passed laws
that routinely allowed young offenders to be tried as adults in criminal court.
Historically their cases were adjudicated by juvenile court judges rather than
by juries. Now some states have provisions under which very young juveniles (in some states as young as 10 years old) can be waived from juvenile to
criminal court and subjected to both the privileges available to and the sanctions imposed on adult defendants. One such privilege is the right to trial by
jury, a "privilege" that was afforded to Jacob Ind who, after allegedly suffering
years of sexual molestation by his stepfather and emotional abuse from his
mother, shot them to death in Colorado in 1992. He was 15 years old at the

time and intended to commit suicide after the killings, but he told a friend about the crime and his friend alerted the school principal. Jurors convicted Jacob on two counts of first-degree murder, unaware that the only possible punishment was life without the possibility of parole. Now in his late 30s, Ind has spent well over half of his life in prison.

This case and others like it raise questions about how, in the adversarial context of a courtroom, jurors judge the actions of a youthful offender. Do they evaluate only the *actus reus* and *mens rea* without also considering the defendant's youthfulness? And which is the more appropriate calculation: judging the nature of the offense and intention of the offender as they would for an adult offender, or factoring into the equation that the defendant is a minor?

These are among the questions we address in this chapter. We describe the tradition and rationale for having separate systems to adjudicate the cases of juvenile and adult defendants. We consider how, in recent decades, the distinct boundaries that existed between those systems for nearly a hundred years in the United States have blurred, and what the public, and by extension lay jurors, think about that development. Finally, we explain how youthful offenders have fared when subjected to the adult criminal court system. At the center of our analysis is the role that jurors and juries play in resolving these cases and the psychological factors that affect their judgments. We reach the paradoxical conclusion that although some jurors evaluate the actions of juvenile offenders in light of their still-developing cognitive and psychosocial capabilities and render verdicts that account for those factors, other jurors adjudicate these youthful offenders even more harshly than adult offenders charged with the same crimes. Jurors' inferences and stereotypes about juvenile offenders seem to explain these discrepancies, at least to some extent. As a result, youth tried in criminal courts may be subjected to harsher sanctions and bleaker futures than those adjudicated for comparable offenses in juvenile courts.

The Rationale of the Juvenile Justice System

Established at the turn of the twentieth century, juvenile courts were founded on the premise that young offenders were developmentally different from adults and that these differences should influence how their criminal conduct was evaluated. So in the early part of the century, juvenile court judges inquired into the social and dispositional backgrounds of delinquent youth and took these factors into account when judging culpability and imposing punishments. Because juvenile offenders were considered malleable and redeemable, rehabilitation was favored over retribution and punishment.

Even at the inception of the juvenile justice system, though, not all youthful offenders were treated with kid gloves. Some juvenile court judges were hesitant to claim jurisdiction over older delinquents who committed serious wrongs, and some states allowed for these juvenile offenders to be tried as adults (Applegate, Davis, & Cullen, 2009). Claims that juvenile courts were coddling offenders became much more common when youth crime rates rose in the 1960s and 1970s, and they reached a feverish pitch in the 1980s and 1990s when the level of serious crimes committed by juveniles increased exponentially (Bishop, Frazier, & Henretta, 1989). Juvenile court caseloads rose 49% between 1987 and 1996, even though the population of juveniles increased by only 11% (Snyder & Sickmund, 1999). As juvenile crimes—particularly violent and other serious crimes—became more frequent, and fear of youthful offenders rose, lawmakers started questioning the effectiveness of the rehabilitation ideal espoused by the juvenile court system. In its place they began to favor more punitive practices for the most serious young offenders.

With the rise in youth crimes came the depiction of some juvenile offenders as "superpredators"—hardened, remorseless delinquents, raised in moral poverty and beyond redemption, who "fear neither the stigma of arrest nor the pain of imprisonment ... [and] so long as their youthful energies hold out will do what comes 'naturally': murder, rape, rob, assault, burglarize, deal deadly drugs and get high" (DiIulio, 1995, p. 26). Compared with deviant youth of the past, juvenile offenders of the 1990s purportedly had "more dangerous drugs in their bodies, more deadly weapons in their hands, and a seemingly more casual attitude about violence" (Fox, 1996, p. 2). The perception of young offenders shifted from naively innocent, malleable, and amenable to rehabilitation to "heinous, vicious, adult-type criminals" (Feld, 1999, p. 162).

In light of these characterizations, as well as the dramatic rise in crime rates involving young offenders and diminished confidence in the juvenile courts to sanction them, changes were afloat in the late 1980s and early 1990s. During this period some state legislatures revised the expressed objective of their juvenile court systems by deemphasizing rehabilitation in preference for public safety (Torbet & Szymanski, 1998), and lawmakers began to mandate severe treatment of juvenile offenders. Among their chief strategies was making it easier to move juvenile cases to criminal courts for an increasing variety of offenses and for younger offenders (Bishop, 2000). Advocates believed that for seriously violent and chronic juvenile offenders, adjudication in adult court was a proportionate response to the nature of their offenses and offered more effective means of deterrence and incapacitation than the juvenile justice system (Bishop, 2000).

But as Steinberg (2009) has pointed out (and as we paraphrase him), this intersection of criminality and youth raised a dilemma: Because we do not expect crimes to be committed by young people or young people to commit crimes, we must either redefine their offenses as noncriminal or redefine them as nonchildren. For most of the twentieth century we opted for the former, treating infractions committed by juveniles as mere delinquent acts to be adjudicated within the juvenile justice system. Waivers and transfers were used sparingly under the assumption that exposing youthful offenders to the adversarial proceedings and harsh punishments of criminal courts would do them irreparable harm (Bishop & Frazier, 2000). But with shifting perspectives on juvenile crime at the end of the century, policymakers increasingly favored the latter approach, redefining young offenders as adults and prosecuting them in the criminal system.

Juvenile Waiver and Transfer

In order to prosecute juvenile offenders as adults, legislatures designated certain crimes for automatic waiver to criminal court, specified other crimes for presumptive waiver, and expanded the authority of prosecutors to review cases and file directly in criminal court. Over time, various procedures developed to facilitate waiver and transfer from juvenile to adult court. Fifteen states now require that juvenile courts automatically waive cases that meet certain criteria regarding offense type, offender age, and criminal history. Criminal courts have exclusive jurisdiction over these cases. For example in New York, 16- and 17-year-old offenders will be tried as adults for any alleged offense. An additional 15 states have defined a set of cases in which waiver to criminal court is presumed appropriate, and juveniles who meet certain age and offense thresholds must present evidence that rebuts that presumption (Griffin, Addie, Adams, & Firestine, 2011).

Another form of transfer involves discretionary waiver: Forty-five states allow juvenile court judges, using their discretion, to waive jurisdiction on a case-by-case basis, typically after a formal hearing on a prosecutor's motion that the juvenile is "not amenable" to treatment in the juvenile justice system. Most states set the minimum age for judicial waiver at 14, but in Kansas the minimum age is 10, and Colorado and Missouri allow transfers for 12-year-olds, paving the way to prosecuting these very young offenders as adults (Griffin et al., 2011).

The use of judicial waivers has decreased in recent years. Data compiled by the Office of Juvenile Justice and Delinquency Prevention showed that the number of cases judicially waived to criminal courts, in jurisdictions with over 81% of the nation's juveniles, dropped by 35% between 1994 and 2007 (Griffin et al., 2011). In its place, other transfer mechanisms continue to operate. For example, in some states prosecutors are entrusted to decide whether to bring a case in juvenile or criminal court with no formal hearing and no opportunity for a defendant to know the basis for that decision. In Montana, 12-year-olds can be subjected to prosecution at the option of the prosecutor, as can 13-year-olds in Wyoming (Griffin et al., 2011).

The overall result of these procedures has been a dramatic increase over the past few decades in the number of adolescent offenders whose cases are moved to criminal court and resolved by juries. One estimate is that approximately 247,000 offenders younger than 18 were referred to criminal courts in

2007 (Griffin et al., 2011). Many juveniles tried in criminal courts are convicted of serious crimes and subjected to adult-like punishment (Cook & Laub, 1998). Historically, the prototypical transferred offender is a 17-year-old African American male who committed an offense against persons (as opposed to property; Snyder & Sickmund, 1999) and who, after being convicted, received a prison sentence of approximately eight years (Strom, 2000).

Thus, over the course of three decades, juvenile justice has been "criminalized," that is, transformed from a benevolent, rehabilitation-focused process to one that encompasses harsh treatment and punitive sanctions, at least for those youthful offenders who commit serious, violent crimes (Feld, 1993). These policies remain largely in place today, even though juvenile crime rates have dropped noticeably since the mid-1990s. For instance, according to FBI data, the number of murders involving a juvenile offender fell 67% between 1994 and 2010 (Sickmund & Puzzanchera, 2014).

Layperson Beliefs About Juvenile Transfer

We can get some hints about how jurors treat juveniles in criminal courts by understanding what the public thinks, generally, of the transfer process and of juveniles who are affected by it. Citizens' attitudes are factored into policymakers' actions—though that process is complicated and tenuous—and can help to define the "boundaries and opportunities regarding what policies might be implemented" (Piquero et al., 2010, p. 189). Transfer laws assume that juvenile courts are ill-equipped to handle offenders who commit serious crimes and that a subgroup of young offenders are as culpable and deserving of punishment as adult criminals. So a reasonable question is whether these policies accurately reflect the views of the public about youthful offenders' amenability to treatment and capacity for change.

Do people generally liken youthful offenders to adult criminals and assume a pessimistic stance on those issues? If so, their beliefs would be inconsistent with the consensus among social scientists that adolescents differ from adults with regard to cognitive, social, and emotional capacities that affect their conduct and culpability. These scholars argue that policies which equate the two groups ultimately do more harm than good for offenders, taxpayers, and public safety (Scott & Steinberg, 2008). They suggest that it is never too early or too late to try to save juvenile offenders from a life of crime (Losel, 2007). We briefly describe what social scientists have learned about the developmental trajectories of most juvenile offenders, what their findings suggest regarding juvenile waiver and transfer, and how the public thinks about those issues.

Developmental trajectories of youthful offenders and implications for culpability judgments. Social scientists are generally optimistic about the time course of juvenile offending because most youthful offenders grow out of their criminal ways. Such sanguinity is informed by Moffitt's (1993) important distinction between adolescence-limited and life-course-persistent offenders, and longitudinal research demonstrating that the vast majority of young offenders will desist from criminal activity as they mature into adulthood (Reppucci, Woolard, & Fried, 1999). According to most studies, only 5%–10% of juvenile offenders become chronic adult offenders (Steinberg, 2009), and criminologists' age–crime curves show that the incidence of criminal activity peaks at just under age 17 for nonviolent crimes and just over age 17 for violent offenses (Piquero, Farrington, & Blumstein, 2003).

These patterns are consistent with well-established changes in cognitive and psychosocial development throughout adolescence and early adulthood: Although many basic cognitive capabilities have matured by age 16, other cognitive competencies and many social and emotional abilities continue to develop in late adolescence and even beyond (Steinberg, 2009). Thus, compared with adults even 18-year-olds are more impulsive and prone to pressure from peers, more likely to focus on rewards rather than risks when making choices, and less likely to ponder the consequences of their actions.

Evidence of these developmental trajectories has led many observers to express concerns about the appropriateness of trying juveniles as adults. They contend that adolescents' underdeveloped psychosocial and emotional maturity impairs their capacity to make rational decisions *not* to engage in wrongful conduct (Steinberg, 2009). They argue that just as the criminal law recognizes diminished judgment in people with mental disorders as mitigating culpability (Morse, 2011), adolescents lacking cognitive and psychosocial maturity are inherently less blameworthy than adult offenders (Cauffman, Woolard, & Reppucci, 1999; Grisso, 1996; Steinberg & Scott, 2003). One implication of these arguments is that in order to make fair and just decisions, jurors who determine guilt and judges who impose punishment must be aware that developmental factors render adolescents inherently less culpable than adults.

Evolving public opinion about juvenile transfer. Have these findings percolated into the mainstream of public knowledge, and if so, have they influenced public perceptions about juvenile offenders? Opinions seem to have changed over time. In the 1990s, when many people viewed juvenile courts as responding too leniently to young offenders, there was general support for transferring serious youthful offenders to the criminal court system (Scott, Reppucci, Antonishak, & DeGennaro, 2006). Data collected in 1995 as part of the National Opinion Survey on Crime and Justice showed that a nationally representative sample of Americans supported the use of waivers: 65% agreed that juvenile offenders should be tried as adults for committing property crimes, as did 70% for drug offenses and 87% for violent crimes (Jan, Ball, & Walsh, 2008). These results mean that the public favored adult-like treatment for juvenile offenders at younger ages than they favored granting adolescents adult-like privileges and autonomy (e.g., holding a job, voting, purchasing alcohol), which is a trend that continues to this day (Reppucci, Scott, & Antonishak, 2009).

Even in the 1990s, though, the public held nuanced beliefs about juvenile transfer, expressing more support for transferring offenders who committed violent crimes, had prior records, had not been abused, used weapons, and harmed strangers (Feiler & Sheley, 1999; Stalans & Henry, 1994). Black offenders were more likely to elicit a preference for transfer than Whites (Feiler & Sheley, 1999), an opinion apparently still held by Whites who hold stereotypical views of delinquency and victimization (Pickett & Chiricos, 2012).

The public's sensitivity to context and to specific details of the crime and the criminal became more apparent during the decade of the 2000s, and support for differential treatment of juvenile and adult offenders grew. Underlying this preference was growing awareness that young offenders' criminal choices are influenced by a lack of developmental maturity (Scott & Steinberg, 2008) and a belief that they can and should be rehabilitated (Cullen, 2006; Piquero et al., 2010). Some findings from this era suggest that support for transfer stemmed not from punitive objectives but from hopes that it would provide individualized attention and lead to reform for serious young offenders (Applegate et al., 2009). Optimism about the prospects of juvenile rehabilitation has, for the most part, continued into the 2010s, reflecting a growing knowledge base and understanding of adolescent development (Trzcinski & Allen, 2012).

But even as the public has returned to endorsing the rehabilitative potential of some youthful offenders, they continue to harbor punitive preferences for the most violent and chronic among them. Data from 470 Florida residents surveyed in 2002 showed that fully two-thirds supported transfer for repeat violent offenders (Applegate et al., 2009), and a large sample of college students questioned by Mears, Pickett, and Mancini (2015) expressed support for both rehabilitation and punishment, depending on the nature of the crime. Get-tough policies are especially likely to be favored by individuals who endorse "superpredator"-like characteristics in young offenders and who value retribution and punishment over rehabilitation and reform (Duke & Greene, 2015; Greene & Evelo, 2013).

Taken together, these findings indicate that the punitive responses to juvenile crime that were present during the 1990s and that resulted in shifting boundaries of criminal court adjudication have generally abated (Scott et al., 2006). The public now seems to be aware of linkages between adolescent immaturity and reduced criminal responsibility. But they still favor a "tough love" approach, desiring accountability and punishment of chronic and violence-prone young offenders but favoring rehabilitation and second chances for less serious offenders who, in all likelihood, will grow out of their criminal ways. In short, they want juvenile transfer and waiver to be available but used sparingly (Applegate et al., 2009).

Some legislative and judicial responses to youthful offenders mirror this softening in attitudes. For example, Delaware legislators ended automatic transfers for certain nonviolent offenders in 2005, and the Connecticut legislature raised the maximum age for juvenile court adjudication from 16 to 18 in 2010. Fewer cases were moved to criminal court via judicial waiver in the mid-2000s than a decade earlier (National Center for Juvenile Justice, 2006), and United States Supreme Court decisions of the past decade (e.g., *Graham v. Florida*, 2010; *Miller v. Alabama*, 2012; *Roper v. Simmons*, 2005) signal a reduction in the harsh treatment of juveniles.

But wavering support for allowing juvenile cases to be moved to criminal court may not be synonymous with lenient judgments of specific offenders. Many legislators, juvenile court judges, and prosecutors still favor waivers and transfer for serious and chronic offenders. Thoughts about the appropriateness of juvenile waivers and transfers may also affect jurors, serving as a filter through which they process evidence and reach verdicts. But how those opinions combine with case evidence to affect jurors' judgments is unclear. General attitudes are not especially predictive of behaviors in a specific situation (Fishbein & Ajzen, 1974), and the particular details of a case generally factor most prominently in jurors' case-related decisions (Devine et al., 2001). We now consider how jurors think about juvenile waivers and transfers and the role that they play in resolving cases involving young offenders.

How Jurors Decide Cases of Juveniles Tried as Adults

When cases are waived, transferred, or filed directly in criminal court, the proceedings are no longer "juvenile adjudications" but rather "trials," and the alleged wrongdoings are no longer "delinquent acts" but rather "crimes." Factfinders are no longer benevolent juvenile or family court judges but rather laypeople acting as jurors and, in bench trials, criminal court judges.

Trial proceedings in criminal court do not generally account for or make accommodations for an offender's age, although the sanctions imposed after a conviction often do. This means that the trial of a 16-year-old defendant in New York will, in almost all respects, look exactly like the trial of a 35-year-old defendant: proceeding from jury selection through opening statements, to the direct and cross-examination of witnesses, closing arguments, jury instructions, deliberations, and issuance of verdicts. How does a defendant's youthfulness affect jurors' and juries' reasoning as these processes unfold?

The first opportunity for the defendant's age to matter is during jury selection, when prospective jurors can be informed that the case has been waived from juvenile court. Analyses of *voir dire* transcripts from criminal trials with juvenile defendants reveal that potential jurors are sometimes questioned about their attitudes concerning waiver and their willingness to convict a young defendant (Danielsen, Levett, & Kovera, 2004). Such questioning has the potential to bias the jury because it indicates that a judge or prosecutor has already examined the defendant's conduct and deemed it worthy of trial in criminal court, potentially signaling the defendant's culpability. Another potentially biasing factor occurs via repeated questioning about the prospect that a youthful offender could be sentenced to adult prison, possibly desensitizing jurors to that concern (Greathouse, Sothmann, Levett, & Kovera, 2011).

Greathouse and her colleagues (2011) tested whether *voir dire* questions asked of jurors affected their perceptions of a youthful defendant's guilt and evaluation of the trial evidence, and whether pretrial biases persist through the presentation of evidence to influence jurors' verdicts. In a series of studies they exposed participants to videotaped mock jury selections in which some participants saw a standard *voir dire* and others saw a "juvenile qualifica-tion" *voir dire*. The latter included questions about whether jurors' ability to be fair and impartial would be affected by knowing that a juvenile was being tried as an adult and, if convicted, could spend time in an adult prison. Participants saw mock jurors in the film who opposed juvenile waivers being dismissed from jury service. Responses to a post–*voir dire* questionnaire showed that participants who watched the juvenile qualification jury selec-tion gave higher estimates of the defendant's guilt than participants who saw the standard *voir dire*. But when, in a follow-up study, researchers also exposed participants to variations in the trial evidence, they found that the effects of juvenile qualifying *voir dire* did not persist through the presenta-tion of evidence: Those who were exposed to the questions about the youthful offender rendered posttrial judgments that were similar to those of partici-pants who saw the standard *voir dire*.

Although potentially biasing effects of questions about juvenile waiver may not linger through the presentation of evidence, Greathouse et al. (2011) point to other reasons that jury selection in these cases could lead to biased judgments. They argue that juvenile qualification, like death qualification in capital cases (see Chapter 11), may reduce the representativeness of the jury, a concern bolstered by the finding that African Americans are more likely than other racial or ethnic groups to oppose trying juveniles as adults (Levett, Danielsen, & Kovera, 2003). They also surmise that the quality of deliberations will be diminished in a juvenile-qualified jury because diver-sity in perspectives and experiences is reduced when jurors hold roughly similar attitudes.

Comparing Trial Outcomes for Juvenile and Adult Offenders

Juvenile offenders whose cases are transferred from the rehabilitation-oriented juvenile system to the punishment-oriented criminal system might be viewed as especially dangerous or chronic offenders who, unless they are incapacitated in some way, are likely to reoffend. By the very fact that the case has been transferred, transferees may be perceived as having commit-ted especially serious offenses. Such negative perceptions have the poten-tial to affect jurors' decision making and verdicts, rendering outcomes that are harsher than the evidence warrants. This situation effectively deprives defendants of their right to an impartial jury as guaranteed by the Sixth Amendment (Levine et al., 2001).

Do empirical data support these concerns? The answer, it seems, is complicated. Many studies assess how the cases of juvenile offenders are resolved and whether youthful offenders' age and maturity influence factfinders' decisions, but their methodologies and conclusions vary substantially. Some involve archival research techniques which compare large numbers of cases involving juvenile and adult offenders across a variety of crime types, whereas others compare cases transferred to criminal court with cases that stay in the juvenile system. Some employ experimental methodology, including a subset that compares dispositions as a function of the offenders' ages (typically varied between approximately 15 and 25) and another subset that evaluates differences that occur when a case is transferred versus resolved in juvenile court. Some studies control for variables that could influence the decision to waive or transfer a case to criminal court (e.g., prior record, demographic information, type of weapon involved in the offense), whereas others do not. The outcome measures also vary, with some studies measuring jury conviction rates, others assessing likelihood of conviction for various crimes, and still others evaluating outcomes as distinct as agreement with the transfer decision and sentencing preferences for transferred versus nontransferred youth. In short, this analysis could easily slip into a comparison of apples and oranges (and bananas), as it is inherently challenging to compare jurors' evaluations of (a) adult offenders, (b) juvenile offenders adjudicated in juvenile court, and (c) transferred juvenile offenders.

Because of this variety of methodologies and measures, discerning clear patterns in responses is difficult. But we have made a concerted effort to compare apples to apples (or, at a minimum, Winesaps to Honeycrisps, i.e., *fairly* similar entities) and to clarify which research findings are merely informative and which are more dispositive on the main question that interests us, namely, whether a young offender whose case is transferred to the criminal court system and resolved by jurors is viewed and treated differently from an adult defendant charged with the same crime. We also compare and assess outcomes for transferred youth and similarly-aged offenders whose offenses are adjudicated in the juvenile system, acknowledging that the latter does not involve trial by jury.

Archival studies. Because they aggregate data across many cases and include plea-bargained verdicts, archival studies are only tangentially relevant to concerns about how jurors evaluate juvenile cases. Still, they can point to trends in citizen responses to youthful offenders, so we provide a brief description of the most relevant findings here.

One objective of transferring chronic and violent offenders to criminal court is to assure that they receive more certain punishment than they would in juvenile court (Myers, 2003). A number of studies found that conviction rates for waived youth are quite high, generally in the range of 75%–95% (e.g., Griffin et al., 2011; Podkopacz & Feld, 1996), which is roughly comparable to conviction rates for adult defendants, though Rainville and Smith's (2003) analysis of felony offenses in 40 U.S. counties showed conviction rates for both adult and juvenile offenders at approximately 67%. Issues like selective referral and regional differences in rates of plea bargains can possibly explain these discrepancies.

Two studies get us somewhat closer to our goal of comparing apples to apples. Eigen (1981) determined that juveniles charged as adults for homicides in Pennsylvania were convicted more often than adults charged with homicides, and they were more likely than their adult counterparts to be handed serious verdicts of first- or second-degree murder. Myers (2003) evaluated a cohort of 557 male juvenile offenders between the ages of 15 and 18 who were arrested in Pennsylvania for robbery, aggravated assault, or both in 1994. Of these, 138 were transferred to criminal court and 419 remained in juvenile court. After controlling for some of the variables that could influence the transfer decision (e.g., prior record), Myers also found that transferred juveniles were more likely than nontransferred juveniles to be convicted, and more likely to be convicted of the targeted offense rather than a lesser charge. These findings suggest that transferees may fare rather poorly in the adult criminal system.

Experimental studies. Experimental studies can provide useful data on the questions of interest because researchers manipulate the evidence presented to participants (often mock jurors), enabling us to determine how the cases of juveniles tried as adults compare with those of adults charged with the same crime. In these studies, researchers manipulated the age of the offender rather than the venue in which the case was tried. Other experimental studies allow us to assess whether youths of a certain age charged with roughly the same crimes are treated differently when tried as adults versus adjudicated as juveniles. In this group of studies, the setting of the trial (i.e., juvenile versus criminal court) was varied while the offenders' age remained constant.

Do laypeople reach differing conclusions about juvenile offenders tried as adults versus adult offenders? How do they evaluate youthful defendants adjudicated in juvenile court and those tried as adults in criminal court? One recent study showed that mock jurors were *less* likely to convict a 16-year-old tried as an adult than a 19-year-old on charges of murder and felony-theft (Tang & Turner, 2013), and a few other studies have found no effect of defendants' age on mock jurors' verdicts when all defendants were tried as adults (e.g., Walker & Woody, 2011; Warling & Peterson-Badali, 2003). Although defendants' age (14-year-old tried as an adult versus 24-year-old) did not influence verdicts in Walker and Woody's study of jurors' responses to a defendant charged with either aggravated robbery or burglary, the data suggested that jurors may perceive a younger and less mature defendant who commits a serious offense as unusually mature for his age and more responsible than an older offender. Whether and how these perceptions of maturity might affect judgments of guilt is unclear.

But several other studies support the notion that laypeople's judgments of juveniles tried as adults may be harsh. For example, Tang, Nuñez, and Bourgeois (2009) asked participants various questions about their perceptions of a crime and a defendant, varying whether the offender was a 16-year-old juvenile adjudicated in juvenile court, a 16-year-old juvenile tried as an adult in criminal court, or a 19-year-old adult tried in criminal court. In two studies they found that participants rated the crime as more serious when it was alleged to have been committed by a juvenile tried as an adult than when it was pinned on the juvenile adjudicated in juvenile court or the adult defendant. Participants also believed that the defendant was a greater danger to society when he was described as a juvenile tried as an adult compared to a juvenile adjudicated in juvenile court or an adult defendant. Finally, ratings of the likelihood that the defendant was a chronic offender were higher for the juvenile tried as an adult than the other two defendants. Although the biases against juveniles tried as adults were present across the board, they were exacerbated in participants classified by researchers as prosecution-biased.

Further evidence of the role of pretrial biases in judgments of youthful offenders comes from a study by Tang and Nuñez (2003). They classified jurors as prosecution-biased or defense-biased according to their scores on the Juror Bias Scale (Kassin & Wrightsman, 1983; Lecci & Myers, 2002) and exposed them to evidence in a first-degree murder trial. The researchers also varied the age of the offender (13, 16, 19), with all defendants being tried in criminal court. (Note that they did not include a juvenile whose case remained in juvenile court, a methodological choice with considerable ecological validity because, as we have noted, lay jurors are not involved in juvenile court cases.) Although defendants' age did not directly influence mock jurors' verdicts, it had an interesting effect when considered in combination with pretrial biases: Prosecution-biased jurors set a lower standard of proof for the 16-year-old than the 19-year-old, supporting the notion that these jurors may hold negative stereotypes of juveniles tried as adults and subject them to harsher outcomes than adult offenders charged with the same or a similar crime.

The unusual situation of seeing a young person prosecuted in criminal court can affect the inferences that jurors make and indirectly influence their verdicts. These points were made clear by Levine and his colleagues (2001), who gave mock jurors minimal information about an 11-year-old tried as an adult for murder and then questioned participants about their impressions of the youth. Participants were asked about the likelihood that the individual had committed crimes in the past, had a criminal record, and had a lot of previous contact with the police, among other things. They were also asked whether knowledge of those characteristics was relevant to and would influence their verdicts. Mock jurors endorsed as likely all of the characteristics we listed (83% said it was likely that the individual had committed crimes in the past, 71% that it was likely the offender had a criminal record, and 68% that the individual likely had previous contact with the police). Most participants said that these factors would be relevant to their verdicts (past crimes = 94%; previous criminal record = 95%; previous police contact = 88%). Of those who agreed that the factor was relevant, most also said that it would affect their verdicts toward guilt (past crimes = 93%; previous record = 97%; previous police contact = 91%).

These findings suggest that people form relatively negative impressions of juvenile offenders tried as adults—particularly with regard to their criminal propensity and history—when they have little specific information about the nature of the offense or the background of the offender. They also suggest that rules barring the disclosure of an offender's criminal record may not be enough to guarantee that person the right to an impartial jury, because jurors may simply assume that such a record exists.

One hint as to why young people accused of crimes are evaluated negatively is that jurors hold them responsible for their offenses, even while acknowledging that they may lack the cognitive and psychosocial maturity to understand the consequences of their actions. For example, Scott et al. (2006) had 789 adults watch a video clip of an armed robbery in which the perpetrator was wearing a face mask. Participants were told that the offender was 12, 15, or 20 years old. Although they rated the teens as less mature than the 20-year-old, they perceived the 15-year-old to be as responsible for committing the crime as the adult offender. Similar findings come from a study by Perry and Stevenson (2010), who told mock jurors that a defendant was either 15 or 35 years old and found that although mock jurors believed the juvenile was more likely than the adult to be rehabilitated, they perceived them to be equally responsible for the crime. A person perceived to be responsible for committing a crime will elicit relatively little sympathy and heightened anger from laypeople (Najdowski & Bottoms, 2012).

Considering these findings as a whole, acknowledging some inconsistencies in the results, and recognizing the apples-and-oranges problem, we can reach tentative conclusions about how jurors are likely to evaluate juveniles in criminal court. We surmise that at least some laypeople are likely to evaluate juvenile offenders tried as adults in a rather harsh light, partly because of the inferences they draw about these offenders. And although waived and transferred cases typically *do* entail more chronic offenders and more serious crimes, not all juveniles tried as adults have prior records, and not all have committed violent offenses. As we noted, some transfers occur automatically because of the nature of the crime, and others occur because states have a "once an adult, always an adult" policy which requires that after an offender has been tried in criminal court, subsequent offenses must also be waived regardless of their severity. Our analysis suggests that some juveniles tried as adults may fare rather poorly when face-to-face with a jury in the context of a criminal trial.

In addition to the negative inferences that laypeople make about youthful offenders, an additional factor is at play here—namely, the stereotypes that laypeople, including prospective jurors, hold of juveniles accused of

committing crimes. Knowing that a juvenile's case has been moved to criminal court may be enough to unleash various stereotypes of youthful offenders, particularly, as we have noted, among the prosecution-oriented subset of
a jury pool. What causes these stereotypes to develop and persist, and how do
they affect jurors' thought processes and judgments?

Jurors' Stereotypes of Juvenile Offenders

Even if jurors are not aware that a case has been moved from the juvenile
system into the criminal courts (they are sometimes but not always informed
of that fact), upon entering the courtroom they will see a young person at the
defendant's table, flanked by attorneys. A natural reaction at that moment
is to categorize the defendant as an adolescent and, more precisely, as an
(alleged) juvenile offender.

Invoking person-related categories or stereotypes leads to assumptions
that people possess characteristics shared by other members of that category.
And though overgeneralized beliefs about particular groups can be unsavory
and lead to biased feelings and treatment of group members, stereotyping
allows for efficient cognitive processing. Clustering people, objects, or ideas
into groups allows us to simplify and organize our environment, an especially useful thing in any information-dense situation. And a trial is nothing
if not an information-dense situation.

So prospective jurors who walk into that courtroom may have ready-
made assumptions about the defendant even without hearing any evidence
in a case. As we will show, laypeople's stereotypes lead them to presume that
a juvenile being tried as an adult has committed more serious offenses, is
more dangerous, and is more likely to have a criminal history than an adult
offender or a juvenile whose case stays in the juvenile court system (Tang
et al., 2009).

As a trial unfolds, jurors actually rely on multiple sources of information
to help construct a narrative that explains the facts of the case, and their stereotypes affect what evidence they attend to, how they interpret and remember the evidence, and how they factor it into their judgments. They rely on
preexisting stereotypes stored in memory as categorical representations of
people, as well as stereotypes that are activated by attorneys' arguments during the trial—both of which affect how the evidence is evaluated. Another
source of information is the evidence presented by witnesses during the trial,
including details that could individuate the defendant, distinguishing him or
her from other members of the category "alleged juvenile offender." How do
these various sources of information compete for jurors' attention and work
synergistically to influence their verdicts?

Certain characteristics of criminal defendants, including their criminal
record and socioeconomic status (SES), are known to influence laypeople's
beliefs and perceptions and to affect the way they interpret the evidence
(Devine & Caughlin, 2014). Stereotypes about juvenile offenders tried as

adults also encompass various demographic details and affect jurors' judgments. For example, juvenile offenders' SES is apparently associated with jurors' blame assessments and guilt determinations. Among adult defendants, those with low SES are perceived to be more blameworthy and guilty than high-SES defendants (Mazzella & Feingold, 1994), and the same beliefs and behaviors apply to juvenile offenders. In their simulation of an aggravated robbery and felony murder trial of a 15-year-old defendant, Farnum and Stevenson (2013) found that, all other things being equal, a low-SES juvenile defendant was seven times more likely to be convicted of felony murder than a high-SES defendant.

Somewhat less clear is whether defendants' race affects laypeople's judgments of juvenile offenders. Also using the facts of an aggravated robbery and felony murder trial, Stevenson and Bottoms (2009) specified that the juvenile was either African American or Caucasian and found that men, but not women, gave higher degree-of-guilt ratings for the murder and were more supportive of trying the case in criminal court when it was attributed to an African American.

Preexisting stereotypes about juvenile offenders are heavily influenced by jurors' knowledge and life experiences, including their understanding of patterns of offending, precursors to offending, and mitigating circumstances, and by their exposure to information about the types of crimes typically committed by young people. Those who understand the developmental trajectories of youthful offenders and the influences on their behavior will encode and interpret the evidence in one way. Jurors who lack that understanding or who believe that violent offending is a Black phenomenon, for example (Rattan, Levine, Dweck, & Eberhardt, 2012), will encode and interpret the evidence in a different, more punitive way (Metcalfe, Pickett, & Mancini, 2015). The latter may include dispositional attributions for offending (especially for young offenders), assumptions about treatment amenability, and the belief that certain juveniles possess adult-like criminal intentions and maturity.

The extent to which people believe that juveniles are responsible for committing most crimes also affects their thoughts about the culpability of young offenders and their policy preferences. Although only 19% of all crimes are committed by juveniles and only 5% of juvenile arrestees are charged with a violent crime (Snyder & Sickmund, 1999), laypeople estimate that the figures are much higher. Participants in one study estimated that 41% of all crimes are committed by juvenile offenders and that 27% of those involve violent acts (Haegerich, Salerno, & Bottoms, 2013). Media coverage is undoubtedly a factor here, since the mass media tend to focus on crimes involving deaths (e.g., murders of parents and siblings) and devote more coverage as the age of the suspect decreases (Pizarro, Chermak, & Gruenewald, 2007). This distorted focus on serious and unusual crimes committed by young offenders may have led to the punitive policy measures that emerged in the late 1980s and 1990s and may have motivated the public to accept harsh treatment for certain young offenders.

People who believe that juvenile crime rates are increasing are also more likely than others to hold young offenders responsible for their crimes and to recommend harsh punishment in order to deter others (Warling & Peterson-Badali, 2003). In one study, researchers asked mock jurors whether they thought juvenile crime in their area had been increasing, decreasing, or staying the same over the past two years, and then presented a videotaped trial of an alleged school shooting by a 15-year-old defendant. Of participants who convicted the defendant, 53% believed that juvenile crime in their community was increasing, whereas among those who acquitted only 20% thought juvenile crime rates were increasing (Camilletti & Scullin, 2012).

"Superpredators" and "wayward youth." Two stereotypes about juvenile offenders in particular have been identified and now dominate scientific research and policy discussions: the cold and calculating *superpredator,* the term originated by DiIulio (1995); and the *wayward youth,* an immature but fundamentally good person who has strayed (Gluck, 1997). As we already noted, the portrayal of a "superpredator" includes a pattern of chronic and serious offending by a young person with an inherently violent nature, who lacks moral character or remorse, has decision-making and judgment processes on par with adults, and is able to manipulate the criminal justice system to avoid accountability. This stereotype encompasses the belief that since there is little chance that "superpredators" can be rehabilitated they should be punished and incapacitated. At the opposite end of a dichotomy the "wayward youth" is described as someone who, as a victim of impoverished social and economic environments and lacking adequate peer and family support and educational opportunities, has fallen prey to criminal conduct. According to this stereotype "wayward youth" are amenable to interventions and can and should be rehabilitated rather than punished.

Recently researchers have theorized that the components of juvenile offender stereotypes include decision-making abilities, competency to understand court procedures, reasons for and patterns of offending, recidivism risks, and potential for rehabilitation (Haegerich et al., 2013). Haegerich and colleagues contend that people view juvenile offenders along these lines and that conceptualizations of "superpredators" and "wayward youth" encompass distinct combinations of these factors.

How, if at all, do these stereotypes affect jurors' reasoning and decisions? The process by which this occurs is now fairly well understood: Jurors attend more carefully to trial information that is consistent with their preexisting stereotypes and retrieve it more easily than stereotype-inconsistent information, which is relatively discounted. Stereotypes can also be activated by attorneys' opening statements and closing arguments during a trial. The filtering of evidence through either preexisting or activated stereotypes ultimately affects jurors' verdict preferences (Bodenhausen, 1988).

Researchers have measured the extent to which mock jurors support the "superpredator" and "wayward youth" stereotypes and how support for them influences beliefs about whether the case should have been transferred and about a juvenile defendant's guilt. Research has also examined whether the two stereotypes can be effectively activated by attorneys' arguments to influence jurors' judgments. Haegerich et al. (2013) first measured support for juvenile offender stereotypes among a group of undergraduate students. A few months later, a subset took part in an ostensibly unrelated mock jury study and read the transcript of a trial involving a 15-year-old African-American male defendant who was charged with aggravated robbery and felony murder. As part of the trial, jurors heard stereotype-activating statements from either the prosecutor (in the Superpredator condition) or the defense attorney (in the Wayward Youth condition), arguing that the defendant was a perfect example of each of those categories of youthful offenders.

In terms of their beliefs about juvenile offenders, on average the student participants favored the "wayward youth" rather than the "superpredator" portrayal. It is important to note, though, that these attitudes may not be representative of community adults who constitute the jury pool, as participants in this study were closer in age to young offenders (and perhaps better able to reflect on their own youthful indiscretions) and better educated than the broader populace.

On the main issue of whether varying stereotypes about juvenile offenders affected case judgments, the data were clear: The more that mock jurors supported the "superpredator" stereotype the more likely they were to convict and to agree that the case should have been tried in criminal court, regardless of stereotype activation condition. And, as expected, participants who had the "superpredator" stereotype activated during the trial were more likely to convict, and participants who had the "wayward youth" stereotype activated were more likely to believe that the case should have stayed in juvenile court, regardless of their preexisting beliefs. There was some indication that the effects of preexisting stereotypes were reduced by jury deliberation, but the effects of activated stereotypes were exacerbated by group discussion.

These findings leave little doubt that jurors have preexisting stereotypes about juvenile offenders that can influence the judgments they render in court. Also, they imply that stereotypes can be triggered by the arguments and emotional appeals that attorneys make during the trial (Haegerich & Bottoms, 2000; see Chapter 12). Importantly, these effects compete with and can eclipse the impact of the evidence on jurors' judgments (Haegerich et al., 2013).

The extent to which laypeople support the "superpredator" and "wayward youth" stereotypes is also predictive of their jurisdictional (i.e., juvenile vs. criminal court) and punishment preferences for juvenile offenders. Duke and Greene (2015) measured the extent to which laypeople endorsed the "superpredator" and "wayward youth" stereotypes and, after providing details about a case in which either a 13-, 17-, or 21-year-old offender was convicted of murdering a stranger, asked participants whether they agreed with the decision to transfer the juvenile case to criminal court and to sentence the offender to life without parole. As support for the "superpredator" stereotype increased, so did participants' agreement with the decision to transfer the case to criminal court, along with their belief that a life sentence was appropriate punishment. In fact, those who strongly agreed with the stereotype deemed a life sentence as appropriate for a 13-year-old as for a 21-year-old, whereas participants who endorsed the "wayward youth" stereotype were much less likely to agree with a life sentence for a 13-year-old than for a 21-year-old offender.

One might reasonably ask whether information that personalizes an individual can effectively eliminate the influence of stereotypes. For example, can trial evidence that shows unambiguously that an individual does not fit the stereotype undermine stereotypic thinking? Although we know of no data that directly address that question with regard to stereotypes of juvenile offenders, findings regarding other stereotypes are instructive and seem to indicate that stereotypes are very difficult to override. Because people solicit stereotype-consistent information and interpret ambiguities in that information in stereotype-consistent ways—in short, because they prefer to confirm rather than disconfirm their stereotypes—these stereotyping effects can be difficult to eliminate. Moreover, at least in the realm of gender stereotypes, people require more compelling evidence to disconfirm than to confirm a stereotype (Biernat, 2003; Biernat & Ma, 2005), and those with strongly held stereotypes tend to have poor recall of individuating information (Gawronski et al., 2003). Thus it is unlikely that individuating information would undermine the assumptions that flow from stereotypic thinking.

Can Jurors' Harsh Judgments of Juvenile Offenders be Remedied?

Jurors' biases against juvenile offenders who are tried as adults may be difficult to remedy if they reflect deep-seated beliefs or experiences, or were formed via exposure to the get-tough rhetoric of some politicians and commentators. But as more is known about the role of cognitive and psychosocial immaturity in juvenile offending, those punitive attitudes may gradually soften. If so, then young offenders, like older offenders, will be judged more by the nature of their actions than by their age.

Some modifications to the trial process can help to achieve that result. One possibility is the sort of juvenile qualification during *voir dire* that we described earlier in this chapter. Greathouse and her colleagues (2011) noted that this line of questioning, and the resultant juror strikes, might reduce the representativeness of the jury. (We address the broader issue of jury representativeness in Chapter 3.) But if *voir dire* questions about an offender's youthfulness are *not* asked, then very punitively oriented jurors potentially could remain on the panel. Because the negative effects of juvenile qualification questioning seem to dissipate as the trial evidence is presented, on balance we think this may be a helpful procedure.

Another potentially useful remedy would be testimony from an expert witness who, in appropriate cases, would have conducted an evaluation of the defendant and could describe that person's psychological, social, and cognitive maturity and the influence of environmental factors on his or her behavior. (In cases involving judicial waiver, someone with this expertise would have already evaluated the offender on these matters and would have prepared a report and possibly testified at a waiver hearing. But the sort of testimony we are proposing here would be directed at the jury during trial rather than the judge prior to trial.) Alternatively, an expert could present "social framework testimony" (Monahan & Walker, 2014), a concept we introduced in Chapter 7. This sort of expert testimony would be based on the results of empirical research studies regarding adolescent development, rather than forensic examination of any particular individual. A respectable body of evidence exists concerning brain maturation, peer influences, risk taking, and temporal perspectives in adolescence (e.g., Steinberg, 2009), and the expert could, in appropriate cases, use that information to provide a context for evaluating the actions of the defendant. As we noted in Chapter 7, social framework testimony has been used in cases of child abuse (Quas, Thompson, & Clarke-Stewart, 2005), spousal abuse (Schuller & Jenkins, 2007), sexual assault (Raitt & Zeedyk, 2000), and employment discrimination (Goodman & Croyle, 1989). In cases with juvenile offenders it might help jurors to understand how and why such a young person could commit such a heinous offense.

At the end of every criminal trial in the United States, jurors are instructed that the defendant is presumed to be innocent and that the presumption continues until the defendant's guilt has been proven beyond a reasonable doubt. Another means of addressing the relatively negative impressions some jurors have of juveniles tried in criminal court is to incorporate a supplementary instruction to the effect that the offender's relative youthfulness has no bearing on his or her guilt (Levine et al., 2001). Although, as we explain in Chapter 14, some instructions of this nature have a boomerang effect by drawing jurors' attention to aspects of the evidence or the proceedings they might not otherwise consider (Steblay, Hosch, Culhane, & McWethy, 2006), there seems to be little downside to such an instruction in trials involving youthful defendants. Inevitably jurors will see for themselves that the defendant is a young person. So rather than allowing their preconceptions and stereotypes to run wild, reminding them via an instruction that the defendant's age is an irrelevant consideration could be a potentially significant safeguard.

Conclusions

Returning to the questions we posed at the beginning of the chapter, we now have some clarity on whether jurors, when they decide the guilt of juvenile offenders, take into account the offender's age, maturity, and developmental status. We can also reach some conclusions about whether, when considering these factors, jurors become more lenient or harsher toward youthful offenders. According to emerging research on cognitive and psychosocial development throughout adolescence, these factors *should* mitigate offenders' culpability since teens below a certain age have difficulty grasping the consequences of their actions, controlling their impulses, and resisting peer influence. Thus, according to Steinberg (2009), one "cannot claim that adolescents 'ought to know better' if, in fact, the evidence indicates that they do not know better, or more accurately, cannot know better, because they lack the abilities needed to exercise mature judgment" (p. 471).

Public attitudes toward juvenile offenders have softened in recent years in light of increasing awareness of adolescent development and evidence of juveniles' amenability to treatment (and, probably, in light of data on the soaring costs of incarcerating large numbers of offenders for many years). But some laypeople still hold relatively harsh and punitive views of juveniles whose cases are waived or transferred to criminal courts. Many generally believe that offenders whose cases warrant transfer are more deviant (Snyder & Sickmund, 1999) and dangerous (Myers, 2003) than those whose cases remain in the juvenile system and adult offenders.

These beliefs also influence jurors' judgments. They factor into the inferences that jurors make about transferred juveniles prior to hearing any evidence, and they inform the stereotypes through which jurors process evidence and determine verdicts. Although the findings are not entirely consistent, several studies suggest that jurors are more likely to convict transferred youthful offenders than adult offenders. This is particularly true for jurors who have pro-prosecution inclinations and who hold harsh stereotypes about juvenile offenders. Thus, considerable evidence suggests that jurors do not treat juvenile defendants fairly.

Although it is not the focus of this chapter, the consequences of broad transfer and waiver policies for juvenile offenders are worth considering briefly. In ruling that a defendant considered for waiver must be accorded due process, including a hearing and the assistance of counsel, the United States Supreme Court has noted that juvenile transfer can have "tremendous consequences for the juvenile" (*Kent v. U.S.*, 1966, p. 554). Among the consequences are the loss of a number of rights and privileges, a lengthy period of incarceration, abuse by older prisoners while in prison, and little opportunity to be rehabilitated. The New Jersey Supreme Court has called waiver to adult court "the single most serious act the juvenile court can perform . . . because once waiver occurs, the child loses all protective and rehabilitative possibilities available" (*State v. R.G.D.*, 1987, p. 835.)

It is now clear that these decisions were correct, at least in one sense: Juveniles sentenced to adult correctional facilities *are* subjected to harsher environments and fewer rehabilitative services than those placed in juvenile facilities (Redding, 2003). It is also clear that for serious crimes like robbery, burglary, and aggravated assault, youth who are transferred are more likely to reoffend, and reoffend more often, than those who are retained in the juvenile system, although for drug offenses and property crimes the effects of transfer are less clear (Redding, 2010). Undoubtedly there are multiple explanations for this statistic, although the lack of access to interventions aimed at rehabilitation is surely a factor. Recidivism occurs in part because subjecting a juvenile to adult sanctions limits the opportunity to reintegrate into the community, obtain employment, and develop other competencies that move one beyond a life of crime. Criminal court adjudication of juvenile offenders seems to diminish rather than enhance community protection and public well-being.

9

Compensatory Damage Awards Are Excessive and Unpredictable

"Pity the civil jury, seen by some as the sickest organ of a sick system"

(Clermont & Eisenberg, 1992, p. 1125).

In March 2006, U.S. Marine Lance Corporal Matthew Snyder was killed in Iraq. Shortly thereafter his father, Albert Snyder, held his funeral in their hometown of Westminster, Maryland. Fred Phelps, founder of Westboro Baptist Church (WBC) in Topeka, Kansas, traveled to Maryland with six other members of his church to picket the funeral. WBC has demonstrated at numerous funerals to air its belief that God is punishing the United States for its tolerance of homosexuality, especially in the military. On public land near the church where the funeral was held and on the route to the cemetery, the WBC protesters held signs reading, among other messages, "Thank God for Dead Soldiers," "Thank God for IEDs," and "God Hates Fags" (*Snyder v. Phelps*, 2008; 2011). WBC also posted similar comments on its website.

Albert Snyder sued Phelps and WBC for defamation, intrusion upon seclusion (i.e., invasion of privacy), publicity given to private life, intentional infliction of emotional distress, and civil conspiracy. The federal court in Maryland granted WBC summary judgment on the claims of defamation and publicity given to private life, and the other three claims proceeded to a jury trial. At trial, Snyder testified that the protest ruined his son's funeral, was a source of ongoing stress, and continued to make him tearful, angry, and physically ill. Expert testimony supported his claim that the protest had disrupted his grieving process, caused severe depression, and exacerbated preexisting health conditions (*Snyder v. Phelps*, 2011). A jury found for Snyder and awarded him $2.9 million in compensation and an additional $8 million in punitive damages. The judge reduced the punitive award to $2.1 million, for a total award of $5 million (*Snyder v. Phelps*, 2008). The Fourth Circuit Court of Appeals subsequently reversed the jury's verdict (*Snyder v. Phelps*, 2009); the reversal was affirmed by the United States Supreme Court on grounds that the First Amendment's free speech clause protected WBC from liability (*Snyder v. Phelps*, 2011).

The *Snyder* case is interesting for a number of reasons: WBC's actions, which many Americans deem abhorrent; its connection to the hot-button issues of homosexuality and U.S. military involvement in Iraq; the scope of protection for free speech and, to a lesser extent, free exercise of religion; and, most relevant for our present purposes, the difficulty of setting a specific damage award in such cases. Why $2.9 million in compensation and not $29,000 or $290 million? Why $8 million in punitive damages and not $8,000 or $8 billion? In most cases the jury is not required to compartmentalize damage awards or explain how it arrived at a specific figure; accordingly, it provided little detail in *Snyder*. The compensatory award was apparently a single lump sum, aggregated across all of the claims and defendants.

The defendants argued that both the compensatory and punitive awards were excessive. The trial court agreed with WBC with respect to punitive damages but not with respect to compensation (*Snyder v. Phelps*, 2008; our focus here is on compensatory damages; we revisit the jury's punitive award in *Snyder* in the next chapter). Although the appellate review focused on legal issues, especially WBC's free speech defense, and not the magnitude of the award, the question remains: How much compensation is appropriate for someone who had to endure the sort of deliberate harm that Albert Snyder experienced, and that in all likelihood will continue to have harmful effects for the remainder of his life? Although $2.9 million is a large and seemingly arbitrary figure, it probably does not strike most people—as it did not strike the trial court—as outlandish. Our suggested alternatives of $29,000 or $290 million, on the other hand, might. Like criminal sentences, jury damage awards contain a fair measure of subjectivity; but unlike most criminal sentences, damage awards are often decided by juries (on jury sentencing, see Chapter 11). Unfortunately, juries receive little guidance in determining a damage award (Greene & Bornstein, 2000).

These features of jury damage awards—subjectivity and a lack of guidance—have pros and cons. On the positive side, they allow juries to tailor their awards to the unique features of a case. But on the negative side, they can introduce unwanted variability, complicate settlement negotiations, and make the task challenging and frustrating for jurors (Greene & Bornstein, 2000; Mott, Hans, & Simpson, 2000). Many reform efforts in the civil arena, such as caps on damages, are motivated by a widespread perception that jury damage awards are excessive and unpredictable—that is, that the civil jury is "the sickest organ of a sick system," as Clermont and Eisenberg (1992, p. 1125) summarized this perception more than 20 years ago. This criticism of the

civil jury has not slackened in the intervening decades. Claims of excessiveness are more common in certain areas of tort law, such as products liability
and medical malpractice, than in others. Indeed, awards in these kinds of
cases, when plaintiffs prevail at trial, can be substantial. Accordingly, those
same areas are especially likely to fuel calls for tort reform (Bornstein &
Robicheaux, 2008). However, as we discuss below, products liability and medical malpractice comprise relatively few cases, and plaintiffs in these cases do
not fare particularly well (Galanter, 2004; Ostrom, Rottman, & Goerdt, 1996;
Seabury, Pace, & Reville, 2004).

Are damage awards excessive and unpredictable? There are two important considerations in addressing this question. The first consideration is
deciding what exactly we mean by terms like "excessive" and "unpredictable." Excessive does not simply mean large. Large awards, even very, very
large awards, can sometimes be justified by the circumstances of the case.
Excessive means more than seems reasonable or appropriate given the particular features of the case; this definition could apply to a small award or a
large one.

To illustrate, suppose that a defendant, Joe, runs a red stoplight and hits
a car driven by Kim. Kim's friend Amy is in the front passenger seat. Both
are wearing seatbelts, Kim is driving her older-model vehicle with a normal
degree of caution, and Joe is clearly negligent but not reckless. The driver's
side airbag deploys; Kim suffers deep bruising on her torso, facial lacerations
from the broken glass, and a broken hand. There is no passenger's side airbag; Amy suffers a cervical fracture and spinal cord injury that leaves her a
paraplegic with limited use of her arms and hands. She also has a fractured
pelvis and ruptured spleen that require surgery. Kim returns to work after
two weeks, and the cast comes off her hand after six weeks; Amy will never
work again. Both sue Joe for pain and suffering as well as their economic
losses (e.g., medical expenses and lost income). At trial, the jury awards each
plaintiff $500,000.

Arguably, Kim's compensation is excessive, whereas Amy's compensation is inadequate. She is likely to need skilled care for the rest of her life,
which can easily cost $100,000/year; renovations to her home; replacement
for her lost income; and extensive physical therapy, not to mention her
ongoing psychological injuries. Without attempting to estimate what "fair"
compensation would be in her case, it seems clear that a multimillion dollar award would not be untoward. Thus very large awards can sometimes be
justified and not excessive at all.

It is just as hard to define "predictable" as it is to define "excessive." Jurors
are human, and human behavior is never perfectly predictable. One sense of
predictability is foreseeability: Damage awards are predictable if the parties
can anticipate the approximate outcome. This sort of predictability is valuable because it informs potential plaintiffs about whether it is worthwhile to
sue, lets plaintiffs' attorneys working on contingency know if it is financially
feasible to take on a client, and helps both plaintiffs and defendants structure

settlement negotiations. However, some of the reliable predictors might not be legally sanctioned ones. For example, if Joe is driving his company car on the way to an appointment at the time of the accident, his company is probably the defendant instead of (or in addition to) Joe as an individual. Research shows that juries tend to have an anticorporate bias, requiring corporate defendants to pay more for the same injury than individual defendants (Greene & Bornstein, 2003; Hans, 2000). Legally, corporations are supposed to be treated the same as individuals, so there is no legal basis for making corporations pay more in compensation for the same injury than individuals; but the parties could predict that it would be the case.

Another sense of predictability, then, is how well damage awards adhere to the relevant legal criteria. With respect to compensation, the overriding (and arguably sole) criterion is the extent of the plaintiff's injury. More severely injured plaintiffs are entitled to greater compensation. This correspondence between compensation and injury severity is often referred to as "vertical equity" (Greene & Bornstein, 2003)—that is, people who are hurt worse deserve to get more. It can be contrasted with "horizontal equity," which is the idea that people who are hurt about the same (i.e., who are at the same horizontal level on a severity scale) deserve to get approximately the same amount. Our discussion of predictability will emphasize these notions of vertical and horizontal equity, and the extent to which damage awards reflect legally relevant criteria as opposed to extralegal factors.

A second important consideration in addressing the appropriateness of damage awards is the category of damages. Generally speaking, damages can be compensatory or punitive.[1] As their names implies, the primary purpose of compensatory damages is restitution—to replace, insofar as possible, the loss caused to the plaintiff by the defendant's wrongful behavior. The primary purpose of punitive damages is punishment—to exact retribution against the defendant and deter the defendant and others from similar behavior in the future. These distinctions are not entirely clear-cut; because

---

[1] Nominal damages are a third category of damages, which "are an inconsequential or trifling sum awarded to a plaintiff when a technical violation of [his/her] rights has occurred but the plaintiff has suffered no actual loss or injury" (Committee on Pattern Jury Instructions, District Judges Association, Fifth Circuit, 2014, §15.6). Nominal damages are relatively rare but can be noteworthy when they occur, such as a jury's award of $1 to the United States Football League (USFL) in its antitrust action against the National Football League (*United States Football League v. National Football League*, 1988). The USFL sought $1.7 billion in damages. Pursuant to antitrust law, the award was trebled to $3—still far short of the plaintiff's alleged losses. Nominal damages could hardly be construed as excessive, though they might be unpredictable. Because our major interest is in how juries determine substantial damage awards, we do not discuss nominal damages further, although we note that much more research needs to be done on how and why juries make such judgments.

defendants typically pay the compensatory damages, and punitive damages typically go to the plaintiff, compensation serves a secondary deterrent function and punitive damages provide additional compensation (American Law Institute, 1965; Epstein & Sharkey, 2012; Sharkey, 2008). However, jurors are not instructed on these secondary purposes of the different categories of damages; they are simply told, in essence, that compensatory damages compensate the plaintiff and punitive damages punish the defendant. For example, the Fifth Circuit Court of Appeals' pattern jury instructions inform jurors:

> If you find that Defendant [name] is liable to Plaintiff [name], then you must determine an amount that is fair compensation for all of Plaintiff [name]'s damages. These damages are called compensatory damages. The purpose of compensatory damages is to make Plaintiff [name] whole—that is, to compensate Plaintiff [name] for the damage that [he/she/it] has suffered. Compensatory damages are not limited to expenses that Plaintiff [name] may have incurred because of [his/her] injury. If Plaintiff [name] wins, [he/she] is entitled to compensatory damages for the physical injury, pain and suffering, and mental anguish that [he/she] has suffered because of Defendant [name]'s wrongful conduct
> (Committee on Pattern Jury Instructions, District Judges
> Association, Fifth Circuit, 2014, §15.2).

We treat punitive damages in detail in Chapter 10; our focus here is on compensatory damages. The bulk of the chapter addresses the two components of the myth about juries posed in the chapter's title: first, are compensatory awards excessive? And second, are they unpredictable? Before we address these questions, we provide a brief overview of the different elements of compensation.

A Compensatory Damages Overview

Different kinds of civil cases can wind up at trial; the most common are torts (61% in a study by Langton & Cohen, 2008) and contract claims (33%; Langton & Cohen, 2008). Within the category of torts, the most common claim by far is for vehicular negligence (Langton & Cohen, 2008; Ostrom et al., 1996). For example, vehicular negligence cases accounted for 35% of all state civil trials in 2005 (Langton & Cohen, 2008). More controversial cases, which are more likely to be featured in media reports and that fuel the tort reform movement, such as medical malpractice and products liability, are considerably less common (e.g., they comprised 9.1% and 1.3%, respectively, of state trials in Langton and Cohen's 2005 sample). As mentioned in Chapter 1, roughly 90% of tort cases that go to trial are decided by a jury (compared to 36% of contract cases; Langton & Cohen, 2008).

Regardless of the type of case, the jury's primary task is to determine if the defendant should be held liable for causing the plaintiff's injury and, if so, how much financial compensation to award the plaintiff. There are multiple ways of compartmentalizing compensatory damages, but the most common categories are economic and noneconomic damages (also referred to as pecuniary and nonpecuniary damages, or special and general damages, respectively). Roughly half of all civil compensation is for noneconomic damages (Vidmar, Gross, & Rose, 1998). Plaintiffs can recover for past losses (i.e., costs incurred between the time of injury and the trial) as well as future losses (i.e., continuing costs moving forward from the time of trial). The calculation of both kinds of damages presents challenges.

Economic damages include things like medical expenses, lost income, and reduced profit or market share (e.g., in commercial cases). Some of these costs may be covered by the plaintiff's insurance, in which case the plaintiff's insurance carrier is often a party to the lawsuit in an effort to recover its expenditures from the defendant (or the defendant's insurer). Past economic damages can often be calculated with a fair degree of precision. In the example used earlier, Kim would have received medical bills from hospitals and doctors for her treatment, and her lost income can be computed simply by multiplying her weekly wage by the two weeks of missed work.

Future economic damages are a good deal more complicated. In Amy's case, what kind of care will she need, and how much will it cost? The care will presumably become more expensive over time, but at what rate? If she is a student who has not yet embarked on a career, toward what kind of career was she most likely headed? If she did work, but we assume that she no longer can, what would her income trajectory (i.e., raises and promotions) have been like over the course of her career? What is her life expectancy? Will her health remain the same over time, improve, or deteriorate? If she has children, will they require childcare, and for how long? Differences in the assumptions underlying these questions can lead to cost estimates that differ by hundreds of thousands and even millions of dollars. These same issues can come up even for much less severe injuries. Kim could expect ongoing problems from her broken hand, requiring further treatment and rehabilitation; depending on her line of work, the broken hand could also negatively affect her job performance and future earnings (e.g., piano tuner, surgeon, professional athlete). If she is unable to continue in her current occupation, can she retrain in another field, and how would those earnings compare to her current salary?

Noneconomic damages are hard to quantify both in past and future terms; it is therefore easier, in some respects, to argue that a certain amount is (or is not) appropriate, which produces more opportunities for horizontal inequity and more controversy and calls for reform (Bornstein & Robicheaux, 2008; Greene & Bornstein, 2003; Wissler, Kuehn, & Saks, 2000). According to the American Tort Reform Association (www.atra.org), "The broad and basically unguided discretion given juries in awarding damages for noneconomic loss is the single greatest contributor to the inequities and inefficiencies of the tort liability system." Noneconomic damages are roughly synonymous with pain and suffering, although they can be broken down further to include the amount and duration of numerous elements (see, generally, Greene & Bornstein, 2003; Wissler et al., 2000; Wissler, Evans, Hart, Morry, & Saks, 1997): physical pain; mental suffering; disfigurement; disability; emotional distress, which encompasses a number of different negative emotional states (e.g., fear, anxiety, embarrassment, depression); loss of enjoyment of life (often referred to as "hedonic damages"; see Greene, Sturm, & Evelo, 2016; Poser, Bornstein, & McGorty, 2003); and loss of consortium or companionship (usually a spouse, child, or parent). In the majority of cases, jurors are not instructed to make separate awards for each of these elements, although they may be (Poser et al., 2003).

A number of features of noneconomic damages, apart from their hard-to-quantify nature, make them difficult to assess. First, with the exception of disfigurement and disability, they are invisible (the consequences of pain, such as grimacing and obvious discomfort, might be visible, but the pain itself is necessarily subjective). Jurors have a hard time understanding, and compensating plaintiffs for, injuries that they cannot see (Hans, 2008; Hans & Vadino, 2000). In part because of their invisibility, psychological injuries are notoriously difficult to assess for forensic purposes (Greenberg, Otto, & Long, 2003).

Accompanying the lack of visibility, all of these elements, except for disfigurement, disability, and pain, are predominantly psychological in nature.[2] The law evinces something of a double standard with respect to physical and psychological injuries, deeming the former more legitimate and compensation-worthy than the latter (Bornstein, 2009; Bornstein & Schwartz, 2009). For example, both kinds of injury are generally compensable for intentional torts; but when the tortfeasor's actions are negligent rather than intentional, psychological injury by itself (i.e., without physical injury) is generally not compensable (e.g., *Twyman v. Twyman*, 1993).

Third, the distinction between physical and psychological elements of noneconomic damages is largely spurious to begin with (Bornstein & Schwartz, 2009). All of the "physical" elements of noneconomic damages have a psychological side; it would be impossible, for instance, to separate the physical and psychological aspects of pain. Moreover, abundant research shows that persistent negative emotional states (e.g., depression, anxiety) have clear physical components (e.g., a neurotransmitter imbalance).

Fourth, although many future economic costs will go up over time (i.e., the same level of medical and skilled nursing care becomes more expensive; one's lost income would be greater the further his or her working life

---

[2] This is not to say that disfigurement, disability, and pain lack psychological components, but those components would generally fall under the rubric of "suffering."

advances), there are good reasons to suspect that future noneconomic costs would actually go down. Individuals habituate to permanent injuries and loss of function (Horgan & MacLachlan, 2004; Riis et al., 2005). In the case of our hypothetical plaintiff Amy, this means that her paralysis would likely cause her less emotional distress 20 years from now than it would today.

Because of the many kinds of data needed to substantiate economic damages and the imprecision of estimating noneconomic damages, claims for both categories of damages frequently involve expert witnesses: economists, accountants, actuaries, medical and mental health professionals, physical and occupational therapists, human resource or organizational consultants, and other professionals with expertise relevant to the facts in issue. Trial consultants may also work with these experts and the attorneys in litigants' attempts to place a dollar figure on and justify a certain damage award (Bornstein & Greene, 2011b). Consultants can work for either side, making the case that an award should be relatively large (for plaintiffs) or small (for defendants). In practice, civil defendants typically argue that they should not be held liable but that even if they are, the plaintiff deserves less than he or she is requesting.

This is not to say that plaintiffs invariably request a specific amount of compensation, known as an *ad damnum*. Rules and customs vary across jurisdictions; some attorneys feel they fare better if they request a specific amount in damages, whereas others prefer not to; and systematic data on the prevalence of *ad damnums* do not appear to exist. Nonetheless, anecdotal evidence suggests that they are common. They are probably more common for economic than for noneconomic damages, as the former are easier to estimate with some degree of precision. Perhaps because of that greater precision and justification, jurors take *ad damnums* for economic damages more seriously than *ad damnums* for noneconomic damages (Diamond, Rose, Murphy, & Meixner, 2011). As we discuss below, the amount of the *ad damnum* can influence the jury's damage awards.

Deliberating on Damages

Whether or not the plaintiff recommends a specific dollar figure, the jury still has the task of deciding on an exact amount. Some jurors enter deliberations with a specific number in mind, whereas others—according to some research the majority (Mott et al., 2000)—do not. Those who do have a number in mind arrive at it by various means: Some employ a holistic, "Gestalt" approach by which they simply choose a figure that seems fair, and others use some sort of calculation strategy that takes into account, for example, discrete components of damages (Greene, 1989; Greene & Bornstein, 2003).

Regardless of whether jurors begin deliberation with a specific figure in mind, a large part of the process involves individual jurors suggesting specific amounts. The jury must then take the dollar figures proposed by individual jurors—which can be quite disparate—and arrive at a single consensus amount. How do they do that? Jurors are explicitly instructed that they should not simply average their individual preferences; rather, they are supposed to come to an agreed-upon value as a result of reasoned deliberation. Consistent with this instruction, explicit averaging is rare, although group awards do tend to converge toward the middle of individual jurors' predeliberation preferences (Diamond & Casper, 1992; Mott et al., 2000). There is some evidence that jurors in the middle of the award range are more persuasive (Diamond & Casper, 1992), but whether more persuasive jurors tend to adopt moderate values or they are more persuasive *because* they adopt more moderate values is difficult to ascertain.

Roughly equal numbers of jurors report that the group picked a fair number without calculation, then adjusted it up or down if it seemed too high or low, or performed some sort of calculation (Mott et al., 2000). The most common method of calculation is to multiply expected earnings by expected work life (Mott et al., 2000). The deliberation process itself tends to inflate compensation awards; that is, mean jury awards are larger than the mean awards of those same individual jurors prior to deliberation (Diamond, Saks, & Landsman, 1998; Greene & Bornstein, 2003), especially for relatively severe injuries (Shea Adams & Bourgeois, 2006). There is also some evidence that deliberation reduces award variability (Diamond et al., 1998; but see Shea Adams & Bourgeois, 2006). In that sense, then, it is an effective safeguard.

Are Compensatory Damage Awards Excessive?

As we noted previously, the excessiveness question is very difficult to address, for the simple reason that many of the things compensation is intended for are intangible and therefore very hard to quantify in dollars. The law provides remedies other than monetary compensation, such as injunctive or declaratory relief (Hasen, 2012); but for the most part, especially in torts and contracts, compensation means money. Average compensation is relatively modest. Langton and Cohen (2008) found that the median final award for all cases in which plaintiffs won (including punitive damages, though these were rare) was $28,000 ($24,000 in tort cases, $35,000 in contract cases), and 62% of plaintiffs received $50,000 or less. Only 4% of winning plaintiffs received $1 million or more.

It is tempting to conclude from the low median value that compensation is hardly excessive. However, that would be an oversimplification—an award of $28,000 is excessive if the plaintiff deserves only $10,000. How, then, to measure excessiveness? When compensation can be quantified—or at least estimated in a more or less concrete manner, as in the case of economic damages—the question can be addressed directly: Do juries award plaintiffs compensation that is commensurate with their actual and estimated costs? Relatedly, we can examine how much plaintiffs actually *receive*, which might or might not correspond to what the jury actually *awards*.

When compensation cannot be easily quantified, as with noneconomic damages, more indirect methods are necessary. Nonetheless, a number of sources of information pertain to the question: Do plaintiffs win (i.e., receive *any* damages) an unreasonable amount of the time? Do they win in some kinds of cases more often than others? Are compensatory awards increasing disproportionately over time? Are jury awards comparable to those determined by judges (we defer this question to Chapter 13)?

It is impossible to say with any degree of certainty how often plaintiffs "should" win, but given the preponderance of evidence standard and the fact that only reasonably close cases make it to trial (otherwise they are dropped, dismissed, or settled), it should probably be somewhere in the neighborhood of 50%. Overall, across different kinds of cases, that is roughly how often plaintiffs do win—50% of the time (e.g., Bovbjerg, Sloan, Dor, & Hsieh, 1991; Devine et al., 2001; Gross & Syverud, 1991; Langton & Cohen, 2008; Ostrom et al., 1996). These same studies show that the plaintiff win rate varies across case type: Plaintiffs win approximately 40% of products liability jury trials and about 20%–30% of medical malpractice jury trials. Vehicular negligence, contracts, and commercial plaintiffs, in contrast, fare comparatively well at trial, winning more than half and in some studies over 60% of the time.

Countering this difference in win rates, damage awards in malpractice and products liability trials (when the plaintiff wins) tend to be higher than in other types of cases (Bovbjerg et al., 1991; Langton & Cohen, 2008; Ostrom et al., 1996; Seabury et al., 2004). The award discrepancy is a direct consequence, at least in part, of the low win rate for these classes of plaintiffs, as well as the relative difficulty and cost in trying these cases (e.g., complex evidence, the need for expert witnesses). That is, if plaintiffs and attorneys are going to invest the necessary resources in trying malpractice and products liability cases, then the potential payoff needs to be large. Thus they are more likely to involve very severely injured plaintiffs. When controlling for injury severity, the difference in compensation across case types is greatly reduced (Bovbjerg et al., 1991).

Compensation necessarily increases over time to some extent, due to factors like inflation and increasing medical costs; but there is little evidence that growth in compensation is disproportionate when taking those factors into account. Seabury and colleagues (2004) analyzed 40 years of civil jury verdicts (1960–1999) in San Francisco and Cook County, Illinois. Although the mean award increased substantially over time, even when adjusted for inflation, the median award did not. This pattern reflected an increase over time in the number of large outliers. Nonetheless, large awards were still rare, and most of the increase was due to increased medical costs and not to noneconomic damages. Higher medical costs can also explain why the increase in awards over time was greater for medical malpractice than for other kinds of cases, although other research has shown a nonsignificant or only marginally significant increase in jury awards in malpractice cases (Black, Silver, Hyman, & Sage, 2005). Awards for vehicular negligence, which are the most common kind of tort case, have not increased (Seabury et al., 2004). Chronological trends do not directly address the question of excessiveness—awards might have always been excessive and simply stayed that way. However, in showing that awards are not becoming larger over time, these trends help to allay concerns that excessive damage awards are a growing problem.

Another way of looking at the excessiveness question is to ask whether plaintiffs' compensation is adequate to meet their costs. Although noneconomic costs are virtually impossible to quantify or estimate precisely, economic costs can be measured (for past costs) and estimated (for future costs). If anything juries tend to *undercompensate* plaintiffs, especially those with relatively serious injuries. This has been documented, for example, in several studies of victims of medical negligence (Black et al., 2005; Sloan & Hsieh, 1990; Sloan & van Wert, 1991). Sloan and colleagues found that for birth-related and emergency room injuries, medical malpractice plaintiffs received only 57% and 80%, respectively, of their estimated costs. The disparity was greatest for plaintiffs who died as a result of their injuries (Sloan & van Wert, 1991).

Reducing Compensation

There are a number of sources of post-verdict "haircuts," meaning that for various reasons plaintiffs might not actually receive the jury's full award, or indeed any of it (Hyman et al., 2007; Vidmar et al., 1998). Most obviously, a defendant might win on appeal. But even in the absence of a victorious appeal, defendants usually pay less than the full amount. In one study of 306 medical malpractice jury trials in which the plaintiff won, 75% had payment less than the adjusted verdict (i.e., verdict plus interest; Hyman et al., 2007). Haircuts were larger and more frequent as the size of the award increased, and they increased over time (the sample included cases from 1988–2003). Post-verdict settlements for insurance policy limits, possibly in response to the threat of appeal or protracted legal wrangling, were especially common. Other reasons for a haircut include a defendant's inability to pay, forcing plaintiffs to take what they can get; an applicable statute capping damages at an amount lower than the jury's verdict; or a posttrial motion for the trial judge to reduce the verdict, a process known as *remittitur*.[3]

---

[3] *Remittitur* is allowed in the federal courts and in most states, although at least one state (Missouri) has abolished the practice (*Firestone v. Crown Center Redevelopment Corp.*, 1985; see, generally, Epstein & Sharkey, 2012). A plaintiff may also move for an increase in the award, known as *additur*. *Additur*, which is allowed in state but not in federal courts, is even less common than *remittitur* (Baldus, MacQueen, & Woodworth, 1995). *Additur/remittitur* can occur on appeal as well as from a ruling by the trial judge.

The premise of caps is straightforward: They limit, or "cap," the amount of damages. In practice, however, they are anything but straightforward, and capping schemes vary considerably across jurisdictions. They can apply to total damages, punitive damages, or noneconomic damages; apply to any civil defendant or only certain categories of tortfeasors (e.g., healthcare providers in cases involving medical liability); vary depending on the severity of the plaintiff's injury or type of defendant (e.g., a higher limit for hospitals than for physicians); and set a fixed dollar amount, an amount that increases incrementally over time, a ratio (e.g., a ratio of punitive to compensatory damages, or noneconomic to economic damages), or an amount that takes the plaintiff's life expectancy into account (e.g., Alaska caps noneconomic damages at the greater of $400,000 or life expectancy x $8,000). Our focus here is on caps for noneconomic damages; we discuss caps on punitive damages in Chapter 10.

Juries are generally not instructed about the existence of a cap—that is, they are "blindfolded" about this rule (Diamond & Casper, 1992), just as they are about things like whether litigants have insurance that will cover some or all of the award, and the role of attorney fees. Nonetheless, jurors might be aware of a cap simply by virtue of general familiarity with the laws in their jurisdiction. If they are unaware of a cap (or know about the cap but award a higher amount anyway), then the judge simply reduces the award to the amount set by the statute. It would therefore seem that caps necessarily lower the amount of noneconomic compensation, and by and large, that is precisely what they do.

A number of states cap noneconomic damages under at least some circumstances. According to data compiled by ATRA (as of June 10, 2015), 30 states had enacted laws setting some sort of cap on noneconomic damages, most in the range of $250,000–$1 million. ATRA itself supports a $250,000 cap. Federal laws in the United States do not impose a cap, although they do in Canada with some exemptions. The Canadian cap was $100,000 when it was established by the Canadian Supreme Court in 1978, but it has since been adjusted for inflation and currently is approximately $360,000 (Bau, 2014). Noneconomic damage caps have been found unconstitutional in some states (e.g., Alabama [*Moore v. Mobile Infirmary Association*, 1991]; Wisconsin [*Petrucelli v. Wisconsin Patients Compensation Fund*, 2005]), but they have been upheld or unchallenged in others. The statutes have been challenged mainly on grounds of equal protection, due process, separation of powers, or right to a jury trial.

The vast majority of jury damage awards fall below the maximum, so caps do not come into play very often, even in cases with relatively severe injuries. For example, Baldus and colleagues (1995) analyzed 461 personal injury cases, from a large number of states, involving infants and children and in which the defendant was found liable. Ninety percent of the plaintiffs suffered one or more severe injuries such as amputation, hearing or sight impairment, paralysis, or intracranial injury. Yet even in these cases, caps were applied only 7% of the time. Nonetheless, the reduction in those cases was substantial, amounting to an average reduction of $1,444,000—more than 70% of the original award. There is also some evidence that caps affect the ultimate damages payout more often in cases where the plaintiff has died (Hyman et al., 2007).

Considering that caps apply most often in cases of very severe and/or long-term injuries, Baldus et al. (1995) argue that the caps potentially result in a significant degree of undercompensation (see also Marder, 2005). Undercompensating the most severely injured plaintiffs reduces vertical equity. And in light of other sources of post-verdict haircuts (e.g., settlement for insurance policy limits), the above-cap amounts might not have been collected anyway (Hyman et al., 2007). Evidence also indicates that when there is a cap on noneconomic damages, plaintiffs' attorneys will simply compensate by seeking larger economic damages (Sharkey, 2005). Jurors who are aware of the cap's existence might display this deliberate crossover effect themselves; but even if they are unaware, they may simply respond to attorneys' efforts to obtain more in economic damages. Thus it is unclear just how effective caps really are.

Caps are also arbitrary in both their amount (e.g., why a $250,000 and not a $500,000 limit?) and, in some states, the cases to which they apply (e.g., why should compensation for a plaintiff injured by medical negligence be restricted, but not compensation for a plaintiff injured by vehicular negligence? Is the former's pain and suffering for the same injury somehow less?). Finally, despite claims that by reducing damage awards in medical malpractice cases, caps will reduce healthcare costs, adverse health outcomes, malpractice insurance rates, and the number and size of claims, the data fail to show much of a relationship between caps and any of these measures (Black et al., 2005; Donohue & Ho, 2007; Paik, Black, Hyman, & Silver, 2012; Yang, Studdert, Subramanian, & Mello, 2012). Thus, although caps might rectify a small number of genuinely excessive awards, on the whole they are a crude approach that lacks benefits to either litigants or society and potentially makes compensation less rather than more fair (i.e., by undercompensating severely injured plaintiffs).

Caps are essentially a legislative reduction in damages. There can also be a judicial reduction. Judges are generally loath to disturb a jury verdict, so the standard for *remittitur* is high. The wording used to describe the *remittitur* threshold varies across jurisdictions, but to be reduced, compensation must usually be "grossly" or "outrageously" excessive, demonstrate a clear "miscarriage of justice," or "shock the conscience" of the court (Baldus, MacQueen, & Woodworth, 1995; Epstein & Sharkey, 2012; *Snyder v. Phelps*, 2008). Consequently, *remittitur* is rare, occurring in approximately 5%–8% of cases in which the plaintiff wins (Hyman et al., 2007; Vidmar et al., 1998). An advantage of *remittitur* compared to caps is that judges can conduct a comparative analysis of awards in similar cases, thereby ensuring a reasonable degree of horizontal equity (Baldus et al., 1995). The selection of appropriate comparison cases, which is no easy feat, is critical.

Neither caps nor *remittitur* directly addresses the allegation that jury awards are excessive: "Correcting" the jury's award by reducing it, by statute or judicial discretion, does not change what the jury did. From a broader perspective, however, the judicious use of *remittitur* (as well as *additur*) preserves the advantages of the civil jury while limiting the risk that defendants will have to pay, and plaintiffs will receive, excessive awards. It can reduce vertical and horizontal inequity and thereby improve the overall fairness of the civil justice system (Baldus et al., 1995).

Excessiveness: A Summary

In the absence of clear metrics to determine what constitutes fair and reasonable compensation, especially for noneconomic damages, it is difficult to answer the question of whether compensatory awards are excessive. However, several lines of evidence imply that they are not. Plaintiffs win about 50% of the time, and the average compensation award is relatively modest, although the win rate and compensation both vary depending on the type of case, with plaintiffs standing to gain more money in cases with a lower probability of winning, such as medical malpractice. There is also little support for the notion that compensatory awards are increasing substantially over time; that is, above and beyond inflation and the ever-growing cost of medical care.

In part because of those costs, many plaintiffs, especially those with very grave injuries, are undercompensated. The risk of undercompensation is compounded further by the multiple sources of post-verdict haircuts, such as caps on damages, settlements for insurance policy limits, and judicial *remittitur*. To be sure, some plaintiffs receive more compensation than they deserve. But it is just as certain that some plaintiffs receive less than they deserve. On the whole we find very little, if any, support for the myth that juries' compensation awards are systematically excessive.

Are Compensatory Damage Awards (Un)predictable?

Just as there are different ways of addressing the excessiveness question, there are different ways of addressing whether compensation awards are predictable. One approach is to examine whether awards appropriately track relevant case characteristics and ignore irrelevant characteristics. The principal, and arguably sole, relevant characteristic is the severity of the plaintiff's injury: Plaintiffs who are hurt worse deserve greater compensation. Hence, vertical equity is a way of addressing whether awards are predictable. There is an infinite number of irrelevant characteristics: nonprobative features of the plaintiff (e.g., race, gender), the identity of the defendant (e.g., an individual or a corporation), the cause of the injury (e.g., an automobile accident or medical negligence), how much compensation the plaintiff requests, and so on.

It is debatable whether predictability is a desirable outcome in and of itself. Suppose, for example, that research showed a linear relationship between a plaintiff's height and compensation, such that taller plaintiffs receive greater compensation.[4] Height therefore predicts compensation, but since height is almost always irrelevant (we say "almost always" because one could envision a case where it is relevant, such as a basketball-playing plaintiff), this sort of predictability is presumably not a good thing. On the other hand, completely random damage awards—that is, with no identifiable predictors—would likely be even worse, and understanding the reliable predictors (desirable or not) is a necessary precursor to designing strategies to enhance "good" predictability and decrease "bad" predictability, such as instructing jurors not to consider a plaintiff's height.

An emphasis on the variables that affect compensation focuses mainly on vertical equity—that is, what factors predict who gets more than others. A second approach focuses more on horizontal equity, that is, variability for comparable injuries. As variability decreases, predictability increases. Statistically speaking, it is easier to predict the probable compensation for a particular plaintiff if we know that the range of compensation for plaintiffs with similar injuries is $180,000–$220,000 than if it is $50,000–$350,000. Some reform efforts are geared toward improving jurors' reliance on relevant factors as opposed to irrelevant ones, whereas others are geared toward reducing variability.

The usual sorts of jury research methods have been employed to study the predictability of damage awards: simulations that manipulate some relevant (e.g., injury severity) or irrelevant factor (e.g., defendant behavior, the *ad damnum*) to see if it makes a difference; archival studies that have coded for these same or similar case characteristics; and studies of jury deliberations (simulated or real) to see which factors jurors talk about during deliberation. Talking about a case feature does not necessarily mean that it influences jurors' decisions, nor does the failure to discuss some aspect of the case mean that it has no effect on their decisions. Nonetheless, the content of deliberations gives an idea of the things that jurors deem important. In the remainder of this section we give an overview of the processes by which relevant and irrelevant case characteristics can influence jurors' decisions, followed by a discussion of some of the factors that should and should not influence their compensation awards.

---

[4] The height effect would be confounded with a gender effect (i.e., on average men are taller than women), which we ignore for purposes of the present hypothetical example.

Damages Decision Making: General Processes

Not surprisingly, jury damage awards are not perfectly "clean" in the sense that they take into account factors that are legally relevant and ignore extraneous factors. In particular, their verdicts can show "fusion," which refers to jurors' tendency to let information that is relevant for one type of legal judgment influence another type of legal judgment for which it is irrelevant (e.g., Bornstein & Greene, 2011; Devine, 2012; Feigenson, 2000; Greene & Bornstein, 2003). Fusion can be seen in a variety of situations. For instance, jurors may consider the outcome of an accident (e.g., an injury to a plaintiff or injury to property) both in awarding compensation—where it *is* relevant— and in determining liability, where it *is not* relevant. If a plaintiff is injured in a car accident, the injury's severity is a key factor in setting any compensation that the plaintiff might receive, but it does not tell the jury who was at fault in the case. Nonetheless, research suggests that mock jurors reliably demonstrate fusion, allowing injury severity to influence both judgments (e.g., Bornstein, 1998; Greene, Johns, & Bowman, 1999; Robbennolt, 2000). In short, more severely injured plaintiffs arouse greater sympathy (Bright & Goodman-Delahunty, 2011), which can spill over into jurors' liability determinations (Bornstein, 1998).

Jurors also demonstrate fusion when they allow information on the plaintiff's comparative fault to influence their damage awards, awarding less compensation to plaintiffs who are partially negligent (Hammitt, Carroll, & Relles, 1985; Zickafoose & Bornstein, 1999). Zickafoose and Bornstein (1999) explain these findings in terms of "hindsight bias," whereby decision makers are unable to ignore, in hindsight, information that they already have (see also Arkes, 1989; Rachlinski, 1998; Smith & Greene, 2005). And, like all decision makers, jurors tend to demonstrate a phenomenon known as "confirmation bias"—that is, they seek out and remember information that is consistent with their verdict preference and scrutinize and reject information that is inconsistent with that preference (Carlson & Russo, 2001).

Thus, research suggests that the various stages in jurors' decision-making process—such as assessing negligence, awarding compensation, and awarding punitive damages—are not independent; rather, each of the judgments influences the others. Leading theories of juror decision making posit that fusion results from fundamental psychological processes that make it difficult, if not impossible, for jurors to compartmentalize their decisions (e.g., Bornstein & Greene, 2011; Devine, 2012). Two theories that point toward this same conclusion are the *story model* of juror decision making and *coherence-based reasoning*.

Hastie and his colleagues have proposed in several articles (for review, see Hastie, 2008; Pennington & Hastie, 1993) that early in a trial, jurors formulate a "story" relating to the facts in issue. As the trial proceeds, they selectively incorporate evidence that is consistent with their initial story and discount inconsistent evidence. Thus, judgments that are made at an earlier stage influence judgments made at a later stage. In most civil jury trials, the jury hears all of the evidence that pertains to all of the judgments they will be asked to make (e.g., liability and, if the defendant is held liable, compensation), and they make all of the decisions at the same time. This format is often referred to as a "unitary" or "all-issues" trial, as opposed to a bifurcated trial, in which the jury hears evidence relevant to one issue (e.g., liability), makes that decision, and then hears evidence relevant to the next issue (e.g., damages) and makes that decision (see Chapter 14). In in all-issues trial, the initial decision (e.g., the determination of negligence) would have great potential to color jurors' subsequent decision regarding damages. Essentially, jurors might judge an injury as relatively severe—and therefore award more money to a particular plaintiff—partly because they have already found the defendant liable. Conversely, knowing that the injury is relatively severe could influence their judgment of the defendant's liability. Consistent with this view, mock jurors often report that their liability judgments are motivated in part by their desire to compensate the plaintiff (Greene, Johns, & Bowman, 1999). In other words, fusion can run both ways: Simply finding a defendant liable can inflate the damage award, and injury severity can influence liability judgments.

A series of studies by Simon (2004) on coherence-based reasoning shows similarly that "fixing" some of these key decisions causes other, related decisions to be biased in the same direction. In other words, in situations where the liability decisions are made in favor of a plaintiff, the other decisions, regarding damages, would have a disproportionate tendency to be in the plaintiff's favor (i.e., larger) as well. Notably, this tendency to fuse judgments occurs outside the conscious awareness of jurors (Simon, 2004). In the remainder of this section, we discuss the extent to which factors that should and should not influence jurors' compensation awards actually do affect their verdicts.

Things That Should Affect Compensation

There is really only one overriding factor that should affect compensation: the severity of the plaintiff's injury. And, overwhelmingly, it does. Injury severity strongly predicts economic damages, noneconomic damages, and total damages. This has been demonstrated in experimental jury simulations (e.g., Bornstein, 1998; Feigenson, Park, & Salovey, 2001; Greene, Hayman, & Motyl, 2008; Greene, Johns, & Smith, 2001; Robbennolt, 2002b), meta-analysis (Robbennolt, 2000), and archival analyses of actual jury verdicts (e.g., Bovbjerg et al., 1991; Vidmar, 1995; Vidmar et al., 1998) across a wide range of case types. Plaintiffs who are hurt worse, by any metric, consistently receive more compensation on average than less severely injured plaintiffs. Malpractice trials have received an especially high degree of scrutiny. As in other kinds of cases, negligence judgments in malpractice jury trials are overwhelmingly determined by legally relevant factors like the strength of the evidence, and compensation awards track the severity of the plaintiff's injury (Landsman, 2008; Marder, 2005; Vidmar, 1995; Vidmar et al., 1998).

What makes an injury more or less severe? In economic terms, more severe injuries are associated with greater medical costs (treatment, hospitalization, rehabilitation, etc.) and lost income (e.g., time off work, disability). In noneconomic terms, more severe injuries cause greater pain, suffering, and related consequences. In a fine-grained analysis of what, exactly, constitutes noneconomic harm, Wissler and colleagues (1997, Experiment 1) presented mock jurors with five different cases whose plaintiffs displayed a range of injuries: a spinal fracture resulting in quadriplegia, a broken leg repaired by several operations and a cast, facial cuts leaving a permanent scar, permanent brain damage with extensive physical and mental impairment, and second- and third-degree burns that required skin grafts and produced scarring. Participants were told that the defendant in each case had been found liable, and the plaintiff's economic costs had been paid; their task was solely to assign noneconomic damages. They also rated each injury for its amount and duration of physical pain; amount and duration of mental suffering; degree of visibility, disability, and disfigurement; effect on everyday life; and overall severity.

Wissler et al. (1997) found that cases with more serious and permanent consequences (i.e., quadriplegia and brain damage) were perceived as more severe and were rated higher on most dimensions than the other cases. More interesting were the relationships among the various dimensions and between the dimensions and noneconomic damages. Disability, mental suffering, and disfigurement were correlated more strongly with the other dimensions than were visibility and pain. Taken together, the specific injury ratings (excluding effect on everyday life) explained 75% of the variance in ratings of overall injury severity, with perceived disability and amount and duration of mental suffering being the strongest predictors. These same dimensions, along with perceived disfigurement, were the strongest predictors of participants' compensation awards. The plaintiff's perceived disability made the largest single contribution to participants' awards. Wissler et al. replicated this same pattern of findings in a second study with a wider range of injuries, leading them to conclude that "Contrary to popular belief, pain and suffering awards were far from random. Instead, they were strongly affected by the severity and duration of the harm suffered by the plaintiff" (pp. 202–203). Simply put, more severe injuries—especially those associated with greater disability and mental suffering—garner greater compensation.

The relationship between injury severity and compensation illustrates vertical equity. Interestingly, however, the relationship is nonlinear, such that deceased plaintiffs—presumably those with the most severe injuries— receive less compensation than the most severely injured plaintiffs who survive their injuries (e.g., Bovbjerg et al., 1991; Vidmar et al., 1998). This "death dip" seems counterintuitive, but it makes normative sense: In many respects, the severely injured but living plaintiff will incur greater economic and noneconomic costs, especially in the future, than the deceased plaintiff (Greene & Bornstein, 2003). Put another way, there might be some fates (e.g., brain damage causing drastically impaired cognitive functioning) worse than death.

Consistent with the strong predictive value of injury severity, studies of jury deliberation show that jurors spend more time talking about the evidence, especially evidence related to the plaintiff's injuries, than anything else. This pattern has been demonstrated in mock jury studies (Greene et al., 2008), posttrial juror interviews (Mott et al., 2000), and analyses of actual jury deliberations (Diamond et al., 2011). For example, Mott and colleagues found that clear majorities of jurors reported considering the plaintiff's past and future medical expenses, factors relevant to lost income (e.g., salary, plaintiff's age, years of future earnings), and factors relevant to noneconomic damages (e.g., loss of consortium, pain and suffering). The seriousness of the plaintiff's injury or loss was the most frequently discussed factor: An average of 78% of the jurors in each case reported discussing or using injury severity during deliberation.

The powerful effect of injury severity on compensation is the good news. The not-so-good news is that the effect is so strong that it spills over onto other judgments, especially liability determinations. Defendants who allegedly caused more severe injuries are more likely to be held liable than when the plaintiff's injuries are relatively less severe, even when the defendant's actions are held constant (Greene & Bornstein, 2003; Robbennolt, 2000).

Things That Should Not Affect Compensation

Although plaintiffs who are hurt worse receive greater compensation than plaintiffs with less severe injuries, there is still considerable variability in compensation for plaintiffs with similar injuries—that is, there is a significant degree of horizontal inequity (Saks et al., 1997). Some of this inequity doubtless results from random variation and idiosyncratic differences among plaintiffs that crude measures of severity fail to capture; however, a portion of the inequity is likely due to the systematic influence of factors that should not affect compensation but nonetheless do. It is beyond the scope of the present chapter to review all of the extralegal factors that have been shown to influence damage awards (for a review, see Devine, 2012; Greene & Bornstein, 2003; Wissler et al., 2000). We discuss a few of these factors for illustrative purposes: a common feature of the plaintiff's case that is unrelated to how much compensation the plaintiff deserves (the *ad damnum*); defendant characteristics that might be relevant to some judgments that juries make but that are not relevant to compensation (the defendant's identity and conduct); and factors that the jury is supposed to ignore but might consider anyway (e.g., attorney fees and insurance).

As mentioned above, many (but not all) cases include an *ad damnum*. When such a value is present, jurors' damage awards tend to skew toward the *ad damnum*. In one of the early demonstrations of this phenomenon, Chapman and Bornstein (1996) presented mock jurors with a personal-injury plaintiff who requested $100, $20,000, $5 million, or $1 billion in non-economic damages for her injury, which consisted of ovarian cancer that led to major surgery, sterility, considerable pain and suffering, and a poor prognosis. The more the plaintiff asked for, the more she received in compensation; moreover, the more likely participants were to judge that the defendant had caused the plaintiff's injury. These results suggest that the mock jurors "anchored" on the *ad damnum* and used it as a starting point in determining their award.

In most demonstrations of anchoring, the numerical anchor is arbitrary and clearly unrelated to the judgment participants have to make (Tversky & Kahneman, 1974). In the civil jury context, jurors might reasonably assume that a plaintiff who requests more has actually been hurt worse; that is, they might use the *ad damnum* as a proxy for relevant information. However, research shows that this is not the case: Chapman and Bornstein (1996) found that the *ad damnum* did not affect participants' overall impression of the plaintiff or their perceptions of her medical expenses (which they were told were completely covered by insurance), suffering, honor, or interest in fighting injustice. In fact, asking for an exorbitant amount of damages creates negative perceptions of the plaintiff, making him or her seem more selfish and less generous (Chapman & Bornstein, 1996). Nonetheless, those same plaintiffs receive more compensation. In some cases a very large *ad damnum* can exert a boomerang effect, leading to such a negative impression of the plaintiff that compensation starts to diminish (Diamond et al., 2011; Marti & Wissler, 2000); but by and large, research supports the conclusion that "the more you ask for, the more you get" (Bornstein & Greene, 2011; Chapman & Bornstein, 1996; Hans & Reyna, 2011; Reyna et al., 2015). Essentially, the cognitive heuristic of anchoring trumps a negative impression.

The anchoring effect on damages is quite robust (Bornstein & Greene, 2011b), possibly because people are especially prone to anchoring when confronting novel judgment tasks or when they lack confidence in their decision-making abilities (Jacowitz & Kahneman, 1995). Both of these features (i.e., a novel task and low confidence) likely characterize civil jurors, most of whom are inexperienced and all of whom receive little guidance. Monetary anchors provided by the defendant (Duke, Hosch, & Duke, 2015; Greene, Downey, & Goodman-Delahunty, 1999; Marti & Wissler, 2000) or an expert witness (Raitz, Greene, Goodman, & Loftus, 1990) function in essentially the same way. It seems probable that anchors provided by one's fellow jurors could raise or lower the group's final award accordingly, although we know of no research that has examined this question.

Anchoring can even occur by varying not only the monetary amount but also the way in which that amount is expressed. For example, McAuliff and Bornstein (2010) presented mock jurors with a plaintiff who consistently asked for the same amount of damages for her pain and suffering over a 2-year period but who expressed it as a request for $10/hour, $240/day, $7,300/month, or a lump sum of $175,000 (this sort of breakdown is typically referred to as a *per diem* argument, as requesting a certain amount of compensation per day is most common; but other units of time may also be used). There was also a control condition containing no *ad damnum*. Participants awarded more when the plaintiff asked for $10/hour or a total of $175,000 than in the other two per diem conditions. This finding could reflect people's natural tendency to find some numbers, especially round ones like $10/hour, to be more meaningful than others (e.g., $240 and $7,300, despite ending in 0, are less common values; see Hans & Reyna, 2011). Anchoring effects are greater for relatively meaningful anchors (Reyna et al., 2015). As in the study by Chapman and Bornstein (1996), the plaintiff's perceived suffering did not vary across conditions.

Anchoring can also be an unintended consequence of caps. As discussed earlier, caps effectively reduce very large awards (i.e., awards that would exceed the cap). But what effect would they have on small awards? Theoretically, caps should have no effect whatsoever on awards that are below the cap threshold. However, Saks et al. (1997) found that if jurors are aware of the existence of a cap, it can actually pull noneconomic damages up for relatively mild or moderate injuries; that is, the cap functions as an anchor. Caps also increased the variability of the damage award for less severe injuries. Thus, a procedure that is explicitly designed to reduce variability and lower awards can have precisely the opposite effects in some cases; and it is worth reiterating that the vast majority of cases involve relatively moderate damages (Langton & Cohen, 2008; Ostrom et al., 1996).

Defendant characteristics, which should be irrelevant to compensation, can also affect compensatory damage awards. Despite a widespread perception that a "deep-pocket" effect exists, research generally fails to show that jurors force wealthier defendants to pay more compensation for the same injury than less well-endowed defendants (Greene & Bornstein, 2003; Greene et al., 2000; Robbennolt, 2002b).[5] Rather, there is an "anticorporate" effect, whereby larger damages are assessed against corporate than against individual defendants (e.g., Diamond & Salerno, 2013; Hans, 2000; MacCoun, 1996). Consistent with this finding, jurors with more pro-business and pro–tort reform attitudes award less compensation in cases involving corporate defendants (Hans, 2000). Of course, wealth and identity might go together: On average, corporations likely have greater financial resources than individuals. Roughly one-third of jurors report discussing whether the defendant was a corporation or could afford a large compensation award (Mott et al., 2000), suggesting that jurors might not cleanly distinguish between the two.

---

[5] One study actually found that judges were influenced more than jurors by the defendant's wealth in awarding compensation (Robbennolt, 2002b). We discuss judicial judgments in Chapter 13.

Nonetheless, when the two characteristics are separated, corporate status matters more than wealth (MacCoun, 1996).

Part of the reason for jurors' anti-corporate bias is an expectation that large corporations, compared to small, independently-owned companies or individuals, are seen as having less respect for consumers and more likely to cause harm to employees or consumers (Bornstein, 1994). In other words, people hold corporations to a higher standard and might therefore be inclined to view certain conduct by a corporation in a more negative light than the same conduct by an individual (Diamond & Salerno, 2013). Several studies have found that, independent of the defendant's identity, the defendant's conduct can exert an effect on compensatory damages, although the effect is somewhat inconsistent. For example, Greene and colleagues have conducted several jury simulation studies using different kinds of cases that manipulated the reprehensibility of the defendant's conduct (Cather, Greene, & Durham, 1996; Greene et al., 2008; Greene, Johns, & Smith, 2001; Greene, Woody, & Winter, 2000). For example, in the products liability case used by Cather et al., the defendant (a lawnmower manufacturer) either had conducted a great deal of safety research and been notified of only a few accidents similar to the plaintiff's, or had conducted less safety research and been notified of many similar accidents. The defendant's conduct did not affect the amount of compensation awarded to the plaintiff (it did affect punitive damages; we discuss this aspect of the research in Chapter 10). Subsequent studies found that evidence of the defendant's conduct affected compensation for some cases but not others (Greene et al., 2000), for relatively mild but not more severe injuries (Greene et al., 2001, 2008), and for deliberating juries as well as individual mock jurors (Greene et al., 2001, 2008). Other researchers have failed to find a direct effect of defendant conduct on compensation awards (e.g., Anderson & MacCoun, 1999; Feigenson et al., 2001), although compensation is correlated with mock jurors' perceptions of the defendant's blameworthiness (Feigenson et al., 2001). Thus there is some evidence that jurors fuse evaluations of the defendant's conduct—relevant to some judgments, such as liability and punitive damages—with their determination of compensatory damages. However, the fusion is subtle and apparently moderated by other variables, such as the type of case and characteristics of the plaintiff's injury.

The examples discussed in this section so far address jurors' inappropriate use of information that they have available to them. In the case of the *ad damnum*, the information is attorney argument, not evidence, whereas in the case of defendant characteristics, it is evidence that is relevant to some judgments but not to compensation. A final category of factors that jurors might rely on concerns taboo factors that are not presented at all, but about which jurors might speculate. This category includes things to which the courts routinely "blindfold" jurors, such as pretrial settlement negotiations, insurance, and attorneys' fees, in an effort to prevent them from considering those factors. In most jurisdictions, rules of evidence bar this information in all or nearly all circumstances. How much do jurors discuss these factors anyway?

The answer to this question is mixed. The bad news is that jury simulations (Greene et al., 2008), analyses of real-world deliberations (Diamond & Vidmar, 2001), and posttrial juror interviews (Mott et al., 2000) all show that forbidden factors arise frequently during deliberation. For example, an average of 77% of jurors interviewed after trial by Mott et al. reported discussing attorney fees, often going as far as specifying the amount (e.g., one-third of the total award); an average of 21% discussed whether the plaintiff's insurance would cover expenses, and 40% discussed the defendant's insurance situation. An analysis of actual jury deliberations likewise found that jurors frequently talked about these issues (Diamond & Vidmar, 2001). Diamond and Vidmar found that at least one juror raised the topic of attorney fees in 83% of the cases in their sample.

The good news is that most jurors who said they discussed the forbidden factors (e.g., attorney fees) claimed that they did not incorporate them into their final award decisions (Mott et al., 2000). Moreover, laboratory research has found little relationship between how much juries talk about forbidden factors and their verdicts (Greene et al., 2008). Nonetheless, the fact that jurors raise these issues as much as they do suggests that blindfolding is an unnecessary source of variability, in that awards could vary depending on whether jurors happen to bring knowledge or expectations about taboo topics into the deliberation room. Thus, "[t]he traditional approach of merely forbidding evidence on certain topics is of limited value when jurors draw on life experiences and peek through their blindfolds" (Diamond & Vidmar, 2001, p. 1915).

Improving Predictability

Several reforms have been proposed to improve predictability, especially by reducing variability. The most common approaches are damages schedules, special verdict forms, and clarified instructions. Proposals for schedules (or "scaling") differ in their particularities; the principal feature they share is providing jurors with benchmarks to help them arrive at a fair compensation award (Baldus et al., 1995; Bovbjerg, Sloan, & Blumstein, 1989; Diamond et al., 1998; Saks et al., 1997). There are multiple ways of constructing schedules, but the benchmarks usually take the form of suggested ranges for different kinds of injury, sometimes taking other plaintiff characteristics into account (e.g., age) or actual awards in other, similar cases. Providing this information to jurors can reduce some of the variability in their awards (Saks et al., 1997).

Although these findings show that schedules are a promising means of reducing variability and thereby enhancing predictability, they are problematic for a number of legal and practical reasons (Baldus et al., 1995). Given the substantial variability associated with the elements of noneconomic injury, a reasonably valid schedule would be extremely difficult to construct. For example, an injury causing nerve damage to several fingers on the nondominant hand would likely cause significantly more suffering and lost enjoyment of life to a plaintiff whose primary hobby is playing the piano than to a plaintiff whose primary hobby is reading. Setting the appropriate dollar ranges and finding representative comparison cases—especially ones that are acceptable to both the plaintiffs' and defense bar—would be challenging. And schedules simultaneously increase the complexity of jurors' task, by requiring them to assimilate additional, somewhat technical information, while also reducing the jury's critical factfinding role.

A less intrusive approach would be for judges to use special verdicts or interrogatories (i.e., posing a series of questions to the jury that require a concrete finding of fact), which are often used in criminal trials as well as in the liability phase of civil trials (Marder, 2005). This sort of framework would help jurors apply "guided discretion" in much the same manner that they do in capital cases, such as determining aggravating and mitigating factors and future dangerousness (see Chapter 11). Relatively little research has been conducted on special verdicts, but what research has been done suggests that they can be beneficial in terms of focusing jurors' attention on legally appropriate factors and lessening their reliance on inappropriate factors (Wiggins & Breckler, 1990). A potential downside to special verdicts, especially ones that require jurors to itemize discrete components of compensation, is that they may lead to higher awards than general (i.e., "lump sum") verdicts. Some research has found this to be the case (Poser et al., 2003; Wiggins & Breckler, 1990). As we have argued elsewhere in this chapter, larger awards are not necessarily worse; nor are they necessarily better. The key question is whether special verdicts facilitate jurors' understanding and application of the law and enable them to do a better job of matching compensation to plaintiffs' deservingness. Zickafoose and Bornstein (1999) found that they do: Requiring mock jurors to itemize the different categories of damages (i.e., lost earnings, medical expenses, bodily harm, and pain and suffering) reduced the extent to which they inappropriately discounted compensation to partially negligent plaintiffs. Future research is needed to confirm this finding and compare the pros and cons of different types of special verdicts (e.g., those using itemization versus those posing interrogatories).

Special verdicts should not be confused with providing jurors a third verdict option, which occurs in certain criminal contexts. The Scottish criminal justice system, for example, allows for a verdict of "not proven" instead of "guilty" or "innocent," and some American jurisdictions allow for a verdict of guilty but mentally ill (Hope et al., 2008; Smithson, Deady, & Gracik, 2007). Special verdict forms, on the other hand, maintain the traditional verdict options but structure the verdict form so as to minimize juror confusion. An advantage of special verdict forms is that they provide structure and guidance to the task of determining damages, where such structure is typically lacking.

Enhanced jury instructions—highlighting the factors that jurors should both consider and ignore in awarding damages—might be able to accomplish this same goal, and some research has explored the possibility (see, generally, Wissler et al., 2000). For example, Wissler, Rector, and Saks (2001) presented mock jurors with a vehicular negligence case that varied the degree of the defendant's responsibility (specifically, how much over the speed limit he was driving and whether he was drunk) and the content of the jury instructions. In the control instruction condition, participants received only general instructions regarding liability and defining the elements of damages. In the "don't discount" condition, participants were additionally told not to let their feelings about the defendant influence their award, and not to reduce their award if they felt the defendant was not completely responsible. The "don't punish" instructions also told participants not to let their feelings influence their award, and not to increase their compensation in order to punish the defendant.[6] In the control condition, noneconomic damage awards (but not economic damages) were higher in the high- than in the low-defendant responsibility condition, demonstrating fusion—that is, mock jurors' evaluation of the defendant's conduct (an irrelevant consideration) influenced their compensation awards. However, this effect was reduced in the two special instruction conditions, especially with the "don't discount" instructions. This result is encouraging, as it suggests that instructions can aid jurors in attending to relevant case characteristics while ignoring irrelevant ones. Similar instructions could target other sources of potential bias, such as the *ad damnum*, explicitly informing jurors that it is merely a suggestion, not evidence, and can therefore be disregarded (Diamond et al., 2011).

Revised instructions are not a panacea by any means. Comprehension of revised instructions is still less than one would desire (often considerably less; see Chapter 14), and rewriting instructions fails to address structural obstacles inherent in the trial process that might impede juror performance (Diamond, Murphy, & Rose, 2012; Wissler et al., 2000). Nonetheless, in light of the limited guidance and high degree of vagueness in civil jury instructions (at least compared to criminal jury instructions), they would be a good place to start. "If [instructions] were used to provide jurors with additional information about determining damages, then jurors would try to follow these instructions, just as they try to follow all of the instructions that the judge gives them" (Marder, 2005, p. 1287, footnote omitted).

Predictability: A Summary

Jury compensation awards are predictable insofar as they systematically reflect variation in identifiable and measurable variables. Much of this

---

[6] A fourth instruction condition consisted of a bifurcation manipulation, which we discuss in Chapter 14.

predictability shows jurors' reliance on legally relevant factors like injury severity, which is the single best predictor of compensatory damages. However, some of the predictability betrays the influence of an array of extralegal factors, such as the *ad damnum*, defendant characteristics, and forbidden factors like attorney fees. To a large extent these extralegal influences are symptomatic of fusion in jurors' decision making. Factors that are relevant to one type of judgment, such as liability or punitive damages, have a tendency to infiltrate other judgments, like compensation, for which they are technically irrelevant. It is also the case that the "good" predictability and the "bad" predictability, taken together, do not explain all of the variance in awards; there is a substantial amount of unexplained, and likely random, variation.

This variation introduces a considerable degree of horizontal inequity, which must be weighed against the substantial vertical equity reflected in the strong correlation between injury severity and awards. It is highly probable that much of the inequity results from the "precious little guidance" (Greene & Bornstein, 2000) that jurors receive in awarding damages. Techniques that have potential for improving predictability exist, such as damages schedules, special verdicts, and enhanced instructions. Unfortunately, little research on these reforms has been conducted, and they have not yet been widely adopted.

Conclusions and Recommendations

Jurors face a daunting task in awarding compensation. It is clear that many plaintiffs, like Albert Snyder, have suffered grievous injury; but it is much less clear how much compensation they deserve, especially for their noneconomic injuries. In arriving at a specific compensatory damage award, jurors might not engage in explicit calculations, but their approach to quantification is, for the most part, rational and evidence-based. Thus there is little support for the claim that jury damage awards are either excessive or unpredictable. This is not to say, however, that there is no room for improvement. Jurors are susceptible to fusion in determining compensation, and extralegal factors can influence their awards.

A number of procedural reforms exist to reduce very large (and potentially, though not necessarily, excessive) awards and to increase predictability: caps, *additur/remittitur*, schedules, special verdict forms, and revised instructions. Although caps on noneconomic damages reduce awards, they are not tailored to individual case characteristics and do little to enhance predictability beyond making otherwise large awards predictably lower; they can also lead to undercompensation in some cases and, paradoxically, can elevate otherwise small awards as well as economic damages. Award reduction by judge, rather than by legislature, has a couple of advantages: Judges can take individual case characteristics into account, and they have knowledge of comparable cases. Thus we favor a system of *additur/remittitur* over caps, as a method of fine-tuning awards and correcting rare instances of grossly inappropriate awards. However, like caps, such a system does nothing to improve jury verdicts, per se.

Unlike judges, jurors lack knowledge of comparable cases. Damages schedules are a means of giving them that knowledge, and they are beneficial in terms of reducing variability. However, schedules are not very practical, at least at this point in time. The remaining reforms—special verdict forms and revised instructions—are more feasible, and there is some evidence that they can improve jurors' decision making. Thus we propose giving jurors more and clearer guidance, in the form of revised instructions and special verdict forms, in conjunction with a system of judicial (and judicious) *additur/remittitur.*

10

Punitive Damage Awards Are Excessive and Unpredictable

"Punitive damages are the hammer of civil justice"
(Scheiner, 1991, p. 142).

Jurors do many things: They determine criminal and civil responsibility, they award civil compensation to injured plaintiffs, and they are occasionally involved in other areas of law, such as family court and civil commitment hearings. One thing that they rarely do, however, is punish. In most jurisdictions, jurors do not determine criminal sentences except in capital cases. Yet even in jurisdictions with the death penalty (currently 31 states and the federal courts), capital trials are rare, and only a small fraction of murder defendants receive death sentences (Blume, Eisenberg, & Wells, 2004). Nonetheless, capital trials attract enormous attention from all branches of government, the media, and special interest groups (e.g., the National Coalition to Abolish the Death Penalty).

Jury-administered civil punishment, in the form of punitive damages, is likewise rare. Juries award punitive damages in only 5%–8% of cases in which the plaintiff wins (e.g., Daniels & Martin, 1990; Eisenberg et al., 1997; Langton & Cohen, 2008; Vidmar & Hans, 2007), leading one observer to conclude that "Punitive damages awards are a teaspoon-sized drop in an ocean of civil litigation" (Rustad, 1992, p. 37). They are especially infrequent in the most common kinds of civil litigation, such as vehicular negligence. Yet despite their rarity, punitive damages, like capital sentencing, receive a great deal of attention from appellate courts (including the United States Supreme Court), state and federal legislatures, special interest groups (e.g., the American Association for Justice, the American Tort Reform Association [ATRA]), and the public.

Why is there so much attention to jury punishment if it is such an infrequent phenomenon? Following the previous chapter on compensatory damages, the present chapter answers that question by reviewing empirical evidence and reform efforts on punitive damages in civil cases, and Chapter 11 addresses jury punishment in criminal cases. Before examining punitive damages in detail, we offer some preliminary observations on juries and punishment, contrasting juries' tasks in civil and criminal trials.

General Thoughts on Juries and Punishment

One reason why punitive damages capture the public imagination is that they receive a great deal of media attention. MacCoun (2006; Bailis & MacCoun, 1996) has shown that very large damage awards, many of which include punitive damages, receive extensive media coverage, whereas more mundane cases with smaller verdicts tend to be ignored. Controversial areas of law that are closely associated with the tort reform movement, such as products liability and medical malpractice, also receive disproportionate media attention (Bailis & MacCoun, 1996; Robbennolt & Studebaker, 2003). This skewed depiction of the civil justice system may be understandable from a media marketing perspective, but it can produce an erroneous impression of the true state of affairs—that is, an expectation that large awards and whopping punitive damages are common. A false impression can influence jurors' verdicts if consumers of biased media representations wind up on juries (Robbennolt & Studebaker, 2003; see the section on juror characteristics below). It can also exacerbate the situation by leading potential plaintiffs to be more likely to file lawsuits in expectation of huge wins and potential defendants to be overly cautious in their behavior (e.g., in product development or medical treatment; see Bornstein & Robicheaux, 2008; Robbennolt & Studebaker, 2003). Issues associated with the death penalty—heinous crimes, capital trials, death row conditions, and executions—likewise receive substantial media coverage (Haney, 2005).

In addition to evidence that media coverage contributes to the tail of the award distribution wagging the dog (MacCoun, 2006), factors inherent in the process of punishment make jury-determined punishment particularly noteworthy. Punishment is an emotional process involving an array of psychological, social, and cultural forces (e.g., Duckitt, 2009). Whether it involves grounding a child, sanctioning an employee, sentencing a defendant to death, or awarding punitive damages, it is very hard to remain dispassionate while punishing another. It is likewise emotional for the punished party—more so than simply having to make restitution—owing to the public censure aspect of punishment. As we discuss in Chapter 12, the emotional component of punishment might or might not be desirable. But regardless of whether legal guidelines carve out a role for emotion in punishment by jury, the emotional element helps to explain why juries' punishment decisions are such a contentious issue.

Another reason for the high degree of attention to jury punishment is that, by reserving this function of juries for the most serious criminal and civil offenses, the stakes are almost unimaginably high. In capital cases it is, quite literally, a matter of life and death. In civil cases it is only a matter of money, but the sums can be astronomical, amounting to billions of dollars— enough to bankrupt sizeable and fiscally sound companies. Punitive damages do not, of course, have to be large, and many punitive awards are quite modest (Langton & Cohen, 2008). Nonetheless, the vast majority of the largest damage awards include a substantial punitive damages component (Hersch & Viscusi, 2004).

Thus, criminal and civil punishment are similar in that they are both emotional, high-stakes decisions; yet in many other respects, they are fundamentally different. For example, contrast the situations of two defendants: Gregory Russeau and Takeda Pharmaceutical. A Texas jury sentenced Russeau to death by lethal injection for the 2001 robbery and beating death of James Syvertson, a 75-year-old auto mechanic.[1] Russeau's jury had to decide a number of issues, most notably whether he posed a risk of future danger (they decided "yes") and whether there were any mitigating circumstances that made him less deserving of the death penalty (they decided "no"; *Russeau v. Stephens*, 2014). Gregory Russeau was executed on June 18, 2015—the most recent execution in the United States at the time of this writing.

One state to the east, a federal jury in Louisiana awarded plaintiff Terrence Allen $1,475,000 in compensation and $9 billion in punitive damages—reportedly the seventh-largest punitive damages award in American history—in his lawsuit against Takeda Pharmaceutical and Eli Lilly. The jury allocated 75% of the responsibility for compensatory damages against Takeda and 25% against Lilly ($1,106,250 and $368,750, respectively); for punitive damages, they assessed $6 billion against Takeda and $3 billion against Lilly (Fackler & Pollack, 2014). The jury found that the companies' diabetes drug had caused Allen's bladder cancer and that they had misled patients, doctors, and regulators about the drug's risks (Fackler & Pollack, 2014; Feeley, 2014). The judge remitted the punitive portion of the award to $36.8 million, a 99.6% reduction (Feeley, 2014). Takeda's jury had to decide a number of issues, most notably whether the drug's warning label was adequate (no) and whether the company's actions were reprehensible (yes).

Clearly, deciding whether a convicted murderer poses a risk of future danger is very different from deciding whether two international pharmaceutical companies acted reprehensibly. In addition, the criminal and civil juries considered categorically different forms of punishment (execution/imprisonment vs. a financial penalty) and applied substantially different standards of proof (beyond a reasonable doubt vs. preponderance of the evidence).

---

[1] Russeau was actually sentenced to death twice, as his first sentence was vacated on appeal (*Russeau v. State*, 2005).

Nonetheless, juries reached verdicts in both cases and many more like them. Granting these powers to juries seems to suggest a belief that they can be fair in administering punishment, including punishment of this magnitude.

However, both capital sentencing (see Chapter 11) and punitive damages have been frequent targets of reform efforts (e.g., Hersch & Viscusi, 2004; Sunstein et al., 2002). As with compensatory damages (see Chapter 9), there exists a popular belief that juries' punitive damage awards are excessive and unpredictable—we address this belief later in the chapter. Although there are also concerns about how well juries can determine criminal sentences, reform efforts in the capital sentencing domain concentrate more on abolishing the death penalty as a form of punishment or helping jurors do better by revising jury instructions (see Chapter 14). In contrast, reform efforts in the context of civil punishment are geared primarily toward curtailing juries' discretion through policies like caps and remittitur, or even removing punishment from civil juries' purview altogether (see Chapter 13). Because of these disparate beliefs about juries' ability to determine civil and criminal punishment, as well as the fundamental differences between the tasks themselves, we discuss civil and criminal punishment separately.

The Punitive Damages Paradox

The Scheiner (1991) quotation at the head of the chapter, which likens punitive damages to a hammer, exemplifies their purpose—to punish, to hurt. In the United States they are allowed under at least some circumstances in nearly all state and federal courts (Robbennolt, 2002a). Louisiana, Massachusetts, Nebraska, New Hampshire, and Washington are the only states to prohibit them completely. When permitted, punitive damages are reserved for instances where the defendant has acted with outrageous, reckless, willful, or wanton indifference to the rights of others. For example, the Fifth Circuit Court of Appeals' pattern jury instructions state:

> You may, [in addition to compensatory damages], award punitive damages if you find that Defendant [name] acted with malice or with reckless indifference to the rights of others. One acts with malice when one purposefully or knowingly violates another's rights or safety. One acts with reckless indifference to the rights of others when one's conduct, under the circumstances, manifests a complete lack of concern for the rights or safety of another. . . . The purpose of punitive damages is to punish and deter, not to compensate. Punitive damages serve to punish a defendant for malicious or reckless conduct and, by doing so, to deter others from engaging in similar conduct in the future. You are not required to award punitive damages (Committee on Pattern Jury Instructions, District Judges Association, Fifth Circuit, 2014, §15.7).

In this context, by "punishment" courts generally mean retribution, as opposed to deterrence (*Cooper Industries, Inc. v. Leatherman Tool Group, Inc.*, 2001). Thus, punitive damages serve mainly to make the defendant suffer (i.e., retribution) and to ensure that neither the defendant nor similarly situated others will act this way in the future (i.e., specific and general deterrence). These goals are clearly very different from the restitutive purpose of compensatory damages.

Punitive damages are something of a paradox. On one hand, they are the focus of a large number of jury reform efforts, making them perhaps the single most controversial topic with regard to civil juries (e.g., Bornstein & Greene, 2003; Bornstein & Robicheaux, 2008; Sharkey, 2003); many observers argue that only judges, rather than juries, should be empowered to award punitive damages (e.g., Hersch & Viscusi, 2004; Sunstein et al., 2002); and they have received significant scrutiny from the United States Supreme Court (e.g., *BMW v. Gore*, 1996; *State Farm Mutual Automobile Insurance Co. v. Campbell*, 2003). On the other hand, study after study shows that they are quite rare, occurring in roughly 5%–8% of civil trials with winning plaintiffs (e.g., Bornstein, Robicheaux, & Thimsen, 2009; Devine et al., 2001; Eisenberg et al., 1997; Langton & Cohen, 2008). As plaintiffs win approximately 50% of the time (with variation across case types; see Chapter 9), juries therefore award punitive damages in only 3%–4% of all civil jury trials. Part of the reason for their low frequency is that, owing to the typically higher burden of proof for recovering punitive damages (discussed more below), most plaintiffs do not seek them. Langton and Cohen (2008) found that only 1,832 plaintiffs in 26,948 cases (6.8%) sought punitive damages; of those, 700 (38.4%) received them. Plaintiffs seeking punitive damages were more likely to get them in contract cases (44.6%) than in tort cases (30.9%).

The question, then, is why there is so much concern—arguably a disproportionate concern—about punitive damages. This question has no easy answer, but we believe it has multiple components. First and foremost is the sheer magnitude of some punitive damage awards. Some awards, such as the $9 billion punitive verdict against Takeda discussed previously, are eye-poppingly large. Enough punitive damage awards exceed $100 million that this subset of "blockbuster" awards has received focused empirical analysis (e.g., Hersch & Viscusi, 2004). Large-scale, low-frequency events are noteworthy (MacCoun, 2006). Earthquakes do not happen often either, but they grab our attention when they do.

A major reason some punitive damage awards are so large is that punitive damages in general—and blockbuster punitive awards in particular—are more likely to be levied against corporate than individual defendants (Eisenberg et al., 1997). Larger awards against corporate defendants may be justified, though they are not necessarily; if corporations are, on average, wealthier or less likely to respond to adverse trial outcomes than individuals, then they might require larger awards to accomplish the goal of deterrence. Businesses also often argue that very large punitive awards have a negative effect on business, as in interfering with innovative product development and reducing profits and market incentives (the extent to which they actually do so is questionable; see Palmer & Sanders, 2010). The greater involvement of corporate defendants leads to the second reason why punitive damages feature so prominently in the tort reform debate—corporations have the financial resources, organizational structure, and political influence to advance an agenda in the debate (Bornstein & Robicheaux, 2008); that is, they have a "dog in the fight."

Third, punitive damages raise complex issues of fairness. Although their principal purpose is punishment, they usually go mostly or entirely to the plaintiff, thereby providing an unfair form of "supercompensation." There are legitimate reasons for this policy: Punitive damages provide an incentive for plaintiffs to file lawsuits against defendants who have acted recklessly but caused relatively little compensable damage (at least individually; the collective damages aggregated across potential or actual plaintiffs might be substantial; see *BMW v. Gore*, 1996). According to this logic, punitive damages might constitute a windfall, but the possibility of such a windfall is necessary for plaintiffs to pursue certain defendants in the civil justice system. In *Gore*, for example, the plaintiff, Dr. Ira Gore, Jr., sued BMW because the new car he purchased for $40,000 had been slightly damaged and repainted. The company did not disclose this information, and he argued that the nondisclosure constituted fraud and that the damage reduced the car's resale value. BMW acknowledged the nondisclosure policy, and Gore introduced evidence that a large number of vehicles were affected. A jury awarded Gore $4,000 in compensation and $4 million in punitive damages (reduced by the Alabama Supreme Court to $2 million, but still adjudged grossly excessive by the United States Supreme Court). If he had only been able to recover the somewhat modest compensation of $4,000, Gore would very likely have been disinclined to undertake the time and expense of going to trial, and BMW could have continued its deceptive practice with impunity.

Fourth, punishment is an emotional process. Emotion is explicitly a part of sentencing in capital cases (e.g., determining the aggravating factor of heinousness; see Chapters 11 and 12); it is explicitly a part of civil punishment as well. To award punitive damages, jurors must conclude that a defendant's actions were willful, wanton, reprehensible, or reckless (the precise terminology varies depending on the jurisdiction). That kind of behavior naturally elicits in jurors a sense of moral outrage (Kahneman, Schkade, & Sunstein, 1998). In Chapter 12 we consider whether jurors' emotional response facilitates or interferes with their ability to follow the law. For present purposes, the emotional aspect of punitive damages helps to explain why they are such a heated and controversial topic.

The frequent claims that juries' punitive damage awards are erratic (e.g., Kahneman et al., 1998) and that judges would do better (e.g., Hersch & Viscusi, 2004) reflect a strong undercurrent of belief that juries cannot determine civil punishment fairly. Can they? Our examination of this question parallels our approach to compensatory damage awards in Chapter 9, namely, whether punitive damage awards are excessive or unpredictable. As discussed in the previous chapter, excessiveness and unpredictability are independent attributes: Awards can meet the criteria for one, both, or neither.

Are Punitive Damage Awards Excessive?

The United States Supreme Court has been very clear that the Fourteenth Amendment's Due Process clause prohibits "grossly excessive" punitive damage awards (e.g., *BMW v. Gore*, 1996, p. 568; see also *Philip Morris USA v. Williams*, 2007; *State Farm Mutual Automobile Insurance Co. v. Campbell*, 2003). The tricky part is in determining what constitutes "grossly excessive" or even "plain old excessive." As with compensation, it is not simply a function of the awards' absolute size. In *BMW v. Gore*, the Court identified three guideposts for courts to use in reviewing punitive awards for possible excessiveness: the reprehensibility of the defendant's conduct, the relationship between the plaintiff's actual or potential harm (i.e., the amount of compensation) and the punitive award, and the relationship between the punitive award and available civil penalties. These guideposts, which have been reaffirmed in the Court's subsequent punitive damages jurisprudence, indicate that larger awards are justified the more reprehensible the defendant's actions, the more severe the plaintiff's injuries, and the greater any other civil sanctions. Because punitive damages serve a deterrent as well as a retributive purpose, the defendant's wealth is generally a relevant factor also, and most states instruct juries accordingly (Epstein & Sharkey, 2012). For example, the Fifth Circuit's pattern instructions tell jurors that the three guideposts "should guide you in fixing the proper amount," and then go on to add that "You may consider the financial resources of Defendant [name] in fixing the amount of punitive damages" (Committee on Pattern Jury Instructions, District Judges Association, Fifth Circuit, 2014, §15.7).

Although the *Gore* guideposts are explicitly used to determine excessiveness on a case-by-case basis, when considered in the context of the population of punitive damage awards, they really speak more to predictability. Do the defendant's conduct, the defendant's wealth, and the plaintiff's injuries predict punitive damage awards? Thus we address the role of these factors in the following section. In the remainder of this section, we describe research on the frequency and size of punitive damage awards in general, the extent to which they vary across case types, and whether they are increasing over time.

The frequency of punitive damage awards varies considerably across case types (Bornstein et al., 2009; Devine et al., 2001; Greene & Bornstein, 2003). They are most common for intentional torts, employment-related torts, fraud, and slander/libel, whereas they are relatively infrequent in vehicular negligence, medical malpractice, and products liability cases (e.g., Eisenberg et al., 1997; Rustad, 1998). For example, slander and libel plaintiffs receive punitive damages in 30% of cases (Rustad, 1998). These case types differ in a number of respects; one important distinction is that those where punitive damages are relatively common (e.g., employment, fraud, slander/libel) tend to involve financial losses, whereas the ones with fewer punitive damage awards (e.g., vehicular negligence, malpractice) more often involve personal injuries (i.e., physical and psychological harm). Research supports this contrast: Punitive damages are more common in cases with financial injuries than in cases with personal injuries (Moller, Pace, & Carroll, 1999). Certain classes of defendants are also overrepresented in the population of blockbuster awards, with companies in the energy and chemical industry (25%), finance and insurance industry (23%), and pharmaceutical and healthcare industry (16%) most likely to find themselves on the paying end of extreme punitive damage awards (Del Rossi & Viscusi, 2010).

Viscusi and colleagues have conducted several studies of blockbuster cases, that is, those with punitive damage awards of at least $100 million (Del Rossi & Viscusi, 2010; Hersch & Viscusi, 2004; Viscusi, 2004). Their most recent analysis included 100 blockbuster awards from 1985—the first time an award exceeded the $100 million mark—through 2008. Such awards are obvious candidates for excessiveness. However, an emphasis on blockbuster awards obscures the fact that the distribution is severely positively skewed. Like compensatory awards, most punitive damage awards are modest (e.g., Ostrom et al., 1996). For example, an analysis of state court data from 1991–1992 found that the median award was $38,000 (Ostrom et al., 1996). In a more recent analysis (of 2005 trial data), Langton and Cohen (2008) found that the median punitive damage award was $64,000, although 27% of the awards exceeded $250,000, and 13% were $1 million or more. They also found that the size of the award varied depending on case type. It was highest for tortious interference (a type of contract case; Mdn = $6,888,000) and medical malpractice (Mdn = $2,835,000; the next highest median award was for employment discrimination, at $115,000). However, punitive damages were rarely sought in these kinds of cases and even more rarely awarded (e.g., malpractice plaintiffs who sought punitive damages received them only 10.7% of the time, much less than the overall recovery rate of 30.9% for tort plaintiffs seeking punitive damages). Punitive damage awards are also higher in federal than in state courts (Eisenberg, Goerdt, Ostrom, & Rottman, 1996).

Although there is some evidence that the sheer number of very large awards is increasing (Hersch & Viscusi, 2004; Viscusi, 2004), these awards constitute a tiny fraction of the total number of punitive damage awards. Consequently, despite the presence of outliers, the overall magnitude of punitive damage awards—like the magnitude of compensatory awards—has remained stable and is not increasing disproportionately over time when adjusted for inflation (Eisenberg et al., 2002, 2006; Eisenberg, Hans, & Wells, 2008). Moreover, the ratio of punitive to compensatory damages is actually decreasing (Del Rossi & Viscusi, 2010). Del Rossi and Viscusi compared blockbuster awards before and after the 2003 *State Farm* decision. In *State Farm* the Supreme Court declined "to impose a bright-line ratio which a punitive damages award cannot exceed" (p. 425), but held that "in practice, few awards exceeding a single-digit ratio between punitive and compensatory damages, to a significant degree, will satisfy due process" (p. 425). This language has been widely interpreted as establishing a 10:1 ratio ceiling for most cases. In the blockbuster cases, the pre–*State Farm* mean ratio was 717.7, compared to a post–*State Farm* mean of 14.3 (the medians were 12.3 and 2.0, respectively; Del Rossi & Viscusi, 2010; see Eisenberg & Heise, 2011, for more equivocal evidence of a *State Farm* effect).

The variability in the frequency and size of punitive damage awards across case types could simply reflect the fact that certain classes of defendants (at least certain classes of defendants who are hauled into court) are more likely to act reprehensibly than others, cause greater damage, and require larger damage awards to achieve the goals of retribution and deterrence. It does not necessarily indicate that awards against some defendants are excessive. In addition, punitive damage awards overall do not appear to be increasing over time. The number of very large awards is increasing, but even those awards are adhering better to legal guidelines (i.e., a moderate punitive-to-compensatory ratio) now than in the past. Thus there is little evidence for the claim that juries' punitive damage awards are excessive.

Are Punitive Damage Awards (Un)predictable?

Eisenberg et al. (1997) anticipate the answer to the predictability question in the title of their article: "The Predictability of Punitive Damages." As we discussed in the previous chapter with respect to compensatory damages, there are positive and negative aspects to predictability. Predictability is desirable if appropriate factors (e.g., reprehensible conduct) predict punitive damages, but it is more problematic (albeit useful to know) if inappropriate factors (e.g., jurors' attitudes) are predictive. Here we review research on the role of the defendant's conduct and characteristics, the severity of the plaintiff's injury, and juror characteristics.

Defendant's Conduct and Characteristics

Several experiments have investigated the effect of the defendant's conduct on mock jurors' punitive damage awards (these same studies also measured compensation awards; see Chapter 9). Judges instruct jurors to consider reprehensible conduct by the defendant in awarding punitive damages, and they do. Compared to defendants who acted in a more benign fashion, defendants who behaved reprehensibly are more likely to have to pay *any* punitive damages (Anderson & MacCoun, 1999), as well as to pay larger awards (Cather et al., 1996; Greene et al., 2000; Greene, Coon, & Bornstein, 2001). This pattern held for several different kinds of tort cases—personal injury, products liability, insurance bad faith, and automobile negligence—but not for medical malpractice (Cather et al., 1996; Greene et al., 2000; Greene, Coon, & Bornstein, 2001).

Consistent with these studies showing an effect of reprehensibility, mock jurors report relying primarily on defendant-focused factors, such as specific and general deterrence, punishment, and ability to pay (Shea Adams & Bourgeois, 2006). They consider the defendant's actions more than any other factor in deciding on punitive damages, and those who say that the defendant's conduct was the most influential factor make higher awards than those who report being most influenced by some other factor (Daftary-Kapur & Berry, 2010). Some research suggests that they are more interested in punishing the defendant's actions (i.e., relying on the goal of retribution) than in deterring the defendant (Greene, Coon, & Bornstein, 2001; Hastie, Schkade, & Payne, 1999a), although large numbers of mock jurors weigh the two goals equally (Hastie et al., 1999a; Robicheaux & Bornstein, 2010). Of course, what jurors report relying on is not a perfect indicator of what they actually do rely on, but these findings suggest that in awarding punitive damages, they concentrate mainly on legally relevant issues like deterrence and punishment (i.e., retribution). Deliberation studies show, however, that a nontrivial minority of deliberating juries fail to discuss legally relevant factors related to the defendant's conduct, such as malice and recklessness, in deciding whether to award punitive damages (Hastie, Schkade, & Payne, 1998).

Mock jurors also respond appropriately to evidence of the defendant's stated or presumed wealth (e.g., as a function of company size) in awarding punitive damages (Greene et al., 2000; Kahneman et al., 1998; Robbennolt, 2002b). For example, Robbennolt presented jury-eligible citizens with a case in which the plaintiff, an HMO patient, experienced side effects and was hospitalized after taking a medication prescribed by the HMO. The case varied in terms of the plaintiff's injury severity (low potential/low actual harm, high potential/low actual harm, or high potential/high actual harm) and the defendant's wealth (low or high, operationalized as a net worth of $11 million or $611 million). Participants were more likely to award punitive damages against the relatively wealthy defendant than against the less wealthy defendant, and their awards were also larger.

Because defendant wealth is difficult to measure and code in real cases, archival analyses of punitive damage awards typically use defendants' corporate status as a proxy for wealth, assuming that corporations, on average, have greater financial resources than individuals. By this measure also, defendant characteristics matter: Punitive awards are higher against corporate than against individual defendants (Eisenberg et al., 1997), and nearly all blockbuster awards involve a corporate defendant (Del Rossi & Viscusi, 2010).

Unlike individual defendants, corporate defendants cannot die (though they can, of course, go bankrupt or out of business altogether, which is probably the equivalent of death in the corporate world). A curious anomaly in the civil punishment arena is that some jurisdictions allow punitive damages against the estates of deceased defendants, on the rationale that such damages continue to serve the goal of general deterrence (most jurisdictions do not allow punitive damages to survive the defendant's death; Robicheaux & Bornstein, 2010). When it is allowed, jurors are just as likely to award punitive damages against a deceased defendant as against a live one, even when the defendant has been severely injured in the tortious event. They also assess equivalent sums of money against living and deceased defendants (Robicheaux & Bornstein, 2010). This seems to go against the law's intent, as requiring deceased defendants to pay punitive damages might accomplish general deterrence, but it cannot accomplish retribution (apart from punishing the defendant's heirs) or specific deterrence. In contrast, requiring living defendants to pay punitive damages can accomplish all of these goals. Despite awarding comparable amounts in the two situations, jurors are somewhat sensitive to this distinction. When the defendant has died, they report being motivated primarily by the goal of deterring others, whereas they also consider retribution and specific deterrence in the case of a living defendant (Robicheaux & Bornstein, 2010).

Injury Severity and the Punitive–Compensatory Relationship

The relationship between injury severity and punitive damages is rather complicated. On one hand, the punishing element of punitive damages is expressly defendant-focused, making the defendant's behavior and financial resources the paramount concerns; that is, the awarding of punitive damages, and their magnitude, should be a function of the reprehensibility of the defendant's conduct and how large a penalty would be necessary to achieve deterrence. Plaintiff characteristics, such as the extent of the plaintiff's injury, would therefore seem to be irrelevant. On the other hand, punitive damages jurisprudence requires there to be a sensible relationship between the amount of punitive damages and the amount of compensation; and compensation, as discussed in the previous chapter, is primarily a function of injury severity. Thus, greater punitive damages for cases involving relatively severe injuries (compared to milder injuries) are not invariably problematic and, indeed, can even be interpreted as a requirement under *Gore* and subsequent cases. The precise nature of the punitive–compensatory relationship is open to interpretation, but the Supreme Court has provided substantial guidance. As noted earlier, in *State Farm Mutual Insurance Co. v. Campbell* (2003), the Court essentially imposed a *de facto* 10:1 ratio in most cases. In some kinds of cases, the upper limit might be even lower; the Court suggested that a maximum ratio of 1:1 might be appropriate in maritime cases (*Exxon Shipping Co. v. Baker*, 2008).

Two lines of research have addressed the punitive–compensatory relationship: experimental simulations investigating the effect of injury severity on mock jurors' punitive damages awards, and archival analyses of cases including punitive damages. The experimental studies on the effect of injury severity have yielded mixed findings. Several studies show that relatively severe injuries lead to larger punitive damage awards than less severe injuries (Kahneman et al., 1998; Robbennolt, 2002b; Robbennolt & Studebaker, 1999), but other studies have failed to find an effect of injury severity on the decision to award punitive damages (Hastie, Schkade, & Payne, 1999b) or on the amount (Cather et al., 1996; Daftary-Kapur & Berry, 2010). Mock jurors report considering injury severity and other plaintiff-focused and compensatory factors, such as medical costs, lost earnings, and pain and suffering, in awarding punitive damages (Greene, Coon, & Bornstein, 2001; Hastie et al., 1999a; Shea Adams & Bourgeois, 2006).

The majority of archival analyses of punitive damage awards have used compensatory awards as a proxy for injury severity rather than coding injury severity directly. However, Rustad (1992) coded injury severity in 260 (non-asbestos) products liability cases in which punitive damages were awarded, using five severity categories: temporary partial disability, permanent partial disability, temporary total disability, permanent total disability, or death. Only 4% of the cases involved temporary partial disability, whereas 60% involved either permanent total disability or death. Thus, cases with punitive damages tend to involve relatively severe injuries to plaintiffs. The size of punitive damages does not decrease when the plaintiff dies (Rustad, 1992), failing to mirror the "death dip" observed for compensatory damages (see Chapter 9). We argued in the previous chapter that the compensatory death dip makes sense, in that a deceased plaintiff's future economic and noneconomic costs are likely less than those of a gravely injured plaintiff. The same argument does not apply to punitive damages; on the contrary, the need for punishment seems greater for a defendant whose recklessness causes death than for one whose recklessness causes "merely" a serious injury.

Studies focusing on the ratio of punitive to compensatory damages generally reach the same conclusion. For example, Eisenberg and colleagues (2008) analyzed multiple datasets of punitive damage awards, which included both blockbuster awards and a broader, more inclusive sample of cases. They found that compensatory awards were a strong predictor of punitive awards, with the former explaining over 50% of the variance in the latter (see also Eisenberg et al., 2002; 2006; Eisenberg & Heise, 2011). There is some evidence that the relationship breaks down at both the upper and lower ends of the distribution (Del Rossi & Viscusi, 2010; Eisenberg et al., 2008; Eisenberg & Heise, 2011; Hersch & Viscusi, 2004; Viscusi, 2004). For example, Del Rossi and Viscusi observed a mean ratio in blockbuster cases of 612.6, which is well in excess of the single-digit ratio recommended by the Supreme Court in *State Farm Mutual Insurance Co. v. Campbell* (2003); there was also an enormous degree of variability (the ratio's standard deviation was 4,464.6). It is worth noting that the majority of these cases involved an individual plaintiff and a corporate defendant, which would effectively impose a reasonable

212 The Jury Under Fire

upper limit on compensation (i.e., only so much is needed to compensate a single individual, even one with very grave injuries); however, to accomplish the goals of punitive damages, especially deterrence, the amount of punishment needed for a large corporation could be quite substantial.

Juror Characteristics

Relatively few studies have addressed the relationship between jurors' background characteristics or attitudes and their punitive damage awards. Demographic variables appear to have little predictive value (Greene & Bornstein, 2003). For example, Hastie et al. (1998) examined the relationship between mock jurors' pre- and post-deliberation verdicts on whether to award punitive damages and their gender, race/ethnicity, age, education level, and income level (they measured only punitive liability judgments and not punitive damage awards). Only income and race/ethnicity predicted verdicts, and though statistically significant, the size of the effects was small (pre-deliberation rs = -.10 and -.13, respectively). Higher income and White participants were less likely to find the defendant liable for punitive damages than lower income and minority participants (see also Hastie et al., 1999b). Another study found that female jurors awarded higher punitive damages than male jurors (Kahneman et al., 1998), but overall, gender and other background characteristics are weak predictors of jurors' damage awards (Greene & Bornstein, 2003).

Jurors' attitudes provide somewhat more useful information. For example, mock jurors with a stronger belief that there is a litigation crisis award less in punitive damages, at least in some kinds of cases (Vinson, Costanzo, & Berger, 2008). Vinson et al. found a relationship between litigation crisis attitudes and punitive awards in a tobacco and a pharmaceutical case, but not in an insurance case. Similarly, the more individuals agree with the notion that "lawyers ask much more in damages than is warranted," the less they award in punitive damages (Hastie et al., 1999a). Hastie et al. also found that case-specific attitudes (e.g., environmental attitudes in a toxic tort with environmental damage case) predicted both mock jurors' willingness to find the defendant liable for punitive damages (Hastie et al., 1999b) and the size of their awards (Hastie et al., 1999a).

Thus, jurors' attitudes are better predictors of their punitive damage awards than their demographic characteristics. This observation is consistent with research on juror characteristics for other kinds of decisions (e.g., civil liability and compensation, criminal guilt; see, generally, Devine, 2012; Devine & Caughlin, 2014; Greene & Bornstein, 2003; Vidmar & Hans, 2007). It is unsurprising that jurors' attitudes and beliefs about certain issues influence their decisions in cases where those issues arise, such as civil cases with the potential for large punitive damage awards. What is surprising, and arguably more problematic, is that many of those attitudes and beliefs—such as a belief that punitive damages are excessive and unpredictable—are misguided. As we observed earlier, the attention paid to punitive damages greatly exceeds what seems merited by the low frequency of cases with punitive damages and the modest amount of punitive damage awards in the vast majority of cases. And the research reviewed here shows that by and large, the factors that most strongly predict punitive damage awards—the defendants' conduct and wealth and the amount of compensatory damages—are precisely those that the law requires.

Punitive Damages Reform and Alternatives

Despite the tepid evidence on whether juries' punitive damage awards are excessive or unpredictable, a number of jurisdictions have considered or implemented a variety of procedures (or taken advantage of existing procedures, such as *remittitur*) to control them.[2] The means of control vary. One approach is simply to reduce the size of the awards through caps or *remittitur*. The rationale for punitive caps and *remittitur* is analogous to the rationale for using these procedures for noneconomic damages (see Chapter 9). A second approach is to raise the threshold for punitive liability, thereby making it harder for plaintiffs to recover any punitive damages. Means of doing this are, for example, raising the standard of proof, elevating the degree of reprehensible conduct necessary for punitive awards to be justified, and requiring a higher degree of consensus among jurors on the issue of punitive damages than for other issues. A reform procedure unique to punitive damages is "split recovery," whereby a portion of the award goes to an entity other than the plaintiff.

   Finally, the trial can be bifurcated. Bifurcation involves splitting the trial into separate stages, whereby evidence on general liability and compensation are presented in the initial stage, and once the jury has made those judgments of fact, evidence relevant to punitive damages (e.g., the defendant's wealth, additional evidence of reprehensible conduct that was not pertinent to liability) is presented in a second stage. Several states (California, Kansas, Missouri, Montana, Nevada, Ohio, and South Carolina) automatically require bifurcation of the compensatory and punitive damages phases in all cases involving a claim for punitive damages, and others require it at the defendant's request. This kind of bifurcated procedure presumably helps jurors follow the law by reducing the likelihood that they will fuse different judgments together. As there are different forms of bifurcation, some of which do not involve punitive damages, we discuss this procedure in Chapter 14; the remainder of the present section focuses on reforms specific to punitive damages. The reforms

---

[2] The American Tort Reform Association is an excellent source of up-to-date information on punitive damages reform efforts across the United States (http://www.atra.org/issues/punitive-damages-reform).

are not, of course, exclusive; a number of states provide for caps and bifurcation or caps and split recovery, and Missouri employs all three reform mechanisms. In addition, judicial *remittitur* is always an option. Thus, states have sought to reform (and some might say, to restrict) juries' punitive damages decision making on multiple fronts.

Reducing the Amount: Caps and *Remittitur*

Similar to noneconomic damages, there are different kinds of punitive damage caps. The most common forms are flat caps, which may or may not increase over time (i.e., indexed for inflation), and proportional caps (i.e., where the punitive amount is some multiplier of the compensation award). The ratio for proportional caps is typically between 3:1 and 5:1 but can be as low as 1:1 (e.g., in Colorado). In most jurisdictions with caps, the two forms are combined (e.g., Alaska caps punitive awards in most types of cases at the greater of $500,000 or three times compensation). According to ATRA, 23 states have enacted statutory caps. The applicability or amount of the cap sometimes varies depending on case and litigant characteristics, such as a business defendant's size (e.g., number of employees) or net worth, the nature (e.g., physical vs. nonphysical injury) or severity of the plaintiff's injury, whether the defendant adhered to governmental regulations (e.g., FDA approval procedures), and the type of case (e.g., whether the case involved discrimination, sexual abuse, or the defendant's financial gain). The logic behind many of these qualifications, such as those pertaining to case type, seems to be that some forms of defendant conduct (e.g., negligence motivated by financial gain) are automatically more reprehensible than others and therefore less deserving of a cap or deserving of a higher cap. The caps have been challenged in a number of jurisdictions; they have been upheld in some but struck down as unconstitutional in others.

Punitive damage caps affect a nontrivial number of cases. One analysis found that they affected 23% of cases with punitive damage awards (Hyman et al., 2007). By and large, caps on punitive damages have the same effects as caps on noneconomic damages (see Chapter 9). They necessarily reduce the size of juries' punitive awards, especially large awards, regardless of whether jurors are informed of the cap or the reduction is imposed by the court after the verdict (Baldus et al., 1995; Greene, Coon, & Bornstein, 2001; Hyman et al., 2007). For example, Greene and colleagues compared mock jurors' damage awards for three different kinds of cases (personal injury, products liability, and insurance bad faith) under one of four punitive damage limit conditions. One group of participants was given no limit, and a second group was not allowed to award punitive damages at all (i.e., they could award only compensatory damages); two other groups were given a punitive damage cap: either a flat amount ($200,000) or a proportional limit (i.e., the punitive award could not exceed the compensatory award). When there was no cap on punitive damages, the mean award (averaged across cases) was $1,579,000, compared to $107,000 in the flat cap and $261,000 in the proportional cap conditions. Awards were significantly higher in the unlimited condition than in the two cap conditions, which did not differ from one another. The absence of a difference between the two cap conditions is likely a function of the particular case facts. In cases with more severe injuries (i.e., substantially exceeding $200,000), a proportional cap would presumably lead to larger awards than a flat cap of $200,000.

However, punitive caps can have unintentional consequences, in a couple of different respects. First, the cap can function as an anchor, in much the same way as a compensatory *ad damnum*. Robbennolt and Studebaker (1999) presented mock jurors with a simulated personal injury case in which they were instructed that there was a cap on punitive damages of $100,000, $5 million, or $50 million; there was also a no-cap control condition. Participants' punitive damage awards increased systematically as the cap increased, and the mean award was even greater in the high-cap than in the no-cap condition. Thus a procedure designed to lower punitive damage awards—which it does for awards that would otherwise exceed the cap—can paradoxically raise awards that would otherwise be lower. In the same way, a plaintiff's asking for a certain amount of punitive damages can serve as an anchor (Daftary-Kapur & Berry, 2010; Hastie et al., 1999a). Whether the "suggested" amount comes from the plaintiff or the state legislature makes no difference—it serves as an anchor for jurors' awards.

A second unintended consequence of caps is that, as the level of the punitive cap increases, the size and variability of compensation awards may increase as well. Robbennolt and Studebaker (1999) found that the highest cap value increased compensatory damages as well as punitive damages. At the other extreme, barring jurors from awarding any punitive damages—effectively a cap of $0—also leads to higher compensation awards (Anderson & MacCoun, 1999; Greene, Coon, & Bornstein, 2001). Not allowing any punitive damages can also lead to more variable compensatory damage awards, especially when the defendant's conduct is not very reprehensible (Greene, Coon, & Bornstein, 2001).

This "crossover" effect of caps is another instance of the fusion of damage awards (see Chapter 9), and it has been replicated in archival analysis of actual jury verdicts in jurisdictions with and without caps (Sharkey, 2008). These data suggest that jurors form an idea of how much a case is worth and make efforts to award that amount, regardless of the label the law places on different categories of damages (i.e., compensatory or punitive). The behavior of plaintiffs' attorneys could play a part as well. The attorneys—who are much more likely than jurors to know about the existence of a cap—might find it less attractive to litigate cases with low expected compensation but high punitive potential when a cap is in place, and they might also make extra efforts to argue for a high compensation award (Sharkey, 2008).

The procedure for punitive damages *remittitur* is essentially the same as for noneconomic damages *remittitur*; it can be performed by either the trial judge or an appellate court when the award is of "conscience shocking" magnitude. Because judges are loath to disturb a jury's verdict, punitive damages *remittitur* is relatively rare, just as with *remittitur* for noneconomic damages (Baldus et al., 1995). Judges do not use *remittitur* to reduce punitive damages in states with caps, presumably because it is simply unnecessary (Hyman et al., 2007). Some states have attempted to increase judicial oversight of punitive damages by requiring judges to review all punitive awards, but such mandatory review, without appropriate deference to the jury's verdict, has generally been deemed unconstitutional (e.g., *Armstrong v. Roger's Outdoor Sports*, 1991).

As noted above, the judge in *Allen v. Takeda* (2014) remitted the jury's $9 billion punitive damage award by more than 99%, to $36,875,000 ($27,656,250 for Takeda and $9,218,750 for codefendant Eli Lilly). Prior to the reduction, the compensatory to punitive ratio was 5424:1 for Takeda and 8136:1 for Lilly; post-*remittitur* the ratio was 25:1 for both defendants. The judge observed that although the final judgment still somewhat exceeded the 10:1 maximum ratio implied by the Supreme Court in its punitive damages jurisprudence, it represented only a small fraction of the companies' net worth and profits from selling the drug in question (*Allen et al. v. Takeda*, 2014). *Takeda* is perhaps the most recent highly publicized instance of *remittitur*, but the most famous example is undoubtedly the McDonald's "hot coffee" case, in which the jury's punitive award was reduced from $2.7 million to $480,000, an 82% decrease (Galanter, 1998; Vidmar & Hans, 2007). In light of the $160,000 that the plaintiff received in compensatory damages for her severe burns, the ratio went from 17:1 to 3:1. The jury in the trial of Albert Snyder against Westboro Baptist Church, discussed in Chapter 9, awarded Snyder $8 million in punitive damages and $2.9 million in compensation. Even though the punitive to compensatory ratio in the jury's original verdict was only 2.8:1, the judge remitted the punitive damages portion of the award to $2.1 million, making the ratio less than 1:1 (*Snyder v. Phelps*, 2008). These cases show that *remittitur* is a very powerful mechanism for making punitive damage awards comport with Supreme Court jurisprudence. However, as we pointed out in the previous chapter, neither *remittitur* nor caps directly improves juries' damages decision making.

Raising the Threshold

The American Tort Reform Association recommends limiting the number of cases that qualify for punitive damages by requiring that a defendant acted with "actual malice" and that such behavior be proven by clear and convincing evidence. The pattern jury instructions cited earlier require the jury to find that the defendant "acted with malice or with reckless indifference to the rights of others. One acts with malice when one purposefully or knowingly violates another's rights or safety. One acts with reckless indifference to the rights of others when one's conduct, under the circumstances, manifests a complete lack of concern for the rights or safety of another" (Committee on Pattern Jury Instructions, District Judges Association, Fifth Circuit, 2014, §15.7). Malice and reckless indifference clearly differ in terms of their degree of intent; that is, acting "purposefully or knowingly" is more deliberate and intentional than acting "recklessly." Other statutes define the punitive damages threshold in terms of "willful" or "wanton" conduct on the part of the defendant. Would juries be less likely to award punitive damages if the defendant had to have acted maliciously than if his behavior merely had to be reckless or willful? Whether jurors can distinguish among these semantic niceties is an open question, but considering that they struggle with understanding a large number of legal terms (see Chapter 14), it seems unlikely.

Requiring a higher standard of proof seems, logically, to be more straightforward. Depending on the jurisdiction, liability for punitive damages must be proved by a preponderance of the evidence, clear and convincing evidence, or beyond a reasonable doubt (Robbennolt, 2002a; Woody & Greene, 2012), whereas the standard of proof for compensatory damages is typically by a preponderance of the evidence. The standard of proof usually applies statewide, although it can vary across jurisdictions within a state (e.g., New York; Lazer & Higgitt, 2009). The majority of jurisdictions use the clear-and-convincing standard for punitive damages, which is higher than a preponderance of the evidence but lower than proof beyond a reasonable doubt. In probability threshold terms, it is usually defined as approximately .70–.80 as compared to .51 for preponderance and approximately .90 for beyond a reasonable doubt (Woody & Greene, 2012). The standard of proof in most other jurisdictions is a preponderance of the evidence (Woody & Greene, 2012).

A heightened standard of proof is a popular reform proposal to guard against juries' perceived irregularity in awarding punitive damages (e.g., Kuhlik & Kingham, 1990; see, generally, the American Tort Reform Association at www.atra.org). Yet despite the fact that most states use a higher standard for punitive liability than for compensatory liability, research shows that varying the standard of proof has no discernible impact on mock jurors' decision to award punitive damages (Woody & Greene, 2012). This finding is consistent with other research showing that jurors have difficulty understanding and applying standards of proof (Devine, 2012).

A final means of raising the threshold is to make the jury's decision rule more stringent (see, generally, Chapter 4). For example, a state might require unanimity in determining the amount of punitive damages, despite having a non-unanimous (e.g., two-thirds) decision rule for other elements of civil cases. Two states (Montana and Texas) have enacted such a reform, but it was subsequently found unconstitutional in Montana (*Finstad v. W.R. Grace & Co.*, 2000). Thus, despite the clear logic in raising the necessary threshold for punitive damages, it is not at all clear that doing so is either feasible or would produce fewer punitive damage awards.

Split Recovery

Alternative distribution mechanisms, commonly referred to as split recovery schemes, "split" the punitive damages award so that a portion goes to the plaintiff and the remainder goes somewhere else. Their rationale is straight-forward: They preserve the retributive and deterrent aspects of the punitive element by requiring defendants to pay more than mere compensation, but they reduce the "windfall" component by which plaintiffs receive damages in excess—often far in excess—of their actual injury (Bornstein et al., 2009; Schwartz, Behrens, & Silverman, 2003; Sharkey, 2003). They also serve to compensate society for the larger harm—often undetected or at least unlitigated—caused by the defendant's actions (Sharkey, 2003).[3] At least 10 states (Alaska, Colorado, Florida, Illinois, Iowa, Indiana, Missouri, New York, Oregon, and Utah) have enacted some form of split recovery. Both the amount and the destination of the nonplaintiff portion of the split award varies. The non-plaintiff portion ranges from 20% (New York) to 75% (Indiana, Iowa) but is usually between one-third and one-half of the award; the destination is most often the state's general fund but can also be some sort of fund providing public medical assistance (e.g., Florida) or civil reparations (e.g., Iowa). As with other reforms, plaintiffs have challenged split recovery schemes in the courts, with mixed results. For example, the Colorado Supreme Court struck down a statute requiring that one-third of any punitive damage award go to the state's general fund, on grounds that it constituted an unlawful taking of property (*Kirk v. Denver Publishing Co.*, 1991); however, similar statutes have been upheld in other states where they have been challenged.

Although most split recovery schemes have a statutory basis, judges have also experimented with them (Martin, 2003; Sharkey, 2003), and some states give judges the discretion to allocate a portion of the award to a recipient other than the plaintiff. For example, in the case of *Dardinger v. Anthem Blue Cross and Blue Shield* (2002), a jury awarded the plaintiff $2.5 million in compensation and $49 million in punitive damages for the defendants' breach of contract and bad faith in their handling of his wife's insurance coverage for treatment of metastatic brain cancer. The Ohio Supreme Court deemed the punitive award excessive and reduced it to $30 million plus interest; further-more, on its own initiative, the court allocated $10 million of the award to the

---

[3] Using this notion of societal damages as a starting point, Sharkey (2003) pro-poses converting split recovery of punitive damages into a new category of societal compensatory damages, whereby the jury would award both individual damages designed to compensate plaintiffs before the court and societal dam-ages designed to compensate third parties who have been harmed but are not before the court. Such a framework, she argues, would serve essentially the same purpose as split recovery while better satisfying the philosophical rationale underlying compensatory and punitive damages, as well as avoiding the polar-izing debate surrounding punitive damages.

plaintiff, with the remainder, after attorney fees, going to "a place that will achieve a societal good, a good that can rationally offset the harm done by the defendants in this case" (*Dardinger*, p. 146). Accordingly, the Ohio Supreme Court held: "In this case we order that the corpus of the punitive damages award go to a cancer research fund, to be called the Esther Dardinger Fund, at the James Cancer Hospital and Solove Research Institute at the Ohio State University" (*Dardinger*, p. 146).

The jurors in *Dardinger* did not know that two-thirds of their punitive damage award would go toward establishing a cancer research fund and not to the plaintiff; just as with caps, jurors are ordinarily blindfolded to any prevailing post-verdict allocation policy. What if the blindfold came off? The likely effect of jurors' knowledge of split recovery is unclear (Schwartz et al., 2003; Sharkey, 2003). On one hand, jurors might have less interest in giving money to the state than to the plaintiff and therefore award less. Indeed, some research suggests that mock jurors are more likely to award punitive damages when they go to the plaintiff than when they go to the state (Anderson & MacCoun, 1999). On the other hand, however, there are several reasons to suspect that split recovery schemes would actually lead to larger awards. Jurors might see themselves, as state citizens, as indirect beneficiaries; they might appreciate the opportunity to contribute to a worthy cause, especially if the nonplaintiff portion goes to a designated fund and not simply to the state treasury; and, if they view punitive damages as serving a compensatory purpose (Greene, Coon, & Bornstein, 2001), they might feel the need to raise their punitive awards to replace the portion unfairly "taken" by the state, as well as to raise their compensatory awards. Although we are unaware of any published empirical research directly addressing the issue, this reasoning, in conjunction with the research on caps discussed above, implies that split recovery could have paradoxical effects. It is quite possible that it would reduce the windfall to plaintiffs while increasing both their compensation and the amount of punishment meted out to defendants.

If research shows that caps and split recovery are ineffective at best and, at worst, unfair or counterproductive, are there other alternatives? One frequently raised alternative is to remove the task from juries and have judges do it (e.g., Hersch & Viscusi, 2004; Sunstein et al., 2002). Unfortunately, research comparing judges' and juries' punitive damage awards finds little difference between the two (see Chapter 13). Our recommendations mirror the ones that we made for compensatory damages in the previous chapter: a judicious use of *remittitur*, revised instructions, and bifurcation (i.e., separating the trial's punitive phase from the liability and/or compensation phase). None of these options is a panacea—for example, revised instructions and bifurcation have yielded some promising results (see Chapter 14), but they are not without their costs (e.g., the time and effort to draft the instructions, longer trials). Nonetheless, these alternatives preserve and potentially improve the jury's function in determining civil punishment, while maintaining judicial oversight as a safety mechanism (Baldus et al., 1995).

Conclusions

The primary function of punitive damages is, as the name implies, to punish. The punishment aim encompasses both retribution and deterrence, of the defendant and others. Because most or all of any punitive damage award goes to the plaintiff, punitive damages also provide extra compensation for plaintiffs. The close connection between compensation and punishment is exemplified further by Supreme Court holdings that there should be a clear relationship between the amounts of the two categories of damages.

Despite being infrequent, punitive damages have received a great deal of attention from the media, researchers, and policymakers. A widespread perception exists that similar to juries' compensatory damage awards, their punitive damage awards are excessive and unpredictable. In the previous chapter we concluded that although they are not perfectly predictable and in accordance with legal guidelines, jurors' compensatory damage awards are mostly rational and evidence-based. The same is true of their punitive damage awards. Although a very small number of punitive damage awards are extremely large, most of them are modest (less than $100,000), and they are not increasing over time. Moreover, some evidence suggests that the vast majority of blockbuster awards receive post-verdict haircuts from procedures like caps and *remittitur*, and the frequency of blockbuster awards appears to be declining as a natural consequence of the Supreme Court's decision in *State Farm* (2003) that the ratio of punitive to compensatory damages should generally not exceed 10:1.

The systematic relationship between punitive and compensatory damages reflects an underlying tendency for juries to use the severity of the plaintiff's injury in awarding punitive damages. But even more than injury severity, juries rely on evidence of the defendant's conduct and financial resources, awarding higher punitive damages against defendants who have behaved in a more reprehensible fashion and against relatively wealthy defendants. The influence of these factors indicates that jurors properly rely on things that should influence their punitive damage awards.

The effects of other defendant characteristics on punitive damages are more problematic. For example, corporate defendants pay more than individual defendants. Compared to individuals, corporations might act more reprehensibly, cause greater damage, or be wealthier, but it is hard to isolate these factors from one another, and they do not necessarily co-occur. Jurors also do not make full allowance for a defendant's demise, even though deceased defendants obviously cannot be punished or deterred. When questioned about their goals in awarding punitive damages, mock jurors report focusing primarily on the defendant's conduct and what kind of an award is necessary to achieve punishment and deterrence, but they do not invariably report relying on those factors, and they consider other factors as well (e.g., aspects of the plaintiff's injury). Jurors' own characteristics are not very predictive of their punitive damage awards, although their attitudes, especially toward civil litigation and issues that might arise in specific cases, can lead to lower or higher awards.

Some of the reforms designed to correct for perceived excessiveness and bias in jurors' punitive damage awards, such as caps and split recovery schemes, can actually have unintended consequences. Under some circumstances they can increase the size and variability of punitive damages, and they can also increase compensatory damages. Other reforms, such as raising the standard of proof or requiring unanimity on punitive damages (but not compensatory damages), seem logical, but little research exists on their effectiveness; what research has been done suggests that they would not have much impact on juries' verdicts. As with noneconomic damages reform, we are more positive about procedures that allow judges to modify a jury's punitive damages award, such as *remittitur* and split recovery. Judges have more knowledge than jurors about comparable cases, and *remittitur* and judicially determined split recovery—unlike caps and split recovery mandated by statute—permit judges to tailor any post-verdict adjustment to the facts and circumstances of the individual case.

Such procedures should, however, be used sparingly. Overall, jurors determine civil punishment fairly well, meaning there is not much need for judges to step in. The next chapter examines whether juries do equally well in determining criminal punishment and reaches a markedly different conclusion.

11

Jurors in Criminal Cases Can Fairly
Punish Wrongdoers

"The prognosis for a fair, equitable, and procedurally sound capital
legal process is grim"

(Lynch, 2009, p. 175).

Although in most states jurors do not sentence the majority of criminal
defendants whom they find guilty, they do determine sentencing for the most
serious crime, namely capital murder, where the importance of their role has
been continually reaffirmed (e.g., *Ring v. Arizona*, 2002; *Hurst v. Florida*,
2016). As of 2015, 19 states and the District of Columbia have abolished the
death penalty, meaning that in those jurisdictions jurors essentially never
punish criminal defendants. In the remaining jurisdictions (i.e., the 31 states
with the death penalty and the federal courts), capital trials are still quite
rare, as they occur only for the most extreme crimes, typically first-degree
murder. The rate of death sentences meted out to known murderers varies
somewhat across jurisdictions, but in no state does it exceed 6% (Blume,
Eisenberg, & Wells, 2004). The low rate is primarily a function of the scarcity
of murder cases in which the death penalty is an option, because either the
suspect pleads guilty or the prosecution does not seek the death penalty. But
even in cases where the jury does choose between life and death, the death
penalty is not that common. For example, a study of federal capital prosecutions found that capital juries imposed death sentences only 34% of the time
(available at the Death Penalty Information Center website; see http://www.
deathpenaltyinfo.org/federal-death-penalty#statutes).

Like punitive damages, then, juries rarely determine criminal punishment. Nonetheless, capital punishment is a prominent issue in the media,

legislative debates, the courts, and general social discourse. As we indicated in the previous chapter, there are good reasons for this high degree of attention to the death penalty: media coverage, which is often misleading and inflammatory (Haney, 2005), though in recent years it has also included publicity surrounding death row inmates who have been exonerated by DNA testing (see www.innocenceproject.org); the emotional element of both the crimes and the jury's and public's reaction to them; and the stakes, which are so high they are scarcely imaginable. Add to this the irreversible nature of the death penalty, amid fears that an innocent person could be executed, along with the gruesome nature of the execution process, and it is clear why the death penalty in general, and juries' role in the prosecution of capital crimes, is so contentious.[1] It is also clear why significant numbers of capital jurors report finding it very difficult, if not impossible, to decide whether a defendant should be given the death penalty and, ultimately, to vote for a penalty of death (e.g., Dillehay & Sandys, 1996). Because capital trials are the most prominent instance of jury punishment, as well as the focus of most empirical research on jury sentencing, we limit our discussion of punishment by criminal juries in the present chapter to capital cases; we briefly consider jury sentencing in noncapital cases in the context of judge–jury differences in Chapter 13.

Capital Sentencing Basics

Many countries, especially Western industrialized nations, have abolished the death penalty. Yet even among countries that retain the death penalty, U.S. trial procedures are relatively unique (Lynch, 2009). American juries have long been involved in recommending or determining the defendant's sentence in capital cases, yet the jury's role has increased over time (Vidmar & Hans, 2007). Specifically, in *Ring v. Arizona* (2002; affirmed in *Hurst v. Florida*, 2016) the United States Supreme Court held that the jury, and not the judge, had to determine the existence of any aggravating factors that would make a defendant eligible for the death penalty. Thus, even in the minority of states where judges nominally decide on the final sentence, the jury is essentially making the decision. Despite jurors' prominent role in capital sentencing, courts, legislators, and researchers have repeatedly expressed

---

[1] States have striven to make executions less gruesome, having progressed from hanging and firing squad through electrocution and the gas chamber to the current standard method of lethal injection. Although it is consistently touted as a more humane procedure, lethal injection is not without its problems. It has recently been involved in several highly publicized "botched" executions, such as the 2014 execution of Oklahoma death row inmate Clayton Lockett. Lockett writhed, struggled against his restraints, opened his eyes, and attempted to speak while he was supposedly sedated during his execution (Stern, 2015).

concerns about how well they are able to perform the task. Indeed, a concern about juries' arbitrariness in capital cases was a major factor in the United States Supreme Court's ban of the death penalty in 1972 (*Furman v. Georgia*). Post-*Furman* laws have sought to provide jurors with enough guidance that any arbitrariness becomes negligible (e.g., *Gregg v. Georgia*, 1976). The Court has also narrowed the scope of the death penalty, finding it unconstitutional for rape (*Coker v. Georgia*, 1977), mentally retarded defendants (*Atkins v. Virginia*, 2002), and persons younger than 18 years of age at the time of the crime (*Roper v. Simmons*, 2005).

The structure of capital trials differs from other criminal jury trials in three main respects: the manner of jury selection, bifurcation of the guilt and sentencing phases of trial, and the form and content of jury instructions. In addition to the usual jury selection procedures (see Chapter 3), capital trials involve a process of *death qualification*, whereby jurors whose personal views toward the death penalty would "prevent or substantially impair the performance of [their] duties" are excluded (*Wainwright v. Witt*, 1985, p. 424; see also *Witherspoon v. Illinois*, 1968). In theory, the procedure eliminates prospective jurors who would automatically sentence a defendant to either death or life imprisonment regardless of the circumstances of the case; but in practice, it mainly excludes jurors with strong objections to the death penalty. Death qualification makes sense—it would be illogical and unfair to have jurors who are unwilling to consider one of the sentencing options decide on a sentence. However, as we describe in the section on juror attitudes below, it can introduce bias, leading to conviction-prone juries. It is also worth noting that the procedure is unique to capital trials. For example, jurors in civil cases where the plaintiff is seeking punitive damages are not asked whether they would automatically award or refuse to award them.

As mentioned in Chapter 10 (and discussed at greater length in Chapter 14), civil trials, such as those involving punitive damages, can be bifurcated. Following the reinstituting of capital punishment in 1976, capital trials are always bifurcated. In the first ("guilt") phase, the jury decides whether the defendant is guilty; if so, they determine the defendant's sentence in the second ("sentencing") phase. In most jurisdictions the alternative to a death sentence is life without parole (LWOP), but life with the possibility of parole may also be an option. In each phase, only evidence relevant to that particular decision is presented, although there is necessarily some overlap. For example, questions about the murderer's identity would be relevant only to guilt; questions about the defendant's harsh upbringing would be relevant only to sentencing; and questions about the victim's identity (e.g., if the victim was a police officer and the perpetrator knew that) would be relevant to both.

Finally, the guided or "channeled" discretion approach to capital sentencing that the Supreme Court currently requires (e.g., *Gregg v. Georgia*, 1976) has resulted in jury instructions that are unusually complex and can run for many pages. Jury instructions inform jurors which factors to consider in deciding whether to sentence a capital defendant to death or life imprisonment. The precise factors vary depending on the jurisdiction, but all instructions distinguish between factors that make the defendant more deserving of the death penalty ("aggravators") and those that make the defendant less deserving of the death penalty ("mitigators"). Aggravators, which must be enumerated by statute, include things like murdering multiple victims, committing the crime against a peace officer or to avoid arrest, heinousness, prior felony convictions, and a high risk of future violence. To sentence a defendant to death, the jury must unanimously agree on the existence of at least one aggravator beyond a reasonable doubt.

Some statutes enumerate possible mitigators as well, such as the absence of a prior criminal history; mental or emotional disturbance; the defendant's age, character, or prior good acts; the victim's willing participation in the crime; and the prospect of rehabilitation. A defendant is also allowed to present "any aspect of a defendant's character or record and any of the circumstances of the offense that the defendant proffers as a basis for a sentence less than death" (*Lockett v. Ohio*, 1978, p. 604). Evidence that falls into this catch-all mitigation category can, quite literally, be anything; common factors include evidence of an abusive childhood, prior drug use, brain damage/low IQ, and good behavior while awaiting trial. Mitigators generally do not require either unanimity or proof beyond a reasonable doubt.

If the jury finds both aggravating and mitigating circumstances to be present, they must then weigh them against one another. They may only impose a death sentence if they unanimously agree that the aggravators outweigh the mitigators. If the mitigators are greater, or they cannot reach unanimity, then they must impose a life sentence. Importantly, they are allowed to sentence the defendant to life even if they determine the aggravators outweigh the mitigators; that is, they are never required to impose the death penalty.

One way to think about jurors' sentencing decisions in death penalty cases is as consisting of two distinct components: a measurement task and a comparison task (Rachlinski & Jourden, 2003). The measurement task, which is specific to each defendant, involves evaluating the evidence to assess the defendant's deathworthiness. Measurement essentially involves placing the individual defendant somewhere on a scale of deathworthiness that ranges from very low to very high. The comparison task then involves comparing that measurement with some absolute threshold that draws the line between life and death. If the scale value falls below the threshold, the sentence is life imprisonment; if it exceeds the threshold, the sentence is death. According to Rachlinski and Jourden (2003, p. 459), "The task in a capital case is surprisingly analogous to determining whether to purchase a used car." What are the car's merits? And are they great enough to justify paying the purchase price?

Like buying a car, sentencing a defendant is a cognitively demanding task. The decision maker has a wealth of information, but that information is still incomplete; extraneous information can influence the decision; and the decision threshold is vague. In the sentencing context, courts' instructions are relevant to both the measurement and comparison tasks, but those instructions are complicated and confuse as much as they illuminate. Thus, both tasks are potential sources of bias. Consider, for example, a capital defendant's race. Jurors might interpret the same conduct (e.g., gratuitous violence) as more heinous when committed by a Black defendant than a White defendant (a measurement bias). They might also apply a lower threshold for sentencing Black defendants to death than White defendants (a comparison bias).

Research on jurors' death penalty decision making makes it clear that their decisions are consistent and legally appropriate in some respects, but that they struggle with both the measurement and comparison components of the task in other respects (for review, see Devine, 2012; Haney, 2005). A number of cognitive (e.g., instruction comprehension), procedural (e.g., death qualification), and attitudinal variables make capital sentencing especially challenging and can introduce bias. These biases have been documented using a variety of empirical approaches: mock juror/jury studies, posttrial interviews of actual jurors, and archival analyses of capital jury verdicts (Haney, 2005; Lynch, 2009). In the remainder of the chapter, we consider the extent to which jurors rely on factors that should affect their decisions in capital cases, as well as those that should not affect their decisions.

Factors that Should Affect Capital Punishment

As described above, the central factors that should affect whether a jury sentences a defendant to death or life imprisonment are aggravators and mitigators, as stated in the jury instructions. However, the instructions do not necessarily define these terms beyond referring to them as circumstances that might favor one sentence over the other; they are not even always categorized into separate lists (Haney, 2005; Haney & Lynch, 1994). In this section we review research on jurors' comprehension of jury instructions on aggravation and mitigation, as well as the impact of several specific aggravating or mitigating factors. We also consider the special case of victim impact evidence.

Aggravation and Mitigation: General Comprehension

In one sense, jurors respond appropriately to aggravating and mitigating evidence. For example, Miller and Bornstein (2006) conducted a mock jury study in which participants made capital sentencing decisions in a murder trial that contained either four aggravators (e.g., the crime was committed for pecuniary gain) and two mitigators (e.g., the defendant confessed and cooperated with authorities) or two aggravators and four mitigators. Participants were significantly less punitive—operationalized as more confident in a sentence of LWOP, as opposed to the death penalty—in the "high mitigators" than in the "high aggravators" condition, at least under some circumstances. This shows that the balance of aggravating and mitigating factors can affect jurors' decisions as the law intends.

Research looking at jurors' understanding of what, exactly, constitutes aggravation or mitigation is less sanguine. Jurors' comprehension of death penalty instructions is not very good, especially for the concept of mitigation (for review, see Alvarez, Miller, & Bornstein, 2016; Haney, 2005; Lieberman, 2009; we also cover jury instructions in Chapter 14). For example, Haney and Lynch (1994) found that only 8% of a sample of college undergraduates could correctly define both aggravation and mitigation, even after hearing the instructions three times. In some cases jurors even use mitigating evidence (e.g., evidence of a defendant's childhood maltreatment or alcohol abuse) as an aggravating factor, especially if they see the factor as controllable and stable (Stevenson, Bottoms, & Diamond, 2010). The mitigating factors that are most likely to occur in actual cases (e.g., a defendant's impaired capacity to appreciate the criminality of his conduct, committing the crime under the influence of a mental or emotional disturbance, acting as an accomplice or minor participant) are the ones most likely to be misunderstood (Haney & Lynch, 1994).

In addition to having trouble with the concepts of aggravation and mitigation individually, jurors struggle with how to weigh them against one another, as required by law. Both simulation studies and posttrial juror interviews have documented this finding (e.g., Haney & Lynch, 1994; Haney, Sontag, & Costanzo, 1994; Wiener, Pritchard, & Weston, 1995). For example, a disturbing number of jurors—as many as one-third or more—incorrectly believe that under some circumstances, such as when aggravation outweighs mitigation, the death penalty is mandatory (Haney & Lynch, 1994; Haney et al., 1994; Luginbuhl & Howe, 1995). In fact, there are *no* circumstances under which a death sentence is legally required. Jurors are also confused by the different standards of proof that many jurisdictions use for mitigating (preponderance of the evidence) and aggravating factors (beyond a reasonable doubt; Eisenberg & Wells, 1993).

The difficulty of understanding capital jury instructions, especially with regard to weighing aggravating and mitigating factors (Lynch & Haney, 2009; Wiener et al., 2004), has led to efforts to revise jury instructions to improve comprehension. In addition to affecting comprehension, instruction revision leads to a higher proportion of life sentences and an enhanced ability to distinguish between aggravating and mitigating factors (e.g., Lynch & Haney, 2009; Patry & Penrod, 2013). We discuss these attempts at instruction revision, and provide further information on instruction comprehension in general, in Chapter 14.

If jurors do not understand the concepts of aggravation and mitigation, then these concepts obviously cannot have their intended effect on sentencing decisions. As we discuss in the following section, specific aggravating and mitigating factors, such as crime heinousness, might also affect guilt judgments, for which they are irrelevant. This effect of case characteristics on guilt judgments would be another illustration of fusion, discussed in previous chapters.

Specific Aggravators and Mitigators

Some research has focused on the impact of specific aggravators or mitigators. Three factors that have garnered research interest are remorse (a mitigator), future dangerousness (an aggravator), and heinousness (an aggravator). Instructions vary across jurisdictions. Remorse may be listed as a specific mitigating factor or fall into the catch-all (i.e., nonenumerated) mitigation category. Heinousness and dangerousness are among the most commonly listed aggravators. Dangerousness is unique in that in some states (Texas is the most noteworthy example), jurors determine future dangerousness as a separate issue, essentially making it the sole aggravator. For instance, in sentencing Gregory Russeau to death (see Chapter 10), the jury concluded that he caused the victim's death and represented a future danger to society, and that there was no mitigating evidence supporting a lesser sentence (*Russeau v. Stephens*, 2014). Coincidentally, several states that make future dangerousness a primary consideration in sentencing are consistently among the states with the highest number of executions (Texas, Virginia, and Oklahoma; see Dorland & Krauss, 2005; Lynch, 2009). Because remorse and heinousness implicate emotion, we defer a lengthier discussion of those factors to Chapter 12; we focus here on the specific aggravating factor of dangerousness.

Future dangerousness is an important consideration in sentencing, and jurors do make an effort to estimate the defendant's future behavior (Blume, Garvey, & Johnson, 2001; Eisenberg & Wells, 1993). The crucial question is, "Dangerous to whom?" Prior to the advent of statutes making LWOP the sole alternative to the death penalty, jurors might have been concerned that a defendant sentenced to life imprisonment would be paroled and could therefore harm other members of society. Now that "life means life" in most jurisdictions with the death penalty, the only risk—barring the extremely small chance of a defendant's escape from prison—is to prison workers and other inmates. The state has an obvious interest in protecting these individuals from harm.[2] Multiple types of evidence can be relevant to future dangerousness: remorse (based on the assumption that a remorseful defendant would be less likely to commit similar acts in the future), evidence of past violence (applying the age-old psychological adage that past behavior is the

---

[2] As a class, capital murderers are not unduly violent while in prison, whether they are sentenced to death or LWOP (Cunningham, Reidy, & Sorensen, 2005). The most influential predictor of prison violence is age at the time of incarceration (Cunningham, Sorensen, & Reidy, 2005).

best predictor of future behavior), and expert testimony from a mental health practitioner who has evaluated the defendant. For example, in Gregory Russeau's (second) punishment hearing, the prosecution presented evidence of the defendant's extensive criminal history, his conduct while in custody, and testimony by three expert witnesses expressing their professional opinion that he posed a future danger to society (*Russeau v. Stephens*, 2014).

As noted earlier (see Chapter 7), predicting future violence is a very imperfect science; it is even less precise when predicting violence in an institutional setting rather than in open society (Dorland & Krauss, 2005). Nonetheless, both sides commonly present expert psychiatric or psychological testimony on the risk of future violence during the sentencing phase of capital trials (Krauss & Sales, 2001; Sundby, 1997). These experts may also address the effects of childhood trauma, the defendant's mental state currently and at the time of the crime, the nature and severity of any mental health disorders, and even the defendant's neurological characteristics. Psychological expert testimony on dangerousness is typically clinical in nature, based on an evaluation of the defendant, as opposed to social framework testimony (see Chapter 7).

The more dangerous jurors perceive a defendant to be, the more likely they are to favor a death sentence (Blume et al., 2001; Edens, Colwell, Desforges, & Fernandez, 2005; Eisenberg & Wells, 1993). Perceptions of dangerousness, in turn, are affected by expert testimony. Mock jurors perceive a capital defendant as more dangerous and are more likely to sentence him to death when an expert testifies that the defendant poses a high risk of future violent behavior (e.g., Lynch, 2009; Saks et al., 2014), although the manner in which the expert presents that testimony can influence their verdicts (see Chapter 7). For example, clinical expert testimony is more persuasive than actuarial expert testimony (e.g., Krauss & Lee, 2003; Krauss et al., 2004). Other aspects of the clinical expert testimony can matter as well. Edens et al. (2005) presented mock jurors with a capital case in which psychological expert testimony described the defendant as psychopathic, psychotic (with symptoms consistent with a diagnosis of schizophrenia), or not mentally disordered. Participants viewed the defendant diagnosed as a psychopath as the most dangerous, and they were also most likely to sentence him to death (60% sentenced him to death in the psychopathy condition versus 38% and 30% in the no disorder and psychosis conditions, respectively). This finding shows that psychiatric labels can be stigmatizing and can lead to negative inferences in the courtroom as well as in everyday contexts (Skinner, Berry, Griffith, & Byers, 1995).

Victim Impact Evidence: Aggravator or Something Altogether Different?

In some cases the prosecution presents evidence of the impact that the crime has had on those close to the victim, commonly known as *victim impact evidence.* This kind of evidence is quite variable (Eisenberg, Garvey, & Wells, 2003; Greene, 1999; Myers & Greene, 2004; Paternoster & Deise, 2011). It usually takes the form of a statement by someone close to the victim, such as a family member, and often includes a description of personal qualities of the victim and the victim's character, as well as how the victim's violent death has affected the survivors. It may also include opinions from the survivors about their preferred punishment.

Victim impact evidence is controversial for a number of reasons (Myers & Greene, 2004; Paternoster & Deise, 2011). The principal concern is that it would do little more than inflame jurors' passions and hence be prejudicial (we explore the emotional implications of victim impact evidence in Chapter 12). It is not listed as an aggravating factor because doing so would convey the message that some victims' lives are more valuable than others; but if it makes some defendants (i.e., those whose crimes had more negative consequences) seem more deathworthy than others, it essentially functions as one. Despite these concerns, the Supreme Court has upheld the right of victims to testify during the penalty phase of capital trials, largely on grounds that victim harm may be relevant to the issue of the defendant's blameworthiness (*Payne v. Tennessee*, 1991), and impact statements are also permitted in noncapital trials in all 50 states (Cassell, 2009). However, victim impact statements are not automatically admissible; the *Payne* court held that their relevance must be weighed against potential prejudice on a case-by-case basis. They can occur as part of any sentencing hearing but are most controversial when offered in the penalty phase of capital trials.

Overall, victim impact statements do tend to affect jurors' sentencing decisions (Myers & Greene, 2004; Myers et al., 2013; Paternoster & Deise, 2011; but see Eisenberg et al., 2003). For example, an early study of the phenomenon found that a victim impact statement increased the percentage of mock jurors voting for death (vs. a prison sentence) from 30% to 67% (Myers & Arbuthnot, 1999). A number of factors affect the impact of victim impact evidence, such as the identity of the witness providing the testimony (e.g., a spouse vs. a coworker of the victim; McGowan & Myers, 2004), the degree of harm to the victim's family (Myers, Lynn, & Arbuthnot, 2002), and juror characteristics (e.g., death penalty attitudes; Butler, 2008).

In *Payne v. Tennessee* (1991), the Supreme Court suggested that victim impact statements should have less of an effect when crime heinousness is high than when it is low, presumably because heinous crimes would already strongly incline jurors toward the death penalty (Myers et al., 2013). However, Myers and colleagues failed to obtain the predicted interaction between heinousness and the presence of victim impact statements on sentencing decisions—each factor independently increased punishment severity in a mock capital murder trial.

In addition to potentially arousing sympathy for the victim and antipathy for the defendant (Myers & Greene, 2004), victim impact evidence can alter jurors' interpretation of the evidence. Greene, Koehring, and Quiat (1998) found that the more respectable victims seemed in victim impact testimony, the more severe the crime seemed and the less heavily mock jurors weighed certain mitigating evidence (i.e., evidence that the defendant had a difficult childhood; see also Eisenberg et al., 2003). Thus, not only does victim impact evidence act like an aggravator when it is not technically an aggravator, but it can also color jurors' evaluation of other evidence. The risk of prejudice is therefore high. Much of the problem results from the fact that "jurors have virtually no direction regarding their use of victim impact evidence" (Myers & Greene, 2004, p. 508). Some jury instructions attempt to distinguish victim impact evidence from evidence of aggravation, but the distinction is subtle, written in complex legal language, and likely to be confusing to jurors (Myers & Greene, 2004). As a result, jurors probably simply weigh victim impact evidence as one more aggravator. In a sense, it is the "hidden aggravator."

Factors that Should Not Affect Capital Punishment

Given the small number of factors that legitimately should affect the sentencing phase of capital trials, there is a very large and potentially infinite number of factors that, theoretically, should not affect jurors' decisions in one or both phases of capital trials. Of these, research has focused primarily on death qualification, one of the distinguishing procedural aspects of capital trials; characteristics of the defendant and victim, particularly their race; and characteristics of the jurors, such as their race, religion, personality, and attitudes.

Death Qualification and Jurors' Attitudes

Death qualification is a procedural matter, but it is one where the principal consideration is jurors' attitudes—namely, their attitude toward the death penalty. Almost by definition, individuals who survive the death qualification process have more positive attitudes toward the death penalty (Haney, Hurtado, & Vega, 1994). Two related lines of research have explored this fact: studies comparing the judgments of death-qualified mock jurors to the judgments of "excludables"—individuals whose opposition to the death penalty precludes them from serving—and studies measuring the correlation between death penalty attitudes and mock jurors' judgments. Some studies include both a general attitude measure and the death qualification procedure.

As described above, the death qualification procedure is relatively straightforward and brief, in theory if not always in practice: Jurors are asked a question or two to determine whether their personal views toward the death penalty would "prevent or substantially impair the performance of [their] duties" (*Wainwright v. Witt*, 1985, p. 424). However, attitudes toward the death penalty are multifaceted and cannot be adequately measured with just one or two items (O'Neil, Patry, & Penrod, 2004). O'Neil and colleagues developed a 15-item scale of death penalty attitudes with five factors: General Support (e.g., "No matter what crime a person has committed executing them is a cruel punishment"), Retribution and Revenge (e.g., "Society has a right to get revenge when murder has been committed"), Death Penalty Is a Deterrent (e.g., "The death penalty does not deter other murderers"), Death Penalty Is Cheaper (e.g., "It is more cost efficient to sentence a murderer to death rather than to life imprisonment"), and Life without Parole Allows Parole (e.g., "Even when a murderer gets a sentence of life without parole, he usually gets out on parole"). The factors are moderately intercorrelated (rs between .17 and .56), but they tap into distinct constructs. The existence of five distinct factors relevant to death penalty attitudes suggests that death qualification might be an overly crude and simplistic process that fails to account for the nuances of jurors' death penalty attitudes.

It is hardly surprising that the more one favors the death penalty, the more likely one is to assign the death penalty in a particular case (indeed, it would be hard to explain the absence of such a relationship). Numerous studies, both jury simulations and posttrial juror interviews, have documented this relationship (Devine et al., 2001; Haney, 2005), which is strongest for general death penalty support, belief that the death penalty is a deterrent, and belief that a murderer sentenced to LWOP nonetheless gets out on parole (O'Neil et al., 2004). Even among those who have survived death qualification as part of the *voir dire* process, jurors with stronger pro–death penalty attitudes are more likely to sentence a capital defendant to death than jurors who are less supportive of the death penalty (Allen, Mabry, & McKelton, 1998; Butler & Moran, 2007b; Lynch & Haney, 2009; Nietzel et al., 1999; O'Neil et al., 2004). Some research indicates that the relationship is actually stronger for jurors who have undergone *voir dire* (Allen et al., 1998). Death qualification is associated not only with a greater willingness to sentence "routine" capital defendants to death, but also with a greater willingness to execute special populations such as juveniles (Butler, 2007a) and the elderly and physically disabled (Butler, 2010). Compared to excludables, death-qualified jurors are also more susceptible to pretrial publicity, despite a greater belief that it would not affect the defendant's right to a fair trial (Butler, 2007b), and less receptive to the insanity defense (Butler & Wasserman, 2006). Thus, death-qualified jurors might be more likely to prejudge defendants in cases where these elements are present.

The effect of attitudes on sentencing verdicts is due at least partially to differing interpretations of the evidence. For example, the more jurors support the death penalty, the less they see potentially mitigating factors as mitigating (Haney et al., 1994; Luginbuhl & Middendorf, 1988; Stevenson et al., 2010), and the more they see potentially aggravating factors as aggravating (Haney et al., 1994; Luginbuhl & Middendorf, 1988). In one study, stronger support for the death penalty was associated with perceiving more intent in the actions of a defendant whose crime was captured by a surveillance camera (Goodman-Delahunty, Greene, & Hsiao, 1998). Similar results have been found for death qualification: Compared to excludables, death-qualified jurors are more likely to find aggravating factors and less likely to find mitigating factors in the same body of evidence (Butler & Moran, 2002; 2007a), and they are affected more by victim impact evidence (Butler, 2008). The relationship between death penalty attitudes and sentencing might also be a comprehension issue; mock jurors who favor capital punishment have poorer comprehension of death penalty instructions than those who oppose it (Haney, 2005), and they are more accepting of ambiguous expert scientific testimony (Butler & Moran, 2007a).

What these studies also show is that as a screening process, death qualification is "badly flawed" (Vidmar & Hans, 2007, p. 251). A substantial minority of capital jurors—all of whom survived death qualification—appear to believe that anyone found guilty in a capital trial deserves death, regardless of the circumstances (Bowers, Sandys, & Steiner, 1998; Dillehay & Sandys, 1996). This means that they must have misrepresented their intentions during jury selection (i.e., they said they could and would consider the possibility of a life sentence, but they didn't mean it); misunderstood the questions they were asked during death qualification; responded to a question about one aspect of their death penalty attitudes which was not entirely consistent with other (unquestioned) aspects of their attitudes (O'Neil et al., 2004); or genuinely believed during jury selection that they could be open-minded, but the trial changed their minds. Regardless of the explanation, a number of jurors decide on the appropriate sentence before deliberation in the sentencing phase even begins, which necessarily tilts the jury toward a death sentence.

Perhaps even more problematic is that juries composed entirely of death-qualified jurors are significantly more likely to convict during the guilt phase than juries that include a small number of jurors who would ordinarily be excluded during death qualification (e.g., Cowan, Thompson, & Ellsworth, 1984; for review, see Allen et al., 1998; Greene & Heilbrun, 2014; Haney, 2005; Vidmar & Hans, 2007). In a meta-analysis of the relationship between death penalty attitudes and guilt verdicts, Allen and colleagues obtained a statistically significant mean effect size of $r = .17$. Although this correlation is relatively small, they estimated—based on an assumption of an overall conviction rate of 50%—that a pro–death penalty juror would be 59% likely to convict, versus 41% for an anti–death penalty juror. Thus a favorable attitude toward the death penalty would translate into a 44% increase (i.e., going from 41% to 59%) in the probability that a juror would favor conviction—a far from trivial change.

There are multiple possible reasons for the conviction-proneness of death-qualified juries (e.g., Haney, 1984; 2005). The procedure might desensitize jurors to capital punishment or lead them to believe that the legal system in general, or the judge—who is, after all, the one conducting the procedure—favors the death penalty in this particular case. Hearing other jurors espouse their support for the death penalty during *voir dire* might exert a subtle form of social influence. Jurors who favor the death penalty might interpret the same evidence as more incriminating and less exculpatory than jurors who oppose it. Pro–death penalty jurors might be more confident and persuasive during deliberation. And jurors who favor the death penalty might implement a lower conviction threshold (i.e., they require less compelling evidence in order to find the defendant guilty) than anti–death penalty jurors. Research has supported all of these possibilities to varying degrees (Haney, 2005).

In addition to the issue of conviction bias, death qualification raises concerns about jury representativeness. On average, women and minorities (particularly Blacks and Hispanics) are less likely to endorse the death penalty than men and Whites (Haney, 2005; O'Neil et al., 2004). Persons with high socioeconomic status and those affiliated with conservative religions (e.g., fundamentalist Christians; see section on juror characteristics below) are also comparatively more likely to favor the death penalty (Bornstein & Miller, 2009; Lynch, 2009). Consequently, death qualification produces juries with fewer women, minorities, poor citizens, and religious liberals. Although the conviction-proneness of death-qualified juries is a robust finding in the empirical literature (Vidmar & Hans, 2007), the Supreme Court has thus far dismissed the research (*Lockhart v. McCree*, 1986).

The relationship between death penalty attitudes and jurors' verdicts is so robust that Devine et al. (2001, p. 675) concluded that "no cluster of attitudes/values has received enough attention to allow firm conclusions to be drawn except for one—attitudes toward capital punishment." And the direction of the relationship is clear: The more pro–death penalty the jurors' attitudes, the more likely they are to convict *and* to sentence a capital defendant to death.

Defendant and Victim Characteristics

Race is perhaps the most contentious issue with respect to the death penalty as currently administered in the United States. According to the conventional wisdom, death rows disproportionately contain people of color. Several studies show that approximately 40% of U.S. inmates on death row are Black, 40% are White, and 12%–13% are Latino (e.g., Blume et al., 2004; see, generally, http://deathpenalty.org/article.php?id=86). According to U.S. census data for 2013, non-Hispanic Whites comprise approximately 63% of the population, with African Americans constituting 13% and Hispanic/Latinos 17% (http://quickfacts.census.gov/qfd/states/00000.html). By this metric, African Americans appear to be overrepresented on death row. Yet a finer-grained analysis shows that African Americans are not more likely than Whites to be sentenced to death. For example, Blume et al. (2004), in a study of nearly 6,000 persons sentenced to death between 1977 and 1999, found that although African Americans committed 51.5% of the country's murders, they comprised only 41.3% of death row inmates. Moreover, the proportion of a state's Black death row inmates was highly correlated with the proportion of Black murder offenders.

Jury simulation research has found a modest effect of defendant race, with Black defendants somewhat more likely to be sentenced to death than White defendants (Lynch & Haney, 2000; 2009). This pattern is especially true for White jurors and after jury deliberation (Lynch & Haney, 2009; 2011; Shaked-Schroer, Costanzo, & Marcus-Newhall, 2008). Rather than simple prejudice it appears to be due to more subtle influences, such as a greater tendency to find aggravating circumstances and an inclination to place less weight on mitigating evidence when the defendant is Black than when the defendant is White (Baldus et al., 1998).

Thus, the role of the defendant's race is somewhat unclear. In part, this might reflect the fluid nature of racial categories (e.g., the U.S. census considers Hispanic to be an ethnicity, so Hispanics can be of any race) and the high degree of variability within races and ethnicities. Supporting this view, Eberhardt, Davies, Purdie-Vaughns, and Johnson (2006) asked undergraduate participants to rate the stereotypicality of male Black capital defendants' appearance. The pictures were of actual capital defendants in Philadelphia, Pennsylvania between 1979 and 1999. Those with a more stereotypically Black appearance (e.g., broad nose, thick lips, dark skin) were more likely to have been sentenced to death than those with a less stereotypically Black appearance. These findings generalize beyond the death penalty—Burch (2015) found that medium- and dark-skinned Blacks receive longer sentences than light-skinned Blacks (and Whites) across a range of felonies.

In the study by Eberhardt et al. (2006), the effect of defendant stereotypicality held for Black defendants convicted of murdering White victims but not for Black defendants convicted of murdering Black victims. This moderating effect of victim race comports with the major conclusion about the role of race in the death penalty: Victim race is a much stronger predictor of capital sentencing than defendant race. Defendants convicted of murdering African-American victims are substantially less likely to receive the death penalty than those convicted of murdering Whites, especially when the murderer is African American (Baldus, Pulaski, & Woodworth, 1983; Baldus, Woodworth, & Pulaski, 1990; Baldus et al., 1998; Blume et al., 2004; Gross & Mauro, 1989; Lynch & Haney, 2000, 2009). Offenders convicted of murdering Latino victims are even less likely to receive the death penalty than offenders who killed African Americans (Pierce & Radelet, 2005). These disparities are a function of both prosecutorial and jury decision making; that is, prosecutors are more likely to seek the death penalty in "minority-on-White" cases, and juries are more likely to give it. Conversely, the death penalty is relatively less likely when the perpetrator and victim are both minorities, as in "Black-on-Black" cases (Blume et al., 2004). Since most murder cases involve victims and defendants of the same race/ethnicity, these two forces combine to produce fewer African Americans on death row than the proportion of murders committed by African Americans would suggest (Blume et al., 2004). Nonetheless, the role played by the race of the victim clearly shows that jurors (as well as prosecutors) are relying on an extraneous factor in making their decisions. When controlling for relevant factors like crime characteristics (e.g., heinousness), dangerousness, and prior offending, any racial disparity in sentencing is reduced but not eliminated (e.g., Baldus et al., 1983). Moreover, it is hard to control for these factors, as the same evidence of aggravating or (even more so) mitigating factors can seem more or less compelling depending on the victim's race (Baldus et al., 1998). Yet despite this evidence, the Supreme Court remains unpersuaded that disparities due to the race of the victim are a major cause for concern (*McCleskey v. Kemp*, 1987).

Juror Characteristics

Various juror characteristics are related to jurors' death penalty attitudes and sentencing decisions. The most consistent effects are for jurors' gender, race, and religion. Jurors are easier to categorize along some of these dimensions than others. The traditional gender categories of male and female ignore transgender people, and simple racial categories ignore or potentially misclassify persons who are biracial or multiethnic. Religion is probably the most problematic demographic variable, as religion is a multifaceted construct that includes, among other things, one's denominational affiliation (e.g., Catholic, Baptist, Muslim), degree of observance (often referred to as "devotionalism"), and specific religious beliefs (e.g., believing that the Bible is the literal word of God). This blurring of category boundaries complicates efforts to identify juror characteristics that predict death penalty decision making; nonetheless, we can draw some general conclusions.

As mentioned above, attitudes toward the death penalty differ as a function of race/ethnicity, with Whites favoring it more strongly than minorities, especially African Americans (e.g., Haney, 2005). Women are also less supportive of the death penalty than men (Haney, 2005; Miller & Hayward, 2008) and less likely to be death qualified (Summers, Hayward, & Miller, 2010). If Blacks and women in general are more likely to be opposed to the death penalty, then they are less likely to survive death qualification, meaning that they might be underrepresented on capital juries. These differences in death penalty attitudes even survive death qualification. For example, a majority of White jurors on death-qualified juries favor the death penalty, whereas a majority of Black jurors favor life imprisonment, even though all of them held views moderate enough that they were not automatically excluded (Bowers, Steiner, & Sandys, 2001). As would seem to follow, then, the more Whites there are on a jury, the more likely the jury is to favor death, especially when the defendant is Black (Bowers et al., 2001; Lynch & Haney, 2009).

At least part of the racial difference reflects differential use of evidence. Both posttrial interviews (Bowers et al., 2001; Fleury-Steiner, 2004) and experimental simulations (Lynch & Haney, 2009) show that Black and White jurors interpret the same trial evidence differently. For example, White male jurors are less responsive than non-White and women jurors to mitigating circumstances (Lynch & Haney, 2009; 2011). However, the effect varies as a function of defendant race. Lynch and Haney (2011) found that White male jurors were significantly less likely to consider several pieces of mitigating evidence for a Black defendant than for a White defendant; conversely, they considered aggravating evidence more for the Black defendant than the White defendant. Defendant race had no effect on the weighing of aggravators and mitigators for women and non-White jurors. This pattern is especially pronounced in cases involving a Black defendant and a White victim (Brewer, 2004). The interaction of juror, defendant, and victim race could be partially due to empathy, a concept we discuss in Chapter 12. Jurors are more likely to sentence a defendant to death when they empathize with the victim than when they do not (Sundby, 2003). On average, jurors might empathize more with victims and defendants of their own race.

Although differential evidence usage explains part of the story with respect to jurors' race and ethnicity, it does not explain all of it; social forces come into play as well (Lynch, 2009). Posttrial interviews of capital jurors suggest that White males tend to dominate jury deliberations (Fleury-Steiner, 2004). They are especially likely to adopt forceful strategies in overcoming resistance to imposing the death penalty by jurors who are women and minorities (Fleury-Steiner, 2004).

Because religion is a central element of many people's self-concept, and the nature and purpose of punishment are core components of most religious belief systems—including, in many cases, an explicit stance on capital punishment (e.g., the Bible's dictum of "an eye for an eye and a tooth for a tooth")—we might reasonably expect religion to be a stronger predictor of jurors' sentencing preferences than other individual difference variables (Bornstein & Miller, 2009). Research investigating the question has found that jurors' religion is a somewhat reliable predictor of both their death penalty attitudes and their verdicts. Although the data are equivocal, Protestants, especially those belonging to fundamentalist or evangelical churches, tend to be more supportive of the death penalty on average, whereas Catholics tend to be less supportive (Bornstein & Miller, 2009; Miller & Hayward, 2008; Unnever & Cullen, 2009). Consistent with these data, jurors with certain religious affiliations (e.g., non-Catholics, Southern Baptists) and religious beliefs (e.g., fundamentalism) are more likely to be death qualified (Summers et al., 2010) and also to favor sentencing defendants to death (Eisenberg, Garvey, & Wells, 2001; Miller & Hayward, 2008).

In addition to demographic variables like race and religious affiliation, death penalty attitudes are associated with a host of other attitude and personality variables. Compared to excludables, death-qualified jurors are more authoritarian (Butler, 2010; Butler & Moran, 2007b), oriented toward the prosecution (Fitzgerald & Ellsworth, 1984), politically conservative (Unnever &

Cullen, 2009), and racist, sexist, and homophobic (Butler, 2007c). They also have lower need for cognition (Butler & Moran, 2007a; but see Summers et al., 2010), a stronger belief in a just world (Butler & Moran, 2007b), and a more internal locus of control (Butler & Moran, 2007b). These characteristics are independently associated with mock jurors' capital sentencing decisions (Butler & Moran, 2007b); in conjunction with death penalty attitudes, they can produce death-qualified juries that are significantly predisposed toward a death sentence—a tendency that could be exacerbated if certain features, such as a gay or minority defendant or complex evidence, are present in a given case.

Jurors may not be challenged during *voir dire* solely on grounds of race (*Batson v. Kentucky*, 1986) or gender (*J.E.B. v. Alabama*, 1994; see Chapter 3). Courts are divided on whether a juror's sexual orientation (see Chapter 3) or religion (Bornstein & Miller, 2009) can be the basis of a peremptory challenge, with some allowing it and others not. Given the racial and gender differences in death penalty attitudes, death qualification would facilitate attorneys' efforts to find a pretext for excluding minorities or women. And the death qualification process also serves to select jurors with a conviction- and punishment-prone constellation of personality attributes. Overall, capital trial procedures virtually ensure a less diverse jury, which reduces the chances that minority viewpoints will be heard.

Alternatives and Reforms

In light of research showing that jurors rely on extralegal factors in sentencing capital defendants, it is worthwhile to consider whether better alternatives exist. One option might be to remove the task from juries altogether and have judges do it; but apart from the fact that little evidence shows judges do much better than juries (see Chapter 13), the Supreme Court has spoken clearly on the matter: Juries, not judges, must recommend a sentence or, at a minimum, make the factual determinations relevant to sentencing (i.e., dangerousness, aggravators/mitigators; see *Ring v. Arizona*, 2002; *Hurst v. Florida*, 2016). In one sense, then, the judicial option is moot. However, judges in some states do not have to accept the jury's recommendation; if they believe it is not warranted by the evidence, judges may contravene a death recommendation and impose a life sentence (and in Alabama they can contravene a life recommendation and impose death). Given the jury's sacrosanct role in death penalty cases, and the fact that judges in many states are elected and therefore vulnerable to public opinion, such a course seems highly unlikely.

Eliminating the death qualification process would address the problem of death-qualified jurors' conviction proneness, but it is not a solution in and of itself. Jurors who are fundamentally opposed to the death penalty obviously cannot participate in the sentencing phase; if they did, it would be impossible for the jury to reach a unanimous verdict of death—which, under nearly all current statutes, effectively means a life sentence. One alternative would be to have separate panels determine guilt and sentencing; an inclusive jury would decide on the defendant's guilt, and a death-qualified jury would then decide on the sentence. This procedure is not without its drawbacks. For one thing, it would be more costly and time-consuming to empanel two juries than one jury. These costs could be ameliorated somewhat by augmenting the original, guilt-phase jury with alternate jurors; death qualification would take place only if the jury convicted the defendant, and the alternate jurors could substitute for original jurors who are excluded for the penalty phase (Haney, 2005). Such a procedure would still entail some additional costs (i.e., taking the time to select a greater number of jurors, conducting death qualification as a separate procedure and not part of the initial *voir dire*, and the time commitment of a greater number of jurors), but it would be much less costly than using two completely separate panels. Moreover, the added costs seem acceptable compared to the benefit of eliminating (or at least reducing) the conviction bias that results from traditional death qualification.

Either solution—separate panels or an augmented jury—would still require the guilt-phase jury to be blind to the fact that the defendant was being tried for a capital crime. Otherwise, it could introduce an acquittal bias. There is some evidence that jurors are less likely to convict as the potential consequences of a conviction become more severe (Devine, 2012). Although the evidence for this "severity–leniency" hypothesis is somewhat equivocal (Devine, 2012; Freedman, Krismer, MacDonald, & Cunningham, 1994), it implies that if jurors, especially those with anti–death penalty attitudes, know that a guilty verdict means the possibility of a death sentence—even if sentencing is done by a completely separate panel—then they might be more likely to acquit than if death were not one of the sentencing options. Is that better or worse than having jurors who are more likely to convict during the guilt phase? And even if one were to conclude that an acquittal bias is better than a conviction bias, such blindfolding might not be feasible, as capital prosecutions involve filing a distinct charge. The death qualification procedure raises complex issues with no easy solution.

The best alternative, and perhaps the only viable one, is to revise death penalty instructions to enable jurors to do a better job of applying the law. As we discuss in Chapter 14, many of the errors that capital jurors make are a direct consequence of comprehension errors. Revising the instructions for greater comprehensibility alleviates those errors to some extent, though it does not eliminate them altogether. Fusion of judgments, such as properly using an aggravating factor (e.g., heinousness) in the penalty phase but improperly using it in the guilt phase, can potentially be lessened by explicitly instructing jurors on which variables are, and are not, relevant to each phase of the trial (Crocker, 1997). Instructions could also emphasize the irrelevance of defendant and victim characteristics such as race, although calling greater attention to those factors could inadvertently make them more salient (Alvarez et al., 2016; Steblay et al., 2006).

Conclusions

Jurors are entrusted with the most portentous decision any jury can make—whether a defendant deserves to die or spend the rest of his or her life in prison. Do capital juries merit that trust? Similar to the weighing process that jurors must undertake in assessing aggravators and mitigators, there are factors that weigh in favor of juries having this power but other factors that weigh against it. On the positive side, jurors respond appropriately to evidence of aggravating circumstances. They are more likely to give a death sentence to defendants whose crimes contain more aggravating circumstances or whom they perceive to pose a high risk of future dangerousness.

On the negative side, jurors' comprehension of death penalty instructions is poor, especially with respect to mitigating circumstances, and poor comprehension is associated with harsher sentences. In addition, a variety of extralegal factors relating to defendant, victim, and juror characteristics can all affect sentencing outcomes. The death qualification process, which produces conviction-prone juries, is particularly problematic. Research documenting the influence of these extralegal factors calls into question the fairness of having juries sentence capital defendants, and whether the errors are correctable. Ultimately, "it may be that the very nature of the task—trying to rationalize the process of determining who deserves to live or die among those who commit murder—makes the realization of a constitutionally sound and fair death penalty system an ideal impossible to fully realize" (Lynch, 2009, p. 176).

This conclusion differs from the one we reached in Chapter 10, namely, that jurors do a reasonably good job of following the law in awarding punitive damages. Why do they do better with civil than with criminal punishment? One explanation has to do with jurors' emotional and moral response. Emotion is involved in both forms of punishment, but it might be qualitatively different in the case of capital punishment, owing both to the nature of the offense and the nature of the penalty. Deciding whether to sentence another person to death is such an unusual and emotional thing to ask jurors to do that the legal system has implemented a number of "mechanisms of moral disengagement" to enable them to perform the task (Haney, 1997; 2005). These mechanisms might facilitate jurors' ability to cross normal psychological barriers (i.e., the barrier against deciding whether another person deserves to live or die), but they might also contribute to suboptimal decision making (the next chapter explores the role of emotion in jurors' decision making in more detail).

Another possible reason why jurors follow the law better in determining civil than criminal punishment is that, as most reviews of capital juries conclude, "death is different" (e.g., Haney, 2005; Vidmar & Hans, 2007). In addition to the divergent ways that the law deals with emotion in the two different punishment contexts, it is simply difficult to compare the many substantive and procedural issues that distinguish the two.

Unfortunately, reform options in this domain are limited. The law of the land insists that juries, not judges, perform this function. Alternatives to death qualification are complicated or infeasible. Revising instructions for greater comprehensibility helps, but comprehension is modest even with rewritten instructions, in part because the legal issues that need to be communicated are unavoidably complex. And even perfect comprehension would not solve the problem. "The jury is a significant factor in the unfairness and caprice, but it is essential to point to other difficulties in capital litigation" (Vidmar & Hans, 2007, p. 263). There are other systemic problems, such as media bias in portraying violent crime, inadequate counsel, racial disparities in who gets prosecuted for capital crimes, insufficient appellate review, courts' (including the Supreme Court's) reluctance to avail themselves of relevant empirical data, and limited resources for defendants with special needs, such as those with intellectual or psychological impairment (Haney, 2005; Vidmar & Hans, 2007).

Regrettably, these problems are no easier to address than the problems with juries. The alternatives are as clear as they are stark: accept the imperfections of a system of jury-determined punishment for the most severe crimes, on the rationale that the benefits of an imperfect system (e.g., preserving a mechanism whereby the public can express the strongest possible condemnation of certain acts) outweigh the costs (e.g., racial disparities); or conclude, as did Supreme Court Justice Harry Blackmun, that "the death penalty experiment has failed" (*Callins v. Collins*, 1994, p. 1145). There are signs, such as some states' moratoria on and repeal of the death penalty (e.g., on the ballot in Nebraska in Nov. 2016), that consensus is moving in the direction of Justice Blackmun's conclusion. But the majority of American states and the United States Supreme Court still subscribe to the myth that juries can be fair in punishing the most serious criminals.

12

Jurors Can Control Their Emotions

"A commitment to public trials based on live witness testimony presented to lay decision makers in an adversarial, often dramatic context means that jurors' emotions will likely play a role in their judgments"

(Feigenson, 2010, p. 46).

On June 17, 2015, a young White man opened fire at Emanuel African Methodist Episcopal Church, a historically Black church in Charleston, South Carolina. Nine people were killed, including the church pastor. Dylann Roof was charged with 33 counts of federal hate crimes, in addition to other federal and state charges (e.g., murder, attempted murder, and weapons charges).[1] In support of the hate crime charges, the federal indictment cited evidence that Roof created a website where he posted racist diatribes and photographs (Neuman, 2015; Shoichet & Perez, 2015).

Few human experiences are as emotionally laden as hate. Thus, by definition, "hate crime" implicates emotion. But whose? Clearly the perpetrator's—to qualify as a hate crime, his actions must have been motivated by hatred toward a particular class of people. Such crimes "are the criminal manifestation of prejudice" (Lawrence, 2007, p. 210). But in evaluating a defendant's actions to determine whether he was, in fact, motivated by prejudice or

---

[1] Most states have hate crime laws, but South Carolina is one of a handful of states that does not (the others are Arkansas, Georgia, Michigan, and Wyoming). As this book went to press (August 2016), Roof's state trial was scheduled to begin in January 2017 and his federal trial in November 2016, but state and federal officials were still consulting on coordinating the trial schedules. Both the state and federal charges carry the death penalty.

hatred, jurors' emotions are likely to be aroused as well. It is hard to imagine that jurors could vote to convict someone of a hate crime without hating him themselves, at least a little.

Emotion and law intersect in myriad ways. Although "law and emotion" as a distinct field of inquiry is of relatively recent vintage (Maroney, 2006), scholarly attention to the topic dates back at least 100 years (Bornstein & Wiener, 2010b), and awareness of the close relationship between emotion and law dates back much further (Blumenthal, 2010). Emotions can and do influence the decision making of numerous legal actors, including jurors, judges, victims, witnesses, attorneys, and police (Bornstein & Wiener, 2010b; Maroney, 2006). Yet the legal system and the study of emotions have a complex relationship (Bornstein & Wiener, 2006; 2010a; Wiener, Bornstein, & Voss, 2006). On the one hand, courts and policymakers often assume that jurors can and do make decisions dispassionately, considering only the factual evidence and checking their emotions at the door (Maroney, 2006). Allowing an emotional response to "trump" the evidence, whether the emotion is elicited by the evidence itself or other aspects of the case (e.g., pretrial publicity), is anathema to the justice system. At the extreme, emotion could lead jurors to disregard the law entirely, as when the jury nullifies a legally appropriate verdict (Hamm, Bornstein, & Perkins, 2013; Kerr, 2010).

Yet on the other hand, there are many instances in which the law allows, and even seems to require, emotion to be part of the decision-making calculus (Feigenson, 2010; Maroney, 2009). For example, perpetrators' emotional state is a fundamental element of deciding whether to prosecute (and convict) an offense as a hate crime (Lieberman, 2010); jurors have expectations about the sorts of emotions that victims and witnesses ought to have, and about how those emotions should influence their behavior (Bornstein et al., 2008; McAuliff & Kovera, 2012; Wessel, Drevland, Eilertsen, & Magnussen, 2006); and a crime's heinousness can make the perpetrator eligible for enhanced punishment, such as the death penalty.

Thus, the law applies something of a double standard to emotion. There are some circumstances in which emotion should not figure into jurors' decisions and other circumstances in which it should. Jurors therefore do not have to set aside their emotions entirely; rather, the law expects them to control their emotions. This means ignoring them altogether in some situations, and in other cases using them only to the extent, and for the purposes, specified by the law. The capacity of emotion to overcome rational human judgment has been known and written about for centuries, featuring extensively in the work of Plato, Aquinas, Descartes, and other protopsychologists (e.g., Hunt, 2007). Emotion can also provide useful cues for decision makers to incorporate into their decisions (e.g., Damasio, 1994; Maroney, 2009); for example, a bad feeling about a particular course of action might be a legitimate reason to avoid that choice. Such "gut feelings," however, go against legal requirements for jurors to base their decisions solely on admissible evidence.

Research suggests that jurors are often unable to control their emotions when making legal judgments (indeed, this is one of the reasons many observers feel that judges would be better decision makers—precisely because judges are presumably more dispassionate and less likely to be swayed by emotion; see Chapter 13). However, it is important to point out that an emotion-driven verdict does not necessarily involve negative emotions or disadvantage one kind of litigant as opposed to another. In many cases it will work to the detriment of defendants, as when there is gruesome evidence of the crime with which a criminal defendant is charged. But in other cases it can work to defendants' advantage, as when juries nullify a law that they believe to be unjust and acquit defendants who should, according strictly to the evidence, be found guilty; or when they opt for life without parole for a remorseful capital defendant. And jurors who feel sympathy for a civil defendant might be less likely to find the defendant liable.

To address the role of emotion in jury decision making, we distinguish between legally relevant and legally irrelevant emotional responses. Although this distinction is an oversimplification, it allows us to consider separately situations where the law explicitly acknowledges some role for emotion (e.g., hate crimes, heinousness in capital sentencing) and those where an emotional response goes above and beyond the evidence. But first, we offer some preliminary observations on emotion and juries.

Emotion and Juries: Preliminary Observations

The Aristotelian and still prevalent view, that law is reason free from emotion, is a legal fiction. Jurors are no more immune to emotional influence than anyone else involved in the civil or criminal justice systems. Indeed, one could argue that because of their unfamiliarity with the role they are asked to play (compared to judges, police, and attorneys), the magnitude of the decisions they are expected to make (substantial financial penalties and loss of liberty and even life), and the nature of the evidence that sometimes arises (e.g., graphic evidence of injury or death, emotional testimony), jurors would be more susceptible to emotional influences than other legal actors.

The challenge is in determining, as Feigenson (2010) put it, how emotion influences jurors' judgments, whether it should, and what to do about it (see also Maroney, 2006; Wiener et al., 2006). These questions require a consideration of the descriptive, normative, and prescriptive aspects of the role of emotion in juror decision making. That is, *does* emotion influence jurors (descriptive); *should* emotion influence jurors, and under what circumstances (normative); and what procedural reforms might improve the ways in which emotion does or does not influence jurors (prescriptive). An additional challenge is in establishing what we mean when we talk about emotion.

In both legal and psychological contexts, emotion is a loose construct without an agreed-upon definition. In this chapter we use the term *emotion* mainly in the broad, colloquial sense, to refer to an affective response in jurors, although at times we will refer to specific emotions (e.g., anger, sadness), as different emotions are associated with different cognitive processes. A variety of terms are used to describe these affective states, including emotions, moods, feelings, sentiments, temperaments, and so on. They differ in a number of ways, such as their antecedents and consequences, duration, underlying physiology, subjective experience, and function; moreover, researchers disagree about what, exactly, each term means and how many varieties there are (e.g., Davidson, 1994; Frijda, 1994). Debates over the nature of emotion and other affective constructs are beyond the scope of the present chapter. For our purposes, we view emotions as relatively brief, functional affective states (i.e., biasing the organism toward a certain action) that are usually accompanied by a distinctive facial expression and physiological state (Davidson, 1994; Ekman, 1994).

Various emotion scholars have proposed different numbers of distinct, basic emotions (e.g., Ekman, 1992; 1994); the emotions most relevant to jury decision making are anger, disgust, fear, and sadness—notably, all negative emotions. Yet despite the fact that they are all negative affective states, these emotions differ in a number of important respects—most importantly, in the jury context, in terms of how individuals experiencing them appraise situations and process information. For example, according to the Appraisal-Tendency Framework (Lerner & Tiedens, 2006; Tiedens & Linton, 2001), the emotion of anger is associated with a sense that one has been offended, a sense of certainty about what has happened and what caused it, a belief that another person (as opposed to the situation or the self) is responsible, and an expectation that one can influence the situation (Lerner & Tiedens, 2006). In contrast, fear is associated with a feeling of uncertainty rather than certainty, and sadness is associated with a belief that situational forces are responsible. Thus the particular negative emotions aroused by trials could influence how jurors process the evidence and the verdicts they reach.

For the most part, a specific emotional response in jurors is elicited by trial evidence or some other aspect of the case, but it need not be. Jurors might arrive at court angry over an argument they had that morning with their spouse, or sad because they recently experienced a bereavement. They might also simply be in a bad mood because they have to do jury duty instead of going about their usual routine (see Chapter 2), the weather is nasty, or any number of other reasons. In this sense, then, emotion can be elicited by a source integral or incidental to jurors' judgment task (Feigenson & Park, 2006). Integral and incidental emotion do not necessarily exert the same effects on decision making; they might operate by different pathways, and the effects of integral emotion would normally be stronger (Feigenson & Park, 2006). Nonetheless, emotion often affects judgments even when people realize that the source of their emotion has nothing to do with the task at hand (Loewenstein & Lerner, 2003). For example, people process information differently depending on whether they are in a good or a bad mood, regardless of how the mood arose (Forgas, 1995; 2010).

Emotion can also influence jurors' judgments either directly or indirectly (Feigenson & Park, 2006). An example of direct influence would be if a juror took emotion as a relevant informational cue (e.g., my feeling angry makes the defendant seem more blameworthy), whereas indirect influence would be if the emotion affected the construal of some information, which then affected judgment (e.g., my feeling angry leads me to process exonerating information less carefully, which makes the defendant seem more blameworthy). These distinctions, among others, make emotional influences on jury decision making a complex and intricate topic that cannot be covered completely in a single chapter (it is also one of the reasons we left it until late in the present volume, as it draws on many of the topics raised previously). In the remainder of the chapter we discuss a number of the ways that emotion affects jurors, both when it should and when it should not.

Legally Relevant Emotion

Jury Nullification

One of the most fundamental ways that jurors can express emotion is in choosing to ignore laws that they dislike, a process known as *jury nullification*. It has been used to explain, for instance, all-White juries' failure to convict defendants charged with crimes against Blacks during the Reconstruction and Civil Rights eras; juries' failure to convict draft dodgers during the Vietnam War period; and, more recently, acquittals in euthanasia and assisted suicide cases. Although courts rarely inform juries of their right to nullify the law and often take steps to minimize the risk of nullification, juries' nullification power is essentially inviolate (*Sparf and Hansen v. United States*, 1865; see Hamm et al., 2013). Nullification is one of the main ways that juries, in refusing to return a verdict demanded by strict application of the law, express community sentiment (Finkel, Hurabiell, & Hughes, 1993; Marder, 1999; Reed & Bornstein, 2015).

For a jury verdict to be properly considered nullification, jurors must understand the law as presented to them and find all elements of the crime met beyond a reasonable doubt, yet acquit the defendant anyway (Hamm et al., 2013; see also Meissner, Brigham, & Pfeifer, 2003). By this standard, nullification is very infrequent, even when jurors are explicitly told they have the power to ignore the law (Hamm et al., 2013; Marder, 1999). Nonetheless, it does occur, and the very prospect of it strikes fear in the hearts of judges and prosecutors. There are a number of reasons why juries might nullify (Horowitz, Kerr, & Niedermeier, 2001; Kerr, 2010): a belief that the defendant's illegal behavior was justifiable or excusable, that the law should be rejected, that the defendant has suffered enough already or is unusually sympathetic, or that the punishment (in the event of a conviction) would be excessive.

Another possible reason for nullification is that the sorts of cases where nullification arises, which tend to involve perceived injustice (e.g., laws that go against the conscience of the community), provoke a strong emotional reaction. Confronting injustice is emotionally arousing (Haidt, 2001; Mikula, Scherer, & Athenstaedt, 1998), and typical nullification instructions even tell jurors to consider their feelings in reaching a verdict (Kerr, 2010). However, these same kinds of cases might also contain emotional properties, such as sympathetic defendants or unsympathetic victims, that jurors should not consider. The presence of emotion originating from different sources could make it difficult for jurors to distinguish between emotional reactions to legally prescribed information (e.g., outrage at an unjust law) and to legally proscribed information (e.g., sympathy or antipathy for the parties involved; Kerr, 2010). In support of this possibility, some evidence suggests that instructing jurors that they have the power to nullify can exacerbate jurors' other emotional biases in trials where nullification is an issue (Horowitz, Kerr, Park, & Gockel, 2006; Kerr, 2010). This finding provides a compelling argument against informing jurors of their nullification power.

Hate Crimes

Laws against hate crimes, also known as bias crimes, provide enhanced punishment for crimes that are motivated by enmity against a protected class of individuals, especially when the offense involves actions that willfully cause bodily injury to another person. Multiple rationales underlie hate crime statutes, but the main ones are that because these crimes are motivated by bias, they cause greater harm—to immediate victims, the target community, and society as a whole—than parallel crimes not motivated by bias against members of a particular group (Kovera, 2007; Lawrence, 2007). Although hate crime laws have been controversial since their inception, they have generally been deemed constitutional (e.g., *Virginia v. Black*, 2003) and are now an established feature of the American criminal justice landscape.

According to the National Gay and Lesbian Task Force, as of June 2013, 45 states and the District of Columbia had enacted some sort of hate crime statute. The statutes vary in the victim characteristics that they cover. All include race, ethnicity, and religion, but they vary in whether they also include gender, disability, sexual orientation and gender identity, age, political affiliation, and homelessness. Many states allow for a civil cause of action in addition to criminal penalties. The most recent federal legislation is the Matthew Shepard and James Byrd, Jr. Hate Crimes Prevention Act (enacted in October 2009), which expanded the previously protected characteristics of a victim's actual or perceived race, color, religion, or national origin to include gender, sexual orientation, gender identity, and disability (18 U.S. Code § 249).

As Kovera (2007) observes, hate crimes do not require that the perpetrator actually experience hatred while committing the crime. Dylann Roof could have been—and by most accounts was—calm and detached that day at Emanuel African Methodist Episcopal Church. But regardless of his emotional state at the time, if he selected his victims based on their race, then his actions meet the definition of a hate crime. It is hard to fathom someone's choosing a victim based on the person's group membership without harboring strong negative feelings toward the group both beforehand and at the time of the crime, but it is theoretically possible.

People generally hold positive attitudes toward hate crime laws, at least in the abstract (e.g., Craig & Waldo, 1996; Dunbar & Molina, 2004; Lieberman, 2010). However, those positive attitudes do not necessarily translate into tougher jury verdicts in hate crime cases, as illustrated by several studies that have examined mock jurors' decision making in hate crime prosecutions. The most fundamental question is how jurors would evaluate the same act depending on whether it is labeled as a hate crime. Plumm and Terrance (2013) explored this question by presenting mock jurors with an assault case in which the alleged victim and perpetrator met at a bar. The victim bought the perpetrator a drink and then asked the perpetrator to dance, whereupon the perpetrator beat the victim unconscious. Victim and perpetrator gender were manipulated, such that either a female perpetrator allegedly assaulted a male victim, or a male perpetrator allegedly assaulted a female victim. The perpetrator made gender bias–related comments (e.g., "I don't dance with dumb bastards [bitches]"), and the victim and witnesses perceived the incident to be bias motivated. Throughout the trial, the transcript referred to the case as either first-degree assault or bias-motivated assault (i.e., a hate crime) based on the victim's gender. Participants in the first-degree assault condition were more likely to find the defendant guilty than those in the hate crime condition, suggesting a reluctance to convict a defendant of a hate crime—at least when the charge involves gender bias.

Although Plumm and Terrance (2013) found a pro-defendant effect of labeling a crime a hate crime, the hate crime label does not always bias juror decisions in the defendant's favor. Research on other motivations for hate crimes has found that the hate crime label, or evidence that the crime was motivated by bias, has no effect when the charge involves sexual orientation bias (Plumm, Terrance, Henderson, & Ellingson, 2010) and can even lead to harsher sentence recommendations (i.e., an anti-defendant effect; see Cramer, Wakeman et al., 2013). These differential effects of labeling an incident a hate crime imply that laypeople perceive some offenses as more typical exemplars of hate crimes than others.

Some research has explored this possibility by comparing mock juror judgments for hate crimes that vary in terms of the victim's identity. For example, Cramer and colleagues compared mock juror sentencing decisions for a second-degree murder hate crime involving an African American, gay, or transgender victim (Cramer et al., 2014; Cramer, Kehn et al., 2013). In one study (Cramer, Kehn et al., Study 2), participants recommended longer sentences when the victim was gay than when the victim was transgender (the African American victim did not differ from either of the other two conditions). In other studies (Cramer et al., 2014; Cramer, Kehn et al., Study 1), recommended sentences were roughly the same for the different victims, regardless of how much participants blamed the victim and their support for hate crime laws. The lone exception was for gay victims among participants who did not support hate crime laws (Cramer et al., 2014). In this situation, victim blame was a strong predictor of sentencing when the victim was gay, but not otherwise.

Other victim and perpetrator characteristics and circumstances of the case matter as well. With respect to race, defendants are perceived as most guilty, and receive the harshest sentences, when the victim is African American and the alleged perpetrator is White, compared to same-race offenses or those with a White victim and African American perpetrator (Marcus-Newhall, Blake, & Baumann, 2002). In addition, Plumm et al. (2010) found that mock jurors blamed the victim more, and the defendant less, in a hate crime case based on sexual orientation when the crime took place in a non–gay bar and the victim allegedly provoked the defendant by putting his arm around him and asking him to dance.

These findings show that not all hate crimes are created equal; rather, laypeople have certain expectations about what constitutes a hate crime. Generally, they view a typical hate crime as involving violence as opposed to a nonviolent offense, directed toward a member of a minority group, and motivated by ignorance, fear, or anger (Craig & Waldo, 1996). The expectation of a fearful or angry perpetrator shows that people are sensitive to hate crimes' emotional component. They also evince considerable evidence of blaming the victim (i.e., not perceiving the victim as innocent; Craig & Waldo, 1996). The extent of victim blaming varies depending on victim type and other case characteristics; the more they blame the victim, the less likely they are to find the defendant guilty and administer a harsh sentence (Cramer et al., 2014).

Emotional Witnesses

A witness's demeanor, including his or her emotional expression, is an important part of the witness's credibility. In other words, it is not only what the witness says that matters, but also how the witness says it. Depictions of trials on television and in movies often make it seem like every witness provides gripping, emotionally laden testimony. Anyone who has sat through an actual trial knows that the cinematic image is an exaggeration; most trials contain a large amount of dry, repetitive, and technical testimony. Nonetheless, some testimony is highly compelling and emotional. Indeed, it is hard to imagine testimony from a victim of a violent crime or a severely injured plaintiff that would not involve some element of an emotional display by the witness, with an accompanying emotional response by the jurors.

In general, jurors expect victims to be emotional while testifying, and emotional witnesses are perceived more sympathetically than less emotional witnesses (Rose, Nadler, & Clark, 2006). However, the impact of witnesses' emotions depends on a number of factors, such as the emotion's fit to the crime, the emotional display's intensity, and its consistency over time. For example, emotional testimony that seems disproportionate to the offense (e.g., sobbing while testifying about a pickpocketing and describing the crime's severe and lasting effects) is looked at askance (Rose et al., 2006). This kind of reaction would fit a victim of a more severe crime, but not a pickpocketing victim.

As described in Chapter 5, jurors' perception of child eyewitnesses is affected by characteristics of the child and the child's memory, such as the child's age and whether the memory (e.g., of CSA) has been repressed or remembered all along. The child's behavior while testifying can also influence juror verdicts. Golding, Fryman, Marsil, and Yozwiak (2003) varied the demeanor of the alleged child victim in a first-degree rape trial so that she was calm, teary, or crying hysterically while on the stand. Mock jurors were more likely to convict the defendant when the girl was teary while testifying than when she was calm or crying hysterically. Apparently they expect child witnesses, especially in sexual assault or CSA cases, to be upset when required to confront the defendant and give testimony in court (Regan & Baker, 1998), but too much emotion can be as damaging to a child witness's perceived credibility as too little (Golding et al., 2003). When child witnesses behave as expected they seem more credible, and jurors are more likely to convict the defendant based on their testimony. These findings have implications not only for working with child witnesses prior to trial (i.e., too much preparation could dull a child's demeanor), but also for possible accommodations to make testimony less stressful, such as closed-circuit television, videotaped testimony, or having a support person present. If these accommodations cause the child's testimonial demeanor to deviate too much from what jurors expect, or if jurors expect the accommodations to alter children's demeanor but they do not, then the child witness's perceived credibility could be adversely affected (McAuliff & Kovera, 2012).

Witness demeanor is also an important determinant of how jurors perceive adult sexual assault victims. As with child victims, people generally expect them to be somewhat (though not overly) emotional when describing the assault (Kaufmann et al., 2003; Klippenstine & Schuller, 2012). Insofar as their actual behavior is congruent with expectations—that is, tearful and struggling to maintain control, as opposed to showing neutral or positive emotion—they come across as more credible when providing a statement to police (Bollingmo et al., 2009; Kaufmann et al., 2003), although the effect of witness demeanor dissipates after group discussion (Dahl et al., 2007). It can also be reduced by providing a cautionary instruction (Bollingmo et al., 2009).

Like most victims, sexual assault victims have to describe on multiple occasions what happened to them—and what impresses jurors, apparently, is the victim's consistency over multiple tellings. Klippenstine and Schuller (2012) investigated the effect of a sexual assault victim's demeanor on two separate occasions: the day following the alleged assault (manipulated as part of her roommate's testimony) and during trial (manipulated as part of her own testimony). What affected mock jurors' verdicts was not so much her demeanor, per se, but the constancy of her demeanor over time. When she was tearful and upset in describing the incident on both occasions, 71% of participants voted to convict the defendant, and 75% voted to convict when she was calm and controlled on both occasions. In contrast, only 25%–30% of participants voted to convict when her demeanor was inconsistent. This result shows that people have expectations about the stability of individuals' emotional reactions over time, as well as about the specific form that those reactions take.

Emotion as Mitigator or Aggravator: Remorse and Heinousness

As described in Chapter 11, emotion is a legitimate factor in criminal sentencing. The emotional evidence can derive from the defendant's testimony (i.e., remorse) or characteristics of the crime itself (i.e., heinousness). Heinousness is a frequent statutory aggravator, whereas remorse is sometimes listed as a mitigating factor and otherwise falls into the catch-all mitigation category. Although the terms are typically not defined for jurors, it is clear that they have an emotional component. Webster's *Third New International Dictionary (Unabridged)* defines *heinous* as "hatefully or shockingly evil; grossly bad; enormously and flagrantly criminal; abominable, execrable."[2] It defines *remorse* as "a gnawing distress arising from a sense of guilt for past wrongs (as injuries done to others); self-reproach." In instructing jurors to consider these factors, the law is very explicitly telling them that emotion matters in the sentencing phase of capital trials. Importantly, though, the law is not telling them that it matters in the guilt phase. Are jurors able to keep these tasks separate and use evidence only for its legally intended purpose? Research on remorse and heinousness suggests that they are not.

There are many different ways of showing remorse. Most often it takes the form of a verbal statement (e.g., "I am sorry for what I did," "I feel badly about it"), but it can also be demonstrated nonverbally. Nonverbal signs of remorse (e.g., crying, looking down, hanging one's head) can have an even greater effect on jurors' perceptions of criminal defendants than verbal expressions (Corwin, Cramer, Griffin, & Brodsky, 2012). Jurors are affected by a defendant's display of remorse or lack thereof. For example, many jurors who favor a life sentence perceive the defendant as remorseful, whereas jurors who vote

---

[2] The word *heinous* comes from the Germanic *hair*, to hate, which seems to imply that hate crimes are necessarily heinous, and vice versa.

for the death penalty cite the defendant's apparent lack of remorse as a factor in their verdict preference (Eisenberg, Garvey, & Wells, 1998; Sundby,
1998). In posttrial interviews of actual jurors, Sundby found that only 9% of
jurors who sentenced the defendant to death believed he was truly sorry for
the crime, compared to 30% of jurors who sentenced the defendant to life.[3]
These relatively low values, even for jurors giving a life sentence, reflect the
fact that despite the apparent benefit of remorse, remorseful capital defendants are rare (or perhaps more accurately, jurors rarely perceive them to be
remorseful; Sundby, 1998). They might genuinely lack remorse; alternatively,
prosecutors might be less likely to seek the death penalty against remorseful
defendants, or defendants might not show it out of fear that jurors will perceive them as insincere. Jurors do often question the genuineness of defendants' display of remorse (Sundby, 1998).

Although remorse can benefit defendants in the penalty phase, it can
work against them in the guilt phase, presumably because a verbal demonstration of remorse is an implicit admission of culpability (Jehle, Miller, &
Kemmelmeier, 2009; Niedermeier, Horowitz, & Kerr, 2001). A nonverbal display of remorse, in contrast, can make defendants seem less guilty (MacLin,
Downs, MacLin, & Caspers, 2009). In a capital case, jurors would ordinarily not hear evidence of a defendant's remorse until the penalty phase; however, nonverbal signs of remorse (or a lack thereof) could be apparent during
the guilt phase (e.g., the defendant's appearing abashed and contrite versus
stony-faced and hostile).

Remorse can play an important role in civil cases also. Remorse, especially when it is accompanied by an apology, reduces anger toward alleged
harmdoers while making them seem more sympathetic (Bornstein, Rung, &
Miller, 2002; Greene, 2008; Robbennolt, 2008). However, it can also make
them seem more culpable. Bornstein et al. (2002) varied the defendant's
behavior in a medical malpractice trial. The physician defendant expressed
remorse at the time of the incident and again at trial, expressed remorse
at trial, explicitly demonstrated a lack of remorse, or made no mention of
remorse (control). Defendants were perceived more positively when they
showed remorse than when they did not, regardless of when they displayed
their remorse; but defendants who showed remorse at the time of the incident
were required to pay more in compensation than defendants in the other
conditions, especially when the plaintiff's injury was relatively severe. This
finding suggests that showing remorse early on in a case with potentially
negligent conduct can make defendants seem more culpable, and jurors
effectively punish them more via compensatory damages. Because apologies

---

[3] These figures combine jurors who responded "Yes, sure he was sorry" or "Yes,
I think he was sorry." Other response options were "Not sure, he acted sorry but
it might have been just a show"; "No, he acted sorry, but it was a show"; and "No,
he didn't even pretend to be sorry" (Sundby, 1998).

and expressions of remorse can make defendants seem more culpable, there is much debate about whether, when, and how they should be offered, and many states now do not allow them into evidence, at least in certain kinds of cases like medical malpractice (Robbennolt, 2008).

Most jury instructions list the crime's being especially heinous or a related construct (e.g., atrocious, wanton) as an aggravating factor. However, these terms are defined loosely, if at all, and they are applied inconsistently (Bornstein & Nemeth, 1999; Kerr, 2010; Rosen, 1986). Depending on the wording of the statute and courts' interpretation of the statute, heinousness can encompass characteristics of the victim (e.g., age, degree of suffering, employment as a peace officer), characteristics of the defendant (e.g., gang or organized crime membership, motivation in committing the crime), or the nature of the crime (e.g., torture, postmortem mutilation). Little research has addressed jurors' perception of these various aspects of heinousness and how they affect their verdicts, and "the empirical literature is a bit of a mess" (Kerr, 2010, p. 120). What research has been done suggests that heinousness (e.g., mutilation, gratuitous violence) leads to more severe sentences in the sentencing phase of capital trials (Appelbaum et al., 2015; Myers, Roop, Kalnen, & Kehn, 2013). For example, Myers et al. manipulated heinousness in terms of a murder's brutality. The perpetrator either killed the victim instantly with a single bullet to the heart or shot him 14 times, pistol-whipped him, and inserted an umbrella into his rectum, causing him to experience extreme pain. Mock jurors were significantly more likely to sentence the defendant to death in the more heinous than in the less heinous condition. As heinousness is an aggravating factor, this is exactly as it should be. Heinousness can even be so powerful as to negate the mitigating effect of remorse (Eisenberg et al., 1998).

Studies examining the effect of heinousness at the guilt phase of a capital trial find that it can also lead to a higher proportion of guilty verdicts (Bornstein & Nemeth, 1999). Heinousness is immaterial to the question of whether the defendant committed the crime; whether he committed the crime for financial gain, dismembered the body, or the victim was a child has no bearing on his guilt.[4] Thus, an effect of heinousness on guilt judgments is another instance of jurors' fusion of judgments (see Chapter 9). To some extent it can be rectified by the normal bifurcation procedure, whereby evidence of heinousness would not be presented until the penalty phase, but some indications of heinousness (e.g., victim characteristics and certain aspects of the crime itself) would necessarily arise during the guilt phase.

Although it is not explicitly referred to as such, heinousness can factor into civil punishment (i.e., punitive damages) as well. Recall that the

---

[4] Some of these features of the case might have a bearing on whether the defendant is charged with capital murder or a less serious form of homicide, but conviction on a lesser charge is generally not an option for juries in capital trials.

language used to explain the type of conduct that must have been present to justify a punitive damage award refers to willful, wanton, reprehensible, or reckless behavior (see Chapter 10). These terms suggest behavior that is likely to elicit an emotional response and is worthy of condemnation, such as a drug company that knowingly exposed consumers to grave health risks without adequate warning (see, e.g., the case of *Allen et al. v. Takeda*, 2014, described in Chapter 10).

Kahneman et al. (1998; see also Kahneman, Schkade, & Sunstein, 2002) demonstrated the close connection between jurors' emotional response to civil defendants' misconduct and their punitive damage awards. According to their "outrage model," a defendant's reckless conduct elicits an attitude of outrage in those who hear about it, such as jurors; this outrage is then associated with a response tendency of punitive intent, which jurors express by awarding punitive damages. To test the model, they presented mock jurors with summaries of a number of different personal injury cases in which the plaintiff sought both compensatory and punitive damages. Jurors were told to assume that the plaintiff had already received $200,000 in compensation, and they then rated the outrageousness of the defendant's conduct, rated how much punishment the defendant deserved, or awarded punitive damages. Kahneman et al. found a high rate of agreement about which cases were more/less outrageous, as well as which ones were more/less deserving of punishment. There was less agreement, though still a substantial amount, about how much money to award in punitive damages. Of greatest relevance to the present discussion, there was considerable agreement among relative judgments of outrage, punishment, and punitive damage awards; that is, the more outrageous participants felt the defendant's behavior was, the more they felt the defendant deserved to be punished and the more they would make the defendant pay. Although they were somewhat variable in terms of translating their outrage into an exact dollar figure, they clearly viewed punitive damages as a vehicle for expressing that outrage.

Emotional evidence of mitigation and aggravation exerts complex effects on jurors' judgments. It can affect both sentencing decisions, where it is relevant, and guilt verdicts, where it is irrelevant. Thus, as in other situations (e.g., the awarding of damages; see Chapters 9 and 10), jury decision making demonstrates fusion: Jurors have a tendency to use evidence for purposes where it is not intended, as well as for legitimate purposes. Because emotional evidence is clearly relevant to some parts of a case, often it is impossible to limit presentation of this potentially biasing evidence. Emotional evidence related to mitigation and aggravation therefore poses a particularly thorny problem.

Emotionally Arousing Evidence

Perhaps the most direct way that emotion could exert an effect on jurors is by the presentation of emotionally arousing evidence. Obvious examples of emotionally arousing evidence are exhibits or testimony that satisfy one or more of the 3 G's: graphic, gruesome, and gory. Technically, these evidentiary features are independent of heinousness, although they often co-occur. The issue is not so much the "what" of the evidence but rather the "how" in the way it is presented. For example, in the trial of a defendant for an unusually brutal murder, the prosecution has a great deal of leeway in the evidence that it introduces to show the crime's brutality, such as pictures of the victim or witnesses' testimony (e.g., an eyewitness, police officer, or forensic examiner).

There is some, albeit mixed, evidence that exposing jurors to gruesome evidence, especially of a visual nature (i.e., pictures as opposed to oral testimony), increases perceptions of the defendant's guilt and the likelihood of conviction (Bornstein & Nemeth, 1999; Devine, 2012; Kerr, 2010). Some evidence suggests that the effect of gruesome evidence is greater when the case against the defendant is relatively weak than when it is relatively strong (Bright & Goodman-Delahunty, 2004). The effect of gruesome evidence could be mediated by jurors' emotional response to the evidence, their perception of other evidence against the defendant (e.g., making it seem more incriminating, or making exonerating evidence seem less exculpatory), their perception of the defendant himself (e.g., making him seem more blameworthy), or even their conviction threshold. For example, graphic photographic evidence of a crime victim's injuries increases mock jurors' negative emotions, such as hostility, vengefulness, anger, disgust, and sadness (Bright & Goodman-Delahunty, 2006; Cush & Goodman-Delahunty, 2006; Douglas, Lyon, & Ogloff, 1997; Kerr, 2010). These feelings, particularly anger, mediate the evidence's effect on verdicts (Bright & Goodman-Delahunty, 2006; Douglas et al.; Kerr, 2010). Gruesome evidence also elicits more compassion for the victim (Cush & Goodman-Delahunty, 2006).

The effect of graphic evidence does not appear to be mediated by inferences about other specific pieces of evidence presented at trial—that is, with occasional exceptions (Bright & Goodman-Delahunty, 2004), it does not bias how jurors process information generally (Cush & Goodman-Delahunty, 2006; Kerr, 2010). Nor does it have much effect on general feelings toward the defendant (Cush & Goodman-Delahunty, 2006). However, there is some evidence that it alters jurors' conviction threshold, with those exposed to gruesome evidence interpreting the degree of certainty required by "beyond a reasonable doubt" as lower than those not exposed (Kassin & Garfield, 1991; but see Thompson & Dennison, 2004).

Although most research on graphic or gruesome evidence has focused on visual evidence, verbal evidence can also be gruesome, as in a coroner's verbal testimony detailing the nature of a murder victim's injuries. Gruesome verbal testimony can bias guilt judgments in a manner similar to pictorial evidence (Bright & Goodman-Delahunty, 2004), but it does not always have this effect (Bright & Goodman-Delahunty, 2006; Thompson & Dennison, 2004), lending support to the adage that a picture is worth a thousand words—that is, gruesome visual evidence is more powerful than gruesome verbal evidence.

Graphic evidence of a plaintiff's injuries produces comparable emotion-mediated effects in civil cases, leading to more pro-plaintiff judgments (Bright & Goodman-Delahunty, 2011; Fishfader, Howells, Katz, & Teresi, 1996). Some evidence indicates that gruesomeness does not affect all judgments equally—emotion mediates the effect of graphic details on liability assessments but not damage awards (Fishfader et al., 1996). In civil cases these effects are mediated at least partially by sympathy for the plaintiff. As discussed in Chapter 9, civil plaintiffs with relatively severe injuries appear more sympathetic, and greater juror sympathy leads to higher compensation (e.g., Bornstein 1998). This effect of emotion is perfectly legitimate—feeling sorrier for a plaintiff, presumably because of a perception that the person's injuries are worse, should lead to greater compensation. Unfortunately, however, injury severity–mediated sympathy can also lead to a greater tendency to find the defendant liable, even when the evidence against the defendant is held constant (see Chapter 9).

Jurors' emotional responses to different parties at trial do not occur in isolation. In civil trials, for example, where the plaintiff and defendant are discrete, readily identifiable entities (albeit not necessarily individuals)—compared to the amorphous state in criminal prosecutions—sympathy for the plaintiff and defendant are reciprocal (Bornstein, 1998). And the angrier jurors feel toward the defendant, the more sympathy they feel toward the plaintiff (Feigenson et al., 2001). Feelings toward the plaintiff and defendant are especially likely to interact when they have both behaved in a blameworthy fashion, as in comparative negligence cases (Feigenson et al., 2001).

Evidence does not even have to be especially graphic to have these effects. Simply handling a weapon that was allegedly used in a crime (and would therefore be entered into evidence at trial) makes jurors perceive a criminal defendant as guiltier than those jurors who merely hear a description of the weapon or also see it but do not handle it (Dienstbier et al., 1998). Dienstbier and colleagues found that this weapon effect was not mediated by changes in mock jurors' mood (e.g., anger), suggesting that emotional evidence like a weapon can bias jurors' judgments by diverse pathways (e.g., via an emotional response or change in schemas and information processing).

Other evidence might influence perceptions of the defendant indirectly, via perceptions of the victim. As described in Chapter 11, victims are allowed to testify during the sentencing phase of capital (and some noncapital) trials, and such victim impact statements tend to lead to harsher sentences (Myers & Greene, 2004; Paternoster & Deise, 2011). The major concern about victim impact statements, to which both courts and jury researchers are sensitive (e.g., Myers & Greene, 2004; *Payne v. Tennessee*, 1991), is that they have the potential to incite jurors' passions while offering little in the way of probative value. Judges often cite the evidence's inflammatory nature in limiting the number of witnesses who can provide such testimony (this occurred, for example, in the sentencing hearings for Timothy McVeigh in the 1995 Oklahoma City bombing and for James Holmes in the 2012 Aurora,

Colorado theater shooting; Myers & Greene, 2004). Even when limited, the testimony can be powerful—the McVeigh jurors wept openly during the victim impact testimony (Myers & Greene, 2004).

Victim impact evidence is likely to elicit a variety of different emotions: anger at the defendant, sadness and sympathy or empathy for the victim and victim's survivors, and possibly even fear that one could be similarly victimized (Myers & Greene, 2004; Paternoster & Deise, 2011). As discussed below in the section on jurors' emotional state, these distinct emotions can have very different effects on how jurors process evidence, so the effect of victim impact evidence will likely vary depending on the particular emotions they happen to elicit. There is some evidence that positive feelings, such as sympathy and empathy for the victim, do more than negative feelings like anger to mediate the effect of victim impact evidence on jurors' sentencing decisions (Myers & Greene, 2004; Paternoster & Deise, 2011).

As Myers and Greene (2004) point out, an emotion-mediated effect of victim impact statements can be both rational and legally appropriate. For instance, jurors could use their emotional response to the testimony as a relevant cue that the defendant has inflicted greater harm, is more blameworthy, and deserves harsher punishment. Indeed, victim impact statements make the victim more sympathetic (Paternoster & Deise, 2011) and also create the impression that the defendant has caused greater suffering (Myers et al., 2013). Although these sentiments are potentially relevant to the decision of what sentence to give, they carry the risk of disparate trial outcomes and raise concerns about whether the law values some victims more than others.

Summary

There are a number of ways in which the law allows—indeed in some cases demands—emotion to be a part of jury decisions. Allowing or even prescribing an emotional element does not, of course, mean that emotion has its intended effect. For example, the law is of two minds with respect to jury nullification: Courts consistently uphold jurors' right to nullify the law, but they generally refuse to make jurors explicitly aware of that right, and they are unhappy when jurors exercise it. And the enhanced penalties sought by labeling something a hate crime are more likely to occur for some categories of victims than others.

Emotional evidence is similarly problematic. A witness's demeanor while testifying is relevant to her credibility, but jurors' expectations about witnesses' emotional displays while on the stand interact with witnesses' actual demeanor. Emotional evidence is often relevant, as in depicting a crime's heinousness, the defendant's remorse, or simply the nature of a gruesome crime. However, the manner of portraying such evidence can make it seem more or less compelling, thereby producing verdicts that are driven more by jurors' emotional reaction to the evidence than by the evidence itself, and producing an effect on both legally relevant and legally irrelevant judgments.

The precise relevance of other emotional evidence, such as victim impact evidence, is not entirely clear, yet it likewise influences jurors' emotions, with resultant effects on their verdicts.

In these situations the judge must balance the evidence's probative value against its potentially prejudicial impact. This is a delicate and challenging task for judges to perform, and the challenges are likely to increase as technological advances make high-resolution, vivid visual evidence more affordable and commonplace. We do not envy judges the job of having to grapple with legally relevant emotion; later in the chapter we discuss possible remedies.

Legally Irrelevant Emotion

The previous section covered legally relevant emotion, which encompasses jurors' emotional responses to the law as a whole (jury nullification), the defendant's state of mind in committing the crime (hate crimes), and various kinds of emotionally arousing evidence (emotional witnesses, evidence of heinousness and remorse, graphic and victim impact evidence, etc.). Jurors' emotional responses in these situations might be problematic if they exceed the role for emotion that the law anticipates, or lead jurors to give the evidence too much (or conceivably too little) weight—but using emotion, in and of itself, is acceptable. In other situations that is not the case. The present section considers situations in which jurors rely on legally irrelevant emotion. A number of sources can contribute to that affect—extraneous information (i.e., not admitted as evidence at trial), jurors' emotional states during trial, and their more stable emotional characteristics.

Nonevidentiary Sources of Emotion

Although our emphasis is on jurors' emotional response to evidence presented during trial, extraneous information can also elicit an emotional response. Three ways that this can occur are through jurors' exposure to pretrial publicity about the case being tried, their attitudes toward certain categories of cases, and emotional displays by trial participants who are not in the witness box.

Pretrial publicity (PTP) has a robust effect on jurors' verdicts (Spano, Groscup, & Penrod, 2011; Steblay, Besirevic, Fulero, & Jimenez-Lorente, 1999). Most PTP research focuses on information that is damaging to criminal defendants, so-called *negative PTP*. But positive PTP can work to criminal defendants' advantage, although its effect is smaller than the effect of negative PTP (Ruva & McEvoy, 2008). PTP can also work to the detriment of civil plaintiffs and defendants (Bornstein, Whisenhunt, Nemeth, & Dunaway, 2002).

Although it is clear that PTP exerts an effect on jurors' decision making, it is less clear why it has that effect. Jurors might consciously treat the

PTP as additional factual information relevant to the case, despite the fact that it came from outside trial; they might confuse PTP with the trial evidence, leading them to incorporate nonevidentiary information into their trial decisions without realizing it; the PTP could distort their processing of subsequent evidence in a direction consistent with the PTP; or PTP could elicit an emotional response, causing jurors to make intuitive rather than evidence-driven decisions or to shift their subjective standard of proof. In an effort to tease apart these possibilities, some research has distinguished between factual PTP, which is unsensational information that would be probative of a fact in issue if introduced at trial—for example, information that incriminates a criminal defendant—and emotional PTP, which would inflame jurors' emotions without speaking directly to facts in the case.

For example, Kramer, Kerr, and Carroll (1990) exposed mock jurors to a videotaped armed robbery trial. Prior to viewing the trial, jurors read and viewed news coverage of the trial that contained only basic information about the case, factually biasing information (e.g., that the defendant had a substantial prior criminal record), emotionally biasing information (e.g., that a car matching the robbery getaway vehicle was involved in a hit-and-run accident in which a 7-year-old girl died, and that the defendant was a suspect in the hit-and-run), or both kinds of PTP. The emotional PTP produced a negative emotional response (e.g., sadness, anger), but the factual PTP did not. Although neither type of PTP affected individual jurors' predeliberation verdicts, emotional PTP made deliberating juries more likely to convict (31% vs. 11%). Factual PTP did not significantly affect the jury conviction rate, suggesting that emotional PTP is more biasing than factual PTP (see also Kerr, 2010).

A limitation of Kramer et al.'s (1990) findings is that although the emotional PTP was more arousing than the factual PTP, jurors might also have perceived it as more factually relevant, even though it was not intended as such. That is, learning that the defendant was a suspect in a hit-and-run accident a few hours after the robbery might have made him seem more likely to be guilty of the robbery. When factual and emotional PTP are equated on diagnosticity—that is, when they are equally likely to incriminate the defendant—but differ in their level of emotional arousal, they exert comparable effects on mock jurors' verdicts (Wilson & Bornstein, 1998). And, just as emotional PTP can be perceived as factually relevant, factual PTP can produce an emotional response. Negative PTP makes jurors angry, and anger partially mediates the effect of PTP on their case judgments (Ruva, Guenther, & Yarbrough, 2011).

Although the prejudicial impact of PTP on jurors' verdicts reflects, to some extent, the PTP's emotional content, that is not terribly surprising. Just as jurors are not very adept at ignoring information they are told to disregard (Steblay et al., 2006), they incorporate pretrial information dealing with the case into their decision, regardless of whether the information elicits an emotional response or not. Somewhat more surprising, jurors can begin trial biased against certain defendants even in the absence of case-specific information. Simply hearing about similar, though completely unrelated, cases can make jurors more likely to convict in a given case (e.g., Greene & Wade, 1988).

This effect is so general that for certain kinds of cases, jurors do not even need to hear about other cases; rather, people might have such strong opinions about certain kinds of offenses that they simply show up at trial having prejudged any defendant who is charged with a certain crime. For example, Vidmar (1997) examined jury selection procedures in 25 Canadian cases involving charges of sexual abuse, most with minor complainants. On average, more than one-third (36%) of prospective jurors were rejected for acknowledging that they could not be impartial in a sexual abuse case. Vidmar (1997) explained such findings in terms of generic (as opposed to case-specific) prejudice, which is prejudice "that may arise from other sources of experience that cause a juror to categorize elements of a case as falling within a particular type regardless of the identities of the particular persons involved" (p. 22). The prejudice might arise from personal experience (e.g., a history of sexual victimization) or simply a general familiarity with a type of offense through community sentiment or media exposure. Thus, as with damage awards in civil cases (see Chapter 9), media coverage could create expectations in prospective jurors that make it harder for litigants to obtain a fair trial.

A variety of offenses might be susceptible to generic prejudice: sexual abuse, sexual assault, domestic violence, insanity, drug crimes, capital crimes, terrorism, and so forth (Vidmar, 1997; 2002; 2003). Generic prejudice can apply to biases based on specific charges (e.g., rape vs. first-degree vs. third-degree sexual assault) or broad crime categories (e.g., any sexual assault crime; Keller & Wiener, 2011; Wiener, Arnot, Winter, & Redmond, 2006).[5] It can also be evoked by other case characteristics, such as a defendant's race, ethnicity, religion, or sexual orientation (Vidmar, 2002; 2003), but it is most likely to occur in cases involving highly stigmatized conduct, such as sexual assault or crimes against unusually vulnerable persons (e.g., children; Wiener et al., 2006). Because CSA involves both sexual assault and a child victim, it is a prime candidate for generic prejudice. When generic

---

[5] With respect to variations in possible prejudice as a function of charge, we note that jurisdictions vary widely not only in the number of "degrees" available for a certain offense (e.g., first-degree vs. second-degree murder or sexual assault), but also in the terminology used to describe roughly comparable crimes. This is especially true with respect to sexual offenses. What qualifies as first-degree sexual assault in one jurisdiction might be labeled rape in another. Although we are unaware of research addressing the effect of crime labels on jury decision making, the issue does sometimes come up at trial. For example, in 2006 a trial judge in Lincoln, Nebraska banned the word "rape" from a sexual assault trial as being unfairly inflammatory and prejudicial (Massey, 2007).

prejudice arises, jurors have a visceral reaction based on the alleged offense that predisposes them against the defendant. Excusing jurors who admit to having such prejudice is doubtless beneficial to efforts to provide defendants with a fair and impartial jury; however, jurors are ill-equipped to evaluate their own impartiality, meaning that prospective jurors who acknowledge their generic prejudice might actually decide the case just fine, whereas others who disavow any prejudice might in fact harbor a bias of which they are unaware (see Chapter 3).

As discussed above, although a witness's emotional expression while testifying is relevant to judging the witness's credibility, the witness's emotion while *not* testifying is not relevant. Many witnesses are in the courtroom when not testifying, especially when they are also victims, plaintiffs, or defendants. Criminal defendants do not even have to testify, but they are still, almost always, present throughout trial. Jurors attend to these key figures and notice how they are responding to the proceedings (Rose & Diamond, 2009). For example, observers of Casey Anthony's trial for the murder of her 2-year-old daughter called attention to the defendant's crying during witness testimony and closing arguments, especially when the evidence dealt with her daughter's death and remains (e.g., Carbone, 2011; Colarossi, 2011). Some commentary raised the possibility that her crying was staged and insincere, as she responded to evidence differently when the jury was and was not present (Colarossi, 2011).[6] We are not aware of any research on criminal defendants' off-the-stand behavior, but considering the prominence of defendants in the courtroom, and evidence that jurors discuss civil litigants' "offstage" behavior (Rose & Diamond, 2009), it is a ripe topic for investigation.

For that matter, jurors might be influenced by emotional displays by anyone in the courtroom: attorneys, judge, reporters, or spectators (Rose & Diamond, 2009). In *People v. Nelson* (2014), for example, the defendant claimed that he was deprived of his right to a fair trial because members of the victim's family wore T-shirts in court with the victim's photo, name, and the words "Remembering" or "Remember." He argued that the shirts improperly elicited sympathy for the victim and were therefore prejudicial and inflammatory. The trial court disagreed; the appellate court, while acknowledging the shirts' potential emotional impact on jurors, affirmed the verdict (*People v. Nelson*, 2014).

In the Anthony case, even the attorneys' emotional reactions became an issue, with the judge admonishing them that they should not show an emotional reaction to the other side's arguments (one attorney was apparently seen trying to stifle a smile while opposing counsel spoke; Carbone, 2011). By virtue of their training and experience, judges are presumably good

---

[6] We are grateful to Jonathan Golding for calling our attention to this aspect of the Casey Anthony trial, and to the general role of defendants' and witnesses' off-the-stand emotional behavior.

at avoiding overt emotional responses to evidence. Nonetheless, they might subtly signal an emotional reaction or indicate how they are leaning through other nonverbal behaviors (Blanck et al., 1985; Rosenthal, 2002; 2003; 2006). For example, Halverson, Hallahan, Hart, and Rosenthal (1997) found that mock jurors were more likely to convict a criminal defendant when the judge believed the defendant was guilty than when the judge believed he was not guilty, presumably because of nonverbal cues that the judge transmitted while reading the jury instructions (see Collett & Kovera, 2003, for similar results in a mock civil trial). However, the judge's overall emotional demeanor (e.g., open and encouraging vs. stern and stoic) does not appear to affect jurors' decisions (Bornstein & Hamm, 2012). One could also ask how emotional behavior by spectators, such as friends or family of crime victims, would affect jurors' decision making.

Jurors' Emotional State

Earlier sections of this chapter covered emotional reactions to specific kinds of trial evidence and information related to trial that is not part of the trial itself (e.g., PTP). Certain trials as a whole are also likely to arouse jurors' emotions. It would only be natural for jurors to feel negative emotions, such as anger, fear, sadness, or disgust, toward civil or criminal defendants who are alleged to have caused—and whom the evidence might show to have perpetrated—injury to others. The most prominent emotion, at least in criminal cases, appears to be anger. Greater juror anger over the course of a trial is associated with harsher sentencing recommendations in capital trials, in part because it makes aggravating evidence seem more important (Nuñez, Schweitzer, Chai, & Myers, 2015) and mitigating evidence seem weaker (Georges, Wiener, & Keller, 2013). As jurors' anger increases, their ability to detect inconsistencies in witness testimony also decreases (Semmler & Brewer, 2002).

Sadness is another emotion that jurors could experience in the normal course of trial—for example, through exposure to emotional witness testimony or to injured and visibly suffering victims or plaintiffs. Sad jurors are better than jurors in a neutral mood at detecting testimonial inconsistencies, and the more inconsistencies they notice, the less credible that witness seems, and the less likely jurors are to reach a verdict favoring the side that called the inconsistent witness (Semmler & Brewer, 2002; as described in Chapter 5, inconsistencies can be either within or between witnesses, and the manipulation by Semmler and Brewer included both types). Assuming it is desirable for jurors to detect testimonial inconsistencies, sadness induces better juror decision making.

We noted in Chapter 11 that "death is different." The expression also applies to the role of emotion in capital trials. In addition to the many ways that emotion factors into capital trials that we have already discussed, especially at the sentencing phase (e.g., heinousness, remorse, victim impact statements, anger), the prospect of deciding that another person deserves to die can elicit a unique emotional response. Haney (1997; 2005) has argued that deciding whether to sentence another person to death is such an extreme, anomalous, and emotional process that the legal system has implemented a number of mechanisms "to bridge the gulf between the deep-seated inhibitions of capital jurors and state-sanctioned violence of the most profound sort" (Haney, 2005, p. 142). Borrowing from Bandura's (2002) theory of moral disengagement, he refers to these as "mechanisms of moral disengagement." According to Haney, the structure and content of capital trials work to dehumanize the defendant; exaggerate the difference between the defendant and the jurors; create a perception that the jury's actions are compelled by self-protection and have only remote, nebulous consequences; and diffuse jurors' sense of personal responsibility (see also Conley, 2013). These mechanisms effectively preempt any chance of positive feelings toward the defendant while nurturing negative sentiment and preventing jurors from fully appreciating the enormity of what they are being asked to do.

These mechanisms of moral disengagement, like many other trial features that trigger an emotional response, are integral to the trial itself. Jurors could also experience completely unrelated emotion. Consistent with predictions of the Appraisal-Tendency Framework that anger would make people more certain and inclined to blame another person (versus the situation), Lerner, Goldberg, and Tetlock (1998) found that angry participants were more punitive toward harmdoers than participants who were emotionally neutral, even when their anger was elicited by a completely separate task. The cases used by Lerner et al. dealt broadly with negligence, but they did not comprise jury simulations. In a task more akin to what jurors are expected to do, Bodenhausen, Sheppard, and Kramer (1994) induced anger, sadness, or neutral affect in student participants before asking them to render judgments in an ostensibly unrelated task involving peer judicial review. The judicial review cases involved allegations of assault and cheating. They also varied whether the student defendant in each case fit the offender stereotype (i.e., Hispanic vs. non-Hispanic in the assault case and an athlete vs. non-athlete in the cheating case). Angry participants' guilt judgments were affected by offense stereotypes (i.e., they perceived the Hispanic and athlete defendants as guiltier than their counterparts), whereas the judgments of sad and neutral participants were not. Analogous research by Curtis (2013) found that like anger, happiness increased mock jurors' reliance on stereotypes in judging a defendant's guilt, whereas anxiety did not.

Another way of manipulating jurors' emotional state via extraneous information is to make them think about their own mortality. According to terror management theory, humans are unique in their awareness of their own mortality, and they protect against death anxiety by developing, sharing, and protecting their self-esteem and cultural worldview (e.g., Burke, Martens, & Faucher, 2010; Greenberg, Solomon, & Pyszczynski, 1997). Thinking about one's mortality exaggerates this natural tendency toward worldview and self-esteem defense. Lieberman, Arndt, Personius, and Cook (2001) manipulated heterosexual, non-Jewish mock jurors' mortality salience by asking some of them to think about their own deaths. Participants for whom mortality was salient punished hate crime defendants less than control participants, presumably because the victims (in two separate cases, a gay or Jewish man) threatened their worldview. What made this finding particularly interesting is that when they were asked about hate crimes in the abstract, mortality salient participants were more supportive of hate crime legislation in general, and enhanced punishment for hate crime offenders, than control participants. In the abstract, "hate crime perpetrators" threaten one's worldview; in a specific case, however, the "deviant" victim can pose the threat. Insofar as the vast majority of hate crime victims are minorities or outsiders—racial/ethnic and religious minorities, LGBT individuals, women, and so on—jurors' tendency to protect their worldview could occur even in the absence of a mortality salience manipulation and could explain some of the victim blaming that takes place in hate crime cases (Lieberman, 2010). In other kinds of trials, especially when victim blame is not an issue and the trial itself raises issues of mortality (e.g., capital sentencing), mortality salience can actually lead to more appropriate use of the evidence (Lieberman, Shoemaker, & Krauss, 2014).

Thus, jurors' emotional state during trial, whether due to the content of the trial itself or outside forces, leads them to process trial information differently. Negative emotions are most likely to be elicited by trial evidence, but not all negative emotions are equal in this regard. Discrete emotions are associated with unique appraisal tendencies, and anger, sadness, and anxiety produce different constellations of effects. One might expect happiness and other positive states to be rare juror emotions—deciding legal disputes is hard work (just ask any judge), and little about being a juror is likely to make them rejoice. However, moods are relatively long-lasting affective states (Davidson, 1994), so it is not at all far-fetched that a juror could arrive in court in a good mood and that the juror's mood could color his or her interpretation of the evidence. A mild positive mood leads to more heuristic and less thorough information processing than a neutral or mildly negative mood (Curtis, 2013; Forgas, 2010). In this sense, then, it might be good that trials do not produce happy jurors.

Jurors' Emotional Characteristics

It is also possible that some jurors, by virtue of their disposition, respond more strongly than others to potentially arousing evidence. Some research shows that mock jurors who are higher in empathy (e.g., perspective taking) issue more guilty verdicts and harsher sentences (e.g., Olsen-Fulero & Fulero, 1997; Dienstbier et al., 1998).[7] Depending on the case facts, empathetic jurors

---

[7] Empathy is a complex construct that has both a trait and a state component (Batson, Turk, Shaw, & Klein, 1995). It is also closely related to, yet distinct from,

might identify with any number of trial participants: victims/plaintiffs, defendants, witnesses, or even the attorneys. In most cases, though, the most "empathizable" figure is likely to be the injured party—a criminal victim or a civil plaintiff. Whether or not the defendant is guilty or liable of causing that person's injury, it is usually (though by no means always) a given that the victim/plaintiff has, in fact, suffered some sort of injury. Thus it is not all that surprising that more empathetic jurors would be tougher on defendants.

Research on juror empathy has used a variety of criminal and civil cases, but the bulk of research has examined the role of empathy in rape trials (e.g., Olsen-Fulero & Fulero, 1997). Multiple scales exist that measure empathy with rape victims, such as the Rape Empathy Scale (Deitz, Blackwell, Daley, & Bentley, 1982) and Rape-Victim Empathy Scale (Smith & Frieze, 2003). The scales measure both victim empathy in the context of rape and endorsement of rape myths. For example, the Rape Empathy Scale requires respondents to choose between pairs of items like "In general, I feel that rape is an act that is provoked by the rape victim" or "In general, I feel that rape is an act that is not provoked by the rape victim." In the Rape-Victim Empathy Scale, respondents rate their (dis)agreement with statements like "I find it easy to take the perspective of a rape victim."

Women are consistently higher than men in empathy for rape victims (Deitz et al., 1982; Osmann, 2011; Smith & Frieze, 2003). Victim and perpetrator gender matter as well: Empathy is greater for female victims and for those raped by a man (Osmann, 2011). People with higher rape empathy perceive rape victims as less responsible for the assault and less blameworthy (Smith & Frieze, 2003); accordingly, they view accused rapists as more responsible, more likely to be guilty, and deserving of harsher sentences (Deitz et al., 1982). The relationship between rape empathy and judgments of rape victims has been demonstrated cross-culturally (e.g., Sakalh-Ugurlu, Yalcin, & Glick, 2007).

Although crime victims are probably the best candidates for empathy in the courtroom setting, they are not the only ones. Some categories of accused crime perpetrators quite likely elicit some degree of empathy, as do most civil plaintiffs, who by definition have suffered an (alleged) injury, and civil defendants who are not entirely at fault (Feigenson et al., 2001). With respect to criminal defendants, research on rape empathy shows that empathizing with rape perpetrators is associated with perceiving victims as more responsible, and men have greater empathy for perpetrators than women (Smith & Frieze, 2003). The most sympathetic defendants are probably those who were victims themselves and who responded to their victimization by harming (in some cases killing) their abusers, as in the case of battered women or children

---

sympathy (Wispe, 1986). Distinguishing between empathy and sympathy, and the subtypes of each construct, either in general or in legal contexts, is beyond the scope of the present work (see Feigenson, 1997).

who kill their abusers. Mock jurors who empathize more strongly with the defendant in such cases perceive the defendant more favorably (Plumm & Terrance, 2009) and are less likely to find the defendant guilty (Haegerich & Bottoms, 2000). Empathy with victims and perpetrators appear to be independent constructs (Smith & Frieze, 2003).

Summary

There are as many sources of irrelevant emotion at trial as there are of relevant emotion. Jurors respond emotionally to a variety of extraevidentiary sources of information, ranging from the courtroom behavior of litigants and others to specific information about the case and general prejudice. Their emotional states, whether affected by the trial itself or extraneous forces, and their emotion-related traits (e.g., empathy) influence how they process trial evidence and, ultimately, their verdicts. Jurors will naturally vary in their emotional dispositions, the mood they are in during trial (which would vary within as well as between jurors), and their reaction to trial evidence. It would be impossible, and arguably undesirable, to empanel a jury of stoics or eradicate all traces of extraneous emotional influence. Nonetheless, these emotional contributions to jury decision making need to be acknowledged, controlled, and in most instances minimized. The following section discusses specific strategies for dealing with emotion at trial.

Recommendations and Reforms

Emotion is such a fundamental part of human decision making—really, of the human condition as a whole—that it would be impossible to eradicate it altogether from the jury process. And, as this chapter has been at pains to show, we would not want to. Nonetheless, we can still ask whether it is possible to improve the ways in which emotion figures into jurors' judgments—so that it stays out when it should be out, and when it may come in, it enters only for the purposes and to the extent that the law intends. Both general and specific strategies exist.

General Debiasing Strategies

Assuming that emotional influence is undesirable because it introduces bias, the reform question becomes one of debiasing. For debiasing of decision making to be successful, "the decision maker must be (i) aware of the unwanted influence; (ii) motivated to correct the bias; (iii) aware of the magnitude and direction of the bias; and (iv) able to adjust the response appropriately" (Feigenson & Park, 2006, p. 156). As Feigenson and Park point out, jurors are quite possibly unaware of the bias, its magnitude, or direction; unmotivated to correct it even when they are aware; and unable to adjust their decision making even if they perceive a need and are motivated to do so. This combination of factors does not bode well for general debiasing efforts.

Nevertheless, we should not simply throw up our hands and walk away. One possible approach, proposed by Feigenson and Park (2006), is to make jurors more accountable. Having to explain and account for one's decision— or merely anticipating having to—leads to better, more rational decisions with less emotional influence (Lerner & Tetlock, 1999). Of course, one of the hallmarks of the jury system is that jurors are explicitly *not* accountable— their decisions are final (though subject to appeal), and they do not have to justify them to anyone. Still, it should be possible to increase jurors' sense of accountability without violating the sanctity and finality of their decisions, perhaps by requiring or at least encouraging them to discuss the case with the judge after they deliver their verdict (as discussed in Chapter 2, such posttrial sessions with the judge have additional advantages in terms of reducing juror stress and increasing their satisfaction with the process). Lerner et al. (1998) found that making participants accountable, by informing them that they would be interviewed about their judgments afterwards by an expert who would examine their responses, reduced the tendency for incidental anger to make them more punitive.

Specific Strategies

One logical approach to dealing with evidence or with extraneous trial information that might bias jury verdicts via emotional influence would be to address the risk in jury instructions. For example, the judge could tell jurors not to be unduly swayed by the content or form of emotionally arousing evidence like gruesome photographs. Empirical evidence conflicts on whether instructing jurors to consider gruesome evidence dispassionately and not to let their emotion influence their verdicts lessens the emotional impact of the evidence (Cush & Goodman-Delahunty, 2006; Thompson & Dennison, 2004). Moreover, even the research finding an effect of such a limiting instruction shows that it is modest and not limited to the graphic evidence. It reduces the overall conviction rate, especially when the instruction comes before (as opposed to after) the evidence; however, the limiting instruction does not specifically reduce the effect of gruesome evidence (i.e., it reduces convictions whether or not gruesome evidence is present; Cush & Goodman-Delahunty, 2006). The limited effectiveness of limiting instructions on graphic evidence might be due to jurors' belief—erroneous, as it turns out—that such evidence would not influence their decisions (Douglas et al., 1997). The ineffectiveness of instructions targeting emotion is consistent with the larger body of research showing that such instructions have only minimal impact on jury decisions (Alvarez et al., 2016; see also Chapter 14).

Victim impact statements pose a somewhat different problem. Currently, this testimony can take various forms (e.g., oral vs. written) and be used for different purposes (e.g., to humanize the victim, compare the victim to others, or express an opinion about the appropriate punishment; Myers & Greene, 2004). Thus the issue is not so much whether to provide instructions that would limit the evidence's use as to provide jurors with general guidance on the purposes and functions of the evidence. Platania and Berman (2006) found that such guidance can effectively mitigate the biasing effect of victim impact evidence. Until this kind of guidance becomes more widespread, victim impact statements should be carefully scrutinized and limited in scope, in order to minimize their potentially biasing effect (Myers & Greene, 2004).

Jurors' own characteristics might likewise seem not to be very malleable, but empathy has both trait and state components (Batson, Turk, Shaw, & Klein, 1995). Although trait empathy is a stable characteristic that is not susceptible to manipulation by transient factors, state empathy is modifiable. Several jury simulation studies have induced empathy by asking jurors to take the defendant's perspective and imagine themselves in the defendant's situation at the time of the crime, with the result that jurors then perceived the defendant more positively (Archer, Foushee, & Davis, 1979; Haegerich & Bottoms, 2000; Plumm & Terrance, 2009). It should even be possible to produce empathy for defendants charged with the most serious crimes, such as capital murder (Conley, 2013). Crossing the "empathic divide" in such cases would help to counter the potentially biasing effects of moral disengagement (Haney, 2004; 2005). Eliciting empathy does not, of course, necessarily make trials fairer, as empathy is not evidence. But it would not be prejudicial to the defendant.

A variety of remedies have been proposed for counteracting possible emotional bias associated with nonevidentiary information like PTP. The most common remedies are individual or extended *voir dire*, change of venue, continuance to allow the publicity to die down or at least fade in jurors' memory, and a judicial admonition instructing jurors to ignore PTP (Spano et al., 2011). Research examining these safeguards has shown that they are generally ineffective at mitigating PTP effects (Kramer et al., 1990; Spano et al., 2011). For example, simply instructing jurors to ignore information learned through PTP does not reduce its effects (e.g., Alvarez et al., 2016; Bornstein et al., 2002), in large part because of the ways that PTP works. If it distorts jurors' interpretation of trial evidence, if they are unable to distinguish between pretrial information and evidence admitted at trial, or if the PTP induces an emotional response that colors jurors' reaction to the case, then they cannot simply set the PTP aside.

Deliberation is another possible safeguard. PTP might arouse individual jurors' emotions and bias their verdicts, but cooler heads would presumably prevail once the group comes together to deliberate. However, the results of empirical studies suggest otherwise. Recall that Kramer et al. (1990) found stronger PTP effects for deliberating mock juries than for individual jurors (see also Steblay et al., 1999). They found, moreover, that PTP exposure made conviction-prone mock jurors more persuasive. Interestingly, these effects occurred despite the absence of a direct relationship between the amount of

PTP discussion during deliberation and jury verdicts, suggesting again that PTP exerts its effects through subtle mechanisms (e.g., biased interpretation of trial evidence).

Remedies proposed for PTP are unlikely to be very effective at dealing with generic prejudice. Even if a continuance did allow emotions associated with a specific case to die down, negative attitudes toward a particular type of offense would persist, and those attitudes are likely to be fairly consistent across venues. As discussed above, *voir dire* could remove jurors with obvious prejudice against a class of defendants—those who are aware of it and willing to admit it—but the remaining jurors might be every bit as biased yet unaware of their biases or disinclined to disclose them (Vidmar, 2002). The only remaining alternatives for combating generic prejudice would appear to be jury instructions, expert testimony, and reminding jurors of their oath to be fair and impartial. In light of instructions' relative ineffectiveness at reducing specific PTP effects (Alvarez et al., 2016; Spano et al., 2011), we are not optimistic that an instruction telling jurors to set aside their attitudes and assumptions toward defendants charged with, say, child sexual abuse would be very effective. Making sure they are aware that allegations of such highly repulsive acts sometimes turn out to be false might be more effective. This information could be provided via jury instructions or expert testimony. Ultimately, as some have observed (Doppelt, 1991), it might be virtually impossible for certain classes of defendants to receive trial by an impartial jury; they might be better off with a bench trial, on the assumption—a reasonable one, though we know of no empirical data on the issue—that judges would be less susceptible to generic prejudice.

Conclusions

Despite the popular portrayal of legal decision making as a dispassionate, evidence-driven process, emotion runs rampantly through it. Not only does the law fail to exclude emotion from jurors' decision making, but in some instances (e.g., jury nullification, use of witnesses' emotion in assessing credibility, aggravating and mitigating circumstances) it explicitly allows a role for emotion. The challenge is in determining the circumstances in which emotion should play a role, the mechanisms and parameters of emotional influence, and what to do if and when emotion has an inappropriate or excessive influence (Feigenson, 2010; Wiener et al., 2006).

Emotion has a proper role to play in jury decision making, just as it has a proper role to play in most human endeavors. And emotion does figure quite prominently in jurors' reasoning. However, the law is often of two minds about whether, why, and how emotion should factor in, such as with regard to jury nullification and victim impact statements. In addition, jurors' emotional response is sometimes excessive, varies depending on case characteristics that objectively should not matter (e.g., the type of hate crime victim), can lead to diverse outcomes depending on the specific emotion they experience or their own emotional characteristics, and sometimes takes irrelevant information (e.g., PTP) into account.

Unfortunately, emotion influences the sorts of decisions that it should not as well as those it should. This fusion of judgments is characteristic of juror decision making, and this makes it difficult to develop effective reforms. Limiting instructions (e.g., "Consider your emotional response for X, but not for Y") might help, but these are subtle distinctions for jurors to make; and other remedies, such as general debiasing strategies or traditional safeguards, may not be much more effective. It would be impossible for jurors to set aside their emotions at trial; alas, getting them to control their emotions does not seem to be any easier.

13

Just Let the Judge Do It

"Juries are more prone to generate large awards than are judges"
(Hersch & Viscusi, 2004, p. 34)

For every jury that acquits O.J. Simpson, there is a judge who sentences a manslaughter defendant to 10 years of attending church services. For every multibillion dollar punitive damage award by a jury, a judge sentences a defendant to 15 years in prison for possessing seven shotgun shells (*United States v. Young*, 2014). For every jury that acquits Casey Anthony, a judge gives a convicted child molester probation instead of jail time because he is too short for prison (5'1"). These examples, which we do not claim are representative or randomly chosen, illustrate that it is just as easy to find instances of "outrageous" judicial behavior as jury behavior (although the truth is often more complex and considerably less outrageous than the media coverage suggests; see Galanter, 1998).

Nonetheless, implicit in most criticisms of the jury is the assumption that judges would do a better job. In fact, this plank of the jury reform platform is often explicit rather than implicit: calls to remove cases from juries' to judges' purview have recurred throughout American history (Jonakait, 2003). The assumption that judges would be more effective decision makers than jurors is a reasonable one, considering that experts in most walks of life, by virtue of their greater knowledge and experience, perform better than novices (Chi, Glaser, & Farr, 2014; Ericsson & Smith, 1991). Judges are trained, experienced factfinders, whereas most jurors are doing the job for the very first time. You would not want someone who has never played basketball shooting free throws with the game on the line, or a person who has never followed the stock market choosing where to invest your money; so why give comparable responsibility to laypeople serving as jurors?

As described in Chapter 1, juries have existed for hundreds of years, and the right to a jury trial is enshrined in the U.S. Constitution; so they offer some advantages compared to dispute resolution by legal professionals like judges (see Landsman, 1993, 2002; Vidmar, 2000a; Vidmar & Hans, 2007). Presumably the disparity between the skills and experience of judges, as compared to lay jurors, was as great in the late eighteenth century, when the Constitution was written, as it is today. Nonetheless, the founding fathers deemed adjudication by one's peers to be important enough that they guaranteed it for all but relatively minor criminal offenses and civil wrongs. Jury trials have been a bedrock of the American justice system ever since. Moreover, although the frequency of jury trials is diminishing in the United States (Galanter, 2004), it is on the rise elsewhere. As we noted in Chapter 1, more than 50 countries currently employ jury systems, with additional countries using some other form of lay participation in the administration of justice (Hans, Fukurai, Ivkovic, & Park, 2017; Kaplan & Martin, 2006; Marder, 2011; Vidmar, 2000b). Several countries, including Russia, Spain, and South Korea, have introduced (or reintroduced after a prior abolition) jury systems in just the last 25 years (Hans et al., 2017).

Threats to the Right to a Jury Trial

There have not really been any serious attempts to take jury trials away from criminal defendants in the United States. On the contrary, for the most severe possible sentence—namely, the death penalty—the United States Supreme Court has taken some of the decision-making authority away from the judge in favor of the jury. Specifically, the Court held in *Ring v. Arizona* (2002) that the jury, and not the judge, had to determine the existence of any aggravating factors that would make a defendant eligible for the death penalty (see also *Hurst v. Florida*, 2016, and Chapter 11 in this volume). There are other respects in which juries appear to have more power than judges in criminal cases. For example, the jury may disregard the judge's instructions on the law altogether and reach a verdict contrary to law, a process known as *jury nullification* (Hamm et al., 2013; see Chapter 12). Courts typically decline to instruct juries on their nullification right, but the right itself has been consistently upheld (e.g., *Sparf and Hansen v. United States*, 1865; see Hamm et al., 2013).

In the civil justice system, on the other hand, the jury has not fared as well, leading Landsman (2002) to conclude that "a slow whittling away at the jury" (p. 905) has resulted in a marginalized jury that is unable to perform the functions envisioned for it by the Seventh Amendment. In civil cases judges may reverse the jury's verdict in either direction by entering a judgment notwithstanding the verdict (or N.O.V., for the Latin *non obstante veredicto*). They can also keep a verdict for the plaintiff but raise (or more often lower, in practice) the amount awarded in damages (referred to as *additur* and *remittitur*, respectively; see Baldus et al., 1995, as well as Chapters 9 and 10 in this volume). *Remittitur* can be substantial. For example, in the first jury trial in the slew of lawsuits initiated by the major record companies in the early 2000s to curtail file sharing, the jury found the defendant liable for infringing copyright on 24 songs and awarded the plaintiff, Capitol Records, $222,000. The defendant, Jammie Thomas-Rasset, obtained a new trial (for reasons unrelated to the damage award) and was again found liable, this time for *$1.92 million*. The judge reduced the award to $54,000; however, the record company refused to accept the *remittitur*, so there was a third trial in which the company was awarded $1.5 million. Again the court reduced it to $54,000. On appeal, the original award of $222,000 was reinstated (*Capitol Records, Inc. v. Thomas-Rasset*, 2012).

In the *Capitol Records* case, there was a jury (three juries to be precise), but the judge altered the jury's decision in two of three trials. Judges should, of course, have the right, in the interest of justice, to raise or lower a grossly disproportionate award. As we discuss in Chapters 9 and 10, *additur* and *remittitur* are effective mechanisms for ensuring vertical and horizontal equity. We leave for the reader to judge whether an award of $1.5–$2 million for illegally sharing 24 songs was grossly disproportionate (as well as whether a range of verdicts from $222,000 to $1.92 million constitutes an abnormal degree of variability). More problematic are reform efforts that would remove the right to a jury trial in certain kinds of civil cases altogether. Most commonly, such proposals arise in cases containing a great amount of complex evidence, such as patent infringement or antitrust litigation, or in those where there is a perception that juries consistently reach verdicts contrary to law or fairness, as in the case of punitive damages.

For example, in *Markman v. Westview Instruments, Inc.* (1996), the United States Supreme Court held that judges, not juries, should evaluate and decide the meaning of the words used in patent claims, because the wording is a matter of law and not a question of fact. Although the holding seems innocuous and arcane enough on the surface, it was predicated, at least in part, on the Court's belief that judges are superior in their "construction of written instruments" such as patents (p. 388). Despite preserving the right to jury trial in patent-infringement cases, it restricts the jury's responsibility for determining the outcome of such cases (Landsman, 2002). Of potentially greater concern, it opens the door for limiting the jury's purview in other types of cases that depend heavily on the construction of written instruments, which are potentially quite numerous (e.g., contracts, insurance policies, financial statements, etc.).

Motivated largely by a perceived increase in "blockbuster" punitive damage awards (Viscusi, 2004), as well as Supreme Court jurisprudence finding some punitive awards to be excessive (*BMW v. Gore*, 1996; *State Farm v. Campbell*, 2003), a number of commentators have proposed that judges or other professional bodies, and not juries, should determine punitive damage awards (e.g., Hersch & Viscusi, 2004; Mogin, 1998; Sharkey, 1996; Sunstein et al., 2002). Indeed, a few states have passed statutes whereby juries retain the ability to determine punitive liability, as well as compensatory liability and the amount of compensation, but the judge then sets the amount of punitive damages (Robbennolt, 2002b; Scheiner, 1991). Such reforms are further evidence of the "whittling away" referred to by Landsman (2002).

Choosing a Bench or a Jury Trial

As intended by the Sixth and Seventh Amendments, jury trials are most common in serious criminal and relatively high-stakes civil cases. They are quite rare in certain types of cases, such as juvenile and family court. Criminal defendants may waive their right to a jury trial and be tried by a judge—commonly referred to as a "bench trial"—but such requests are not always automatically granted, sometimes requiring agreement from the judge and prosecutor (see *Singer v. United States*, 1965).

There are many reasons why one might prefer a bench or jury trial. All else being equal, bench trials are shorter, simply because there is no need for jury selection, and judges can rule on motions in open court without having to excuse and call back the jury. For this reason alone, criminal defendants or civil litigants who are in a hurry to have their case resolved might prefer a bench trial. By contrast, a verdict rendered by one's peers might feel more appropriate and meaningful than a verdict delivered by a government employee, even a skilled and impartial one. Most of the reasons boil down, of course, to a judgment of which factfinder is most likely to produce a "fair" or "favorable" verdict (and although these are not necessarily the same thing, presumably they are in the minds of most litigants).

There is a great deal of attorney "folklore" about whether to opt for a jury or a bench trial, most of which draws on common stereotypes about judges being more rational and dispassionate and juries being more easily swayed by emotion or community sentiment. This "cultural script of judicial dispassion" (Maroney, 2011, p. 629) persists despite a lack of evidence demonstrating that judges really are all that dispassionate, as well as the existence of evidence showing that emotion, in some circumstances, can actually benefit legal (as well as other kinds of) decision making (e.g., Bornstein & Wiener, 2006; 2010a; Maroney, 2011; for a discussion of emotion and jurors, see Chapter 12).

Exemplars of the cultural script of judicial dispassion (Maroney, 2011), and the accompanying script of jury irrationality and volatility, are easy to find. One law firm's website, under the heading "Should I Waive a Jury Trial and Instead Have a Bench Trial?" says: "In many cases, especially when the crime is publicly scorned (i.e. DUI, domestic violence, animal cruelty, sex offenses) yet a bona-fide defense exists, one should consider waiving a jury trial. The case is then tried to only the judge. This can make it easier to focus the case on evidence and argument that matters most toward a not guilty verdict, rather than spending a lot of time and effort persuading twelve jurors to put aside their biases" (http://www.greghillassociates.com/lawyer-attorney-1940462.html).

The power of litigants, in consultation with their attorneys, to choose whether to have a bench or jury trial means that to some extent, judges and juries are trying different kinds of cases. This selection effect confounds attempts to compare judge and jury verdicts in actual cases (Clermont & Eisenberg, 1992; Vidmar, 1994). If there are systematic differences in the kinds of cases that wind up before the two categories of decision makers, then those differences alone, and not the identity of the decision maker, could explain any discrepancies in outcomes.

Despite the overall decline in trials—which most commentators attribute to the proliferation of alternative dispute resolution mechanisms (e.g., Galanter, 2004)—litigants are still taking advantage of their constitutional right to a jury trial. For example, Langton and Cohen (2008) analyzed civil trials held in state courts during 2005. They found that 68.3% of the trials overall involved juries. However, the rate varied quite a bit depending on the kind of case. Ninety percent of tort cases had juries, compared to 36% of contract cases and 26.4% of real property cases. The rate also varies widely in felony criminal trials, depending on the jurisdiction (Jonakait, 2003). There is even evidence that the ratio of jury to bench trials is increasing; put another way, the number of trials is vanishing more rapidly for bench than for jury trials, at least in federal civil cases (Clermont & Eisenberg, 2002; see also Chapter 1).

Comparing Judges and Juries

Whether judges or juries are "tougher" or "more lenient" depends, of course, on one's side. If judges convict more often than juries, then judges are tougher from the criminal defendant perspective. If they are similarly more likely to find against civil defendants, then judges are tougher from the civil defendant perspective but more lenient when viewed from the plaintiff side.

A number of empirical studies have compared the decisions of judges and juries (Greene & Wrightsman, 2003). These studies generally fall into one of three categories (Bornstein, 2006): archival studies, which compare trial outcomes in jury versus bench trials in similar kinds of cases; studies of judge–jury agreement, which poll judges on the verdict they would have reached in jury trials over which they preside; and experimental vignette studies, which assess judge and jury (more often individual juror) decisions in hypothetical case scenarios created by the experimenters. Our focus in the present chapter is on trial judges, as their task is most similar to that of jurors; for that reason they are both often referred to as "factfinders," though judges perform additional functions that jurors do not (e.g., interpreting the law). There is also a sizeable psychological literature on the decision making of appellate judges (e.g., Simon, 1998; Wrightsman, 2006), which we do not review here, with one or two exceptions (see below).

Archival Comparisons

In one of the earliest and largest studies, Clermont and Eisenberg (1992) compared plaintiff win rates and recoveries in federal civil cases (primarily tort and contract cases) tried before either juries or judges over an 11-year period (1979–1989). In products liability and medical malpractice cases—as described in Chapter 1, two of the most contentious areas of law and those that have spurred significant reform efforts—the results ran against the stereotype that juries are swayed more by sympathetic plaintiffs, such as those alleging harm caused by defective products or negligent physicians. Products liability and malpractice plaintiffs prevailed at trial at a higher rate before judges (48% and 50%, respectively) than they did before juries (28% and 29%). Plaintiffs also prevailed more often before judges in motor vehicle and negotiable instrument cases, although these differences were less dramatic than for products liability and malpractice cases. In two other types of cases—federal employers' liability (for which there were relatively few cases) and marine personal injury—plaintiffs had a higher win rate in jury trials than in bench trials.

In criminal cases, a New York City study of felony trials from 2006 through 2010 found that judges convicted less often than juries, 61% to 67% (El-Ghobashy, 2011). A Canadian study of a particular type of crime, historic child sexual abuse (defined as at least two years between the end of the alleged offense and the trial date), obtained similar findings: Judges convicted in 68.6% of cases compared to 93.1% for juries (Read et al., 2006). Read et al. also found that judges and juries responded to somewhat different features of the case. Both groups were influenced by the complainant's relationship to the accused and the presence of experts at trial. However, judges (but not juries) were sensitive to length of the delay between the alleged offense and trial, severity of the offense, and claims of repression; whereas juries (but not judges) were sensitive to age of the complainant when the alleged abuse began and the presence of threats by the alleged perpetrator.

Judges also give lighter sentences (King & Noble, 2005; Weninger, 1994). Although most states permit jury sentencing only in capital cases, several states authorize jury sentencing for other crimes as well, resulting in approximately 4,000 noncapital felony sentences meted out by juries per year (King & Noble, 2005). Military courts also allow jury sentencing, even, at the accused's request, after a guilty plea (Breen, 2011). King and Noble analyzed sentencing data for felony convictions in 1995–2001 from two of these states, Arkansas and Virginia. They compared average sentences after jury trial to average sentences after bench trial, as well as to average sentences after a guilty plea. Juries' sentences were significantly longer than judges' sentences (whether after trials or guilty pleas) in both states, a pattern that was more pronounced for relatively less severe offenses. They also found that jury sentences were significantly more variable, which they attributed largely to sentencing guidelines with narrow recommended ranges that were provided to judges but not to juries (and despite these guidelines, nontrivial disparities in judicial sentencing persist; Lovegrove, 1984; Saks & Hastie, 1986).

As King and Noble (2005) point out, a number of factors could underlie the disparity between judges' and juries' sentences in noncapital cases. Judges might offer a sentencing "discount" to defendants who opt for the more efficient bench trial. Juries might have less mitigating information available, and they might not be allowed to suspend sentences or place defendants on probation, which they are prevented from doing in Arkansas and Virginia. Juries might overestimate the likelihood of judges' reducing their sentences and therefore deliver harsher sentences in anticipation of such a reduction, in order to achieve an outcome they consider fair in the end. Regardless of the reason for it, King and Noble argue that greater jury punitiveness could pose yet another threat to community involvement via jury trials in criminal adjudication, if it ultimately leads more defendants to waive their right to a jury trial.

Such an outcome seems unlikely, however, in light of a judge–jury comparison in capital cases conducted by Hans and colleagues (2015), who found that judges gave harsher, rather than more lenient, sentences. Hans et al. conducted a historical analysis of sentencing outcomes in all capital trials in Delaware from 1977–2007 ($n = 146$). Statutory changes during this period meant that there was an era in which juries made sentencing decisions, followed by an era in which judges did, followed by a third "hybrid" era in which juries determined the presence of any aggravating factors beyond a reasonable doubt, but judges retained the ultimate sentencing authority (the hybrid system was declared unconstitutional by the Delaware Supreme Court in August 2016, following the United States Supreme Court's decision in *Hurst v. Florida*, 2016). Death sentences were significantly more common in the judge era (53%) than in the jury era (19%; the hybrid era was in between, at 39%). Thus, when it comes to the most severe possible penalty, judges are more punitive. Judicial sentences are also more severe than jury sentences in military courts (Breen, 2011). Overall, then, archival comparisons of criminal trial outcomes yield somewhat mixed results. Civilian juries are tougher than judges in noncapital cases, being more likely to convict and award harsher sentences; but they are less likely to sentence defendants to death versus life in prison, and military juries are also more lenient than military judges.

An especially controversial area of law is punitive damages (see Chapter 10), and not surprisingly it is also an area where researchers have compared judge and jury verdicts. As with any transfer of power from jury to judge, the reasons why the matter is controversial with respect to punitive damages are relatively straightforward. On the one hand, judges, by virtue of their greater experience and presumed objectivity, might be fairer. On the other hand, the Seventh Amendment's right to a jury trial would seem to encompass defendants exposed to punitive liability. In addition, cases involving punitive damages—where the defendant has allegedly acted wantonly or recklessly—are arguably precisely the kinds of cases where community sentiment, as expressed by a jury of one's peers, is essential (Reed & Bornstein, 2015; Scheiner, 1991).

We reviewed research on how well juries can set punitive damage awards in Chapter 10; here we examine the handful of studies, conducted largely by the same researchers, that address whether judges do any better. Before presenting the studies, we note that (1) the studies are contradictory, and (2) much of the disagreement revolves around the particular methods and statistical assumptions and techniques employed by the researchers. Our goal in reviewing these studies is to present a balanced overview without going into a wealth of technical detail (for which we refer the reader to the original studies).

On the "judges are better" side of the debate, Hersch and Viscusi (2004) analyzed jury and judge verdicts from the Civil Justice Survey of State Courts for 1996, which included over 9,000 cases in 45 state courts selected from the nation's 75 most populous counties. Plaintiffs were actually more likely to win before judges than juries, 62% versus 47%. Although both groups awarded punitive damages infrequently, in only 4% of cases, the mean punitive damage award was larger for juries ($1.8 million) than for judges ($557,000; the difference between the median awards was smaller, but it still favored juries). Moreover, Hersch and Viscusi found that the relationship between punitive and compensatory damage awards—an essential consideration according to the United States Supreme Court, which has held that under most circumstances, the punitive to compensatory ratio should typically not exceed a single digit (i.e., it should be less than 10:1; see *State Farm v. Campbell*, 2003)—was weaker for juries than it was for judges. The average ratio was 4.6 for juries and 1.25 for judges, meaning that judges' punitive awards tracked their compensatory awards more closely (importantly, the average ratio was less than 10:1 for both groups).

Hersch and Viscusi (2004) also identified 63 "blockbuster" cases, defined as those with punitive damage awards greater than $100 million, for the period 1985–2003 (see also Del Rossi & Viscusi, 2010; Viscusi, 2004). They found that juries were more likely than judges to make these extremely large awards, with only three of the 63 blockbuster verdicts awarded by judges. They conclude that "[t]his world of blockbuster awards is almost exclusively the province of juries" (p. 34).

On the "it ain't necessarily so" side of the debate, Eisenberg and colleagues (Eisenberg et al., 2002; 2006; Eisenberg & Heise, 2011) analyzed similar but larger datasets, and they used different statistical assumptions. For example, Eisenberg et al. (2006) included the same Civil Justice Survey 1996 data, as well as data from 1992 and 2001. They replicated Hersch and Viscusi's findings that judges and juries awarded punitive damages at about the same rate (4%–5%), juries' mean punitive awards were larger ($3 million vs. $461,000), and a higher percentage of jury awards were large (12% exceeded $1 million vs. 3% for judges, which, they point out, means that even for juries the vast majority of awards were less than $1 million). But according to these authors, judges and juries imposed roughly the same punitive to compensatory ratio (see also Del Rossi & Viscusi, 2010, who found no difference in the ratios for judges and juries); the ratio remained steady over time for both groups; and compensatory awards were the strongest predictor of punitive awards for both groups. In addition, judges' and juries' propensity to award punitive damages varied depending on the type of case, with judges more likely to award punitive damages in cases with bodily injury, but juries more likely to do so in cases with financial injury.

More recent research by Eisenberg and Heise (2011) did find that the punitive to compensatory ratio was higher for juries than for judges in the most recent cases in their dataset (2005). Rather than concluding that juries are becoming less rational than judges in awarding punitive damages or that *State Farm* is affecting judges more than juries, they attribute the difference to case selection effects (i.e., strategic decision making by litigants about whether to opt for a bench or jury trial). Overall, they found little difference in the punitive damages decision making of judges and juries.

Eisenberg et al. (2006) also found that juries' punitive awards were more variable. As we mentioned previously, greater variability is potentially problematic, as it raises the risk of horizontal inequity and maybe even vertical inequity as well. However, greater variability is a virtually inevitable consequence of dealing with higher values overall, which Eisenberg et al. attribute to nonrandom case routing; that is, high-stakes cases are more likely to wind up before juries than judges. In support of this interpretation they note that juries were more likely than judges to see cases with corporate defendants. Taken as a whole, the conclusions of Eisenberg and colleagues' research (2006; see also Eisenberg et al., 2002; Eisenberg & Heise, 2011) fail to provide much support for the argument that juries cannot rationally determine punitive damages—or at least the related argument that judges would do a better job of it. Indeed, this conclusion characterizes the archival comparisons as a whole. In civil cases, judges find for plaintiffs more often in some kinds of cases but less often in others, whereas in criminal cases, evidence suggests that juries are more likely to convict and are tougher in sentencing for some types of cases but not others.

Judge–Jury Agreement

The seminal study of judge–jury agreement was conducted approximately 50 years ago by Harry Kalven and Hans Zeisel (1966). Kalven and Zeisel asked a sample of 555 judges to report, for over 3,500 jury trials, both the jury verdict and the verdict that they themselves would have reached. They assessed both liability and damages in civil trials, and guilt/innocence in criminal trials. The results across case types were strikingly similar, with judges agreeing with the jury 75%–80% of the time on civil defendants' liability and 75%–78% of the time on criminal defendants' guilt (the ranges reflect slight differences depending on how they treated hung juries). In civil cases, judges would have awarded less than the jury's actual award in 52% of trials and more than the jury's award in 39% of trials. The take-home point from the Kalven and Zeisel study is a matter of perspective. On the one hand, judges and juries agreed much more often than would be expected by chance, suggesting that both sets of decision makers are responding to the same kinds of evidence. On the other hand, they disagreed in roughly one out of every four trials, a nontrivial rate, and the disagreement rate might have been suppressed by judges' knowledge of the jury's verdict and desire to be consistent with it.

Of perhaps greater interest than the sheer rate of (dis)agreement is the directionality of those disagreements and the reasons for them. Kalven and Zeisel (1966) found that criminal juries were somewhat more lenient than judges; that is, in instances of disagreement, they were more likely to acquit when judges would have convicted than vice versa. This, combined with judges' preference for smaller damage awards in civil cases, suggests that judges on the whole are tougher: They award less money and convict more often. Although it runs counter to King and Noble's (2005) finding that judges impose lighter sentences, this interpretation accords well with judges' own impression of why they sometimes disagreed with juries, namely, that juries were more responsive to defendant characteristics capable of producing sympathy (e.g., age, attractiveness, remorse, etc.). When it comes to sentencing, perhaps juries are more responsive to sympathy-arousing victim characteristics, leading them to be tougher on criminal defendants.

At least two subsequent studies have replicated Kalven and Zeisel's (1966) findings, in both civil (Sentell, 1991) and criminal trials (Eisenberg et al., 2005). Eisenberg and colleagues improved on Kalven and Zeisel's methodology by asking not only judges, but also jurors and attorneys, a number of questions, most notably their evaluations of evidence strength and case complexity. Their sample included over 300 criminal trials in the counties of Los Angeles (CA), Maricopa (AZ), and the Bronx (NY), as well as the District of Columbia. Their agreement rate was virtually identical to that obtained by Kalven and Zeisel: 70%–75% (again depending on the treatment of hung juries). They observed the same asymmetry in judge–jury disagreements (i.e., judges would convict when juries acquitted more often than the other way around), but in examining the reasons for judge–jury disagreements they found that evidence strength—especially as perceived by the judge—played a significant role. Consistent with the overall pattern, judges were more likely than juries to convict when the judges viewed the evidence as medium or strong; but they were actually more likely to acquit when they viewed the evidence against the defendant as weak. Unlike evidentiary strength, differences in legal complexity did not explain judge–jury disagreement.

Overall, then, the judge–jury agreement studies suggest two conclusions. First, judges agree with jury verdicts much more often than not, about three-quarters of the time. Second, one cannot say, on balance, that one kind of arbiter is easier or tougher than the other. There is some evidence that judges treat civil plaintiffs and criminal defendants more harshly, but this tendency depends on such factors as the strength of the evidence.

Experimental Studies

As the other chapters in this volume make clear, a substantial jury simulation literature has developed over the last several decades. Parallel to this jury simulation literature exists a much smaller body of work on "judge simulations" in which real judges read or view hypothetical cases and give their impressions, typically including a verdict. The pros and cons of such experimental studies are the same as for jury simulations (see Chapter 1), with the additional complication that judges are a less available sample than college undergraduates or even community members. Nonetheless, researchers have taken this approach in several studies, some of which focus on whether judges are susceptible to the same sorts of cognitive biases as jurors, whereas others focus directly on mock verdicts (sentencing or damage awards).

As an example of the latter approach, Diamond and Stalans (1989) asked Illinois state court judges and laypeople (both students and individuals summoned for jury duty but who did not serve) to recommend sentences in four different case vignettes: trials of a burglar, a cocaine seller, a purse snatcher, and an aggravated batterer (stabbing). The results varied slightly depending on the case and the judges' jurisdiction (Cook County vs. elsewhere in the state), but overall, the judges' sentences were somewhat more severe. For instance, in the case of the defendant who was convicted of selling 11 grams of cocaine, 30% of judges favored a prison sentence (as opposed to straight probation or probation and jail), compared to 5% of student mock jurors and 16% of nonstudent mock jurors. These findings are the opposite of those obtained by King and Noble (2005, discussed above), who found that judges' sentences in actual cases in Arkansas and Virginia were more lenient than jurors' sentences. The pattern of greater judicial leniency has also been found in research comparing Dutch judges' recommended sentences to those recommended by Dutch laypeople (de Keijser & Elffers, 2009).

Experimental comparisons of judges and jury-eligible citizens in civil cases have yielded fewer differences. Their awards for punitive damages are of comparable size and variability, and they both make proper use of relevant legal factors, such as the actual and potential severity of the plaintiff's injury and the defendant's wealth (Robbennolt, 2002b). In awarding general (e.g., pain and suffering) damages, jurors award somewhat more compensation—but this tendency is due, at least in part, to jurors viewing the same injury as more severe than judges (Wissler, Hart, & Saks, 1999). Wissler and colleagues found that the awards of both judges and jurors closely tracked their assessment of how severely the plaintiff had been injured.

Guthrie and colleagues (Guthrie, Rachlinski, & Wistrich, 2001) assessed judges' susceptibility to five widespread and robust cognitive biases, including anchoring, framing, and hindsight effects. These biases have been amply demonstrated in the population as a whole, as well as in mock jurors (Devine, 2012; Greene & Bornstein, 2003; Vidmar & Hans, 2007). Participants were 167 federal magistrate judges, who were drawn from a group of judges attending an educational conference. The sample comprised nearly one-third of all the federal magistrate judges in the country at the time.

On three of the five biases, judges' reasoning was just as flawed as laypeople's. They were less susceptible to the other two biases, but they still showed evidence of suboptimal reasoning. Like jurors (Steblay et al., 2006), judges are incapable of completely disregarding information that they are aware of but that has been ruled inadmissible (Landsman & Rakos, 1994; Wistrich, Guthrie, & Rachlinski, 2005). Overall, most of the research on cognitive biases shows that judges are, by and large, just as susceptible to them as jurors or other laypeople (Simon, 1998; for an exception, see Viscusi, 2001). This stands to reason, considering that the biases reflect fundamental decision-making processes that are adaptive in many (though not all) circumstances and that are notoriously hard to monitor and change, even among decision makers with a great deal of experience in some domain (e.g., Ariely, 2009; Hastie & Dawes, 2009). Perhaps recognizing the potential for bias among judges as well as jurors, Sunstein and colleagues (2002, p. 258)—who are quite critical of juries, at least with respect to the awarding of punitive damages—conclude that "perhaps the ideal system of punitive damages awards would not involve juries or even judges, but specialists [from a regulatory agency] in the subject matter at hand, who would be able to create clear guidelines for punitive awards." Clear guidelines certainly would not hurt, but expecting specialists with even more expertise than judges to be immune to fundamental reasoning biases seems more wishful than realistic.

Although the common expectation is that judges would be less susceptible to cognitive biases than jurors, they might actually be *more* susceptible. Rachlinski (2000) distinguishes between insider versus outsider perspectives on cognitive illusions. What this means is that it is easier to identify cognitive biases in others than in oneself. When it comes to decision making at trial, then, "judges are more likely to adopt an outsider perspective to decision making by juries than by themselves or other judges" (Rachlinski, 2000, p. 66). Consequently, judges are more likely to recognize and adapt to jurors' decision-making biases, whereas they tend to ignore their own biases. According to this view, rather than simply assuming that judges will do better, we have reason to expect that, at least in some respects, they might actually do worse—not because they are more susceptible to bias but because they are just as susceptible to bias, yet unlikely to do anything about it.

Indirect Judge–Jury Comparisons

The previous comparisons of judge and jury decision making can be thought of as direct comparisons, in that they examine judgments made by the two different kinds of factfinders about either the same stimuli, as in the agreement studies and experimental comparisons, or about comparable stimuli. Another approach to the question is to ask whether judges and juries are affected similarly by various factors, which might be appropriate legal considerations (e.g., evidence) or extralegal factors. Such indirect comparisons can inform us whether judges and juries show the same pattern with regard to certain variables.

Although the category of legal considerations that should influence trial judgments is fairly well circumscribed (by, e.g., rules of evidence and procedure), the category of extralegal factors, which has attracted a great deal of social scientific research (Devine, 2012), is virtually infinite. Among other things, it includes features of the decision maker (e.g., age, gender, race/ethnicity, religion), characteristics of the parties involved at trial (e.g., litigants, attorneys, witnesses), and extraneous situational variables (e.g., stress). For exemplary purposes, we review two variables where research has examined both groups of decision makers: religion and stress (for reviews of the role of extralegal factors in judges' decision making generally, see Ashenfelter, Eisenberg, & Schwab, 1995; Cohen, 2014; Schubert, 1964; Segal & Spaeth, 1993; Spohn, 2002).

Religion

Although many individual characteristics can exert an effect on legal decision makers' reasoning, religion is unique in that it is so intimately tied up with the sorts of moral judgments that legal situations frequently demand (Bornstein & Miller, 2009). For example, some religions prescribe certain stances on social issues that might come up at trial (e.g., capital punishment, family planning, sexual behavior) in ways that other social classifications do not. Women, racial and ethnic minorities, rich people, and members of other groups might be more or less likely to hold certain positions on these issues, but there is no official "party line," so to speak. Religious beliefs can, and in some cases do, lead to exemptions for judges and jurors alike—judicial recusals and juror challenges for cause during *voir dire*. More often, however, individuals from diverse religious backgrounds participate in the trial process, allowing for an examination of the relationship between decision makers' religion—either affiliation or adherence to specific beliefs—and trial outcomes. For the most part, neither judges nor jurors are allowed to invoke religious beliefs explicitly in making their decisions, but the law on these matters is somewhat murky (Bornstein & Miller, 2009). In any case, such instances are relatively rare; rather, religion might lead individuals to decide a certain way without their being aware of it.

Studies of trial judges' religion have found that it is not a strong predictor of their verdicts (Ashenfelter et al., 1995; Bornstein & Miller, 2009; George, 2001), although there is some evidence that Catholic judges are more liberal on race issues (Vines, 1964). Religion exerts a greater effect on appellate judges' decision making (for review, see Bornstein & Miller, 2008–2009; 2009). As appellate judges typically make decisions as members of a tribunal, rather than fully empowered solitary decision makers, most studies examine individual judges' votes rather than the tribunal's decision. Jewish appellate judges, including those on the United States Supreme Court, tend to be more liberal, whereas evangelical judges tend to be more conservative. Catholic appellate judges are less predictable, being more liberal on some issues (e.g., gender discrimination) but more conservative on others (e.g., obscenity, gay rights). One study, which included federal trial (district) as well as appellate courts, went so far as to conclude that "the single most prominent, salient, and consistent influence on judicial decision making was religion—religion in terms of affiliation of the claimant, the background of the judge, and the demographics of the community" (Sisk, Heise, & Morriss, 2004, p. 614).

Jurors' religion likewise correlates with their verdict preferences, albeit not in precisely the same way that it does for judges, nor always in the way that attorney intuition and folklore suggest (Bornstein & Miller, 2009). For example, some trial advocacy manuals claim that Catholics and Jews will respond more to emotional appeals (e.g., Goldstein, 1935)—a broad and, to our knowledge, unsubstantiated (and arguably unsubstantiable) stereotype. However, some attorney beliefs with respect to religion appear to have a basis in fact. There is a popular belief among many members of the bar that Jews and Catholics are less likely than adherents of other faiths to favor a death sentence in capital trials (Murphy, 2005). Indeed, most Jewish organizations oppose the death penalty, as does the Catholic church (Drinan, 2000). Not surprisingly, some (though not all) studies find that Catholics and Jews are less supportive of the death penalty, and less likely to vote for it as a sentencing option in capital cases, than Protestants, especially fundamentalist Christians and Southern Baptists (Bornstein & Miller, 2009; Eisenberg et al., 2001).

In other sorts of cases the role of jurors' religion varies depending on the type of case, as with judges (Bornstein & Miller, 2009). It might exert a larger impact in capital cases than in more routine trials, given the polarization in views on the death penalty in society at large and the salience of the death penalty, among other social issues, in religious discourse. Nonetheless, the data show that neither judges nor jurors are completely able to set their religious views aside when deciding cases.

Stress

Both groups are also susceptible to stressors that accompany trial. As described in Chapter 2, a number of procedural and evidentiary variables can make jury duty a challenge. Judges must deal with many of the same sorts of variables, such as long trials and complex or gruesome evidence (e.g., Chamberlain & Richardson, 2013; Flores et al., 2008–2009). Other stressors that jurors face do not concern judges, such as unfamiliarity with the situation and disruption to their daily lives (Miller & Bornstein, 2013); for judges, deciding cases *is* their daily life.

On the other hand, judges face stressors that do not concern jurors, such as managing courtroom personnel, directing the trial, juggling heavy workloads, and dealing with public and media scrutiny. Both groups might have safety concerns, especially for certain kinds of trials (e.g., racketeering, gang trials), but given jurors' comparative anonymity, safety concerns are likely greater for judges. Indeed, there has been a spate of cases in recent years involving violence against judges or their families. For example, in 2005 a defendant on trial for rape in Atlanta overpowered a deputy sheriff, stole her handgun, used it to shoot (and critically injure) her, then went to the courtroom where his trial was taking place and shot Fulton County Superior Court judge Rowland Barnes and the court reporter, killing them both. After leaving the courtroom, he shot and killed another deputy. In a 2009 California case, a murder defendant left the stand to attack the judge, who had just announced a recess; deputies shot and killed the defendant, David Paridiso, while Judge Cinda Fox was relatively unharmed. Judges are very aware of these incidents, leading many of them to fear for their safety (Flores et al., 2008–2009).

In addition to safety concerns, judges experience stress from secondary traumatic stress and burnout (Chamberlain & Miller, 2009; Chamberlain & Richardson, 2013). Secondary traumatic stress, which can result from exposure to others' trauma (e.g., crime victims), is associated with a host of negative physical and psychological symptoms (Chamberlain & Miller, 2009), and it can affect jurors as well as judges (Miller & Bornstein, 2013). As most jurisdictions now require jurors to serve only one day or on a single trial, burnout is unlikely to be an issue for jurors except for the occasional very long trial, or for grand jurors, a little-studied group who serve for lengthy periods. However, judges demonstrate a number of symptoms of burnout (e.g., depression, negative attitudes toward work) due to factors like media scrutiny, work overload, inadequate resources, and workplace conflict (Chamberlain & Richardson, 2013). Thus, despite the popular image of judges as aloof, dispassionate arbiters, they are susceptible to stress in the same manner as jurors. Some of the stressors judges face are the same as those that jurors encounter, while others are different; but the potential effects on judges' well-being and the administration of justice are comparable.

Conclusions

The myth of judicial superiority raises a number of questions, both descriptive and normative. The descriptive question is simply whether judges and juries reach different trial outcomes. Although it is simple in the asking, the answer is bedeviled by data limitations and methodological concerns. Nonetheless, studies that have compared the two sets of decision makers, either directly or indirectly, show few systematic or straightforward patterns. In many respects they do not differ (e.g., overall agreement, susceptibility to cognitive biases), whereas in other respects the existence or direction of differences depends on how one analyzes and interprets the data (e.g., punitive damages) or the particular methodology used (e.g., archival vs. experimental comparisons of criminal sentencing). Furthermore, the most plausible explanations for any observed differences focus on the weight attributed to legal and procedural variables, such as differential evidence (in terms of either its availability or its utilization) and decision options (e.g., sentencing), more than on differences in individual characteristics, attitudes, or reasoning ability.

Apart from the descriptive question—which is complicated enough—there is a pair of more normative, philosophical issues. The first is, what constitutes *better* decision making in this context? The problem here is that judges are often held up as the gold standard in the justice system, but it is not a given that if judges and juries disagree, then juries are necessarily inferior (Bornstein & Greene, 2011a). For example, the agreement studies show that when judges and juries disagree, juries have a tendency to be more lenient (setting aside the moderating effect of evidence strength). Archival comparisons, on the other hand, show that judges, at least in criminal cases, tend to be the more lenient ones for many but not all (i.e., capital) kinds of cases. Is either pattern necessarily a bad thing? For instance, rather than juries being too lenient, perhaps judges are being too harsh.

"Better" in the trial context is hard to define, but it might include things like closer adherence to the law (hence an absence of jury nullification), more appropriate use of evidence (e.g., verdicts more in line with evidence strength), and less variability in outcomes (i.e., comparable treatment of similarly situated litigants). By these metrics, there is slight, but not overwhelming, evidence in favor of judges. Juries do occasionally, albeit rarely, ignore the evidence and refuse to apply the law (Hamm et al., 2013). However, judges might nullify too—we just don't hear about it—and it hardly seems fair to malign the jury for exercising a right that has consistently been upheld (*Sparf and Hansen v. United States*, 1865).

This point goes to the second aspect of the normative question, namely: Is it desirable for judge and jury verdicts to be totally in sync? As King and Noble (2005, p. 332) aptly observe, "Indeed, the right to a jury trial itself . . . is premised in part on the likelihood of a different outcome when a jury decides instead of a judge." Put another way, if juries behave exactly like judges, then juries are in some ways redundant. Because they are also inefficient—requiring twelve people to do the job of one, who remains part of the process anyway, plus adding to the length of trials—they should arguably be discarded. There could well be legitimate reasons, such as citizen engagement, to retain juries even if they function merely as judicial clones. But if the right to jury trial incorporates other values, such as the expression of community sentiment—as opposed to the sentiment of a small class of professional, highly educated, and well-paid adjudicators—then we should embrace the jury's autonomy and resulting disparities from judicial decisions. These values appear to be part of the reason why other countries have adopted juries or other lay adjudication systems (Hans et al., 2017).

To be clear, we are not encouraging juries to flout the law, nor are we diminishing judges' importance to the administration of justice in both jury and bench trials. But we see no great cause for concern about occasional judge–jury disagreement, even when it appears, as it inevitably will, that juries have reached an objectively "wrong" verdict. Acceptance of these infrequent errors is a small price to pay for the many benefits that a jury system provides, especially in light of the very scant evidence that judges do the job any better.

14

Jurors Don't Need Any Special Help

> "It seemed to me that we are all taught to write things down, especially if they are important, so we will not forget; and, if we do not understand, to ask a question. These two things were preached to us starting in grade school; so why is it we throw that common sense out of the window in jury trials?"
>
> (Ferrara, 2008, p. 330)

As the preceding chapters illustrate, jurors struggle with many aspects of their jury service. They often feel lost and confused, unsure of their proper role, and they may struggle with understanding the evidence or the law; all of these things can impair their ability to reach a proper verdict. Just because juries rarely flout the law by blatantly disregarding it (Hamm et al., 2013), that does not mean that they fully understand it and apply it as legislators and judges intend. For many years courts tended to assume that jurors are equipped to do their duty without much assistance. Recently, research showing that they have difficulty in understanding certain kinds of evidence, as well as both procedural and substantive instructions, has led to a number of procedural innovations designed to help jurors. Chapter 2 described innovations before and after trial, such as juror education, orientation, and debriefing programs, and the subsequent chapters addressed area-specific reform efforts. The present chapter focuses on general strategies that can be implemented throughout trial, such as clarifying the legal instructions, modifying the trial structure, and allowing jurors to ask questions, take notes, and discuss the case prior to deliberation. It also presents a few novel possibilities for enhancing jurors' factfinding and decision making.

Traditional Versus Innovative Safeguards

When questions arise about jurors' ability to interpret evidence and apply the law properly, courts often invoke a number of traditional "safeguards": *voir dire*, cross-examination, closing arguments, jury instructions, and deliberation. We refer to these safeguards as "traditional" ones because they are part and parcel of any jury trial. To this list we would add expert testimony, which can serve the purpose of aiding jurors in their use of other evidence presented at trial, as in the case of expert testimony about eyewitness memory or confessions. Although expert testimony does not occur in every trial, it is fairly commonplace and does not involve a departure from standard procedure. As described in Chapter 7, it generally does have an effect on jurors' decisions, though not always in the manner intended.

The other traditional safeguards are doubtless beneficial with respect to their primary purpose. *Voir dire* identifies clearly biased jurors, cross-examination highlights weaknesses or inconsistencies in a witness's testimony, closing arguments summarize each side's case, instructions present the applicable law, and deliberation ensures some degree of group consensus. But beyond that, do they help? There are several ways of answering this question. First, a safeguard might increase jurors' knowledge or understanding of a particular procedure or kind of evidence. For example, deliberation might allow some jurors to correct other jurors' misunderstandings and thereby increase their overall comprehension of the evidence or law. Second—and perhaps as a direct or indirect consequence of better comprehension—a safeguard could facilitate jurors' use of the evidence or application of the law. For example, expert testimony on eyewitness memory might help jurors to do a better job of discriminating between eyewitnesses whose memory likely varies in strength (the data on whether eyewitness expert testimony has such an effect is mixed; see Chapter 7). And third, a safeguard might make jurors simply feel better about their jury service without having any discernible effect on the trial outcome. They might like the court's efforts to weed out biased jurors during *voir dire*, or value the process of deliberating to a unanimous verdict, as opposed to simply taking a vote and going with the majority (see Chapter 4 for a discussion of jury decision rules). Juror satisfaction is important because of its relationship to failure-to-appear rates and civic engagement more broadly (see Chapter 2).

Various studies of safeguards focus on one or more of these different consequences. As discussed in Chapter 5, extensive *voir dire*, cross-examination, and closing arguments do relatively little to enhance jurors' performance in eyewitness cases (Devenport et al., 2009; van Wallandael et al., 2007). For example, closing arguments that call attention to the limitations of eyewitness testimony have occasionally been found to sensitize jurors to variations in witnessing conditions (Laub et al., 2016), but more often they merely make jurors more skeptical about eyewitness evidence

290 The Jury Under Fire

(Geiselman et al., 2002; Geiselman & Mendez, 2005) and can even elimi-nate the positive effects of expert testimony (Geiselman et al., 2002). And using extensive *voir dire* to identify jurors who will respond to certain kinds of evidence has not proven to be particularly effective (Crocker & Kovera, 2011; Devenport & Cutler, 2004).

Deliberation would seem to offer great potential for improving com-prehension, following the maxim that two heads (or six, or twelve) are bet-ter than one. In theory, if one juror forgets or misremembers some aspect of the evidence or law, then other jurors could set the record straight. However, collaborative recall can also have inhibitory effects or lead to the spreading of false recollections (Salerno & Diamond, 2010). Although deliberation can be contentious, the process—especially under a unani-mous decision rule—does make jurors feel better about the work they are doing (see Chapters 2 and 4) and more confident in the accuracy of their verdicts (Davis et al., 1993).

Some studies of deliberation show that it also improves comprehension of jury instructions (e.g., Diamond et al., 2012; Greene & Johns, 2001) and that instructions have a greater effect on verdicts after deliberation than before (Wheatman & Shaffer, 2001); however, a number of other studies have found that neither individual jurors' self-reported (Devine et al., 2007) nor their actual comprehension improves much from pre- to post-deliberation (Ellsworth, 1989; Landsman et al., 1998; Lynch & Haney, 2009). Some evi-dence suggests that deliberation helps jurors understand the evidence more than it helps them understand the law (Ellsworth, 1989), at least under some circumstances (e.g., when they are instructed prior to hearing the evidence; see Bourgeois, Horowitz, ForsterLee, & Grahe, 1995), and that it aids in com-prehension of the law on some issues but not others (Diamond & Levi, 1996). In the absence of any authoritative documentation, such as a trial transcript or written instructions from the judge, it might be just as easy for a mistaken juror to persuade a correct one as the other way around; and if most jurors have it wrong, then a juror who is the lone voice of reason faces an uphill battle (Diamond & Levi, 1996).

In part because of the failure of traditional safeguards to have much of a salutary effect on jurors' decision making, courts and legislatures have increasingly adopted a number of more innovative techniques to accomplish this purpose. The remainder of this chapter reviews research on the effective-ness of those innovations. We include jury instructions as one such innova-tion because, although instructions are "traditional" in the sense that they are a necessary part of all jury trials, efforts to revise instructions for greater comprehension are of relatively recent vintage. We follow our discussion of jury instructions with sections on bifurcation and the effectiveness of allow-ing jurors to take notes, ask questions, and discuss the case with one another prior to deliberation. Finally we consider some novel, relatively untested proposals to reform jury trials and enhance the quality of jurors' decision making.

Jury Instructions

Many courts and legal commentators have a strong preference for using jury instructions, rather than other methods, as a means of enhancing trial fairness (Marder, 2006; *New Jersey v. Henderson*, 2011; Sheehan, 2011; Turgeon et al., 2014). There are many reasons for this preference. Instructions are less costly and time-consuming than remedies like expert testimony and bifurcation; and because the judge delivers the instructions (albeit often with attorney input), they have an aura of authority and impartiality that more attorney-driven safeguards, such as *voir dire* and cross-examination, lack. Some studies show that jurors feel they do not have a good grasp of what the instructions mean (e.g., Greene & Bornstein, 2000), whereas jurors in other studies report understanding the law quite well (e.g., Devine et al., 2007). Still other studies show that jurors struggle to understand the law in some respects but "get it right" in many others (Diamond et al., 2012). This discrepancy might reflect variability in comprehension across different kinds of cases, as well as the vagaries of self-report. Jurors might believe they understand the instructions without actually understanding or being able to apply them, in much the same way that an eyewitness can be certain about an identification that turns out to be mistaken; and the opposite can be true as well (i.e., understanding the instructions without appreciating that fact). Studies of actual comprehension speak more directly to the issue.

The effectiveness of jury instructions has been studied in a number of different ways. For example, comprehension levels have been studied in real and mock jurors, with and without exposing them to a trial, pre-deliberation and post-deliberation, and using a variety of test formats (e.g., multiple choice, true/false, or open-ended items; for review, see Alvarez et al., 2016; Daftary-Kapur, Dumas, & Penrod, 2010; Devine, 2012; Lieberman, 2009; Ogloff & Rose, 2005). Not surprisingly, jurors' comprehension levels vary depending on the nature of the instructions and means of assessment, but they often fail to exceed 50% and are poor for both procedural and substantive legal matters, even including bedrock legal concepts like the burden of proof (e.g., Daftary-Kapur et al., 2010; Lieberman, 2009; Marder, 2006; Ogloff & Rose, 2005). Smith and Haney (2011, p. 339) aptly summarize this literature by stating that "in virtually all of the reported research—regardless of the participant demographics, methodology employed, or specific legal context—jurors' comprehension of the legal instructions that are supposed to guide their decision making appears to be very low."

There are different sources of comprehension errors, with the most common being misunderstanding of legal terms (i.e., "legalese"), structural weaknesses in the instructions, and omission errors (Diamond et al., 2012). One analysis found that more than half of jurors' comprehension errors resulted from omissions, where the instructions did not explicitly cover some topic or issue (e.g., whether attorneys' fees were compensable; Diamond et al., 2012). The low level of comprehension occurs across different types of civil

(Greene & Bornstein, 2000) and criminal cases (Alvarez et al., 2016) and has been documented in empirical studies going back more than three decades (Charrow & Charrow, 1979; Elwork, Sales, & Alfini, 1982; Severance & Loftus, 1982). Reflecting this modest level of comprehension, instructions (compared to no instructions at all) do not generally have a sizeable effect on jurors' decisions (e.g., Nietzel et al., 1999; Patry & Penrod, 2013).

In some respects comprehension is an end in itself—jurors who feel that they do not understand what they are supposed to do end their jury service feeling frustrated and dissatisfied (Greene & Bornstein, 2000). Even more importantly, poor comprehension can impair the administration of justice. Some studies show that jurors who understand the law poorly reach different (and typically more punitive) verdicts from those who understand it well (e.g., Patry & Penrod, 2013; Shaked-Schroer et al., 2008; Wheatman & Shaffer, 2001; Wiener et al., 2004; Wiener et al., 1995). In large part this reflects problems jurors have with understanding key concepts, such as mitigation in capital cases (e.g., Haney & Lynch, 1994; Lynch & Haney, 2011).

A substantial body of literature has examined whether rewriting jury instructions, primarily to simplify their language, improves comprehension. These efforts use a number of different techniques, such as substituting more common words for "legalese," shortening sentences, and simplifying syntax. For the most part, revising instructions along these lines does increase comprehension, typically on the order of 10%–30% (Daftary-Kapur et al., 2010; Devine, 2012; Marder, 2006). In one of the earliest instruction revision efforts, Charrow and Charrow (1979) increased comprehension on their most stringent measure from 32% to 43% by simplifying vocabulary, shortening sentences and reducing the use of passive voice, removing negations, and similar techniques (using a less stringent measure, performance improved from 45% to 59%). Providing written instructions in addition to delivering them orally, including visual aids like flowcharts or decision trees, and instructing jurors at both the outset and conclusion of trial can also benefit comprehension, as well as juror satisfaction (Daftary-Kapur et al., 2010; Diamond et al., 2012; Lieberman, 2009; Marder, 2006; Ogloff & Rose, 2005).

These findings have contributed to the adoption by several states of "plain language" instructions (Marder, 2006; Tiersma & Curtis, 2008). Consider, for example, California's revised instructions, which were approved in 2003 (civil) and 2005 (criminal). The old instruction on the burden of proof in civil cases read: "'Preponderance of the evidence' means evidence that has more convincing force than that opposed to it. If the evidence is so evenly balanced that you are unable to say that the evidence on either side of an issue preponderates, your finding on that issue must be against the party who had the burden of proving it" (California Jury Instructions: Civil [BAJI] No. 2.60; see Tiersma & Curtis, 2008, p. 243). The new instruction reads: "When I tell you that a party must prove something, I mean that the party must persuade you, by the evidence presented in court, that what he or she is trying to prove is more likely to be true than not true. This is sometimes referred to as 'the burden of proof' " (Civil Jury Instructions [CACI] No. 200; see Tiersma & Curtis, 2008, p. 244). Tiersma and Curtis found that mock jurors were better able to understand and apply the new instructions than the old ones. The American Bar Association (2005) recommends that "The court should instruct the jury in plain and understandable language regarding the applicable law and the conduct of deliberations" (Principle 14, pp. 20–21).

Several studies of jury instructions have investigated whether instructions concerning a particular type of evidence or element of the law are effective. As with research on overall comprehension, the results of such studies are generally disappointing. For example, jurors who are explicitly instructed to disregard some piece of information—either formally presented evidence that has been ruled inadmissible or extraneous information like pretrial publicity—still use the information in reaching a verdict (Alvarez et al., 2016; Daftary-Kapur et al., 2010; Steblay et al., 2006). In some circumstances the instruction can even call more attention to the inadmissible evidence (Steblay et al., 2006). Evidence can be, and is, ruled inadmissible in all kinds of trials. Many other jury instructions are naturally tailored to particular kinds of cases. The two types of cases in which specific instructions have probably received the closest scrutiny are those involving eyewitnesses and the death penalty.

Instructions on Eyewitness Testimony

As described in Chapter 5, the fallibility of eyewitness memory has recently become a major public policy concern, in large part due to its role in false convictions. Because instructions are a traditional safeguard, many efforts by courts and legislatures to address the limitations of eyewitness testimony have focused on instructions (e.g., *New Jersey v. Henderson*, 2011; for review, see Bornstein & Hamm, 2012; Jones, Bergold, Dillon, & Penrod, 2016; Turgeon et al., 2014). The precise instructions used vary across jurisdictions, but the most common ones are modeled on the *Telfaire* instruction (*United States v. Telfaire*, 1972), which calls jurors' attention to several factors (e.g., opportunity to observe the perpetrator, time between the crime and the identification) that might have a bearing on eyewitness performance. The critical issue, as with expert testimony on eyewitness issues (see Chapter 7), is whether enhanced instructions can sensitize jurors to variations in the strength of eyewitness evidence. Sensitization means that instructions enable jurors to do a better job of discriminating—especially in terms of their verdicts—among witnesses who are likely to be more or less accurate; that is, more guilty verdicts in cases with "good" eyewitnesses than in cases with "bad" ones.

Several studies have addressed this issue, with inconsistent results. Some studies have found that instructions from the judge cautioning jurors about problems and limitations of eyewitness testimony do sensitize jurors to meaningful differences in the eyewitness testimony itself (i.e., relatively good vs. relatively poor eyewitnesses, based on various characteristics of the witness, perpetrator, and situation; Geiselman & Mendez, 2005; Ramirez, Zemba, & Geiselman, 1996). However, other studies have found that such instructions merely make jurors more skeptical about eyewitnesses (i.e., they convict less; see Greene, 1988; Katzev & Wishart, 1985), and still others find no effect of instructions on verdicts whatsoever (e.g., Bornstein & Hamm, 2012; Cutler et al., 1990; Greene, 1988; Jones et al., 2016; Laub et al., 2016; Martire & Kemp, 2009; Paterson, Anderson, & Kemp, 2013). The ineffectiveness of instructions occurs not only for visual (eyewitness) identifications, but also for auditory (earwitness) identifications (Bornstein & Hamm, 2012; Laub et al., 2016). A recent meta-analysis by Berman and Penrod (2012) found that compared to no instruction at all, some sort of instruction on eyewitness issues tended to reduce the number of guilty verdicts (i.e., it produced skepticism) irrespective of the nature of the eyewitness instruction, but it did not produce sensitization.

The inconsistency, especially in terms of finding a sensitization effect, is likely due to the high variability in the content of specialized instructions about eyewitness testimony in both jury simulations and real-world trials involving eyewitnesses. The instructions range from broad admonitions that eyewitnesses may be less accurate than they think they are, to referencing any number of specific factors (e.g., length of exposure time, eyewitness confidence) without specifying how those factors relate to eyewitness performance (the approach taken in *Telfaire*), to an empirically based summary of the relationship (e.g., longer exposure leads to better performance, confidence is usually not a strong predictor of accuracy). The challenge in designing effective instructions on eyewitness testimony is to determine just how much information to provide without appearing to introduce new evidence and encroaching on the judge's neutrality.

Death Penalty Instructions

Capital jury instructions are notorious for being especially complicated, and instruction comprehension—more precisely, the alleged lack thereof—has been the basis of a number of death penalty appeals (Diamond & Levi, 1996; Haney, 2005). Among the potentially confusing aspects of the instructions are the definitions of aggravating and mitigating factors (see Chapter 11), especially mitigators, as jurors are typically allowed to consider mitigators other than those listed by statute (in contrast, they may consider only statutorily enumerated aggravators); the decision rule for determining the presence of aggravators and mitigators; the ambiguous structure of the sentencing process itself (i.e., how jurors should weigh aggravators and mitigators relative to one another in translating the aggravator–mitigator calculus into a verdict); and lack of clarity regarding the non–death penalty option (e.g., whether "life" really means life imprisonment or the possibility exists for parole).

Studies measuring jurors' comprehension of the unique instructions used in capital cases yield essentially the same findings as other jury instruction studies, namely that comprehension is relatively poor. Depending on the measure and topic, performance generally ranges from 25%–70% accuracy (Alvarez et al., 2016; Haney, 2005; Lynch, 2009). Jurors are especially likely to struggle with central concepts like aggravation and mitigation, in some cases even interpreting mitigators erroneously as aggravators and vice versa (Haney & Lynch, 1994; Lynch & Haney, 2009). Revising the instructions by simplifying the language and reducing ambiguity improves comprehension considerably (e.g., Diamond & Levi, 1996; Patry & Penrod, 2013; Shaked-Schroer et al., 2008; Smith & Haney, 2011; Wiener et al., 1995). For example, Diamond and Levi found that revised instructions increased mock jurors' average comprehension from 50% to 65% correct.

Diamond and Levi's (1996) finding—that simplifying instructions helps, but that comprehension even with revised instructions still leaves a lot to be desired (e.g., a score of 65% would barely be passing in most academic settings)—is fairly typical. Clearly more can and should be done to improve comprehension. Smith and Haney (2011) tested the effectiveness of so-called "pinpoint instructions," which contained case-specific examples in addition to simplified, plain-language instructions. For example, the instructions referred to the defendant by name and covered only factors that were relevant to, and had occurred in, the present case. The pinpoint instructions improved comprehension above and beyond that for the simplified instructions.

As noted above, poorer comprehension is often associated with a greater tendency to give the death penalty (Diamond & Levi, 1996; Lynch & Haney, 2009; Patry & Penrod, 2013; Wiener et al., 1995; 2004), although not all studies have obtained this relationship (e.g., Smith & Haney, 2011). Inferior comprehension can also exacerbate discrimination against Black defendants (Lynch & Haney, 2000; 2009; Shaked-Schroer et al., 2008). Without opening the Pandora's Box of debating whether more or fewer death sentences are desirable as a matter of public policy, it seems irrefutable that any sentence should reflect proper understanding of the instructions and should be applied fairly across different classes of defendants. Continued efforts to revise jury instructions in capital cases, as well as criminal and civil trials in general, therefore seem highly worthwhile.

Modifying the Trial Structure via Bifurcation

Why Bifurcate? Fusion of Judgments at Trial

As discussed in a number of the previous chapters (see especially Chapters 9–12), a commonly considered issue in research on jury decisions is erroneous "fusion," by which jurors let information that is relevant for one type of legal judgment influence another type of legal judgment, for which it is irrelevant (Bornstein & Greene, 2011a; Devine, 2012; Feigenson, 2000; Greene & Bornstein, 2003). For example, injury severity can influence judgments of liability (e.g., Bornstein, 1998; Greene, Johns, & Bowman, 1999; Robbennolt, 2000) and the size of punitive damage awards (Robbennolt, 2002b; Robbennolt & Studebaker, 1999, Experiment 2); outrageous conduct by a defendant can lead to higher compensatory damage awards (Greene, Johns, & Smith, 2001; Greene et al., 2000); and information on the plaintiff's comparative fault can produce lower damage awards (Hammitt et al., 1985; Zickafoose & Bornstein, 1999).

Thus, research suggests that the various "stages" in jurors' decision-making process, such as assessing negligence, awarding compensation, and awarding punitive damages in civil cases, are not independent; rather, each of the judgments influences the others. As criminal jurors rarely sentence except in capital cases, there is usually only one "stage," namely, the determination of guilt (there might, of course, be discrete issues that comprise the guilt determination). Thus there is theoretically less opportunity for fusion in criminal than in civil trials. And when criminal juries do sentence, the guilt and sentencing phases are explicitly separate, or bifurcated. Criminal bifurcation comes up most commonly in serious felony (especially capital) trials, where a jury (or occasionally separate juries) hears evidence and makes decisions in one phase about the defendant's guilt and in a second phase about the defendant's sentencing (e.g., Horowitz & Seguin, 1986; Rodriguez & Berry, 2009). Although the two phases are nominally distinct, evidence that is most pertinent to one phase unavoidably appears in the other phase. For example, heinousness is a common aggravating factor in capital sentencing; but evidence of heinousness, such as extreme violence (e.g., torture, mutilation of the body), would ordinarily appear in the guilt phase, too, as part of the prosecution's case linking the defendant to the crime. Some evidence suggests that heinousness affects conviction rates as well as sentencing, although research manipulates heinousness in different ways and the data are inconsistent (see Chapter 12).

The norm for civil trials, on the other hand, is to present evidence relevant to liability and damages as part of the same proceeding, following which jurors determine both issues at the same time. Civil rules of procedure in most jurisdictions also allow for bifurcation, whereby liability and damages (or different kinds of damages) are determined in separate trial phases rather than all at the same time. In addition to potentially reducing fusion, bifurcation can save courts time and alleviate congested dockets, in that plaintiffs who lose on the issue of liability in a bifurcated trial do not present evidence on issues related to damages, whereas plaintiffs who lose in a traditional, or "unitary" trial still do. These savings significantly outweigh any increase in trial length in bifurcated trials that do go on to the damages phase (Zeisel & Callahan, 1963).

Research on Bifurcation

A number of experimental jury simulations have addressed the effects of bifurcation in civil trials. Studies of civil bifurcation vary in terms of which judgments, exactly, are being separated (i.e., liability vs. compensation, or liability + compensation vs. punitive damages; for review, see Devine et al., 2001; Greene & Bornstein, 2003). For example, Horowitz and Bordens (1990) had six-person mock juries reach a verdict in a simulated toxic tort case. They made their decisions in either a unitary trial format, where they heard all the trial evidence before making any decisions, or a bifurcated format, where they heard evidence on, and rendered a decision about, trial issues separately. They found that unitary juries were significantly more likely to find for the plaintiff (85.4% pro-plaintiff verdicts) than bifurcated juries (68.6% pro-plaintiff verdicts). Smith and Greene (2005) similarly found that bifurcated juries were significantly less likely than unitary juries (69% v. 100%) to find that a vehicular negligence defendant had caused the plaintiff's injury (see also Zeisel & Callahan, 1963). In addition, individual mock jurors who participated in a bifurcated trial format perceived the defendant as less negligent than did those in a unitary trial format (Smith & Greene, 2005). Although not all studies comparing bifurcated to unitary juries have found a difference in terms of liability verdicts or fault allocation (e.g., Wissler et al., 2001), the studies as a whole suggest that bifurcation in civil trials reduces the number of pro-plaintiff verdicts with regard to the defendant's liability/negligence. This presumably occurs because bifurcation lessens the influence on those judgments of extraneous injury-related information.

The findings are less clear with respect to the effect of bifurcation on damage awards when jurors first find the defendant liable. In the Horowitz and Bordens (1990) study, bifurcated mock juries awarded more compensation than unitary mock juries. In contrast, Smith and Greene (2005) found the opposite result: Both individual mock jurors and deliberating juries in the bifurcated trial condition awarded plaintiffs less compensation than those in the unitary trial condition. Finally, Wissler and colleagues (2001) found no difference in general damages between bifurcated and nonbifurcated mock jurors.

Additional research has found that bifurcating compensatory and punitive damages can reduce defendants' chances of being held liable (Landsman et al., 1998) and the size of the compensatory award (Shea Adams & Bourgeois, 2006), suggesting that eliminating testimony relevant to punitive damages—which typically goes to the defendant's reckless or wanton conduct—can reduce possible prejudice in the liability and compensation phases of trial. However, bifurcation can also make the defendants more likely to be held liable for punitive damages and raise the punitive award compared to a nonbifurcated condition (Greene et al., 2000; Landsman et al., 1998). For example, Landsman et al. found that punitive awards made by both individual jurors and deliberating juries in bifurcated trials were nearly four times those for jurors in unitary trials.

Research on bifurcation within the damages phase of trial shows that it does little to improve jurors' comprehension of either evidence or instructions (Landsman et al., 1998), but it can decrease variability in compensatory damage awards (Shea Adams & Bourgeois, 2006). Reduced variability for the same injury is a clear improvement in jury performance, as it means that similarly situated plaintiffs receive comparable outcomes. Shea Adams and Bourgeois also found that mock jurors reported using evidence more appropriately when their decisions were bifurcated. Specifically, compared to participants in a unitary trial, participants in a bifurcated trial reported relying more on the cost of treating the plaintiff's injuries and reimbursing the plaintiff for medical costs when determining compensation. Conversely, they reported relying less on the defendant's actions when determining compensation. Although these data are participants' own self-reports, they suggest that bifurcation facilitates jurors' ability to attend to relevant evidence and disregard irrelevant evidence; in other words, it inhibits fusion.

A variant on these bifurcation procedures involves a damages phase followed by a liability phase. This procedure, referred to as "reverse bifurcation," is commonly used in class-action asbestos trials. Its purpose is to narrow the range of compensation in the event of a full trial and thereby induce settlements. A settlement after the first phase would eliminate the need to determine defendants' liability, which in asbestos cases is typically complex and time consuming. Michelle White (2002; 2003) compiled data on approximately 5,500 asbestos trials conducted in several states from 1987–2002. According to her results, bifurcation resulted in a 29% increase in the plaintiff's probability of winning compared to unitary trials, and a $628,000 increase in compensatory damages. She also found that plaintiffs in bifurcated trials were 54% more likely to receive punitive damages, although the amount of any punitive damages did not increase significantly. Combining the greater probability of winning and the larger compensation award if a plaintiff did win, she showed that, on average, plaintiffs in bifurcated trials received an average of $1.2 million more.

These observed tendencies for reverse bifurcated trials to result in a greater likelihood of a plaintiff's verdict and higher compensatory damages are understandable in psychological terms, as illustrated by the research on fusion described previously. Specifically, if jurors are first asked to assess damages, they are likely to take it for granted that someone—especially someone who is also involved in the proceedings, like the defendant—caused the damage, leading them to elaborate a story about how the plaintiff's injury occurred. An a priori assessment of damages strongly implies a causal nexus, leading to a higher estimation that the defendant's actions caused the plaintiff's injury. Once jurors determine that an injury has occurred and evaluate the extent of that injury, hindsight would lead them to see the injury as relatively more foreordained (Rachlinski, 1998)—in this context, that means an inflated estimation that the defendant was liable for causing the injury.

In summary, traditional trials that require jurors to consider different evidence for different judgments (e.g., guilt vs. sentencing, liability vs. damages) pose a considerable risk of fusion, whereby evidence that is relevant for one judgment influences a separate judgment. Fusion can be prejudicial to one side or another. Bifurcation alleviates this prejudice to some extent, by keeping the focus on one judgment at a time. However, bifurcation can have paradoxical effects, such as reducing civil defendants' liability and compensatory damages but increasing their punitive liability and punitive damages (e.g., Landsman et al., 1998); and different bifurcation procedures can yield very different outcomes (White, 2002; 2003).

Moreover, bifurcating issues before a single jury is simpler in theory than it is in practice. For instance, it would be impossible for jurors in a personal injury case not to have some knowledge of the extent of the plaintiff's injuries while deciding liability; even without testimony detailing the injuries, the plaintiff is physically present in court throughout the trial. Similarly, capital juries deciding on a defendant's guilt would know, by virtue of the death qualification process, that the death penalty is an option, along with some of the circumstances of the case that make it an option. The only clear way to avoid this sort of biasing effect would be to have the two issues—damages and liability, or guilt and sentencing—determined by entirely different panels (see, e.g., Horowitz & Seguin, 1986). Such a procedure is usually not practical.

Note Taking

Allowing jurors to take notes would seem to be a matter of common sense (Ferrara, 2008). Prominent jurists like Supreme Court Justice Sandra Day O'Connor have advocated juror note taking (O'Connor, 1997), and courts have considered the matter at least as far back as 1900 (Robbennolt, Penrod, & Heuer, 1999). Note taking is a tried and true memory aid, and by facilitating comprehension, it might also increase juror satisfaction. However, until quite recently, most jurisdictions did not allow jurors to take notes; the majority now do, but the practice is not universal (Ferrara, 2008; Marder, 2006). Even where statutes permit it, judges usually have discretion either to allow the practice or not, producing considerable variability both across and within jurisdictions, and even within individual courtrooms depending on the particular trial (Marder, 2006). The principal concerns are that jurors' notes might be incomplete or erroneous (one might ask, unlike their memories?), leading to a distorted view of the case; note taking would be distracting, time-consuming, or too hard to do effectively; notes could favor one side of the case; and jurors with more detailed notes would dominate jury deliberations (Heuer & Penrod, 1994a; Larsen, 1996; Robbennolt et al., 1999).

Heuer and Penrod (1988, 1989, 1994a, 1994b) conducted some of the earliest, and still arguably the best, research on juror note taking.[1] For example, they conducted a national field experiment in which jurors in 160 civil and criminal trials from 33 states were randomly assigned to either a note-taking or a non-note-taking condition (Heuer & Penrod, 1994a; see also Heuer & Penrod, 1994b). Most jurors who were allowed to take notes did so (87%), but their notes were not extensive (an average of 14.4 pages in civil trials, which lasted longer, and 7.1 pages in criminal trials). Allowing jurors to take notes had no effect on their verdicts or the rate of judge–jury agreement.

Laboratory studies have found that note taking can affect verdicts under some circumstances. For instance, Horowitz and Bordens (2002) found that note-taking juries awarded less compensation than juries whose members were not allowed to take notes, but only for six-person (vs. 12-person) juries under high information load, which they operationalized as multiple plaintiffs (see also Horowitz & ForsterLee, 2001). Six-person, non-note-taking juries under high information load also awarded the highest punitive damages. These results suggest that allowing jurors to take notes can reduce possible bias introduced by trial complexity or jury size. Research shows that note taking has either no effect on the length of deliberations (Ferrara, 2008; Heuer & Penrod, 1994a) or produces a slight increase, possibly due to more jurors participating or their bringing forth more evidence (Horowitz & Bordens, 2002).

Field research shows that neither note takers themselves nor other jurors perceived the practice as distracting or unduly influential during deliberation (Heuer & Penrod, 1994a). In these same field studies, note taking affected neither jurors' objective comprehension of jury instructions (Heuer & Penrod, 1988) nor their subjective sense of how well or how easily they remembered the evidence (Heuer & Penrod, 1994a). The failure of note taking to confer a memory advantage is surprising, considering that it is a useful mnemonic technique in many other contexts (Kiewra, 1989). Several jury simulation studies have found that note taking does enhance memory and comprehension (e.g., ForsterLee & Horowitz, 1997; ForsterLee, Kent, & Horowitz, 2005; Horowitz & Bordens, 2002; Horowitz & ForsterLee, 2001; Rosenhan, Eisner, & Robinson, 1994), suggesting that studies failing to find an effect might simply have used measures that were not sufficiently tailored to the individual cases (Robbennolt et al., 1999). Some research has also found a positive correlation between the amount and accuracy of notes taken and the accuracy of evidence recall (e.g., ForsterLee & Horowitz, 1997; Rosenhan et al., 1994).

More important than whether note taking has an overall effect on comprehension or verdicts is whether it enables jurors to do a better job of applying the law. Horowitz and ForsterLee (2001) addressed this issue by

---

[1] These same studies also examined juror questions; those results are included in the next section.

presenting mock juries with a complex civil trial involving multiple plaintiffs who varied in terms of their injury severity. Note-taking juries were better able to distinguish among the differentially worthy plaintiffs; that is, their compensation awards more closely tracked differences in the severity of the plaintiffs' injuries than did the awards of non-note-taking juries. This benefit of note taking can be enhanced still further by providing note-taking juries with jury instructions prior to the evidence (ForsterLee & Horowitz, 1997) or with nonevaluative, written summaries of expert testimony prior to trial and during deliberation (ForsterLee et al., 2005).

Research on note taking's effect on how jurors feel about their jury service is mixed. Some studies have found little effect of the practice on how satisfied jurors are with the trial, deliberation process, or verdict (Heuer & Penrod, 1994a; Horowitz & Bordens, 2002), whereas other studies have found that note taking increases jurors' satisfaction with the trial process and their perception of how efficiently the jury worked together as a group (ForsterLee et al., 2005; Horowitz & ForsterLee, 2001). Jurors also overwhelmingly feel that their notes are valuable records of the evidence presented during trial (Heuer & Penrod, 1994a).

There's No Such Thing as a Stupid Question . . .

A number of states now permit jurors to ask questions, although the precise procedure varies across jurisdictions (Marder, 2010; Mott, 2003). Jurors do not simply have *carte blanche* to ask any question they want of any witness; rather, the question must first be vetted by the judge (and in some jurisdictions, the attorneys). Hence there is no such thing as a stupid question, as long as the judge approves the question for presentation to the witness. Allowing juror questions has a number of potential pros and cons. The consequences pertain to jurors' own well-being, lawyers' litigation strategy, and the pursuit of justice. On the plus side they can help jurors understand the case, "buy into" their role, and stay focused; the questions can give attorneys insight into what is on jurors' minds; and jurors who can ask questions are less likely to try and find answers on their own, outside of court. On the minus side, questions could lengthen trials and raise issues for appeal if an inappropriate question is asked, disrupt attorneys' trial strategy and cause them to lose control of the process, and turn into juror advocacy if the questions begin to take on a partisan flavor.

Studies of the topic show that jurors do not ask that many questions; the questions they do ask are overwhelmingly relevant and reasonable, and the procedure adds minimally, if at all, to the length of trials (e.g., Ferrara, 2008; Heuer & Penrod, 1994a; Mott, 2003). Questions directed to general and expert witnesses are most common, especially in civil cases, as are questions about evidence, motive, and what constitutes a reasonable person for legal purposes. Jurors ask more questions of witnesses for the prosecution or plaintiff than defense witnesses (Heuer & Penrod, 1994a), and they ask more questions in criminal than in civil cases (Mott, 2003).

It is unclear how much juror questions enhance comprehension or lead to better verdicts, but judges, jurors, and lawyers, especially prosecutors, are generally positive about the practice (Ferrara, 2008; Mott, 2003). For example, Heuer and Penrod (1994a) found that jurors felt questions were helpful for clarifying the evidence, clarifying the law, and getting to the truth; the more questions asked, the more helpful they found the practice to be. Oddly, though, allowing juror questions did not increase jurors' satisfaction with the trial or the verdict (perhaps partly because satisfaction with both was high regardless of condition).

Overall, then, even though allowing juror questions may not have clear-cut objective advantages in terms of better comprehension or verdicts, it does appear to confer subjective benefits (i.e., jurors and other trial participants feel better about the process) while adding little in the way of costs (e.g., trial duration). Although judges and attorneys do not feel that juror questions give them much useful information about a particular trial (Heuer & Penrod, 1994a), questions can still provide them with valuable feedback about the operation of the justice system (Ferrara, 2008). Thus, it is a worthwhile reform.

Nonetheless, questions remain, as even proponents of the procedure are quick to point out (e.g., Marder, 2010). Should the policy change come about by statute, case law, or a state Supreme Court rule change? Should questions be permitted for all cases or only certain kinds (e.g., those with complex evidence; see Heuer & Penrod, 1994b)? Should questions be asked by the judge or by the jurors themselves (after judge approval)? Should jurors be allowed to ask follow-up questions? Should attorneys have an opportunity to object, either before or after a question is asked? Most importantly, as Marder observes, permitting is not the same as encouraging or doing. In most jurisdictions that allow questions, it is not a matter of right; rather, like note taking, judges have the discretion to employ the procedure or not in individual cases. This means that even when juror questions are technically acceptable, they are likely to be underutilized.

Predeliberation Discussion

Jurors are instructed not to discuss the case until the presentation of evidence ends, they have been instructed on the law, and the deliberation phase officially commences. Not surprisingly, jurors often report after trial that they discussed the case with one another prior to deliberation (Diamond et al., 2003; Hannaford, Hans, & Munsterman, 2000), and the prohibition is virtually impossible to enforce. The major concern about predeliberation discussion is that it could lead jurors to form a premature judgment, which could lead to selective interpretation and recall of evidence, which could in turn constrain an open and full deliberation. Discussion could also confer undue influence on highly vocal, opinionated jurors too early in the game; could make jurors feel freer to discuss the case with nonjurors; or could allow influence by alternate jurors who would not be a part of the final decision-making body (Diamond et al., 2003).

On the other hand, there are a number of potential objective and subjective benefits to predeliberation discussion, such as better comprehension, greater juror motivation and involvement, addressing questions or concerns in a timely manner, reducing jurors' need or desire to discuss the case with others outside of court, and giving them an opportunity to vent (Diamond et al., 2003). It would facilitate greater familiarity with one another, which would increase their comfort level (a subjective benefit) and facilitate a more rational selection of the jury foreperson when deliberation begins (an objective benefit).

Two Arizona studies compared discuss and no-discuss civil juries: one study by surveying jurors after trial (Hannaford et al., 2000; see also Hans, Hannaford, & Munsterman, 1999), and one by recording and analyzing the content of actual jury deliberations (Diamond et al., 2003). The two studies included 161 and 50 cases, respectively; in both samples the largest number of cases involved motor vehicle accidents with individual plaintiffs, with most of the remainder being other kinds of torts. Because of practical constraints, assignment to the discuss and no-discuss conditions was not perfectly random, but the cases were highly comparable across conditions.

Most juries allowed to discuss the case did so, although significant minorities did not (31% in the Hannaford study and 11% in the Diamond study). The disparity could simply reflect the retrospective nature of the Hannaford study: It is possible that the jurors had discussions, but they were not meaningful or salient enough to remember. The data from the Diamond study confirm this interpretation, as many comments about the case were brief. Those who were allowed to discuss the case did not always follow the court's rules, frequently discussing the case when not all jurors were present, as well as discussing the case with nonjurors. Both studies found that the rate of talking to nonjurors (e.g., family and friends) was about the same in the discuss and no-discuss conditions (11% vs. 14% of juries in the Hannaford study, and 15% vs. 10% of jurors in the Diamond study). Importantly, neither study found much evidence of prejudgment among jurors who were allowed to discuss the case, although jurors allowed to discuss were more likely to express a verdict preference before the presentation of evidence had concluded. Apart from violating the prohibition against discussing the case unless all jurors were present, then, the discussion process appears to have worked more or less as intended. The next question, then, is how it affected jurors: their comprehension, their verdicts, and their feelings about their jury service.

Jurors reported understanding the evidence and the law equally well in the two conditions (Hannaford et al., 2000), and Diamond and colleagues

(2003) identified numerous instances where discussion resulted in the correction of one or more jurors' lack of knowledge or misunderstanding. This provides strong evidence that discussion can enhance jurors' understanding of the evidence (because the analysis concerned discussion during trial, they had not yet received their final instructions on the law). Discussion had no effect on the frequency of asking questions (Diamond et al., 2003).

Juries allowed to discuss were less likely to reach a unanimous verdict in one of the two studies (Hannaford et al., 2000). On the other hand, Diamond et al. (2003) found no effect on unanimity (in fact, there was a nonsignificant trend in the opposite direction); juries that discussed were less likely to hang (0% vs. 8%), and they spent somewhat less time deliberating (Ms of 91 minutes vs. 117 minutes; these comparisons were not statistically significant, likely due to the high variability and small sample size). There was scant evidence that the direction of verdicts differed across conditions. For example, juries in the Diamond et al. study found for the plaintiff in 64% of trials with discussion and 67% of trials without discussion. Hannaford et al. found that discussion decreased the likelihood of a defense verdict, but the effect was smaller (and only marginally significant) when controlling for other factors, especially whether or not the jury actually engaged in discussion. Judges in both studies were roughly as likely to agree with the jury's verdict regardless of whether or not they were allowed to discuss the case prior to deliberation. On the whole, then, discussion does not appear to have an effect on trial outcomes.

Jurors who were allowed to discuss found the discussions helpful at improving their understanding of the evidence (Hannaford et al., 2000; Hans et al., 1999) and in facilitating their comprehension of expert testimony (Diamond et al., 2003). Most jurors supported the policy, especially after experiencing discussion (Hans et al., 1999). Moreover, most of the jurors who were not allowed to discuss the evidence wished that they could (Hans et al., 1999). Although discussion did not, for the most part, increase their satisfaction with various aspects of the trial or the deliberation process (Diamond et al., 2003; Hannaford et al., 2000), it clearly did not have adverse consequences for jurors' feelings about the experience.

Thus, allowing jurors to discuss the case prior to deliberation offers a number of potential benefits. As with some of the other innovative safeguards, such as question asking and note taking, *allowing* it does not necessarily mean *doing* it—but most jurors allowed to discuss the case take advantage of the opportunity. Although discussion does not affect the frequency with which juries talk about the case out of court, they appear to find it hard to follow the admonition to discuss the case only when all of the jurors are present. This could simply be because prior to the deliberation phase, there are relatively few instances when they are all together in the jury room (e.g., during a break individual jurors might leave to make a phone call, smoke a cigarette, etc.).

The Newest Reforms

Progress marches on in reforming jury trials to enhance decision making and produce outcomes that are more predictable and equitable. At the forefront of innovations, a few trial judges—particularly federal judges who have lifetime appointments and can afford to take risks—have made changes in the way they conduct jury trials, and a smattering of commissions and panels have collected data on the outcomes of various innovations. But because these reforms have not yet been subjected to rigorous empirical scrutiny, we do not know whether and how they actually enhance jurors' experiences and affect verdicts. Still, they are worth mentioning as they represent the next wave in jury reforms. We describe three such reforms: providing substantive jury instructions prior to the presentation of evidence, allowing attorneys to present interim arguments, and having expert witnesses testify back to back.

Earlier in the chapter we discussed how revised jury instructions can, in many circumstances, lead to improved comprehension. In addition to simplifying and clarifying the language and concepts included in the instructions, revised instructions—particularly regarding the relevant law—could be provided at both the beginning of the trial, which would be a novel procedure, and at the end, as is customary. What advantages might derive from preliminary substantive jury instructions? The answer is rather straightforward: Just as first-time observers of a debate or a sports event need to know the rules of the competition in order to know who won, so too do jurors need to know the relevant laws they will apply to the evidence they hear during the trial. Learning about the law only at the end of trial requires jurors to retroactively reexamine the evidence in that light, which can be a daunting task if the trial lasts for any length of time. When this reform was assessed by the Seventh Circuit Bar Association (2008) in approximately three dozen trials, over 80% of the jurors exposed to substantive preliminary instructions said it enhanced their understanding of the law. This reform might be utilized more often if, at the start of the trial, judges knew exactly what instructions they would deliver at the end. Unfortunately, because the issues in trials can evolve as the trial goes on, they often do not.

In lengthy or complex trials it might be useful for attorneys to give arguments akin to closing arguments in the middle of trial, as well as at the end. These so-called "interim arguments" summarize the evidence for jurors and can, for example, help them make sense of technical or complicated expert testimony, explain how a witness's testimony meshes with other evidence, and remind them of the law they will need to apply during deliberations. Although interim arguments are rarely given (Hannaford-Agor, 2015), interviews conducted as part of the Seventh Circuit Project (2008) revealed that 80% of jurors thought they aided comprehension.

As we explained in Chapter 7, one of the most vexing tasks for jurors is understanding and using testimony given by expert witnesses. Various features of expert testimony contribute to its complexity; in addition to its technical or scientific nature, because of the way that trials are structured, expert testimony from opposing sides can be quite disjointed, both substantively and temporally. As a result, jurors have to recall the testimony of experts who testified earlier in the trial when evaluating the opinions of those who testify later on the same issue. This makes it difficult to discern whether there are areas of agreement, on what topics, and how and why the experts disagree.

Would it make sense to have the experts testify in immediate sequence— or even, in a radical departure from tradition, to allow them to testify together, questioning each other about their assumptions and conclusions? In terms of jury comprehension, the answer is probably yes. But these reforms have, with only a handful of exceptions, never been implemented in the United States (Wood, 2007), probably because they represent such a drastic move away from traditional adversarial trial procedures. For that reason judges may be hesitant to restructure trials to allow back-to-back or conversing experts, making it difficult to assess whether those reforms could enhance jury decision making.

Conclusions and Recommendations

It is decidedly not easy being a juror, and any belief to the contrary is a myth. In addition to the disruption to one's daily life associated with serving on a jury, many of the substantive and procedural aspects of trials make it difficult for jurors to follow the law and do their job properly. In particular, their comprehension of evidence and legal instructions is limited, and their decisions are subject to fusion, according to which they use evidence relevant to one kind of judgment for other judgments. Fortunately, the justice system is beginning to recognize this fact, and courts are increasingly implementing innovative techniques that have the potential to help jurors. These techniques include revised instructions, bifurcation, and allowing jurors to take notes, ask questions, or discuss the case with one another prior to deliberation. Precise data are hard to come by, but the available evidence suggests that the prevalence of the innovations varies quite a bit. Most jurisdictions currently permit note taking, and a substantial number allow juror questions and have revised their jury instructions; but bifurcation, except when mandated as in capital cases, is relatively uncommon, and predeliberation discussion is very rare. In addition, judges often have the final say, meaning that a procedure might be permissible but not necessarily widely implemented. All of these innovations are promising, but none of them is a panacea; they help in different ways, with some improving jurors' objective performance (i.e., better comprehension and/or more just verdicts) and others improving their subjective experience (i.e., a sense of understanding the law or evidence better and greater satisfaction with the trial process). Although largely untested at this point, newer reforms such as substantive pretrial instructions, interim arguments, and sequential expert testimony also have the potential to enhance jurors' decision making.

Attempts to revise instructions improve jurors' subjective comprehension, and there is some evidence, albeit mixed, that revised instructions also lead to better verdicts in terms of less racial discrimination and more appropriate use of the evidence (e.g., discriminating between relatively good and bad eyewitnesses, more appropriate use of mitigating evidence in capital cases). Although jurors' subjective comprehension and satisfaction are laudable goals, there is clearly room for further improvement. That improvement is likely to require systematic, substantive, and structural changes, as opposed to piecemeal interventions, no matter how well intentioned (Diamond et al., 2012), as well as a consideration of jurors' cognitive abilities and predispositions broadly construed (Diamond, 1993b).

Similarly, jurors in bifurcated trials feel that they are doing a better job, and the research also suggests that bifurcated trials are fairer in the sense of facilitating jurors' ability to use evidence—and only evidence—that is relevant to a particular decision. Nonbifurcated trials, on the other hand, introduce the possibility of bias due to the natural psychological processes involved in human decision making. This necessarily produces differences in verdicts between bifurcated and nonbifurcated trials, but the effects do not clearly favor one side or the other. Plaintiffs in bifurcated trials fare worse on liability but better on punitive damages, with the data on compensatory damages inconsistent; and they fare better in reverse bifurcated trials.

Several of the innovations involve tweaks to juror behavior, as opposed to structural changes to the trial itself. These procedures—note taking, question asking, and predeliberation discussion—have little if any effect on the direction of verdicts, although there is some evidence that they can help jurors reach more legally appropriate verdicts (e.g., the beneficial effect of note taking on damage awards as a function of injury severity; ForsterLee & Horowitz, 1997; Horowitz & ForsterLee, 2001). For the most part, jurors perceive these procedures to be helpful, and several studies show that they actually do improve jurors' understanding of the evidence, but the procedures do not produce large gains in juror satisfaction. There is also substantial variability in the extent to which jurors use the procedures as intended. Jurors take advantage of all of them, but some jurors take advantage more than others, and no procedure is used all that extensively (e.g., the amount of notes and number of questions in most trials is modest). Moreover, although their notes and questions are generally relevant and properly executed, jurors often do not follow court rules in discussing the case (e.g., they have discussions without all members present).

Each of the nontraditional trial innovations reviewed in the present chapter has a number of potential advantages and disadvantages. Research shows that for the most part, the feared disadvantages (e.g., longer trials, negative effects on verdicts) have failed to materialize. The same research shows that the hoped-for benefits, while not overwhelming, are not trivial. The absence of negative outcomes and promising evidence of benefits in terms of jurors' subjective impressions, better comprehension, and improved adherence to the law is encouraging. We are also optimistic that greater benefits are still to come, as instructions continue to be revised for better comprehensibility, bifurcation procedures are compared and refined, more judges who are in a position to allow greater juror participation actually do it, and new models for reform emerge. As courts continue to look for ways to help jurors follow the law, we encourage them to adopt these innovations and to experiment with others. Therein lies progress.

15

Conclusion

"Myths which are believed in tend to become true"
(Orwell, 1947/1968, p. 6).

The jury is an easy target. Jury verdicts are a matter of public record, and with rare exceptions, jurors' identities are public as well. No one, especially both sides in an adversarial system, is going to agree with every jury decision. But in most cases at least one party agrees with the verdict, and more often than not (roughly 75% of the time), the judge does, too. The American justice system, like those in other countries, has its flaws and limitations, but it is a gross exaggeration to lay all of those problems at the feet of the jury. Juries are not the sole, or even the major, contributor to large-scale problems like over-incarceration, false convictions, rising insurance premiums, and soaring health care costs, any more than smoking cigarettes is the major cause of global warming. Yet juries receive a disproportionate share of criticism for the failings of the legal system. As we observed in Chapter 1, if the jury is not truly endangered, it is definitely threatened. Why?

A major reason for criticism of the jury is the persistence of jury myths. This book has explored a number of those myths and presented the empirical evidence showing that they are just that—myths, beliefs without a sound empirical foundation. In this final chapter we take a step back and speculate on some of the larger questions related to jury myths: Where do they come from? Why do they persist? How do we correct them? Following our discussion of myths, we summarize the various jury reforms reviewed in the book, distinguishing among reforms that have a solid empirical basis, reforms that seem promising but need research documenting their effectiveness, and reforms that have adverse consequences and should be discarded. Finally, we briefly consider the most pressing and promising areas for future research.

The Origins and Persistence of Jury Myths

Myths in general have their place. For millennia they have helped people make sense of the world and have provided comfort and meaning (e.g., Campbell, 1988; Freud, 1928/1961). Many myths, such as creation myths, are relatively harmless, perhaps because they are basically impossible to disprove. Yet other myths, which are directly contradicted by evidence—and jury myths fall into this category—can do considerable harm. As George Orwell observed in the above quotation, myths can create a self-fulfilling prophecy whereby they reshape the world in their image.

Consider, for example, the myth raised in Chapter 2, that people dread jury duty. Setting aside the question of the belief's truth (and as we showed, it is largely unfounded), what are the consequences of holding that belief? If people believe that jury duty is unpleasant and something to be avoided at all costs, they will try to get out of it, which not only could lead to a contempt of court citation and fine, but would also deprive them of the benefits of participating in the adjudication process. Courts will respond by summoning many more jurors than they actually need, causing inefficiency and unnecessary inconvenience. Jurors who "get stuck" with jury duty will enter it with a resentful attitude, which could color their task performance. Lawyers and their clients, anticipating the hassle of empaneling a jury, might be more inclined to opt for a bench trial, even though, in certain cases, they would fare better before a jury. The worse everyone's experience with juries is, the truer the myth becomes.

Or consider another example, raised in Chapter 9, that juries' compensatory damage awards are excessive. If people believe very large awards are the norm, then jurors will feel like they have to award large amounts in order to be fair. If judges subscribe to the myth, then their awards will likewise be large. Potential plaintiffs, expecting substantial windfalls, will be more litigious and less willing to settle. Potential defendants will go overboard to avoid the risk of lawsuits (e.g., issuing excessive product warnings) and will be more inclined to settle or opt for a bench trial. Again, the myth becomes reality. On the other hand, if people believe awards are excessive—that is, very large but undeservedly so—then as factfinders (jurors or judges) they might actually undercompensate plaintiffs. Plaintiffs would still be reluctant to settle (admittedly, it is hard to imagine a plaintiff perceiving an award as undeservedly large), and defendants would still be overly willing to settle. This scenario does little to further the aims of justice.

Myths about the jury system are not only common, but they are also resistant to change: "Despite years of research that rebuts stereotypes about juries, every day lawyers and policymakers act on the basis of those stereotypes. Why are such misperceptions about the legal system so resilient? Why do the misperceptions not eventually undergo correction, as lawyers repeatedly observe the consequences of their misperceptions?" (Clermont & Eisenberg, 2002, p. 146). One might expect that jury myths would break apart on the shoals of jury reality. Why don't they? There are no doubt many reasons underlying the persistence of jury myths. Four that are particularly troublesome are distortion of the facts by self-serving special interest groups, media bias, fundamental cognitive processes, and the intuitive nature of many of the myths.

The tort reform movement is a prominent example of how special interest groups perpetuate jury myths (Bornstein & Robicheaux, 2008). For example, the most vocal and effective tort reform organization, the American Tort Reform Association (ATRA), was cofounded in 1986 by the American Medical Association and the Council of Engineering Companies. These groups, which are well funded and politically powerful, understand-ably seek to further the interests of their constituents, who are physicians and product manufacturers, respectively. One way of furthering their inter-ests is to limit physicians' and manufacturers' expenses. ATRA attributes a large share of those expenses, which include insurance and product devel-opment costs, to the tort system in general and jury verdicts in particular, despite the facts that as civil defendants, physicians and product manufac-turers fare comparatively well at trial, and scant evidence shows a connec-tion between these factors (e.g., medical malpractice insurance premiums) and trial verdicts (see Chapter 9). Part of ATRA's strategy is to call attention to blockbuster jury verdicts, even though such verdicts are extremely rare and not representative of the civil justice system as a whole.

It is not our aim to demonize ATRA or the tort reform movement in general. Neither the civil nor the criminal justice system functions optimally, and reforms—assuming they are evidence-based—can yield large benefits. Moreover, we are in full agreement with portions of ATRA's agenda, such as the promotion of jury service, sound science in the courtroom, and contin-gent fee reform. But in highlighting unrepresentative cases with very high awards and promoting caps on damages, ATRA is perpetuating the myth that jury damage awards are excessive and unpredictable.

The tort reform movement's tendency to emphasize unrepresentative cases is symptomatic of the second reason underlying myth persistence—media bias. Blockbuster awards receive disproportionate media coverage (Bailis & MacCoun, 1996; Robbennolt & Studebaker, 2003), as do death pen-alty cases in the criminal context (Haney, 2005).[1] As we discuss in earlier chapters, this bias creates unrealistic expectations among all of the players—jurors, attorneys, judges, and litigants. These expectations and their accom-panying behavior mean that, as Orwell observed, the myths ultimately become the truth.

---

[1] We take no position on whether disproportionate media coverage drives reform efforts, the reform movement drives the media coverage, or both result from some underlying systemic factor. Regardless, media bias in covering juries is very real.

It is tempting to see the actions of special interest groups and the media as part of a grand conspiracy to discredit the jury. Although we cannot rule that out, we are not so cynical as to posit such a conspiracy. Rather, we suspect that both of these phenomena reflect, to a large extent, fundamental cognitive processes—the third reason why jury myths persist. It is natural to give greater attention to abnormal, low-frequency events, such as blockbuster civil verdicts, than to ordinary and mundane happenings (MacCoun, 2006). The abnormal cases then stand out in memory and are taken as more "normal" than they actually are (Tversky & Kahneman, 1974). Isolated, aberrant events come to be viewed as typical, thereby confirming the myth.

Finally, several of the myths have a great deal of intuitive appeal. Of course jurors understand eyewitness and confession evidence; of course they treat juveniles in an age-appropriate manner; of course they control their emotions; of course they follow the law, especially when making life-or-death decisions, the biggest and gravest decisions imaginable. Why wouldn't they? Humans are naturally overconfident about their knowledge and abilities (e.g., Bornstein & Zickafoose, 1999) and have limited insight into their own decision-making processes (Nisbett & Wilson, 1977). Absent direct evidence to the contrary—and bear in mind that most Americans rarely, if ever, serve on a jury (Rose et al., 2012)—people have little reason to question beliefs that seem to make so much sense.

The perpetuation of jury myths by special interest groups and the media, our natural cognitive processes, and the myths' intuitive appeal make them extremely hard to dispel. These factors work together: The myths make more sense than the alternatives, we are more likely to encounter confirming than disconfirming information, and we are more likely to notice and remember confirming than disconfirming information. Myths would not be myths if they were easily changed, and jury myths are hardly an outlier; psychological myths abound (e.g., Lilienfeld, Lynn, Ruscio, & Beyerstein, 2010).

But as we have been at pains to demonstrate, much of what people think they know about the jury is simply wrong. To affect the law and influence jury performance, we need to change commonsense (mis)understandings of how juries work. Public education is one means of accomplishing this objective. Growing awareness of false convictions has brought attention to particularly problematic kinds of evidence, such as eyewitness testimony and confessions. The media, along with courts and other government entities themselves, could also do more to educate the public about jury service (it's not that bad, really!) and to implement procedural innovations to help juries do their job better. Researchers have a role to play as well. In legal contexts, it is incumbent on policymakers contemplating reforms to rely on data rather than myths. In the face of enough data, even the most firmly entrenched myths will eventually crumble. After all, remember when the world was flat?

Jury Reform: Summary and Evaluation

Each of the preceding chapters covers numerous reforms, some of which have been around for a while, and some that are new and relatively (in some cases completely) untested. Table 15.1 provides an evaluative summary of jury reforms. We break down the reforms into three categories based on the extent of empirical support each has garnered: (1) evidence shows the reform is effective; (2) evidence shows the reform is ineffective and maybe even counterproductive; and (3) the reform makes sense, but evidence of its effectiveness is mostly lacking. This categorization raises the question of how much evidence is necessary to move a reform from the "unknown" to the "effective" or "ineffective" category. There is no straightforward answer to this question, which comes up in any discussion of justice system reform. Relevant criteria for judging whether a research literature provides an adequate basis for establishing new policies, or reforming existing ones, include a consistent and substantial body of research findings that derive from diverse methods, provide extensive coverage of the research domain, relate clearly to applicable real-world contexts (e.g., actual juries), and reflect a high degree of consensus in the scientific community (Malpass et al., 2008). Many of these criteria contain a subjective element (e.g., how many studies constitute a "substantial" amount of research), but because reforms to the justice system are often time-consuming, costly, and disruptive to implement, we should undertake them based on, at minimum, a series of studies and not just one or two (Malpass et al., 2008). Consequently, some of the topics in the "Unknown" category in Table 15.1 have been investigated, but we are not confident in recommending their adoption yet, either because insufficient research has been conducted or the results are too equivocal.

As we described in discussing various reforms in depth in the preceding chapters, there are multiple ways of measuring a reform's effectiveness. It could improve jurors' understanding of the law or evidence presented at trial, lead to more consistent and legally appropriate verdicts by enabling jurors to place more weight on legally relevant factors while ignoring legally irrelevant ones, or simply make jurors feel more satisfied with their jury service. For present purposes, we employ a liberal operationalization of effectiveness—if a reform helps in any of these respects, while not producing negative consequences, we consider it a success.

A superficial inspection of Table 15.1 might seem to give cause for optimism—after all, the table lists more than twice as many effective as ineffective reforms currently in use. This is promising news, but any optimism must be tempered by the fact that although some of the effective reforms are becoming increasingly widespread (e.g., videotaping of confessions, juror note taking), several others are used only sparingly (e.g., jury duty reminders, individualized *voir dire*, bifurcation, predeliberation discussion). Still others, like revised instructions, vary enormously across jurisdictions, and

Table 15.1 Summary of Jury Reforms

Effective	Pretrial questionnaires of prospective jurors[2,3]
	Jury duty reminders[2]
	Juror orientation programs[2]
	Individualized *voir dire*[2,3]
	Posttrial debriefing (esp. for high-stress trials)[2]
	Showing jurors videotaped interrogations/confessions[6]
	Revised jury instructions to increase comprehension and clarify difficult legal matters (e.g., awarding damages, capital punishment, victim impact statements)[9,11,12,14]
	Letting jurors take notes[14]
	Letting jurors ask questions[14]
	Bifurcation[14]
	Predeliberation discussion[14]
Ineffective	Punishing no-show jurors[2]
	Juries with fewer than 12 members[4]
	Non-unanimous juries[4]
	Juvenile waiver and transfer[8]
	Caps on damages[9,10]
Unknown	Increasing compensation and user-friendliness of jury service[2]
	Public education about jury service[2]
	Limiting or eliminating peremptory challenges[3]
	Educating judges on juror bias (esp. implicit bias)[3]
	Voir dire opening statements and expanded, more open-ended *voir dire*[3,5]
	Educating jurors and legal professionals about problematic evidence (e.g., a pretrial tutorial on eyewitnesses; continuing legal education)[5,6]
	Expert testimony about problematic evidence (e.g., eyewitnesses, confessions)[6,7]
	Jury instructions about possible bias or problematic evidence (e.g., eyewitnesses, confessions, a defendant's youth, gruesome evidence)[6,8,12]
	Increased use of judicial *additur/remittitur*[9]
	Preliminary substantive jury instructions[14]
	Scheduling damages[9]
	Special verdict forms[9]
	Raising the threshold for punitive damages liability[10]
	Split recovery of punitive damages[10]
	Modifying the death qualification procedure[11]
	Increasing jurors' accountability[12]
	Helping jurors cross the empathic divide[12]
	Interim attorney arguments[14]
	Back-to-back expert testimony[14]

Note. Superscripts refer to the chapter in which a reform is discussed in more detail.

despite leading to significant improvements in comprehension, they still fall short of their goal (Diamond et al., 2012).

And although some of the ineffective reforms (e.g., punishing no-show jurors) exist in only a few jurisdictions, others—particularly small and non-unanimous juries, juvenile waiver, and caps on damages—are pervasive. On a daily basis, these reforms are having negative consequences for both the juror experience and the administration of justice in jurisdictions across the United States. For some reforms, the direct consequences may be relatively benign—no-show penalties are typically rather modest, and trial outcomes for smaller and non-unanimous juries are roughly comparable to those for 12-person, unanimous juries. However, the indirect consequences in these cases are substantial, as they diminish the legitimacy of the jury and have negative effects on the jury's decision-making process (e.g., by reducing diversity and stifling dissent). Moreover, the direct consequences of other reforms are far from trivial—reforms like juvenile transfer and caps on damages can have adverse, and arguably unjust, consequences for the parties involved. We therefore conclude that these ineffective reforms should be, at a minimum, modified to eliminate these adverse consequences and maybe even abolished altogether.

Should courts adopt all the reforms with demonstrated effectiveness? Not necessarily, for two reasons. First, even in the case of effective reforms, some uncertainty remains. What should be included in pretrial questionnaires, juror orientation materials, and individualized *voir dire*? Should reminders be sent by email, text, phone call, or post, and what should be the content of the reminder message? Who should debrief jurors, and how? What camera perspective should be used to videotape interrogations? Without additional empirical data on these matters, courts and policymakers cannot know how to implement the reforms to achieve maximum impact.

Second, in making this decision, it is important to consider not only the benefits of a reform but also its costs (Miller & Bornstein, 2013). Who benefits from a given reform, and how, varies depending on the nature of the reform. It could be the jurors, who experience less stress and greater satisfaction; court administrators, who have fewer no-shows and disgruntled jurors; attorneys, who are less anxious about unpredictable jury verdicts and consequently do a better job of counseling their clients; judges, who oversee a more smoothly functioning process; litigants, who experience more predictable and consistent (and therefore more just) trial outcomes, as well as fairer procedures; and even society as a whole, which benefits from citizens' greater and more positive involvement with this aspect of democratic governance. Although some of these potential benefits are more tangible than others, they are all worth striving for.

Nevertheless, jury reforms—even effective ones—carry costs in terms of time, money, and possible inefficiencies (at least in the short term) caused by any disruption to the status quo. Reminding jurors of their duty to serve, creating juror orientation materials, compensating mental health professionals to debrief jurors after high-stress trials, paying for video recording equipment (for interrogations), and even juror notebooks all entail very concrete, and often nontrivial, financial expenditures. The time investment of court personnel can be substantial in sending reminders; conducting juror orientation, individualized *voir dire*, bifurcated trials, and debriefing; collecting (and possibly examining) jurors' notes; and allowing juror questions. And any innovation that requires attorneys, judges, and other court personnel to change their way of doing business is likely to meet with some degree of initial confusion. if not outright opposition. By and large, judges have considerable control over trial procedures in their own courtrooms and cannot be compelled to adopt a new procedure. Many judges are open to modifying trial procedures to improve the process (e.g., Kaye, 2008; Kozinski, 2015), but the temptation to continue business as usual is doubtless as strong in the courtroom as in any other context.

As the large number of entries in the bottom section of Table 15.1 makes clear, many innovative and potentially useful measures are either untried or lack sufficient data, in quantity or clarity, to afford a strong recommendation for their adoption. Most are either untested or have been tried in only a handful of studies or jurisdictions, making it hard to draw strong conclusions. A few, such as expert testimony on eyewitness memory and instructions on specific kinds of evidence, have attracted a great deal of research interest, but with mixed results. It is hard to know the reason for these inconclusive findings; they are likely due, at least in part, to methodological variations across studies. In the case of relatively untested reforms, as with reforms already known to work, decisions must be made both to try a measure in the first place and to examine how to make the reform most effective.

One thing is clear: Opportunities to improve jury performance abound. The importance of testing the effect of reforms prior to their widespread adoption cannot be overstated, as implementation of reforms that make sense on the surface but have not been subjected to empirical scrutiny can lead to wasted effort and expense or, worse, adverse consequences for the parties involved. The number of reforms that have already been tried is substantial, yet it is exceeded by those still in the development phase, and no doubt there are countless others waiting to be imagined. This richness bodes well for the future of juries and those who study them.

Future Research Needs

The significant number of reforms in need of empirical assessment (see Table 15.1) points to one obvious research need, namely, more studies testing reforms' effectiveness. Even among the reforms that already have some degree of empirical support, many have been tested using only a single research approach or in a very limited fashion (e.g., a single study in a single jurisdiction). Because evidentiary rules and trial procedures vary somewhat across jurisdictions and because of the possibility of spurious findings, we can be more confident in concluding that a reform really works if it is replicated in multiple jurisdictions.

The field of jury research is dominated by experimental simulations. This is not necessarily a bad thing, as the experimental method confers a number of advantages (e.g., rigorous experimental control, causal inferences; see Bornstein, 2017). Yet we can be more confident about research results if they arise from multiple methodologies. It is especially important to confirm findings from experimental simulations with one of the methods using real jurors (Diamond, 1997). No simulation, regardless of its realism, can capture all of the complexity and consequences of an actual trial (Bornstein & McCabe, 2005). Very often, of course, it will not matter—the results will converge on the same conclusions regardless of the studies' verisimilitude (Bornstein, 2017). But we cannot simply assume that they will be the same.

To that end, we applaud the growth of the empirical legal studies movement, which relies heavily on archival analyses (Eisenberg, 2011; Suchman & Mertz, 2010). We also encourage more courts to allow researchers to conduct field studies in which real juries are assigned to different experimental conditions. As we described in Chapter 14, field studies of juries on topics like note taking, question asking, and predeliberation discussion have yielded important insights into jury behavior, but these studies are the exception rather than the rule. The growing number of individual judges (e.g., Kaye, 2008; Kozinski, 2015), as well as state supreme courts and bar associations, that are open to trial innovations is a very positive sign for the future. Such efforts require the coordination of judges and other court employees (e.g., court clerks), legal scholars and social scientists, and public officials (e.g., jury commissioners). In some cases they might even require enabling legislation (e.g., caps on damages are a statutory reform).

Bringing these many constituencies together is no easy task, but many organizations are trying. To mention just two examples, the National Center for State Courts regularly tracks and tests innovative trial procedures (Hannaford-Agor, 2015). And one of the main focuses of the recently established Civil Jury Project at New York University School of Law is to "undertake an empirical assessment of the current role of the jury in our civil justice system" (http://civiljuryproject.law.nyu.edu/about/), in large part via field studies.[2] Field studies can be an incredibly powerful research tool, and we hope to see more of them.

In some instances, research yields conflicting results as a function of methodology, such as studies on judge–jury differences in sentencing (Diamond & Stalans, 1989; King & Noble, 2005; see Chapter 13). In such situations the temptation is often either to ignore the research altogether

---

[2] Disclosure: Both authors are academic advisors to the NYU Civil Jury Project, which is led by Stephen Susman, Samuel Issacharoff, and Catherine Sharkey.

(analogous to throwing up one's hands in response to opposing expert testimony; see Chapter 7) or to go with the "better" research method. Although these reactions are understandable, and easier than the hard work of carefully scrutinizing the conflicting studies and assessing their respective strengths and weaknesses, they are shortsighted and unproductive. As we argued in Chapter 1, every jury research technique has its pros and cons; none is simply better than the others across the board (see, generally, Kovera, 2017). If empirical studies are going to be discounted, it should only be because they lack scientific merit in some respect, and not merely because their findings diverge from those of other studies.

Finale

At the end of our previous book on juries (Greene & Bornstein, 2003), we asked whether the glass of jury behavior was half empty or half full. We concluded that it was half (if not even three-quarters) full. A dozen years later, we see no reason to change our minds. The standard for judging jury decisions is not whether the jury reached the "right" or even the "best possible" decision, but whether its decision was reasonable in light of the evidence (Bornstein & Greene, 2011a). By that standard juries fare quite well, as attested to by the infrequency with which judges enter a judgment notwithstanding the jury's verdict, impose *additur* or *remittitur,* or reverse a jury verdict on appeal. The jury is much more than a vestigial remnant of an outmoded system; rather, it is a system of lasting and proven value.

   Nonetheless, half (or even three-quarters) full does not mean completely full, without any spillage whatsoever. Like any social institution, even one that has evolved over 900 years, the jury system is imperfect. Some innocent criminal defendants are falsely convicted, and some blameless civil defendants are required to pay damages; by the same token, both criminal and civil wrongdoers are sometimes not held accountable for their actions, which not only leaves victims and plaintiffs without a remedy but also leaves the wrongdoers free to harm others. More subtly, jury decisions are more variable than they should be. Although no two cases are identical, parties with highly similar circumstances, evidence, and applicable laws can receive widely divergent outcomes. Of course, if juries were perfectly predictable, then they would be superfluous—we could simply enter all of the relevant facts into a preprogrammed formula and obtain the result, which would be the same every time. That might contribute to the goal of consistent and predictable verdicts, but it would detract from the jury's other functions, such as serving as a vehicle for participatory democracy and as a check on governmental authority. A jury verdict's consequences for those directly involved are undoubtedly important, but they are not the sole criterion by which a jury system should be judged.

It is therefore important to do what we can to ensure that jury decisions are as accurate as possible, while bearing in mind that the jury system transcends the decisions of individual juries. Fortunately, we have the means at our disposal to improve jury decisions. We will never make them error-free. But evidence-based jury reforms offer a way to debunk the myths, lower the volume on the controversies, and foster justice.

References

Abdel-Monem, T., Bingham, S., Marincic, J., & Tomkins, A. (2010). Deliberation and diversity: Perceptions of small group discussions by race and ethnicity. *Small Group Research, 41*, 746–776.

Abramson, J. (1994). *We, the jury: The jury system and the ideal of democracy.* New York: Basic Books.

Abshire, J., & Bornstein, B.H. (2003). Juror sensitivity to the cross-race effect. *Law and Human Behavior, 27*, 471–480.

Allen v. Hardy, 478 U.S. 255 (1986).

Allen et al. v. Takeda Pharmaceuticals North America, Inc. et al. (2014). Memorandum ruling on defendants' Rule 59 motion for new trial. Available at https://docs.justia.com/cases/federal/district-courts/louisiana/lawdce/6:2012cv00064/121414/729.

Allen, M., Mabry, E., & McKelton, D.-M. (1998). Impact of juror attitudes about the death penalty on juror evaluations of guilt and punishment: A meta-analysis. *Law and Human Behavior, 22*, 715–731.

Allison, M., & Brimacombe, C.A.E. (2010). Alibi believability: The effect of prior convictions and judicial instructions. *Journal of Applied Social Psychology, 40*, 1054–1084.

Alonzo, J.D., & Lane, S.M. (2010). Saying versus judging: Assessing knowledge of eyewitness memory. *Applied Cognitive Psychology, 24*, 1245–1264.

Alvarez, M.J., Miller, M.K., & Bornstein, B.H. (2016). It will be your duty . . .": The psychology of criminal jury instructions. In M.K. Miller & B.H. Bornstein (Eds.), *Advances in psychology and law* (Vol. 1) (pp. 119–158). New York: Springer.

Amar, A.R. (1998). *The Bill of Rights: Creation and reconstruction.*

American Bar Association (2005). *Principles for juries and jury trials.* Washington, DC: Author.

American Law Institute (1965). *Restatement (second) of torts.* St. Paul, MN: American Law Institute.

American Psychological Association (2013a). Brief for amicus curiae American Psychological Association in support of appellant (*People v. Thomas*, Court of Appeals, State of New York). Retrieved from http://www.apa.org/about/offices/ogc/amicus/thomas.pdf.

American Psychological Association (2013b). Specialty guidelines for forensic psychology. *American Psychologist, 68,* 7–19.

American Publishing Company v. Fisher, 166 U.S. 464 (1897).

Anderson, C., Lepper, M., & Ross, L. (1980). Perseverance of social theories: The role of explanation in the persistence of discredited information. *Journal of Personality and Social Psychology, 39,* 1037–1049.

Anderson, M.C., & MacCoun, R.J. (1999). Goal conflict in juror assessments of compensatory and punitive damages. *Law and Human Behavior, 23,* 313–330.

Apodaca v. Oregon, 406 U.S. 404 (1972).

Appelbaum, P.S., Scurich, N., & Raad, R. (2015). Effects of behavioral genetic evidence on perceptions of criminal responsibility and appropriate punishment. *Psychology, Public Policy, and Law, 21,* 134–144.

Appleby, S., Hasel, L., & Kassin, S. (2013). Police-induced confessions: An empirical analysis of their content and impact. *Psychology, Crime & Law, 19,* 111–128.

Appleby, S., & Kassin, S. (2011). *When confessions trump DNA: Relative impacts of self-report and DNA evidence on juror decisions.* Paper presented at American Psychology-Law Society, Miami, FL.

Applegate, B., Davis, R., & Cullen, F. (2009). Reconsidering child saving: The extent and correlates of public support for excluding youths from the juvenile court. *Crime and Delinquency, 55,* 51–77.

Archer, R.L., Foushee, H.C., & Davis, M.H. (1979). Emotional empathy in a courtroom simulation: A person-situation interaction. *Journal of Applied Social Psychology, 9,* 275–291.

Ariely, D. (2009). *Predictably irrational: The hidden forces that shape our decisions* (revised and expanded). New York: Harper Perennial.

Arizona Supreme Court Committee on More Effective Use of Juries (1994). *Jurors: The power of 12.* Phoenix, AZ: Author.

Arizona v. Fulminante, 499 U.S. 279 (1991).

Arkes, H.R. (1989). Principles in judgment/decision-making research pertinent to legal proceedings. *Behavioral Sciences & the Law, 7,* 429–456.

Arkes, H. (1991). Costs and benefits of judgment errors: Implications for debiasing. *Psychological Bulletin, 110,* 486–498.

Armstrong v. Roger's Outdoor Sports, Inc., 581 So.2d 414 (Ala. 1991).

Ashenfelter, O., Eisenberg, T., & Schwab, S. (1995). Politics and the judiciary: The influence of judicial background on case outcomes. *Journal of Legal Studies, 24,* 257–281.

Associated Press (2014, Dec. 29). *5 things about Americans' slipping sense of civic duty.* Retrieved from http://nypost.com/2014/12/29/5-things-about-americans-slipping-sense-of-civic-duty/

Atkins v. Virginia, 536 U.S. 304 (2002).

Bailis, D.S., & MacCoun, R.J. (1996). Estimating liability risks with the media as your guide: A content analysis of media coverage of tort litigation. *Law and Human Behavior, 20*, 419–429.

Baldus, D.C., MacQueen, J.C., & Woodworth, G. (1995). Improving judicial oversight of jury damages assessments: A proposal for the comparative additur/remittitur review of awards for nonpecuniary harms and punitive damages. *Iowa Law Review, 80*, 1109–1267.

Baldus, D.C., Pulaski, C., & Woodworth, G. (1983). Comparative review of death sentences: An empirical study of the Georgia experience. *Journal of Criminal Law and Criminology, 74*, 661–753.

Baldus, D.C., Woodworth, G., & Pulaski, C. (1990). *Equal justice and the death penalty: A legal and empirical analysis.* Boston: Northeastern University Press.

Baldus, D.C., Woodworth, G., Zuckerman, D., Weiner, N.A., & Broffitt, B. (1998). Race discrimination and the death penalty in the post-*Furman* era: An empirical and legal overview with recent findings from Philadelphia. *Cornell Law Review, 83*, 1638–1770.

Ballew v. Georgia, 435 U.S. 233 (1978).

Banaji, M., & Greenwald, A. (1995). Implicit gender stereotyping in judgments of fame. *Journal of Personality and Social Psychology, 68*, 181–198.

Bandura, A. (2002). Selective moral disengagement in the exercise of moral agency. *Journal of Moral Education, 31*, 101–119.

Bank, S.C., & Poythress, N.G. (1982). The elements of persuasion in expert testimony. *Journal of Psychiatry and Law, 10*, 173–204.

Bargh, J. (2006). *Social psychology and the unconscious: The automaticity of higher mental processes.* Philadelphia: Psychology Press.

Bar-Hillel, M. (1980). The base rate fallacy in probability judgments. *Acta Psychologica, 44*, 211–233.

Batson v. Kentucky, 476 U.S. 79 (1986).

Batson, C.D., Turk, C.L., Shaw, L.L., & Klein, T.R. (1995). Information function of empathic emotion: Learning that we value others' welfare. *Journal of Personality and Social Psychology, 68*, 300–313.

Bau, L. (2014). *The history and treatment of damages in Canada.* Retrieved from http://www.lindsayllp.ca/articles/the-history-and-treatment-of-damages-in-canada/.

Bazerman, M., Giuliano, T., & Appelman, A. (1984). Escalation of commitment in individual and group decision making. *Organizational Behavior and Human Performance, 32*, 141–152.

Becker, G.S. (1968). Crime and punishment: An economic approach. *Journal of Political Economy, 76*, 169–217.

Bedau, H., & Radelet, M. (1987). Miscarriages of justice in potentially capital cases. *Stanford Law Review, 40*, 21–179.

Bell, B.E., & Loftus, E.F. (1988). Degree of detail of eyewitness testimony and mock juror judgments. *Journal of Applied Social Psychology, 18*, 1171–1192.

Belli, R.F. (2012). *True and false recovered memories: Toward a reconciliation of the debate.* New York: Springer.

Bellin, J., & Semitsu, J. (2011). Widening *Batson's* net to ensnare more than the unapologetically bigoted or painfully unimaginative attorney. *Cornell Law Review, 96*, 1075–1130.

Bennett, M. (2010). Unraveling the Gordian knot of implicit bias in jury selection: The problems of judge-dominated voir dire, the failed promise of Batson, and proposed solutions. *Harvard Law and Policy Review, 4,* 149–171.

Benton, T.R., McDonnell, S., Ross, D.F., Thomas, N., & Bradshaw, E. (2007). Has eyewitness research penetrated the American legal system? A synthesis of case history, juror knowledge, and expert testimony. In R.C.L. Lindsay, D.F. Ross., J.D. Read, & M.P. Toglia (Eds.), *The handbook of eyewitness psychology (Vol. 2): Memory for people* (pp. 453–500). Mahwah, NJ: Erlbaum.

Benton, T.R., Ross, D.F., Bradshaw, E., Thomas, W.N., & Bradshaw, G.S. (2006). Eyewitness memory is still not common sense: Comparing jurors, judges, and law enforcement to eyewitness experts. *Applied Cognitive Psychology, 20,* 115–130.

Berman, G.L., & Cutler, B.L. (1996). Effects of inconsistencies in eyewitness testimony on mock-juror decision making. *Journal of Applied Psychology, 81,* 170–177.

Berman, G.L., Narby, D.J., & Cutler, B.L. (1995). Effects of inconsistent eyewitness statements on mock-jurors' evaluations of the eyewitness, perceptions of defendant culpability and verdicts. *Law and Human Behavior, 19,* 79–88.

Berman, M.K., & Penrod, S.D. (2012). Judicial instruction on eyewitness identification: A meta-analysis. Unpublished manuscript.

Bernstein, D.E. (1996). Junk science in the United States and the Commonwealth. *Yale Journal of International Law, 21,* 123–182.

Biernat, M. (2003). Toward a broader view of social stereotyping. *American Psychologist, 58,* 1019–1027.

Biernat, M., & Ma, J. (2005). Stereotypes and the confirmability of trait concepts. *Personality and Social Psychology Bulletin, 31,* 483–495.

Bishop, D.M. (2000). Justice offenders in the adult criminal justice system. In M. Tonry (Ed.), *Crime and justice: A review of research* (Vol. 26, pp. 81–167). Chicago: University of Chicago Press.

Bishop, D.M., & Frazier, C.E. (2000). Consequences of transfer. In J. Fagan & F. E. Zimring (Eds.), *The changing borders of juvenile justice: Transfer of adolescents to the criminal court* (pp. 227–276). Chicago: University of Chicago Press.

Bishop, D.M., Frazier, C.E., & Henretta, J.C. (1989). Prosecutorial waiver: Case study of questionable reform. *Crime and Delinquency, 35,* 179–201.

Black, B., Silver, C., Hyman, D.A., & Sage, W.M. (2005). Stability, not crisis: Medical malpractice claim outcomes in Texas, 1988-2002. *Journal of Empirical Legal Studies, 2,* 207–259.

Blackstone, W. (1979). *Commentaries on the Laws of England: Of the rights of persons.* Chicago: University of Chicago Press.

Blanck, P.D., Rosenthal, R., & Cordell, L.H. (1985). The appearance of justice: Judges' verbal and nonverbal behavior in criminal trials. *Stanford Law Review, 38,* 89–164.

Blandón-Gitlin, I., Sperry, K., & Leo, R. (2011). Jurors believe interrogation tactics are not likely to elicit false confessions: Will expert witness testimony inform them otherwise? *Psychology Crime & Law, 17,* 239–260.

Block, S.D., Shestowsky, D., Segovia, D.A., Goodman, G.S., Schaaf, J.M., & Alexander, K.W. (2012). "That never happened": Adults' discernment of children's true and false memory reports. *Law and Human Behavior, 36,* 365–374.

Bloeser, A., McCurley, C., & Mondak, J. (2012). Jury service as civic engagement: Determinants of jury summons compliance. *American Politics Research, 40,* 179–204.

Blume, J.H., Eisenberg, T., & Wells, M.T. (2004). Explaining death row's population and racial composition. *Journal of Empirical Legal Studies, 1,* 165–207.

Blume, J.H., Garvey, S., & Johnson, S. (2001). Future dangerousness in capital cases: Always "at issue." *Cornell Law Review, 86,* 397–410.

Blumenthal, J.A. (2010). A moody view of the law: Looking back and looking ahead at law and the emotions. In B.H. Bornstein & R.L. Wiener (Eds.), *Emotion and the law: Psychological perspectives* (pp. 185–210). New York: Springer.

BMW v. Gore, 517 U.S. 559 (1996).

Boatright, R. (1999). *Improving citizen response to jury summonses.* Chicago: American Judicature Society.

Boatright, R. (2001). Generational and age-based differences in attitudes toward jury service. *Behavioral Sciences and the Law, 19,* 285–304.

Bodenhausen, G.V. (1988). Stereotypic biases in social decision making and memory: Testing process models of stereotype use. *Journal of Personality and Social Psychology, 55,* 726–737.

Bodenhausen, G.V., Sheppard, L.A., & Kramer, G.P. (1994). Negative affect and social judgment: The differential impact of anger and sadness. *European Journal of Social Psychology, 24,* 45–62.

Boeri, D., & Sobel, Z. (2015, March 3). Judge's quest to find a 'fair and impartial' Tsarnaev jury in Boston finally comes to a close. *WBUR News.* Retrieved from http://www.wbur.org/2015/03/03/tsarnaev-jury-boston-judge-otoole.

Bolivar County Circuit Court Task Force (2014). June 19 public forum to focus on jury service in Bolivar County. Retrieved from https://courts.ms.gov/news/2014/BOLIVAR%20COUNTY%20CIRCUIT%20COURT%20TASK%20FORCE.pdf.

Bollingmo, G., Wessel, E., Sandvold, Y., Eilertsen, D.E., & Magnussen, S. (2009). The effect of biased and non-biased information on judgments of witness credibility. *Psychology, Crime & Law, 15,* 61–71.

Bond, C., & DePaulo, B. (2006). Accuracy of deception judgments. *Personality and Social Psychology Review, 10,* 214–234.

Bornstein, B.H. (1994). David, Goliath, and Reverend Bayes: Prior beliefs about defendants' status in personal injury cases. *Applied Cognitive Psychology, 8,* 233–258.

Bornstein, B.H. (1998). From compassion to compensation: The effect of injury severity on mock jurors' liability judgments. *Journal of Applied Social Psychology, 28,* 1477–1502.

Bornstein, B.H. (1999). The ecological validity of jury simulations: Is the jury still out? *Law & Human Behavior, 23,* 75–91.

Bornstein, B.H. (2004). The impact of different types of expert scientific testimony on mock jurors' liability verdicts. *Psychology, Crime & Law, 10,* 429–446.

Bornstein, B.H. (2006). Judges vs. juries. *Court Review, 43,* 56–58.

Bornstein, B.H. (2009). Physical v. mental pain: A legal double standard? *APA Monitor, 40*(2), 18.

Bornstein, B.H. (2017). Jury simulation research: Pros, cons, trends and alternatives. In M.B. Kovera (Ed.), *The psychology of juries: Current knowledge and a research agenda for the future.* Washington, DC: American Psychological Association.

Bornstein, B.H., & Greene, E. (2011a). Jury decision making: Implications for and from psychology. *Current Directions in Psychological Science, 20,* 63–67.

Bornstein, B.H., & Greene, E. (2011b). Consulting on damage awards. In R.L. Wiener & B.H. Bornstein (Eds.), *Handbook of trial consulting* (pp. 281–295). New York: Springer.

Bornstein, B.H., & Hamm, J.A. (2012). Jury instructions on witness identification. *Court Review, 48,* 48–53.

Bornstein, B.H., & McCabe, S.G. (2005). Jurors of the absurd? The role of consequentiality in jury simulation research. *Florida State University Law Review, 32,* 443–467.

Bornstein, B.H., & Miller, M.K. (2008-2009). Does judges' religion influence their decision making? *Court Review, 45,* 112–115.

Bornstein, B.H., & Miller, M.K. (2009). *God in the courtroom: Religion's role at trial.* New York: Oxford University Press.

Bornstein, B.H., Miller, M., Nemeth, R., Page, G., & Musil, S. (2005). Juror reactions to jury duty: Perceptions of the system and potential stressors. *Behavioral Sciences and the Law, 23,* 321–346.

Bornstein, B.H., & Muller, S.L. (2001). The credibility of recovered memory testimony: Exploring the effects of alleged victim and perpetrator gender. *Child Abuse and Neglect, 25,* 1415–1426.

Bornstein, B.H., & Nemeth, R.J. (1999). Jurors' perception of violence: A framework for inquiry. *Aggression and Violent Behavior, 4,* 77–92.

Bornstein, B.H., O'Bryant, S., & Zickafoose, D.J. (2008). Intuitions about arousal and eyewitness memory: Effects on mock jurors' judgments. *Law and Psychology Review, 32,* 109–129.

Bornstein, B.H., & Robicheaux, T.R. (2008). Crisis, what crisis? Perception and reality in civil justice. In B.H. Bornstein, R.L. Wiener, R. Schopp, & S. Willborn (Eds.), *Civil juries and civil justice: Psychological and legal perspectives* (pp. 1–19). New York: Springer.

Bornstein, B.H., Robicheaux, T.R., & Thimsen, S. (2009). Punitive damages: A vehicle for punishment in civil cases. In M.E. Oswald, S. Bieneck, & J. Hupfeld-Heinemann (Eds.), *Social psychology of punishment of crime* (pp. 193–209). Chichester: Wiley-Blackwell.

Bornstein, B.H., Rung, L.M., & Miller, M. (2002). Should physicians apologize for their mistakes? The role of remorse in a simulated malpractice trial. *Behavioral Sciences & the Law, 20,* 393–409.

Bornstein, B.H., & Schwartz, S.L. (2009, March). Injured body, injured mind: Dealing with damages for psychological harm. *The Jury Expert, 21(2),* 33–39.

Bornstein, B.H., Tomkins, A.J., Neeley, E.M., Herian, M.N., & Hamm, J.A. (2013). Reducing courts' failure-to-appear rate by written reminders. *Psychology, Public Policy, & Law, 19,* 70–80.

Bornstein, B.H., Whisenhunt, B., Nemeth, R.J., & Dunaway, D. (2002). Pretrial publicity effects in a civil trial: A two-way street? *Law and Human Behavior, 26,* 3–17.

Bornstein, B.H., & Wiener, R.L. (2006). Special issue on emotion in legal judgment and decision making. *Law and Human Behavior, 30(2)*.

Bornstein, B.H., & Wiener, R.L. (2010a). *Emotion and the law: Psychological perspectives*. New York: Springer.

Bornstein, B.H., & Wiener, R.L. (2010b). Emotion and the law: A field whose time has come. In B.H. Bornstein & R.L. Wiener (Eds.), *Emotion and the law: Psychological perspectives* (pp. 1–12). New York: Springer.

Bornstein, B.H., & Zickafoose, D.J. (1999). "I know I know it, I know I saw it": The stability of the confidence-accuracy relationship across domains. *Journal of Experimental Psychology: Applied, 5*, 76–88.

Bottoms, B.L., Golding, J.M., Stevenson, M.C., Wiley, T.R.A., & Yozwiak, J.A. (2007). A review of factors affecting jurors' decisions in child sexual abuse cases. In M.P. Toglia, J.D. Read, D.F. Ross, & R.C.L. Lindsay (Eds.), *The handbook of eyewitness psychology (Vol. 1): Memory for events* (pp. 509–543). Mahwah, NJ: Erlbaum.

Bourgeois, M.J., Horowitz, I.A., ForsterLee, L., & Grahe, J. (1995). Nominal and interactive groups: Effects of preinstruction and deliberations on decisions and evidence recall in complex trials. *Journal of Applied Psychology, 80*, 58–67.

Bovbjerg, R.R., Sloan, F.A., & Blumstein, J.F. (1989). Valuing life and limb in tort: Scheduling "pain and suffering." *Northwestern University Law Review, 83*, 908–976.

Bovbjerg, R.R., Sloan, F.A., Dor, A., & Hsieh, C.R. (1991). Juries and justice: Are malpractice and other personal injuries created equal? *Law and Contemporary Problems, 54*, 5–42.

Bowers, W.J., Sandys, M., & Steiner, B.D. (1998). Foreclosed impartiality in capital sentencing: Jurors' predispositions, attitudes and premature decision-making. *Cornell Law Review, 83*, 1476-

Bowers, W.J., Steiner, B.D., & Sandys, M. (2001). Death sentencing in Black and White: An empirical analysis of the role of jurors' race and jury racial composition. *University of Pennsylvania Journal of Constitutional Law, 3*, 171–274.

Bowler, S., Esterling, K., & Holmes, D. (2014). GOTJ: Get out the juror. *Political Behavior, 36*, 515–533.

Boyce, M., Beaudry, J., & Lindsay, R.C.L. (2007). Belief of eyewitness identification evidence. In R.C.L. Lindsay, D.F. Ross., J.D. Read, & M.P. Toglia (Eds.), *The handbook of eyewitness psychology (Vol. 2): Memory for people* (pp. 501–525). Mahwah, NJ: Erlbaum.

Bradfield, A.L., & Wells, G.L. (2000). The perceived validity of eyewitness identification testimony: A test of the five *Biggers* criteria. *Law and Human Behavior, 24*, 581–594.

Bradshaw, G., Ross, D., Bradshaw, E., Headrick, B., & Thomas, W. (2005). Juror reactions to jury duty: Perceptions of the system and potential stressors. *Law and Human Behavior, 29*, 457–467.

Breen, P.D. (2011). The trial penalty and jury sentencing: A study of Air Force courts-martial. *Journal of Empirical Legal Studies, 8*, 206–235.

Brekke, N.J., & Borgida, E. (1988). Expert psychological testimony in rape trials: A social-cognitive analysis. *Journal of Personality and Social Psychology, 55*, 372–386.

Brewer, N., & Burke, A. (2002). Effects of testimonial inconsistencies and eyewitness confidence on mock-juror judgments. *Law and Human Behavior, 26,* 353–364.

Brewer, T.W. (2004). Race and jurors' receptivity to mitigation in capital cases: The effect of jurors', defendants', and victims' race in combination. *Law and Human Behavior, 28,* 529–545.

Brigham, J.C. (1981). The accuracy of eyewitness evidence: How do attorneys see it? *The Florida Bar Journal, 55,* 714–721.

Brigham, J.C., & Wolfskeil, M.P. (1983). Opinions of attorneys and law enforcement personnel on the accuracy of eyewitness identification. *Law and Human Behavior, 7,* 337–349.

Bright, D.A., & Goodman-Delahunty, J. (2004). The influence of gruesome verbal evidence on mock juror verdicts. *Psychiatry, Psychology and Law, 11,* 154–166.

Bright, D.A., & Goodman-Delahunty, J. (2006). Gruesome evidence and emotion: Anger, blame and jury decision-making. *Law and Human Behavior, 30,* 183–202.

Bright, D.A., & Goodman-Delahunty, J. (2011). Mock juror decision making in a civil negligence trial: The impact of gruesome evidence, injury severity, and information processing route. *Psychiatry, Psychology and Law, 18,* 439–459.

Broda-Bahm, K. (2013). Getting beyond "Can you be fair?" Framing your cause questions. *The Jury Expert, 25*(4), 1–3.

Brodsky, S.L. (2009). *Principles and practice of trial consultation.* New York: Guilford.

Brodsky, S.L., Griffin, M.P., & Cramer, R.J. (2010). The Witness Credibility Scale: An outcome measure for expert witness research. *Behavioral Sciences & the Law, 28,* 892–907.

Brodsky, S.L., Neal, T.M.S., Cramer, R.J., & Ziemke, M.H. (2009). Credibility in the courtroom: How likeable should an expert witness be? *Journal of the American Academy of Psychiatry and the Law, 37,* 525–532.

Brodsky, S.L., & Pivovarova, E. (2016). The credibility of witnesses. In C. Willis Esqueda & B.H. Bornstein (Eds.), *The witness stand and Lawrence S. Wrightsman, Jr* (pp. 41–52). New York: Springer.

Broeder, D. (1965). Voir dire examinations: An empirical study. *Southern California Law Review, 38,* 503-

Brown, R. (1994). Peremptory challenges as a shield for the pariah. *American Criminal Law Review, 31,* 1203–1212.

Brown, T., & Murphy, E. (2010). Through a scanner darkly: Functional neuroimaging as evidence of criminal defendant's past mental states. *Stanford Law Review, 62,* 1119–1208.

Brunell, T., Dave, C., & Morgan, N. (2009). Factors affecting the length of time a jury deliberates: Case characteristics and jury composition. *Review of Law and Economics, 5,* 555–578.

Burch v. Louisiana, 441 U.S. 130 (1979).

Burch, T. (2015). Skin color and the criminal justice system: Beyond Black-White disparities in sentencing. *Journal of Empirical Legal Studies, 12,* 395–420.

Bureau of Justice Statistics (2001). *Civil Justice Survey of State Courts.* Report ICPSR03957-v.3. Washington, DC: U.S. Department of Justice, Office of Justice Programs.

Burke, B.L., Martens, A., & Faucher, E.H. (2010). Two decades of terror management theory: A meta-analysis of mortality salience research. *Personality and Social Psychology Bulletin, 14,* 155–195.

Burns, N., Schlozman, K., & Verba, S. (2001). *The private roots of public action: Gender, equality and political participation.* Cambridge, MA: Harvard University Press.

Butler, B. (2007a). The role of death qualification in capital trials involving juvenile defendants. *Journal of Applied Social Psychology, 37,* 549–560.

Butler, B. (2007b). The role of death qualification in jurors' susceptibility to pretrial publicity. *Journal of Applied Social Psychology, 37,* 115–123.

Butler, B. (2007c). Death qualification and prejudice: The effect of implicit racism, sexism, and homophobia on capital defendants' right to due process. *Behavioral Sciences & the Law, 25,* 857–867.

Butler, B. (2008). The role of death qualification in venirepersons' susceptibility to victim impact statements. *Psychology, Crime & Law, 14,* 133–141.

Butler, B. (2010). Moving beyond *Ford, Atkins,* and *Roper*: Jurors' attitudes toward the execution of the elderly and the physically disabled. *Psychology, Crime & Law, 16,* 631–647.

Butler, B., & Moran, G. (2002). The role of death qualification in venirepersons' evaluations of aggravating and mitigating circumstances in capital trials. *Law and Human Behavior, 26,* 175–184.

Butler, B., & Moran, G. (2007a). The role of death qualification and need for cognition in venirepersons' evaluations of expert scientific testimony in capital trials. *Behavioral Sciences & the Law, 25,* 561–571.

Butler, B., & Moran, G. (2007b). The impact of death qualification, belief in a just world, legal authoritarianism, and locus of control on venirepersons' evaluations of aggravating and mitigating circumstances in capital trials. *Behavioral Sciences & the Law, 25,* 57–68.

Butler, B., & Wasserman, A.W. (2006). The role of death qualification in venirepersons' attitudes toward the insanity defense. *Journal of Applied Social Psychology, 36,* 1744–1757.

Cacioppo, J.T., Petty, R.E., Feinstein, J.A., & Jarvis, W. (1996). Dispositional differences in cognitive motivation: The life and times of individuals varying in need for cognition. *Psychological Bulletin, 119,* 197–253.

Callins v. Collins, 510 U.S. 1141 (1994).

Camilletti, C., & Scullin, M. (2012). Attorney and lay beliefs about factors affecting jurors' perceptions of juvenile offender culpability. *Psychology, Crime & Law, 18,* 113–128.

Campbell, J. (1988). *The power of myth.* New York: Doubleday.

Capitol Records, Inc. v. Thomas-Rasset, 692 F.3d 899 (8th Cir. 2012).

Carbone, N. (2011, July 3). Casey Anthony trial: Laughing and crying during closing arguments. *Time.* Available at http://newsfeed.time.com/2011/07/03/casey-anthony-trial-laughing-and-crying-during-closing-arguments/.

Carlson, K., & Russo, J. (2001). Biased interpretation of evidence by mock jurors. *Journal of Experimental Psychology: Applied, 7,* 91–103.

Cassell, P.G. (2009). In defense of victim impact statements. *Ohio State Journal of Criminal Law, 6*, 611–648.

Cather, C., Greene, E., & Durham, R. (1996). Plaintiff injury and defendant reprehensibility: Implications for compensatory and punitive damage awards. *Law and Human Behavior, 20*, 189–205.

Cauffman, E., Woolard, J., & Reppucci, N.D. (1999). Justice for juveniles: New perspectives on adolescents' competence and culpability. *Quinnipiac Law Review, 18*, 403–420.

Chamberlain, J., & Miller, M.K. (2009). Evidence of secondary traumatic stress, safety concerns, and burnout among a homogeneous group of judges in a single jurisdiction. *Journal of the American Academy of Psychiatry and the Law, 37*, 214–224.

Chamberlain, J., & Richardson, J.T. (2013). Judicial stress: A topic in need of research. In M.K. Miller & B.H. Bornstein (Eds.), *Stress, trauma, and wellbeing in the legal system* (pp. 269–290). Oxford: Oxford University Press.

Champagne, A., Shuman, D.W., & Whitaker, E. (1992). Expert witness in the courts: An empirical examination. *Judicature, 76 (June-July)*, 5–10.

Chapman, G., & Bornstein, B.H. (1996). The more you ask for the more you get: Anchoring in personal injury verdicts. *Applied Cognitive Psychology, 10*, 519–540.

Charrow, R.P., & Charrow, V. (1979). Making legal language understandable: A psycholinguistic study of jury instructions. *Columbia Law Review, 79*, 1306–1374.

Chi, M.T.H., Glaser, R., & Farr, M.J. (2014). *The nature of expertise.* Psychology Press.

Chojnacki, D., Cicchini, M., & White, L. (2008). An empirical basis for the admission of expert testimony on false confessions. *Arizona State Law Journal, 40*, 1–45.

Christianson, S-A., & Hübinette, B. (1993). Hands up! A study of witnesses' emotional reactions and memories associated with bank robberies. *Applied Cognitive Psychology, 7*, 365–379.

Clark, H.L., & Nightingale, N.N. (1997). When jurors consider recovered memory cases: Effects of victim and juror gender. *Journal of Offender Rehabilitation, 25*, 87–104.

Clark, M., Anand, V., & Roberson, L. (2000). Resolving meaning: Interpretation in diverse decision-making groups. *Group Dynamics, 4*, 211–221.

Clark, S. (2014). The juror, the citizen, and the human being: The presumption of innocence and the burden of judgment. *Criminal Law and Philosophy, 8*, 421–429.

Clermont, K.M., & Eisenberg, T. (1992). Trial by jury or judge: Transcending empiricism. *Cornell Law Review, 77*, 1124–1177.

Clermont, K.M., & Eisenberg, T. (2002). Litigation realities. *Cornell Law Review, 88*, 119–154.

Cohen, J. (2014). *Blindfolds off: Judges on how they decide.* Chicago: American Bar Association.

Coker v. Georgia, 433 U.S. 584 (1977).

Colarossi, A. (2011, June 10). Casey Anthony trial: Video shows Caylee morphing into skull with duct tape over mouth. *Orlando Sentinel.* Available at http://articles.orlandosentinel.com/

2011-06-10/news/os-casey-anthony-trial-day-15-20110610_1_ duct-tape-casey-anthony-caylee-marie.

Colgrove v. Battin, 413 U.S. 149 (1973).

Collett, M.E., & Kovera, M.B. (2003). The effects of British and American trial procedures on the quality of juror decision-making. *Law and Human Behavior, 27*, 403–422.

Colorado v. Connelly, 479 U.S. 157 (1986).

Committee on Pattern Jury Instructions, District Judges Association, Fifth Circuit (2014). *Pattern jury instructions (civil cases)*. Thomson Reuters.

Commonwealth v. Alicia, No. 27 EAP 2012 (Pa. 2014).

Commonwealth v. DiGiambattista, 813 N.E. 2d 516 (Mass. 2004).

Conley, R. (2013). Living with the decision that someone will die: Linguistic distance and empathy in jurors' death penalty decisions. *Language in Society, 42*, 503–526.

Connolly, D.A., & Read, J.D. (2006). Delayed prosecutions of historic child sexual abuse: Analyses of 2064 Canadian criminal complaints. *Law and Human Behavior, 30*, 409–434.

Connolly, D.A., & Read, J.D. (2007). Canadian criminal court reports of historic child sexual abuse: Factors associated with delayed prosecution and reported repression. In M.-E. Pipe, M.E. Lamb, & Orbach, & A.-C. Cederborg (Eds.), *Child sexual abuse: Disclosure, delay, and denial* (pp. 195–217). Mahwah, NJ: Erlbaum.

Connors, E., Lundregan, T., Miller, N., & McEwen, T. (1996). *Convicted by juries, exonerated by science: Case studies in the use of DNA evidence to establish innocence after trial*. Washington, DC: Department of Justice.

Consolini, P. (1992). *Learning by doing justice: Jury service and political attitudes* (Doctoral dissertation). University of California Berkeley, Berkeley, CA. http://www.la1.psu.edu/cas/jurydem/Consolini_Dissertation.pdf.

Cook, P., & Laub, J. (1998). The unprecedented epidemic in youth violence. In M. Tonry & M. Moore (Eds.), *Crime and justice: A review of research* (Vol. 24, pp. 27–64). Chicago: University of Chicago Press.

Cooper Industries, Inc. v. Leatherman Tool Group, Inc., 532 U.S. 424 (2001).

Cooper, J., Bennett, E.A., & Sukel, H.L. (1996). Complex scientific testimony: how do jurors make decisions? *Law and Human Behavior, 20*, 379–394.

Cooper, J., & Neuhaus, I.M. (2000). The "hired gun" effect: Assessing the effect of pay, frequency of testifying, and credentials on the perception of expert testimony. *Law and Human Behavior, 24*, 149–171.

Cooper, M., & Wood, M. (1974). Effects of member participation and commitment in group decision making on influence, satisfaction, and decision riskiness. *Journal of Applied Psychology, 59*, 127–134.

Cornwell, E., & Hans, V. (2011). Representation through participation: A multilevel analysis of jury deliberations. *Law and Society Review, 45*, 667–698.

Correll, J., Park, B., Judd, C., & Wittenbrink, B. (2002). The police officer's dilemma: Using ethnicity to disambiguate potentially threatening individuals. *Journal of Personality and Social Psychology, 83*, 1314–1329.

Corwin, E.P., Cramer, R.J., Griffin, D.A., & Brodsky, S.L. (2012). Defendant remorse, need for affect, and juror sentencing decisions. *Journal of the American Academy of Psychiatry and the Law, 40*, 41–49.

Costanzo, M., Blandón-Gitlin, I., & Davis, D. (2016). The content, purpose, and effects of expert testimony on interrogations and confessions. In B.H. Bornstein & M.K. Miller (Eds.), *Advances in psychology and law* (Vol. 2). New York: Springer.

Costanzo, M., Krauss, D., & Pezdek, K. (2006). *Expert psychological testimony for the courts.* London: Psychology Press.

Costanzo, M., & Leo, R. (2007). Research findings and expert testimony on police interrogations and confessions to crimes. In M. Costanzo, D. Krauss, & K. Pezdek (Eds.), *Expert psychological testimony for the courts* (pp. 69–98). Mahwah, NJ: Erlbaum.

Costanzo, M., Shaked-Schroer, N., & Vinson, K. (2010). Juror beliefs about police interrogations, false confessions, and expert testimony. *Journal of Empirical Legal Studies, 7,* 231–247.

Coughlan, P. (2000). In defense of unanimous jury verdicts: Mistrials, communication, and strategic voting. *American Political Science Review, 94,* 23–35.

Cowan, C.L., Thompson, W.C., & Ellsworth, P.C. (1984). The effects of death qualification on jurors' predispositions to convict and on the quality of deliberation. *Law and Human Behavior, 8,* 53–79.

Craig, K.M., & Waldo, C.R. (1996). "So what's a hate crime anyway?" Young adults' perceptions of hate crimes, victims, and perpetrators. *Law and Human Behavior, 20,* 113–129.

Cramer, R.J., Clark, J.W., Kehn, A., Burks, A.C., & Wechsler, H.J. (2014). A mock juror investigation of blame attribution in the punishment of hate crime perpetrators. *International Journal of Law and Psychiatry, 37,* 551–557.

Cramer, R.J., Kehn, A., Pennington, C.R., Wechsler, H.J., Clark, J.W., & Nagle, J. (2013). An examination of sexual orientation—and transgender-based hate crimes in the post-Matthew Shepard era. *Psychology, Public Policy, and Law, 19,* 355–368.

Cramer, R.J., Wakeman, E.E., Chandler, J.F., Mohr, J.J., & Griffin, M.P. (2013). Hate crimes on trial: Judgments about violent crime against gay men. *Psychiatry, Psychology and Law, 20,* 202–215.

Crocker, C.B., & Kovera, M.B. (2011). Systematic jury selection. In R.L. Wiener & B.H. Bornstein (Eds.), *Handbook of trial consulting* (pp. 13–31). New York: Springer.

Crocker, P.L. (1997). Concepts of culpability and deathworthiness: Differentiating between guilt and punishment in death penalty cases. *Fordham Law Review, 66,* 21–86.

Cronin, P. (1958). Six-member juries in district courts. *Boston Bar Journal, 4,* 27–29.

Cullen, F. (2006). It's time to reaffirm rehabilitation. *Criminology and Public Policy, 5,* 665–672.

Cunningham, M., Reidy, T., & Sorensen, J. (2005). Is death row obsolete? A decade of mainstreaming death-sentenced inmates in Missouri. *Behavioral Sciences and the Law, 23,* 307–320.

Cunningham, M., Sorensen, J., & Reidy, T. (2005). An actuarial model for assessment of prison violence risk among maximum security inmates. *Assessment, 12,* 40–49.

Curtis, G.J. (2013). Don't be happy, worry: Positive mood, but not anxiety, increases stereotyping in a mock-juror decision-making task. *Psychiatry, Psychology and Law, 20,* 686–699.

Cush, R.K., & Goodman Delahunty, J. (2006). The influence of limiting instructions on processing and judgments of emotionally evocative evidence. *Psychiatry, Psychology and Law, 13,* 110–123.

Cutler, B.L., Dexter, H.R., & Penrod, S.D. (1989). Expert testimony and jury decision making: An empirical analysis. *Behavioral Sciences & the Law, 7,* 215–225.

Cutler, B.L., Dexter, H.R., & Penrod, S.D. (1990). Nonadversarial methods for sensitizing jurors to eyewitness evidence. *Journal of Applied Social Psychology, 20,* 1197–1207.

Cutler, B., & Hughes, D. (2001). Judging jury service: Results of the North Carolina Administrative Office of the Courts Juror Survey. *Behavioral Sciences and the Law, 19,* 305–320.

Cutler, B.L., & Kovera, M.B. (2011). Expert psychological testimony. *Current Directions in Psychological Science, 20,* 53–57.

Cutler, B.L., Penrod, S.D., & Dexter, H.R. (1989). The eyewitness, the expert psychologist, and the jury. *Law and Human Behavior, 13,* 311–332.

Cutler, B.L., Penrod, S.D., & Dexter, H.R. (1990). Juror sensitivity to eyewitness identification evidence. *Law and Human Behavior, 14,* 185–191.

Cutler, B.L., & Wells, G.L. (2009). Expert testimony regarding eyewitness identification. In K.S. Douglas & J.L. Skeem (Eds.), *Psychological science in the courtroom: Consensus and controversy* (pp.100–123). New York, NY: Guilford Press.

Daftary-Kapur, T., & Berry, M. (2010). The effects of outcome severity, damage amounts and counterfactual thinking on juror punitive damage award decision making. *American Journal of Forensic Psychology, 28,* 21–45.

Daftary-Kapur, T., Dumas, R., & Penrod, S.D. (2010). Jury decision-making biases and methods to counter them. *Legal and Criminological Psychology, 15,* 133–154.

Dahl, J., Enemo, I., Drevland, G.C.B., Wessel, E., Eilertsen, D.E., & Magnussen, S. (2007). Displayed emotions and witness credibility: A comparison of judgments by individuals and mock juries. *Applied Cognitive Psychology, 21,* 1145–1155.

Damasio, A.R. (1994). *Descartes' error: Emotion, reason, and the human brain.* New York: Avon Books.

Daniels, S., & Martin, J. (1990). Myth and reality in punitive damages. *Minnesota Law Review, 75,* 1–64.

Danielsen, E., Levett, L., & Kovera, M.B. (2004). *When juveniles are tried as adults: What happens during voir dire?* Paper presented at the American Psychology-Law Society, Scottsdale, AZ.

Dardinger v. Anthem Blue Cross and Blue Shield, 781 N.E.2d 121 (Ohio 2002).

Daubert v. Merrell Dow Pharmaceuticals, 509 US 579, 113 S. Ct. 2786 (1993).

Davidson, R.J. (1994). On emotion, mood, and related affective constructs. In P. Ekman & R.J. Davidson (Eds.), *The nature of emotion: Fundamental questions* (pp. 51–55). New York: Oxford University Press.

Davis v. Ayala, U.S. Supreme Court No. 13–1428 (2015).

Davis, D. Leo, R., & Williams, M. (2014). Disputed interrogation techniques in America: True and false confessions and the estimation of valuation of Type I and Type II errors. In S. Cooper (Ed.), *Controversies in innocence cases in America*. Burlington, VT: Ashgate Publishing Company.

Davis, J.H., Au, W., Hulbert, L., Chen, X., & Zarnoth, P. (1997). Effects of group size and procedural influence on consensual judgments of quality: The example of damage awards and mock civil juries. *Journal of Personality and Social Psychology, 73*, 703–718.

Davis, J.H., Kerr, N., Atkin, R., Holt, R., & Meek, D. (1975). The decision processes of 6—and 12-person mock juries assigned unanimous and 2/3 majority rules. *Journal of Personality and Social Psychology, 32*, 1–14.

Davis, J.H., Stasson, M.F., Parks, C.D., Hulbert, L., Kameda, T., Zimmerman, S.K., & Ono, K. (1993). Quantitative decisions by groups and individuals: Voting procedures and monetary awards by mock civil juries. *Journal of Experimental Social Psychology, 29*, 326–346.

Deffenbacher, K.A., Bornstein, B.H., Penrod, S.D., & McGorty, E.K. (2004). A meta-analytic review of the effects of high stress on eyewitness memory. *Law and Human Behavior, 28*, 687–706.

Deffenbacher, K.A., & Loftus, E.F. (1982). Do jurors share a common understanding concerning eyewitness behavior? *Law and Human Behavior, 6*, 15–30.

Deitz, S.R., Blackwell, K.T., Daley, P.C., & Bentley, B.J. (1982). Measurement of empathy toward rape victims and rapists. *Journal of Personality and Social Psychology, 43*, 372–384.

de Keijser, J.W., & Elffers, H. (2009). Punitive public attitudes: A threat to the legitimacy of the criminal justice system? In M.E. Oswald, S. Bieneck, & J. Hupfeld-Heinemann (Eds.), *Social psychology of punishment of crime* (pp. 55–74). Chichester: Wiley-Blackwell.

Del Rossi, A.F., & Viscusi, W.K. (2010). The changing landscape of blockbuster punitive damages awards. *American Law and Economics Review, 12*, 116–161.

Desmarais, S.L., Price, H.L., & Read, J.D. (2008). "Objection, your honor, Television is not the relevant authority!" Crime drama portrayals of eyewitness issues. *Psychology, Crime and Law, 14*, 225–243.

Desmarais, S.L., & Read, J.D. (2011). After 30 years, what do we know about what jurors know? A meta-analytic review of lay knowledge regarding eyewitness factors. *Law and Human Behavior, 35*, 200–210.

Devenport, J.L., & Cutler, B.L. (2004). Impact of defense-only and opposing eyewitness experts on juror judgments. *Law and Human Behavior, 28*, 569–576.

Devenport, J.L., Kimbrough, C.D., & Cutler, B.L. (2009). Effectiveness of traditional safeguards against erroneous conviction arising from mistaken eyewitness identification. In B.L. Cutler (Ed.), *Expert testimony on the psychology of eyewitness identification* (pp. 51–68). New York: Oxford University Press.

Devenport, J.L., Stinson, V., Cutler, B.L., & Kravitz, D.A. (2002). How effective are the cross-examination and expert testimony safeguards? Jurors' perceptions of the suggestiveness and fairness of biased lineup procedures. *Journal of Applied Psychology, 87*, 1042–1054.

Devine, D.J. (2012). *Jury decision making: The state of the science.* New York, NY: New York University Press.

Devine, D.J., Buddenbaum, J., Houp, S., Stolle, D.P., & Studebaker, N. (2007). Deliberation quality: A preliminary examination in criminal juries. *Journal of Empirical Legal Studies, 4,* 273–303.

Devine, D.J., Buddenbaum, J., Houp, S., Stolle, D.P., & Studebaker, N. (2009). Strength of evidence, extraevidentiary influence and the liberation hypothesis: Data from the field. *Law and Human Behavior, 33,* 136–148.

Devine, D.J., & Caughlin, D.E. (2014). Do they matter? A meta-analytic investigation of individual characteristics and guilt judgments. *Psychology, Public Policy, and Law, 20,* 109–134.

Devine, D.J., Clayton, L.D., Dunford, B.B., Seying, R., & Pryce, J. (2001). Jury decision making: 45 years of empirical research on deliberating groups. *Psychology, Public Policy, and Law, 7,* 622–727.

DeWitt, J.S., Richardson, J.T., & Warner, L.G. (1997). Novel scientific evidence and controversial cases: a social psychological examination. *Law and Psychology Review, 21,* 1–27.

Dexter, H.R., Cutler, B., & Moran, G. (1992). A test of voir dire as a remedy for the prejudicial effects of pretrial publicity. *Journal of Applied Social Psychology, 22,* 819–832.

Diamond, S.S. (1993a). What jurors think: Expectations and reactions of citizens who serve as jurors. In R. Litan (Ed.), *Verdict: Assessing the civil jury system* (pp. 282–305). Washington, DC: Brookings Institution.

Diamond, S.S. (1993b). Instructing on death: Psychologists, juries, and judges. *American Psychologist, 48,* 423–434.

Diamond, S.S. (1997). Illuminations and shadows from jury simulations. *Law and Human Behavior, 21,* 561–571.

Diamond, S.S. (2003). Truth, justice, and the jury. *Harvard Journal of Law and Public Policy, 26,* 143–155.

Diamond, S.S. (2006). Beyond fantasy and nightmare: A portrait of the jury. *Buffalo Law Review, 54,* 717–763.

Diamond S.S. (2013, July 15). Zimmerman trial: Time to reconsider six-member jury. *Miami Herald.*

Diamond, S.S., & Casper, J.D. (1992). Blindfolding the jury to verdict consequences: Damages, experts, and the civil jury. *Law & Society Review, 26,* 513–563.

Diamond, S.S., & Levi, J.N. (1996). Improving decisions on death by revising and testing jury instructions. *Judicature, 79,* 224–232.

Diamond, S.S., Murphy, B., & Rose, M.R. (2012). The "kettleful of law" in real jury deliberations: Successes, failures, and next steps. *Northwestern University Law Review, 106,* 1537–1608.

Diamond, S.S., Rose, M., & Murphy, B. (2006). Revisiting the unanimity requirement: The behavior of the non-unanimous civil jury. *Northwestern University Law Review, 100,* 201–230.

Diamond, S.S., Rose, M.R., Murphy, B., & Meixner, J. (2011). Damage anchors on real juries. *Journal of Empirical Legal Studies, 8*(S1), 148–178.

Diamond, S.S., Saks, M.J., & Landsman, S. (1998). Juror judgments about liability and damages: Sources of variability and ways to increase consistency. *DePaul Law Review, 48,* 301–325.

Diamond, S.S., & Salerno, J.M. (2013). Empirical analysis of juries in tort cases. In J. Arlen (Ed.), *Research handbook on the economics of torts* (pp. 414–435). Cheltenham, UK: Edward Elgar Publishing.

Diamond, S.S., & Stalans, L.J. (1989). The myth of judicial leniency in sentencing. *Behavioral Sciences & the Law, 7*, 73–89.

Diamond, S.S., & Vidmar, N. (2001). Jury room ruminations on forbidden topics. *Virginia Law Review, 87*, 1857–1915.

Diamond, S.S., Vidmar, N., Rose, M., Ellis, L., & Murphy, B. (2003). Juror discussions during civil trials: Studying an Arizona innovation. *Arizona Law Review, 45*, 1–81.

Dienstbier, R.A., Roesch, S.C., Mizumoto, A., Hemenover, S.H., Lott, R.C., & Carlo, G. (1998). Effects of weapons on guilt judgments and sentencing recommendations for criminals. *Basic and Applied Social Psychology, 20*, 93–102.

DiIulio, J.J. (1995, Nov. 27). The coming of the superpredators. *Weekly Standard*, 23–28.

Dillehay, R.C., & Sandys, M.R. (1996). Life under *Wainwright v. Witt*: Juror dispositions and death qualification. *Law and Human Behavior, 20*, 147–165.

Donohue, J.J., & Ho, D.E. (2007). The impact of damage caps on malpractice claims: Randomization inference with difference-in-differences. *Journal of Empirical Legal Studies, 4*, 69–102.

Doppelt, J.C. (1991). Generic prejudice: How drug war fervor threatens the right to a fair trial. *American University Law Review, 40*, 821–836.

Dorland, M., & Krauss, D. (2005). The danger of dangerousness in capital sentencing: Exacerbating the problem of arbitrary and capricious decision-making. *Law and Psychology Review, 29*, 63–105.

Douglas, K.S., Lyon, D.R., & Ogloff, J.R.P. (1997). The impact of graphic photographic evidence on mock juror decisions in a murder trial: Probative or prejudicial? *Law and Human Behavior, 21*, 485–501.

Douglass, A.B., Neuschatz, J.S., Imrich, J., & Wilkinson, M. (2010). Does post-identification feedback affect evaluations of eyewitness testimony and identification procedures? *Law and Human Behavior, 34*, 282–294.

Douglass, A.B., & Steblay, N. (2006). Memory distortion in eyewitnesses: A meta-analysis of the post-identification feedback effect. *Applied Cognitive Psychology, 20*, 859–869.

Dovidio, J.F., & Gaertner, S.L. (1998). On the nature of contemporary prejudice: The causes, consequences, and challenges of aversive racism. In J.L. Eberhardt & S.T. Fiske (Eds.), *Confronting racism: The problem and the response* (pp. 3–32). Thousand Oaks, CA: Sage.

Drinan, R.F. (2000). Religious organizations and the death penalty. *William and Mary Bill of Rights Journal, 9*, 171–177.

Drizin, S., & Leo, R. (2004). The problem of false confessions in the post-DNA world. *North Carolina Law Review, 82*, 891–1007.

Dror, I., & Charlton, D. (2006). Why experts make errors. *Journal of Forensic Identification, 56*, 600–616.

Duckitt, J. (2009). Punishment attitudes: Their social and psychological bases. In M.E. Oswald, S. Bieneck, & J. Hupfeld-Heinemann (Eds.), *Social psychology of punishment of crime* (pp. 75–92). Chichester: Wiley-Blackwell.

Duke, L, & Greene, E. (2015). *Beliefs about causes of juvenile crime affect attitudes regarding punishment.* Paper presented at American Psychology-Law Society, San Diego.

Duke, M.C., Hosch, H.M., & Duke, B. (2015). The effect of liability stipulation on damage awards in a personal injury case. *Psychology, Public Policy, and Law, 21*, 265–279.

Dunbar, E., & Molina, A. (2004). Opposition to the legitimacy of hate crime laws: The role of argument acceptance, knowledge, individual differences, and peer influence. *Analyses of Social Issues and Public Policy, 4*, 91–113.

Dunbar, R., Duncan, N., & Nettle, D. (1995). Size and structure of freely forming conversational groups. *Human Nature-an Interdisciplinary Biosocial Perspective, 6*, 67–78.

Duncan v. Louisiana, 391 U.S. 145 (1968).

Dustin, D. (1986). *How to avoid jury duty: A guilt free guide.* Retrieved from http://www.amazon.com/How-Avoid-Jury-Duty-Guilt/dp/0961562609.

Eberhardt, J.L., Davies, P.G., Purdie-Vaughns, V.J., & Johnson, S.L. (2006). Looking deathworthy: Perceived stereotypicality of Black defendants predicts capital-sentencing outcomes. *Psychological Science, 17*, 383–386.

Edens, J.F., Colwell, L.H., Desforges, D.M., & Fernandez, K. (2005). The impact of mental health evidence on support for capital punishment: Are defendants labeled psychopathic considered more deserving of death? *Behavioral Sciences and the Law, 23*, 603–625.

Edmonson v. Leesville Concrete Co., 500 U.S. 614 (1991).

Ehrlinger, J., Gilovich, T., & Ross, L. (2005). Peering into the bias blind spot: People's assessments of bias in themselves and others. *Personality and Social Psychology Bulletin, 31*, 680–692.

Eigen, J.P. (1981). Punishing youth homicide offenders in Philadelphia. *Journal of Criminal Law and Criminology, 72*, 1072–1093.

Eisenberg, T.E. (2011). The origins, nature, and promise of empirical legal studies and a response to concerns. *University of Illinois Law Review, 2011*, 1713–1738.

Eisenberg, T., Garvey, S.P., & Wells, M.T. (1998). But was he sorry? The role of remorse in capital sentencing. *Cornell Law Review, 83*, 1599–1637.

Eisenberg, T., Garvey, S.P., & Wells, M.T. (2001). Forecasting life and death: Juror race, religion, and attitude toward the death penalty. *Journal of Legal Studies, 30*, 277–311.

Eisenberg, T., Garvey, S.P., & Wells, M.T. (2003). Victim characteristics and victim impact evidence in South Carolina capital cases. *Cornell Law Review, 88*, 306–342.

Eisenberg, T., Goerdt, J., Ostrom, B., & Rottman, D. (1996). Litigation outcomes in state and federal courts: A statistical portrait. *Seattle University Law Review, 19*, 433–453.

Eisenberg, T., Goerdt, J., Ostrom, B., Rottman, D., & Wells, M.T. (1997). The predictability of punitive damages. *Journal of Legal Studies, 26*, 623–660.

Eisenberg, T., Hannaford-Agor, P., Hans, V., Waters, N., Munsterman, G., Schwab, S., & Wells, M. (2005). Judge-jury agreement in criminal cases: A partial replication of Kalven and Zeisel's *The American Jury. Journal of Empirical Legal Studies, 2*, 171–206.

Eisenberg, T., Hannaford-Agor, P.L., Heise, M., LaFountain, N., Munsterman, G.T., Ostrom, B., & Wells, M.T. (2006). Juries, judges, and punitive damages: Empirical analyses using the Civil Justice Survey of State Courts 1992, 1996, and 2001 data. *Journal of Empirical Legal Studies, 3,* 263–295.

Eisenberg, T., Hans, V.P., & Wells, M.T. (2008). The relation between punitive and compensatory awards: Combining extreme data with the mass of awards. In B.H. Bornstein, R.L. Wiener, R.F. Schopp, & S.L. Willborn (Eds.), *Civil juries and civil justice: Psychological and legal perspectives* (pp. 105–115). New York: Springer.

Eisenberg, T., & Heise, M. (2011). Judge-jury difference in punitive damages awards: Who listens to the Supreme Court? *Journal of Empirical Legal Studies, 8,* 325–357.

Eisenberg, T., LaFountain, N., Ostrom, B., Rottman, D., & Wells, M.T. (2002). Juries, judges, and punitive damages: An empirical study. *Cornell Law Review, 87,* 743–779.

Eisenberg, T., & Wells, M.T. (1993). Deadly confusion: Juror instructions in capital cases. *Cornell Law Review, 79,* 1–17.

Ekman, P. (1992). An argument for basic emotions. *Cognition and Emotion, 6,* 169–200.

Ekman, P. (1994). All emotions are basic. In P. Ekman & R.J. Davidson (Eds.), *The nature of emotion: Fundamental questions* (pp. 15–19). New York: Oxford University Press.

Ekman, P., & O'Sullivan, M. (1991). Who can catch a liar? *American Psychologist, 46,* 913–920.

El-Ghobashy, T. (2011, Aug. 8). Judges acquit more often than juries. *Wall Street Journal.* Available at: http://online.wsj.com/news/articles/ SB10001424053111903454504576490702326607610?mod=googlen ews_wsj&mg=reno64-wsj&url=http%3A%2F%2Fonline.wsj.com% 2Farticle%2FSB10001424053111903454504576490702326607610. html%3Fmod%3Dgooglenews_wsj.

Ellsworth, P.C. (1989). Are twelve heads better than one? *Law and Contemporary Problems, 52,* 207–224.

Elwork, A., Sales, B.D., & Alfini, J.J. (1982). *Making jury instructions understandable.* Charlottesville, VA: Michie.

Epstein, J. (2009). Expert testimony: Legal standards for admissibility. In B.L. Cutler (Ed.), *Expert testimony on the psychology of eyewitness identification* (pp. 69–89). Oxford: Oxford University Press.

Epstein, R.A., & Sharkey, C.M. (2012). *Cases and materials on torts* (10th ed.). Aspen.

Ericsson, K.A., & Smith, J. (1991). *Toward a general theory of expertise: Prospects and limits.* Cambridge: Cambridge University Press.

Exxon Shipping Co. v. Baker, 554 U.S. 471 (2008).

Fackler, M., & Pollack, A. (2014, April 9). Jury awards $9 billion in damages in drug case. *New York Times,* p. B3. Available at http://www.nytimes.com/ 2014/04/09/business/international/japanese-drug-maker-ordered-to-pay-6- billion-over-cancer-claims.html?_r=0.

Faigman, D.L. (1999). *Legal alchemy: The use and misuse of science in the law.* New York: Freeman.

Faigman, D.L., & Baglioni, A.J. (1988). Bayes' Theorem in the trial process: instructing jurors on the value of statistical evidence. *Law and Human Behavior, 12,* 1–17.

Faigman, D.L., Blumenthal, J., Cheng, E., Mnookin, J., Murphy, E., & Sanders, J. (2014). *Modern scientific evidence: The law and science of expert testimony*. Eagan, MN: Thomson Reuters/West.

Farnum, K., & Stevenson, M. (2013). Economically disadvantaged juvenile offenders tried in adult court are perceived as less able to understand their actions, but more guilty. *Psychology, Crime and Law, 19*, 727–744.

Feeley, J. (2014, Oct. 27). Takeda, Lilly win 99.6% cut in Actos punitive damages. *Bloomberg Business*. Available at http://www.bloomberg.com/news/articles/2014-10-27/takeda-lilly-get-9-billion-actos-award-cut-99-percent.

Feigenson, N. (1997). Sympathy and legal judgment. *Tennessee Law Review, 65*, 1–78.

Feigenson, N. (2000). *Legal blame: How jurors think and talk about accidents*. Washington, DC: American Psychological Association.

Feigenson, N. (2010). Emotional influences on judgments of legal blame: How they happen, whether they should, and what to do about it. In B.H. Bornstein & R.L. Wiener (Eds.), *Emotion and the law: Psychological perspectives* (pp. 45–96). New York: Springer.

Feigenson, N., & Park, J. (2006). Emotions and attributions of legal responsibility and blame: A research review. *Law and Human Behavior, 30*, 143–161.

Feigenson, N., Park, J., & Salovey, P. (2001). The role of emotions in comparative negligence judgments. *Journal of Applied Social Psychology, 31*, 576–603.

Feiler, S.M., & Sheley, J.F. (1999). Legal and racial elements of public willingness to transfer juvenile offenders to adult court. *Journal of Criminal Justice, 27*, 55–64.

Feld, B.C. (1993). Criminalizing the American juvenile court. In M. Tonry (Ed.), *Crime and justice: A review of research* (Vol. 17, pp. 197–280). Chicago: University of Chicago Press.

Feld, B.C. (1999). *Readings in juvenile justice administration*. New York: Oxford University Press.

Ferguson, A. (2013). *Why jury duty matters: A citizen's guide to constitutional action*. New York: NYU Press.

Ferrara, A.J. (2008). Lessons learned from jurors' questions about evidence during trial. *Journal of Court Innovation, 1*, 329–343.

Finkel, N.J., Hurabiell, M.L., & Hughes, K.C. (1993). Right to die, euthanasia, and community sentiment: Crossing the public/private boundary. *Law and Human Behavior, 17*, 487–506.

Finstad v. W.R. Grace & Co., 8 P.3d 778 (Mont. 2000).

Firestone v. Crown Center Development Corp., 693 S.W.2d 99 (Mo. 1985).

Fishbein, M., & Ajzen, I. (1974). Attitudes toward objects as predictive of single and multiple behavioral criteria. *Psychological Review, 81*, 59–74.

Fisher, R.P., Mello, E.W., & McCauley, M.R. (1999). Are jurors' perceptions of eyewitness credibility affected by the cognitive interview? *Psychology, Crime & Law, 5*, 167–176.

Fishfader, V.L., Howells, G.N., Katz, R.C., & Teresi, P.S. (1996). Evidential and extralegal factors in juror decisions: Presentation mode, retention, and level of emotionality. *Law and Human Behavior, 20*, 565–572.

Fiske, S.T., & Borgida, E. (2008). Providing expert knowledge in an adversarial context: Social cognitive science in employment discrimination cases. *Annual Review of Law and Social Science, 4*, 123–148.

Fitzgerald, R., & Ellsworth, P. (1984). Due process v. crime control: Death qualification and jury attitudes. *Law and Human Behavior, 8*, 31–51.

Fleury-Steiner, B. (2004). *Jurors' stories of death: How America's death penalty invests in inequality*. Ann Arbor, MI: University of Michigan Press.

Flores, D.M., Miller, M.K., Chamberlain, J., Richardson, J.T., & Bornstein, B.H. (2008–2009). Judges' perspectives on stress and safety in the courtroom: An exploratory study. *Court Review, 45*, 76–89.

Flowe, H.D., Finklea, K.M., & Ebbesen, E.B. (2009). Limitations of expert psychology testimony on eyewitness identification. In B.L. Cutler (Ed.), *Expert testimony on the psychology of eyewitness identification* (pp. 201–221). Oxford: Oxford University Press.

Fordham, J. (2006). Illuminating or blurring the truth: Jurors, juries, and expert evidence. In B. Brooks-Gordon & M. Freeman (Eds.), *Law and psychology: Current legal issues* (Vol. 9) (pp. 338–360). Oxford: Oxford University Press.

Forgas, J.P. (1995). Mood and judgment: The Affect Infusion Model (AIM). *Psychological Bulletin, 116*, 39–66.

Forgas, J.P. (2010). Affect in legal and forensic settings: The cognitive benefits of not being too happy. In B.H. Bornstein & R.L. Wiener (Eds.), *Emotion and the law: Psychological perspectives* (pp. 13–44). New York: Springer.

Forrest, K., Woody, W.D., Brady, S., Batterman, K., Stastny, B., & Bruns, J. (2012). False-evidence ploys and interrogations: Mock jurors' perceptions of ploy type, deception, coercion, and justification. *Behavioral Sciences and the Law, 30*, 342–364.

ForsterLee, L., & Horowitz, I.A. (1997). Enhancing juror competence in a complex trial. *Applied Cognitive Psychology, 11*, 305–319.

ForsterLee, R., Horowitz, I.A., Ho, R., ForsterLee, L., & McGovern, A. (1999). Community members' perceptions of evidence: The effects of gender in a recovered memory civil trial. *Journal of Applied Psychology, 84*, 484–495.

ForsterLee, L., Kent, L., & Horowitz, I.A. (2005). The cognitive effects of jury aids on decision-making in complex civil litigation. *Applied Cognitive Psychology, 19*, 867–884.

Foster v. Chatman, 578 U.S. ___ (2016).

Fox, J.A. (1996). *Trends in juvenile violence: A report to the United States Attorney General on current and future rates of juvenile offending*. Bureau of Justice Statistics: U.S. Department of Justice.

Fox, S.G., & Walters, H.A. (1986). The impact of general versus specific expert testimony and eyewitness confidence upon mock juror judgment. *Law and Human Behavior, 10*, 215–228.

Frazier v. Cupp, 394 U.S. 731 (1969).

Freedman, J.L., Krismer, K., MacDonald, J.E., & Cunningham, J.A. (1994). Severity of penalty, seriousness of the charge and mock jurors' verdicts. *Law and Human Behavior, 18*, 189–202.

Freud, S. (1928/1961). *The future of an illusion* (orig. published as *Die Zukunft einer Illusion*, J. Strachey, transl.). New York: W.W. Norton.

Friedman, H. (1972). Trial by jury: Criteria for convictions, jury size and type I and type II errors. *The American Statistician, 26*, 21–23.

Frijda, N.H. (1994). Varieties of affect: Emotions and episodes, moods, and sentiments. In P. Ekman & R.J. Davidson (Eds.), *The nature of emotion: Fundamental questions* (pp. 59–67). New York: Oxford University Press.

Fulero, S.M. (2001, May). Recent cases focus on false confessions and expert testimony. *APA Monitor, 32*(5), 20.

Fulero, S.M. (2010). Tales from the front: Expert testimony on the psychology of interrogations and confessions revisited. In G.D. Lassiter & C. Meissner, (Eds.), *Police interrogations and false confessions: Current research, practice, and policy recommendations.* Washington, DC: American Psychological Association.

Furman v. Georgia, 408 U.S. 238 (1972).

Gabora, N.J., Spanos, N.P., & Joab, A. (1993). The effects of complainant age and expert psychological testimony in a simulated child sexual abuse trial. *Law and Human Behavior, 17,* 103–119.

Gabriel, R. (2015, Aug. 28). Thank and excuse: Five steps toward improving jury selection. Retrieved from http://www.thejuryexpert.com/2015/08/thank-and-excuse-five-steps-toward-improving-jury-selection/.

Galanter, M. (1987). Jury shadows: Reflections on the civil jury and the "litigation explosion." In *The American civil jury* (pp. 15–42). Washington: Roscoe Pound-American Trial Lawyers Foundation.

Galanter, M. (1998). An oil strike in hell: Contemporary legends about the civil justice system. *Arizona Law Review, 40,* 717–752.

Galanter, M. (2004). The vanishing trial: An examination of trials and related matters in federal and state courts. *Journal of Empirical Legal Studies, 1,* 459–570.

Galanter, M., & Frozena, A. (2011). The continuing decline of civil trials in American courts. *Pound Civil Justice Institute–2011 Forum for State Appellate Court Judges.* Retrieved on July 20, 2015 from: http://www.poundinstitute.org/sites/default/files/docs/2011%20judges%20forum/2011%20Forum%20Galanter-Frozena%20Paper.pdf.

Garrett, B.L. (2010). The substance of false confessions. *Stanford Law Review, 62,* 1051–1119.

Garrett, B.L. (2011). *Convicting the innocent: Where criminal prosecutions go wrong.* Cambridge, MA US: Harvard University Press.

Gastil, J., Burkhalter, S., & Black, L. (2007). Do juries deliberate? A study of deliberation, individual difference, and group member satisfaction at a municipal courthouse. *Small Group Research, 38,* 337–359.

Gastil, J., Deess, E.P., Weiser, P., & Simmons, C. (2010). *The jury and democracy: How jury deliberation promotes civic engagement and political participation.* New York: Oxford University Press.

Gauchat, G. (2012). Politicization of science in the public sphere: A study of public trust in the United States, 1974 to 2010. *American Sociological Review, 77,* 167–187.

Gawronski, B., Ehrenberg, K., Banse, R., Zukova, J., & Klauer, K. (2003). It's in the mind of the beholder: The impact of stereotypic associations on category-based and individuating impression formation. *Journal of Experimental Social Psychology, 39,* 16–30.

Geiselman, R.E., & Mendez, B.A. (2005). Assistance to the fact finder: Eyewitness expert testimony versus attorneys' closing arguments. *American Journal of Forensic Psychology, 23,* 5–15.

Geiselman, R.E., Putman, C., Korte, R., Shahriary, M., Jachimowicz, G., & Irzhevsky, V. (2002). Eyewitness expert testimony and juror decisions. *American Journal of Forensic Psychology, 20,* 1–16.

General Electric Co. v. Joiner, 522 U.S. 136 (1997).

George, T.E. (2001). Court fixing. *Arizona Law Review, 43,* 9–62.

Georges, L.C., Wiener, R.L., & Keller, S.R. (2013). The angry juror: Sentencing decisions in first-degree murder. *Applied Cognitive Psychology, 27,* 156–166.

Georgia v. McCollum, 505 U.S. 42 (1992).

Geraerts, E., Raymaekers, L., & Merckelbach, H. (2008). Recovered memories of childhood sexual abuse: Current findings and their legal implications. *Legal and Criminological Psychology, 13,* 165–176.

Gibson, S.C., & Greene, E. (2013). Assessing knowledge of elder financial abuse: A first step in enhancing prosecutions. *Journal of Elder Abuse and Neglect, 25,* 167–182.

Gilbert, D., & Hixon, J.G. (1991). The trouble of thinking: Activation and application of stereotypic beliefs. *Journal of Personality and Social Psychology, 60,* 509–517.

Gilovich, T. (1991). *How we know what isn't so: The fallibility of human reason in everyday life.* New York: The Free Press.

Gluck, S. (1997). Wayward youth, super predator: An evolutionary tale of juvenile delinquency from the 1950's to the present. *Corrections Today, 59,* 52–646.

Golding, J.M., Dunlap, E., & Hodell, E.C. (2009). Jurors' perceptions of children's eyewitness testimony. In B.L. Bottoms, C.J. Najdowski, & G.S. Goodman (Eds.), *Children as victims, witnesses, and offenders: Psychological science and the law* (pp. 188–208). New York, NY: Guilford Press.

Golding, J.M., Fryman, H.M., Marsil, D.F., & Yozwiak, J.A. (2003). Big girls don't cry: The effect of child witness demeanor on juror decisions in a child sexual abuse trial. *Child Abuse & Neglect, 27,* 1311–1321.

Golding, J.M., Sanchez, R.P., & Sego, S.A. (1996). Do you believe in repressed memories? *Professional Psychology: Research and Practice, 27,* 429–437.

Golding, J.M., Sanchez, R.P., & Sego, S.A. (1997). The believability of hearsay testimony in a child sexual assault trial. *Law and Human Behavior, 21,* 299–325.

Golding, J.M., Sanchez, R.P., & Sego, S.A. (1999). Age factors affecting the believability of repressed memories of child sexual assault. *Law and Human Behavior, 23,* 257–268.

Golding, J.M., Stewart, T.L., Yozwiak, J.A., Djadali, Y., & Sanchez, R.P. (2000). The impact of DNA evidence in a child sexual assault trial. *Child Maltreatment, 5,* 373–383.

Goldstein, I. (1935). *Trial technique.* Chicago: Callaghan.

Gomes, D., Stenstrom, D., & Calvillo, D. (2012). *Expert testimony is more effective than jury instructions in increasing sensitivity to disputed confession evidence.* Poster presented at American Psychology-Law Society, San Juan, Puerto Rico.

Goodman, G.S., Golding. J.M., Helgeson, V., Haith, M., & Michelli, J. (1987). When a child takes the stand: Jurors' perceptions of children's eyewitness testimony. *Law and Human Behavior, 11,* 27–40.

Goodman, J., & Croyle, R.T. (1989). Social framework testimony in employment discrimination cases. *Behavioral Sciences & the Law, 7,* 227–241.

Goodman-Delahunty, J., Cossins, A., & O'Brien, K. (2010). Enhancing the credibility of complainants in child sexual assault trials: The effect of expert evidence and judicial directions. *Behavioral Sciences & the Law, 28,* 769–783.

Goodman-Delahunty, J., Greene, E., & Hsiao, W. (1998). Construing motive in videotaped killings: The role of jurors' attitudes toward the death penalty. *Law and Human Behavior, 22,* 257–271.

Gordon, S.G. (2015). All together now: Using principles of group dynamics to train better jurors. *Scholarly Works.* Paper 896. Retrieved from http://scholars.law.unlv.edu/facpub/89.

Graham v. Florida, 560 U.S. 48 (2010).

Granhag, P.A., Strömwall, L.A., & Hartwig, M. (2005). Eyewitness testimony: Tracing the beliefs of Swedish legal professionals. *Behavioral Sciences and the Law, 23,* 709–727.

Graziano, S.J., Panter, A.T., & Tanaka, J.S. (1990). Individual differences in information processing strategies and their role in juror decision making and selection. *Forensic Reports, 3,* 279–301.

Greathouse, S., Sothmann, F., Levett, L., & Kovera, M.B. (2011). The potentially biasing effects of voir dire in juvenile waiver cases. *Law and Human Behavior, 35,* 427–439.

Greenberg, J., Solomon, S., Pyszczynski, T. (1997). Terror management theory of self-esteem and cultural worldviews: Empirical assessments and conceptual refinements. In M.P. Zanna (Ed.), *Advances in experimental social psychology* (pp. 61–139). San Diego, CA: Academic Press.

Greenberg, S.A., Otto, R.K., & Long, A.C. (2003). The utility of psychological testing in assessing emotional damages in personal injury litigation. *Assessment, 10,* 411–419.

Greene, E. (1988). Judge's instructions on eyewitness testimony: Evaluation and revision. *Journal of Applied Social Psychology, 18,* 252–276.

Greene, E. (1989). On juries and damage awards: The process of decision making. *Law and Contemporary Problems, 52,* 225–246.

Greene, E. (1999). The many guises of victim impact evidence and effects on jurors' judgments. *Psychology, Crime & Law, 5,* 331–348.

Greene, E. (2008). "Can we talk?" Therapeutic jurisprudence, restorative justice, and tort litigation. In B.H. Bornstein, R.L. Wiener, R.F. Schopp, & S.L. Willborn (Eds.), *Civil juries and civil justice: Psychological and legal perspectives* (pp. 233–256). New York: Springer.

Greene E., & Bornstein, B.H. (2000). Precious little guidance: Jury instruction on damage awards. *Psychology, Public Policy, and Law, 6,* 743–768.

Greene, E., & Bornstein, B.H. (2003). *Determining damages: The psychology of jury awards.* Washington, DC: American Psychological Association.

Greene, E., & Cahill, B. (2012). Effects of neuroimaging evidence on mock juror decision making. *Behavioral Sciences and the Law, 30,* 280–296.

Greene, E., Coon, D., & Bornstein, B.H. (2001). The effects of limiting punitive damage awards. *Law and Human Behavior, 25,* 217–234.

Greene, E., Downey, C., & Goodman-Delahunty, J. (1999). Juror decisions about damages in employment discrimination cases. *Behavioral Sciences & the Law, 17,* 107–121.

Greene, E., & Evelo, A.J. (2013). Attitudes regarding life sentences for juvenile offenders. *Law and Human Behavior, 37,* 276–289.

Greene, E., & Evelo, A.J. (2015). Cops and robbers (and eyewitnesses): A comparison of lineup administration by robbery detectives in the USA and Canada. *Psychology, Crime & Law, 21,* 297–313.

Greene, E., Hayman, K., & Motyl, M. (2008). "Shouldn't we consider . . .?" Jury discussions of forbidden topics and effects on damage awards. *Psychology, Public Policy, and Law, 14,* 194–222.

Greene, E., & Heilbrun, K. (2014). *Wrightsman's psychology and the legal system* (8th ed.). Belmont, CA: Wadsworth/Cengage.

Greene, E., & Johns, M. (2001). Jurors' use of instructions on negligence. *Journal of Applied Social Psychology, 31,* 840–859.

Greene, E., Johns, M., & Bowman, J. (1999). The effects of injury severity on jury negligence decisions. *Law and Human Behavior, 23,* 675–693.

Greene, E., Johns, M., & Smith, A. (2001). The effects of defendant conduct on jury damage awards. *Journal of Applied Psychology, 86,* 228–237.

Greene, E., Koehring, H., & Quiat, M. (1998). Victim impact evidence in capital cases: Does the victim's character matter? *Journal of Applied Social Psychology, 28,* 145–156.

Greene, E., Sturm, K.A., & Evelo, A.J. (2016). Affective forecasting about hedonic loss and adaptation: Implications for damage awards. *Law and Human Behavior, 40,* 244–256.

Greene, E., & Wade, R. (1988). Of private talk and public print: General pre-trial publicity and juror decision-making. *Applied Cognitive Psychology, 2,* 123–135.

Greene, E., Woody, W.D., & Winter, R. (2000). Compensating plaintiffs and punishing defendants: Is bifurcation necessary? *Law and Human Behavior, 24,* 187–205.

Greene, E., & Wrightsman, L.S. (2003). Decision making by juries and judges: International perspectives. In D. Carson & R. Bull (Eds.), *Handbook of psychology in legal contexts* (2nd ed.) (pp. 401–422). Chichester, UK: Wiley.

Greenwald, A.G., McGhee, D., & Schwartz, J. (1998). Measuring individual differences in implicit cognition: The Implicit Association Test. *Journal of Personality and Social Psychology, 74,* 1464–1480.

Greenwald, A.G., Nosek, B.A., & Banaji, M.R. (2003). Understanding and using the Implicit Association Test: I. An improved scoring algorithm. *Journal of Personality and Social Psychology, 85,* 197–216.

Gregg v. Georgia, 428 U.S. 153 (1976).

Griffin, P., Addie, S., Adams, B., & Firestine, K. (2011). *Trying juveniles as adults: An analysis of state transfer laws and reporting.* Washington, DC: U.S. Department of Justice, Office of Justice Programs, Office of Juvenile Justice and Delinquency Prevention.

Grisso, T. (1996). Society's retributive response to juvenile violence: A developmental perspective. *Law and Human Behavior, 20,* 229–247.

Gross, S.R. (1991). Expert evidence. *Wisconsin Law Review, 1991,* 1113–1232.

Gross, S.R. (1996). The risks of death: Why erroneous convictions are common in capital cases. *Buffalo Law Review, 44,* 469–500.

Gross, S.R., Jacoby, K., Matheson, D.J., Montgomery, N., & Patil, S. (2005). Exonerations in the united States 1989 through 2003. *Journal of Criminal Law & Criminology, 95,* 523–560.

Gross, S.R., & Mauro, R. (1989). *Death and discrimination: Racial disparities in capital sentencing*. Boston: Northeastern University Press.

Gross, S.R., & Syverud, K.D. (1991). Getting to no: A study of settlement negotiations and the selection of cases for trial. *Michigan Law Review, 90*, 319–393.

Gudjonsson, G. (2003). *The psychology of interrogations and confessions: A handbook*. Chichester, England: John Wiley and Sons.

Gudjonsson, G., & MacKeith, J.A. (1982). False confessions: Psychological effects of interrogation. In A. Trankell (Ed.), *Reconstructing the past: The role of psychologists in criminal trials* (pp. 253–269). Deventer, The Netherlands: Kluwer.

Guthrie, C., Rachlinski, J.J., & Wistrich, A.J. (2001). Inside the judicial mind. *Cornell Law Review, 86*, 777–830.

Guy, L., & Edens, J. (2003). Juror decision-making in a mock sexually violent predator trial: Gender differences in the impact of divergent types of expert testimony. *Behavioral Science and the Law, 21*, 215–237.

Guy, L., & Edens, J. (2006). Gender differences in attitudes towards psychopathic sexual offenders. *Behavioral Sciences and the Law, 24*, 65–85.

Haederle, M. (2010, March-April). Trouble in mind: Will the new neuroscience undermine our legal system? *Miller-McCune*, 70–79.

Haegerich, T.M., & Bottoms, B.L. (2000). Empathy and jurors' decisions in trials involving child sexual assault allegations. *Law and Human Behavior, 24*, 421–448.

Haegerich, T., Salerno, J., & Bottoms, B. (2013). Are the effects of juvenile offender stereotypes maximized or minimized by jury deliberation? *Psychology, Public Policy, and Law, 19*, 81–97.

Haidt, J. (2001). The emotional dog and its rational tail: A social intuitionist approach to moral judgment. *Psychological Review, 108*, 814–834.

Halverson, A.M., Hallahan, M., Hart, A.J., & Rosenthal, R. (1997). Reducing the biasing effects of judges' nonverbal behavior with simplified jury instruction. *Journal of Applied Psychology, 82*, 590–598.

Hamilton, M., Lindon, E., Pitt, M., & Robins, E. (2014). The ubiquitous practice of "prehabilitation" leads prospective jurors to conceal their biases. *The Jury Expert, 26*, 48–65.

Hamm, J.A., Bornstein, B.H., & Perkins, J. (2013). Jury nullification: The myth revisited. In D. Fung (Ed.), *The psychology of policy-making* (pp. 49–71). Hauppauge, NY: Nova Science Publishers.

Hammitt, J.K., Carroll, S.J., & Relles, D.A. (1985). Tort standards and jury decisions. *Journal of Legal Studies, 14*, 751–762.

Haney, C. (1984). On the selection of capital juries: The biasing effects of the death-qualification process. *Law and Human Behavior, 8*, 121–132.

Haney, C. (1997). Violence and the capital jury: Mechanisms of moral disengagement and the impulse to condemn to death. *Stanford Law Review, 49*, 1447–1486.

Haney, C. (2004). Condemning the other in death penalty trials: Biographical racism, structural mitigation, and the empathic divide. *DePaul Law Review 53*, 1557–1589.

Haney, C. (2005). *Death by design*. Oxford: Oxford University Press.

Haney, C., Hurtado, A., & Vega, L. (1994). "Modern" death qualification: New data on its biasing effects. *Law and Human Behavior, 15*, 619–633.

Haney, C., & Lynch, M. (1994). Comprehending life and death matters: A preliminary study of California's capital penalty instructions. *Law and Human Behavior, 18,* 411–436.

Haney, C., Sontag, L., & Costanzo, S. (1994). Deciding to take a life: Capital juries, sentencing instructions, and the jurisprudence of death. *Journal of Social Issues, 50,* 149–176.

Hannaford, P., Hans, V., & Munsterman, G. (2000). Permitting jury discussions during trial: Impact of the Arizona reform. *Law and Human Behavior, 24,* 359–382.

Hannaford-Agor, P. (2012). A new option for addressing juror stress? *The Court Manager, 26,* 50–52.

Hannaford-Agor, P. (2015). *But have we made any progress? An update on the status of jury improvement efforts in state and federal courts.* Retrieved from http://www.law.nyu.edu/sites/default/files/upload_documents/But-have-we-made.pdf.

Hannaford-Agor, P., Hans, V., Mott, N., & Munsterman, G. (2002). *Are hung juries a problem?* Report No. NCJ 201096. Washington, DC: U.S. Department of Justice, National Institute of Justice.

Hannaford-Agor, P., & Waters, N. (2004). *Examining voir dire in California.* San Francisco: Administrative Office of the Courts, Judicial Council of California.

Hans, V.P. (1978). 1The Effects of the Unanimity Requirement on Group Decision Processes in Simulated Juries (Unpublished Ph.D. dissertation, University of Toronto).

Hans, V.P. (1993). Attitudes toward the civil jury: A crisis of confidence? In R. Litan (Ed.), *Verdict: Assessing the civil jury system* (pp. 248–281). Washington, DC: Brookings Institution.

Hans, V.P. (2000). *Business on trial: The civil jury and corporate responsibility.* New Haven, CT: Yale University Press.

Hans, V.P. (2001). The power of twelve: The impact of jury size and unanimity on civil jury decision making. *Delaware Law Review, 4,* 1–31.

Hans, V.P. (2008). Faking it? Citizen perceptions of whiplash injuries. In B.H. Bornstein, R.L. Wiener, R.F. Schopp, & S.L. Willborn (Eds.), *Civil juries and civil justice: Psychological and legal perspectives* (pp. 131–150). New York: Springer.

Hans, V.P. (2013). Jury jokes and legal culture. *DePaul Law Review, 62,* 391–413.

Hans, V.P. (2014). What's it worth? Jury damage awards as community judgments. *William & Mary Law Review, 55,* 935–969.

Hans, V.P., Blume, J.H, Eisenberg, T., Hritz, A.C., Johnson, S.L., Royer, C.E., & Wells, M.T. (2015). The death penalty: Should the judge or the jury decide who dies? *Journal of Empirical Legal Studies, 12,* 70–99.

Hans, V.P., & Eisenberg, T. (2011). The predictability of juries. *DePaul Law Review, 60,* 375–396.

Hans, V.P., Fukurai, H., Ivkovic, S.K., & Park, J. (in press). Global juries: A plan for research. In M.B. Kovera (Ed.), *The psychology of juries: Current knowledge and a research agenda for the future.* Washington, DC: American Psychological Association.

Hans, V.P., Gastil, J., & Feller, T. (2014). Deliberative democracy and the American civil jury. *Journal of Empirical Legal Studies, 11,* 697–717.

Hans, V.P., Hannaford, P.L., & Munsterman, G.T. (1999). The Arizona jury reform permitting civil jury trial discussions: The views of trial participants, judges, and jurors. *University of Michigan Journal of Law Reform, 32,* 349–377.

Hans, V.P., & Jehle, A. (2003). Avoid bald men and people with green socks? Other ways to improve the voir dire process in jury selection, *Chicago-Kent Law Review, 78,* 1179–1201.

Hans, V.P., Kaye, D.H., Dann, M., Farley, E.J., & Albertson, S. (2011). Science in the jury box: Jurors' comprehension of mitochondrial DNA evidence. *Law & Human Behavior, 35,* 60–71.

Hans, V.P., & Reyna, V.F. (2011). To dollars from sense: Qualitative to quantitative translation in jury damage awards. *Journal of Empirical Legal Studies, 8(S1),* 120–147.

Hans, V.P., & Vadino, N. (2000). Whipped by whiplash? The challenges of jury communication in lawsuits involving connective tissue injury. *Tennessee Law Review, 67,* 569–586.

Hanson, R., & Morton-Bourgon, K. (2009). The accuracy of recidivism risk assessments for sex offenders: A meta-analysis of 118 predictive studies. *Psychological Assessment, 21,* 1–21.

Hartwig, M., Granhag, P., Stromwall, L., & Kronkvist, O. (2006). Strategic use of evidence during police interviews: When training to detect deception works. *Law and Human Behavior, 30,* 603–619.

Hasel, L., & Kassin, S. (2009). On the presumption of evidentiary independence: Can confessions corrupt eyewitness identifications? *Psychological Science, 20,* 122–126.

Hasen, R.L. (2012). *Examples & explanations: Remedies* (3rd ed.). Aspen.

Hastie, R. (1991). Is attorney-conducted voir dire an effective procedure for the selection of impartial juries? *American University Law Review, 40,* 703–726.

Hastie, R. (2008). What's the story? Explanations and narratives in civil jury decisions. In B.H. Bornstein, R.L. Wiener, R.F. Schopp, & S.L. Willborn (Eds.), *Civil juries and civil justice: Psychological and legal perspectives* (pp. 23–34). New York: Springer.

Hastie, R., & Dawes, R.M. (2009). *Rational choice in an uncertain world: The psychology of judgment and decision making* (2nd ed.). Sage Publications.

Hastie, R., Penrod, S.D, & Pennington, N. (1983). *Inside the jury.* Cambridge, MA: Harvard University Press.

Hastie, R., Schkade, D.A., & Payne, J.W. (1998). A study of juror and jury judgments in civil cases: Deciding liability for punitive damages. *Law and Human Behavior, 22,* 287–314.

Hastie, R., Schkade, D.A., & Payne, J.W. (1999a). Juror judgments in civil cases: Effects of plaintiff's requests and plaintiff's identity on punitive damage awards. *Law and Human Behavior, 23,* 445–470.

Hastie, R., Schkade, D.A., & Payne, J.W. (1999b). Juror judgments in civil cases: Hindsight effects on judgments of liability for punitive damages. *Law and Human Behavior, 23,* 597–614.

Henkel, L., Coffman, K., & Dailey, E. (2008). A survey of people's attitudes and beliefs about false confessions. *Behavioral Sciences and the Law, 26,* 555–584.

Hernandez v. New York, 500 U.S. 352 (1991).

Hersch, J., & Viscusi, W.K. (2004). Punitive damages: How judges and juries perform. *Journal of Legal Studies, 33,* 1–36.

Heuer, L., & Penrod, S. (1988). Increasing jurors' participation in trials: A field experiment with jury notetaking and question asking. *Law and Human Behavior, 12*, 231–262.

Heuer, L., & Penrod, S. (1989). Instructing jurors: A field experiment with written and preliminary instructions. *Law and Human Behavior, 13*, 409–430.

Heuer, L., & Penrod, S. (1994a). Juror notetaking and question asking during trials: A national field experiment. *Law & Human Behavior, 18*, 121–150.

Heuer, L., & Penrod, S. (1994b). Trial complexity: A field investigation of its meaning and its effects. *Law & Human Behavior, 18*, 29–51.

Hoffman, M.B. (1997). Peremptory challenges should be abolished: A trial judge's perspective. *The University of Chicago Law Review, 64*, 809–871.

Hoffman, M.B. (2000). Peremptory challenges: Lawyers are from Mars, judges are from Venus. *Green Bag 2d, 3*, 135–447.

Holcomb, M.J., & Jacquin, K.M. (2007). Juror perceptions of child eyewitness testimony in a sexual abuse trial. *Journal of Child Sexual Abuse: Research, Treatment, & Program Innovations for Victims, Survivors, & Offenders, 16*, 79–95.

Hope, L., Greene, E., Memon, A., Gavisk, M., & Houston, K. (2008). A third verdict option: Exploring the impact of the Not Proven verdict on mock juror decision making. *Law and Human Behavior, 34*, 241–252.

Horgan, O., & MacLachlan, M. (2004). Psychological adjustment to lower-limb amputation: A review. *Disability and Rehabilitation, 26*, 837–850.

Horowitz, A. (1990). *Ross v. Oklahoma*: A strike against peremptory challenges. *Wisconsin Law Review, 1990*, 219–239.

Horowitz, I.A., & Bordens, K.S. (1990). An experimental investigation of procedural issues in complex tort trials. *Law and Human Behavior, 14*, 269–285.

Horowitz, I.A., & Bordens, K.S. (2000). The consolidation of plaintiffs: The effects of number of plaintiffs on jurors' liability decisions, damage awards, and cognitive processing of evidence. *Journal of Applied Psychology, 85*, 909–918.

Horowitz, I.A., & Bordens, K. (2002). The effects of jury size, evidence complexity, and note taking on jury process and performance in a civil trial. *Journal of Applied Psychology, 87*, 121–130.

Horowitz, I.A., Bordens, K.S., Victor, E., Bourgeois, M.J., & ForsterLee, L. (2001). The effects of complexity on jurors' verdicts and construction of evidence. *Journal of Applied Psychology, 86*, 641–652.

Horowitz, I.A., & ForsterLee, L. (2001). The effects of note-taking and trial transcript access on mock jury decisions in a complex civil trial. *Law and Human Behavior, 25*, 373–391.

Horowitz, I.A., ForsterLee, L., & Brolly, I. (1996). Effects of trial complexity on decision making. *Journal of Applied Psychology, 81*, 757–768.

Horowitz, I.A., Kerr, N.L., & Niedermeier, K.E. (2001). Jury nullification: Legal and psychological perspectives. *Brooklyn Law Review, 66*, 1207–1249.

Horowitz, I.A., Kerr, N.L., Park, E.S., & Gockel, C. (2006). Chaos in the courtroom reconsidered: Emotional bias and juror nullification. *Law and Human Behavior, 30*, 163–181.

Horowitz, I.A., & Seguin, D.G. (1986). The effects of bifurcation and death qualification on assignment of penalty in capital crimes. *Journal of Applied Social Psychology, 16*, 165–185.

Hosch, H.M., Beck, E.L., & McIntyre, P. (1980). Influence of expert testimony regarding eyewitness accuracy on jury decisions. *Law and Human Behavior, 4*, 287–296.

Houston, K.A., Hope, L., Memon, A., Read, J.D. (2013). Expert testimony on eyewitness evidence: In search of common sense. *Behavioral Sciences & the Law, 31*, 637–651.

Howell, S. (1998). *Citizen evaluation of the Louisiana courts: A report to the Louisiana Supreme Court.* New Orleans: University of New Orleans.

Huang, K., & Lin, C. (2014). Mock jury trials in Taiwan—Paving the ground for introducing lay participation. *Law and Human Behavior, 38*, 367–377.

Huber, P. (1991). *Galileo's revenge: Junk science in the courtroom.* New York: Basic Books.

Hunt, M. (2007). *The story of psychology (updated and revised).* New York: Anchor.

Hurst v. Florida, 577 U.S. ___ (2016).

Hurwitz, S.D., Miron, M.S., & Johnson, B.T. (1992). Source credibility and the language of expert testimony. *Journal of Applied Social Psychology, 22*, 1909–1939.

Hyman, D.A., Black, B., Zeiler, K., Silver, C., & Sage, W.M. (2007). Do defendants pay what juries award? Post-verdict haircuts in Texas medical malpractice cases, 1988–2003. *Journal of Empirical Legal Studies, 4*, 3–68.

Inbau, F., Reid, J., Buckley, J., & Jayne, B. (2001). *Criminal interrogation and confessions* (4th ed.). Gaithersberg, MD: Aspen.

Innocence Project (2008). A false confession in Missouri? Retrieved from http://www.innocenceproject.org/a-false-confession-in-missouri/

Ivkovic, S.K., & Hans, V.P. (2003). Jurors' evaluations of expert testimony: Judging the messenger and the message. *Law & Social Inquiry, 28*, 441–482.

Jackson v. Louisiana, 134 S. Ct. 1950 (2014).

Jackson v. State, 5 So. 3d 1144 (Miss. Ct. App. 2008).

Jacowitz, K.E., & Kahneman, D. (1995). Measures of anchoring in estimation tasks. *Personality and Social Psychology Bulletin, 21*, 1161–1167.

Jan, I., Ball, J., & Walsh, A. (2008). Predicting public opinion about juvenile waivers. *Criminal Justice Policy Review, 19*, 285–300.

J.E.B. v. Alabama ex rel. T.B., 511 U.S. 127 (1994).

Jehle, A., Miller, M.K., & Kemmelmeier, M. (2009). The influence of accounts and remorse on mock jurors' judgments of offenders. *Law and Human Behavior, 33*, 393–404.

Johnson v. Louisiana, 406 U.S. 356 (1972).

Johnson, C., & Haney, C. (1994). Felony voir dire: An exploratory study of its content and effect. *Law and Human Behavior, 18*, 487–506.

Johnson, S.L. (1985). Black innocence and the white jury. *Michigan Law Review, 83*, 1611–1708.

Jonakait, R.N. (2003). *The American jury system.* New Haven, CT: Yale University Press.

Jones, A.M., Bergold, A.S., Dillon, M., & Penrod, S.D. (2016). Sensitizing jurors to factors influencing the accuracy of eyewitness identification: Assessing the effectiveness of the *Henderson* instructions. Manuscript submitted for publication.

Jones, O.D., Wagner, A.D., Faigman, D.L., & Raichle, M.E. (2013). Neuroscientists in court. *Nature Reviews Neuroscience, 14,* 730–736.

Jones, S. (1987). Judge-versus attorney-conducted voir dire: An empirical investigation of juror candor. *Law and Human Behavior, 11,* 131–146.

Judicial Council of California (2009). *Jury sanctions: 2008 Report to the legislature, California Code of Civil Procedure Section 209.* San Francisco: California Administrative Office of the Courts.

Kaasa, S.O., Peterson, T., Morris, E.K., & Thompson, W.C. (2007). Statistical inference and forensic evidence: Evaluating a bullet lead match. *Law and Human Behavior, 31,* 433–447.

Kahneman, D., Schkade, D., & Sunstein, C. (1998). Shared outrage and erratic awards: The psychology of punitive damages. *Journal of Risk and Uncertainty, 16,* 47–84.

Kahneman, D., Schkade, D.A., & Sunstein, C.R. (2002). Shared outrage, erratic awards. In C.R. Sunstein, R. Hastie, J.W. Payne, D.A. Schkade, & W.K. Viscusi (Eds.), *Punitive damages: How juries decide* (pp. 31–42). Chicago, IL: University of Chicago Press.

Kahneman, D., & Tversky, A. (1973). On the psychology of prediction. *Psychological Review, 80,* 237–251.

Kalven, H., & Zeisel, H. (1966). *The American jury.* Boston: Little, Brown.

Kang, J., Bennett, M., Carbado, D., Casey, P., Dasgupta, N., Faigman, D., . . . & Mnookin, J. (2012). Implicit bias in the courtroom. *UCLA Law Review, 59,* 1124–1186.

Kaplan, M.F., & Martin, A.M. (2006). *Understanding world jury systems through social psychological research.* New York: Psychology Press.

Kaplan, M.F., & Miller, C. (1987). Group decision making and normative vs. informational influence: Effects of type of issue and assigned decision rule. *Journal of Personality and Social Psychology, 53,* 306–313.

Kassin, S. (2005). On the psychology of confessions: Does *innocence* put *innocents* at risk? *American Psychologist, 60,* 215–228.

Kassin, S. (2008). Expert testimony on the psychology of confessions: A pyramidal framework of the relevant science. In E. Borgida & S. Fiske (Eds.), *Beyond common sense: Psychological science in the courtroom* (pp. 195–218). Malden, MA: Blackwell Publishing.

Kassin, S.M., & Barndollar, K.A. (1992). The psychology of eyewitness testimony: A comparison of experts and prospective jurors. *Journal of Applied Social Psychology, 22,* 1241–1249.

Kassin, S.M., Drizin, S., Grisso, T., Gudjonsson, G., Leo, R., & Redlich, A. (2010). Police-induced confessions: Risk factors and recommendations. *Law and Human Behavior, 34,* 3–38.

Kassin, S.M., Ellsworth, P.C., & Smith, V.L. (1989). The "general acceptance" of psychological research on eyewitness testimony: A survey of the experts. *American Psychologist, 44,* 1089–1098.

Kassin, S.M., & Garfield, D.A. (1991). Blood and guts: General and trial specific effects of videotaped crime scenes on mock juror verdicts. *Journal of Applied Social Psychology, 21,* 1456–1472.

Kassin, S.M., & Gudjonsson, G.H. (2004). The psychology of confessions: A review of the literature and issues. *Psychological Science in the Public Interest, 5,* 33–67.

Kassin, S.M., Leo, R., Crocker, C., & Holland, L. (2003). *Videotaping interrogations: Does it enhance the jury's ability to distinguish between true and false confessions?* Paper presented at International Conference on Psychology and Law, Edinburgh, Scotland.

Kassin, S.M., Leo, R., Meissner, C., Richman, K., Colwell, L., Leach, A.-M., & La Fon, D. (2007). Police interviewing and interrogation: A self-report survey of police practices and beliefs. *Law and Human Behavior, 31,* 381–400.

Kassin, S.M., Meissner, C., & Norwick, R. (2005). "I'd know a false confession if I saw one": A comparative study of college students and police investigators. *Law and Human Behavior, 29,* 211–227.

Kassin, S.M., & Neumann, K. (1997). On the power of confession evidence: An experimental test of the fundamental difference hypothesis. *Law and Human Behavior, 21,* 469–484.

Kassin, S.M., Reddy, M.E., & Tulloch, W.F. (1990). Juror interpretations of ambiguous evidence: The need for cognition, presentation order, and persuasion. *Law and Human Behavior 14,* 43–55.

Kassin, S.M., & Sukel, H. (1997). Coerced confessions and the jury: An experimental test of the "harmless error" rule. *Law and Human Behavior, 21,* 27–46.

Kassin, S.M., Tubb, V.A., Hosch, H.M., & Memon, A. (2001). On the "general acceptance" of eyewitness testimony research: A new survey of the experts. *American Psychologist, 56,* 405–416.

Kassin, S.M., & Wrightsman, L. (1980). Prior confessions and mock juror verdicts. *Journal of Applied Social Psychology, 10,* 133–146.

Kassin, S.M., & Wrightsman, L. (1983). The construction and validation of a juror bias scale. *Journal of Research on Personality, 17,* 423–442.

Katzev, R.D., & Wishart, S.S. (1985). The impact of judicial commentary concerning eyewitness identifications on jury decision making. *Journal of Criminal Law & Criminology, 76,* 733–745.

Kaufmann, G., Drevland, G.C.B., Wessel, E., Overskeid, G., & Magnussen, S. (2003). The importance of being earnest: Displayed emotions and witness credibility. *Applied Cognitive Psychology, 17,* 21–34.

Kawakami, K. Dovidio, J., & Van Kamp, S. (2007). The impact of naïve theories related to strategies to reduce biases and correction processes on the application of stereotypes. *Group Processes and Intergroup Relations, 10,* 141–158.

Kaye, D. H. and Koehler, J.J. (1991). Can jurors understand probabilistic evidence? *Journal of the Royal Statistical Society A, 154,* 75–81.

Kaye, J.S. (1999). Rethinking traditional approaches. *Alabama Law Review, 62,* 1491–1498.

Kaye, J.S. (2008). Why juries? Looking back, looking ahead. *Journal of Court Innovation, 1,* 185–188.

Keller, S.R., & Wiener, R.L. (2011). What are we studying? Student jurors, community jurors, and construct validity. *Behavioral Sciences and the Law, 29,* 376–394.

Kent v. U.S., 383 U.S. 541 (1966).

Kerr, N.L. (2010). Explorations in juror emotion and juror judgment. In B.H. Bornstein & R.L. Wiener (Eds.), *Emotion and the law: Psychological perspectives* (pp. 97–132). New York: Springer.

Kerr, N.L., Atkin, R., Stasser, G., Meek, D., Holt, R., & Davis, J. (1976). Guilt beyond a reasonable doubt: Effects of concept definition and assigned decision rule on the judgments of mock jurors. *Journal of Personality and Social Psychology, 34*, 282–294.

Kerr, N.L., Kramer, G.P., Carroll, J.S., & Alfini, J. (1991). On the effectiveness of voir dire in criminal cases with prejudicial pretrial publicity: An empirical study. *American University Law Review, 40*, 665–701.

Kerr, N.L., & MacCoun, R. (1985). The effects of jury size and polling method on the process and product of jury deliberation. *Journal of Personality and Social Psychology, 48*, 349–363.

Kiewra, K.A. (1989). A review of notetaking: The encoding storage paradigm and beyond. *Educational Psychology Review, 1*, 147–172.

King, I., & Nesbit, T. (2009). The empirical estimation of the cost-minimizing jury size and voting rule in civil trials. *Journal of Economic Behavior and Organization, 71*, 463–472.

King, N.J., & Noble, R.L. (2005). Jury sentencing in noncapital cases: Comparing severity and variance with judicial sentences in two states. *Journal of Empirical Legal Studies, 2*, 331–367.

Kirk v. Denver Publishing Co., 818 P.2d 262 (Colo. 1991).

Klippenstine, M.A., & Schuller, R. (2012). Perceptions of sexual assault: Expectancies regarding the emotional response of a rape victim over time. *Psychology, Crime & Law, 18*, 79–94.

Koehler, J.J. (1992). Probabilities in the courtroom: an evaluation of the objections and policies. In D.K. Kagehiro & W.S. Laufer (Eds.), *Handbook of psychology and law* (pp. 167–184). New York: Springer-Verlag.

Koehler, J.J. (1996). The base rate fallacy reconsidered: descriptive, normative, and methodological challenges. *Behavioral and Brain Sciences, 19*, 1–53.

Koehler, J.J. (2001).When are people persuaded by DNA match statistics? *Law and Human Behavior, 25*, 493–513.

Koehler, J.J. (2011). Misconceptions about statistics and statistical evidence. In R.L. Wiener & B.H. Bornstein (Eds.), *Handbook of trial consulting* (pp. 121–133). New York: Springer.

Koehler, J.J., Chia, A., & Lindsey, J.S. (1995). The random match probability (RMP) in DNA evidence: Irrelevant and prejudicial? *Jurimetrics Journal, 35*, 201–219.

Koehler, J.J., & Shaviro, D. (1990). Veridical verdicts: Increasing verdict accuracy through the use of overtly probabilistic evidence and methods. *Cornell Law Review, 75*, 247–279.

Kovera, M.B. (2007). Implications of automatic and controlled processes in stereotyping for hate crime perpetration and litigation. In R.L. Wiener, B.H. Bornstein, R. Schopp, & S.L. Willborn (Eds.), *Social consciousness in legal decision making: Psychological perspectives* (pp. 227–246). New York: Springer.

Kovera, M.B. (2017). *The psychology of juries: Current knowledge and a research agenda for the future.* Washington, DC: American Psychological Association.

Kovera, M.B., Levy, R.J., Borgida, E., & Penrod, S.D. (1994). Expert testimony in child sexual abuse cases: Effects of expert evidence type and cross-examination. *Law and Human Behavior, 18*, 653–674.

Kovera, M.B., Gresham, A.W., Borgida, E., Gray, E., & Regan, P.C. (1997). Does expert psychological testimony inform or influence juror decision making? A social cognitive analysis. *Journal of Applied Psychology, 82*, 178–191.

Kovera, M.B., & McAuliff, B.D. (2000). The effects of peer review and evidence quality on judge evaluations of psychological science: Are judges effective gatekeepers? *Journal of Applied Psychology, 85*, 574–586.

Kovera, M.B., McAuliff, B.D., & Hebert, K.S. (1999). Reasoning about scientific evidence: effects of juror gender and evidence quality on juror decisions in a hostile work environment case. *Journal of Applied Psychology, 84*, 362–375.

Kozinski, A. (2015). Criminal law 2.0. *Georgetown Law Journal Annual Review of Criminal Procedure, 44*, iii-xliv. Available at http://georgetownlawjournal. org/files/2015/06/Kozinski_Preface.pdf.

Kramer, G.P., Kerr, N.L., & Carroll, J.S. (1990). Pretrial publicity, judicial remedies, and jury bias. *Law and Human Behavior, 14*, 409–438.

Krauss, D.A., & Lee, D. (2003). Deliberating on dangerousness and death: Jurors' ability to differentiate between expert actuarial and clinical predictions of dangerousness. *International Journal of Law and Psychiatry, 26*, 113–137.

Krauss, D.A., Lieberman, J.D., Olson, J. (2004). The effects of rational and experiential information processing of expert testimony in death penalty cases. *Behavioral Sciences and the Law, 22*, 801–822.

Krauss, D.A., McCabe, J.G., & Lieberman, J.D. (2012). Dangerously misunderstood: Representative jurors' reactions to expert testimony on future dangerousness in a sexually violent predator trial. *Psychology, Public Policy and Law, 18*, 18–49.

Krauss, D.A., & Sales, B.D. (2001). The effects of clinical and scientific expert testimony on juror decision making in capital sentencing. *Psychology, Public Policy and Law, 7*, 267–310.

Krauss, E. (2005). Jury trial innovations in New York State: Improving jury trials by improving jurors' comprehension and participation. *New York State Bar Association Journal, 77*, 22–27.

Krieger, L.H., & Fiske, S.T. (2006). Behavioral realism in employment discrimination law: Implicit bias and disparate treatment. *California Law Review, 94*, 997–1008.

Kuhlik, B., & Kingham, R. (1990). The adverse effects of standardless punitive damage awards on pharmaceutical development and availability. *Food Drug Cosmetic Law Journal, 45*, 693–708.

Kukucka, J., & Kassin, S. (2014). Do confessions taint perceptions of handwriting evidence? An empirical test of the forensic confirmation bias. *Law and Human Behavior, 38*, 256–270.

Kumho Tire Co. v. Carmichael, 526 U.S. 137 (1999).

Kunda, Z., Davies, P., Adams, B., & Spencer, S. (2002). The dynamic time course of stereotype activation: Activation, dissipation, and resurrection. *Journal of Personality and Social Psychology, 82*, 283–299.

Lamb, M.E., Sternberg, K.J., Orbach, Y., Hershkowitz, I., & Horowitz, D. (2003). Differences between accounts provided by witnesses and alleged victims of child sexual abuse. *Child Abuse & Neglect, 27*, 1019–1031.

Landsman, S. (1993). The civil jury in America: Scenes from an unappreciated history. *Hastings Law Journal, 44*, 579–619.

Landsman, S. (1995). Of witches, madmen, and products liability: An historical survey of the use of expert testimony. *Behavioral Sciences and the Law, 13,* 131–157.

Landsman, S. (1999). The civil jury in America. *Law and Contemporary Problems, 62,* 285–304.

Landsman, S. (2002). Appellate courts and civil juries. *University of Cincinnati Law Review, 70,* 873–911.

Landsman, S. (2008). Reflections on juryphobia and medical malpractice reform. In B.H. Bornstein, R.L. Wiener, R. Schopp, & S. Willborn (Eds.), *Civil juries and civil justice: Psychological and legal perspectives* (pp. 151–174). New York: Springer.

Landsman, S., Diamond, S., Dimitropoulos, L., & Saks, M.J. (1998). Be careful what you wish for: The paradoxical effects of bifurcating claims for punitive damages. *Wisconsin Law Review, 1998,* 297–342.

Landsman, S., & Rakos, R.F. (1994). A preliminary inquiry into the effect of potentially biasing information on judges and jurors in civil litigation. *Behavioral Sciences and the Law, 12,* 113–126.

Lane, K., Kang, J., & Banaji, M. (2007). Implicit social cognition and law. *Annual Review of Law and Social Science, 3,* 427–451.

Langton, L., & Cohen, T. (2008). *Civil bench and jury trials in state courts, 2005.* Bureau of Justice Statistics Special Report (NCJ 223851). Washington, DC: U.S. Department of Justice.

Larsen, S. (1996). Taking and use of trial notes by jury. *American Law Reports, 36,* 1–254.

Lassiter, G.D. (2010). Videotaped interrogations and confessions: What's obvious in hindsight may not be in foresight. *Law and Human Behavior, 34,* 41–42.

Lassiter, G.D., & Geers, A. (2004). Bias and accuracy in the evaluation of confession evidence. In G.D. Lassiter (Ed.), *Interrogations, confessions, and entrapment* (pp. 197–214). New York: Kluwer/Plenum.

Lassiter, G.D., Geers, A.L., Handley, I.M., Weiland, P.E., & Munhall, P.J. (2002). Videotaped interrogations and confessions: A simple change in camera perspective alters verdicts in simulated trials. *Journal of Applied Psychology, 87,* 867–874.

Lassiter, G.D., & Irvine, A. (1986). Videotaped confessions: The impact of camera point of view on judgments of coercion. *Journal of Applied Social Psychology, 16,* 268–276.

Lassiter, G.D., Ware, L., Lindberg, M., & Ratcliff, J. (2010). Videotaping custodial interrogations: Toward a scientifically based policy. In G.D. Lassiter & C. Meissner (Eds.), *Police interrogations and false confessions: Current research, practice, and policy recommendations* (pp. 143–160). Washington, DC: American Psychological Association.

Lassiter, G.D., Ware, L.J., Ratcliff, J.J., & Irvin, C.R. (2009). Evidence of the camera perspective bias in authentic videotaped interrogations: Implications for emerging reform in the criminal justice system. *Legal and Criminological Psychology, 14,* 157–170.

Laub, C.E., Kimbrough, C.D., & Bornstein, B.H. (2016). Mock juror perceptions of eyewitnesses vs. earwitnesses: Do safeguards help? Manuscript submitted for publication.

Lawrence, F.M. (2007). The hate crime project and its limitations: Evaluating the societal gains and risks in bias crime law enforcement. In R.L. Wiener, B.H. Bornstein, R. Schopp, & S.L. Willborn (Eds.), *Social consciousness in legal decision making: Psychological perspectives* (pp. 209–226). New York: Springer.

Lazer, L.D., & Higgitt, J.R. (2009). Ascertaining the burden of proof for an award for punitive damages in New York? Consult your local appellate division. *Touro Law Review, 25,* 725–737.

Lecci, L., & Myers, B. (2002). Examining the construct validity of the original and revised JBS: A cross-validation of sample and method. *Law and Human Behavior, 26,* 455–463.

Leichtman, M.D., & Ceci, S.J. (1995). The effects of stereotypes and suggestions on preschoolers' experiences. *Developmental Psychology, 31,* 568–578.

Leippe, M.R., & Eisenstadt, D. (2007). Eyewitness confidence and the confidence-accuracy relationship in memory for people. In R.C.L. Lindsay, D.F. Ross., J.D. Read, & M.P. Toglia (Eds.), *The handbook of eyewitness psychology (Vol. 2): Memory for people* (pp. 377–425). Mahwah, NJ: Erlbaum.

Leippe, M.R., & Eisenstadt, D. (2009). The influence of eyewitness expert testimony on jurors' beliefs and judgments. In B.L. Cutler (Ed.), Expert testimony on the psychology of eyewitness identification (pp. 169–199). Oxford: Oxford University Press.

Leippe, M.R., Manion, A.P., & Romanczyk, A. (1992). Eyewitness persuasion: How and how well do fact finders judge the accuracy of adults' and children's memory reports? *Journal of Personality & Social Psychology, 63,* 181–197.

Leippe, M.R., & Romanczyk, A. (1987). Children on the witness stand: A communication/persuasion analysis of jurors' reactions to child witnesses. In S.J. Ceci, M.P. Toglia, & D.F. Ross (Eds.), *Children's eyewitness memory* (pp. 155–177). New York: Springer-Verlag.

Lempert, R. (1993). Civil juries and complex cases: Taking stock after twelve years. In R.E. Litan (Ed.), *Verdict: Assessing the civil jury system.*

Leo, R. (2008). *Police interrogation and American justice.* Cambridge, MA: Harvard University Press.

Leo, R., & Davis, D. (2010). From false confession to wrongful conviction: Seven psychological processes. *Journal of Psychiatry and Law, 38,* 9–55.

Leo, R., & Liu, B. (2009). What do potential jurors know about police interrogation techniques and false confessions? *Behavioral Sciences and the Law, 27,* 381–399.

Leo, R., Neufeld, P., Drizin, S., & Taslitz, A. (2013). Promoting accuracy in the use of confession evidence: An argument for pretrial reliability assessments to prevent wrongful convictions. *Temple Law Review, 85,* 759–837.

Leo, R., & Ofshe, R. (1998). The consequences of false confessions: Deprivations of liberty and miscarriages of justice in the age of psychological interrogation. *Journal of Criminal Law and Criminology, 88,* 429–496.

Lerner, J.S., Goldberg, J., & Tetlock, P. (1998). Sober second thought: The effects of accountability, anger, and authoritarianism on attributions of responsibility. *Personality and Social Psychology Bulletin, 24,* 563–574.

Lerner, J.S., & Tetlock, P.E. (1999). Accounting for the effects of accountability. *Psychological Bulletin, 125,* 255–275.

Lerner, J.S., & Tiedens, L.Z. (2006). Portrait of the angry decision maker: How appraisal tendencies shape anger's influence on cognition. *Journal of Behavioral Decision Making, 19,* 115–137.

Levett, L., Danielsen, E., & Kovera, M.B. (2003). *Racial differences in attitudes toward juvenile waiver to adult court.* Paper presented at the Psychology and Law International Conference, Edinburgh, Scotland.

Levett, L.M., & Kovera, M.B. (2008). The effectiveness of opposing expert witnesses for educating jurors about unreliable expert evidence. *Law and Human Behavior, 32,* 363–374.

Levine, M., Williams, A., Sixt, A., & Valenti, R. (2001). Is it inherently prejudicial to try a juvenile as an adult? *Behavioral Sciences and the Law, 19,* 23–31.

Levine, T., Kim, R., & Blair, J. (2010). Inaccuracy at detecting true and false confessions and denials: An initial test of a projected motive model of veracity judgments. *Human Communication Research, 36,* 81–101.

Lieberman, J.D. (2009). The psychology of the jury instruction process. In J.D. Lieberman & D.A. Krauss (Eds.), *Jury psychology: Social aspects of trial processes: Psychology in the courtroom, Vol. 1* (pp. 129–155). Burlington, VT: Ashgate Publishing.

Lieberman, J.D. (2010). Inner terror and outward hate: The effects of mortality salience on bias motivated attacks. In B.H. Bornstein & R.L. Wiener (Eds.), *Emotion and the law: Psychological perspectives* (pp. 133–155). New York: Springer.

Lieberman, J.D., Arndt, J., Personius, J., & Cook, A. (2001). Vicarious annihilation: The effect of mortality salience on perceptions of hate crimes. *Law and Human Behavior, 25,* 547–566.

Lieberman, J.D., Carrell, C.A., Miethe, T.D., & Krauss, D.A. (2008). Gold versus platinum: Do jurors recognize the superiority and limitations of DNA evidence compared to other types of forensic evidence? *Psychology, Public Policy, and Law, 14,* 27–62.

Lieberman, J.D., Krauss, D.A. (2009). The effects of labelling, expert testimony, and information processing mode on juror decisions in SVP civil commitment trials. *Journal of Investigative Psychology and Offender Profiling, 6,* 25–41.

Lieberman, J.D., Krauss, D.A., Kyger, M., & Lehoux, M. (2007). Determining dangerousness in sexually violent predator evaluations: Cognitive-experiential self-theory and juror judgments of expert testimony. *Behavioral Sciences and the Law, 25,* 507–526.

Lieberman, J.D., Shoemaker, J., & Krauss, D.A. (2014). The effects of mortality salience and evidence strength on death penalty sentencing decisions. *Psychology, Crime & Law, 20,* 199–221.

Lilienfeld, S.O. (2012). Public skepticism of psychology: Why many people perceive the study of human behavior as unscientific. *American Psychologist, 67,* 111–129.

Lilienfeld, S.O., Lynn, S.J., Ruscio, J., & Beyerstein, B.L. (2010). *Fifty great myths of popular psychology: Shattering widespread misconceptions about human behavior.* Chichester, England: Wiley-Blackwell.

Lindsay, R.C.L. (1994). Expectations of eyewitness performance: Jurors' verdicts do not follow from their beliefs. In D.F. Ross, J.D. Read, & M.P. Toglia (Eds.), *Adult eyewitness testimony: Current trends and developments* (pp. 362–384). Cambridge, UK: Cambridge University Press.

Lindsay, R.C.L., Lim, R., Marando, L., & Cully, D. (1986). Mock-juror evaluations of eyewitness testimony: A test of metamemory hypotheses. *Journal of Applied Social Psychology, 16*, 447–459.

Lindsay, R.C.L., Wells, G.L., & O'Connor, F.J. (1989). Mock-juror belief of accurate and inaccurate eyewitnesses: A replication and extension. *Law and Human Behavior, 13*, 333–339.

Lindsay, R.C.L., Wells, G.L., & Rumpel, C.M. (1981). Can people detect eyewitness-identification accuracy within and across situations? *Journal of Applied Psychology, 66*, 79–89.

Liptak, A. (2015, Nov. 2). Supreme Court to decide if Georgia went too far in excluding black jurors. Retrieved from http://www.nytimes.com/2015/11/03/us/politics/supreme-court-to-decide-if-georgia-went-too-far-in-excluding-black-jurors.html?_r=0.

Litan, R.E. (Ed.) (1993). *Verdict: Assessing the civil jury system.* Washington, DC: The Brookings Institution.

Lockett v. Ohio, 438 U.S. 586 (1978).

Lockhart v. McCree, 476 U.S. 162 (1986).

Loewenstein, G., & Lerner, J. (2003). The role of affect in decision making. In R. Davidson, K. Scherer, & H. Goldsmith (Eds.), *Handbook of affective sciences* (pp. 619–642). Oxford: Oxford University Press.

Loftus, E.F., Weingardt, K.R., & Hoffman, H.G. (1993). Sleeping memories on trial: Reaction to memories that were previously repressed. *Expert Evidence, 2*, 51–59.

Losel, F. (2007). It's never too early and never too late: Towards an integrated science of developmental interventions in criminology. *The Criminologist, 32*, 1–8.

Losh, S., & Boatright, R. (2002). Life-cycle factors, status, and civic engagement: Issues of age and attitudes toward jury service. *Justice System Journal, 23*, 221–234.

Losh, S., Wasserman, A., & Wasserman, M. (2000). "Reluctant jurors:" What summons response reveals about jury duty attitudes. *Judicature, 83*, 304–310.

Lovegrove, S.A. (1984). Structuring judicial sentencing discretion. In D.J. Müller, D.E. Blackman, & A.J. Chapman (Eds.), *Psychology and law* (pp. 301–317). John Wiley & Sons.

Luginbuhl, J., & Howe, J. (1995). Discretion in capital sentencing instructions: Guided or misguided? *Indiana Law Journal, 70*, 1161–1181.

Luginbuhl, J., & Middendorf, K. (1988). Death penalty beliefs and jurors' responses to aggravating and mitigating circumstances in capital trials. *Law and Human Behavior, 12*, 263–281.

Luppi, B., & Parisi, F. (2013). Jury size and the hung-jury paradox. *Journal of Legal Studies, 42*, 399–422.

Lynch, M. (2009). The social psychology of capital cases. In J.D. Lieberman & D.A. Krauss (Eds.), *Jury psychology: Social aspects of trial processes* (pp. 157–181). London: Ashgate.

Lynch, M., & Haney, C. (2000). Discrimination and instructional comprehension: Guided discretion, racial bias, and the death penalty. *Law and Human Behavior, 24*, 337–358.

Lynch, M., & Haney, C. (2009). Capital jury deliberation: Effects on death sentencing, comprehension, and discrimination. *Law & Human Behavior, 33*, 481–496.

Lynch, M., & Haney, C. (2011). Mapping the racial bias of the White male capital juror: Jury composition and the "empathic divide." *Law & Society Review, 45,* 69–101.

Maass, A., Brigham, J.C., & West, S.G. (1985). Testifying on eyewitness reliability: Expert advice is not always persuasive. *Journal of Applied Social Psychology, 15,* 207–229.

MacCoun, R.J. (1989). Experimental research on jury decision-making. *Science, 244,* 1046–1050.

MacCoun, R.J. (1996). Differential treatment of corporate defendants by juries: An examination of the "deep-pockets" hypothesis. *Law and Society Review, 30,* 121–161.

MacCoun, R.J. (2006). Media reporting of jury verdicts: Is the tail (of the distribution) wagging the dog? *DePaul University Law Review, 55,* 539–562.

MacCoun, R.J. (2015). The epistemic contract: Fostering an appropriate level of public trust in experts. In B.H. Bornstein & A.J. Tomkins (Eds.), *Motivating cooperation and compliance with authority: The role of institutional trust* (pp. 191–214). New York: Springer.

MacCoun, R., & Kerr, N. (1988). Asymmetric influence in mock jury deliberation: Jurors' bias for leniency. *Journal of Personality and Social Psychology, 54,* 21–33.

MacLean, C.L., Brimacombe, C.A.E., Allison, M., Dahl, L.C., & Kadlec, H. (2011). Post-identification feedback effects: Investigators and evaluators. *Applied Cognitive Psychology, 25,* 739–752.

MacLin, M.K., Downs, C., MacLin, O.H., & Caspers, H.M. (2009). The effect of defendant facial expression on mock juror decision-making: The power of remorse. *North American Journal of Psychology, 11,* 323–332.

Macpherson, S. (2013, August 19). Mini-openings set the stage for jury selection. *Deliberations.* Retrieved from http://jurylaw.typepad.com/deliberations/2013/08/index.html.

Macpherson, S. (2014). Why do we ask jurors to promise that they will do the impossible? *The Jury Expert, 26,* 33–35.

Magnussen, S., Melinder, A., Stridbeck, U., & Raja, A.Q. (2010). Beliefs about factors affecting the reliability of eyewitness testimony: A comparison of judges, jurors and the general public. *Applied Cognitive Psychology, 24,* 122–133.

Magnussen, S., Safer, M.A., Sartori, G., & Wise, R.A. (2013). What Italian defense attorneys know about factors affecting eyewitness accuracy: A comparison with U.S. and Norwegian samples. *Frontiers in Psychiatry, 4,* 1–6.

Magnussen, S., Wise, R.A., Raja, A.Q., Safer, M.A., Pawlenko, N., & Stridbeck, U. (2008). What judges know about eyewitness testimony: A comparison of Norwegian and US judges. *Psychology, Crime & Law, 14,* 177–188.

Mallett, R., Wilson, T., & Gilbert, D. (2008). Expect the unexpected: Failure to anticipate similarities leads to an intergroup forecasting error. *Journal of Personality and Social Psychology, 94,* 265–277.

Malloy, L., Shulman, E., & Cauffman, E. (2014). Interrogations, confessions, and guilty pleas among serious adolescent offenders. *Law and Human Behavior, 38,* 181–193.

Malpass, R.S., Ross, S.J., Meissner, C.A., & Marcon, J.L. (2009). The need for expert psychological testimony on eyewitness identification. In B.L. Cutler (Ed.), *Expert testimony on the psychology of eyewitness identification* (pp. 3–27). Oxford: Oxford University Press.

Malpass, R.S., Tredoux, C.G., Schreiber Compo, N., McQuiston-Surrett, D., MacLin, O.H., Zimmerman, L.A., & Topp, L.D. (2008). Study space analysis for policy development. *Applied Cognitive Psychology, 22*, 789–801.

Mancini, D.E. (2011). The CSI effect reconsidered: Is it moderated by need for cognition? *North American Journal of Psychology, 13*, 155–174.

Marcus-Newhall, A., Blake, L.P., & Baumann, J. (2002). Perceptions of hate crime perpetrators and victims as influenced by race, political orientation, and peer group. *American Behavioral Scientist, 46*, 108–135.

Marder, N.S. (1999). The myth of the nullifying jury. *Northwestern University Law Review, 93*, 877–923.

Marder, N.S. (2005). The medical malpractice debate: The jury as scapegoat. *Loyola of Los Angeles Law Review, 38*, 1267–1296.

Marder, N.S. (2006). Bringing jury instructions into the twenty-first century. *Notre Dame Law Review, 81*, 449–511.

Marder, N.S. (2010). Answering jurors' questions: Next steps in Illinois. *Loyola University Chicago Law Journal, 41*, 727–752.

Marder, N.S. (2011). An introduction to comparative jury systems. *Chicago-Kent Law Review, 86*, 453–456.

Marder, N.S. (2012). *Batson* revisited. *Iowa Law Review, 97*, 1585–1612.

Marder, N.S. (2013). The changing composition of the American jury. In L.B. Andrews & S.K. Harding (Eds.), *Then & now: Stories of law and progress* (pp. 66–74). Chicago: Chicago-Kent College of Law.

Marder, N.S. (2015). Juror bias, voir dire, and the judge-jury relationship. *Chicago-Kent Law Review, 90*, 927–956.

Markman v. Westview Instruments, Inc., 517 U.S. 370 (1996).

Markman, K., & Hirt, E. (2002). Social prediction and the "allegiance bias." *Social Cognition, 20*, 58–86.

Maroney, T.A. (2006). Law and emotion: A proposed taxonomy of an emerging field. *Law and Human Behavior, 30*, 119–142.

Maroney, T.A. (2009). Emotional common sense as constitutional law. *Vanderbilt Law Review, 62*, 851–917.

Maroney, T.A. (2011). The persistent cultural script of judicial dispassion. *California Law Review, 99*, 629–681.

Marti, M.W., & Wissler, R.L. (2000). Be careful what you ask for: The effect of anchors on personal injury damage awards. *Journal of Experimental Psychology: Applied, 6*, 91–103.

Martin, C.J. (2003). *Dardinger v. Anthem Blue Cross & Blue Shield*: Judicial redistribution of punitive damage awards. *San Diego Law Review, 40*, 1649–1670.

Martire, K.A., & Kemp, R.I. (2008). Knowledge of eyewitness identification issues: Survey of public defenders in New South Wales. *Psychiatry, Psychology and Law, 15*, 78–87.

Martire, K.A., & Kemp, R.I. (2009). The impact of eyewitness expert evidence and judicial instruction on juror ability to evaluate eyewitness testimony. *Law and Human Behavior, 33*, 225–236.

Martire, K.A., & Kemp, R.I. (2011). Can experts help jurors to evaluate eyewitness evidence? A review of eyewitness expert effects. *Legal and Criminological Psychology, 16*, 24–36.

Martire, K.A., Kemp, R.I., Watkins, I., Sayle, M.A., & Newell, B.R. (2013). The expression and interpretation of uncertain forensic science evidence: Verbal equivalence, evidence strength, and the weak evidence effect. *Law and Human Behavior, 37*, 197–207.

Massey, M. (2007, July 23). Putting the term "rape" on trial. *Time*. Available at http://content.time.com/time/nation/article/0,8599,1646133,00.html.

Mazzella, R., & Feingold, A. (1994). The effects of physical attractiveness, race, socioeconomic status, and gender of defendants and victims on judgments of mock jurors: A meta-analysis. *Journal of Applied Social Psychology, 24*, 1315–1344.

McAuliff, B.D., & Bornstein, B.H. (2010). All anchors are not created equal: The effects of per diem versus lump sum requests on pain and suffering awards. *Law and Human Behavior, 34*, 164–174.

McAuliff, B.D., & Bornstein, B.H. (2012). Beliefs and expectancies in legal decision making: An introduction to the Special Issue. *Psychology, Crime & Law, 18*, 1–10.

McAuliff, B.D., & Kovera, M.B. (2008). Juror need for cognition and sensitivity to methodological flaws in expert evidence. *Journal of Applied Social Psychology, 38*, 385–408.

McAuliff, B.D., & Kovera, M.B. (2012). Do jurors get what they expect? Traditional versus alternative forms of children's testimony. *Psychology, Crime & Law, 18*, 27–47.

McAuliff, B.D., Kovera, M.B., & Nunez, G. (2009). Can jurors recognize missing control groups, confounds, and experimenter bias in psychological science? *Law & Human Behavior, 33*, 247–257.

McAuliff, B.D., Nemeth, R.J., Bornstein, B.H., & Penrod, S.D. (2003). Juror decision making in the 21st century: confronting science and technology in court. In D. Carson and R. Bull (Eds.), *Handbook of psychology in legal contexts* (2d ed.) (pp. 303–327). Chichester, UK: Wiley.

McCabe, D.P., Castel, A.D., & Rhodes, M. (2011). The influence of fMRI lie detection evidence on juror decision-making. *Behavioral Sciences and the Law, 29*, 566–577.

McCabe, J.G., & Krauss, D.A. (2011). The effect of acknowledging mock jurors' feelings on affective and cognitive biases: It depends on the sample. *Behavioral Sciences and the Law, 29*, 331–357.

McCabe, J.G., Krauss, D.A., & Lieberman, J.D. (2010). Reality check: A comparison of college students and community samples of mock jurors in a simulated sexual violent predator civil commitment. *Behavioral Sciences and the Law, 28*, 730–750.

McCauley, M.R., & Parker, J.F. (2001). When will a child be believed? The impact of the victim's age and juror's gender on children's credibility and verdict in a sexual-abuse case. *Child Abuse & Neglect, 25*, 523–539.

McCleskey v. Kemp, 107 S. Ct. 1756 (1987).

McGowan, M.G., & Myers, B. (2004). Who is the victim anyway? The effects of bystander victim impact statements on mock juror sentencing decisions. *Violence and Victims, 19*, 357–374.

Mears, D.P., Pickett, J.T., & Mancini, C. (2015). Support for balanced juvenile justice: Assessing views about youth, rehabilitation, and punishment. *Journal of Quantitative Criminology, 31,* 459–479.

Meissner, C.A., Brigham, J.C. and Pfeifer, J.E. (2003). Jury nullification: The influence of judicial instruction on the relationship between attitudes and juridic decision-making. *Basic and Applied Social Psychology, 25,* 243–254.

Meissner, C.A., Redlich, A., Michael, S., Evans, J., Camilletti, C., Bhatt, S., & Brandon, S. (2014). Accusatorial and information-gathering interrogation methods and their effects on true and false confessions: A meta-analytic review. *Journal of Experimental Criminology, 10,* 459–486.

Meissner, C.A., Sporer, S.L., & Schooler, J.W. (2007). Person descriptions as eyewitness evidence. In In R.C.L. Lindsay, D.F. Ross., J.D. Read, & M.P. Toglia (Eds.), *Handbook of Eyewitness Psychology (Vol. 2): Memory for people* (pp. 1–34). Mahwah, NJ: Erlbaum.

Melilli, K.J. (1996). *Batson* in practice: What we have learned about *Batson* and peremptory challenges. *Notre Dame Law Review, 71,* 447–503.

Melinder, A., & Magnussen, S. (2015). Psychologists and psychiatrists serving as expert witnesses in court: What do they know about eyewitness memory? *Psychology, Crime & Law, 21,* 53–61.

Melton, G.B., Petrila, J., Poythress, N.G., & Slobogin, C. (2007). *Psychological evaluations for the courts: A handbook for mental health professionals and lawyers* (3rd ed.). New York: Guilford Press.

Mesmer-Magnus, J., & DeChurch, L. (2009). Information sharing and team performance: A meta-analysis. *Journal of Applied Psychology, 92,* 535–546.

Metcalfe, C., Pickett, J, & Mancini, C. (2015). Using path analysis to explain racialized support for punitive delinquency policies. *Journal of Quantitative Criminology, 31,* 699–725.

Mikula, G., Scherer, K.R., & Athenstaedt, U. (1998). The role of injustice in the elicitation of differential emotional reactions. *Personality and Social Psychology Bulletin, 24,* 769–783.

Miller v. Alabama, 132 S. Ct. 2455 (2012).

Miller, C. (1985). Group decision making under majority and unanimity decision rules. *Social Psychology Quarterly, 48,* 51–61.

Miller, M.K. (2006). *Religion in criminal justice.* New York: LFB Publishing.

Miller, M.K., & Bornstein, B.H. (2006). The use of religion in death penalty sentencing trials. *Law and Human Behavior, 30,* 675–684.

Miller, M.K., & Bornstein, B.H. (2013). The experience of jurors: Reducing stress and enhancing satisfaction. In M.K. Miller & B.H. Bornstein (Eds.), *Stress, trauma, and wellbeing in the legal system* (pp. 247–267). New York: Oxford University Press.

Miller, M.K., & Hayward, R.D. (2008). Religious characteristics and the death penalty. *Law and Human Behavior, 32,* 113–123.

Miller, M.K., Wood, S.M., & Chomos, J.C. (2014). Relationships between support for the death penalty and cognitive processing: A comparison of students and community members. *Criminal Justice and Behavior, 41,* 732–750.

Miller-El v. Dretke, 545 US 231 (2005).

Mize G., & Hannaford-Agor, P. (2008). Building a better voir dire process. *The Judge's Journal, 47.*

Mize, G., Hannaford-Agor, P., & Waters, N. (2007). *The state-of-the-states survey of jury improvement efforts: A compendium report.* Williamsburg, VA: National Center for State Courts. Retrieved from http://www.ncsc-jurystudies.org/State-of-the-States-Survey.aspx.

Moffitt, T.E. (1993). Life-course-persistent and adolescence-limited antisocial behavior: A developmental taxonomy. *Psychological Review, 100,* 674–701.

Mogin, P. (1998). Why judges, not juries, should set punitive damages. *University of Chicago Law Review, 65,* 179–223.

Moller, E., Pace, N., & Carroll, S. (1999). Punitive damages in financial injury jury verdicts. *Journal of Legal Studies, 28,* 283–339.

Monahan, J., & Walker, L. (2014). *Social science in law: Cases and materials* (8th ed.). New York: Foundation Press.

Moore v. Mobile Infirmary Association, 592 So. 2d 156 (Ala. 1991).

Morrison, C.M. (2014). Negotiating peremptory challenges. *The Journal of Criminal Law and Criminology, 104,* 1–58.

Morse, S.J. (2011). Mental disorder and criminal law. *Journal of Criminal Law and Criminology, 101,* 885–968.

Mott, N.L. (2003). The current debate on juror questions: "To ask or not to ask, that is the question." *Chicago-Kent Law Review, 78,* 1099–1125.

Mott, N.L., Hans, V.P., & Simpson, L. (2000). What's half a lung worth? Civil jurors' accounts of their award decision making. *Law and Human Behavior, 24,* 401–419.

Munsterman, T., Munsterman, J., & Penrod, S. (1990). *A comparison of the performance of eight-and twelve-person juries.* Arlington, VA: National Center for State Courts.

Murphy, D.E. (2005, March 16). Case stirs fight on Jews, juries, and execution. *The New York Times,* p. A1.

Musick, M., Rose, M., Dury, S., & Rose, R. (2015). Much obliged: Volunteering, normative activities, and willingness to serve on juries. *Law and Social Inquiry, 40,* 433–460.

Myers, B., & Arbuthnot, J. (1999). The effects of victim impact information on the verdicts and sentence recommendations of mock jurors. *Journal of Offender Rehabilitation, 29,* 95–112.

Myers, B., & Greene, E. (2004). The prejudicial nature of victim impact statements: Implications for capital sentencing policy. *Psychology, Public Policy, and Law, 10,* 492–515.

Myers, B., Lynn, S.J., & Arbuthnot, J. (2002). Victim impact testimony & juror judgments: The effects of harm information and witness demeanor. *Journal of Applied Social Psychology, 32,* 2393–2412.

Myers, B., Roop, A., Kalnen, D., & Kehn, A. (2013). Victim impact statements and crime heinousness: A test of the saturation hypothesis. *Psychology, Crime & Law, 19,* 129–143.

Myers, D.L. (2003). Adult crime, adult time: Punishing violent youth in the adult criminal justice system. *Youth Violence and Juvenile Justice, 1,* 173–197.

Myers, J.E., Redlich, A., Goodman, G., Prizmich, L., & Imwinkelried, E. (1999). Jurors' perceptions of hearsay in child sexual abuse cases. *Psychology, Public Policy, & Law, 5,* 388–419.

Nagel, S., & Neef, M. (1975). Deductive modeling to determine an optimum jury size and fraction required to convict. *Washington University Law Quarterly,* 933–978.

Najdowski, C. (2010). Jurors and social loafing: Factors that reduce participation during jury deliberations. *American Journal of Forensic Psychiatry, 31,* 49–76.

Najdowski, C., & Bottoms, B. (2012). Understanding jurors' judgments in cases involving juvenile defendants: Effects of confession evidence and intellectual disability. *Psychology, Public Policy, and Law, 18,* 297–337.

Nance, D.A., & Morris, S.B. (2005). Juror understanding of DNA evidence: An empirical assessment of presentation formats for trace evidence with a relatively small and quantifiable random match probability. *Journal of Legal Studies, 34,* 395–444.

Narby, D.J., & Cutler, B.L. (1994). Effectiveness of voir dire as a safeguard in eyewitness cases. *Journal of Applied Psychology, 79,* 724–729.

National Academy of Sciences (2014). *Identifying the culprit: Assessing eyewitness identification.* Retrieved from https://public.psych.iastate.edu/glwells/NAS_Eyewitness_ID_Report.pdf.

National Center for Juvenile Justice (2006). *National juvenile court data archive: Juvenile court case records 1985–2003.* Pittsburgh, PA: Author.

National Center for State Courts (1998). *Through the eyes of the juror: A manual for addressing juror stress.* Williamsburg, VA: National Center for State Courts. Retrieved from http://www.ncsc-jurystudies.org/What-We-Do/~/media/Microsites/Files/CJS/What%20We%20Do/THROUGH%20THE%20EYES%20OF%20THE%20JUROR.ashx.

National Center for State Courts (2007). *State-of-the-states survey of jury improvement efforts: A compendium report.* Williamsburg, VA: National Center for State Courts. Retrieved from http://www.ncsc-jurystudies.org/State-of-the-States-Survey.aspx.

National Center for State Courts (2014). *Jury management.* Williamsburg, VA: National Center for State Courts. Retrieved from http://www.ncsc.org/Services-and-Experts/Areas-of-expertise/Jury-management.aspx.

National Center for State Courts (2015). *Civil justice initiative: The landscape of civil litigation in state courts.* Williamsburg, VA: National Center for State Courts. Available at http://www.ncsc.org/~/media/Files/PDF/Research/CivilJusticeReport-2015.ashx?utm_source=iContact&utm_medium=email&utm_campaign=Communications&utm_content=1115+%40The+Center.

Neal, T.M.S. (2014). Women as expert witnesses: A review of the literature. *Behavioral Sciences and the Law, 32,* 164–179.

Neal, T.M.S., & Brodsky, S.L. (2008). Expert witness credibility as a function of eye contact behavior and gender. *Criminal Justice and Behavior, 35,* 1515–1526.

Neal, T.M.S., Christiansen, A., Bornstein, B.H., & Robicheaux, T.R. (2012). The effects of mock jurors' beliefs about eyewitness performance on trial judgments. *Psychology, Crime & Law, 18,* 49–64.

Neal, T.M.S., & Grisso, T. (2014). Assessment practices and expert judgment methods in forensic psychology and psychiatry: An international snapshot. *Criminal Justice and Behavior, 41,* 1406–1421.

Neil v. Biggers, 409 U.S. 188 (1972).

Neilson, W.S., & Winter, H. (2005). The elimination of hung juries: Retrials and nonunanimous verdicts. *International Review of Law and Economics, 25,* 1–19.

Nemeth, C. (1977). Interactions between jurors as a function of majority vs. unanimity decision rules. *Journal of Applied Social Psychology, 7*, 38–56.

Neuman, S. (2015, July 31). Dylann Roof pleads not guilty to federal hate crime charges. *National Public Radio.* Available at http://www.npr.org/sections/thetwo-way/2015/07/31/428139323/dylann-roof-pleads-not-guilty-to-federal-hate-crime-charges.

Neuschatz, J.S., Lawson, D.S., Swanner, J.K., Meissner, C.A., & Neuschatz, J.S. (2008). The effects of accomplice witnesses and jailhouse informants on jury decision making. *Law and Human Behavior, 32*, 137–149.

Neuschatz, J.S., Wilkinson, M.L., Goodsell, C.A., Wetmore, S.A., Quinlivan, D.S., & Jones, N.J. (2012). Secondary confessions, expert testimony, and unreliable testimony. *Journal of Police and Criminal Psychology, 27*, 179–192.

Newcombe, P.A., & Bransgrove, J. (2007). Perceptions of witness credibility: Variations across age. *Journal of Applied Developmental Psychology, 28*, 318–331.

New Jersey v. Henderson, 208 N. J. 208, 27 A. 3d 872 (2011).

Niedermeier, K.E., Horowitz, I.A., & Kerr, N.L. (2001). Exceptions to the rule: The effects of remorse, status, and gender on decision making. *Journal of Applied Social Psychology, 31*, 604–623.

Niedermeier, K.E., Kerr, N.L., & Messé, L.A. (1999). Jurors' use of naked statistical evidence: exploring bases and implications of the Wells effect. *Journal of Personality and Social Psychology, 76*, 533–542.

Nietzel, M.T., McCarthy, D.M., & Kerr, M.J. (1999). Juries: The current state of the empirical literature. In R. Roesch, S.D. Hart, & J.R.P. Ogloff (Eds.), *Psychology and law: The state of the discipline* (pp. 23–52). New York: Kluwer.

Nisbett, R.E., & Wilson, T.D. (1977). Telling more than we can know. *Psychological Review, 84*, 231–259.

Noon, E., & Hollin, C.R. (1987). Lay knowledge of eyewitness behaviour: A British survey. *Applied Cognitive Psychology, 1*, 575–593.

Norton, M.I., Sommers, S.R., & Brauner, S. (2007). Bias in jury selection: Justifying prohibited peremptory challenges. *Journal of Behavioral Decision Making, 20*, 467–479.

Norton, M.I., Vandello, J., & Darley, J. (2004). Casuistry and social category bias. *Journal of Personality and Social Psychology, 87*, 817–831.

Nosek, B., Smyth, F., Hansen, J., Devos, T., Lindner, N., Ranganath, K., . . . & Banaji, M. (2007). Pervasiveness and correlates of implicit attitudes and stereotypes. *European Review of Social Psychology, 18*, 36–88.

Nuñez, N., Gray, J., & Buck, J.A. (2011). Educative expert testimony: A one-two punch can affect jurors' decisions. *Journal of Applied Social Psychology, 42*, 535–559.

Nuñez, N., Schweitzer, K., Chai, C.A., & Myers, B. (2015). Negative emotions felt during trial: The effect of fear, anger, and sadness on juror decision making. *Applied Cognitive Psychology, 29*, 200–209.

O'Brien, K., Goodman-Delahunty, J., Clough, J., & Pratley, J. (2008). Factors affecting juror satisfaction and confidence in New South Wales, Victoria and South Australia. *Trends and Issues in Crime and Criminal Justice* (No. 354). Canberra, Australia: Australian Institute of Criminology.

O'Connor, S.D. (1997). Juries: They may be broken, but we can fix them. *Federal Lawyer, 44*, 20–25.

Ofshe, R., & Leo, R. (1997). The decision to confess falsely: Rational choice and irrational action. *Denver University Law Review, 74*, 979–1122.

Ogletree, C. (1994). Just say no!: A proposal to eliminate racially discriminatory uses of peremptory challenges. *American Criminal Law Review, 31*, 1099–1151.

Ogloff, J.R.P., & Rose, G. (2005). The comprehension of judicial instructions. In N. Brewer & K.D. Wilson (Eds.), *Psychology and law: An empirical perspective* (pp. 407–444). New York: Guilford Press.

Ogloff, J.R.P., & Vidmar, N. (1994). The impact of pretrial publicity on jurors. *Law and Human Behavior, 18*, 507–525.

Ogloff, J.R.P., Wallace, D.H., & Otto, R.K. (1992). Competencies in the criminal process. In D. K. Kagehiro and W. S. Laufer (Eds.), *Handbook of psychology and law* (pp. 343–360). New York: Springer-Verlag.

Ohtsubo, Y., Miller, C., Hayashi, N., & Masuchi, A. (2004). Effects of group decision rules on decisions involving continuous alternatives: The unanimity rule and extreme decisions in mock civil juries. *Journal of Experimental Social Psychology, 40*, 320–331.

Olczak, P., Kaplan, M., & Penrod, S. (1991). Attorneys' lay psychology and its effectiveness in selecting jurors: Three empirical studies. *Journal of Social Behavior and Personality, 6*, 431–452.

Olsen-Fulero, L., & Fulero, S.M. (1997). Commonsense rape judgments: An empathy-complexity theory of rape juror story making. *Psychology, Public Policy, and Law, 3*, 402–427.

O'Neil, K.M., Patry, M.W., & Penrod, S.D. (2004). Exploring the effects of attitudes toward the death penalty on capital sentencing verdicts. *Psychology, Public Policy, and Law, 10*, 443–470.

Orwell, G. (1947/1968). The English people. In S. Orwell & I. Angus (Eds.), *As I please (1943-1945): The collected essays, journalism and letters of George Orwell* (Vol. 3, pp. 1–38). New York: Harcourt, Brace & World, Inc.

Osmann, S.L. (2011). Predicting rape empathy based on victim, perpetrator, and participant gender, and history of sexual aggression. *Sex Roles, 64*, 506–515.

Ostrom, B.J., Rottman, D.B., & Goerdt, J.A. (1996). A step above anecdote: A profile of the civil jury in the 1990s. *Judicature, 79*, 233–241.

Overby, L., Brown, R., Bruce, J., Smith, C., & Winkle, J. (2005). Race, political empowerment, and minority perceptions of judicial fairness. *Social Science Quarterly, 86*, 444–462.

Pacini, R., & Epstein, S. (1999). The relation of rational and experiential processing styles to personality, basic beliefs, and the ratio-bias problem. *Journal of Personality and Social Psychology, 76*, 972–987.

Page, A. (2005). Batson's blind spot: Unconscious stereotyping and the peremptory challenge. *Boston University Law Review, 85*, 155–262.

Paik, M., Black, B.S., Hyman, D.A., & Silver, C. (2012). Will tort reform bend the cost curve? Evidence from Texas. *Journal of Empirical Legal Studies, 9*, 173–216.

Palmer, M., & Sanders, T.B. (2010). Surprise! Most blockbuster jury awards are ignored by the stock market. *Review of Law & Economics, 6*, 145–166.

Paternoster, R., & Deise, J. (2011). A heavy thumb on the scale: The effect of victim impact evidence on capital decision making. *Criminology, 49,* 129–161.

Paterson, H.M., Anderson, D.W.M., & Kemp, R.I. (2013). Cautioning jurors regarding co-witness discussion: The impact of judicial warnings. *Psychology, Crime & Law, 19,* 287–304.

Patry, M.W., & Penrod, S.D. (2013). Death penalty decisions: Instruction comprehension, attitudes, and decision mediators. *Journal of Forensic Psychology Practice, 13,* 204–244.

Pawlenko, N.B., Safer, M.A., Wise, R.A., & Holfeld, B. (2013). A teaching aid for improving jurors' assessments of eyewitness accuracy. *Applied Cognitive Psychology, 27,* 190–197.

Payne v. Tennessee, 111 S. Ct. 2597 (1991).

Payne, B.K. (2001). Prejudice and perception: The role of automatic and controlled processes in misperceiving a weapon. *Journal of Personality and Social Psychology, 81,* 181–192.

Pearce, M.W. (2011). The admissibility of expert witness testimony. In R.L. Wiener & B.H. Bornstein (Eds.), *Handbook of trial consulting* (pp. 137–172). New York: Springer.

Pennington, N., & Hastie, R. (1993). The story model for juror decision-making. In R. Hastie (Ed.), *Inside the juror* (pp. 192–221). Cambridge: Cambridge University Press.

People v. Nelson, NY Slip Op. 09019 (New York App. Div., 2nd Jud. Dept. 2014).

Perillo, J.T., & Kassin, S.M. (2011). Inside interrogation: The lie, the bluff, and false confession. *Law and Human Behavior, 35,* 327–337.

Perry, S., & Stevenson, M. (2010). *Investigating the effects of defendant age on jurors' sentencing preferences.* Unpublished manuscript.

Petrucelli v. Wisconsin Patients Compensation Fund, 701 N.W.2d 440 (Wis. 2005).

Petty, R.E., & Cacioppo, J.T. (1986). The elaboration likelihood model of persuasion. In L. Berkowitz (Ed.), *Advances in experimental social psychology* (Vol. 19; pp. 123–203). New York: Academic Press.

Philip Morris USA v. Williams, 549 U.S. 346 (2007).

Pickel, K., Warner, T., Miller, T., Barnes, Z. (2013). Conceptualizing defendants as minorities leads mock jurors to make biased evaluations in retracted confession cases. *Psychology, Public Policy, and Law, 19,* 56–69.

Pickett, J.T., & Chiricos, J. (2012). Controlling other people's children: Racialized views of delinquency and whites' punitive attitudes toward juvenile offenders. *Criminology, 50,* 673–710.

Pierce, G., & Radelet, M. (2005). The impact of legally inappropriate factors on death sentencing for California homicides, 1990–1999. *Santa Clara Law Review, 46,* 1–47.

Piper, A., Lillevik, L., & Kritzer, R. (2008). What's wrong with believing in repression? A review for legal professionals. *Psychology, Public Policy, & Law, 14,* 223–242.

Piquero, A., Cullen, F., Unnever, J., Piquero, N., & Gordon, J. (2010). Never too late: Public optimism about juvenile rehabilitation. *Punishment & Society, 12,* 187–207.

Piquero, A., Farrington, D., & Blumstein, A. (2003). The criminal career paradigm: Background and recent developments. *Criminal Justice, 30,* 359–506.

Pizarro, J., Chermak, S., & Gruenewald, J. (2007). Juvenile "super-predators" in the news: A comparison of adult and juvenile homicides. *Journal of Criminal Justice and Popular Culture, 14*, 84–111.

Platania, J., & Berman, G.L. (2006). The moderating effect of judge's instructions on victim impact testimony in capital cases. *Applied Psychology in Criminal Justice, 2*, 84–101.

Plumm, K.M., & Terrance, C.A. (2009). Battered women who kill: The impact of expert testimony and empathy induction in the courtroom. *Violence Against Women, 15*, 186–205.

Plumm, K.M., & Terrance, C.A. (2013). Gender-bias hate crimes: What constitutes a hate crime from a potential juror's perspective? *Journal of Applied Social Psychology, 43*, 1468–1479.

Plumm, K.M., Terrance, C.A., Henderson, V.R., & Ellingson, H. (2010). Victim blame in a hate crime motivated by sexual orientation. *Journal of Homosexuality, 57*, 267–286.

Podkopacz, M.R., & Feld, B.C. (1996). The end of the line: An empirical study of judicial waiver. *Journal of Criminal Law and Criminology, 86*, 449–492.

Pornpitakpan, C. (2004). The persuasiveness of source credibility: A critical review of five decades evidence. *Journal of Applied Social Psychology, 34*, 243–281.

Poser, S., Bornstein, B.H., & McGorty, E.K. (2003). Measuring damages for lost enjoyment of life: The view from the bench and the jury box. *Law and Human Behavior, 27*, 53–68.

Posey, A.J., & Wrightsman, L.S. (2005). *Trial consulting.* Oxford: Oxford University Press.

Pozzulo, J.D., & Dempsey, J.L. (2009). Witness factors and their influence on jurors' perceptions and verdicts. *Criminal Justice and Behavior, 36*, 923–934.

Pozzulo, J.D., Dempsey, J.L., & Crescini, C. (2010). Factors affecting juror decisions in historic child sexual abuse cases involving continuous memories. *Criminal Justice and Behavior, 37*, 951–964.

Pozzulo, J.D., Lemieux, J.M.T., Wells, E., & McCuaig, H.J. (2006). The influence of eyewitness identification decisions and age of witness on jurors' verdicts and perceptions of reliability. *Psychology, Crime, & Law, 12*, 641–652.

Price, P.C., & Stone, E.R. (2004). Intuitive evaluation of likelihood judgment producers: Evidence for a confidence heuristic. *Journal of Behavioral Decision Making, 17*, 39–57.

Pronin, E., Gilovich, T., & Ross, L. (2004). Objectivity in the eye of the beholder: Divergent perceptions of bias in self versus others. *Psychological Review, 111*, 781–799.

Purkett v. Elem, 514 U.S. 765 (1995).

Quas, J.A., Thompson, W.C., & Clark-Stewart, K.A. (2005). Do jurors "know" that it's so about child witnesses? *Law and Human Behavior, 29*, 425–456.

Rachlinski, J.J. (1998). A positive psychological theory of judging in hindsight. *University of Chicago Law Review, 65*, 571–625.

Rachlinski, J.J. (2000). Heuristics and biases in the courts: Ignorance or adaptation? *Oregon Law Review, 79*, 61–102.

Rachlinski, J.J., Johnson, S., Wistrich, A., & Guthrie, C. (2009). Does unconscious racial bias affect trial judges? *Notre Dame Law Review, 84*, 1195–1246.

Rachlinski, J.J., & Jourden, F. (2003). The cognitive components of punishment. *Cornell Law Review, 88*, 457–485.

Rainville, G., & Smith, S. (2003). *Survey of 40 counties, 1998: Juvenile felony defendants in criminal courts.* Washington, DC: U.S. Department of Justice, Office of Justice Programs, Bureau of Justice Statistics.

Raitt, F., & Zeedyk, M. (2000). *The implicit relation of psychology and law: Women and syndrome evidence.* London: Routledge.

Ramirez, G., Zemba, D., & Geiselman, R. (1996). Judges' cautionary instructions on eyewitness testimony. *American Journal of Forensic Psychology, 14*, 31–63.

Ratcliff, R., & McKoon, G. (1981). Automatic and strategic priming in recognition. *Journal of Verbal Learning and Verbal Behavior, 20*, 204–215.

Rattan, A., Levine, C., Dweck, C., & Eberhardt, J. (2012). Race and the fragility of the legal distinction between juveniles and adults. *PLoS ONE, 7.*

Read, J.D., Connolly, D.A., & Welsh, A. (2006). An archival analysis of actual cases of historic child sexual abuse: A comparison of jury and bench trials. *Law and Human Behavior, 30*, 259–285.

Read, J.D., & Desmarais, S.L. (2009). Lay knowledge of eyewitness issues: A Canadian evaluation. *Applied Cognitive Psychology, 23*, 301–326.

Reagan, R.T., Mosteller, F., & Youtz, C. (1989). Quantitative meanings of verbal probability expressions. *Journal of Applied Psychology, 74*, 433–442.

Redding, R.E. (2003). The effects of adjudicating and sentencing juveniles as adults: Research and policy implications. *Youth Violence and Juvenile Justice, 1*, 128–155.

Redding, R. (2010). *Juvenile transfer laws: An effective deterrent to delinquency?* Washington, DC: Office of Juvenile Justice and Delinquency Prevention. Retrieved from https://www.ncjrs.gov/pdffiles1/ojjdp/220595.pdf.

Reed, K., & Bornstein, B.H. (2015). Using mock jury studies to measure community sentiment toward child sexual abusers. In M.K. Miller, J.A. Blumenthal, & J. Chamberlain (Eds.), *Handbook of community sentiment* (pp. 57–68). New York: Springer.

Regan, P.C., & Baker, S.J. (1998). The impact of child witness demeanor on perceived credibility and trial outcome in sexual abuse cases. *Journal of Family Violence, 13*, 187–195.

Reisberg, D. (2014). *The science of perception and memory: A pragmatic guide for the justice system.* New York: Oxford University Press.

Reppucci, N.D., Scott, E., & Antonishak, J. (2009). Political orientation and perceptions of adolescent autonomy and judicial culpability. *Behavioral Sciences and the Law, 27*, 29–34.

Reppucci, N.D., Woolard, J.L., & Fried, C.S. (1999). Social, community, and preventive interventions. *Annual Review of Psychology, 50*, 387–418.

Reyna, V.F., Hans, V.P., Corbin, J.C., Yeh, R., Lin, K., & Royer, C. (2015). The gist of juries: Testing a model of damage award decision making. *Psychology, Public Policy, and Law.* Advance online publication. http://dx.doi.org/10.1037/law0000048.

Riis, J., Loewenstein, G., Baron, J., Jepson, C., Fagerlin, A., & Ubel, P. (2005). Ignorance of hedonic adaptation to hemodialysis: A study using ecological momentary assessment. *Journal of Experimental Psychology: General, 134*, 3–9.

Rijnbout, J., & McKimmie, B. (2014). Deviance in organizational decision making: Using unanimous decision rules to promote the positive effects and alleviate the negative effects of deviance. *Journal of Applied Social Psychology*, *44*, 455–463.

Ring v. Arizona, 536 U.S. 584 (2002).

Riordan, K. (2012). Ten angry men: Unanimous jury verdicts in criminal trials and incorporation after *McDonald*. *Journal of Criminal Law and Criminology*, *101*, 1403–1433.

Robbennolt, J.K. (2000). Outcome severity and judgment of "responsibility": A meta-analytic review. *Journal of Applied Social Psychology*, *12*, 2575–2609.

Robbennolt, J.K. (2002a). Determining punitive damages: Empirical insights and implications for reform. *Buffalo Law Review*, *50*, 103–203.

Robbennolt, J.K. (2002b). Punitive damage decision making: The decisions of citizens and trial court judges. *Law and Human Behavior*, *26*, 315–341.

Robbennolt, J.K. (2008). Apologies and civil justice. In B.H. Bornstein, R.L. Wiener, R.F. Schopp, & S.L. Willborn (Eds.), *Civil juries and civil justice: Psychological and legal perspectives* (pp. 195–231). New York: Springer.

Robbennolt, J.K., Penrod, S., & Heuer, L. (1999). Assessing and aiding civil jury competence. In A.K. Hess & I.B. Wiener (Eds.), *The handbook of forensic psychology* (2nd ed.) (pp. 273–301). New York: Wiley.

Robbennolt, J.K., & Studebaker, C.A. (1999). Anchoring in the courtroom: The effects of caps on punitive damages. *Law and Human Behavior*, *23*, 353–373.

Robbennolt, J.K., & Studebaker, C.A. (2003). News media reporting on civil litigation and its influence on civil justice decision making. *Law and Human Behavior*, *27*, 5–27.

Robertson, C., Yokum, D., & Palmer, M. (2013). The inability of jurors to self-diagnose bias. *Arizona Legal Studies Discussion Paper No. 12–35*. University of Arizona College of Law.

Robertson, N., Davies, G., & Nettleingham, A. (2009). Vicarious traumatisation as a consequence of jury service. *Howard Journal of Criminal Justice*, *48*, 1–12.

Robicheaux, T.R., & Bornstein, B.H. (2010). Punished, dead or alive: Empirical perspectives on awarding punitive damages against deceased defendants. *Psychology, Public Policy, & Law*, *16*, 393–417.

Rodriguez, D.N., & Berry, M.A. (2009). Dissonance reduction in jurors' post-verdict decisions. *American Journal of Forensic Psychology*, *27*, 5–17.

Roper v. Simmons, 543 U. S. 551 (2005).

Rose, M.R. (2003). A *voir dire* of *voir dire*: Listening to jurors' views regarding the peremptory challenge. *Chicago-Kent Law Review*, *78*, 1061–1098.

Rose, M.R. (2005). A dutiful voice: Justice in the distribution of jury service. *Law and Society Review*, *39*, 601–634.

Rose, M.R., & Diamond, S.S. (2008). Judging bias: Juror confidence and judicial rulings on challenges for cause. *Law and Society Review*, *42*, 513–548.

Rose, M.R., & Diamond, S.S. (2009) Offstage behavior: Real jurors' scrutiny of non-testimonial conduct. *DePaul Law Review*, *58*, 311–342.

Rose, M.R., Diamond, S.S., & Musick, M.A. (2012). Selected to serve: An analysis of lifetime jury participation. *Journal of Empirical Legal Studies*, *9*, 33–55.

Rose, M.R., Ellison, C., & Diamond, S. (2008). Preferences for juries over judges across racial and ethnic groups. *Social Science Quarterly*, *89*, 372–391.

Rose, M.R., Nadler, J., & Clark, J. (2006). Appropriately upset? Emotion norms and perceptions of crime victims. *Law and Human Behavior, 30,* 203–219.

Rosen, R.A. (1986). The "especially heinous" aggravating circumstance in capital cases—the standardless standard. *North Carolina Law Review, 64,* 941–992.

Rosenhan, D.L., Eisner, S.L., & Robinson, R.J. (1994). Note taking can aid juror recall. *Law and Human Behavior, 18,* 53–61.

Rosenthal, R. (2002). Covert communication in classrooms, clinics, courtrooms, and cubicles. American Psychologist 57, 839–849.

Rosenthal, R. (2003). Covert communication in laboratories, classrooms, and the truly real world. *Current Directions in Psychological Science, 12,* 151–154.

Rosenthal, R. (2006). Applying psychological research on interpersonal expectations and covert communication in classrooms, clinics, corporations, and courtrooms. In S.I. Donaldson, D.E. Berger, & K. Pezdek (Eds.), *Applied psychology: New frontiers and rewarding careers* (pp. 107–118). Mahwah, NJ: Lawrence Erlbaum Associates.

Ross, D.F., Dunning, D., Toglia, M.P., & Ceci, S. (1990). The child in the eyes of the jury: Assessing mock jurors' perceptions of the child witness. *Law and Human Behavior, 14,* 5–23.

Ross, D.F., Jurden, F.H., Lindsay, R.C.L., & Keeney, J.M. (2003). Replications and limitations of a two-factor model of child witness credibility. *Journal of Applied Social Psychology, 33,* 418–431.

Ross, L. (1977). The intuitive psychologist and his shortcomings: Distortions in the attribution process. *Advances in Experimental Social Psychology, 10,* 174–221.

Rottman, D. (1998). On public trust and confidence: Does experience with the courts promote or diminish it? *Court Review, Winter,* 14–22.

Rottman, D., Hansen, R., Mott, N., & Grimes, L. (2003). *Perceptions of the courts in your community: The influence of experience, race and ethnicity.* Williamsburg, VA: National Center for State Courts. Retrieved from www.ncjrs.gov/pdffiles1/nij/grants/201302.pdf.

Rottman, D., & Strickland, S. (2006). *State Court Organization 2004.* Report NCJ 212351. Washington, DC: Bureau of Justice Statistics, Office of Justice Programs, U.S. Department of Justice.

Royal, K., & Hofman, D. (2013). Impaneled and ineffective: The role of law schools and constitutional literacy programs in effective jury reform. *Denver University Law Review, 90,* 959–975.

Russeau v. State, 171 S.W.3d 871 (Tex. Crim. App. 2005).

Russeau v. Stephens, slip op. #13–70005 (5th Cir. 2014).

Rustad, M. (1992). In defense of punitive damages in products liability: Testing tort anecdotes with empirical data. *Iowa Law Review, 78,* 1–88.

Rustad, M. (1998). Unraveling punitive damages: Current data and further inquiry. *Wisconsin Law Review, 1998,* 15–69.

Ruva, C.L., & McEvoy, C. (2008). Negative and positive pretrial publicity affect juror memory and decision making. *Journal of Experimental Psychology: Applied, 14,* 226–235.

Ruva, C.L., Guenther, C.C., & Yarbrough, A. (2011). Positive and negative pretrial publicity: The roles of impression formation, emotion, and predecisional distortion. *Criminal Justice and Behavior, 38,* 511–534.

Sakalh-Ugurlu, N., Yalcin, Z.S., & Glick, P. (2007). Ambivalent sexism, belief in a just world, and empathy as predictors of Turkish students' attitudes toward rape victims. *Sex Roles, 57*, 889–895.

Saks, M.J. (1989). Legal policy analysis and evaluation. *American Psychologist, 44*, 1110–1117.

Saks, M.J. (1992a). Do we really know anything about the behavior of the tort litigation system—and why not? *University of Pennsylvania law Review, 140*, 1147–1293.

Saks, M.J. (1992b). Normative and empirical issues about the role of expert witnesses. In D.K. Kagehiro & W.S. Laufer (Eds.), *Handbook of psychology and law* (pp. 185–203). New York: Springer-Verlag.

Saks, M. (1996). The smaller the jury, the greater the unpredictability. *Judicature, 79*, 263–265.

Saks, M.J., & Hastie, R. (1986). Social psychology in court: The judge. In H.R. Arkes & K.R. Hammond (Eds.), *Judgment and decision making* (pp. 255–274). Cambridge: Cambridge University Press.

Saks, M.J., Hollinger, L.A., Wissler, R.L., Evans, D.L., & Hart, A.J. (1997). Reducing variability in civil jury awards. *Law and Human Behavior, 21*, 243–256.

Saks, M., & Marti, M. (1997). A meta-analysis of the effects of jury size. *Law and Human Behavior, 21*, 451–467.

Saks, M.J., Schweitzer, N.J., Aharoni, E., & Kiehl, K.A. (2014). The impact of neuroimages in the sentencing phase of capital trials. *Journal of Empirical Legal Studies, 11*, 105–131.

Saks, M.J., & van Duizend, R. (1983). *The use of scientific evidence in litigation.* Williamsburg, VA: National Center for State Courts.

Saks, M.J., & Wissler, R.L. (1984). Legal and psychological bases of expert testimony: Surveys of the law and of jurors. *Behavioral Sciences & the Law, 2*, 435–449.

Salerno, J.M., & Diamond, S.S. (2010). The promise of a cognitive perspective on jury deliberation. *Psychonomic Bulletin & Review, 17*, 174–179.

Salerno, J.M., & McCauley, M.R. (2009). Mock jurors' judgments about opposing scientific experts: Do cross-examination, deliberation and need for cognition matter? *American Journal of Forensic Psychology, 27*, 1–24.

Sams, D., Neal, T., & Brodsky, S. (2013). Avoiding jury duty: Psychological and legal perspectives. *The Jury Expert, 25*, 4–8.

Scheiner, A.H. (1991). Judicial assessment of punitive damages, the Seventh Amendment, and the politics of jury power. *Columbia Law Review, 91*, 142–226.

Schklar, J., & Diamond, S.S. (1999). Juror reactions to DNA evidence: Errors and expectancies. *Law and Human Behavior, 23*, 159–184.

Schubert, G. (1964). *Judicial behavior: A reader in theory and research.* Chicago: Rand McNally & Co.

Schuller, R.A. (1992). The impact of battered woman syndrome evidence on jury decision processes. *Law and Human Behavior, 16*, 597–620.

Schuller, R.A., & Jenkins, G. (2007). Expert evidence pertaining to battered women: Limitations and reconceptualizations. In M. Costanzo, D. Krauss, & K. Pezdek (Eds.), *Expert psychological testimony for the courts* (pp. 203–225). Mahwah, NJ: Erlbaum.

Schuller, R.A., Kazoleas, V., & Kawakami, K. (2009). The impact of prejudice screening procedures on racial bias in the courtroom. *Law and Human Behavior, 33,* 320–328.

Schuller, R.A., Terry, D., & McKimmie, B. (2001). The impact of an expert's gender on jurors' decisions. *Law & Psychology Review, 25,* 59–79.

Schwartz, V.E., Behrens, M.A., & Silverman, C. (2003). I'll take that: Legal and public policy problems raised by statutes that require punitive damages awards to be shared with the state. *Missouri Law Review, 68,* 525–558.

Schweitzer, N.J., & Saks, M.J. (2007). The CSI Effect: Popular fiction about forensic science affects the public's expectations about real forensic science. *Jurimetrics, 47,* 357–364.

Schweitzer, N.J., & Saks, M.J. (2009). The gatekeeper effect: The impact of judges' admissibility decisions on the persuasiveness of expert testimony. *Psychology, Public Policy, and Law, 15,* 1–18.

Schweitzer, N.J., & Saks, M.J. (2011). Neuroimage evidence and the insanity defense. *Behavioral Sciences and the Law, 29,* 592–607.

Schweitzer, N.J., Saks, M.J., Murphy, E.R., Roskies, A.L., Sinnott-Armstrong, W., & Gaudet, L.M. (2011). Neuroimages as evidence in a *mens rea* defense: No impact. *Psychology, Public Policy, and Law, 17,* 357–393.

Scott, E., Reppucci, N.D., Antonishak, J., & DeGennaro, J. (2006). Public attitudes about the culpability and punishment of young offenders. *Behavioral Sciences and the Law, 24,* 815–832.

Scott, E., & Steinberg, L. (2008). *Rethinking juvenile justice.* Cambridge, MA: Harvard University Press.

Scurich, N. (2015). The differential effect of numeracy and anecdotes on the perceived fallibility of forensic science. *Psychiatry, Psychology and Law, 22,* 616–623.

Scurich, N., Krauss, D.A., Reiser, L., Garcia, R.J., & Deer, L. (2015). Venire jurors' perceptions of adversarial allegiance. *Psychology, Public Policy, and Law, 21,* 161–168.

Seabury, S.A., Pace, N.M., & Reville, R.T. (2004). Forty years of civil jury verdicts. *Journal of Empirical Legal Studies, 1,* 1–25.

Segal, J.A., & Spaeth, H.J. (1993). *The Supreme Court and the attitudinal model.* Cambridge: Cambridge University Press.

Seltzer, R. (1999). The vanishing juror: Why are there not enough available jurors? *The Justice System Journal, 20,* 203–218.

Semmler, C., & Brewer, N. (2002). Effects of mood and emotion on juror processing and judgments. *Behavioral Sciences & the Law, 20,* 423–436.

Sentell, R.P. (1991). The Georgia jury and negligence: The view from the bench. *Georgia Law Review, 26,* 85–178.

Seventh Circuit American Jury Project (2008). *Final report.* Retrieved from www.uscourts.gov/file/3467/download.

Severance, L.J., & Loftus, E.F. (1982). Improving the ability of jurors to comprehend and apply criminal jury instructions. *Law and Society Review, 17,* 153—198.

Shafir, E., Simonson, I., & Tversky, A. (1993). Reason-based choice. *Cognition, 49,* 11–36.

Shaked-Schroer, N., Costanzo, M., & Marcus-Newhall, A. (2008). Reducing racial bias in the penalty phase of capital trials. *Behavioral Sciences and the Law, 26,* 603–617.

Sharkey, C.M. (2003). Punitive damages as societal damages. *Yale Law Journal,* *113,* 347–453.

Sharkey, C.M. (2005). Unintended consequences of medical malpractice damages caps. *New York University Law Review, 80,* 391–512.

Sharkey, C.M. (2008). Crossing the punitive-compensatory divide. In B.H. Bornstein, R.L. Wiener, R. Schopp, & S. Willborn (Eds.), *Civil juries and civil justice: Psychological and legal perspectives* (pp. 79–104). New York: Springer.

Sharkey, L.M. (1996). Judge or jury: Who should assess punitive damages? *University of Cincinnati Law Review, 64,* 1089–1139.

Shaw, J.S., Garcia, L.A., & McClure, K.A. (1999). A lay perspective on the accuracy of eyewitness testimony. *Journal of Applied Social Psychology, 29,* 52–71.

Shea Adams, C.M., & Bourgeois, M.J. (2006). Separating compensatory and punitive damage award decisions by trial bifurcation. *Law and Human Behavior, 30,* 11–30.

Sheehan, C. (2011). Making the jurors the "experts": The case for eyewitness identification jury instructions. *Boston College Law Review, 52,* 651–693.

Sherman, J.W., Stroessner, S.J., Conrey, F.R., & Azam, O.A. (2005). Prejudice and stereotype maintenance processes: Attention, attribution, and individuation. *Journal of Personality and Social Psychology, 89,* 607–622.

Shestowsky, D., & Horowitz, L. (2004). How the Need for Cognition Scale predicts behavior in mock jury deliberations, *Law and Human Behavior, 28,* 305–337.

Shestowsky, D., Wegener, D., & Fabrigar, L. (1998). Need for cognition and interpersonal influence: Individual differences in impact on dyadic decisions. *Journal of Personality and Social Psychology, 74,* 1317–1328.

Shoichet, C.E., & Perez, E. (2015, July 22). Dylann Roof faces hate crime charges in Charleston shooting. CNN. Available at http://www.cnn.com/2015/07/22/us/charleston-shooting-hate-crime-charges/.

Shuman, D.W., Champagne, A., & Whitaker, E. (1996). Assessing the believability of expert witnesses: Science in the jurybox. *Jurimetrics Journal, 37,* 23–33.

Shuman, D., & Hamilton, J. (1992). Jury service: It may change your mind. *Southern Methodist University Law Review, 46,* 449–479.

Shuman, D., Hamilton, J., & Daley, C. (1994). The health effects of jury service. *Law and Psychology Review, 18,* 267–307.

Sicafuse, L., Chomos, J., & Miller, M. (2013). Promoting positive perceptions of jury service: An analysis of juror experiences, opinions, and recommendations for courts. *Justice System Journal, 34,* 85–106.

Sickmund, M., & Puzzanchera, C. (Eds.) (2014). *Juvenile offenders and victims: 2014 National Report.* Pittsburgh, PA: National Center for Juvenile Justice. Retrieved from http://www.ojjdp.gov/ojstatbb/nr2014/downloads/NR2014.pdf.

Simon, D. (1998). A psychological model of judicial decision making. *Rutgers Law Journal, 30,* 1–142.

Simon, D. (2004). A third view of the black box: Coherence in legal decision-making. *University of Chicago Law Review, 71,* 511–586.

Simon, D. (2012). *In doubt: The psychology of the criminal justice process.* Cambridge, MA: Harvard University Press.

Simon, D., Stenstrom, D., & Read, S. (2008). *Jurors' background knowledge and beliefs.* Paper presented at American Psychology-Law Society, Jacksonville, FL.

Simon, S., & Marcus, D. (1991, July 3). Jurors don't mind duty, survey finds. *Wall Street Journal*, B3.

Singer v. United States, 380 U.S. 24 (1965).

Sisk, G.C., Heise, M., & Morriss, A.P. (2004). Searching for the soul of judicial decisionmaking: An empirical study of religious freedom decisions. *Ohio State Law Journal, 65*, 491–594.

Skilling v. United States, 561 U.S. 358 (2010).

Skinner, L.J., Berry, K.K., Griffith, S.E., & Byers, B. (1995). Generalizability and specificity of the stigma associated with the mental illness label: A reconsideration twenty-five years later. *Journal of Community Psychology, 23*, 3–17.

Sloan, F.A., & Hsieh, C.R. (1990). Variability of medical malpractice payments: Is the compensation fair? *Law and Society Review, 24*, 997–1039.

Sloan, F.A., & van Wert, S.S. (1991). Cost and compensation of injuries in medical malpractice. *Law and Contemporary Problems, 54*, 131–168.

Smalarz, L., & Wells, G.L. (2014). Post-identification feedback to eyewitnesses impairs evaluators' abilities to discriminate between accurate and mistaken testimony. *Law and Human Behavior, 38*, 194–202.

Smith v. Phillips, 455 U.S. 209 (1982).

Smith, A., & Saks, M. (2008). The case for overturning *Williams v. Florida* and the six-person jury: History, law, and empirical evidence. *Florida Law Review, 60*, 441–470.

Smith, A.C., & Greene, E. (2005). Conduct and its consequences: Attempts at debiasing jury judgments. *Law and Human Behavior, 29*, 505–526.

Smith, A.E., & Haney, C. (2011). Getting to the point: Attempting to improve juror comprehension of capital penalty phase instructions. *Law & Human Behavior, 35*, 339–350.

Smith, B.C., Penrod, S.D., Otto, A.L., & Park, R.C. (1996). Jurors' use of probabilistic evidence. *Law and Human Behavior, 20*, 49–82.

Smith, C., De Houwer, T., & Nosek, B.A. (2013). Consider the source: Persuasion of implicit evaluations is moderated by source credibility. *Personality and Social Psychology Bulletin, 39*, 193–205.

Smith, C.A., & Frieze, I.H. (2003). Examining rape empathy from the perspective of the victim and the assailant. *Journal of Applied Social Psychology, 33*, 476–498.

Smith, D. (1997). Structural and junctional aspects of the jury: Comparative analysis and proposals for reform. *Alabama Law Review, 48*, 441–522.

SmithKline Beecham Corp dba GlaxoSmithKline v. Abbott Laboratories (No. 11-17373, 9th Cir. 2014).

Smithson, M., Deady, S., & Gracik, L. (2007). Guilty, not guilty, or . . .? Multiple options in jury verdict choices. *Journal of Behavioral Decision Making, 20*, 481–498.

Snortum, J., Klein, J., & Sherman, W. (1976). The impact of an aggressive juror in six—and twelve-member juries. *Criminal Justice and Behavior, 3*, 255–262.

Snyder v. Phelps, 533 F. Supp. 2d 567 (U.S. D. Maryland 2008).

Snyder v. Phelps, 580 F. 3d 206 (4th Cir. 2009).

Snyder v. Phelps, 131 S. Ct. 1207 (2011).

Snyder, H.N., & Sickmund, M. (1999). *Juvenile offenders and victims: National report 1999*. Washington, DC: U.S. Department of Justice, Office of Justice Programs, Office of Juvenile Justice and Delinquency Prevention.

Solomon, J.M. (2012). The political puzzle of the civil jury. *Emory Law Journal, 61,* 1331–1395.

Sommers, S.R. (2006). On racial diversity and group decision-making: Identifying multiple effects of racial composition on jury deliberations. *Journal of Personality and Social Psychology, 90,* 597–612.

Sommers, S.R., & Kassin, S.M. (2001). On the many impacts of inadmissible testimony: Selective compliance, need for cognition, and the overcorrection bias. *Personality and Social Psychology Bulletin, 27,* 1368–1377.

Sommers, S.R., & Norton, M.I. (2007). Race-based judgments, race neutral justifications: Experimental examination of peremptory use and the *Batson* challenge procedure. *Law and Human Behavior, 31,* 261–273.

Sommers, S.R., & Norton, M. (2008). Race and jury selection: Psychological perspectives on the peremptory challenge debate. *American Psychologist, 63,* 527–539.

Spano, L.M., Groscup, J.L., & Penrod, S.D. (2011). Pretrial publicity and the jury: Research and methods. In R.L. Wiener & B.H. Bornstein (Eds.), *Handbook of trial consulting* (pp. 217–244). New York: Springer.

Spanos, N.P., Myers, B., DuBreuil, S.C., & Pawlak, A.E. (1992–93). The effects of polygraph evidence and eyewitness testimony on the beliefs and decisions of mock jurors. *Imagination, Cognition and Personality, 12,* 103–113.

Sparf and Hansen v. United States, 156 U.S. 51 (1865).

Speegle, C. (2012–13). The socially unpopular verdict: A post-Casey Anthony analysis of the need to reform juror privacy policy. *Cumberland Law Review, 43,* 259–310.

Spohn, C.C. (2002). *How do judges decide? The search for fairness and justice in punishment*. Thousand Oaks, CA: Sage.

Sporer, S.L., Penrod, S., Read, D., & Cutler, B. (1995). Choosing, confidence, and accuracy: A meta-analysis of the confidence-accuracy relation in eyewitness identification studies. *Psychological Bulletin, 118,* 315–327.

Stalans, L., & Henry, G. (1994). Societal views of justice for adolescents accused of murder: Inconsistency between community sentiment and automatic legislative transfers. *Law and Human Behavior, 18,* 675–696.

Stanovich, K.E., & West, R.F. (1998). Who uses base rates and P(D/~H)? An analysis of individual differences. *Memory & Cognition, 26,* 161–179.

Stasser, G., Kerr, N., & Bray, R. (1982). The social psychology of jury deliberations: Structure, process, and product. In N. Kerr & R. Bray (Eds.), *The psychology of the courtroom* (pp. 221–256). New York: Academic Press.

State v. Crawford, 873 So. 2d 768 (La. Ct. App. 2004).

State v. McClendon, 730 A.2d 1107 (Conn. 1999).

State v. R.G.D., 527 A.2d 834 (N.J. 1987).

State v. Tyler, 2006 WL 264631 (Tenn. Crim. App. 2006).

State Farm Mutual Automobile Insurance Co. v. Campbell, 538 U.S. 408 (2003).

Steblay, N.M., Besirevic, J., Fulero, S.M., & Jimenez-Lorente, B. (1999). The effects of pretrial publicity on juror verdicts: A meta-analytic review. *Law and Human Behavior, 23,* 219–235.

Steblay, N.M., Hosch, H.M., Culhane, S.E., & McWethy, A. (2006). The impact on juror verdicts of judicial instruction to disregard inadmissible evidence: A meta-analysis. Law and Human Behavior, 30, 469–492.

Steinberg, L. (2009). Adolescent development and juvenile justice. Annual Review of Clinical Psychology, 5, 459–485.

Steinberg, L., & Scott, E. (2003). Less guilty by reason of adolescence: Developmental immaturity, diminished responsibility, and the juvenile death penalty. American Psychologist, 58, 1009–1018.

Stern, J.E. (2015, June). The cruel and unusual execution of Clayton Lockett. The Atlantic. Available at http://www.theatlantic.com/magazine/archive/2015/06/execution-clayton-lockett/392069/.

Stevenson, M.C., & Bottoms, B.L. (2009). Race shapes perceptions of juvenile offenders in criminal court. Journal of Applied Social Psychology, 39, 1660–1689.

Stevenson, M.C., Bottoms, B.L., & Diamond, S.S. (2010). Jurors' discussions of a defendant's history of child abuse and alcohol abuse in capital sentencing deliberations. Psychology, Public Policy, and Law, 16, 1–38.

Stinson, V., Devenport, J.L., Cutler, B.L., & Kravitz, D.A. (1996). How effective is the presence-of-counsel safeguard? Attorney perceptions of suggestiveness, fairness, and correctability of biased lineup procedures. Journal of Applied Psychology, 81, 64–75.

Stinson, V., Devenport, J.L., Cutler, B.L., & Kravitz, D.A. (1997). How effective is the motion-to-suppress safeguard? Judges' perceptions of the suggestiveness and fairness of biased lineup procedures. Journal of Applied Psychology, 82, 211–220.

Strodtbeck, F., James, R., Hawkins, C. (1957). Social status in jury deliberations. American Sociological Review, 22, 713–719.

Strom, K. (2000). Profile of state prisoners under age 18. Washington, DC: U.S. Department of Justice, Office of Justice Programs, Bureau of Statistics.

Suchman, M.C., & Mertz, E. (2010). Toward a new legal empiricism: Empirical legal studies and new legal realism. Annual Review of Law and Social Science, 6, 555–579.

Sue, S., Smith, R., & Pedroza, G. (1975). Authoritarianism, pretrial publicity, and awareness of bias in simulated jurors. Psychological Reports, 37, 1299–1302.

Suggs, D., & Sales, B.D. (1981). Juror self-disclosure in the voir dire: A social science analysis. Indiana Law Journal, 56, 245–271.

Sullivan, T. (2004). Police experiences with recording custodial interrogations. Chicago: Northwestern University School of Law, Center on Wrongful Convictions.

Sullivan, T. (2006). The time has come for law enforcement recordings of custodial interviews, start to finish. Golden Gate University Law Review, 37, 175–190.

Sullivan, T. (2012). A compendium of state and federal statutes, court rulings, departmental practices, national organizations' policy statements, and law review articles regarding electronic recording of custodial interviews of felony suspects. Judicature, 95, Whole No. 5.

Summers, A., Hayward, R.D., & Miller, M.K. (2010). Death qualification as systematic exclusion of jurors with certain religious and other characteristics. Journal of Applied Social Psychology, 40, 3218–3234.

Sundby, S. (1997). The jury as critic: An empirical look at how capital juries perceive expert and lay testimony. *Virginia Law Review, 83*, 1109–1189.

Sundby, S. (1998). The capital jury and absolution: The intersection of trial strategy, remorse and the death penalty. *Cornell Law Review, 83*, 1557–1598.

Sundby, S. (2003). The capital jury and empathy: The problem of worthy and unworthy victims. *Cornell Law Review, 88*, 343–381.

Sunstein, C. (2002). The law of group polarization. John M. Olin Law and Economics Working Paper No. 91. University of Chicago Law School.

Sunstein, C.R., Hastie, R., Payne, J.W., Schkade, D.A., & Viscusi, W.K. (2002). *Punitive damages: How juries decide.* Chicago: University of Chicago Press.

Swann, W., & Read, S. (1981). Acquiring self-knowledge: The search for feedback that fits. *Journal of Personality and Social Psychology, 41*, 1119–1128.

Tang, C., & Nuñez, N. (2003). Effects of defendant age and juror bias on judgment of culpability: What happens when a juvenile is tried as an adult? *American Journal of Criminal Justice, 28*, 37–52.

Tang, C., Nuñez, N., & Bourgeois, M. (2009). Effects of trial venue and pretrial bias on the evaluation of juvenile defendants. *Criminal Justice Review, 34*, 210–225.

Tang, C., & Turner, K. (2013). Defendant age, pretrial bias, and crime severity influence the judgment of juvenile waiver cases. *American Journal of Forensic Psychology, 31*, 5–25.

Taylor-Thompson, K. (2000). Empty votes in jury deliberations. *Harvard Law Review, 113*, 1261–1320.

Tenney, E.R., MacCoun, R.J., Spellman, B.A., & Hastie, R. (2007). Calibration trumps confidence as a basis for witness credibility. *Psychological Science, 18*, 46–50.

Thompson v. Utah, 170 U.S. 343 (1898).

Thompson, C.M., & Dennison, S. (2004). Graphic evidence of violence: The impact on juror decision-making, the influence of judicial instructions and the effect of juror biases. *Psychiatry, Psychology and Law, 11*, 323–337.

Thompson, W.C., Kaasa, S.O., & Peterson, T. (2013). Do jurors give appropriate weight to forensic identification evidence? *Journal of Empirical Legal Studies, 10*, 359–397.

Thompson, W.C., & Newman, E.J. (2015). Lay understanding of forensic statistics: Evaluation of random match probabilities, likelihood ratios, and verbal equivalents. *Law and Human Behavior, 39*, 332–349.

Thompson, W.C., & Schumann, E.L. (1987). Interpretation of statistical evidence in criminal trials: the prosecutor's fallacy and the defense attorney's fallacy. *Law and Human Behavior, 11*, 167–187.

Thompson-Cannino, J., Cotton, R., & Torneo, E. (2009). *Picking Cotton: Our memoir of injustice and redemption.* New York: St. Martin's Griffin.

Tiedens, L.Z., & Linton, S. (2001). Judgment under emotional certainty and uncertainty: The effects of specific emotions on information processing. *Journal of Personality and Social Psychology, 81*, 973–988.

Tiersma, P., & Curtis, M. (2008). Testing the comprehensibility of jury instructions: California's old and new instructions on circumstantial evidence. *Journal of Court Innovation, 1*, 231–261.

Tindale, R., Smith, C., Thomas, L., Filkins, J., & Sheffey, S. (1996). Shared representations and asymmetric social influence processes in small groups.

In E. Witte & J. Davis (Eds.), *Understanding group behavior* (Vol. 1, pp. 81–104). Mahwah, NJ: Erlbaum.

Tinsley, Y. (2002). Jury decision-making: A look inside the jury room. *British Society of Criminology Journal, 4.* Retrieved from http://britsoccrim.org/volume4/004.pdf.

Torbet, P., & Szymanski, L. (1998). *State legislative responses to violent juvenile crime: 1966-97 update.* Washington, DC: U.S. Department of Justice.

Tribe, L.H. (1971). Trial by mathematics: Precision and ritual in the legal process. *Harvard Law Review, 84,* 1329–1393.

Trzcinski, E., & Allen, T. (2012). Justice towards youth: Investigating the mismatch between current policy and public opinion. *Children and Youth Services Review, 34,* 27–34.

Turgeon, J., Francis, E., & Loftus, E. (2014). Crafting model jury instructions for evaluating eyewitness testimony. *The Pennsylvania Lawyer, Sept/Oct 2014,* 49–52.

Tversky, A., & Kahneman, D. (1974). Judgment under uncertainty: Heuristics and biases. *Science, 185,* 1124–1131.

Twyman v. Twyman, 855 S.W.2d 619 (Tex. 1993).

Tyler, T.R., & Jackson, J. (2014). Popular legitimacy and the exercise of legal authority: Motivating compliance, cooperation, and engagement. *Psychology, Public Policy, and Law, 20,* 78–95.

Uelmen, G. (1996). Jury-bashing and the O.J. Simpson verdict. *Harvard Journal of Law and Public Policy, 20,* 475–481.

United States v. Blaylock, 421 F.3d 758 (7th Cir. 2005).

United States v. Hall, 93 F.3d 1337 (7th Cir. 1996).

United States v. Young, No. 13-5714 (6th Cir. 2014).

United States v. Telfaire, 469 F.2d 552 (D.C. Cir. 1972).

United States Football League v. National Football League, 842 F.2d 1335 (2nd Cir. 1988).

United States Sentencing Commission (2015). Guilty pleas and trial rates: Fiscal years 2010-2014. Retrieved from http://www.ussc.gov/research/2015-sourcebook/archive/sourcebook-2014

Unnever, J.D., & Cullen, F.T. (2009). Public opinion and the death penalty. In M.E. Oswald, S. Bieneck, & J. Hupfeld-Heinemann (Eds.), *Social psychology of punishment of crime* (pp. 113–133). Chichester: Wiley-Blackwell.

Van Dyke, J. (1977). *Jury selection procedures: Our uncertain commitment to representative panels.* Cambridge, MA: Ballinger Publishing Co.

Van Wallendael, L.R., Cutler, B.L., Devenport, J., & Penrod, S. (2007). Mistaken identification = erroneous conviction? Assessing and improving legal safeguards. In R. C. L. Lindsay, D. F. Ross, J. D. Read, & M. P. Toglia (Eds.), *Handbook of eyewitness psychology.* Mahwah, NJ: Erlbaum.

Van Wallendael, L.R., Surace, A., Hall Parsons, D., & Brown, M. (1994). "Earwitness" voice recognition: Factors affecting accuracy and impact on jurors. *Applied Cognitive Psychology, 8,* 661–677.

Velasco, P.D. (1995). The influence of size and decision rule in jury decision-making. In G. Davies, S. Lloyd-Bostock, & McMurran, & C. Wilson (Eds.), *Psychology, law, and criminal justice: International developments in research and practice* (pp. 344–348). Berlin: Walter De Gruyter.

Vidmar, N. (1994). Making inferences about jury behavior from jury verdict statistics: Cautions about the Lorelei's Lied. *Law and Human Behavior, 18,* 599–617.

Vidmar, N. (1995). *Medical malpractice and the American jury: Confronting the myths about jury incompetence, deep pockets, and outrageous damage awards.* Ann Arbor, MI: University of Michigan Press.

Vidmar, N. (1997). Generic prejudice and the presumption of guilt in sex abuse trials. *Law and Human Behavior, 21,* 5–25.

Vidmar, N. (2000a). A historical and comparative perspective on the common law jury. In N. Vidmar (Ed.), *World jury systems* (pp. 1–52). New York: Oxford University Press.

Vidmar, N. (2000b). *World jury systems.* Oxford: Oxford University Press.

Vidmar, N. (2002). Case studies of pre–and midtrial prejudice in criminal and civil litigation. *Law and Human Behavior, 26,* 73–105.

Vidmar, N. (2003). When all of us are victims: Juror prejudice and "terrorist" trials. *Chicago-Kent Law Review, 78,* 1143–1171.

Vidmar, N. (2008). Civil juries in ecological context: Methodological implications for research. In B.H. Bornstein & R.L. Wiener (Eds.), *Civil juries and civil justice: Psychological and legal perspectives* (pp. 35–65). New York: Springer.

Vidmar, N., Gross, F., & Rose, M. (1998). Jury awards for medical malpractice and postverdict adjustments of those awards. *DePaul Law Review, 48,* 265–299.

Vidmar, N., & Hans, V.P. (2007). *American juries: The verdict.* Amherst, NY: Prometheus Books.

Vines, K. (1964). Federal district judges and race relations cases in the South. *Journal of Politics, 26,* 337–357.

Vinson, K.V., Costanzo, M.A., & Berger, D.E. (2008). Predictors of verdict and punitive damages in high-stakes civil litigation. *Behavioral Sciences and the Law, 26,* 167–186.

Virginia v. Black, 538 U.S. 343 (2003).

Viscusi, W.K. (2001). Jurors, judges, and the mistreatment of risk by the courts. *Journal of Legal Studies, 30,* 107–142.

Viscusi, W.K. (2004). The blockbuster punitive damages awards. *Emory Law Journal, 53,* 1405–1455.

Vollrath, D., & Davis, J. (1980). Jury size and decision rule. In R. Simon (Ed.), *The jury: Its role in American society* (pp. 73–106). Lexington, MA: Heath.

Vollrath, D., Sheppard, B., Hinsz, V., & Davis, J. (1989). Memory performance by decision-making groups and individuals. *Organizational Behavior and Human Decision Processes, 43,* 289–300.

Vrij, A. (2008). *Detecting lies and deceit: Pitfalls and opportunities.* (2nd ed.). London: Wiley. *Wainwright v. Witt,* 469 U.S. 412 (1985).

Walker, C., & Woody, W.D. (2011). Juror decision making for juveniles tried as adults: The effects of defendant age, crime type, and crime outcome. *Psychology, Crime and Law, 17,* 659–675.

Wallace, W. (2010). Police deception during interrogation and its surprising influence on jurors' perceptions of confession evidence (Wayne Wallace responds). *The Jury Expert, 22,* 20–22. Retrieved from http://www.thejuryexpert.com/2010/11/police-deception-during-interrogation-and-its-surprising-influence-on-jurors-perceptions-of-confession-evidence/

Waller, B., Hope, L., Burrowes, N., & Morrison, E. (2011). Twelve (not so) angry men: Managing conversational group size increases perceived contribution by decision makers. *Group Processes and Intergroup Relations, 14,* 835–843.

Wallsten, T.S., Budescu, D.V., Rapoport, A., Zwick, R., & Forsyth, B. (1986). Measuring the vague meanings of probability terms. *Journal of Experimental Psychology: General, 113,* 348–365.

Warden, R., (2003). *The role of false confessions in Illinois wrongful murder convictions since 1970.* Evanston, IL: Northwestern University School of Law, Center on Wrongful Convictions.

Warden, R. (2004). *The snitch system: How incentivized witnesses put 38 innocent Americans on death row.* Chicago: Northwestern University School of Law, Center on Wrongful Convictions.

Warling, D., & Peterson-Badali, M. (2003). The verdict on jury trials for juveniles: The effects of defendant's age on trial outcomes. *Behavioral Sciences and the Law, 21,* 63–82.

Watkins, M. (2014, June 23). Skip jury duty and you'll pay, if judges in Dallas County get their way. Retrieved from http://www.dallasnews.com/news/metro/20140623-skip-jury-duty-and-youll-pay-if-judges-in-dallas-county-get-their-way.ece.

Weinstock, M. (2005). Cognitive bases for effective participation in democratic institutions: Argument skill and juror reasoning. *Theory and Research in Social Education, 33,* 73–102.

Weitzer, R., Tuch, S., & Skogan, W. (2008). Police-community relations in a majority-black city. *Journal of Research in Crime and Delinquency, 45,* 398–428.

Wells, G.L. (1992). Naked statistical evidence of probability: Is subjective probability enough?. *Journal of Personality and Social Psychology, 62,* 739–752.

Wells, G.L., & Lindsay, R.C.L. (1983). How do people infer the accuracy of eyewitness memory? Studies of performance and a metamemory analysis. In S.M.A. Lloyd-Bostock & B.R. Clifford (Eds.), *Evaluating witness evidence* (pp. 41–55). Chichester, U.K.: John Wiley & Sons.

Wells, G.L., Lindsay, R.C.L., & Tousignant, J.P. (1980). Effects of expert psychological advice on human performance in judging the validity of eyewitness testimony. *Law and Human Behavior, 4,* 275–286.

Wells, G.L., Memon, A., & Penrod, S.D. (2006). Eyewitness evidence: Improving its probative value. *Psychological Science in the Public Interest, 7,* 43–75.

Wells, G.L., & Quinlivan, D.S. (2009). Suggestive eyewitness identification procedures and the Supreme Court's reliability test in light of eyewitness science: 30 years later. *Law and Human Behavior, 33,* 1–24.

Wells, T., & Leo, R. (2008). *The wrong guys: Murder, false confessions, and the Norfolk Four.* New York: New Press.

Weninger, R.A. (1994). Jury sentencing in noncapital cases: A case study of El Paso County, Texas. *Washington University Journal of Urban & Contemporary Law, 45,* 3–40.

Wessel, E., Drevland, G.C.B., Eilertsen, D.E., & Magnussen, S. (2006). Credibility of the emotional witness: A study of ratings by court judges. *Law and Human Behavior, 30,* 221–230.

Wetmore, S., Neuschatz, J., & Gronlund, S. (2014). On the power of secondary confession evidence. *Psychology, Crime and Law, 20*, 339–357.

Wevodau, A., Cramer, R.J., Clark, J.W., & Kehn, A. (2014). The role of emotion and cognition in juror perceptions of victim impact statements. *Social Justice Research, 27*, 45–66.

Wheatman, S.R., & Shaffer, D.R. (2001). On finding for defendants who plead insanity: The crucial impact of dispositional instructions and opportunity to deliberate. Law and Human Behavior, 25, 167–183.

White, M.J. (2002). Explaining the flood of asbestos litigation: Consolidation, bifurcation and bouquet trials. National Bureau of Economic Research working paper.

White, M.J. (2003). Resolving the "elephantine mass." *Regulation, Summer 2003*, 48–54.

Whyte, G. (1993). Escalating commitment in individual and group decision making: A prospect theory approach. *Organizational Behavior and Human Decision Processes, 54*, 430–455.

Wiener, R.L., Arnot, L., Winter, R., & Redmond, B. (2006). Generic prejudice in the law: Sexual assault and homicide. *Basic and Applied Social Psychology, 28*, 145–155.

Wiener, R.L., Bornstein, B.H., & Voss, A. (2006). Emotion and the law: A framework for inquiry. *Law and Human Behavior, 30*, 231–248.

Wiener, R.L., Rogers, M., Winter, R., Hurt, L., Hackney, A., Kadela, K., . . . & Morasco, B. (2004). Guided jury discretion in capital murder cases: The role of declarative and procedural knowledge. *Psychology, Public Policy & Law, 10*, 516–576.

Wiener, R.L., Pritchard, C.C., & Weston, M. (1995). Comprehensibility of approved jury instructions in capital murder cases. *Journal of Applied Psychology, 80*, 455–467.

Wigboldus, D., Sherman, J., Franzese, H., & Van Knippenberg, A. (2004). Capacity and comprehension: Spontaneous stereotyping under cognitive load. *Social Cognition, 22*, 292–309.

Wiggins, E.C., & Breckler, S. (1990). Special verdicts as guides to decision making. *Law and Psychology Review, 14*, 1–41.

Wiggins, E.C., & Breckler, S.J. (1992). Management of complex civil litigation. In D. K. Kagehiro and W. S. Laufer (Eds.), *Handbook of psychology and law* (pp. 77–94). New York: Springer-Verlag.

Wilder, D. (1977). Perception of groups, size of opposition, and social influence. *Journal of Experimental Social Psychology, 13*, 253–268.

Wilder, D. (1990). Some determinants of the persuasive power of in-groups and out-groups: Organization of information and attribution of independence. *Journal of Personality and Social Psychology, 59*, 1202–1213.

Williams v. Florida, 399 U.S. 78 (1970).

Wilson, J.R., & Bornstein, B.H. (1998). Methodological considerations in pretrial publicity research: Is the medium the message? *Law and Human Behavior, 22*, 585–597.

Wilson, T., & Brekke, N. (1994). Mental contamination and mental correction: Unwanted influences on judgments and evaluations. *Psychological Bulletin, 166*, 117–142.

Wilson, T., & Gilbert, D. (2003). Affective forecasting. In M.P. Zanna (Ed.), *Advances in experimental social psychology* (Vol. 35, pp. 345–411). San Diego, CA: Academic Press.

Wirthman, L. (2015, April 25). The personal cost of civic duty for jurors in high-profile cases. Retrieved from http://www.denverpost.com/2015/04/24/wirthman-the-personal-cost-of-civic-duty-for-jurors-in-high-profile-cases/

Wise, R.A., Fishman, C., & Safer, M.A. (2009). How to analyze the accuracy of eyewitness testimony in a criminal case. *Connecticut Law Review, 42*, 435–513.

Wise, R.A., Gong, X., Safer, M.A., & Lee, Y.-T. (2010). A comparison of Chinese judges' and US judges' knowledge and beliefs about eyewitness testimony. *Psychology, Crime & Law, 16*, 695–713.

Wise, R.A., Pawlenko, N.B., Safer, M.A., & Meyer, D. (2009). What U.S. prosecutors and defence attorneys know and believe about eyewitness testimony. *Applied Cognitive Psychology, 23*, 1266–1281.

Wise, R.A., & Safer, M.A. (2004). What U.S. judges know and believe about eyewitness testimony. *Applied Cognitive Psychology, 18*, 427–443.

Wise, R.A., Safer, M.A., & Maro, C.M. (2011). What U.S. law enforcement officers know and believe about eyewitness factors, eyewitness interviews and identification procedures. *Applied Cognitive Psychology, 25*, 488–500.

Wispe, L. (1986). The distinction between sympathy and empathy: To call forth a concept, a word is needed. *Journal of Personality and Social Psychology, 50*, 314–321.

Wissler, R.L., Evans, D.L., Hart, A.J., Morry, M.M., & Saks, M.J. (1997). Explaining "pain and suffering" awards: The role of injury characteristics and fault attributions. *Law and Human Behavior, 21*, 181–205.

Wissler, R.L., Hart, A.J., & Saks, M.J. (1999). Decision-making about general damages: A comparison of jurors, judges, and lawyers. *Michigan Law Review, 98*, 751–826.

Wissler, R.L., Kuehn, P.F., & Saks, M.J. (2000). Instructing jurors on general damages in personal injury cases: Problems and possibilities. *Psychology, Public Policy, and Law, 6*, 712–742.

Wissler, R.L., Rector, K.A., & Saks, M.J. (2001). The impact of jury instructions on the fusion of liability and compensatory damages. *Law and Human Behavior, 25*, 125–139.

Wistrich, A.J., Guthrie, C., & Rachlinski, J.J. (2005). Can judges ignore inadmissible information? The difficulty of deliberately disregarding. *University of Pennsylvania Law Review, 153*, 1251–1345.

Witherspoon v. Illinois, 391 U.S. 510 (1968).

Wojdacz, M. (2009). Jury dodgers: What really happens if you ignore your summons? Retrieved from https://www.legalzoom.com/articles/jury-dodgers-what-really-happens-if-you-ignore-your-jury-summons.

Wood, L.C. (2007). Experts in the tub. *Antitrust American Bar Association, 21*, 95–101.

Woody, W.D., & Forrest, K.D. (2009). Effects of false-evidence ploys and expert testimony on jurors' verdicts, recommended sentences, and perceptions of confession evidence. *Behavioral Sciences and the Law, 27*, 333–360.

Woody, W.D., Forrest, K., & Yendra, S. (2014). Comparing the effects of explicit and implicit false-evidence ploys on mock jurors' verdicts, sentencing recommendations, and perceptions of police interrogation. *Psychology, Crime and Law, 20,* 603–617.

Woody, W.D., & Greene, E. (2012). Jurors' use of standards of proof in decisions about punitive damages. *Behavioral Sciences & the Law, 30,* 856–872.

Wrightsman, L.S. (2006). *The psychology of the Supreme Court.* Oxford: Oxford University Press.

Yang, Y.T., Studdert, D.M., Subramanian, S.V., & Mello, M.M. (2012). Does tort law improve the health of newborns, or miscarry? A longitudinal analysis of the effect of liability pressure on birth outcomes. *Journal of Empirical Legal Studies, 9,* 217–245.

Yarmey, A.D., & Jones, H.P. (1983). Is the psychology of eyewitness identification a matter of common sense? In S. Lloyd-Bostock & B.R. Clifford (Eds.), *Evaluating witness evidence* (pp. 13–40). Chichester, UK: Wiley.

Zeisel, H. (1971). And then there were none: The diminution of the federal jury. *University of Chicago Law Review, 38,* 710–724.

Zeisel, H., & Callahan, T. (1963). Split trials and time saving: A statistical analysis. *Harvard Law Review, 76,* 1606–1625.

Zeisel, H., & Diamond, S.S. (1974). "Convincing empirical evidence" on the six member jury. *University of Chicago Law Review, 41,* 281–295.

Zeisel, H., & Diamond, S.S. (1978). The effect of peremptory challenges on jury and verdict: An experiment in a federal district court. *Stanford Law Review, 30,* 491–531.

Zickafoose, D.J., & Bornstein, B.H. (1999). Double discounting: The effects of comparative negligence on mock juror decision-making. *Law and Human Behavior, 23,* 577–596.

About the Authors

Brian H. Bornstein, PhD, is Professor of Psychology and Courtesy Professor of Law at the University of Nebraska-Lincoln, where he serves as Director of the country's oldest Law and Psychology Program. His research interests include jury decision making, the reliability of eyewitness memory, and the application of decision-making principles to everyday judgment tasks. He has authored or edited 16 books and over 150 journal articles and book chapters. He has received grant funding for his research from several agencies, including the National Science Foundation and the National Institute of Justice. Professor Bornstein teaches courses on human memory, psychology and law, decision making, and history of psychology at the graduate and undergraduate levels. He has received research and mentoring awards from the University of Nebraska-Lincoln and the American Psychology-Law Society.

Edie Greene, PhD, is Professor of Psychology, Director of Psychological Sciences Training, and Director of the Graduate Sub-Plan in Psychology and Law at the University of Colorado, Colorado Springs. Her research focuses on legal decision making, beliefs about the causes and consequences of crime, eyewitness memory, and psychological issues in elder law. She has authored four editions of *Psychology and the Legal System*, the leading textbook in her field, two other books, and approximately 100 journal articles or chapters. She has received both college and campus-wide research awards and a teaching and mentoring award from the American Psychology-Law Society, of which she is a past president. She has received federal and foundation funding to support her research and has consulted with attorneys on hundreds of cases involving jury decisions and eyewitness memory.

Index

accidents, 188
accountability, 122, 267
acquittal bias, 239
actus reus, 153
ad damnum. *See* compensation;
  damages
additur, 5, 183n3, 186, 198–99,
  272–73, 318
adolescent development, 170, 171
African Americans, 4, 28, 30, 42, 63, 87
  capital punishment and, 234–35
  juveniles and, 160
age
  bias and, 170
  convictions and, 159, 161–62
  of defendant, 15, 59, 152–72
  disposition and, 161
  of incarceration, 228n2
  voir dire and, 159–60
  of witnesses, 93, 94, 95–96, 97
age-crime curves, 157
aggravating factors
  in capital punishment, 226–29,
  240, 272

defining, 227, 294
emotion and, 251–54
heinousness as, 205, 228,
  251–54, 296
judges and, 277
Allen, Terrence, 202, 216
Allen v. Takeda, 202, 216
American Tort Reform Association
  (ATRA), 178–79, 184, 200, 213n2,
  214, 216–17, 311
anchoring effect, on damages, 192–93
anger, 263, 267
Anthony, Casey, 261, 271
anticorporate effect, 176, 193–94
Apodaca, Robert, 73, 74, 81
Apodaca v. Oregon, 73, 81
appeals, 183n3
Appraisal-Tendency Framework, 263
apps, for jurors, 32
Arizona v. Fulminante, 111–12
ATES. *See* Attitudes Toward
  Eyewitnesses Scale
ATRA. *See* American Tort Reform
  Association

attire, 40, 51
Attitudes Toward Eyewitnesses Scale
    (ATES), 102
attorneys, 48
    bias and, 49
    closing arguments of, 102–3
    fees, 194
    folklore, 274
    interim arguments of, 305
    judges and, 51–52
    jurors and, 49, 53, 56
    peremptory challenges and, 49–51
    witness memory and, 99–100
attribution errors, 117–18
Aurora, Colorado theater shooting, 24
Australia, 29–30
awards, 15. *See also* compensation;
    compensatory damages; damages
    appropriateness of, 176
    bifurcation and, 297–98
    "blockbuster" cases, 204, 207–9, 211,
        220, 273, 278
    in civil cases, 68
    discrepancy, 182
    excessive, 175, 181–83, 206–8,
        273, 310–11
    inappropriate, 199
    injuries and, 175–76, 179, 181–99,
        206–11, 214–15, 218, 220
    judges and, 271, 278–82
    majority-rule and, 79–80
    nominal damages, 176n1
    predictability of, 175–76,
        186–87, 189–91, 195–98, 206,
        208, 211–13, 220
    subjectivity of, 174

Ballew v. Georgia, 61, 63
Barnes, Rowland, 285
Barro, Josh, 17
base-rate fallacy, 139
Batson framework, 49–51, 52, 53
battered woman syndrome, 149
beliefs, *See also* bias; religion
    behavior and, 18

about confessions, 109–10
false confessions and, 109–10
about interrogations, 109–10
jurors and, 39, 54, 56, 104, 116–21
about juvenile offenders, 156–58,
    167–171
of laypeople, 86–87
of legal professionals, 98–101
punitive damages and, 212–13
questionnaire about
    witnesses, 84–88
race and, 50
religion and, 283
voir dire and, 43
witnesses and, 84–94, 100, 105
witnesses' decisions versus, 93–94
about witness memory, 84, 90, 93
Bennett, Mark, 41
bias, 4, 38. *See also* implicit bias
    acquittal, 239
    age and, 170
    anticorporate, 176
    attorneys and, 49
    blind spots, 47
    capital punishment and, 224, 226
    confessions and, 116
    confirmation, 45, 109, 120–21, 188
    conviction, 234, 239
    cultural, 18
    debiasing strategies, 266–69
    emotion and, 247, 267
    explicit, 40–41, 54
    gender, 13, 48, 50, 248
    hate crime and, 242–44, 247–49,
        257–58, 264
    hindsight, 188
    identification, 100
    identification and, 100
    judges and, 54, 281–82
    jury selection and, 39–40
    juveniles and, 163
    media, 241, 311, 311n1, 312
    memory, 11, 82–84
    peremptory challenges and, 50–51
    PTP, 163, 258–59

racial, 13, 48, 49, 56, 224, 226
self-assessment of, 43, 46
from semantic memory, 45
sexual orientation, 248
trials and, 13
truth, 117
voir dire and, 289
of witnesses, 100
bifurcation, of trial, 197n6, 213–14,
    224, 253, 290, 295–99, 306, 308
Biggers factors, 103–4
Bill of Rights, 1, 3
Blackmun, Harry, 241
Blackstone, W., 60, 73
blame, 263–64
"blockbuster" cases, 204–5, 207–9, 211,
    220, 273, 278, 312
BMW v. Gore, 205, 206
Boston Marathon bombing, 24,
    43–44, 45
brain maturation, 170
Breyer, Stephen, 51
brutality, emotion and, 255
Buchella, Marty, 20
Burch v. Louisiana, 74
burden of proof, 292, 293
burnout, of judges, 285
businesses, punitive damages
    and, 204–5
Byrd, James, Jr., 247
bystanders, victims versus, 94–97

capital punishment, 74, 142, 145, 222,
    292. *See also* death penalty
African Americans and, 234–35
aggravating factors in, 226–29,
    240, 272
appeals, 294
attitudes, 231–34, 237–38
ban on, 224
bias and, 224, 226
comparison task in, 225
comprehension and, 295
death qualification process
    and, 231–34

decision threshold in, 226
defendant, 225–26
defendant characteristics
    and, 234–36
deservingness and, 225
emotion and, 251, 262–63
factors that should affect, 226–29
factors that should not affect, 231–40
gender and, 236
hate crime and, 242n1
heinousness and, 243–44
instructions, 294–95
instructions and, 227, 233, 239
judges and, 238
juror characteristics and, 236–38
jurors' attitudes and, 231–34
measurement task in, 225
media and, 222–23
methods of, 223n1
mitigating factors in, 226–29, 240
race and, 234–36
reform, 238–40
religion and, 237, 284
remorse and, 228, 251–52
selection and, 224
sentencing and, 223–26, 233, 238–39
victim characteristics and, 234–36
victim impact evidence, 229–31
voir dire and, 232
Capitol Records, Inc.
    v. Thomas-Rasset, 273
caps, 199
anchoring and, 193
"crossover" effect of, 215
injuries and, 215
on noneconomic damages, 184–85,
    198, 214–16
punitive damages and, 214–16
remittitur and, 185–86, 214–16
case types, compensation and, 182
casuistry, 50
celebrities, 35
Center for Jury Studies, 31
Central Park Five, 115
challenges for cause, 13, 43–48

charitable groups' activities, 30
childcare, 33
childhood, 152, 229
child maltreatment, 95
child sexual abuse (CSA), 95–97, 250, 260, 276
Cisneros, Michael, 137, 139
citizenship, 10
civic attitudes, 29–31
civic duty, 32
civic engagement, 1, 29–31
civic involvement, 29–31
civic virtues, 23
civil cases. *See also* awards;
    "blockbuster" cases; punitive
    damages; verdicts
    compensatory damages in, 173–199
    decision rule in, 217
    decline of, 8
    emotion and, 244, 252, 254, 256, 265
    expert testimony in, 129, 131
    gridlock in, 69
    international, 9
    judges and, 279–80
    legislation and, 4
    punitive damages in, 200–221
    remorse in, 252
    Seventh Amendment and, 35, 60
    types of, 177
    verdicts in, 75, 173–99, 200–221
civil commitment hearings, 200
civil rights, 22–23
clinical psychological
    testimony, 143–45
Clinton, Bill, 140
closing arguments, 102–3
cognitive processes, emotion and, 245
cognitive processing style, 144–45
coherence-based reasoning, 188–89
Cole, Timothy, 82–83, 98, 105
Colgrove v. Battin, 60, 61
Colorado v. Connelly, 108
Commentaries (Blackstone), 60, 73
Commonwealth v. DiGiambattista, 125–26

community, 10, 67, 72, 278
comparative probabilities, 146n3
compensation, 15, 33, 173–99. *See also* awards
    anchoring effect on, 192–93
    average, 181
    bifurcation and, 297, 298
    case types and, 182
    categories of, 178
    defendant characteristics and, 193
    deservingness and, 196, 198
    excessive, 175, 181–83, 206–8, 273, 310–11
    extralegal factors in, 198
    fairness of, 175, 177
    factors that should affect, 189–91
    factors that should not affect, 191–95
    injuries and, 189–92, 195, 198
    noneconomic damages
        and, 182, 186
    overview of, 177–80
    predictability of, 186–87
    punitive damages and, 204, 207–8, 210–12, 219–20, 278–79, 296
    reasonable, 186
    reducing, 183–86
    supercompensation, 205
    sympathy and, 256
    undercompensation, 183, 186, 198
    unemployment, 31
    verdicts and, 189
complexity exception, 128
compliance rates, 19, 21
composition of jury, 3, 4, 11, 23
comprehension, 5, 12, 226–28
    ambiguity and, 295
    capital punishment and, 295
    deliberations and, 290
    discrimination and, 295
    errors, 291
    expert testimony and, 305–6
    increasing, 292
    instructions and, 290–95, 298, 300, 305, 307
    interim arguments and, 305

juror questions and, 298, 300, 302, 305, 307
levels, 291–92
note taking, 299–301
predeliberation discussions and, 303
confessions, 12, 14, 106–27. *See also* false confessions
beliefs about, 109–10
bias and, 116
confirmation bias and, 121
contested, 108
contextual details of, 118–20
convictions and, 111, 113–14
electronic recordings of, 122–24
evidence and, 108–9, 118–19
experts, 148–50
instructions and, 126
interrogations and, 106–10, 117–19, 125, 126, 148–49
jurors and, 109–21, 148
of minorities, 124
overreliance on, 121–26
police and, 115–16
primary versus secondary, 113–14
on real juries, impact of, 114–16
screening, 122
witnesses and, 150
confirmation bias, 45, 109, 120–21, 188
Constitution, U.S., 3, 13–14, 53, 56, 59, 61, 71, 272
consultants, damages and, 180
convictions
age and, 159, 161–62
bias, 239
confessions and, 111, 113–14
erroneous, 4, 79, 82–83, 87, 99, 115–16, 148, 312
expert testimony and, 139, 147–49
false confessions and, 114–15
heinousness and, 253, 296
juvenile transfer and, 161–62
corporations, 4, 176, 204–5, 209–10
credibility
assumption of, 135
emotion and, 250–51, 262

of expert testimony, 128–51
false confessions and, 119
of witnesses, 82–105, 125, 133, 147, 249–50
crime labels, 260n5
cross-examination, 88, 102, 291
cross-race effect, 87, 94
CSA. *See* child sexual abuse
CSI Effect, 129
cultural barriers, jurors and, 22
cultural bias, 18

damages, 79–80, 173–99, 200–221. *See also* awards; compensation; compensatory damages; noneconomic damages; punitive damages
Dardinger v. Anthem Blue Cross and Blue Shield, 218–19
Daubert v. Merrell Dow Pharmaceuticals, 130, 146
David, Larry, 20
death penalty, 74, 142, 145, 222–41. *See also* capital punishment
death qualification process, 15–16, 224, 231–34, 238–39
debiasing strategies, 266–69
decision rule, 11, 14, 30, 58–81
in civil cases, 72–73, 75, 78–79, 217
deliberation and, 76–80
5/6, 75, 79
gridlock and, 80
historical context of, 73
liability judgments and, 79–80
status quo regarding, 74–75
Supreme Court, U.S., and, 73–74
3/4, 75
2/3, 75
defendants. *See also* juveniles
age of, 15, 159
behavior of, 228–29
of "blockbuster" cases, 207, 209
capital punishment, 222–41
characteristics, capital punishment and, 234–36

defendants (*Cont.*)
  characteristics and
    compensation, 193
  conduct of, 194, 197, 208–10, 216–17,
    220, 227
  criminal history of, 229
  deceased, 210
  emotion of, 251–53, 261
  identity of, 194
  insurance of, 194
  jurisdiction of, 68–69
  juvenile, 152–72
  leniency effect, 79
  "offstage" behavior of, 261
  punitive damages and, 200–221
  race of, 235–36, 237
  wealth of, 193n5, 206, 209, 213, 220
deliberations
  comprehension and, 290
  contamination of, 70
  content of, 187, 303
  on damages, 180–81, 187, 191,
    195, 209
  decision rule and, 76–80
  emotion and, 268
  equal participation in, 65
  evidence and, 77
  forbidden factors of, 194
  injuries and, 191
  length, 76
  majority-rule and, 72–81
  opinion and, 70
  predeliberation discussion,
    302–4, 306
  process, 70, 304
  selection and, 70
  size and time of, 64–65
  subjectivity of, 75
  voting requirements and, 75–76
delinquency, 153–54, 158
demeanor
  false evidence, 112
  of jurors, 47–48
  of witnesses, 249–50
deterrence, 210, 212, 220
direct mail methods, 32

direct observation, 11
disability, 179n2, 190, 211, 247
discrimination, 49–50, 53, 295
disfigurement, 179n2, 190
disposition, age and, 161
diversity, 28–29, 35, 63–64, 70, 78
DNA evidence, 120, 121, 132, 135,
    137–40, 138
DNA exonerations, 107, 115, 138
DNA tests, 12, 83, 115, 135, 137n2, 223
due process, 206, 208

earwitness. *See* witnesses
economic damages, 178, 185, 189. *See*
    also compensatory damages
educative testimony, 143
Edward III (King), 73
electrocution, 223n1
electronic recordings, of
    interrogations, 122–24
emotion, 144, 242–70. *See also*
    heinousness; remorse
  aggravating factors and, 251–54
  behavior and, 254
  bias and, 247, 267
  brutality and, 255
  capital punishment and, 251, 262–63
  civil cases and, 256
  cognitive processes and, 245
  credibility and, 250–51, 262
  decision-making and, 244,
    266, 269–70
  of defendant, 261
  definition of, 244–45
  deliberations and, 268
  evidence and, 254–58
  hate crime and, 242
  judges and, 244, 261–62
  judgments and, 245–46
  jurors and, 16, 240–41, 242–70
  legally irrelevant, 258–66
  legally relevant, 246–58
  mitigating factors and, 251–54
  mood and, 245–46, 262
  mortality and, 263–64
  negative, 245, 262

nonevidentiary sources of, 258–62
nullification and, 246–47
preliminary observations of, 244–46
PTP and, 258–59, 268–69
punishment and, 201–2, 205, 240–41
punitive damages and, 254
rationality and, 243
reform and, 266–69
sympathy and, 256
victim impact evidence and, 250, 256–57
witnesses and, 249–51
empathy, 257, 264–65n7, 264–68
empirical legal studies, 12
Employee Assistance Program, 34
Endangered Species Act, 10
equality, of women, 22–23
Equal Protection Clause, 49–50, 51
Erickson, Chuck, 106
ethnicity, 22, 28, 30. *See also* race
evasion, of jury duty, 20–24
evidence, 12, 71
anecdotal, 136
confession and, 108–9, 118–19
deliberations and, 77
demeanor false, 112
DNA, 120, 121, 132, 135, 137–40, 138
emotion and, 254–58
false, 112–13
fit and helpfulness of, 130–31
forensic, 129, 131
graphic, 255–56, 267
gruesome, 255–56, 267
inadmissible, 282, 293
interim arguments, 305
interpretation of, 232
neuroscientific, 140–42
opinions and, 45
probabilistic, 137–40
punitive damages and, 209, 213, 217
recall of, 65, 67, 134, 290, 300, 302, 306
social framework, 143
statistical, 136, 139–40
unanimity and, 77

victim impact, 229–31, 256–57, 267–68, 269
visual, 141
executions, 223n1, *See also* capital punishment
exonerations, DNA, 107, 115, 138
experimental simulations, 10–12, 281–82, 317
experts and expert testimony, 128–51, 229, 289
acceptance of, 132
admissibility of, 130–31
in civil cases, 129, 131
clinical psychological, 143–45
complexity of, 128–29, 134–35
comprehension and, 305–6
confessions and, 148–50
credibility of, 128–51
defining, 129, 130
effect of, 136
gender and, 133
interrogations and, 124–25, 148
judges and, 134, 276
jurors and, 124–25, 128–51
Need for Cognition and, 136–37
neuroscientific evidence, 140–42
nonpsychological, 137–42
perception and, 128–51
probabilistic and DNA evidence, 137–40
psychological, 142, 143t, 149–50
reasons for including, 130–31
relevance of, 131
scientific, 130–31, 133–34, 138, 144, 149–50
social framework testimony, 145–48
understanding, 305–6
explicit bias, 40–41, 54
extremism, 64, 81
eyewitnesses. *See* witnesses

"failed" polygraph, 112
fair cross-section requirement, 78
fairness
of compensation, 175, 177
instructions and, 291

fairness (*Cont.*)
  of punishment, 205–6
  of punitive damages, 205
false confessions, 106–27, 148
  beliefs and, 109–10
  confirmation bias and, 120–21
  convictions and, 114–15
  credibility and, 119
  hallmarks of, 106
  interrogations and, 106–27
  jurors and, 106–27
  prevalence rates of, 107
  recognizing and distinguishing,
    108–9, 126
  reducing, 122, 127
  reform and, 14, 121–26
false convictions, 4, 99, 312
fanaticism, 64
federal employers' liability, 276
Federal Rules of Evidence, 130, 131
Ferguson, A., 36
Ferguson, Ryan, 106–7, 127
First Amendment, 174
fit and helpfulness, of evidence, 130–31
fMRI. *See* functional magnetic
    resonance imaging
forbidden factors, jurors and, 194
forensic evidence, 129, 131
foreperson, 303
Foster, Timothy, 52
Foster v. Chatman, 52–53
Fourteenth Amendment, 49–50, 206
Fox, Cinda, 285
free speech, 174
functional magnetic resonance
    imaging (fMRI), 140–41
fusion, 188–89, 194, 197–98, 215, 228,
    239, 253–54, 270, 295–99
future dangerousness, 228, 229
future economic damages, 178

game-theoretic approaches, 79
gas chamber, 223n1
gender, 247
  bias, 13, 48, 50, 248

capital punishment and, 236
expert testimony and, 133
of jurors, 51
peremptory challenges and, 51–52
rape and, 265
Gore, Ira, Jr., 205
government, 31, 32
Graf, Ed, 72
gridlock, 64, 69–70, 80
group cohesion, 67
group dynamics, 65–66
group polarization, 69
group solidarity, 67
group theory, 77
guilty plea, 8

hate crime, 258
  bias and, 247
  capital punishment and, 242n1
  definition of, 248
  emotion and, 242, 247–49
  heinousness and, 251n2
  laws, 242n1, 248, 249, 264
  race and, 249
  sexual orientation and, 247–49
Hate Crimes Protection Act, 247
HB 39 Bill, 60
heinousness, 16, 24, 170
  as aggravating factor, 205, 228,
    251–54, 296
  bifurcation of trial and, 253
  capital punishment and, 243–44
  hate crime and, 251n2
  instructions and, 253
  punishment and, 253–54
Heitholt, Kent, 106
Henry II (King), 60
heterogeneity, in criminal juries, 63
heuristics, 47–48
hindsight bias, 188
Hispanics, 28, 49, 63, 234–35, 263
Holmes, James, 256–57
homosexual abuse, 97
homosexuality, 173–74
honesty, of witnesses, 96

horizontal equity, 176, 178, 185, 186,
191, 198, 279
humor, 5
hung juries. *See* gridlock
Hurst v. Florida, 223, 277

identification, witness, 82–105, 294
accuracy of, 88–89, 133
bias and, 100
description and, 92
manipulation of, 91
misidentification, 82–83, 99
postidentification feedback
on, 89–90
procedures, 98, 103
reliability of, 82–105, 126
I-I-Eye, 103–4
illusory causation, 123
image, of jury system, 34–35
impartiality, 13, 37, 39, 41, 43, 269
Constitution and, 56
gauging, 45–47
judge's use of heuristics for, 47–48
opinions related to publicity and, 47
prejudice and, 261
implicit bias
of attire, 51
challenges for cause and role of, 43–48
judges and, 54, 282
in peremptory challenges, 48–53
race and, 50
selection and, 42–43
incarceration, age of, 228n2
inclusiveness, unanimity and, 77
income, 21–22, 33, 212
Ind, Jacob, 152–53
indirect judge-jury comparisons, 283
individual assessment, 143
Industrial Revolution, 4
inflation, 182, 186, 207
injuries, 173–99
awards and, 175–76, 183
bifurcation and, 298–99
caps and, 184–86, 193, 198,
213–16, 219–21

compensation and, 189–92, 195, 198
damages and, 184–85, 186
damages and psychological, 179
deliberations and, 191
noneconomic damages and, 189, 193
punitive damages and, 207, 209,
210–12, 215, 296
severity of, 134, 176, 182, 184,
186–91, 198, 208–11
injustice, 247
innocence, presumption of, 41, 43, 45
Innocence Project, 107, 115, 119
instructions, 28, 34, 101–2, 177, 199, 290
capital punishment, 294–95
capital punishment and, 227, 233, 239
comprehension and, 290–95, 298,
300, 305, 307
confessions and, 125–26
content of, 197, 291–95
effectiveness of, 291, 293, 294,
290–95, 305–06
enhanced, 125–26, 197, 293
fairness and, 291
heinousness and, 253
jurisdiction and, 228, 293
language of, 292
nullification, 247
pinpoint, 295
punitive damages and, 203, 219
revising, 203, 305, 307
sensitization versus
skepticism, 293–94
simplification of, 295
structural weaknesses in, 291
substantive, 305
witnesses, 293–94
written, 292
insurance policy limits, 183
interrogations
attribution errors in, 117–18
beliefs about, 109–10
camera position in, 123–24
coercive, 106–8, 110–14, 116, 117,
123, 125
confessions and, 106–27, 148–49

interrogations (*Cont.*)
  confirmation bias and, 120
  dearth of knowledge and, 117
  electronic recordings of, 122–24
  expert testimony and, 124–25, 148
  illusory causation in, 123
  police, 106–9, 112, 148
  psychological pressure in, 110
  transparency of, 122–24
intimidation, of jurors, 40, 66
intuition, witness memory and, 147
Ito, Lance, 1n1

Jackson v. Louisiana, 74
jargon, 40
Johnson v. Louisiana, 73, 77, 79, 81
jokes about jury, 20
judge-jury agreements, 279–81, 287
judge-jury comparisons, 275–85
judges, 271–87
  aggravating factors and, 277
  attorneys and, 51–52
  awards and, 271, 278–282
  bench or jury trials, 274–75
  bias and, 54, 281–82
  "blockbuster" cases and, 278
  burnout of, 285
  capital punishment and, 223,
    238, 241
  civil cases and, 279–80
  comparison of juries and, 275–85
  decision-making of, 271–287
  emotion and, 244, 261–62
  experimental simulations
    and, 281–82
  expert testimony and, 134
  indirect judge-jury
    comparisons, 283
  jurisdiction of, 281
  nullification and, 286
  objectivity of, 277–78
  outsider perspective of, 282
  punitive damages and, 278–79, 281–82
  reasoning of, 282
  religion of, 283–84
  remittitur and, 214, 216, 221

  safety of, 285
  sentencing and, 276–77, 281
  stress of, 283–85
  use of heuristics, 47–48
  witness memory and, 100
judgment notwithstanding the
    verdict, 272–73
judicial dispassion, 274
jurisdiction
  bifurcation and, 296
  of defendant, 68–69
  instructions and, 228, 293
  of judges, 281
  of juvenile courts, 155
  prejudice and, 260n5
  punitive damages and, 217
  research on, 316–17
  Sixth Amendment and, 73
jurors. *See specific entries*
jury. *See specific entries*
jury duty, 17–36
  avoidance of, 13, 17–18, 23, 35
  evasion of, 20–24
  failure to appear for, 23
  as inconvenient, 21
  innovations for enhancing
    experience of, 33–34
  jokes about, 20
  jurors' opinion of, 26–27
  mandatory, 32
  public perception of, 17–36
  reputation and, 35
  Tweets about, 20
juveniles, 15, 152–72. *See also* age
  adolescent development, 170, 171
  African Americans and, 160
  age-crime curve of, 157
  bias and, 163
  cognitive capabilities of, 157
  courts, 154, 155
  crime rates, 156
  crimes, severity of, 154, 156
  criminal record of, 164
  defendants, 152–53, 171
  developmental trajectories
    of, 156–57, 170, 171

harsh treatment of, 159
justice system, 153–56
negative impressions of, 164
public attitudes toward, 171
punishment of, 156, 158–59
recidivism of, 172
rehabilitation of, 153–54, 156, 158, 164, 171–72
in Sixth Amendment, 152
stereotypes of, 153, 158, 163, 165–69, 171
as superpredators, 154
transfer, 154–59, 161, 162, 171, 315
voir dire and, 160, 169
waiver, 154–56, 158–59, 171, 277

Kafka, Franz, 10n4
Kagan, Elena, 52
Kaye, Judith, 35
Knowledge of Eyewitness Behavior Questionnaire (KEBQ), 86
Kumho Tire Co. v. Carmichael, 130

Latinos. *See* Hispanics
Law and Order, 1
law enforcement. *See* police
laws
  adherence to, 286
  for damages, 184
  disregarding, 246–47, 288
  emotion and, 243
  hate crime, 242n1, 248, 249, 264
  juror's understanding of, 303–4
  remittitur, 183n3
  tort, 175
leading questions, 103
legal professionals, 98–101. *See also* attorneys
legislation, 317
  civil cases and, 4
legitimacy, 81, 315
Leo, Richard, 106
lethal injection, 223n1
Lewinsky, Monica, 140
liability. *See* Chapters9 and 10

libel, 207
Lilly, Eli, 202, 216
lineups, 93, 98, 101, 103, 121
Lockett, Clayton, 223n1

Macpherson, Susan, 55
majority-rule. *See also* Chapter4; decision rule
  consequences of, 58
  deliberations and, 72–81
  pressure in, 61
malice, 216–17
Mallin, Michele, 82–83, 98
Markman v. Westview Instruments, Inc., 273
Marshall-Brennan Constitutional Literacy Project, 35
Martin, Trayvon, 6, 59
McVeigh, Timothy, 256–57
measurement task, in capital punishment, 225
media, 7, 201, 222–23, 241, 249, 260, 311, 311n1, 312
medical costs, 178, 182, 186
medical malpractice, 47, 128, 129, 175, 177, 182–83, 185, 186, 189, 201, 206, 207, 209, 252–53, 276
memory bias, 11, 82–84
mens rea, 153
mental health, 144, 229
mental impairment, 190
Miller-El v. Dretke, 51
minorities, 63, 72, 78, 124. *See also* African Americans; Hispanics; women
misidentifications, 82–83, 89
mitigating factors
  in capital punishment, 226–29, 240
  defining, 227, 294
  emotion and, 251–54
  remorse as, 253
mixed tribunals, 9
mood, emotion and, 245–46, 262
moral disengagement, 240, 263
mortality, emotion and, 263–64

National Center for State Courts
(NCSC), 54
need for cognition (NFC), 136–37
negative character testimony, 111
Neil v. Biggers, 103–4. *See also Biggers*
factors
neuroscientific evidence, 140–42
NFC. *See* need for cognition
nominal damages, 176n1
noneconomic damages, 178–80,
182–85, 190–93, 197
assigning, 190
calculation of, 178–79, 180
caps on, 184–85, 198, 214–16
defining, 179
features of, 179
psychological components of, 179
reform, 221
remittitur and, 213
nonpsychological experts, 137–42
normative social influences, 69
note taking, jurors, 299–301, 306
nullification, 10, 20, 246–47, 258, 269,
272, 286
NYU Civil Jury Project, 317n2

oath of jury service, 43
Obama, Barack, 6
objectivity, 44, 277–78. *See also*
impartiality
Occam's Razor, 150
O'Connor, Sandra Day, 299
Office of Juvenile Justice and
Delinquency Prevention, 155
Oklahoma City bombing, 256–57
operative decision rule, 78
orientation programs for jurors, 33
Orwell, George, 309, 310
O'Toole, George, 43–44, 45

Paridiso, David, 285
parole, 232
participation, jury service, 31–32, 65–67
past economic damages, 178
patent claims, 273
Payne v. Tennessee, 230

peer review, 130
per diem argument, 193
peremptory challenges, 13–14, 39, 46–53
autonomy, 48–49
perpetrator characteristics, 249
Perry, Rick, 83
Phelps, Fred, 173
physical handicaps of jurors, 22
plea bargains, 161–62
police, 51, 110, 123
confessions and, 115–16
interrogations, 106–9, 112, 148
witness memory and, 98–99
political engagement, 22
polygraph examination, 110, 112, 131,
132, 141
postidentification feedback
paradigm, 90
posttrial interviews of jurors, 24, 135
post-verdict allocation policy, 219
post-verdict settlements, 183
predeliberation discussion, 302–4, 306
predictability
of awards, 175–76, 186–87, 189–91,
195–98, 206, 208, 211–13, 220
of compensatory damages, 186–87
improving, 195–97
of punitive damages, 208–13
variability and, 195
"prehabilitation," of jurors, 44–45, 57
prejudice, 41, 46, 47, 231. *See also*
hate crime
generic, 260, 269
impartiality and, 261
jurisdiction and, 260n5
media and, 260
pretrial publicity (PTP), 47, 163,
258, 268–69
Principles for Juries and Jury Trials,
37–38, 54
probabilistic evidence, 137–40
products liability cases, 211, 276
professional jurists, 7
proof
burden of, 292, 293
standards of, 202, 217

psychological expert testimony, 142,
143*t*, 149–50
psychological injuries, damages
and, 179
PTP. *See* pretrial publicity
public perception of jury duty,
17–19, 34–35
punishment. *See* capital punishment;
punitive damages
punitive damages, 177, 184, 193, 198,
200–221
beliefs and, 212–13
bias and, 221
bifurcation and, 297
bifurcation of trial
and, 213–14
"blockbuster" cases and, 207–8
businesses and, 204–5
caps and *remittitur*, 214–16
case types and, 206, 208
corporations and, 204–5, 209–10
defendants and, 208–10
emotion and, 254
excessiveness and, 175, 181–83,
206–8, 273, 310–11
income, 212
inflation and, 207
infrequency of, 200–201
instructions and, 203, 219
judges and, 278–79, 281–82
jurisdiction and, 217
jurisprudence, 206, 210
magnitude of, 204, 206–8, 211,
212, 214
media attention to, 201
paradox of, 203–6
predictability of, 208–13
primary function of, 220
punishment and, 220
purpose of, 203
raising threshold on, 216–17
reform and, 203, 204, 213–19, 221
relation to compensatory damages,
204, 207–12, 215, 219–20,
278–79, 296
remittitur, 215–16

split recovery, 213, 218–19,
218n3, 221
as supercompensation, 205
variability of, 208
punitive liability, 213

questionnaires, of jurors, 21, 31,
54–57, 84–88
questions, of jurors, 301–2, 306

race, 28, 30
beliefs and, 50, 110
capital punishment and, 234–36
cross-race effect, 85*t*, 87, 94
of defendant, 226, 235–36, 237
hate crime and, 247–49
implicit bias and, 42, 50
of jurors, 23, 28, 30, 49–52, 212,
235, 236–38
peremptory challenges and, 14,
48, 50–53
religion and, 284
size of jury and, 63
of victim, 235–36, 237
voir dire and, 56
witnesses and, 87, 92
race-neutral explanations, 51–52
racial bias, 13, 48, 49, 56
rape, 260n5, 265
rationality, emotion and, 243
Rational versus Experiential Inventory
(RVEI), 144–45
recidivism, of juveniles, 167, 172
reform. *See* Chapter15; *specific entries*
rehabilitation, 15
of jurors, 44, 54, 57
of juveniles, 153–54, 156, 158,
164, 171–72
religion, 236, 237, 283–84
remittitur, 198–99, 219, 221, 273, 318
caps and, 185–86, 214–16
increased use of, 15
laws, 183n3
noneconomic damages, 213
punitive damages, 215–16
standard for, 185

remorse, 228, 251–54, 252n3
representativeness of juries, 23, 58, 63, 70, 160, 169, 234
repression, 97
research
  future needs in, 316–18
  methodology, 10–13, 318
retribution, 153, 158, 176, 204, 208–10, 220
reverse bifurcation, 298
right to jury trial, 272–74
Ring v. Arizona, 223, 272
Roof, Dylann, 242, 248
Rosendich, Dan, 20
Roughing It (Twain), 4n2
Russeau, Gregory, 202, 228
Russia, 272
RVEI. *See* Rational versus Experiential Inventory

sadness, 119, 245, 255, 257, 259, 262–63, 264
safeguards, 5, 14, 16, 113, 147, 268
  for jurors, 88, 100–4, 170, 293
  traditional versus innovative, 122, 289–90
  voir dire as, 53, 102, 103
safety, juror, 25, 285
sampling theory, 67–69, 80
SB 94 Bill, 60
scientific testimony, 14, 130–31, 133–35, 138, 150
secondary confessions, 113–14
selection of jury, 13–14, 37–57, 159, 260. *See also voir dire*
  bias and, 39–40
  capital punishment and, 224
  deliberations and, 70
  effectiveness of, 54
  implicit bias and, 42–43
  process, 44
  race and, 52
  structural defects in, 57
self-disclosure, 41
self-incriminations, 122
semantic memory, bias from, 45

sensitization and skepticism, 21, 293–94
sentencing, 200, 222, 228n2
  bifurcation of trial and, 224
  capital punishment and, 223–26, 233, 238–39
  future dangerousness and, 228
  heinousness and, 296
  judges and, 276–77, 281
Seventh Amendment, 3, 35, 37, 60, 73, 272, 274, 278
sex offenders, 144
sexual abuse, 260, 260n5
sexual assault victims, 250–51
sexually violent perpetrator (SVP), 144
sexual orientation, 50, 238, 247–49
Shepard, Matthew, 247
Simpson, O. J., 1n1, 271
simulation studies, 103, 123, 144
  experimental, 10–12, 281–82, 317
  judges and experimental, 281–82
  witnesses and, 90–93
Sixth Amendment, 3, 37, 59, 60–61, 73, 152, 161
size of jury, 2, 3, 11, 14, 30, 58–72
  Constitution, U.S., and, 59, 61, 71
  decision making and, 63–70
  diversity and, 63–64, 70
  efficiency and, 69
  gridlock and, 69–70
  historical context of, 60
  juror participation and, 66–67
  minorities and, 63
  optimal, 70–71
  policy, 62
  power and, 68
  quality and, 61, 64–65
  race and, 63
  requirements in Florida, 74
  Seventh Amendment and, 60
  Sixth Amendment and, 60–61
  status quo regarding, 62
  Supreme Court and, 60–62
  time of deliberations and, 64–65
Skilling v. United States, 47
slander, 207
Snyder, Albert, 173–74, 216

Snyder, Matthew, 173–74
Snyder v. Phelps, 173–74
social framework testimony, 143,
    145–48, 170, 229
social influence, 11
social loafing, 66–67
societal damages, 218n3
socioeconomic status, 21, 28, 40, 234
South Korea, 272
Spain, 272
special interest groups, 311, 312
split recovery, 15, 213, 218–19,
    218n3, 221
State Farm Mutual v. Campbell, 210,
    211, 220, 278–79
"State-of-the-States" project, 76
statistical evidence, 129, 135–36, 139–40
statute of limitations, 82–83
stereotypes of juveniles, 153–54, 158,
    163, 165–69, 171
story model of decision making, 188
Street Law, Inc, 35
stress
    of judges, 283–85
    of jurors, 24–26, 34, 267, 285
    of witnesses, 98
subjectivity
    of awards, 174
    of deliberations, 75
suffering, 179n2, 190, 193, 246
summons, 18, 19, 21, 23, 31
Sunstein, Cass, 64
superpredators, 154
Supreme Court, U.S.
    decision rule and, 73–74
    jurisprudence, 103–4, 216, 273
    size of jury and, 60–62
SVP. *See* sexually violent perpetrator
sympathy, 164, 256, 265n7, 280
Syvertson, James, 202

Takeda Pharmaceutical, 202, 216
terror management theory, 263
testimonial false evidence, 112
testimony. *See* confessions; experts and
    expert testimony; witnesses

text messages, for jurors, 31
Thomas-Rasset, Jammie, 273
Thompson v. Utah, 60
Timothy Cole Act, 83
Timothy Cole Advisory Panel on
    Wrongful Convictions, 83
transfers of juveniles, 154–59, 161, 162,
    171, 315
transparency of interrogations, 122–24
The Trial (Kafka), 10n4
trials, *refer to specific topics*
truth bias, 117
Tsarnaev, Dzhokhar, 43–44, 45
Twain, Mark, 4n2
tweets, 20

ultimate opinion testimony. *See* social
    framework testimony
unanimity, 72–81
    evidence and, 77
    murder and, 74
    requirements, 74–75, 77, 79
undercompensation, 183, 186, 198
underrepresentation, 72
unemployment compensation, 31
United States Football League
    v. National Football League, 176n1
urban legends, 7

values, of jurors, 181
vehicular negligence, 182–83
venirepersons, 49
verdicts. *See specific topics*
vertical equity, 176, 185, 186, 190,
    198, 279
victims, 158
    blame of, 264
    bystanders versus, 94–97
    characteristics, 234–36, 247, 253, 280
    emotion of, 250
    empathy for, 265–66
    impact evidence, 229–31, 256–57,
    267–68, 269
    race of, 235–36, 237
    sexual assault, 250–51
    sexual orientation of, 248–49

violence, 144, 229, 296. *See also*
    evidence; heinousness
visual evidence, 141
voir dire, 25, 27, 33, 37–57, 291
    age and, 159–60
    beliefs and, 43
    bias and, 289
    capital punishment and, 232
    effectiveness of, 46
    goals of, 37–40
    individual, 54
    juveniles and, 160, 169
    race and, 56
    as safeguard, 102, 103
    selection and, 55
    structure of, 41, 47
voting, 30
voting requirements, deliberations
    and, 75–76

waivers, juveniles, 154–56, 158–59,
    171, 277
Webster, George, 6–7
Westboro Baptist Church (WBC),
    173–74, 216
Why Jury Duty Matters (Ferguson), 36
Wi-Fi, 33
Williams, Johnny, 59
Williams v. Florida, 59, 60–61, 69, 71
Witherspoon v. Illinois, 224
witnesses/eyewitnesses. *See also*
    Chapter 5; identification, witness
    accuracy of, 83, 88–90, 91, 92, 100, 103
    age of, 93, 94, 95–96, 97
    arousal, 94
    attention of, 92
    Attitudes Toward Eyewitnesses
        Scale, 102
    beliefs and, 84–94, 100, 105
    bias of, 100
    bystanders versus victims, 94–97
    categories of, 132

    child, 94–97, 250
    conditions, 88–89
    confessions and, 150
    confidence of, 83, 88–89, 91, 93
    contradictory statements of, 92
    convictions and, 89
    credibility of, 90, 91, 92, 94, 95–96,
        125, 133, 147, 249–50
    cross-examination of, 102, 291
    decisions versus beliefs, 93–94
    demeanor of, 249–50
    emotion and, 249–51
    experts, 146–47
    honesty of, 96
    I-I-Eye, 103–4
    inconsistency, 92–93
    instructions on, 293–94
    interviews, 91, 98
    legal professionals in other countries
        and, 100–101
    mistakes of, 82
    performance of, 88–90, 94, 97,
        98, 143
    postidentification feedback
        paradigm, 90
    quality of, 147
    questions to, 34
    race and, 87
    reliability of, 85, 102
    repression of victims, 97
    simulation studies and, 90–93
    stress of, 98
    variables of, 90–92, 96
    verdict and, 88, 91
women, 4, 22–23
wrongful convictions, 79, 82–83, 87,
    109, 114–16

young offenders. *See* juveniles
young people, 21, 23

Zimmerman, George, 6–7, 59

Printed in the USA
CPSIA information can be obtained
at www.ICGtesting.com
CBHW071439020324
4901CB00005B/269

9 780190 201340